The Jews of the Middle East and North Africa in Modern Times

The Jews of the Middle East and North Africa in Modern Times

*Reeva Spector Simon,
Michael Menachem Laskier,
and Sara Reguer, Editors*

Columbia University Press
New York

Columbia University Press
Publishers Since 1893
New York Chichester, West Sussex

Library of Congress Cataloging-in-Publication Data

The Jews of the Middle East and North Africa in modern times / Reeva Spector Simon, Michael Menachem Laskier, and Sara Reguer, editors
p. cm.
Includes bibliographical references and index.
ISBN 0-231-10796-X (cl. : alk. Paper) — ISBN 0-231-10797-8 (pbk. : alk. Paper)
1. Jews—Middle East—History—Congresses. 2. Jews—Africa, North—History—Congresses. I. Simon, Reeva S. II. Laskier, Michael M., 1949- III. Reguer, Sara, 1953-

DS135.L4 J49 2002
956'.004924—dc21 2002073451

∞

Columbia University Press books are printed on permanent and durable acid-free paper.
Printed in the United States of America
c 10 9 8 7 6 5 4 3 2 1
p 10 9 8 7 6 5 4 3 2 1

Contents

PART 2. COUNTRY-BY-COUNTRY SURVEY

Introduction

This volume began with an informal discussion by the three editors at the annual meeting of the American Historical Association in 1992. Recognizing the proliferation in the United States of college and university departments in both Middle Eastern and Jewish history, we noted the increasing interest in the role of Middle Eastern and North African Jews in shaping their societies. However, even with the significant monographs that have appeared since the 1980s highlighting aspects of the history and culture of the Jews in the Ottoman Empire, Eretz Israel (Palestine), Iran, North Africa, and their successor states of the twentieth century, we, like many of our colleagues, were frustrated that no one had done a coherent synthesis to present to our students in our courses on Jews of the modern Middle East.

This lacuna in both Jewish and Middle Eastern studies is partly because general histories of the region write Jews out of the standard narrative. As part of the religious and ethnic mosaic that was traditional Islamic society, Jews were but one among numerous minorities. As *dhimmis,* they played a subordinate role in the dominant Muslim society and appear intermittently, most notably as individuals who participated in certain economic niches.

Until modern times the story of the Jews in the region appeared in travelers' accounts and responsa literature (decisions from rabbis in response to submitted queries). With the development in the West of a scientific approach to the study of the Jewish people, however, Jewish historians of the nineteenth century analyzed their society in the context of the "Jewish question" posed by the Christian West. From a Eurocentric perspective the Jews, along with the non-Christian peoples in the Middle East and Asia, were perceived as the Other.

But just as European Christians touted the superiority of the West over the "Orient," European Jews examined their own history Eurocentrically and praised the aristocrats of European Jewry, the Sephardim who achieved parity in multicultural medieval Spain, and in turn lamented the plight of Ashkenazi Jewry, persecuted and exiled from community to community. European Jews marginalized the other (non-European) Jews and Sephardim who settled in Europe and examined them in all their Otherness and exoticism. This orientation has continued, even in Israel—the locus of the majority of Sephardic and Middle Eastern Jewry today—in the context of the dominant Ashkenazi culture. We hope that this book will counteract the stereotype that has evolved of Middle Eastern Jews as primitive premodern people and recast them as possessors of densely textured and creative public and private intellectual lives. This volume is an attempt to reclaim modern Middle Eastern Jewish material, cultural, and spiritual existence, not just to prove that such a history existed. To that end we invited leading scholars in their fields to an international conference at Columbia University, where they presented their papers, discussed them, and ultimately submitted them as chapters of this book.

The communities under discussion lived in the Islamic world. Although this is the political and cultural context in which the Jews lived, our emphasis in this book is specifically on Jewish society. A community subordinate to the dominant Muslim elite, Jews had economic mobility despite their lack of political power. Thus until two centuries ago Jews were at the bottom of the political and religious hierarchy, but at times and in some places they could be better off economically than the Muslim majority, who were primarily peasants in a largely agricultural society. Spain exiled both Jews and Muslims in 1492. Other societies did not always impose discriminatory practices, which also varied in time and place. While Jews in Morocco and Iran at the beginning of the twentieth century were in dire straits, those in Cairo and Baghdad flourished.

The faith-based communities of Muslims, Christians, and Jews had limited interaction. Men dominated all segments of society, and these groups interacted only in public spaces such as the marketplace and the coffee shop. Home and family were private. Jewish religious and educational institutions and social welfare organizations were under the aegis of the community, which over time had developed the means for surviving in the Diaspora.

Exiled from their religious and cultural center in Eretz Israel after the destruction of the First Temple (586 B.C.E.), Jews lived primarily in Babylonia (Mesopotamia). By the time they returned to Eretz Israel at the time of the ancient Persian Empire, they had developed some tools of survival as a minority group. They used these tools when Rome destroyed the Second Temple, and they began their long diasporic history. One branch went from Eretz Israel to Rome, north to the Rhineland, and then east through Germany to Eastern Europe. This is the Ashkenazi branch of Jews. Others stayed in the Middle East. Faith continued to be their way of life, the community was centered on the rabbi and the synagogue, and all normative

Jews used the same Torah (written law), Talmud (oral law), and methodology for solving halakhic (legal) problems. Hebrew became the language of scholarship and prayer. Vernacular dialects such as Judeo-Arabic developed based on the language of the community, interspersed with Hebrew and Aramaic words and phrases; this is paralleled in Eastern Europe by the development of Judeo-German (Yiddish).

Their faith, Judaism, signifies a mode of life based on adherence to the teachings of the Torah given by God. Traditional Jews accept that the Torah came in written form with oral interpretation. The latter evolved through the millennia into a vast sea of legal, ethical, and philosophical writings based mainly on the Talmud, which determined the lifestyle of the Jews wherever they lived. The commonality of law was modified by local and regional customs or praxis, which reflected both the acculturation of the Jews and the realities of life as a minority group. Popular religion, always paralleling rabbinic norms, manifested itself in part in the Hasidic movement in Eastern Europe and in "saint worship" in the Middle East. In the Middle East, a region where living areas are determined by religion, ethnic group, tribe, or occupation, Jews were not really a people who lived apart, as they had in Europe, where they were the dominant minority and singled out under Christian rule as a people who lived apart.

Persian rule had already established an autonomous way of life for communities to enable them to practice their religions. Religious law was to decide personal status issues, an arrangement maintained under Islamic rule well into modern times. The period of the Enlightenment in Europe, changes wrought by the French Revolution and the Napoleonic Wars, and the period of reform in the Ottoman Empire (Tanzimat), accompanied by the stresses of modernization, colonialism, imperialism, and nationalism, affected Jewish communities not only in Europe but in the Middle East as well. How these societies coped with these changes is the subject of this book.

To address these issues we take a double approach. The country chapters, which cover history and politics, economic life, society, and culture, analyze local diversity. Thematic chapters, on the other hand, cut across the region to highlight trends and overarching generalizations of sameness. The two parts of the book complement each other to provide a picture of life in a region where transnational threads remain despite the creation of nation-states, which in many cases occurred less than a century ago, and extend to Europe, the Far East, and the Americas.

The definition of the Middle East and North Africa that we use here is a traditional one and includes the Arabic-speaking lands, the Ottoman

Empire, Turkey, and Iran and Afghanistan. We did not include the former Soviet republics or India because in recent times they shared little of the common history of the Middle East; their main connection is that of Islam. Furthermore, they were politically separated from the region in the twentieth century. Although Middle Eastern Jews form the majority of the population in Israel, their story requires a separate discussion, as do the communities of Middle Eastern and North African Jewry in France, Australia, and the Americas. An examination of the role of Middle Eastern and North African Jewry in Eretz Israel until 1948, however, is integral to this study because the standard histories of the period before the Ashkenazi immigration and the Zionist period neglect Middle Eastern Jews and their contributions to language, economics, and political life.

A note on transliteration. We wrote the book with the American reader in mind and designed it to be user friendly. For commonplace names and those of people often in the news, we have generally used standard American usage, according to *Merriam Webster's Collegiate Dictionary.* Thus we refer to the president of Egypt as Nasser instead of Abd al-Nasir. Hebrew words usually conform to the *Encyclopedia Judaica.* For Arabic, Persian, and Turkish we used the transliteration system of the *International Journal of Middle East Studies* and that adopted by the *Encyclopedia of the Modern Middle East.* For North Africa we maintained French transliteration for names of people and organizations. Arabic terms in the Ottoman context have maintained Turkish transliteration. Unless otherwise noted, the contributors did their own translations of material that they have quoted.

This book would not have been possible without the pioneering work of many scholars from whom we have learned. Only a few of the important works are *A Mediterranean Society* and the numerous studies of the Jews of the region by S. D. Goitein; *The Jews of the Middle East* by Hayyim J. Cohen and his and Zvi Yehuda's bibliography; and Norman Stillman's two volumes of documents, *The Jews of Arab Lands* and *The Jews of Arab Lands in Modern Times.* Others are represented by the authors who have graciously contributed to this book.

This book would also not have been possible without the generous support of the Maurice Amado Foundation, American Friends of the Alliance Israélite Universelle, Ashkelon Academic College of Israel (under the academic auspices of Bar-Ilan University), Brooklyn College of the City University of New York, the Center for Israel and Jewish Studies of Columbia University, the consul general of Israel, the Lucius N. Littauer Foundation, the Memorial Foundation for Jewish Culture, the Middle East Institute of

Columbia University, Jamie and Mickey Shamah of the Raphael Foundation, and the Ezra Zilkha Foundation. We owe a special thanks to Richard Bulliet, Martha Goldstein, Mehrdad Izady, Sheila A. Spector; to Michael Glatzer and Sarit Noy of the Ben-Zvi Institute; and to Polly Kummel, Anne Routon, Peter Dimock, Ron Harris, and Kate Wittenberg of Columbia University Press.

A final note. This book is geared to a varied audience. It is for scholars. It is for teachers in secondary schools as well as college and university professors who wish to teach about all cultures of the mosaic that once existed in the Middle East and to teach about all Jews, to study them comparatively, and to place the "Others" on the same playing field as the now dominant European majority. It is for the people of the communities who are eager for their stories to be told. And it is for the children and grandchildren of Jews of Sephardic and Middle Eastern origin who now live in Europe, the Americas, and Israel and who come to our classes aching to learn about their culture and their history.

Contributors

Ammiel Alcalay teaches at Queens College, New York. His books include *After Jews and Arabs: Remaking Levantine Culture* (1993), *The Cairo Notebooks* (1993), *Keys to the Garden: New Israeli Writing* (1996), and *Memories of Our Future: Selected Essays 1982–1999* (1999). He has also edited and translated numerous books from Bosnia, including *Sarajevo: A War Journal* (1993), by Zlatko Dizdarevic; *The Tenth Circle of Hell* (1996), by Rezak Hukanovic; and *Sarajevo Blues* (1998), by Semezdin Mehmedinovic.

Eliezer Bashan teaches in the Department of Jewish History at Bar-Ilan University in Israel. His major works include *Captivity and Ransom in the Mediterranean: Jewish Society, 1391–1830* (1980), *Studies in the History of the Jews in the Orient and North Africa* (1996), *The Anglican Missions and the Jews of Morocco in the Nineteenth Century* (1991), *The Taragano Family: Jewish Diplomats in the Dardanelles, 1699–1817* (1999), and *The Jews of Morocco: Their Past and Culture* (2000).

Issachar Ben-Ami is a senior researcher and lecturer in the Department of Jewish and Comparative Folklore at the Hebrew University of Jerusalem. He is the author of several books, including *Moroccan Jewry: Ethno-Cultural Studies* (Hebrew and French), *Jewish Holy Men of Morocco and Their Miracles* (Hebrew, 1994), *Thousand and One Jewish Proverbs from Morocco* (Hebrew, 1975), and *Saint Veneration Among the Jews in Morocco* (English, 1998).

David M. Bunis teaches in the Department of Romance Studies and Jewish Languages at the Hebrew University of Jerusalem. Among his many studies published recently are "The Language of the Sephardim: An Historical Overview," in Haim Beinhart, ed., *The Sephardi Legacy* (1992); *A Lexicon of the Hebrew and Aramaic Elements in Modern Judezmo* (1993); and *Voices from Jewish Saloniki* (1999).

Joseph Chetrit is vice rector of the University of Haifa, where he teaches linguistics and is director of the Center for the Study of Jewish Culture in Spain and Muslim Countries. He is the editor of *Miqqedem Umiyyam* and the author of *Piyyut and Hebrew Poetry in Morocco* (1999) and *Diversité* *intra-linguistique à discours: Etudes socio-pragmatiques sur des langues Juives* (in press).

David Cohen is a senior research fellow at the Institute for Research of Pioneer and Zionist Movements in Muslim Lands at the Yad Tabenkin Foundation, Ramat Ef 'al. He has written numerous studies on the Jews of France, Algeria, and Morocco, including *La promotion des Juifs en France a l'époque du second empire, 1852–1870* (1980).

Jane S. Gerber is professor of Jewish history and director of the Institute for Sephardic Studies at the Graduate Center of the City University of New York. She is the author of *Jewish Society in Fez: 1450–1700* (1980), and *The Jews of Spain: A History of the Sephardic Experience* (1992), for which she won the National Jewish Book Award in 1993.

Joseph B. Glass lectures in the Department of Geography at the Rothberg International School and is the academic coordinator of the Halbert Centre for Canadian Studies, both at the Hebrew University of Jerusalem. He has written on the role of Sephardi entrepreneurs in the development of Eretz Israel and is the author of *From New Zion to Old Zion: American Jewish Immigration and Settlement in Palestine, 1917–1939* (2002).

Harvey E. Goldberg teaches in the Department of Sociology and Anthropology at the Hebrew University of Jerusalem. He is author of *Jewish Life in Muslim Libya: Rivals and Relatives* (1990) and editor of *Sephardi and Middle Eastern Jewries: History and Culture in the Modern Era* (1996).

George E. Gruen has taught at Columbia University and Brooklyn College and was the director of Middle East Affairs at the American Jewish Committee from 1962 to 1990. His publications include "Dynamic Progress in Turkish-Israeli Relations," *Israel Affairs* 2 (1995); "Turkey and the Middle East after Oslo I," in Robert O. Freedman, ed., *The Middle East Peace Process After the Oslo Agreements* (1998); and "Defining Limits on Religious Expression in Public Institutions: The Turkish Dilemma," *Jewish Political Studies Review* 11 (1999).

Esther Juhasz teaches in the Department of Jewish and Comparative Folklore at the Hebrew University of Jerusalem. Her publications include *Sephardi Jews in the Ottoman Empire: Aspects of Material Culture* (1989).

Ruth Kark teaches in the Geography Department at the Hebrew University of Jerusalem. She is the author of sixteen books, including *American Consuls in the Holy Land, 1832–1914* (1994), *Land and Settlement in Eretz Yisrael:*

Selected Papers (1995), and *Jerusalem and Its Environs: Quarters, Neighborhoods, Villages, 1800–1948* (2001).

Mark Kligman is associate professor of Jewish musicology at Hebrew Union College–Jewish Institute of Religion, New York, where he specializes in the liturgical traditions of Middle Eastern Jewish communities. His publications include "Music in Judaism" in *The Encyclopedia of Judaism* (2000). He was editor of the Jewish terms for *Workshop Music: A Concise Dictionary* (2000), which covers liturgical music.

Bat-Zion Eraqi-Klorman teaches history at the Open University of Israel. Her recent publications include *The Jews of Yemen in the Nineteenth Century: A Portrait of a Messianic Community* (1993); "Jewish Immigration from Yemen to Palestine during the 1920s and 1930s," *Miqqedem Umiyyam* (2000); and "The Forced Conversion of Jewish Orphans in Yemen," *International Journal of Middle East Studies* 33 (2001).

Jacob M. Landau is professor emeritus of political science at the Hebrew University of Jerusalem. He has published widely in the field of Middle Eastern and Islamic studies. His recent books are *The Politics of Pan-Islam: Ideology and Organization* (1993), *Jews, Arabs, Turks* (1993), *Pan-Turanism: From Irredentism to Cooperation* (1995), and *Politics of Languages in the Ex-Soviet Muslim States* (with Barbara Kellner-Heinkele, 2001).

Michael Menachem Laskier teaches in the Department of Middle East History at Bar-Ilan University, Ramat-Gan, and chairs the Political Science Department at Ashqelon Academic College in Israel. He has written 130 articles and eight books, including *Israel and the Arab World: Israeli-Maghrebi Mutual Interests, Encounters, and the Arab-Israeli Conflict* (forthcoming).

Jean-Marc Ran Oppenheim has written on cultural imperialism in the Middle East and on sports. He was born in Egypt, lived through the Suez Crisis, and emigrated shortly thereafter. He teaches at New York University, Fordham, and Brooklyn College of the City University of New York.

Sara Reguer chairs the Department of Judaic Studies of Brooklyn College of the City University of New York, publishes in the fields of Jordan River politics, the history of Jewish women, World War I, and Palestine under the British mandate. Her publications include "Pinchas Rutenberg and the Jordan River," *Middle Eastern Studies* 31 (1995); "Controversial Waters," *Middle Eastern Studies* 29 (1993); and "Churchill's Role in the Dardanelles Campaign," *British Army Review* 108 (1994).

Aron Rodrigue is the Eva Chernov Lokey Professor of Jewish Studies and professor of history at Stanford University. His recent publications include *Images of Sephardi and Eastern Jewries in Transition, 1860–1939* (1993), *French Jews, Turkish Jews: The Alliance Israélite Universelle and the Politics of Jewish Schooling in Turkey, 1860–1925* (1990), and (with Esther Benbassa) *Sephardi Jewry: The Judeo-Spanish Community, Fourteenth–Twentieth Centuries* (2000).

Haim Saadoun is dean of students at the Open University of Israel and teaches at Haifa University. His publications include *Zionism in Tunisia: 1918–1948* (1992), *Zionist Underground Activity in Muslim Countries* (1997), and *Open and Secret Mass Immigration to Israel from Muslim Lands, 1948–1967* (1999). He is chief editor of the voluminous Middle Eastern Communities Project at the Ben-Zvi Institute.

Haideh Sahim specializes in ancient Iranian linguistics and worked on the *Encyclopaedia Iranica* from 1989 to 1998. Among her publications are "The Dialects of the Jews of Iran" (in Persian), in *Terua 1: The History of Contemporary Iranian Jews* (1996); "The Dialect of the Jews of Hamadan," *Irano-Judaica* (1994); and "Memoirs of Iranian Jews" (in Persian), *Iran Nameh* (1997); and "Iranian Jews in the Qajar Period," *Proceedings of the Conference on Religion and Society in Qajar Iran* (in press).

Reeva Spector Simon is the author of *Iraq Between the Two World Wars* (1986) and the forthcoming *Terrorists, Fanatics, and Spies: The Middle East in Twentieth-Century Thrillers and Detective Novels.* She is coeditor of *The Origins of Arab Nationalism* (1991) and the *Encyclopedia of the Modern Middle East* (1996). Since 1993 she has been the assistant director of the Middle East Institute, Columbia University.

Rachel Simon is an independent scholar at Princeton University. She publishes widely on the Middle East and North Africa. Her publications include *Libya Between Ottomanism and Nationalism* (1987) and *Change Within Tradition Among Jewish Women in Libya* (1992).

Zvi Zohar is a senior research fellow at the Shalom Hartmen Institute of Advanced Judaic Studies in Jerusalem and at Bar-Ilan University; he is also a founding faculty member of Paideia—The European Institute for Jewish Studies in Sweden. His most recent book is *The Luminous Face of the East: Studies in the Legal and Religious Thought of Sephardic Rabbis of the Middle East* (2001).

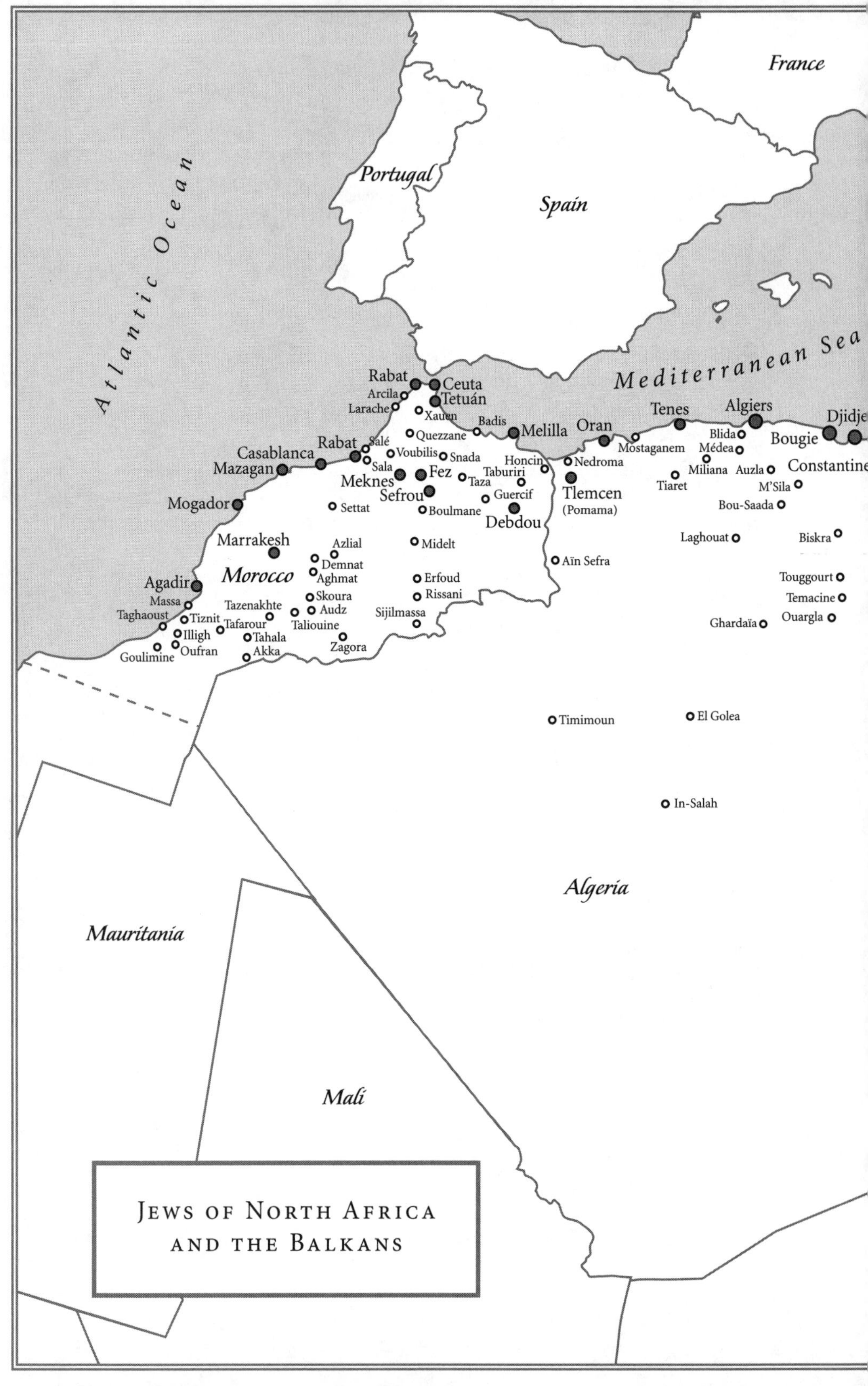

Jews of North Africa and the Balkans

Hungary
Romania
Bosnia
Sarajevo
Italy
Yugoslavia
Black Sea
Bulgaria
Sofia
Skopje
Macedonia
Albania
Salonika
Greece
Ioanina
Turkey
Mateur
Bizerta
Utica
Tunis
Souk ed Arba
Soliman
Le Kef
Nabeul
Kairouan
Sousse
Monastir
Mahdia
Malta
Hadjeb el Aioun
Gafsa
El Guettar
Sfax
Tozeur
Gabés
Djerba
Zarzis
Mediterranean Sea
Ben-Gardane
Zuara
Tripoli
Tunisia
Khoms
Yefran
Nalut
Mesallara
Misurata
Jado
Ghuryan
Benghazi
Derna
Sirte
Tripolitania
Cyrenaica
Fezzan
Zawilah
Matzuk
Libya
Egypt
Niger
Chad
Sudan

Jews of the Middle East
Macedonia
Albania
Greece
Black Sea
Ukraine
Georgia
Armenia
Edirne
Kirkareli
Istanbul
Gallipoli
Ankara
Bursa
Eskisehir
Edremit
Bergama
Menemen
Izmir
Tire
Milas
Baskale
Urmla
Adana
Antep
Kilis
Mersin
Alexandretta
Aleppo
Zakho
Mosul
Arbil
Sulaimaniya
Halabja
Kirkuk
Saqqiz
Cyprus
Latakia
Hama
Tartus
Homs
Syria
Tripoli
Baalbek
Lebonan
Beirut
Damascus
Sidon
Tyre
Safed
Acre
Haifa
Irbid
Mafraq
Jaffa
Nablus
Tel Aviv
Jerusalem
Hebron
Amman
Ma'an
Israel
Jordan
Mediterranean Sea
Tigris River
Euphrates
Khanaqin
Hilla
Ramadi
Baghdad
Iraq
Amara
River
Nasiriya
Alexandria
Rosetta
Damietta
Port Said
Damanhour
Tanta
Mansura
Ismailia
Cairo
Libya
Fayum
Tigris River
Asyut
Egypt
Nile River
Luxur
Aswan
Saudi Arabia
Red Sea
Port Sudan
Sudan
Najran
Sa'dah
Maydi
Amran
Luhayyah
Kaukaban
San'a
Eritrea
Hudaydah
Dhamar
Ibb
Mukha
Qa'baba
Ethiopia

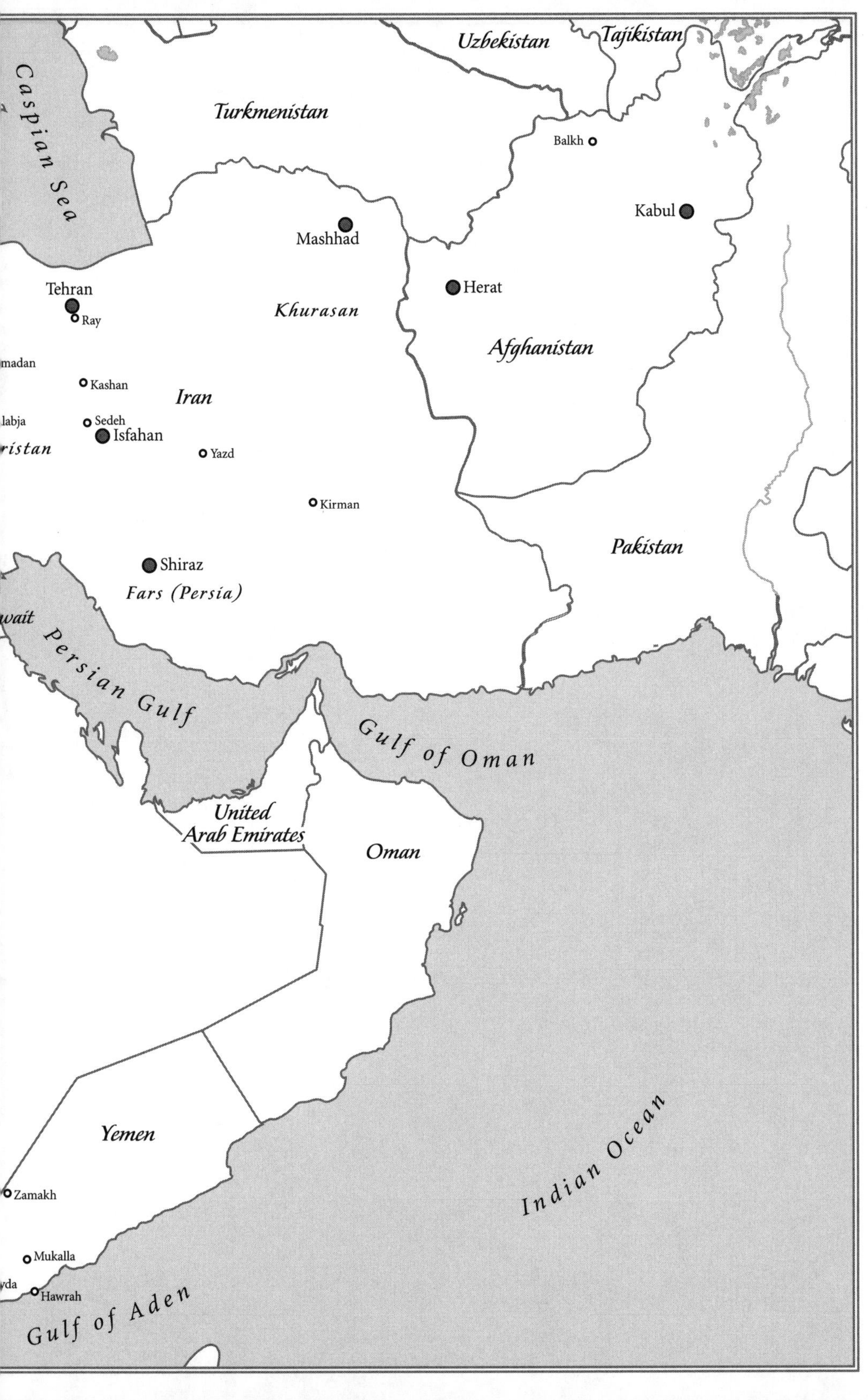

Uzbekistan
Tajikistan
Caspian Sea
Turkmenistan
Balkh
Kabul
Mashhad
Tehran
Ray
Herat
Khurasan
Afghanistan
Kashan
Iran
Sedeh
Isfahan
Yazd
Kirman
Pakistan
Shiraz
Fars (Persia)
Persian Gulf
Gulf of Oman
United
Arab Emirates
Oman
Yemen
Zamakh
Indian Ocean
Mukalla
Hawrah
Gulf of Aden

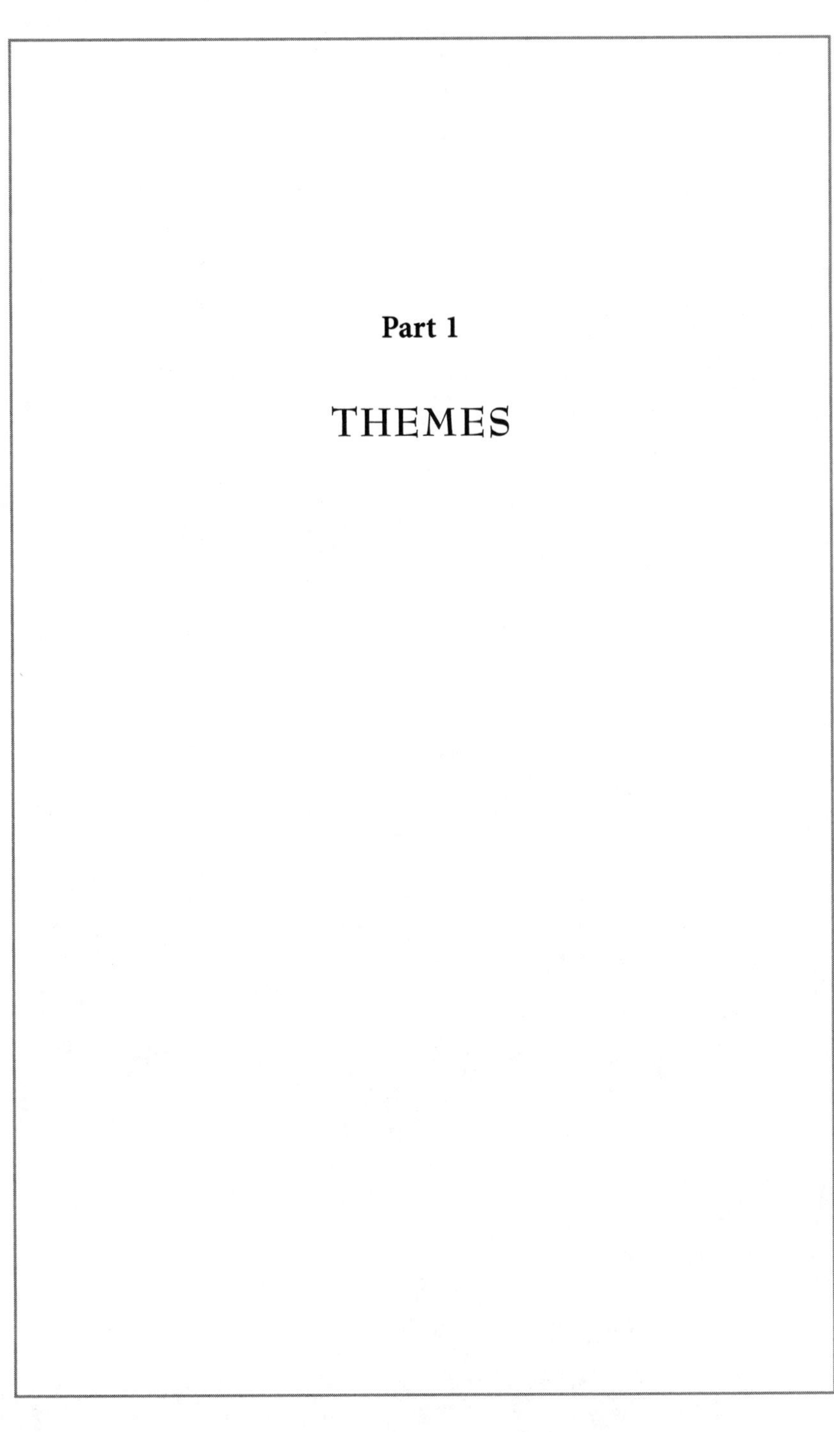

Part 1

THEMES

CHAPTER

1

History of the Jews in the Middle East and North Africa from the Rise of Islam Until 1700

Jane S. Gerber

On the eve of the birth of Islam most of world Jewry lived under Byzantine or Persian rule in the lands of the Mediterranean basin. Although Jews languished in those empires, they formed a lively presence on the Arabian Peninsula, with some Jewish tribes holding conspicuous power in important oases where the prophet Muhammad would preach his new message. Muhammad (571–632 C.E.) was familiar with and impressed by Jewish traditions, such as the indivisibility of the One God, the urgency of repentance before a Day of Judgment dawned, the centrality of prayer and charity in the individual's dealings with other human beings, and the honored place of Abraham and Moses as Lawgivers. Muhammad reached out to the Jews as potential followers, offering himself as the seal of prophecy. When ignored or rebuffed by the Jews, Muhammad's passionate new religion began to differentiate itself from Judaism and Christianity, vociferously condemning the Jews. Although he found it expedient to retain a sense of the partial legitimacy of Judaism, Muhammad was harsh and decisive in his day-to-day dealings with the Jewish tribes of Arabia, subjugating some, deporting or decapitating all males in others. Such precedents born out of the fledgling faith's daily encounters with the older and more established tradition would be embodied in the Qur'an and the traditions of the Prophet and thereby incorporated in the hallowed faith of Islam. In this literature of polemics, as enunciated in the core of Muhammad's exchanges with the Jews, the Jewish people were vilified as "corrupters of Scripture," "accursed by Allah," and consigned to a fate of "perpetual humiliation and wretchedness."

After Muhammad's death in 632, militant Muslim forces surged out of Arabia, conquering vast territories from the Byzantines and Persians. The Muslim forces did not seek the conversion of Jews and Christians; instead, the Muslims found Jews and Christians to be vital to the administration and prosperity of their emerging empire and hoped both to employ Christians and Jews and have them fill the coffers of state. The Muslims soon began to create a policy of toleration, on a low level, that would accomplish these goals. They gradually devised a system of protections that were combined with disabilities (legal disqualifications) in a series of decrees that eventually, though erroneously, became known as the "Covenant" or the "Pact of Umar."

Islam viewed the world as divided in two, the world of Islam and the world of war. Everything not under Islam was to be subdued in battle or through capitulation and surrender. But Islam carved out a niche within the world of Islam for the so-called protected peoples (*dhimmis*), the Jews and Christians, whose Scriptures assured them of some legitimacy and protection. The Muslim toleration of the Jews would soon prove to be ambiguous, the terms of the Pact of Umar varying over time and space. On the one hand, Muslims guaranteed Jews the vital recognition of their faith and the assurance that they would not be forced to accept Islam; on the other, Muslims enjoined Jews to submit to the dominant faith, to pay tribute, and to be humbled. In time Muslim jurists worked out an elaborate system of symbols and signs that was intentionally degrading. For example, they required *dhimmis* to wear distinguishing and at times ridiculous clothing. Muslims expected synagogues and churches to be modest and their rites inconspicuous. Christians and Jews could not bear arms or ride horses and had to pay special discriminatory taxes in the form of a head tax (*jizya*) as well as a land tax. While implementation of the various details of the Pact of Umar was subject to the whims of local leaders and regional variations, it served as a compelling guide. Too great a deviation could provoke religious reformers and fundamentalist outrage. In general, during the early centuries of Islam, while the Muslim world was expanding and its civilization was dynamic, Jews enjoyed a fairly liberal interpretation of their legal disqualifications. During the later centuries of Islam, a growing intolerance marked Muslim policy toward Jews. Throughout, discriminatory taxes and extortionate levies remained a constant bane of Jewish existence.

On balance, the "protected status" of *dhimmi* had offered the Jews several important concessions. Islam permitted the Jews to live according to their own laws and customs, recognizing the right of *dhimmis* to travel freely throughout the Muslim world, except in the Arabian Peninsula. Most occupations and professions were open to Jews and Christians, even ones that accorded esteem and wealth to their practitioners. Synagogues and churches were not to be vandalized, although they should not be too grand in scale. In general, the disabilities that the *dhimmis* encountered were related to questions of status and prestige; thus, for example, *dhimmis* should not hold public office, nor should they serve in positions of authority over Muslims. The second-class status accorded the Jews was not really onerous within the medieval context. In fact, the blend of religious guarantees and subtle discriminations did not strike the Jews as particularly menacing, and the emerging affluence of the world of Islam soon proved to be a magnet. From the eighth through the twelfth centuries fully 85 percent of world Jewry resided in Muslim lands. As economic and political conditions of the Muslim world deteriorated in the later Middle Ages, the harsh features of Islam vis-à-vis *dhimmis* became pronounced, compounding the insecurity of Jewish communities.

JEWISH ECONOMY AND SOCIETY UNDER MEDIEVAL ISLAM

The rapid conquests by Islam in the seventh and eighth centuries brought most of the Mediterranean region and beyond under Muslim rule. When the dust of battle finally settled, the world of Islam stretched from Spain and Morocco in the west to the Indian subcontinent, Central Asia, and the Gobi Desert in the east. With the initial period of dynamic expansion completed by the eighth century, Muslims had established a virtual free-trade zone in the Mediterranean. New cities such as Fez, Kairouan, Fustat (Cairo), Ramla, and Baghdad soon emerged from the nuclei of Muslim garrisons. Trade quickened, and people released pent-up energies as they repaired old routes of commerce and established new avenues of trade. A new economic unity of the Mediterranean emerged, and Jewish settlements began to flourish in the growing centers of Muslim worship and trade. In the case of older cities, such as Alexandria and Antioch, the Jewish communities revived and expanded. In each new or expanded Jewish community people built or restored synagogues, a clear indication that Muslims only gradually articulated and sporadically implemented the disabilities of the Pact of Umar.

The medieval Muslim city was a mosaic of peoples and trades. No exclusively Jewish neighborhoods were compulsory in the Muslim towns during the high Middle Ages, although areas of Jewish residential concentration were common; in fact, in the heyday of Islam the residential concentration of the various religious or ethnic groups was common. Generally speaking,

Jews preferred to live for security reasons in walled neighborhoods with gates that they could bar. Such residential segregation was not necessarily discriminatory, because Middle Eastern cities had, from their beginnings, been organized socially and economically along kinship or tribal lines. Nevertheless, Jews, Muslims, and Christians often lived side by side, sometimes even around the same courtyard. Compulsory Jewish residential quarters, or ghettos (the *haras* and *mellahs* of North Africa), were not introduced until the fifteenth century, causing a severe economic blow and source of great hardship.

Trade was fundamental to Islam from its beginning, in some measure because Muhammad had been a merchant in Mecca. Muslim tradition consequently accorded high esteem to the profession of merchant. In addition, other forces began to propel Jews out of agriculture and into commerce. Because Jews were subjected to discriminatory taxes on their agricultural produce (the *kharaj*), and observed self-imposed regulations (such as letting the land lie fallow during the seven-year cycle of cultivation), competing with Muslims in agriculture became increasingly difficult. Jews would abandon their homesteads rather than change their religion in order to avoid taxation. Thus soon after the Arab conquests around 650 C.E., particularly in Iran and Iraq, Jews emerged as an urban minority in the new commercial centers of Islam.

As Muslims began to chart land routes and secure freedom of passage on the seas by the ninth century, Jews also circulated freely over long distances with a remarkable degree of casualness. Greater safety en route was only one reason for the quickening of Jewish commerce. Jews could call upon their widespread coreligionists in business, both throughout the Mediterranean and beyond, because they shared a common language, Hebrew, and a common legal system. Under medieval Muslim law, the law was personal, not territorial, so people were judged by the jurists of their religious community. For almost one thousand years before the rise of Islam, Jews had lived according to their own legislative system, building an elaborate self-governing code of law, the Talmud. The Muslims' recognition of Jewish autonomy merely bolstered an already established fact of Jewish life. Hospitality to itinerant coreligionists facilitated Jews' travel over vast distances; as a result Jewish merchants were intrepid, secure in the knowledge that they could board safely in Jewish homes or would be ransomed by other Jews should they be captured by the ubiquitous pirates in the Mediterranean, Red Sea, or Indian Ocean.

The Muslim conquests opened a new world of mobility and adventure for Jews, who began to commute regularly between Spain, Sicily, Egypt, Aden, and the Indian Ocean, aided by the books of geography flowing from the pens of Arab scholars. Jewish documents spanning almost one thousand years, preserved in an old synagogue in Fustat (and known as the Cairo Geniza), reveal how natural it was for Jews to be on the move. The people who wrote the Geniza documents were fairly oblivious to political boundaries. Jewish merchant families moved back and forth between the rival kingdoms of Islam and Christendom, becoming standardbearers of the new cosmopolitan Mediterranean civilization, in direct contact with other Jews over vast areas and possessing shared tastes and technologies. The religious calendar determined the rhythm of Jewish life everywhere, including the comings and goings of itinerant Jewish merchants. As one Geniza correspondent wrote, "The synagogue is desolate, for the Maghrebis [North Africans] have left."

Jewish documents in the Cairo Geniza are striking for the enormous variety of goods mentioned as manufactured or traded by Jews. All forms of textiles, spices, staples, and luxuries passed through Cairo on their way east and west, as well as north and south. From such documentary evidence it appears that Jews were the first to grasp the importance of credit and its utility in long-distance trade, devising instruments of credit (known by the Persian term *suftaja*) for trade over long distances in the eighth or ninth centuries. Jewish bankers at the court of the caliphs in Baghdad were instrumental in devising these new modes of economic exchange.

From a ninth-century Arabic account we learn incidentally of the remarkable commercial activities of a Jewish international trading firm, known as the Radanites, that stretched across several continents. The Radanites' representatives spoke a variety of languages and followed four distinct land and sea routes through Europe and the Middle East, all the way to China. Because dangers of shipwreck or piracy always lurked, Jewish merchants often provided provisional divorces to their wives. Among the most fascinating trading posts reached by the Radanites was the kingdom of the Khazars, which emerged in the Crimean area of Khazaria in the eighth century. The conversion of its king to Judaism may have represented a calculated political declaration of neutrality for a kingdom wedged between the borders of warring Byzantium and Islam. Nevertheless, this foothold in the Caucasus encouraged a growing diaspora of Persian-speaking Jews in Central Asia, and they continued to live in the region long after the fall of the Jewish kingdom in the tenth century.

The international traders were undoubtedly the most high-profile members of the Jewish community under Islam, but most Jews followed more modest professions, earning a living as local merchants, craftsmen, or artisans. Petty trade and modest professions were the mainstay of Jewish economic endeavor. In the early years of Islam Jewish craftsmen were distinguished for their high degree of intricate specialization, especially within the textile and silk trade. From the Geniza cache, the historian S. D. Goitein has identified more than 350 occupations that Jews engaged in during the height of Islam. Some, such as gold- and silversmithing, remained a monopoly of Jewish craftsmen until the modern era, the secrets of the trade transmitted from father to son for generations.

Because Jews considered the family to be the ideal form of business partnership, they moved far and wide for the sake of contracting marriages for their offspring while also establishing or consolidating branches of business. Jewish women were also economic agents, playing roles in manufacturing and, to a lesser extent, in commerce. Marriage contracts often stated that the woman was entitled to retain her earnings, usually gained through spinning or weaving. In contrast to Muslim women, most of whom were secluded in their homes, Jewish female brokers circulated freely, serving as vendors to Muslim women confined to the home or the palace in Fatimid Egypt in the eleventh century and in Ottoman Turkey in the sixteenth century. Some Jewish women were physicians and even occasionally teachers and scribes. Some obtained literacy through parental instruction, others through eavesdropping as their brothers were tutored at home. A few Geniza documents were composed and transcribed by women, not dictated to men. A Bible codex penned by a woman is known from fourteenth-century Yemen. In the colophon the calligrapher, daughter of a scribe, apologizes that her work is of such poor quality, explaining that she was nursing a child while working. Women frequently played a decisive role in the rearing and education of their children. Barred from any role in the synagogue or the school, the source of honor and prestige in the Jewish community, Jewish women were nonetheless listed in the Geniza as donors to charity and synagogue buildings, a clear indication of their status as independent owners of property.

In the early centuries of Islam Jews engaged in virtually every occupation, but poverty was also common. During the Middle Ages approximately one-quarter of the Jewish community depicted in the Cairo Geniza could be categorized as beggars. After the twelfth century poverty increased among the Jews, as did the number of men and women engaged in modest handicrafts and petty commerce. The abundant Geniza charitable lists testify to the vicissitudes of wealth and misfortune, as well as the recognition of the importance of communal solidarity.

Every Muslim country produced its share of Jewish physicians, fathers bequeathing their knowledge and clientele to their sons and occasionally to their daughters. Medicine formed a prominent part of the curriculum of a young man's schooling in medieval Spain and North Africa. Service as a physician at court often opened the doors to leadership in the Jewish community, as in the cases of Hasdai ibn Shaprut in tenth-century Ummayad Spain and Moses Hamon in sixteenth-century Istanbul. The first official heads of the Jewish community of Fatimid Egypt (tenth through twelfth centuries) were Tunisian doctors who had arrived with the conquerors from the west. The trusted physician frequently became an administrator, organizing taxes and customs duties. As late as 1618 forty Jewish physicians served at the sultan's court in Istanbul, even though the Jewish community of the Ottoman Empire had passed the apex of its power and influence. Some Jews gained access to the court through their verbal skills. Thus, for example, Samuel ibn Nagrela, the poet and halakhist (exegete and legal scholar) in eleventh-century Spain, is said to have risen from a modest position as a royal secretary to the position of vizier and commander of troops in the medieval princedom of Granada. Such prominence was not without dangers; when ibn Nagrela's less talented son, Joseph, succeeded his father, Joseph's high-handedness provoked a pogrom in Granada in 1066. One complaint was that an infidel Jew should not wield power over Muslims.

By the thirteenth century the Geniza records reflect a palpable change in the economic life of the Jews. Terrorized at an earlier date by the Almohades, an Islamic movement of puritanical fundamentalists in Spain and North Africa, barred from Muslim guilds, pushed out of overseas commerce by the Italian city-states, and increasingly subjected to the strictures of the Pact of Umar, the Jews of the Middle East were gradually reduced to petty trade (peddling) and simple manufacturing. Only with the arrival of the Sephardic exiles after the persecutions and expulsions from Spain of 1391 and 1492 did the economic profile of the Jews experience a temporary upswing.

JEWISH COMMUNAL AND INTELLECTUAL LIFE IN MUSLIM LANDS

Medieval Jews lived in societies where one's religion dictated everything. The larger Muslim community expected Jews to live according to their own laws and to pay their taxes through their community. Indeed, the fiscal structure of the empire enhanced Jewish self-government, because the Muslim authorities were primarily interested in the minorities as a tribute-paying population. As the Muslim conquerors moved into the heart of the ancient Persian Empire, they formally recognized the old, weak institutions of Jewish leadership, lending them a new prestige. In Iraq, Muslims recognized the institution of the exilarch as the head of the Jews there and, by extension, of the Jews in the entire Abbasid Empire. The exilarch sat in the royal council of the caliph in Baghdad and exercised great authority over the Jews; he shared his power with the heads of the two main seats of intellectual power in Iraq, the academies of learning (yeshivas) of Sura and Pumbedita, which were transferred to Baghdad during the period of the Abbasid caliphate. Palestine's yeshiva also received a new lease on life with the Arab conquest and the revival of Jewish life in Jerusalem in the eighth and ninth centuries.

Everywhere in the Islamic world, local Jewish communities ruled themselves, a practice that was in accordance with ancient precedents. Power resided in scholarly leaders who were frequently joined by marriage to merchant families. Courts of Jewish law adjudicated all matters affecting the Jewish people. Because actual copies of the Talmud were quite rare, and local Jewish learning was often inadequate to meet the needs of the people, scholars and laypeople alike would travel to the ancient seats of learning in Iraq. The Muslim conquests and the pacification of routes helped strengthen the spread of Jewish learning. Travel for the sake of knowledge was an honored tradition among Muslims and Jews. In addition, traveling merchants would carry queries to the *geonim* (interpreters of Jewish law and heads of the academies of Sura and Pumbedita) in Baghdad, transmitting their answers to the ports of origin and occasionally leaving copies of these precious documents along their travel route. These questions and answers (known as the responsa literature) formed the basis for the spread of some uniformity in tradition and practice among the far-flung Jewish communities.

Financial contributions from world Jewry flowed into the coffers of the academies of Iraq together with the halakhic queries. For several crucial centuries world Jewry turned to the Baghdad *geonim* for enlightenment, confident that the *geonim* were heirs to an ancient chain of tradition dating to the Babylonian exile. Thus a uniform Judaic tradition gradually emerged in the Mediterranean basin, and the precedents emanating from Iraq's scholars became the shared tradition of Jews from Spain to the Indian Ocean, as Sephardic and Middle Eastern Jews found themselves in one cultural orbit. So important was the work of the *geonim* in this process that the whole of the Middle Ages is sometimes known as the geonic period in Jewish history. By the time the routes of trade and communication broke down in the later Middle Ages, Middle Eastern Jewry had succeeded in developing its own cadre of local rabbinic leadership that could guide widely scattered and autonomous communities with a good degree of uniformity.

The Arab conquerors not only spread Islam but imparted their zeal for the language of their Scriptures, Arabic. The Arab claim that the truth of Islam lay in the beauty of the Arabic Qur'an presented a challenge to the Jews. For the first time they sought to explain the origins and definitions of the Hebrew vocabulary, to demonstrate that Hebrew was every bit as rich and supple as Arabic was. As Hebrew grammarians described the structure of the Hebrew language, they laid the foundations for revolutionary studies of the biblical literature and the birth of medieval Hebrew poetry, setting the stage for the golden age of Hebrew poetry that burst forth in tenth-century Muslim Spain and North Africa.

Between the tenth and the twelfth centuries the most fruitful encounter of Arab culture and the Jewish imagination was that which emerged in the courts of several dazzling centers of Islamic civilization in Spain. Vying with one another as patrons of the arts, Jewish courtiers mirrored Arab cultural tastes and lifestyle. The poetry of the convivial golden age was embedded in a materialistic way of life that allowed for the coexistence of religious and worldly impulses; a class of sophisticated Jewish intellectuals and poets served as communal leaders, religious bards, and arbiters of taste. Equally at home in the composition of charming poetry on frivolous themes and works of profound religious sensibility, the poetry of the golden age of Spain marked the high point of the Jewish immersion in Arab culture. Love of language was evident: Moses ibn Ezra, Solomon ibn Gabirol, Samuel ibn Nagrela, and Judah Halevi are among the most famous of the hundreds of poets who practiced their craft. The Islamic civilization in Spain also profoundly influenced Jewish art, architecture, leisure activities, and even modes of religious devotion. Andalusia was not alone in such development: Jews in Egypt, North Africa, and Sicily followed the Iberian cues with their own circles of Hebrew poets.

The Jews of the Middle East adopted Arabic and for the first time were profoundly exposed to the classics of antiquity, which inquisitive Muslim caliphs had commissioned for translation from Greek or Syriac. Gaining access to the new philosophical vocabulary of the Arabs meant gaining access to new theological concepts previously unfamiliar to the Jews. Whereas Jews had shunned the theological baggage of Hellenism, they now discovered in it an approach that was both attractive and challenging. In addition, because the Arabic language of culture and the language of the street were sufficiently similar, access to one provided access to the other as Jews began to share many aspects of Arab popular culture. Great Jewish thinkers like Saadia Gaon (tenth-century Baghdad) and Moses Maimonides (twelfth-century Spain, Morocco, and Egypt) mined the ancient and medieval classics to present Judaism as a rational body of beliefs, much in the spirit of the Muslim theologians of their day. In imitation of their neighbors the *geonim* began to codify and systematize Jewish tradition. Compilations of liturgy and philosophic introductions to Talmudic tractates provided a new texture to rabbinic civilization.

Islamic civilization was both religious and secular. Educated men of all faiths were exposed to a broad curriculum, with many neutral or semineutral cultural spheres, such as science, philosophy, and mathematics. Jews could share in these unself-consciously. Islamic civilization was especially compelling to Middle Eastern and Iberian Jewry during those centuries of its growth and accomplishment. The exciting cultural synthesis of Jewish thought with medieval Islam ended in the twelfth century, when the Almohades overran Spain and North Africa. Similar threats to Jewish survival also occurred on the peripheries of Islam, in Yemen. The Yemenis' sectarian policy of forced conversion, rare in the annals of Islam, forced the Jews into flight or into crypto-Judaism. As Jews from Spain and North Africa fled, they carried the fruits of the golden age with them to new centers of Jewish life. At the same time the breakdown in the unity of the Muslim empire allowed for growing regional variations of religious expression, some of which would also find resonances in Jewish life. Thus the local traditions of miracle workers, known as marabouts, in North African Islam would resonate among North African Jews.

INTELLECTUAL DISSENT IN JEWISH LIFE UNDER ISLAM

Remnants of ancient Judaic heterodoxy persisted in the Middle East alongside mainstream rabbinic Judaism. Even while the *geonim* and the exilarchs succeeded in creating a modicum of uniformity among the far-flung Jewries of the Muslim world, local customs continued to prevail. The sectarian conflicts that convulsed Islam in its early centuries of rule also affected the Jews. For example, militant messianic movements and shadowy messianic figures began to arise in remote areas of Iraq and Iran, preaching armed struggle against both Jewish and Muslim authority. Figures such as Abu Isa of Isfahan and his disciple Yudghan (d. 776) offered their naive rural followers a mixed message of messianic revolt, asceticism, and a blend of Jewish and Muslim practices. None of these movements posed a serious threat to the Jewish authorities, who quickly suppressed them with the military assistance of the Muslims. But the militant messianic pretenders played upon the deep yearning of the Jews to end their exile and found receptive audiences in provinces wracked by Muslim rebellions.

More serious than the ephemeral messianic movements was the ideological challenge posed by Karaism, a movement that had begun with a religious reformer, Anan ben David, in eighth-century Iraq. He eschewed the Talmud as written by mortals, and he raised serious questions about the validity of the rabbinic tradition and its expounders. He recommended that Jews seek legal guidance directly in the Bible, rather than through the rulings of the rabbis, based on Talmudic and geonic tradition. Anan ben David's adherents spread rapidly, stimulating a powerful response from the rabbis. To counter the Karaite challenge the *geonim* expanded their studies of the Bible and the Hebrew language. The Karaite call for a return to Zion, while embedded in unaccustomed asceticism and mourning, encouraged waves of Jews to settle anew in Jerusalem. While the rabbis ultimately contained the Karaite challenge, and rabbinic opposition eventually forced most Karaites to leave the world of Islam for Byzantium, a significant group of Karaites remained in Egypt until the twentieth century.

REVIVAL AND RENEWAL IN THE LATER MIDDLE AGES: THE SEPHARDIC INFLUX

Jewish life in Islamic lands entered a long period of decline following the Almohad persecutions. The military despotisms of Islamic rulers disrupted urban life, and trade declined precipitously. Then, pushed out of international trade by the ascendant seafaring Italian republics, and subjected to increasingly extortionate levies, Jewish communities suffered and decreased in the thirteenth and fourteenth centuries. The Islamic environment was no longer stimulating to Jewish intellectual life. The great academies of learning in Iraq and Palestine had long ceased to function, destroyed by the decay wrought by invading Mongols and crusaders. Then thousands of Sephardic Jews from Iberia and Majorca came into the region in the fourteenth, fifteenth, and sixteenth centuries, bringing a renewal of Jewish life.

In 1391 Catholics subjected the Jews of Spain to an orgy of violence for an entire year. When the pogroms ceased and an accounting of the slaughter was made, it became clear that tens of thousands of Jews had been murdered, tens of thousands had been forcibly converted to Christianity, and thousands more had fled. Entire circles of scholars and their students, such as Zemah Duran and his son Simon ben Zemah (1361–1444), reached the shores of North Africa. Algeria was their first port of call, but it was not the only one to receive the Sephardim. The victims of 1391 settled wherever they could: Albania, Crete, the Venetian Islands in the Dodecanese, Egypt, Syria, and Palestine. Their arrival was not a one-time event. Throughout the fifteenth century, culminating in the great expulsions of 1492 and 1497, wave after wave of Sephardim turned to the world of Islam.

The Sephardic exiles of 1492 infused new life and much controversy into the Middle Eastern Jewish communities. They tenaciously practiced and affirmed the superiority of their ancestral customs and precedents, introducing these into their new lands of residence. Yet decades of persecution had altered many practices, raising serious questions about the halakhic propriety of their marriages and divorces. Friction immediately broke out between local Jews (*toshavim*) and the Spanish exiles (*megorashim*) in Morocco. Parallel institutions, for the indigenous populations and for the newcomers, became common.

Wherever they arrived, the Sephardim would quickly assume the reins of leadership in politics and the economy. Their knowledge of Europe and European languages made them attractive business partners and diplomatic agents for local Muslim rulers. Jews' experience in the courts of Spain eased their entrée into local politics. To the delight of their Ottoman overlords many Jewish refugees had a practical knowledge of Europe and harbored deep resentment about the treatment they had received from Catholic Spain. Their loyalty to the Ottomans could scarcely be questioned. Sephardic craftsmen knew European technology and brought to the cities of Islam a welcome and valuable artisan supplement to the existing warrior and agrarian classes. Because the Sephardim settled everywhere in Ottoman lands, they began to develop a new Sephardic network, linking the dispersed refugees in North Africa with their coreligionists in Europe, the New World, and Asia. Their Castillian language could be heard alongside the Judeo-Arabic, Berber, or Greek of the native Jews of the Mediterranean rim. Eventually, Ladino, Castillian written in Hebrew script, would become the common tongue of much of Ottoman Jewry.

To the Sephardic exiles the most important destination was the ascendant Ottoman Empire. By the sixteenth century it seemed as if no force could stop the expansion of the Turkish forces into Europe. By that century's end almost half the Jews in the world found themselves under the rule of the Ottoman Turks. Ottoman imperial policy not only welcomed Jews but sought to increase their numbers in specific areas by requiring them to move. Some Jews were transferred from Thrace, Anatolia, and Rumelia to Istanbul; others were settled in Salonika, Rhodes, and Cyprus. Contemporaries deplored this policy of forced relocation, known as *sürgün,* for the cruelty and hardship that it inflicted. In the long run the combined imperial policy of conquest and deportation dispersed the Jews among the empire's leading new commercial centers. Salonika and Istanbul emerged as the prime Jewish communities in this new era. By 1550 Salonika, soon to be known as the Jerusalem of the Balkans, led all other Ottoman cities in Sephardic population, number and variety of congregations, diversity of talent, and abundance of rabbinic leaders. The older communities, such as Cairo, Jerusalem, and Aleppo, were also revitalized as the native Arabic-speaking Jews (*mustaʿarabin*) and the Sephardim intermingled. The population mix soon became even more complex as waves of émigrés from Italy, Germany, and Hungary also intermingled in the Balkans and Asia Minor.

The Ottoman system of local autonomy enabled the Jews to work out their own questions of language and cultural reconstruction. They founded a plethora of synagogues that bore the names of Italian provinces and many cities of Iberia. With so many congregations the multitude of Sephardic scholars who had made Istanbul, and especially Salonika, their home were able to find employment. For the first time the Ashkenazic Jews of Europe and the Sephardim of the Iberian Peninsula were thrown together, adding more frictions and ferment among the Jews. In time the initial divisions became muted. The great yeshiva established in Salonika in 1520 was a leveler; so too was the widely accepted code of law known as the *Shulhan Arukh* that was created by a Sephardic scholar, Rabbi Joseph Caro (1488–1575).

Despite the internal dissent caused by the heterogeneity of Ottoman Jewry, Jews tended to close ranks to assist the secret Jews in Iberia (many pretending to be Christian and known as Marranos or Conversos) or Jews in distress elsewhere. When Venice decided to expel its Jews in 1550, Salonika's leaders immediately invited the homeless families to live with them on a trial basis. When former Conversos were burned at the stake in the Italian port of Ancona in 1555, the great Ottoman Jewish leader Doña Grácia Mendés (1510–66) managed to organize a temporary Jewish economic boycott of that Italian port.

Perhaps the greatest innovation that the Sephardim brought to the world of Islam was the movable Hebrew type that they had recently introduced in Iberia. When they settled in Istanbul and Salonika, refugee printers from Spain and Italy established Hebrew presses. Soon a voluminous literature of rabbinic responsa flowed from the presses of Salonika and Istanbul. The early printings included editions of many rare manuscripts written by the last generation of scholars in Spain, saving these works from oblivion. Through the dissemination of Sephardic works in print, the cultural ideals of the Iberian elite survived the Jews' transition to the more culturally placid Levant. The relative affluence of a small Sephardic elite provided libraries, endowments for students, and subsidies for printing, thereby assuring the preservation of their tradition. The Ottoman Hebrew presses helped disseminate new currents of thought, such as the emergent school of mysticism known as Lurianic cabala, which emanated from Safed in Palestine. Long after all ties with Iberia were broken, the Hebrew and Ladino presses remained an active cultural force in Turkey, keeping abreast of ongoing literary trends in Madrid. The Ladino renaissance culminated in the creation in the eighteenth century of an encyclopedia of Bible stories and folktales known as the *Me-am Loᶜez.* A striking feature of Jewish intellectual life in the Ottoman Empire was that little exchange seems to have developed with the surrounding Turkish culture. The sole exception was music, with Jews adopting and adapting Turkish musical traditions for their own needs.

INTELLECTUAL CURRENTS IN THE OTTOMAN EMPIRE: MYSTICISM AND MESSIANISM

The image of restless vitality presented by Jewish economic and communal conditions during the sixteenth-century Ottoman Empire was only one face of the Jewish people. Behind the renewal and rebuilding, the Jews of Islam were torn by doubts about themselves and questions about why so many had converted in Spain and why God had subjected them to such enormous suffering. From their perspective the events continuing to rock Europe (especially the mighty Ottoman conquests in the heart of Christendom and the great battles of religious reformation in Christendom, with the continuing horrors of the Inquisition in Portugal) were surely part of some grand plan. Thus messianic stirrings once again animated the Jews. Paradoxically, these stirrings accelerated just as the Sephardim were settling down in new places—in the Atlas Mountains of Morocco, the Saharan reaches of Algeria, the steppes of Central Asia, the Galilee town of Safed, and the cosmopolitan commercial city of Izmir in Anatolia, in the heart of the empire. Just beneath the surface of the network of new communities were long-suppressed tensions of waiting for redemption and building in the present, hope and despair, that could easily prove volatile.

During the sixteenth century scholars from all over the Mediterranean gathered in the town of Safed in Palestine and studied mystical lore. Led by Isaac Luria (1534–72), Jewish mysticism assumed a new structure and was infused with messianic meaning. In Luria's view the suffering of the Jews was not a divine punishment; rather, it mirrored the divine state of exile. He taught that Jews were in a unique position, scattered everywhere, to assist God in restoring the wholeness of the universe if only they would understand events "properly" and act accordingly. The basic motif of Lurianic kabbalah was the notion of exile, with God experiencing the pains of exile with His people. Luria's comforting, albeit ambiguous, message began to spread to Izmir and Salonika as the printing press of Safed disseminated his ideas and those of his students. The Jews of Ottoman Turkey were ripe for a messianic explosion, and in the seventeenth century Shabbetai Zevi (1626–76) began his ill-fated career as the messiah, or so he was pronounced by a follower in 1665. His deeds provoked a messianic frenzy that soon spread into Europe. As Jewish commerce came to a halt in the bazaars of Istanbul and Izmir, the Ottoman authorities intervened and arrested the "false messiah," offering him the choice of conversion to Islam or death. He chose conversion and continued to preach messianism for the next decade.

The debacle of his conversion left the agitated Jewish world in a state of crisis. Many of his followers repented, appalled that they had been duped. Others continued to believe in his messiahship even after his death in 1676. Belief in Shabbetai Zevi became a burning issue in Turkey, with some rabbis maintaining their belief in his mission for decades. The paradox of a messiah who takes on a religion in which he does not believe was not lost on former Conversos; Shabbetai Zevi's conversion seemed to be a poignant reflection of their own haunted past. Turkish rabbinical authorities, fearful of renewed messianic outbursts, became extremely suspicious of innovation. The recurrence of messianism had to be carefully contained and returned to its legitimate place in daily prayers.

With the failure of the Sabbatean movement, and the conservative rabbinical response in its aftermath, the Jews of Muslim lands entered a new phase. The Ottoman Empire had begun its prolonged decay in the late sixteenth century, when the era of vigorous sultans ended in 1566 with Suleiman's death. New trade routes introduced by the voyages of the Dutch, Spaniards, and Portuguese were bypassing the Mediterranean commercial centers. Europe remained unaware of the pervasive decay of all layers of Ottoman society until 1683, when the Ottoman military failed for the second time to capture Vienna. Soon thereafter the Ottomans relinquished their choicest conquests in Europe, including Hungary and Serbia. The Muslim world, for various reasons, and the Jews of Islam, as a direct result of Ottoman decay, were soon in a state of stagnation.

The Jews remained a minority of diminishing importance in the world of Islam after the seventeenth century. Travelers to the region were struck by the abject poverty and disease rampant in the teeming Jewish quarters. Their golden ages under Umayyads, Abbasids, and the early Ottomans were but a distant memory—if they were remembered at all. As the European powers began to colonize some of North Africa and Arabian ports, the Jews began to look to Europe, hoping that an ascendant European Jewry could offer them the protection they now found wanting. At this juncture historians speak of the end of medieval times and the dawn of the modern era for the Sephardic and Middle Eastern Jews.

CHAPTER

2

Europe in the Middle East

Reeva Spector Simon

By the beginning of the eighteenth century, the Ottoman Empire, which had ruled much of the Muslim heartland, was on the decline militarily and economically. The Ottoman Turks, at war in the east against the newly emergent Safavi dynasty of Persia, whose adopted state religion of Shiite Islam was at odds with the Ottomans' Sunni Islam, barely controlled the border area of Iraq. The Ottomans had conquered this area in the sixteenth century and had left it to a local dynasty of military governors to rule. In North Africa the Ottomans ruled only Libya; Morocco, never under Ottoman authority, was ruled in part by a member of the Sharifian dynasty and in part by tribal warlords; authority in Tunisia, Algeria, and Egypt remained with local rulers who paid nominal obeisance to Istanbul. The expanding Habsburg and Russian empires gradually took Ottoman territories in Europe and Central Asia from the imperial corpus. The disintegration of Ottoman authority between the center, with its state bureaucracy, and the quasi-independent periphery destabilized the Islamic peace that had characterized the region during its golden age.

In the face of the European onslaught the Ottomans recognized their inherent military weakness and looked first to spiritual and then to temporal remedies. Loath in the past to interact even diplomatically with the Christian West, the authorities in Turkey and later in Tunisia and Persia now had to deal with Europe's obvious military superiority. Yet purchasing Western weapons and military expertise took capital that was in increasingly short supply. Governments could barely afford to pay the European mercenaries that they hired to train their armies or to buy the guns that the troops needed. Inflation caused by the flood of silver from the Spanish Americas, the depletion of local mines, the end of conquest and its accompanying infusion of wealth, and the failure to industrialize forced the Ottomans to borrow from Europe to pay for the arms that the Europeans supplied. As such interaction increased, European businessmen and diplomats took up residence in Muslim countries and were granted consular privileges and economic concessions. As Europe industrialized, it looked to the Middle East for new markets and agents who could facilitate trade.

When Napoleon Bonaparte stepped onto Egyptian soil in 1798, handing out leaflets proclaiming "Liberté, Egalité, et Fraternité," his military and scholarly expedition reflected Europe's new interest in the Middle East. He was sent to the Levant with troops to interfere with British economic hegemony from the Mediterranean to India. Like Alexander the Great, he took with him a corps of scholars—in this case to study the area that had produced Europe's Near Eastern roots. A by-product of the expedition was the discovery of the Rosetta Stone, which made deciphering hieroglyphics possible, thus creating the field of Egyptology. A similar breakthrough in reading ancient cuneiform came from British scholar-diplomats in Persia. These discoveries, along with a resurgence of Protestant evangelicalism in Britain and the United States during the early part of the nineteenth century, revived European interest in the Holy Land and the biblical Jews.

Though Napoleon failed to dislodge the British, France revived its medieval role as protector of Christians in the Holy Land and supported new educational and missionary initiatives in Syria and North Africa. Missionaries from England, most notably the London Society for the Promotion of Christianity Amongst the Jews, spread the Gospel. Various American Protestant groups and the Jesuits founded schools that were to be conduits of Westernization throughout the Ottoman Empire and Iran. Both Christians and Jews, primarily from wealthy families with international connections, began to attend these schools. Some Christian groups also exported European notions of anti-Semitism.

European military conquest followed economic and cultural intrusion. By World War I the political map of the Middle East had changed, as Algeria came under French rule outright in 1830; Tunisia (1881) and Morocco (1912) became French protectorates; and Egypt, which became virtually independent of the Ottoman Empire in the wake of Napoleon's invasion—to the point of occupying Syria from 1830 to 1840—was occupied by Britain in 1882. Britain had colonized Aden in 1829, and British fleets stopped at entrepôts in the Persian Gulf and Arabia that linked both economic and military interests from the Mediterranean to India. Russia and Austria-Hungary took over more Persian and Ottoman lands in the Balkans and the Crimea, and Italy occupied Libya.

During this process life for Jews in these areas changed. Their lives in Iran, Yemen, and Morocco remained stagnant or worsened, with the resuscitation of the most degrading *dhimmi* regulations and instances of forced conversion to Islam. Travelers reported overcrowded Jewish quarters, dilapidated synagogues, and lives of extreme poverty and disease. Nevertheless, while most Jews were poor, the community had always had an overlay of wealthy families that engaged in the monetary dealings that Islam forbade for Muslims. These families often acted also as economic middlemen between the rulers and the Europeans and between the Jewish communities and the local overlords. Whether as the sultan's merchants in Morocco or as trading families operating in the Persian Gulf, these Jews first competed with and later became agents for European economic interests. Their knowledge of Western languages facilitated entry into new niches created by European intrusion into the region. The Europeans needed translators, "fixers," intermediaries with the local authorities, and consular representatives, so Jews and Christians competed for these roles as protégés in Aleppo, Basra, and Jaffa. In exchange for their services they requested and sometimes received diplomatic protection from the European governments that they served, and later they received British, French, Italian, or Russian passports.

Western European Jewry was just coming into its own in the nineteenth century, with the process of emancipation—that of achieving political rights and equal justice under law—well under way in France, England, and some German principalities. At midcentury some Jews had come out of isolated tradition-bound communities; they had participated in revolutions, were members of the French Assembly, would soon be seated in the British Parliament, and would become mayors of cities and cabinet ministers, standing for election not as Jews but as citizens of the country. Some mingled with the literati in Paris and London and were part of the intelligentsia. Some advocated a Jewish version of secular education (Haskalah, or Enlightenment), a process that began in eighteenth-century Western Europe and gradually spread throughout the Jewish world. Just as Western Europeans viewed the peoples of the Middle East as exotic, these Jews viewed their brethren to the east and in Asia in the same way. The development of steamship travel and the proliferation of newspapers brought hitherto isolated regions to Europe's door. Jewish travelers and reporters visited the Middle East, reported on the state of their coreligionists, and deplored what they saw. Looking to their own successes in Western Europe, Jews galvanized their resources to try to emancipate their brethren.

When on February 5, 1840, a Capuchin friar disappeared in Damascus with his Muslim servant, and local Christians blamed the Jews for his death, leaders of Western Jewry took up the cause. The "blood libel," relatively rare in the Middle East but well known from medieval Europe, was an accusation that Jews murdered Christians to use their blood for the baking of matzo for Passover. The French consul supported the accusation that Jews had killed the missing friar because he had been under the consul's jurisdiction. Damascus authorities arrested, tortured, and exacted confessions from prominent Jews; several died and one converted to Islam.

Moses Montefiore of England and Adolphe Crémieux of France not only attempted to intercede with the Ottoman and Egyptian authorities but launched an international campaign to rescue the Jews. Montefiore (1784–1885) was a prominent British Jew who served as president of the Jewish Board of Deputies, the organization that represented Jewish interests in Britain. Crémieux (1796–1880) was a French attorney and advocate of Jewish causes who was a member of the Jewish Consistory of France, a quasi-governmental body that represented the interests of French Jews. The Jews were released in August, but the Egyptian authorities who were then ruling Syria refused to exonerate the Jews; the Ottoman sultan Abdülmecid I then denounced the blood libel and specified that the Jews were to be included in reforms that were under way in the empire.

The blood libel, known as the Damascus Affair of 1840, created new ties between Eastern Jewry and the Western powers. Where the French asserted their declared long-standing protective relationship with Middle Eastern Christians, Britain now supported the Jews. Whether because of political or religious motivations, Lord Ashley Cooper, later the seventh earl of Shaftesbury and the major supporter of Christian evangelicalism in England, advocated protection of the Jews and their return to Palestine as the required precursors for the Second Coming of Jesus. Many Middle Eastern Jews became British protégés, and they brought the Jewish community into the mainstream of Ottoman imperial reform.

In exchange for British support during the Ottoman Empire's economic and military travails, reform-minded Ottoman bureaucrats imposed Western-inspired reforms (Tanzimat) on their empire (these later were adopted in one form or another in North Africa). In the Hatt-i Sherif of Gülhane reform of 1839, issued when the British were supporting the Turks against Egyptian incursions in northern Syria, the Ottoman government granted equal rights to all citizens of the empire and guaranteed their lives, religious freedom, and property without religious distinction; this reform also made everyone eligible for military service.

The Imperial Rescript of 1856 (*hatt-i humayun*), issued after the British supported the Ottomans against the Russians in the Crimean War (1854–56) and the subsequent entry of the empire into the European family of nations, renewed and expanded these rights. Not only were Ottoman Jews citizens but they could be admitted to political office, government service, and civil and military schools. Acceding to Jewish distaste for serving in the military and Muslim repugnance at the thought of serving under infidel commanders, the Ottomans allowed citizens to pay a tax in lieu of service. The Turks repealed this law by World War I, which made everyone eligible for military service. By the end of the nineteenth century statutes requiring people to wear distinguishing clothing had been repealed in many places; men had replaced the turban with the fez, and Jewish corporate autonomy had been centralized in the "Organizational Regulations of the Rabbinate," issued in 1865. A chief rabbi for the empire, *hakham bashi,* was to head the Jewish *millet* (an autonomous self-governing religious community) and was now to be assisted by elected but government-approved lay and religious councils. The councils' duties included supervision and management of communal affairs and liaison between the Jewish community and the authorities. When, for example, the military academies had a Jewish quota, the *hakham bashi* in Istanbul interceded to gain a relaxation of the quotas. Although Jewish courts were to adjudicate personal status issues, reality was more fluid. Jews and Muslims took their differences to Islamic or Ottoman government courts where the litigants thought their interests could be served best. Even with the reforms in place, Jews who held European passports did not give them up, because Europeans and their protégés still maintained extraterritorial judicial rights and economic privilege.

The Montefiore-Crémieux mission to the Middle East also helped to crystallize the new relationship between Western and Middle Eastern Jewry. Despite the success of Montefiore and Crémieux in 1840, issues of forced conversion in Iran in 1839 and Italy in 1858 (the Mortara case) inspired similar work to aid Jews in the Ottoman Empire, Morocco, and Iran to "work toward the emancipation and moral progress of the Jews," according to the mission statement of the Alliance Israélite Universelle (AIU). The AIU was established in May 1860 by a group of French Jewish professionals and community activists that included Crémieux; Narcisse Leven, a lawyer active in French municipal politics; the poet Eugene Emmanuel; and Charles

Netter, a prominent merchant. Its goals were to work on behalf of Jews everywhere and to provide aid for those suffering because they were Jews. Mindful of the efficacy of the press, the AIU encouraged publication of abuses to bring about the end of Jewish suffering. It used its own publications, the French press, and the London *Jewish Chronicle* to publicize the plight of Jews in Iran and Morocco.

The most far-reaching legacy of the AIU came through the establishment of a network of schools in the Middle East and North Africa, where French-educated teachers taught the French language—and in in some cases English and Hebrew—and a curriculum of secular subjects that included history, mathematics, and hygiene. The AIU also undertook vocational training, apprenticeship programs, and schools for girls. From 1862 through the midtwentieth century these schools pulled Jews from Morocco to Iran into the Western orbit. Jews also read newspapers and periodicals of the Haskalah, knew about a new movement called Zionism, and relaxed religious practice instead of reforming it or confronting the rabbinate outright. Educated to be Europeans, Jews who attended AIU schools emerged a generation or so ahead of Muslims in the race to westernization. Muslims mostly attended the state public schools and later entered the state bureaucracies in the Ottoman Empire, Egypt, and Tunisia, but Jews and Christians filled the new niches in the professions. Jews were also tied to the European powers as business agents for foreign companies and the new colonial bureaucracies, so that during the later struggles between nationalism and colonialism, they were caught in the middle politically.

Business opportunities came with the opening of the Suez Canal in 1869, the 1860s cotton boom in Egypt that resulted from the American Civil War, European colonization and economic control of the region, and European Zionist immigration to Eretz Israel. These led to migrations from the Mediterranean countryside to port cities and the spread of Jewish family economic networks from Iraq and Syria to Egypt, North Africa, and India. A renewed influx of Italians, Russians, and Central European Ashkenazim to Istanbul and to such Mediterranean cities as Casablanca, Alexandria, Tripoli, and Jaffa contributed to the cosmopolitanism that was to define the Levantine Jewish culture of the colonial period through World War II; the new immigrants also associated with the foreign non-Arab residents of the cities. The Jewish upper crust had little integration with the indigenous *mustaʿarab* Jews. At the same time the collapse of local industry because of the influx of inexpensive European imports, economic deprivations, Jewish military casualties (although most Jews avoided the draft into the Ottoman army), and the accompanying famine and loss of life in the area during World War I led to emigration from the region. Jews from Syria and Iraq moved to North and South America, England, India, and the Far East. Messianic movements and the lure of a better life led Yemenite Jews to Eretz Israel.

The political map of the region changed again after World War I. French occupation of Morocco in 1912 presaged European rule of the Middle East as a result of the peace treaties at Versailles and San Remo. Dissolved at the end of the war, the Ottoman Empire became an independent Turkey, with Palestine, including Transjordan, and Iraq under British mandate and Syria/Lebanon under French mandate. Granting conflicting promises to Jews for a homeland in Palestine; to Arabs for an Arab state from Arabia to Syria and Iraq, which the Arabs assumed included Palestine; and to themselves, the British and the French set the stage for a nationalist struggle that contributed to the disappearance of most Jewish communities in the region through emigration about thirty years later.

Under Western tutelage the new Middle Eastern states nominally adhered to League of Nations standards of human rights, citizenship, and equality. From Morocco to Iran secularly educated Jews who came of age in the 1920s identified themselves as culturally Western, religiously Jewish, and nationally as citizens of the state of their residence (except for Algerian Jews, who had been granted French citizenship in 1870). Yet aside from Turkey, where Jews were Turkish citizens of the Jewish faith, Jews retained minority status, albeit with designated seats in parliaments where they existed.

This new bourgeoisie strolled the wide boulevards and promenades of the colonial planned cities, lived in new ethnically mixed suburbs, dressed fashionably, dined in restaurants, went to the cinema and the race track, and mingled at social clubs. At home they spoke French or English or the Jewish vernacular, disdaining the local Arabic or Persian, and they gave their children European names. In Iraq some Jews identified with Arab culture to the extent that they joined the nascent Iraqi Arab intelligentsia and were key participants in the development of modern Arabic literature. In Turkey, Judezmo (Judeo-Spanish) was losing out to the Turkish language because of government-required attendance at state schools and state-sponsored cultural homogenization programs.

Religiously Jewish, the middle class fasted on Yom Kippur and observed life cycle religious events. Rabbinic scholarly work declined, because families opted to send their children to universities. They wanted to prepare their children for success in business and the professions in the Levantine world of the interwar era, which combined Mediterranean cosmopolitanism and

European colonialism. Yet in the old neighborhoods of Cairo and Baghdad, in the *mellahs* of North Africa, and in the countryside of Yemen and Kurdistan, Jews continued to live their premodern traditional culture. Only the change of regime in Iran in the 1920s brought westernization and hitherto inaccessible economic and educational opportunities for Jews.

With all the optimism of the 1920s the political reality was still sobering. In Morocco (except for Tangier), Tunisia, Iran, and Yemen, Jews were still *dhimmis.* Where they were citizens of a country, Jews were no longer a protected autonomous ethnicity, nor were they equal. They had become minorities in states that were in the process of adopting national identities. In countries that had political parties, Jews could stand for election as individuals only in Tunisia (if they had French citizenship) and in Turkey; Iraq's Parliament had designated seats for minorities. In Egypt, and later in Morocco, Jews worked in politics behind the scenes, contributing financially to political parties and writing for newspapers. Generally, they were apolitical and loyal, as always, to the regime in power.

The nature of politics began to change in the 1930s. With the independence of Iraq in 1932 the government could implement the hitherto theoretical political ideology of Arab nationalism. Iraq had adopted the ideology of Arab nationalism as the focus of loyalty for all Iraqis, and it was propagated in the schools. Attracting adherents from Iraq to Egypt, this secular approach to Arab unity redefined national identity and advocated the unity of all Arab peoples in a nation that included Egypt, the Arabian Peninsula, and the countries of the Fertile Crescent, including Palestine. The definition of who was an Arab, however, was debatable. While the major theoreticians of the ideology identified as Arab all who spoke Arabic and who identified with the culture of the Arabs regardless of religious affiliation, it soon became clear that Arabness could include Muslims and Christians but not Jews. This was partly because a part of the Arab people, the Palestinian Arabs, were in direct confrontation over Palestine with not only the British colonizers but also the Zionist Jews. This territorial struggle had direct ramifications for the Jewish communities in the region because—despite their protestations and pleas to be viewed as Jewish citizens of their various countries—the terms *Jew* and *Zionist* began to blur as more Middle Eastern countries adopted support for the Palestinian Arabs in their foreign policies. During the Arab Revolt of 1936–39 in Palestine, the governments of a number of countries asked Jews to support the Arabs of Palestine and the Jews complied.

Until World War II, however, political Zionism had little effect on the Jews of the region. Clearly, religion motivated the decision to settle in Eretz Israel, and Jews from Yemen and Morocco did so throughout the nineteenth and early twentieth centuries. When the holy cities of Jerusalem, Safed, Tiberius, and Hebron were under Ottoman rule, individuals made pilgrimages there, students learned in the yeshivas, and rabbis traveled and taught throughout the region. Westernized Jews read Modern Hebrew periodicals and contributed to the cause, but the Zionist leadership evinced little interest in Middle Eastern Jewry and did not send emissaries to the region until Jewish soldiers in the Allied armies made contact with their coreligionists in Iraq and North Africa during World War II. On the one hand, the war and Vichy rule over part of the region sparked some Jewish activism—vociferous boycotts of German goods in Egypt, direct assistance to the Allies in North Africa, and the intervention by Persian Jews to save children escaping from Poland. Jews became disillusioned with the West as the Germans exterminated communities from the Balkans and sent Jews from Libya to concentration camps and from Tunisia to labor camps. On the other hand, in 1941 Jews feared not only that the Axis powers would overrun the Middle East but that the Axis would also support an Arab uprising (led by the Jerusalem mufti al-Hajj Amin al-Husseini and his pro-Axis Arab nationalist supporters). This led to a reassessment of Jewish identity issues and political engagement, sparking movements for self-defense.

Pogroms in Baghdad and Basra in 1941 were wake-up calls for Iraqi Jewry, and the establishment of the State of Israel in 1948 and the process of decolonialization throughout the region after the war led to new political realities and reassessments of Jewish life in the countries verging on independence. The rising nationalism that in most cases left Jews not as equal citizens but as precarious minorities engendered the same kinds of debate about the future that had engulfed Eastern European Jews before the Holocaust. Communal and generational tensions regarding the future of the communities—whether to remain apolitical, join the nationalist parties, become Jewish nationalists or Zionists, or to become active in the universal socialist movements—were short-lived. Events soon overtook political considerations. Anti-Jewish riots in most Middle Eastern and North African countries after the establishment of the State of Israel 1948, and subsequent outbursts of anti-Jewish fervor that accompanied Israeli victories over the Arab states, ultimately led to the emigration of entire communities indigenous to the Middle East and North Africa since ancient times. Equally significant were economic measures aimed at sequestering or nationalizing non-Muslim–owned companies in such countries as Egypt and Iraq, which were moving toward nationalist economies. For some, decisions concerning relocation were obvious. For those who had European passports and liquid assets, Europe and North and South America seemed logical destinations. In countries where property was sequestered, where Jews were denationalized and without the passports required for immigration to other countries, or where windows of opportunity for emigration arose, they were airlifted en masse to Israel. Secularly educated French-speaking North African Jews mainly went to France and Canada; many Algerian Jews already held French citizenship and emigrated to France after Algeria's independence in 1962.

For Jews who remained, whether by choice or by economic necessity, life in the Middle East and North Africa during the last quarter of the twentieth century remained precarious. The monarchs of Morocco and Iran protected Jews; these rulers had covert relations with Israel and were assisted by Jewish social service institutions, such as the Jewish Colonization Association of London and the American Jewish Joint Distribution Committee or educational organizations like Otzar ha-Torah (founded by Syrian-American Jews to run religious schools in Iran and Morocco). With the change of regime in Iran in 1979, much of the Jewish community left for the United States and Canada, unwilling to live under the Islamic republic. In Syria, a state in direct confrontation with Israel, the fate of that Jewish community was linked to Syrian foreign policy and its eroding relations with the United States. Relatives ransomed Syrian Jews and brought them to the West in the 1990s.

Throughout the 1970s and 1980s Jews steadily left the countries they had called home for millennia. They emigrated openly when they could and stealthily when they had to, paying off government officials and local tribesmen and walking great distances over rugged terrain. By the end of the twentieth century most Middle Eastern and North African Jews had settled in Israel, with viable communities remaining only in Turkey, Morocco, and Iran.

CHAPTER

3

Economic Life

Michael Menachem Laskier and Reeva Spector Simon

Bordered by the Atlantic and Indian Oceans, the Black Sea, and the Sahara, the region that we define as the Middle East and North Africa is an area of few navigable rivers and a generally dry climate. Large-scale agriculture in this region, which is heavily dependent upon irrigation, has not been arable since antiquity. By Ottoman times sustained income in the Middle East was historically derived from taxes on the produce of grants of land given to imperial military subordinates. Peasant agriculture often existed in a patron-client relationship. Aside from oil in modern times, natural resources have not been plentiful.

Because of their geographic location, the countries of the Middle East and North Africa have, since ancient times, been the conduits for ideas and commodities among Europe, Africa, and Asia. Southwest Asia was the land bridge for the continents of Europe and Asia, and Asia and Africa—and the nexus for China, India, and Europe, as well as sub-Saharan Africa and southern Europe, and Iraq and Central Europe. The Silk Road that began in China passed west through Afghanistan, Iran, and Iraq, ending on the coast of Syria or Turkey. Merchants shipped spices from Africa, Asia, and the Spice Islands to Arabia that then were brought by land north to Damascus or northwest along the Red Sea and overland to Cairo. Traders brought gold, ivory, ostrich feathers, and slaves from sub-Saharan Africa via the Sudan to Egypt. From cities along the shores of the Mediterranean, traders also exported to Europe leather goods, hides, wax, olive oil, grains, figs, dates, tobacco, silk cloth, and cloth from the hinterlands of North Africa and Anatolia. A continuous bicoastal trade endured despite centuries of war between Muslim and Christian societies.

Inland cities on the trade routes, such as Fez, Marrakesh, Cairo, Aleppo, and Baghdad, attracted settlement and became entrepôts for the caravan traffic that traversed the region. Centers for the transshipment of goods, they provided food and accommodations for the men, camels, mules, and donkeys that carried the loads; they also evolved into important regional economic hubs with significant Jewish populations. The caravans transported textiles and metalwork from Mosul and Damascus through Aleppo to Alexandretta or through Izmir to the Mediterranean coast, where Venetian ships, and later French and British ships, brought the goods and raw materials to Europe.

URBAN AND RURAL PREMODERN ECONOMICS UNDER ISLAMIC RULE

On the eve of the modern era the Jews in the Middle East and North Africa can best be described as a population of primarily urban dwellers, generally poor, a community of petty traders, peddlers, pawnbrokers, and moneylenders to the poor, as well as some midlevel artisans and craftsmen, with a thin stratum of wealthy entrepreneurs and international traders. Travelers to the region and teachers employed by the Alliance Israélite Universelle (AIU) almost always described Jewish communities as impoverished and degraded. As late as 1910, the British wrote that 60 percent of the Jewish population of Baghdad were indigent and 5 percent were beggars. This situation was common to most Jewish communities in the Middle East and North Africa but would change dramatically by the midtwentieth century.

Historically, Islamic tradition and local economic necessity conditioned any Jewish role in the economies of Muslim lands. Unlike Christian Europe, where Jewish landownership became virtually impossible under feudalism, Muslim rule provided a variety of economic parameters. When the Muslim armies invaded Iraq in the seventh century, they found Jews both as landowners and as peasants. New land grants, however, were given only to Muslim soldiers of the conquering armies and not to local minorities. As time passed, Jews tended to opt out of agriculture, because the double taxation—both on land (*kharaj*) and on Jews as *dhimmis* (*jizya*)—proved too onerous. By the sixteenth and seventeenth centuries, as more land came under the rule of the Ottoman Empire, the state owned huge tracts or granted some to officials, and little evidence exists of Jews' playing a role in agriculture, other than as tax collectors, except for a few communities of Jewish farmers in Iraqi, Iranian, and Turkish Kurdistan; in rural Morocco,

Libya, and Yemen; and later in eastern Syria, where they worked on the land for others in patron-client relationships.

Jews worked at specific crafts and occupations mainly because these were related to Jewish religious practices, filled niches in the local economy that were abhorrent to Muslims, or required skills that local authorities needed. In addition to purely religion-based occupations, such as ritual slaughterer (*shohet*) or scribe (*sofer*), Jews worked in all aspects of food and clothing production. Because of Jewish dietary laws they have always worked in the food industry, especially in the processing of cheese, preparation of meat, and production and sale of wine (sacerdotal to Jews but forbidden to Muslims). Muslims permitted Jews to run inns and taverns: seventeenth-century Cairo taxed Jewish tavern owners, but Brusa, Turkey, did not. Jewish butchers and cheese and yogurt makers produced not only for the Jewish community but for the public at large.

Similarly, the Jewish association with the textile industry has religious roots. Because of the Jewish observance of the biblical proscription against mixing linen and wool, Jewish agents purchased wool in the countryside, and Jews spun, dyed, wove, and finished the cloth. In the midnineteenth century seventy of the five thousand Jews of Damascus were dyers of cloth, a Jewish occupation renowned from Central Asia to North Africa. In Salonika Jewish textiles were in such demand by the Ottoman sultan's janissaries that their annual delivery of one thousand blue and two hundred red pieces of fabric (to be sewn into military uniforms) replaced the *jizya* tax on *dhimmis.* As the numbers of troops increased with time, Jewish community leaders had to renegotiate the quota of goods, converting it to a monetary tax, because production for the corps became too onerous an obligation for the community to support.

Work in the textile industry resulted in employment for many Jews in related fields; they became spinners and weavers, dyers and producers of silk thread, and manufacturers of buttons and trimmings. As small-scale entrepreneurs, both men and women sold handkerchiefs and other items in the marketplace. Jewish women were purveyors of clothing and accessories to Muslim women, who did not leave the house in many locales. Jewish women established lists of clients, from women in the sultan's harem to wives of officials, whom they visited on a regular basis. Jewish tailors were also working throughout the region. When Muslims began to dress in Western style after the Crimean War (1854–56), the demand for European tailors was such that many tailors from Eastern and Central Europe settled in Istanbul, considerably augmenting that city's Ashkenazic Jewish population.

Jews were also involved in the production of leather goods and in the export of hides; they were leather tanners and dyers, occupations deemed unclean for Muslims. Jews of the Balkans and Morocco dried, salted, and exported hides to Spain, Portugal, and Gibraltar. They also made saddles, harnesses, and shoes. In 1899 Algiers supported forty-five Jewish tanners and 730 Jewish shoemakers. Throughout Muslim lands Jews were also musicians and entertainers, professions generally considered to be non-Muslim occupations. In areas where Jews were persecuted, such as Yemen, Iran, and Morocco, they were also the sanitation workers. Yet Jews also worked in the trade and processing of precious stones. Until the British East India Company diverted the diamond trade from India to London, Jewish merchants, cutters, and polishers in Egypt, the Maghreb, and southern Europe dominated the industry. As late as the nineteenth century, Livornese Jews in Italy traded in coral and used it as capital.

The Islamic proscriptions against working with metals and charging interest on loans left a number of occupational areas for non-Muslims. In Morocco and Yemen Jews in rural areas worked as blacksmiths and made and repaired tools in exchange for agricultural products; many Jews were also engaged in the refining of gold and the production of gold and silver jewelry. In Egypt, Iraq, Iran, and throughout the Maghreb their workmanship was in high demand. In Yemen Jews created jewelry for the Muslim elite and were sorely missed when they emigrated to Israel in the early 1950s. Yemen also appointed Jews and Christians to administer the minting of coins and to ensure accurate weights and measures. Libya entrusted Jews with fixing the karat weight and installing the karat seal on jewelry. Jews ran the coinage mints from North Africa to Iraq and often became the financial advisers (*sarrafs*) to local and imperial rulers. The halakhic opinions regarding usury—which allowed Jews to purchase bonds, charge commissions for securing credit for any borrower, and appear as silent partners in commercial enterprises—enabled them to receive legitimate profits as investors, brokers, and international traders.

Although Muslims controlled commerce in the Asian interior, by the sixteenth century, primarily because of the influx of Jews who had been expelled from Spain, the number of Jewish commercial agents was increasing. Their connections with indigenous Jewish traders along the Silk Road made them indispensable middlemen for the growing commerce with Europe. The Spanish exiles who settled in Muslim lands during the fifteenth and sixteenth centuries brought with them skills in medicine, banking, armaments production, nautical technology, diplomacy, and European languages and contacts with coreligionists in Europe. They were able to draw upon centuries of experience in international commerce because Spain under Moorish control had traded both with Christian Europe and Muslim lands. The Spanish Jews' knowledge of commodity and money markets, and the use of bills of exchange and checks, as well as their skilled workmanship in the production of luxury goods, provided valuable expertise to the new Ottoman elite. Because commerce carried no stigma under Islam, as it had under Christianity, the Sephardim who arrived in the Ottoman Empire—some not only with capital that they had transferred before they were expelled but with connections to coreligionists in the Italian city-states and other European commercial centers—put their talents to good use in their new homelands along the Mediterranean.

From the fifteenth century through the end of the eighteenth century, the age of merchant capital, these exiles from the Iberian Peninsula made good use of family and international connections. These were broadened geographically once the exiles made their way to Europe, the New World, and later to Asia. Their contacts with Jews in the European commercial cities of Antwerp, Hamburg, and Amsterdam and their knowledge of Western languages produced a Sephardic entrepreneurial elite that occupied leading positions in the commerce of Cairo, Alexandria, Aleppo, Tripoli [Syria], Salonika, Istanbul, and Izmir in the east to Algiers and Mogador in the west. They also had commercial links to peripheral areas of the Ottoman Empire.

In 1571 the city council of Venice decided not to expel the Jews and to allow Ottoman Jews to live outside the city's Jewish ghetto because of their value as merchants to the Levant. This decision probably led to the establishment of the Italian city of Livorno (Leghorn) as a free commercial center in 1593, in order to attract merchants who were Jewish and New Christians (Jewish converts). Granted protection by the dukes of Tuscany—as their subjects after only a day's residence—Iberian Jews could live there free from the Inquisition, able to trade, finance their transactions, and store their goods in a centrally located economic hub from which they networked with coreligionists throughout the Mediterranean and beyond. These new Christians were known as Francos in Syria and Grana or Gorneyim in Tunisia, but most reverted to Judaism. Some Sephardic families—the Montels in Tunisia, and Valensis, Busnachs, and Bacris in Algiers—used their Livornese connections to penetrate markets in Christian lands and to extend these connections to Aleppo in Syria and lands to the east. Often Jewish firms took Christian partners or adopted Christian names to facilitate trade and avoid customs dues in Christian countries.

After the Ottoman authorities—and later the North Africans and Iranians—granted trade concessions to Europeans in the sixteenth century, the interests of Jewish and European merchants merged, becoming at once both symbiotic and competitive. In addition to reductions in customs duties, the Ottomans extended certain rights, called capitulations, to Europeans. The capitulations provided that Europeans involved in litigation would be accompanied at trial by a representative of the European government that protected them or could have the venue changed to a European court. When European companies began to establish commercial bases in Mediterranean port cities, they hired local personnel who spoke Arabic or Turkish and a European language or two as translators. They also hired physicians, some craftsmen, and translators as employees of the diplomatic missions to connect with the authorities and to facilitate commerce. Using local personnel who later paid for the privilege of protection was less expensive than staffing these small offices with Europeans. The savings supported many a French consulate in the Middle East.

Jews brokered transactions for the Ottomans as they imported manufactured products and luxury items from Europe and exported less in finished goods but more in raw materials, such as wool, silk, hides, olive oil, and dried fruits. Jews in ports such as Algiers, Tunis, Alexandria, Izmir, and Salonika acted as agents for the French in particular, because the British, fearing Jewish competition, appointed Christians to purchase and transport commodities to the port, where European vessels conveyed them to Europe, as stipulated either in Ottoman regulation or later in British law. These brokers traveled to the interior of the empire, organized the sale and shipment of goods, and served as mediators between the shippers, local notables, and producers of the wheat, cotton, and silk; the brokers received commissions from the European firms and from the local exporter. If the brokers became bonafide protégés of the European government that they served, the Jewish brokers, and later members of their families, received a *berât,* a document giving them the special status of a subject of a European state and shielding them from Ottoman jurisdiction. In some places these Jewish brokers were also exempt from the *dhimmi* restrictions and lived in the emerging European sections of town as European, rather than local, Jews.

In 1682, the same year that France expelled the Jews from Marseilles (because French traders resented Jewish competition in North Africa), the French gave Jewish merchants their protection in Aleppo. Centrally located, Aleppo served as the transit point for goods from Central Asia, Iran, and the Persian Gulf, either to the Ottoman capital at Istanbul or to the

Mediterranean ports of Alexandretta and Izmir. The role of the Aleppan Jews and the Livornese Franco merchant families who lived in Aleppo (not as *dhimmis* but as protected French nationals) was such that by the end of the eighteenth century, it was said that trade in Aleppo ceased on Jewish fasts and feasts. In 1784 a member of the Franco Picciotto family, Raphael Picciotto, was appointed the Austrian consul in Aleppo. By that time Tuscany and other provinces of Italy had become part of the Habsburg Empire.

In the Middle Eastern hinterland the economic situation was changing. The dislocation caused by the Mongol conquest of the fourteenth century and the almost constant warfare between successor states of the Golden Horde, the Ottoman Empire, and Safavi dynasty in Persia had retarded the development of the area. Ottoman authority rarely penetrated beyond provincial centers until the midnineteenth century; therefore, the nomadization of large areas in eastern Turkey, Syria, and Iraq affected trade. Adding to the insecurity were rebellions against authority and attacks against minority populations, banditry that jeopardized the land trade routes, and local rulers in Jerusalem and Cairo who extorted large sums of money and seized Jewish property and goods at will. The Ottoman government's lack of concern with economic issues was reflected in the construction of few bridges and hostels, the deterioration of harbors, and the paucity of roads. By the eighteenth century, as Europe turned from the Mediterranean to the Atlantic, to sea routes in preference to land—and as Bengali silk became less expensive than that from Iran, and New World coffee replaced Yemeni mocha—the commercial importance of the Near East dissipated. Ottoman defeats on the battlefield by Russia, almost constant war with Persia, and retreat in the Balkans increased the deficits in the imperial treasury. As the Ottomans imported more, inflation grew from the dumping of Spanish silver into the Mediterranean economy, private parties were taking over grain exports (formerly the responsibility of government), and the empire was failing to industrialize. The result was that the Ottoman government had to borrow more and more money in order to stay solvent.

In the eastern Mediterranean, as the Sephardic emigrant elite died out (their descendants did not have the cutting-edge skills in languages and medicine), they left a vacuum that was soon filled by Greek Christian minorities who benefited from their own expertise in European languages, study in Italy, and the preference of European governments to employ coreligionists. The competition between Jews and Christians for the post of *sarraf* in Basra at the end of the eighteenth century and later in Damascus may have played a role in the spate of blood libel incidents in the early nineteenth century. Despite constant maneuvering, the Greek Bahri family was unable to dislodge the Jewish Farhi family from its dominant position in trade and finance in both Damascus and Acre. In North Africa, where no Greeks and Armenians lived, the Jewish commercial elite still held sway.

In 1725 more than 70 percent of the firms doing business with Livorno and Amsterdam were Jewish. The Livornese were involved in the grain, wool, and spice trades. They had commercial interests in Tunisia and in Gibraltar, the gateway from the Mediterranean to England, and were competing successfully with the merchants of Marseilles, whom the French government had granted a monopoly of trade between France and Algeria.

In North Africa the Livornese Jews became agents of the local rulers (deys, beys), who financed them and awarded the Jews monopolies on the import and export of specific commodities. In Morocco the sultan founded the Atlantic seaport of Essaouira (Mogador) as a royal entrepôt that would not only control trade with Europe but would limit European access to the Moroccan countryside. In Essaouira both Muslim and Jewish *tujjar al-sultan* (royal merchants), whose caravans were often funded by the sultan, distributed the imported tea, sugar, metals, gunpowder, and tobacco and had the monopoly on the export of wheat, hides, cereals, and wool.

Jews also participated in selling off the booty brought in by the corsairs that sustained the regimes in the Maghreb. Until its suppression in North Africa, and in the Atlantic and Persian Gulf in the early nineteenth century, piracy was a lucrative commercial endeavor for the sea captains and privateers who acted as independent adventurers or even as unofficial agents of their governments. Whether as English pirates attacking Spanish ships, French pirates operating in the Atlantic, or the Barbary pirates of North Africa who acted in collusion with the rulers, privateers operated in contravention of the self-declared Spanish monopoly of trade in the Atlantic or as predators where the power of the state was weak.

In Algiers the governing elite and merchants equipped these privateering ships in return for a share in the profits from the sale of captured goods and the ransoming of captives. Algiers was not the center of ancient urban culture nor of a wealthy indigenous middle class, but it was dominated by janissaries brought into the area from eastern parts of the Ottoman Empire, as well as sea captains, many of whom were European, and merchants, many of whom were Jews. They ransomed the captives and disposed of goods captured by the corsairs through the Italian seaport of Livorno.

The Busnach and Bacri families, Livornese who settled in Algiers at the end of the eighteenth century, were protégés of the dey, who gave them a virtual monopoly of Algerian commerce. These families broke the British blockade to supply France with wheat during the Napoleonic Wars and established a presence in Marseilles, competing with the Marseilles merchants for trade with the French hinterland. The ships of these families, which at one point numbered as many as 170, sailed under the Algerian flag to major ports in the Mediterranean and to the New World. The Busnachs and Bacris lent money both to the dey and the French government. It was said that the reluctance of the French government to repay the family and the dey led to the French invasion of Algeria in 1830.

Trade in the Persian Gulf and the Indian Ocean became increasingly more significant as commerce in spices arriving via the Red Sea route slowed by the midseventeenth century, after the Portuguese defeated Muslim fleets. Until then Persian Jews traded in horses and silk and operated from commercial bases established at the Straits of Hormuz, which linked Persia and India with Asia Minor. In the eighteenth century Iraqi Jews living in Hamadan conducted trade with Tehran, and those in Basra competed with Cairo merchants, shipping pharmaceuticals, perfumes, precious stones, spices, indigo, and cloth from India and the Persian Gulf via Aleppo to the Mediterranean. For a brief period Jewish brokers had their own fleets and traded independently of the British. Once the British became dominant in India between the second half of the nineteenth century and World War I, however, some Iraqi Jews, most notably from the Sassoon family, began to trade through Bombay and the Far East, eventually establishing family branches of their commercial interests in Hong Kong and émigré communities in England.

Headed by Sheikh Sassoon ben Salih, the family held the position of chief *sarraf* in the eighteenth century for many of the Mamluk governors of Baghdad. When Da'ud Pasha dismissed the son of the sheikh, the Sassoon family established itself first in Bombay and later in points east. David Sassoon (1792–1864) and his family established an economic empire that had centers in Bombay, Calcutta, Rangoon, Hong Kong, Shanghai, and England. Known as the Rothschilds of the Middle East, the Sassoons (who later married into the Rothschild family) exported British textiles to Iraq and Persia, imported textiles and products from the Middle East, and resold them in Britain and India. Sassoons traded in Bombay yarn and English piece goods and extended their interest to Central Asia and southern China. The Sassoons built textile factories in India, established banks, and engaged in extensive philanthropic activities—building schools, hospitals, and orphanages in Baghdad and in sites throughout the British Empire, where most of their business ventures were located. At the beginning of the nineteenth century, they and other Iraqi Jewish merchants were mainly involved in textiles and banking. Other commodities included indigo, rugs, horses, opium, rosewater, and gems.

Many other families set up trading connections first in India and by 1831 in Singapore, where there emerged a large expatriate Jewish community that remained connected to coreligionists and family in Baghdad. The Yehudah and Ezra families settled in Calcutta, and, like the Sassoons, members of these families who left Iraq for Bombay and Asia in the early nineteenth century set up businesses in England so that they could trade directly. More than twenty Jewish firms of Baghdad origin, such as the Sassoon, Shaasha, and Zuluf families, had houses in Manchester; the Bikhor and Salih families operated in Bombay and London; and Sir Elly S. Kadoorie had firms in Hong Kong, Shanghai, and London. By the twentieth century Baghdad Jews and their descendants were a major force in international commerce.

INFLUENCE OF OTTOMAN REFORMS AND EUROPEAN DOMINATION OF THE REGION

The period of reform that dominated the Ottoman Empire and Egypt throughout most of the nineteenth century had serious economic ramifications for minorities. Commercial treaties signed with European countries—most notably, the Convention of Balta Liman in 1838—gave British firms access to the Asian interior for the first time and accelerated the infusion of British textiles into the Ottoman domestic market. In addition, Ottoman minorities made a gradual shift to agricultural cash crops for world markets that led to an economic partnership with European commercial interests that lasted through the first half of the twentieth century. Though few Jews entered the Ottoman civil service when positions became available to minorities in the midnineteenth century, many Jews sought the secular educational opportunities that the Ottomans provided, learning the linguistic and administrative skills that were needed by both the colonial administrations and the European companies that emerged with the French, Italian, and British domination of the region. Economic opportunity motivated Jewish identification with the European powers. Jews maintained these positions until decolonialization after World War II, when a generation of Muslims had been educated to replace them.

European commerce sparked investment in the Middle East. European capital, including infusions by European Jewish economic interests, and

European expertise were instrumental in building the infrastructure for shipping raw materials from the hinterland and for orienting commerce to the coasts of the Mediterranean Sea and the Atlantic and Indian Oceans. Telegraph links were established in 1840. Roads were built and wheeled transport was reintroduced in places where camels and donkeys had trod for centuries. Railroads built from Morocco to Iran led to new or revitalized ports. Grain, cereals, hides, olives, and rice from Mogador, Oran, Tangier, Algiers, Tripoli, Beirut, Port Said, Alexandria, Jaffa, Beirut, Izmir, and Salonika were unloaded for export to cities in the Mediterranean littoral. After 1850 steamship connected these port cities. The opening of the Suez Canal in 1869 and steamship travel on the Tigris and Euphrates Rivers soon reconnected Baghdad and the Persian Gulf to Europe.

Port cities drew many away from small towns in the interior of Syria, Egypt, Morocco, and Algeria, and a general internal migration increased from the end of the nineteenth century through the midtwentieth. As the trans-Saharan trade dried up, Jews left the caravan towns in North Africa for the cities on the coast. Jews from small towns in Morocco looked to Casablanca and Tangier, cities where a European presence meant security. Later, Jewish educational facilities in Casablanca and Tangier provided vocational training as well as scholarly education. Port cities and free-trade zones established in the eighteenth and nineteenth centuries, such as Melilla, Ceuta, and Gibraltar (later under Spanish and British control), drew Jewish capital and expertise. In Iran persecuted Jews left small towns for large cities or moved east to Afghanistan or Central Asia. Where handicrafts suffered from competition from inexpensive European imports and where population increases and natural disaster caused unemployment, the unskilled and the semiskilled moved to the larger cities, working at home as shoemakers, tailors, barbers, and leather workers. Some eked out a living shining shoes or by renting stalls for the day in the marketplace to sell food, matches, or whatever they could buy wholesale or inexpensively. Some women began to work outside the home as domestics for wealthy Jewish families.

Government pacification of the countryside made peddling a more secure endeavor for poor Jews. In North Africa, Kurdistan, and Yemen Jewish peddlers struck out for the countryside, returning home for the Sabbath and holidays. In Morocco they began to settle in market towns, where they were protected by Muslim partners. As minorities, or in Persia as *najis* (the ritually impure), Jews were allowed into Muslim homes where they dealt directly with women—trading spices, cosmetics, henna, matches, thread, needles, mirrors, and other merchandise for grain, olives, oil, figs, butter, and wool.

As Jews, they were considered either totally trustworthy or unmasculine because of their implicit *dhimmi* status and dominated this aspect of rural commerce for a long period. Perhaps it was also of little importance to Muslims because the trade was not very profitable. In Persia and in western Morocco Jews continued to serve as conduits of goods to the countryside until the early twentieth century when modern roads were built and the accessibility to markets was ensured.

Where Jewish interests as provisioners of and moneylenders to the military were tied to the old regime, as in Istanbul and the Balkans, the destruction of the Janissaries in 1826 meant economic disaster until the Jewish community could reorient itself. The principal *sarraf* to the Janissaries, Bekhor Isaac Carmona, was killed, and the Jews lost control of the economy to local Greeks and the Armenians. Jews were dominant as rug merchants and antiquities dealers, and some were haberdashers; most were peddlers, match vendors, shoe shiners, and beggars; a very few were bankers. Turkish Jewry never regained its former economic splendor but almost a century later recovered somewhat, when thousands of Greeks left with the establishment of the Republic of Turkey in 1922. Salonika, on the other hand, became a major boom town linked to the Balkan hinterland, rivaling Beirut for commercial prominence not only at the end of the nineteenth century but continuing into the twentieth century. By World War II a Jewish-dominated industrial infrastructure that had developed in the city included more than twenty-three hundred Jewish-owned businesses. In Damascus Jews who had invested in treasury bonds lost money to the huge deficits in the Ottoman treasury. The opening of the Suez Canal and the shift in trade routes, added to treasury bond losses, led many Aleppan Jews to relocate to Beirut, Cairo, and Alexandria. After Morocco signed commercial treaties with Britain in 1856, the *tujjar al-sultan* lost out to a new group of independent Jewish merchants (*simsar*) and then to European settlers. By the turn of the twentieth century, as Essaouira became less important, Jews transferred their commercial interests to Tangier and Casablanca.

Jewish emigration from the region was fast becoming desirable by the turn of the twentieth century. With periodic economic depressions in the 1890s; the Balkan, Moroccan, and Libyan wars during the first decade of the twentieth century; economic hardship and famine; avoidance of conscription during World War I; and the disruption of trade connections with the creation of borders and new states such as Turkey, Syria, and Iraq after the war, many Jews in the former Ottoman Empire and some in North Africa reassessed their options. Syrian Jews left for New York, Mexico City, and Buenos Aires. Turks went to Seattle, Algerians and Tunisians to France, and Moroccans found themselves in Brazil, Argentina, and North America. Jews from the Middle East and North Africa established Diaspora communities in the New World and the Far East and sent money back home to build institutions and support family. Migration to Israel would occur about fifty years later.

For the majority who remained, port cities attracted not only Jews from the area but also hundreds of thousands of French, Spaniards, Italians, and Ashkenazi Jews. They came to the southern shore of the Mediterranean in search of economic opportunity. In the 1860s the Egyptian cotton boom, brought about by the disruption of exports from the United States during the Civil War, drew Syrian Jews and Ashkenazim to Egypt. Jews built cotton gins and knitting, weaving, and yarn factories and soon controlled half the cotton exports to Europe. In the 1870s ostrich feathers for ladies' hats generated economic growth. In this Jewish-controlled industry caravans brought the feathers from sub-Saharan Africa to Tripoli, where Libyan Jews, primarily women, cleaned and dyed the feathers, which were then shipped to Livorno and on to European fashion houses. By 1907 the boom was over, and many young Libyan women became unemployed.

Nineteenth-century *sarrafs* and commercial middlemen not only used their accumulated capital to establish private banks that now served the local rulers but also became commercial bankers until the establishment of national banks in the midtwentieth century. The Abraham de Camondo family, a significant financial force in nineteenth-century Istanbul, with close connections to European bankers, financed the Ottoman effort in the Crimean War. Of the forty private banks in Istanbul in 1912, eight were Jewish. Jews from Aleppo, Baghdad, and Izmir settled in Cairo and Alexandria in response to changing nineteenth-century trade routes and economic conditions. The Mosseris, Menasces, and Cattawis built fortunes through moneylending and banking services and served on boards or as directors of Egyptian companies. Jews were among the founders of Egypt's Banque Misr, and members of seventeen Jewish families, some of whom had Egyptian citizenship and others of whom had retained foreign nationality, sat on the boards of joint stock companies that ran banks, a railway, the water company, a bus company, an electric firm, and five land development companies. In Tangier the Jewish-owned Banque Pariente and Banque Hassan were important to the basic economy of the Mediterranean basin.

Iraq produced two international banking houses. As the Sassoons followed the British Empire east and finally to London, the Zilkhas went west. In 1899 the Zilkha family was able to parlay a moneylending business into a financial banking house, with branches in Cairo, Alexandria, Beirut, Damascus, and eventually New York. The Zilkhas' assets were worth ten million pounds sterling in 1948, or about $900 million today. The Zilkha Bank, the Sion Aboodie bank (which opened in 1900), and the Edward Aboodie bank (which opened in 1938) handled Iraqi government transactions. The Zilkha bank even handled Iraq's contribution to the Arab League through its branch in Cairo until doing so became politically untenable in the late 1940s, by which time government banks were already established. Most of the *sarrafs* who worked in Baghdad during the 1930s, providing small business loans and credit, were Jews.

Middle Eastern Jewish bankers, in partnership with European merchant bankers, provided the capital for the establishment of Middle Eastern factories and investment opportunities. One of the earliest factories was an olive oil refining plant built by Eugenio Lumbroso in Tunisia in 1892. A citizen of Italy and a resident of Tunisia, Lumbroso was part of a modern transnational Jewish merchant elite that invested in the region. This elite was composed of Italian and Sephardic Jews, many of whom had married into the local Jewish merchant elite of North Africa and Syria; they invested in cotton gins, tobacco, sugar refining, and railways in Egypt and in distilleries, flour mills, the cloth industry, and a cigarette factory in Salonika.

Though Jews had opportunities to own land in the region after 1858, albeit in limited fashion, few purchased large tracts of land. Among those that did was the Daniel family in southern Iraq near Hilleh, and Shaul Shashuah, who invested outside Baghdad and near Basra and Kerbala. Rather, Jews bought urban real estate and property. They invested in the construction of new suburbs in Baghdad, built the Sisli and Nisantas areas in Istanbul, and Maadi and Garden City in Cairo. Libyan Jews began to purchase land in the late 1930s, until they were restricted by the Italian colonial authorities. Jewish concerns bought state land in Giza, formed joint stock companies in Egypt, and established the Kom Ombo land development company, which produced sugarcane for the Egyptian Sugar Company and agricultural materials for industry. Middle Eastern Jews from Jaffa and Jerusalem purchased land for Zionist settlement when the Ottoman government would not allow Europeans to own land in the empire.

In 1907 one-quarter of the population of Alexandria was non-Egyptian. Until the period of decolonialization after World War II, cities along the Mediterranean continued to attract a polyglot and diverse population of Jews, Christians, and Muslims, who joined the French, British, and Italian soldiers and administrators stationed throughout North Africa, the Levant, and Iraq, adding to the region's cosmopolitanism. Many Jews who migrated were European and maintained their European citizenship. They lived in the new suburbs and rarely mixed with the indigenous *mustaʿarab* (Arabic-speaking) Jews, who were generally poor. They remained in the Jewish quarters by choice or, in Morocco and Iran, by government fiat. In Egypt and North Africa the new economic elite, a merger of the indigenous and the wealthy Sephardic families, formed a new haute bourgeoisie that considered itself European—they sent their children to European schools, shopped in Cairo in the Jewish Cicurel or Chemla department stores, attended the new movie theaters, purchased automobiles from Jewish franchises, dressed à la mode, and dined in the new restaurants.

The banks and commercial establishments founded to service this newly wealthy, westernized clientele generated employment opportunities for people with modern skills. The result was the creation of a Jewish middle class, educated in Alliance schools, that was prepared to take the white-collar jobs available in both the European-based firms and the colonial bureaucracy. Beginning in Egypt, Iraq, Algeria, and Tunisia, and then later in Morocco, Turkey, and Iran, these Jews were a generation or more ahead of the Muslim population in acquiring the Western languages and administrative skills required to fill new posts in the colonial administrations. Jews by the tens of thousands got jobs as salaried white-collar workers and as low-to mid-level administrators in the bureaucracies, banks, and foreign firms. They were the stockbrokers, insurance agents, and bank personnel in Egypt and worked in transport, banks, and foreign companies in Iraq. Many Jews had posts in the Iraqi civil service, ran the port of Basra, and worked for the railways and the Iraq Petroleum Company. In North Africa, despite the increasing Jewish literacy in French and the creation of a Gallicized Jewish elite, most jobs went to the French and Italian settlers.

In Tangier, designated an international city in 1923 until Morocco annexed it in 1956, Jews maintained a strong commercial dominance that predated the twentieth century; they worked primarily in banking. As a free port, Tangier attracted Jews from French and Spanish Morocco and European Jewish refugees from the Dodecanese Islands and Central Europe. In Tangier Jews were mainly craftsmen, bank officials, agents of trading companies, or merchants; they controlled exports to England and the United States of leather goods, skins, and eggs and imports to the Spanish protectorate of Morocco of textiles, automobiles, furniture, flour, and spices.

Jews were also attending universities and professional schools, graduating as physicians, engineers, attorneys, pharmacists, and teachers. Among the graduates from Iraq, Libya, and Tunisia were significant numbers of women. By the 1950s, until these countries placed quotas on the number of Jews allowed in higher education, Jews graduated in far greater proportion than their percentage of the population. Although business and commerce remained highly regarded, Jews also began taking degrees in the natural and applied sciences.

At the same time the Alliance Israélite Universelle and the Organization for Rehabilitation through Training (ORT), an organization founded in Russia in 1880 to provide vocational training, worked to raise the economic level of Jews who continued to work in the older, more traditional occupations. In keeping with its goal of Europeanizing Middle Eastern Jewry, the AIU trained Jews for occupations that were not traditionally considered Jewish. In Turkey Jews worked in carpentry, shoemaking, and chair making, as coppersmiths and dentists, but they also became picture-frame makers, heating mechanics, watchmakers, lithographers, marble masons, joiners, haberdashers, pharmacists, painters, bookbinders, woodcarvers, upholsterers, and typographers. Women were being trained to be milliners, dressmakers, launderers, needleworkers, and lace workers. ORT provided vocational training programs, technical assistance, and small business loans in Algeria, Morocco, Tunisia, and Iran. After World War II ORT taught such trades as mechanics, bookkeeping, stenography, plumbing, and modern dressmaking as means to economic independence. With the emigration of educated and wealthy Jews in the 1950s and 1960s to Europe and to Israel, these organizations and the American Jewish Joint Distribution Committee continued to work in the region, providing a safety net for the poor who remained.

Jewish artisans were employed in small ateliers, and Jewish workers were hired for the factories that were becoming significant components of the new Middle Eastern economic structure. There is evidence that since the early Ottoman period some workers were organized in guilds, professional associations that also operated as mutual aid societies. Guilds were generally organized along ethnoreligious lines. For example, Jews had their own guilds for goldsmiths and tailors in Tripoli and for butchers and cheese and yogurt makers in Brusa, Turkey. Members of the society of Jewish boat owners in eighteenth-century Istanbul were the first to ferry people across the Golden Horn; they were later joined by workers in associated occupations, such as fishermen, fruit vendors, and wine sellers, all of whom were dependent upon boat transport. The organization also provided aid for families of men lost at sea.

By the beginning of the twentieth century, a Jewish working class was already evident in Salonika, Libya, Morocco, and Tunisia. In Salonika about ten thousand Jews worked in the tobacco industry, with many women employed in textile, cigarette, and brick factories. Jewish-owned breweries did not employ Jews because the plant had to run twenty-four hours a day, seven days a week. In 1909 Jewish porters in Salonika organized to save their jobs when the government made plans to connect the rail line directly to the port, thus obviating the need to carry cargo the one kilometer from the railhead to the dock. The porters lost and had to find other jobs. During World War II Jewish women working in British military laundries in Libya struck for higher wages, as did clerks in Jewish department stores in Cairo. In Morocco Jewish women were members of the Moroccan Labor Union (Union Marocaine de Travail). Though not founders of most of the Communist parties in the region, Jews were prominent members. Jews still worked as porters, peddlers, and sellers of bread in the market, and many lived a hand-to-mouth existence in the rural areas, but a much higher percentage made up the middle- and upper-class society that Middle Eastern Jewry was becoming in the midtwentieth century.

These gains did not shield most Jews in the Middle East and North Africa from the effects of World War II. Where the Axis scored victories and Vichy rule was in effect in much of North Africa and Syria, Jews were at risk. In Iraq Jews were killed and property destroyed in the 1941 Farhud (pogrom). Where Jews were French citizens, as in Algeria, they were stripped of their citizenship and relegated to subject status. Laws of economic and social discrimination and of confiscation, excessive taxation, and quotas on professions were applied in Algeria, Morocco, and Tunisia, in varying degrees. Jews were allowed to engage in crafts and wholesale trading but could not work in real estate, moneylending, and banking. They were sent to labor camps and conscripted to battalions to dig fortifications. Because breadwinners could not earn a living, the community was in dire straits, especially in those areas where stateless Jewish European refugees had found their way out of Nazi domination and had to be supported. The Turkish government, though a neutral in the war, exacted economic penalties on the Jewish community via the Varlik Vergisi of 1942, creating economic setbacks from which the community was never to recover. Though a few wealthy Jewish industrialists live in Istanbul and Izmir, today's Turkish Jews tend to be small-scale entrepreneurs, the poor having emigrated to Israel after 1949.

With Allied victories in North Africa from 1943 to 1945 came economic stability but lingering apprehension. French-speaking, educated North African Jews worked to regain their French citizenship and emigrated to

France. The return of the British to Iraq in 1941, the establishment of the Mideast Supply Center there, and the British military presence both in Libya and in Egypt all were economic incentives for many Jews to remain. Yet anti-Jewish riots in Egypt, Libya, and Syria in 1945; in Bahrein, Aleppo, and Aden in 1947; and growing nationalist tides in Syria and in many countries after the United Nations declared the partition of Palestine in 1947 became reasons for Jews to emigrate. Their local association with the colonial powers, and the Palestine issue, rapidly made Jews and other minorities targets during the postwar decolonialization. In an era of intense nationalism the role of Jews in the economy—the privileges they had gained through capitulations and their positions in the civil service—came under scrutiny. Soon Muslims began replacing Jews in government jobs; professional schools instituted quotas for Jewish admissions; and socialist governments sequestered or nationalized businesses. Noting the growing signs of danger, those Jews who could transferred their liquid assets and emigrated to Europe and the Americas, leaving those with economic roots in the country and the indigent to await the political dénouement.

In 1935 Iraq began to weed Jews from the bureaucracy to make room for "real" Iraqis; by 1950 few Jews remained in government jobs, quotas were in place for professional opportunities for employment, and import licenses were restricted, requiring Jews to work with Muslim partners. The Egyptian Company Law of 1947, amended in 1954, stipulated that 75 percent of the employees, 90 percent of the laborers, and 50 percent of the capital in a company had to be Egyptian. As most Jews then in Egypt had foreign passports or were stateless, these nominal Egyptians had to be replaced with real Egyptians, and Jews lost their jobs. In Morocco, however, where Jews were recognized as an important source of profit, taxes, and administrative staffing, for a time after the departure of the colonialists (1956–61) the authorities prevented Jews from leaving. They considered Jewish emigration detrimental to the young Moroccan economy.

The newly independent regimes were also concerned with the flight of capital. In Iraq the restrictions on Jewish employment and excessive retroactive taxation led many to register to leave the country in 1950–51, even though they knew that they would lose their Iraqi citizenship. The government made the sale of Jewish property the responsibility of the Ministry of Defense, which confiscated property and restricted sales. Jewish banks that helped to alleviate the economic stress in the community lost their licenses. In Egypt those Jews who remained after the revolution of 1952 soon left in the wake of the 1956 Suez War, but they were allowed to take with them only a few pounds sterling ($10–$12). Thus in Iraq and Egypt alone, today's value of that seized or sequestered Jewish property is in the billions of dollars.

Whereas in Egypt, Iraq, or Syria sequestration and confiscation were frequently directed against Jews, postwar nationalization policies inspired by socialist trends in Tunisia, Morocco, Syria, or Algeria were imposed on all privileged ethnic and religious groups, including the Muslim majority. Nationalization measures of the Abdallah Ibrahim government of Morocco (1958–60); Nasser's nationalization campaign in Egypt in the 1960s; Ahmad Ben Bella's *autogestion* (self-management) and takeover of European businesses and farms as well as the properties and assets of Jews who left Algeria following independence (1962–65); Tunisia's Neo-Destour socialist policies under Habib Bourguiba; and currency restrictions and nationalization in Syria under the Syro-Egyptian Union (1958–61) and under the Baʿth regime (1960s) affected all the affluent. These policies prompted Jews and non-Jews to emigrate immediately. While the less affluent, who were mostly employees or small-scale entrepreneurs, usually emigrated to Israel, the affluent opted for resettlement in Europe and the Americas. Those privileged elements that preferred to stay and weather the crisis, or to postpone their departure, often smuggled their capital to European banks or to financial institutions in Beirut.

Like many Iraqi Jews who remained in Baghdad until the 1970s, Jews from several communities in Morocco, Tunisia, and Algeria also delayed leaving partly because they owned property worth many millions of dollars. These properties were registered with the Ministry of the Interior, and Jews could not sell without its permission; the proceeds of the sales had to be kept in the country, either in cash in banks or reinvested in other property. In Syria, which made it difficult for Jews to leave until 1992, mainly in connection with the Arab-Israeli conflict, some Jews decided not to sneak out because they could not sell their property—they needed official approval to buy or sell property.

Only a few unusually influential Jews survived nationalization, managing to gain a position in the economies of several Arab states, especially in Turkey, Morocco, and Tunisia. Jewish financiers such as Robert Assaraf, Serge Berdugo, and André Azoulay worked with King Hassan II of Morocco to develop business partnerships, to increase Jewish and Israeli tourism to Morocco, and, together with Israeli Foreign Minister Shimon Peres, to organize the first regional economic summit at Casablanca in October 1994. Others have played similar roles in Turkey and in Tunisia.

At the end of the twentieth century the Middle East and North Africa were more religiously homogeneous than ever. Economic cooperation between Jews and Muslims was likely to be based in the growing global economy that operates from Paris, London, and New York. What is to be done about the Jewish assets and property that were nationalized by Middle Eastern regimes remains to be resolved.

RECOMMENDED READING

Benbassa, Esther and Aron Rodrigue. *Sephardi Jewry: A History of the Judeo-Spanish Community, Fourteenth–Twentieth Centuries.* Berkeley: University of California Press, 2000.

Issawi, Charles. *An Economic History of the Middle East and North Africa.* New York: Columbia University Press, 1982.

Laskier, Michael M. *The Jews of Egypt, 1920–1970: In the Midst of Zionism, Anti-Semitism, and the Middle East Conflict.* New York: New York University Press, 1992.

Rosenstock, Morton. "The House of Bacri and Busnach: A Chapter from Algeria's Commercial History." *Jewish Social Studies* 14 (1952): 343–64.

Schroeter, Daniel J. *Merchants of Essaouira: Urban Society and Imperialism in Southwestern Morocco, 1844–1886.* New York: Cambridge University Press, 1988.

CHAPTER

4

Community Leadership and Structure

Michael Menachem Laskier,
Sara Reguer, and Haim Saadoun

Jewish community life in the Diaspora centered on the synagogue and its related functions. The house of worship, the school, the *mikveh* (bathhouse), the inn or hostelry, and in some cases the hospital were often all housed in the synagogue complex—the larger the community, the more diverse the functions.

By the time of the seventh-century Muslim conquests, the Jews of the Middle East and North Africa had already experienced centuries of autonomous living in small communities, and thus their adjustment to the newly imposed *dhimmi* status was not difficult. Because religion defined identity, and Jewish law determined personal status issues, the rabbis dominated Jewish life. Although dynasties of rabbinic families emerged in many cities, similar to the clerical families in the world of Islam, talent could also catapult an unknown individual into a prominent position. He would usually be quickly married into the rival center of community power, that of the rich lay leader.

When the Ottoman Turks took over in the fourteenth to sixteenth centuries, the Jewish community continued its internal autonomy. The Ottomans imposed some controls but left the community to administer its own religious affairs, as well as courts of justice, education, slaughter houses, hospitals, philanthropic institutions, cemeteries, sanitation, and lighting. The leaders would collect taxes, as set by the authorities, and forward them to the government. The main revenue sources included taxes on wine and kosher meat; birth, marriage, and death registration; income derived from rental of community real estate holdings; and monies from wills, inheritance, and donations of the rich. Among the numerous charities were those that collected donations of food and clothing to provide dowries for poor brides, helped and visited the sick, obtained loans for the needy, buried the poor, ransomed captives and slaves, and aided penurious pupils. The community also had to maintain its buildings and pay the salaries of various functionaries, such as the *mikveh* lady, ritual slaughterer, grave digger, synagogue cleaner, and teacher.

Because the Jewish communities of the Ottoman Empire had different backgrounds—such as Greek-speaking Romaniotes, Ashkenazim, and Sephardim in Istanbul—they had many congregations, each organized by common geographical origins that selected its own officiating rabbis and managed its own internal affairs. The heads of the various congregations maintained contact with one another, as well as with the town authorities and other Ottoman officials. Each community, often in its own quarter of the city, was also responsible for street cleaning, lighting, and patrolling to prevent fires and robberies.

The rabbi was the community's highest official; he led the services in the synagogue, officiated at life cycle events, headed the religious court, and sometimes taught in the school. In the cities other judges helped him in the court; in smaller towns he was likely to make unilateral decisions. Because he was also concerned with secular matters, he often had the help of lay leaders (*parnasim*), for example, in appointing teachers or regulating Jewish taxes. Depending on the wealth of the *parnasim* and the individuals involved, the *parnasim* and the rabbis were often rival centers of power. The community enforced its internal laws through internal pressures, such as by refusing to give a synagogue honor to a man who had broken an internal law, or through punishment.

With the Tanzimat reforms of the Ottoman Empire in the mid-nineteenth century, the Ottoman authorities attempted to overhaul the *millet* system in general (the *millet* was a self-governing religious community), to bring about a uniform format and centralized administrative system. While many Jewish communities had elected their own head rabbi, in 1835 the Ottomans conferred the title of chief rabbi (*hakham bashi*) on their choice in Istanbul. The chief rabbi received official sanction through the granting of a special diploma of appointment (*berât*), thus making him a representative figure before the authorities. By 1900 the nomination for chief rabbi was the focus of power struggles between those who supported the status quo and those who favored modernization.

The Tanzimat called for overhauling the *millet*'s lay leadership as well, by establishing a 120-delegate general council that would elect both a seven-rabbi spiritual council and a nine-member lay council to carry out the day-to-day work. If legal autonomy dissipated somewhat after the Tanzimat decree was implemented on February 18, 1856, religious pluralism did continue, and lay leaders did not abandon their autocratic tendencies. The corporate entity of the *millet* basically remained intact, albeit functioning under the guise of an elected leadership.

The Tanzimat reforms affected only those Jewish communities within Ottoman control. This included communities in Turkey, Iraq, Syria, Lebanon, and Palestine. In the Balkans, as the Ottomans lost control to newly emerging nationalist countries, the communal structures came under close supervision of the new state bureaucrats. Morocco, Iran, and Afghanistan, never under Ottoman control, continued their traditional approach to community autonomy for religious minorities until these communities came into contact with European Jews, who began to interfere.

In the nineteenth century North Africa came under French, Italian, and Spanish colonial control. Although the occupations by Western powers occurred at different times, the generalization can be made that all treated local Jewish community structures in a similar fashion. In 1918 in French Morocco the authorities reorganized the rabbinic tribunals into seven lower courts and one supreme rabbinic tribunal in Rabat, appointed the chief rabbi, and paid *dayyanim* (religious court judges). The rabbis still enjoyed autonomy in civil and religious matters, however, and many viewed them—and the reorganized lay councils, whose terms were now limited to two years—as puppets of the regime. The lay councils came under the administration of the French-appointed inspecteur des institutions Israélites.

Not until 1945–47 did France implement another communal reform, creating the Central Council of Jewish Communities (CCJC) in Morocco, which was aimed at centralizing all the communities and their councils, thereby making them more efficient and modern. Yet the CCJC was plagued by internal rivalries and was subservient to the French until Morocco gained independence. Moreover, the Jewish communities of Spanish Morocco and the international zone of Tangier had separate leadership institutions, which were subordinate to the authorities there. Only after independence in 1956 did these communities join the CCJC. Beginning in the mid-1950s the community councils affiliated with the CCJC included numerous government-appointed Jewish leaders, several of whom advocated total integration of the Jews into the new Morocco. They opposed aliyah (immigration to Israel), which was in line with Moroccan government policy, called for the nationalization of the schools of the Alliance Israélite Universelle (AIU), and sought to destroy community institutions—opting for drastic communal reforms in the name of "national integration." Their outlook stirred tensions within the Jewish leadership hierarchy, particularly among those who were Zionist or who realized that communal self-liquidation through emigration to France, Canada, and Israel constituted the best solution to the problems of remaining in Morocco. The fervent Jewish integrationists were members or affiliates of the major political parties, among them the Istiqlal, the National Union of Popular Forces, and the National Democratic Party for Independence. In due course the Jewish integrationists reduced their opposition to communal self-liquidation and sided with the proponents of moderate community reforms.

In Tunisia the internal rivalries of the Tunisian community were based on the division between the indigenous Jews (the Touansa) and the Livornese immigrants of the seventeenth and eighteenth centuries (the Grana). The Grana tried to preserve their Sephardic cultural and political ties to Livorno. A 1710 agreement between the two gave the Grana full community autonomy, but the head of the Jews (*qa'id*) remained of Touansa origin. The two communities had their own autonomous rabbinic and lay organizations, but the Grana were Italian subjects and were European in dress and outlook. This traditional community structure remained intact, as in Morocco, even after the establishment of the French protectorate (1881–1956). The French created the office of the chief rabbi and instituted a nine-man assembly of notables, but this was merely an attempt by the French to supervise the Jewish community closely. The major community reforms implemented by the French took place in 1921 with the creation in the three urban centers of Tunis, Sousse, and Sfax of the Conseil de la Communauté Israélite, to which eligible voters democratically elected notable men. Electoral campaigns for the council reflected the internal political forces of the Tunisian Jews—namely, Zionists versus French assimilationists. Despite these lay organizations, the Jews retained internal community authority, and they continued to squabble even after World War II and the creation of two competing federations of Jewish communities. The return to a single Jewish federation in 1955 hardly engendered communal unity. As long as the French were in charge, they maintained a balance of power between the two. However, after independence in 1956 the Tunisian authorities dissolved the community federations and councils, as well as the welfare funds. New temporary Jewish management committees (Comités Provisoires de Gestion), which still existed in 1999, restricted the community organizations to holding religious services, overseeing Jewish education, and running concomitant philanthropic endeavors. As in Morocco, the authorities occasionally replaced Tunisian Jewish leaders with those they regarded as sufficiently Tunisian in culture and outlook.

Libya, which came under direct Ottoman rule in 1835, became an Italian colony in 1911. It remained under Italy's control until the Axis defeat during World War II. The Jewish community structure in Libya had been similar to that of other traditional Ottoman autonomous communities, with Ottoman reforms only touching their surface. The Ottoman government appointed Jewish magistrates to local provincial courts and paid their salaries, but because each religious community continued to be governed by its own laws and officials, the rabbinic rulings got government sanction. In 1916 Italy legally formalized the Jewish community structure in Libya. As time passed, this community too split between the modernizers and the traditionalists, but the competition never reached the level that emerged in the other countries.

The Jews of Egypt were a heterogeneous group, divided by regional origin and socioeconomic realities. Although Egypt originally was part of the Ottoman Empire, the Turks ceded Egypt to Muhammad Ali and his dynasty in the early nineteenth century, to be replaced unofficially by the British in 1882. Jewish community structure followed an autonomous tradition, with the smaller groups usually obeying decisions made by either the Cairo or the Alexandria rabbinate. Yet lay leadership gradually grew powerful. As early as the 1850s the Alexandria lay leaders established an elected five-member body approved by the authorities to administer community monies without rabbinic intervention. This power grew in the 1870s and was emulated by the Cairo lay leadership on the eve of World War I. The reason given for the changes was efficiency, but the community's autonomous structure essentially remained intact. The British occupiers, like the French, stayed out of internal community affairs.

The only Jewish communities in North Africa to experience sweeping reforms were those of Algeria. When France conquered Algeria in 1830, the authorities continued the custom of choosing the *muqaddam* (autocratic head of the Jews) from among the affluent merchant families, yet the authorities began divesting the rabbinic court of its absolute power, limiting its authority to personal status matters. In 1841 the French decided that French civil courts would hear all Jewish affairs, and they limited rabbis' role to leading worship and life rituals.

The most significant transformation of the old lay-and-rabbinic community system occurred after the mid-1840s. Following the intervention of France in Algerian community matters, the model of the Jewish consistory system was introduced into Algeria. The main function of the consistory was to encourage Jews to exercise modern vocational trades and adapt to modernization through French education; the consistory had become the official organization of the Jews in France in 1808. By the 1850s consistories existed in Algiers, Oran, and Constantine, the three main regional administrative zones of French Algeria. Because Algeria became an integral part of France, the new Algerian community bodies became subordinate to the Central Consistory, which was headquartered in Paris.

The Algerian consistory councils—whose ranks included chief rabbis imported from France, lay presidents, and vice presidents—were elected by a secret ballot to a term of no more than eight years. To become eligible a candidate had to be at least twenty-five years old and a French national. From 1870, when Algerian Jews were granted French citizenship by virtue of the Crémieux Decree, and served in the military, the consistory also stressed military service as a sacred duty.

The new consistory system in Algeria helped the poor, organized public worship, set up synagogues, administered ritual slaughter of animals, supervised nurseries, named the rabbis, provided religious instruction, and maintained the cemeteries. The rabbis became civil servants, their salaries and other expenses covered by the public (not the community) budget, and they had to swear allegiance to France. Unlike the preconsistory period, community leadership now encouraged Jewish youth to enter the productive trades and accept aspects of European lifestyles. After World War II, to make their work more effective the consistories of Algeria organized themselves into a community umbrella organization, the Fédération des Communautés Israélites d'Algérie (FCIA), in April 1947; the elected representatives of the consistories of Algiers, Oran, and Constantine elected the FCIA board from among their number.

A principal decision of the FCIA at its inception was to fight against the indifference of the middle class to their Jewishness, as well as to install a network of social agencies, in an effort to resist the trend toward assimilation that was noticeable in the mixed marriages with local non-Jewish Europeans. The budgets of the FCIA and the consistories depended on the same sources: membership fees; revenues from goods, properties and synagogues; taxes on kosher wine and meat; and a tax on religious ceremonies. The FCIA allocated a substantial portion of its receipts to the Rabbinical College, created in 1948 at Algiers, which trained rabbis and teachers. Emigration in the 1960s and 1970s ended the community, and most communal organizations ceased to exist for the few remaining Jews in Algeria.

If Algeria can be seen as the most modern of Jewish communities in the region, Yemen, Iran, and Afghanistan would be the most traditional. Yemen had neither lay councils nor a centralized structure for community affairs; the authorities placed these responsibilities in the hands of a leading personality who kept in touch with the local ruler. Real authority in Yemen's capital, Sanᶜa, lay in the rabbinic council (*bet-din*), whose decisions were accepted throughout Yemen. During the brief Ottoman occupation there, from 1872 to 1918, the Turks tried to bring Yemen into line with the other provinces of the empire, by appointing a *hakham bashi,* but this was a fleeting reform, and the Yemenite spiritual leaders (*mori*) continued to lead their Jewish communities, both in the synagogue and the *bet-din.* This remained the situation until the final emigration to Israel in 1949.

The Jewish communities of Persia (Iran) and Afghanistan used the same traditional structure found in Yemen, with the rabbi (mullah) serving as the main decision maker in religious and personal status affairs. The lay leadership, organized in a *hevrah* (society), took care of community needs. Even the *jizya* (head tax) continued through the early reign of Reza Shah Pahlavi (1923–41), although he allowed personal status matters to continue under religious autonomy. The *hevrah* then became more modernized and became known by a new term, *anjoman* (society), with one such body for each city. Centralizing charity and community needs led to the creation of new Iranian Jewish organizations in the twentieth century, but the community autonomy remained intact, as it had in pre-Pahlavi times, with no powerful all-Iranian Jewish community organization coming into existence. After the Islamic Revolution of 1979, Iran's *anjomans* were challenged by young Jewish reformists who, despite their secular outlook, identified with the new regime to the point of sharing its anti-Israel policies. The reformists gradually achieved representation within the community councils and soon realized the impossibility of coexisting with the Islamists. The ayatollahs closed down the Jewish reformists' once dynamic newspaper, *Tammuz,* because it criticized the government's appropriation of Jewish schools and the pressure on Jews to adhere to new dress codes.

The European colonial powers left their imprint on the Jewish communities of North Africa, from Morocco to Egypt, and on Iraq, Palestine, Syria, and Lebanon in the interwar period. Only Turkey escaped European occupation, as Mustafa Kemal Atatürk shaped the modern Turkish Republic of the 1920s; in that period Jews became Turkish citizens, and the practice of Judaism was a private concern.

In Ottoman Palestine the Jewish community was divided not only by ethnic, cultural, and linguistic origins but, after 1882 and the first Zionist migration to Israel, also by religious and secular concerns. After World War I the end of Ottoman rule meant the end of traditional internal autonomy for Jewish communities and Istanbul-centered control of traveling *hakham bashis,* but the fragmented community organizations continued. The British tried to introduce modern government organization in Palestine but found it more convenient to perpetuate the Ottoman *millet* system of semiautonomous communities. The Jews there used this to set up a modern quasi-government, with an elected assembly, to run their affairs. In Palestine, then, as a result of the large number of secular Ashkenazi Jews arriving from Eastern Europe, community organization, rabbinic leadership, and traditional life became inextricably bound to the Western, Ashkenazic-powered politics of the Yishuv as it moved toward independence and the establishment of a modern state. The other country to come under British mandate rule was Iraq. The Tanzimat reforms of the Ottoman government had affected Iraq's Jewish communities as it had in all other provinces. Baghdad's *hakham bashi* was the chief religious figure, assisted by both a religious and a lay council. Again, as in most communities the personality and power conflicts were many. Under the British mandate, as well as after independence, Iraqi Jews were citizens with minority status. Their traditional community structures remained intact, supplemented by new independent philanthropic societies.

The French ran their mandates in the same way as the British in regard to Jewish community structure. The real difference was in the attitude of the lay leadership, which became a modernized, educated group that did not look to the rabbinic elite for direction. Political and economic instabilities affected French mandate communities; as poverty increased, so did emigration. In Syria, with independence from France (1941) and anti-Israel feelings among Syrians, the Jewish community plunged into such chaos that the traditional organizations could not easily cope. Many Syrian Jews escaped to Lebanon where the Beirut community institutions assisted them. It was only a matter of time before the Lebanese Jews too closed their community organizations and emigrated.

Modern life and the changes it brought intensified community dissent. In premodern times the lay authority vied with the religious leadership regarding various controls; modernity intensified those conflicts. Soon the influence of Zionism, generational disputes, and Jewish community participation in local and national politics became points of dissension, as were the types of education to give one's children.

Changes in the community structure and leadership also came from outside the Middle East, from Western organizations that existed alongside the traditional. The traditional leadership fought all these changes, but inevitably modernization and westernization won. The new organizations promoted education, welfare, advocacy, social reforms, Zionism, and nationalism. Yet not every new idea affected all these communities, nor did they affect these communities equally.

European and American Jewish organizations had become active on behalf of the Jews of the region in the latter half of the nineteenth century. These organizations became an essential part of regional Jewish life, and they generated reform and modernization. Some are still active in Morocco and Iran, where Jewish communities continue. The Alliance Israélite Universelle (AIU) came to the Ottoman Balkans, Turkey, and Arab lands as early as the 1860s. In addition to promoting French educational interests, this organization fought vigorously for the political rights of Jews in Morocco, Iran, Syria, and Lebanon. The AIU's central committee in Paris, well connected with the Quai d'Orsay, and the AIU teachers and principals on the local level, struggled to lift restrictions imposed by the Islamic *ulama* (religious elite), the regional governors, or the colonial authorities.

The school principals monitored the perpetration of abuses and apprised the European consuls and the AIU leadership in Paris. Consequently, Middle Eastern and North African regimes removed many anti-Jewish measures. Further, AIU personnel in such major centers as Tangier, Casablanca, Algiers, Istanbul, Izmir, Jerusalem, Salonika, Damascus, and Beirut were influential in Jewish community politics. They participated in council sessions, lobbied for curricular and social reforms of the rabbinic schools, and fortified links between local Jews and Jews in Europe.

Since the 1940s other external organizations that have affected internal community developments in the Middle East and North Africa, include the schools of the Organization for Rehabilitation through Training (ORT; founded in Russia to promote vocational training); OSE (the European-based Oeuvre de Secours aux Enfants, which extended its medical clinics); Otzar ha-Torah (a Sephardic organization established by American Jews of Syrian origin that operated religious schools in Morocco and Iran); Ohale Yosef-Yitshaq (religious classes and yeshivas under the sponsorship of the World Lubavitch Organization); the WJC (World Jewish Congress, whose branches became active in North Africa); the AJC (American Jewish Committee, which entered the North African arena through its European office in Paris); the AJDC (American Jewish Joint Distribution Committee, which was created by American Jews to finance community institutions and Jewish emigration, and to provide welfare assistance using money from the United Jewish Appeal); and the Jewish Agency for Palestine (to organize aliyah).

The post–World War II contribution to community service afforded by the World Jewish Congress, the AJDC, and the Jewish Agency deserve some attention. The World Jewish Congress opened sections in North Africa led by local Jewish intellectuals, some of whom sat on community councils and the Moroccan CCJC. Its sections in Algeria, Tunisia, and Morocco (the main North Africa bureau was headquartered in Algiers), in conjunction with the organization's Geneva, London, Paris, and New York offices, monitored anti-Semitism. Together they pressured colonial administrations to grant Jewish populations greater equality with the Muslim and European populations.

The World Jewish Congress could not open offices in the Middle East, given the suspicion of Arab regimes toward organizations of this type. Such obstacles did not deter its European representatives from following closely the measures adopted against Jews, such as banning emigration, the confiscation of financial and immovable assets, and the arrest or prosecution of community leaders, especially in Iraq, Egypt, and Syria. In post-independence Morocco (i.e., after 1956) the sections of the World Jewish Congress prodded the authorities to bestow official recognition upon the CCJC. They tried to influence, albeit unsuccessfully, the Bourguiba regime in Tunisia not to reduce the powers of community institutions. From 1956 to 1961, when Morocco prevented large-scale aliyah to Israel, the congress's Moroccan sections and its London bureau courted the government, with limited success, to liberalize emigration policies. Even the appointment of Dr. Leon Benzaquen, a Jewish community leader, to a cabinet post in Morocco's first independent government was partly accomplished because of intervention by the World Jewish Congress.

The American Jewish Joint Distribution Committee has many achievements to its credit in the Jewish communities since the end of World War II. Once it opened and staffed offices in the Maghreb, it provided money to augment the scope of the AIU and other educational institutions. It pressured Morocco's and Tunisia's outmoded rabbinic schools to modernize and offer general education, persuaded school principals to teach more Hebrew and thus prepare the youth for aliyah, and subsidized OSE clinics, youth summer camps, and community loan associations. In Algeria the AJDC induced the Fédération des Communautés Israélites d'Algérie and consistories to set up social service departments. In the 1950s the AJDC introduced into the Maghreb the notion of social workers and community service in the American sense. Experienced AJDC staff members who had graduated from the Paul Baerwald School of Social Work in Jerusalem trained Algerian and Tunisian community social workers. The new social workers made an immense contribution to community leadership and to the poor and needy. When Israel began organizing emigrations from North Africa and applying social and health criteria in selecting immigrants, the AJDC, in collaboration with community leaders, gave health and welfare assistance to those who were rejected in an effort to make them eligible for emigration.

In Syria and Egypt, where the AJDC could not operate locally, the organization funneled money to the communities through third parties. To get money into Syria the AJDC first transferred funds to banks in Beirut and then to Damascus and Aleppo. From 1956 the AJDC cooperated with Egypt-based representatives of the International Committee of the Red Cross to help Cairo's Jews in four ways. The first was assisting emigrants; this included all pre-emigration expenses, paid by the Jewish community of Cairo and reimbursed with AJDC funds by the Red Cross upon presentation of monthly accounts. The second was assisting the communities; the AJDC channeled money through the Red Cross to the Cairo community council, contributing to its budget. The third was assistance to needy people through the rabbinate in Cairo, paid for by the Red Cross with money from the AJDC upon presentation of monthly accounts. The fourth was helping the communities deal with the paperwork required by reimbursement programs that demanded detailed accounts of income and expenditures to justify the subsidies.

From the 1950s on, the Jewish Agency for Palestine became an important component of community service in French North Africa. The colonial presence there, and the special relationships developed after 1949 between Israel and France, enabled Israeli activity within the Maghreb to enjoy semilegality. In addition to organizing aliyah, and supported by the Alliance, ORT, and AJDC, the Jewish Agency established departments of Youth and Pioneer, Middle Eastern Jewry, Youth Aliyah, and Torah Education, and all were active educationally among the youth in paving the way for community emigration. Following Morocco's independence, the authorities banned aliyah, so Israeli-sponsored Zionism resumed clandestinely. In Tunisia and Algeria the aliyah continued uninterrupted.

Various volunteer organizations and movements had either been initiated locally or were branches of worldwide movements. They functioned separately from the local governing community councils, although the volunteers occasionally received financial aid from the councils. Among the noted voluntary organizations were the pro-Zionist Charles Netter group and the

Magen David Association of young adults, both headquartered in Casablanca. The Charles Netter group traces its existence to the 1930s. It cooperated with Israeli emissaries, beginning in the 1940s, to launch legal and clandestine aliyah, and, together with the Magen David Association, spread Modern Hebrew and contemporary Israeli culture. Both had several thousand members in the early 1950s. Movements with pro-Zionist leanings had emerged after 1920 in Egypt, Tunisia, Syria, and Lebanon under the names of Maccabee, Union Universelle de la Jeunesse Juive, Hapo^cel, Hatekhiya, and Kadima. Some were movements of high school and college students.

The most impressive of the youth and young adult voluntary and scouting movements in modern Morocco were the Eclaireurs Israélites de France (EIF), known since 1956 as Eclaireurs Israélite du Maroc (EIM), and the Département Educatif de la Jeunesse Juive (DEJJ). The EIF was a scouting movement headquartered in France that extended its activity throughout North Africa and obtained official recognition from the authorities. Unlike the barely tolerated and small Israeli-style pioneering movements, the colonial administration allowed the EIF to function publicly in all its community endeavors and permitted members to wear their movement's uniforms. In 1958 the movement had eighteen hundred uniformed male scouts and enjoyed the full support of the newly created Moroccan Youth Ministry.

Created by French-educated young adults and financed by the AJDC, the DEJJ stressed the importance of cooperating with the Moroccan Muslim Youth Movement; this included joint summer cultural programs in several major cities or the Atlas Mountains, under the sponsorship of the colonial administration until 1956, and under the aegis of the Youth Ministry in independent Morocco. During the 1950s the DEJJ established community centers in the *mellahs* (quarters) of Casablanca, Fez, Meknès, Rabat, and Marrakesh. Hundreds of young adults took part in the centers' activities, which, among other programs, included rudimentary vocational training. To forge better ties with the veteran community leadership, the DEJJ, whose main leaders had been recruited from the ranks of the EIF/EIM, became increasingly involved in wider community responsibilities. Patterned after community centers in the United States, the centers began serving adults, holding free discussions and lectures on Jewish issues. They regularly invited Muslim community leaders to explore matters related to Judeo-Muslim coexistence. In 1958 the DEJJ served more than six thousand youths and young adults and extended into various spheres, such as social work among the underprivileged, assistance to delinquent youngsters, social dances, sports, and shabbat gatherings. AJDC money underwrote special classes in French and general education in the *mellahs* that the DEJJ organized for those youth not enrolled at the AIU and other primary day-school networks. In the late 1950s the number of such children surpassed twenty-seven hundred.

No less dynamic was the Comité Juif Algérien d'Etudes Sociales (CJAES), formed by the most prominent French-educated Jews in French Algeria in 1917 and subsequently reorganized. Active mainly in Algiers, the CJAES worked to maintain Jewish civil liberties and collaborated with the World Jewish Congress to do so. This extracommunity organization, like the Ligue Contre l'Antisémitisme Allemand (LICA), which functioned in the Egyptian Jewish communities during the 1930s and 1940s, struggled against anti-Semitism and anti-Jewish newspapers in France and Algeria. When the Vichy government in Algeria temporarily deprived the Jews of their French citizenship, the CJAES fought for its restoration. At the height of the Algerian national revolution (1954–62), the CJAES protected the Jews and their organizations from attacks by French and Muslim factions, each of which was pressuring Jews to join their ranks. Realizing that Jewish organizations were positioned between the French hammer and the Algeria anvil, the CJAES contended that the consistories and the FCIA could not take sides in the Franco-Algerian war; the consistories and FCIA were concerned with religious practices and the administration of other Jewish affairs. Taking the role of the community's advocate, the CJAES tried without success not to alienate either the French or the Algerian rebels. Speaking with the voice of neutrality, it said that although France had to remain in Algeria, the Muslim majority deserved greater political and social liberties; the Jews would coexist with both the Muslim and European communities.

While Algeria remained French, the CJAES used its journal, *Information Juive,* and other forums to call for an interfaith dialogue among the Muslim, European, and Jewish communities. Like the DEJJ, it organized meetings that attracted audiences of several hundred, often including government officials and other non-Jews. It held annual commemorative meetings on the anniversary of the Warsaw Ghetto Uprising and on Israel's Independence Day.

The B'nai B'rith entered several Jewish communities in the Middle East. The oldest of the Jewish fraternal and service organizations, B'nai B'rith extended its influence to Egypt through local Ashkenazi émigrés and affluent Sephardim. The Maimonides Lodge opened in Cairo in 1887 and in Alexandria in 1891. B'nai B'rith founded lodges in Istanbul and Edirne before World War I and in Aleppo, Beirut, and Damascus during or before the French mandate period. In the 1920s the Turkish B'nai B'rith lodges led the campaign in Kemal Atatürk's new republic for Jews to embrace Turkish as their primary language, and it promoted Turkish-language societies. In Egypt B'nai B'rith implemented educational and welfare reforms. Its campaign to dissolve the Cairo community council, whose members B'nai B'rith accused of having undemocratic outlooks, failed. Conversely, the Cairo B'nai B'rith initiative to limit the term of community president and to create more welfare organizations and clinics proved successful. In the 1930s B'nai B'rith and LICA led the anti-Nazi campaign of the Alexandria and Cairo communities, calling for the boycott of German-made products. In Syria and Lebanon B'nai B'rith led the secularization and modernization campaign. In Aleppo B'nai B'rith members served on the community council, while in Beirut and Aleppo, B'nai B'rith worked to expand girls' education as a countermeasure to Christian missionary schools.

The procedure for founding B'nai B'rith lodges in Damascus and Beirut aroused little or no opposition. This was not the case in Aleppo, the heartland of Syrian Jewish traditionalism. In the 1920s the rabbinic elite led by Rabbi Ezra Hammaoui questioned the legitimacy of the lodges. B'nai B'rith enlisted Yaʿakov Meir, a leading Sephardic rabbi, and Hayyim Bijarano, then chief rabbi of Turkey, to intercede on its behalf before the Aleppan spiritual leaders. Aleppo's rabbis regarded B'nai B'rith as an outgrowth of Freemasonry that was influenced by the teachings and practices of this movement's secret fraternal lodges. Although the Freemasons were anticlerical, B'nai B'rith members were dedicated Jews whose goal was to foster community life. Despite rabbinic opposition, B'nai B'rith survived in Aleppo, because of the support it received from lay community leaders who feared the strength of the rabbis and saw B'nai B'rith as an ally in the drive toward modernization.

Zionist youth movements, like the kibbutz-oriented Dror, Ha-Shomer Ha-Tsaʿir, Habonim, and B'nai Akiva, and Jewish Palestine–style political parties—Mapai, Mapam, Herut, and Mizrachi/Ha-Poʿel Ha-Mizrachi—became somewhat prominent in several key communities, notably in Morocco, Tunisia, and Egypt. Zionist federations and associations also sprang up, some as early as the late 1890s, others in the mid-1920s. They developed either as local initiatives or as a result of external interference by Ashkenazim from Palestine and Eastern Europe who settled there. The Zionist federations that emerged in the Maghreb, the Balkans, Turkey, Egypt, and Iran included the Fédération Sioniste de France/Section du Maroc, the Union Sioniste Algérienne, and the Fédération Sioniste de Tunisie. They existed as legal or semilegal organizations, depending on the political climate in those countries. In Yemen and Syria Jews could not organize formal Zionist associations and federations. But several remote semirural communities, including Djerba and Gabès in southern Tunisia, had Zionist associations.

Before 1939 most Zionist organizations and movements worldwide were philanthropic. They raised money for settling European Jews in Palestine but were not generally oriented toward aliyah. Few promoted Modern Hebrew and modern culture. Often they had no backing from governing councils or the rabbinate. Community lay leadership in the Middle East and North Africa included groups that were non-Zionist or anti-Zionist, and among the latter were those who regarded Zionist activism as a plan to deplete community resources by highlighting the centrality of the Yishuv at the expense of local communities. Community leaders also thought that Zionists had set out to limit the lay leadership and offer an alternative leadership. That attitude changed gradually in the 1940s and especially in the 1950s as communities had to prepare for major emigration to Israel. With the founding of the State of Israel in 1948, and the war with Arab nations that continued into 1949, Israeli-sponsored underground Zionist movements became part of Jewish reality in the region. Underground Israeli emissaries and local activists frequently expressed discontent with local Jewish leaders, reproaching them for servility to Arab regimes. Together the activists hoped to counter the entrenched community elite and win adherents to the idea of community self-liquidation. Among the underground movements that trained youth in self-defense and organized clandestine aliyah and Zionist education were the Tnuᶜa (Movement) in Iraq, the Egyptian Zionist underground, and Morocco's Misgeret (Framework). In association with the envoys from Mossad le-Aliya Bet (Organization for Illegal Immigration), the Iraqi Tnuᶜa directed the major aliyah operation called Ezra and Nehemiah in 1950 and 1951, as well as some earlier rescue programs there. The Egyptian underground, dominated by the local Ha-Shomer Ha-Tsaᶜir pioneer movement, took charge of much of the Egyptian aliyah—more than fourteen thousand Jews in 1948–50. It too had been linked to the Mossad le-Aliya Bet. The Mossad, Israel's spy service, sponsored the Moroccan Misgeret underground during the postcolonial era, after Morocco's decision was to curb Jewish emigration. The Misgeret organized the secret aliyah of Moroccan Jewry to Israel from 1956 to 1961.

In challenging the influence of some of the region's community notables and offering themselves as alternatives, the underground forces believed that decolonization, the Arabization of schools, the marginalization of Jews in the new national economies, and the effect of the Arab-Israeli conflict made aliyah inevitable for Jews of those countries. Therefore, they needed to challenge the reluctance of Jewish community leaders and their governments to permit aliyah and worked to win over the Jewish people through propaganda strategies and by stirring anxiety among potential emigrants, that is, by resorting to various tactics of psychological warfare.

Community leaders in those countries gradually cooperated with underground activists. In Iraq in 1950 they realized that emigration to Israel would provide their best alternative. The Baghdad Jewish leadership worked with the Iraqi regime to determine a formula that would accelerate emigration. In Egypt the Cairo community leadership forged ties with the Zionist underground and helped to finance the mass emigration in 1949–50. Several important Moroccan community lay leaders and noted rabbis joined ranks with the Misgeret in the late 1950s; Moroccan Zionists and non-Zionists ultimately concurred that the political and economic future of the Jews required large-scale community-wide departures.

RECOMMENDED READING

Benbassa, Esther and Aron Rodrigue. *Sephardi Jewry: A History of the Judeo-Spanish Community, Fourteenth–Twentieth Centuries.* Berkeley: University of California Press, 2000.

Krämer, Gudrun. *The Jews in Modern Egypt, 1914–1952.* Seattle: University of Washington Press, 1989.

Laskier, Michael M. *North African Jewry in the Twentieth Century: The Jews of Morocco, Tunisia, and Algeria.* New York: New York University Press, 1994.

Marcus, Abraham. *The Middle East on the Eve of Modernity: Aleppo in the Eighteenth Century.* New York: Columbia University Press, 1989.

CHAPTER

5

Religion: Rabbinic Tradition and the Response to Modernity

ZVI ZOHAR

Arguably, the nineteenth and twentieth centuries were the most dynamic and rapidly changing years of human history. For Judaism, as for many other religions, the central challenge of these years was secularization—the marginalization of religion in social and individual life. Science and technology posed another significant challenge. On a philosophical level science seemed to enable the understanding of nature without a need for the divine; on a more practical level ever more rapid technological advances led to correspondingly rapid change in patterns of everyday life, creating gaps between religion and social reality.

In the eighteenth century the Jewish communities of Western and Central Europe were the first to face the consequences of modernity's challenge to traditional religion. By the midnineteenth century, however, the Jews of most Muslim lands also were feeling the consequences of developments in Europe. By the eve of World War I modernity was significantly affecting Jews in North Africa and the Middle East in direct proportion to their economic status, their level of education, and their urban location. That is to say, a wealthy Jew who had been educated by the Alliance Israélite Universelle (AIU) and who was living in a newly built quarter of Cairo was quite modernized, whereas modernization had little effect on the life of a lower-class Jew educated in a *kuttab* (religious school for young children) and living in a Kurdish village. The interwar years saw the extension of modernization to large sectors of the Jewish middle and lower-middle classes. After the midtwentieth century, finding any Jew in these regions whose lifestyle and mind-set remained unaffected by modernity would have been extremely difficult.

Halakhah, or religious law, is the encompassing Jewish normative framework that was created to provide religiously legitimated guidance for almost all aspects of life. From the second century B.C.E. the guardians and trustees of Judaism in general and of halakhah in particular have been the rabbis. As scholars they study the written and the oral Torah, which are the sources of halakhah, interpret them, and apply them. As leaders the rabbis educate their community to want to follow halakhah and teach congregants how to do so. In ages of stability and tradition the primary task of rabbis is maintenance and refinement. In times of change the given is no longer self-evident, and rabbis must use a more activist strategy to face the challenges of dynamic new realities.

This chapter focuses on the rabbis of the Middle East and North Africa during the nineteenth and twentieth centuries (excluding Israel since 1948). First, the chapter surveys the fortunes of the rabbinic class during these two centuries. Then it present an overview of their response to modernity, especially as reflected in their halakhic writings.

THE VICISSITUDES OF THE RABBINIC CLASS IN MODERN TIMES

The very definition of *rabbi* is problematic; while study of Torah was a central cultural-religious ideal in Judaism, Jews were ambivalent about deriving economic gain and social preeminence through Torah. Thus throughout Jewish history many individuals recognized by their communities and by their peers as qualified to fill rabbinic positions earned their living by other means, either by choice or by necessity.

The very phrase "rabbinic position" covers a wide range. Major urban communities developed an array of high-status rabbinic posts, including those of *rav ha-kollel* (chief rabbi of the community), *dayyan* (rabbinic judge), and *rosh yeshiva* (head of an academy of Torah learning). Candidacy for such posts was frequently international. The Jewish community of Cairo or Baghdad might well invite a prominent scholar from Jerusalem or Aleppo to serve as its *rav ha-kollel,* although a leading local scholar, perhaps also related by marriage to a community lay leader, might well have an advantage over "foreign" competitors. Low-status rabbinic positions, which required a measure of rabbinic scholarship, included teachers, scribes, and slaughterers; local talent usually filled these positions.

As a result of Tanzimat reforms in the Ottoman Empire, governments in the Middle East and North Africa began to create posts of chief rabbi (*hakham bashi*) on both the national and district levels. This trend began in 1835, when the sultan appointed Avraham Levi *hakham bashi* of the empire's Jewish *millet.* Government recognition of such "official" rabbis created new possibilities for tension between these appointees and other holders of authority in the community, both rabbinic and lay. A prime example in this context is Rabbi Haim Nahoum (1872–1960), who served as *hakham bashi* of the Ottoman Empire (1908–18) and then as *hakham bashi* of Egypt (1925–60). Although those governments regarded Nahoum as representing all Jews under their jurisdiction, other rabbis considered his rabbinic achievements as mediocre. As a result he gained a reputation as the "best rabbi of the diplomats and best diplomat of the rabbis."

To achieve a high level in rabbinic learning required years of study. Typically, after completing elementary education, an aspiring student would enter an advanced Torah academy, known as a yeshiva in some communities, as a midrash in others. Alternatively, or in addition, he could study as an individual under a practicing rabbi. Travel to far-off yeshivas seems to have been the exception. Most rabbis seem to have received *semikhah* (accreditation to serve as a rabbi) locally from one or several rabbis. Often such scholars were members of rabbinical families, with sons learning from grandfathers and fathers, such as the Ibn Danans and Sarfatis of Fez, the Berdugos and Toledanos of Meknès, and the Abitbuls of Sefrou. They had their family synagogues in their hometowns, and they had hereditary social positions and sources of material support. During their years of study rabbinical students were generally unable to earn a living and required support by others; thus the possibility of becoming a *hakham* (a man of wisdom, the term used in the Middle East and North Africa for a Torah expert) was partly contingent upon economic factors. The economic decline of Muslim lands in recent centuries became a salient factor in the decline of higher Torah study there, because communities, patrons, and families were less and less able to fund students through years of Torah study.

In addition, economic status and modernization were closely linked. Wealthy parents, who in earlier centuries might have sent a gifted son to study for the rabbinate, now tended to prefer a Western education. In premodern times a family might have considered a brilliant young scholar as a prime candidate for the hand of their daughter and therefore would support the young couple economically, enabling him to devote further years to study. With the change in social ideals, and the beginnings of Western education for girls, many parents considered such young men to be less desirable matches. Moreover, the increased complexity of economic activity in modern times and the growing professionalization of occupations made it difficult to regard Torah study as a primary vocation while earning a living through another occupation.

In many cases even the sons of rabbis, formerly considered the most appropriate candidates for a rabbinic career, often preferred other careers. With the advent of Western-style education, the diversification of professional possibilities, and new cultural horizons, a young man endowed with intellectual capabilities realized that he had many more options. The cadre of talent diverted to other channels could not but negatively influence the overall quality and number of candidates for Torah study and a rabbinic career. Modernization thus reinforced a decline in Torah study and rabbinic learning that began in the eighteenth century and became even more pronounced during the nineteenth and twentieth centuries. While we have no data on the number of rabbis living in Muslim lands during those centuries, at no point were there more than a few thousand, from Morocco in the west to Persia in the east, who had achieved a sufficiently high command of halakhic learning to be considered a *hakham.* Although the overall Jewish population of these lands increased during the nineteenth and twentieth centuries, the overall number of *hakhamim* probably decreased after 1900, reaching its lowest point in the late 1940s. This also contributed to a decrease in the number of cultural and literary works in the various genres of rabbinic writing, especially after World War I.

Several communities tried to grapple with these problems. In 1840 Rabbi Abdallah Somekh of Baghdad (1813–89) persuaded a leading Iraqi-Jewish businessman, who had amassed a fortune in colonial India, to endow a yeshiva in Baghdad; this institution, Beit Zilkha, produced most of Iraq's rabbis until World War II; its establishment led to a renaissance in Torah learning in Iraq during the second part of the nineteenth century, yet even its student population gradually declined during that period. However, Iraq's other great scholar of modern times, Rabbi Yosef Hayyim (d. 1909), did not study there; he learned from his father and other scholars and was then supported by his wealthy brothers.

Aleppo in northwestern Syria had been famous as a center of Torah study since the high Middle Ages. In the first half of the nineteenth century, rabbis and certain well-to-do individuals initiated a communal fund for the support of Torah scholars and promising students; the fund was augmented in 1891. Despite these measures, by 1933 only one yeshiva existed in Aleppo, attended by no more than twenty students, most of whom did not intend to serve as rabbis. At that time Aleppo had only ten rabbis, three of whom served as members of the rabbinical court. In Tunisia, long known as a center of Torah study, the yeshivas dwindled dramatically during the nineteenth and twentieth centuries, and the only remaining center of rabbinic learning was on the remote island of Djerba. Algerian Jewry had been in crisis since the eighteenth century; the French conquest and annexation led to a further decrease in Torah learning, with even the well-known midrashim of Constantine in decline. Thus the description of the situation in Morocco in 1912 by Rabbi Yosef Mesas (1892–1975) in *Otzar Ha-Mikhtavim* (Collected Correspondence) in 1912 may be regarded as an expression of a broad phenomenon:

> From the day that the French came to our city, there began a new era in the orders of life. He who calls it a good era—is not in error; and he who calls it a bad era—is not in error. For peace and quiet did increase in the land; but the calm and relaxation which had been in peoples' hearts, so that each felt happiness in his portion whether good or bad—completely vanished. For in all that men have need of, luxuries increased: in clothing and in livelihood, in housing and in utensils; this was especially so with regard to the women and girls, in whose noses rose powerfully the scent of new times. All this led to the increase of bother, toil and work, and involvement in all fields of commerce—accompanied by envy and competitiveness, and by the lust to ascend the rungs of wealth and pleasure. Therefore, all hearts and all minds were filled with many thoughts, both deep and simple, to devise artifices, to cunningly act, to craftily deceive—so as to fill one's hands with reams of money, by hook or by crook, to satisfy the belly of the times which always hungers and thirsts for luxuries, saying: "Give! Give!" to all that the era beneficently offers every day anew.
>
> And also those engaged in Torah began to leave their mother's bosom, and to go out each one to make his profit; for their souls too yearned to taste of the new era's delicacies. And so the pillars of Torah began to weaken—and there was no-one to prop them up, to support them or to admonish at the gate.
>
> (LETTER 212)

At this crucial junction, wrote Mesas in his *Otzar Ha-Mikhtavim,* a dramatic intervention took place: an unknown rabbi, Ze'ev Wolff Halperin, born in Russia and hailing from London, appeared one day in the *mellah* (Jewish quarter) of Meknès. After sizing up the scene for several days, he asked a young rabbi to convene all the young Torah scholars of the city in a synagogue early on a Saturday afternoon: "And I, too came there with the others invited. And he delivered in our ears a beautiful speech about Torah and Worship; and his pleasant speech aroused our hearts to love him and to cleave to him and to heed his voice. And he determined the establishment of a permanent Yeshiva, in which Talmud and the Codes would be studied every evening, in accordance with the regulations which he set out" (letter 212). Soon after, Rabbi Halperin gathered together all the city's elementary school teachers and set out new modes of teaching for them to follow; before long he convened a meeting of the town's merchants and artisans, encouraging them to participate in evening Torah classes for laymen. A month or two later he began convincing these same laymen to each donate a modest weekly sum and thus support a full-day yeshiva program for young Torah scholars. By midsummer the yeshiva was a reality, supported by money that an enthusiastic public committee collected.

This chronicle of events in Meknès describes an influence of the rabbinic world of Europe upon the rabbinic culture of Muslim lands in modern times. During the nineteenth century this influence was primarily by means of the written word, as scholarly Torah publications printed in Europe became increasingly available throughout North Africa and the Middle East. In the twentieth century European and North American Orthodox rabbis and organizations became involved in Torah-study institutions there. Of particular importance were post–World War II attempts by ultra-Orthodox rabbis to recruit young men from North Africa to replenish the student bodies of the Eastern European–style yeshivas that had been decimated by the Holocaust. Almost all men of Moroccan extraction who have qualified for the rabbinate since World War II have received their advanced Torah training at such institutions. This has had profound implications for the character of Jewish life in contemporary France and Israel.

SEPHARDIC RABBINIC CULTURE AND MODERNITY

Before 1950 the influence of European Orthodox Judaism upon the basic ethos of Sephardic rabbinic culture was quite limited. Generally speaking, the response of Sephardic rabbis to the challenges of modernity was different, in significant and interesting ways, from that of their Ashkenazic peers. These differences stem from two synergetic factors: differences between European and Islamic lands in the experience of modernization, and the cultural heritage of the Sephardic rabbinic elite.

In the eighteenth and nineteenth centuries European Jewry underwent processes of Haskalah (Enlightenment) and secularization, accompanied by intense internal social and ideological tensions. Many rabbis felt that these changes threatened the very existence of traditional Judaism, and to counter these threats they formulated a strategy that became known as Orthodoxy. The goal of Orthodoxy was to oppose the radical movements of Jewish modernists, which were seen as endangering the future of true Jewish life. The strategy of Orthodoxy, as formulated by its leaders, was to deny the legitimacy of all modernist innovations, stating that halakhah was an eternal, fixed corpus of normative directives. The Orthodox slogan "Torah prohibits the new" encapsulated this view of halakhah; however, this move was a double-edged sword because that assertion undermines the validity not only of "dangerous" innovations but also of any new halakhic ruling. In other words, although Orthodoxy was, first and foremost, a rejection only of Reform Judaism and Haskalah, the internal logic of its rejectionist strategy severely impaired the ability of Orthodox rabbis to respond to other aspects of modernity in a creative halakhic manner.

Several variables made modernization in North Africa and the Middle East different from that of Europe. One was the absence of Islamic anticlericalism; even Muslims who criticized the current sociopolitical and cultural situation of their society chose to characterize the sought-for changes as compatible with the norms and spirit of Islam. Likewise, Islamic religious leaders in these countries did not respond to modernity by forming radically different forms of Islamic religious life. In this respect Jews of Islamic lands were similar to their Muslim compatriots. Attacking rabbis as backward and criticizing halakhic Judaism as obscurantist was not acceptable, and movements that advocated the abandonment of rabbinic Judaism in favor of some new definition of Jewish identity did not develop. In general, even those sectors of the Jewish community whose lifestyle reflected the commandments of the Torah in only the most minimal way—including those who advocated the modern political ideologies of socialism, communism, or secular Zionism—did not seek to bolster their position by insulting the community's rabbis or traditions.

Other political-legal differences between Europe and the Middle East and North Africa were significant as well. In Europe during the Middle Ages different law systems applied to members of different social groups; in that context rulers were content to endorse the application of halakhah by Jewish communities and courts with regard to cases involving only Jews. In modern times European political thought sought to establish the state as the only framework entitled to make and enforce law and denied the notion of different laws for different social groups. Accordingly, the state discontinued recognition of the decisions of Jewish courts and rabbis, thus depriving them of an important aspect of their status and authority. In most of the Middle East and North Africa a dialectical development occurred in modern times: state legal reforms transferred civil cases from religious to state courts, yet for the first time state authorities empowered rabbinic courts (as well as those of other religions) in the realm of marriage, divorce, and family law in their community. In addition, chief rabbis of major cities were recognized as state functionaries. Thus, while the actual field of law ceded to the rabbis by the state was narrowed, the political and legal status of city rabbis and rabbinical court judges increased. Concomitantly, while a central theme of modern political thought in Europe was the separation of church and state, this idea was either not accepted or accepted in only a limited way in the Middle East and North Africa.

In the absence of Jewish ideological attacks upon Judaism or rabbinic authority in Muslim lands, and in the context of continued—and even increased—sociopolitical recognition of the status of official rabbis, the rabbis faced little external impetus to formulate a policy stating that the "Torah prohibits the new" or to refrain from reaching novel halakhic decisions if warranted by sociohistorical developments. An examination of the writings of such prominent rabbis of the nineteenth and twentieth centuries shows their prevailing attitude was that no immanent features in halakhah require rabbis to refrain from formulating new rulings. In consonance with Sephardic cultural heritage the rabbis held that the greatness and eternal vitality of halakhah was its capacity to express Judaism's noble values in a variety of forms, as appropriate to changing circumstances. In nineteenth-century Europe, for example, some called for the revision of Maimonides' Thirteen Principles of Jewish Faith. They suggested that the principle affirming belief in the absolute eternalness of the Torah be rephrased or deleted, so as to provide Jews with the capability of accommodating Judaism to modern conditions. Rabbi Eliyahu Hazan (1847–1908), born in Izmir and educated in Jerusalem, served as rabbi of Tripoli and then of Alexandria. He responded that the Torah as we have it requires no change at all in order to respond to contemporary historical developments. The reason, he wrote in *Zikhron Yerushalayim* (Remembrance of Jerusalem, 1874), is that

> Since the Holy Torah was given to physical human beings, who are always subject to changes stemming from differences in history and

> time, in rulers and decrees, in nature and climate, in states and realms—therefore, all Torah's words were given in marvelous, wise ambiguity; thus, they can receive any true interpretation at any time.... Indeed, the Torah of Truth, inscribed by God's finger, engraved upon the Tablets—will not change nor be renewed, for ever and ever. (57)

In other words, the words of the holy Torah are eternal, yet the eternalness of the Torah is manifested specifically in its inexhaustible capacity to yield multiple meanings, each appropriate to a different human reality.

A second example is Rabbi Ben-Zion Meir Hai Uzziel (1880–1953), born in the Old City of Jerusalem to an ancient and illustrious Sephardic family. From 1912 to 1939 he served as Sephardic rabbi of Jaffa and Tel Aviv and from 1939 until his death as chief Sephardic rabbi of Israel. In the introduction to the first volume of his collected responsa, *Mishpetei Uzziel* (1935), he totally rejects the central premise of European Orthodoxy and stresses that halakhah must respond to modern developments:

> In every generation, conditions of life, changes in values, and technical and scientific discoveries—create new questions and problems that require solution. We may not avert our eyes from these issues and say "Torah prohibits the New," i.e., anything not expressly mentioned by earlier sages is ipso facto forbidden. A-fortiori, we may not simply declare such matters permissible. Nor, may we let them remain vague and unclear, each person acting with regard to them as he wishes. Rather, it is our duty to search halakhic sources, and to derive, from what they explicate, responses to currently moot issues. . . . In all my responsa, I never inclined towards leniency or strictness according to my personal opinions; rather, my intention and striving were always to search and discover the truth. To the extent that my understanding enabled me, I walked in the light of earlier halakhic masters, whose waters we drink and whose light enlightens us; With this holy light, which issues from the source of the hidden, concealed Light, I illuminated my eyes. (ix–x)

Thus Uzziel rejects the path of both Orthodoxy and Reform. He states that halakhah can and should develop through hermeneutics and analogy, as applied by halakhists deeply motivated to discover the truth. Uzziel sees halakhah as far from a finite set of normative dicta; rather, he requires halakhists to discover anew how Jews should relate to developments in human life, values, and science, following the light contained in earlier rabbinic writings, in order to illuminate thought on contemporary issues.

A third example is Rabbi Hayyim David Ha-Levi, born in Jerusalem in 1924 and educated in Jerusalem's Sephardic yeshivas. He became a member of Israel's Chief Rabbinate Council in 1964 and served as chief rabbi of Tel Aviv from 1973 until his death in 1998. In response to criticism directed against him by an unnamed Orthodox rabbi, Ha-Levi rejected that rabbi's assertion that commitment to Judaism entails refraining from halakhic creativity. Because all legislation requires nearly constant revision due to "changes in the conditions of life," how is it, asks Ha-Levi, that the laws of the Holy Torah, revealed to Moses thousands of years ago, can still function and guide Jews today? He responds:

> This is possible only because permission was given to Israel's sages in each generation to renew halakha as appropriate to the changes of times and events. Only by virtue of this was the continuous existence of Torah in Israel possible, enabling Jews to follow the way of Torah. . . . There is nothing so flexible as the flexibility of Torah. . . . It is only by virtue of that flexibility that the People of Israel, through the many novel and useful rulings innovated by Israel's sages over the generations, could follow the path of Torah and its commandments for thousands of years.
>
> (186)

The similarity between Ha-Levi and Uzziel is striking: the same Torah can serve as the basis of Jewish life for thousands of years, despite far-reaching changes in society, history, science, and culture, because of the flexibility inherent in its words, whose potential is realized through the creative endeavors of the rabbis of each generation. Perennial renewal is a sine qua non of authentic halakhah. Clearly, the basic orientation of Sephardic rabbis, as reflected in these passages from Hazan, Uzziel, and Ha-Levi, differs from that of Ashkenazic Orthodoxy.

CONTINUITY AND CRITIQUE

In certain cases Sephardic rabbis of the first rank stated outright that contemporary Jewish orientations characteristic of secularized modernists more fully express valid Judaic values than do attitudes advocated by rabbinic leaders of the past. An example may be found in the writings of Rabbi

Ya'akov Moshe Toledano (1880–1960) who related to contemporary self-defense activities by Zionist Jews.

Toledano was born in Tiberias of an illustrious Sephardic family of Meknès, served as rabbi in Malta, Cairo, and Alexandria; he returned to Eretz Israel and served as Sephardic chief rabbi of Tel Aviv from 1942 until he died. For a brief period toward the end of his life, he also served as the minister for religious affairs of the government of Israel. Many yeshiva students were murdered during the 1929 riots in Palestine, while other Jews engaged in organized self-defense. Rabbi Toledano was asked which way was better: traditionalist passivity in the face of violence or secular Zionist self-defense? His response reflects a deeply religious critique of the guidance that many rabbis had offered to their communities in the past. According to Toledano, a theologically and morally mistaken understanding of the notion of exile had come to prevail in European rabbinic circles; as a consequence these rabbis preached that Judaism advocated a passive-submissive response to persecution. The Jewish masses had followed the teachings of these rabbis, reacting to pogroms not by self-defense but by allowing themselves and their families to be slaughtered for the sanctification of the Divine Name. Toledano believed that although stating the truth outright is not easy, it must be said: those rabbis bear direct and unequivocal responsibility for the Jewish blood that was spilled unnecessarily because of their misguidance:

> Many of our great rabbis, both in former generations and in current times, erred—and misguided the simple masses of our people—in the belief, that as long as we are in this hard Exile we are forbidden to lift up our head. Rather, we are commanded to bow ourselves down before every tyrant and ruler, and to give "our backs to the smiters and our cheeks to them that pluck off hair" (Isa. 50:6); as if the blood of Israel had been forfeited, and as if He—blessed be He—had decreed that "Jacob be given for a spoil and Israel to the robbers" (Isa. 42:24). They thought, that the decree of Exile and servitude to the nations included slavery and lowliness, and that—as a matter of sanctifying the Name even at the price of one's life—a Jew must forfeit his life and surrender himself like a slave or prisoner of war to Israel's enemies, even in a situation in which it would have been possible to resist them and to retaliate in kind.
>
> Let me, then, state outright, that—begging their pardon—they caused the loss of individual lives and of entire communities of the Jewish people, who in many instances might have saved themselves from death and destruction, had the leaders and rabbis of the generation

> instructed them that they were obligated to defend themselves against aggressors, according to the rule "If a person comes to murder you—kill him first."
>
> (1929:180)

Rabbi Toledano felt that, paradoxically, the behavior of the young generation of secular Zionist Jews exemplified the values of the Torah:

> Let me praise the flowers of this new generation who "awoke and wakened" to revive oppressed hearts, to engirdle themselves with a courageous spirit, and to restore the crown of Israel's honor to its pristine glory. And it is with regard to this that the Bible says: "And I will give you a new heart, and instill in you a new spirit" (Ezek. 36:26).
>
> (182)

For Toledano the dynamic of halakhah can thus enable a Jew to critique specific rabbinic attitudes of the past without in any way relinquishing a sense of continuity and authenticity.

POSITIVE REGARD FOR MODERN SCIENCE AND TECHNOLOGY

Another instance in which a Sephardic rabbi advocates what appears to be a radical recasting of the norms of halakhah is to be found in a discussion of electrical lighting, in which Rabbi Mesas refers to the link between religious ritual, technology, and social reality. Writing in 1935, he permitted the use of electric bulbs in Hanukkah candelabra, instead of the traditional lights (oil or candles) in use since antiquity. Furthermore, he added in his work *Ner Mitzvah* (Candle of Commandment, 1939),

> I hold it to be clear and simple that, if electrical lighting had been extant in Temple times, most certainly it would have been employed in the Temple candelabrum. For it is inconceivable that we should illuminate our private homes with that great, wonderful electric light, which is verily after a heavenly model—and yet illuminate God's holy palace with olive-oil, which even the poorest of the poor despise in our time. It is therefore obvious that we shall illuminate the future Temple, may it be built speedily in our days, with electrical lights. Amen.
>
> (15)

The implications of this brief passage are rich, indeed. First, while electrical light is "after a heavenly model," it was unknown in antiquity and invented only in modern times; thus modern science uncovers sublime aspects of creation hitherto hidden from humankind. Second, an understandable ratio exists between God's "home" (the temple) and the homes of ordinary folk. The temple must deeply impress the pilgrims who make their way to it from all corners of the earth and therefore must be at least the equal of the most outstanding architectural feats of humanity. Thus a situation in which human dwellings are more advanced than God's temple is patently untenable. It follows that advances in science and technology that affect mundane social reality must also find expression in the design of the temple and its equipment.

A third implication flows from what Mesas says. Extensive passages in the Torah and in rabbinic sources discuss the structure of the temple candelabrum, the preparation of pure olive oil for use therein, and the manner in which to clean the old wicks from the candelabrum and light the new wicks and oil. All these passages, it now transpires, are technologically contingent. Their underlying significance is that the temple should be illuminated by the best and most impressive light available to humanity. Thus true commitment to the Torah entails that the halakhic details of temple illumination be redetermined from time to time, in accordance with technological progress.

SUPPORT FOR INTEGRATION OF SECULAR STUDIES INTO THE JEWISH CURRICULUM

In premodern times the traditional Jewish elementary curriculum focused on the mastery of reading and language skills that were necessary for participating in synagogue life. A major issue in modern Jewish history was the reform of the elementary curriculum in order to include secular subjects. By and large, Sephardic rabbis favored such an integrated program.

When the director of a community school asked Rabbi Yoseph Hayyim about a plan for the Baghdad Talmud-Torah that would give children lessons in arithmetic, Arabic, and commercial correspondence in addition to the traditional program of Torah studies, he supported it. Yet he ruled that students could not learn the new subjects inside the synagogue's hall of prayer, where classes in Torah subjects were held. Rabbi Hayyim clearly advocated that Baghdad Jews follow the modern academic model of schools as a community institution that are physically differentiated from the sites of prayer and Torah study. He also saw no problem with regard to the curriculum change. The gap between his position and that of the heads of the great yeshiva of Volozhin, who in 1891 decided to close down the institution rather than agree to the inclusion of secular topics in the curriculum, as required by Russian authorities, is striking.

Significantly, Hayyim presents his position as "stringent" relative to the ruling of another leading Sephardic rabbi, Israel Moshe Hazan (1808–63). Israel Moshe Hazan grew up in Jerusalem and became a member of its rabbinic court around 1840; he then served as chief rabbi of Rome, Corfu, and Alexandria. Hazan supported the conduct of an integrated program of Torah and secular studies inside the synagogue itself. Furthermore, he also wrote in *Sh'erit ha-Nahalah* (Remnants of Inheritance, 1862) that if non-Jewish parents insisted on sending their children to such a Jewish study program, the school could accept them.

SOLIDARITY WITH CONTEMPORARY SOCIETY AND NON-JEWISH STATES

Both emerging nationalism and emancipation attracted many Jewish adherents. For some, Jewish nationalism was expressed in political Zionism, while emancipation seemed to be leading to Jewish equality in the non-Jewish body politic. Many Middle Eastern rabbis expressed positive regard for both changes. In some cases they considered emancipation to entail halakhic consequences. Rabbi Abdallah Somekh, the founder of Baghdad's yeshiva, Beit Zilkha, was highly regarded as a halakhic authority not only by Jews living in Iraq but also by Jews of Iraqi ancestry worldwide. He received a query in 1885 from an Iraqi Jewish community in Bombay, asking whether it was permissible to hire a non-Jew whose job definition would include extinguishing of the synagogue's gas lighting after Friday evening services. (The halakhah forbids the lighting and extinguishing of fire by Jews on the Sabbath.) Rabbinic sages of late antiquity decreed that Jews may not employ non-Jews to circumvent the original rule, to perform on their behalf actions forbidden to Jews. Nevertheless, many medieval halakhists interpreted this leniently, thus creating the institution known in Europe as "Shabbes goy," a non-Jew employed by Jews to assist them on the Sabbath by performing acts that Jews were forbidden, such as the lighting of heating stoves in northern Europe. The Bombay congregation added that the chief rabbi of Jerusalem had permitted them to employ such a worker and had based his ruling on a precedent, a responsum by Rabbi Jacob Poppers of Frankfurt (1718–40). Poppers had reasoned that failure to extinguish synagogue lighting might cause a fire to spread to surrounding homes of non-Jews, who might then accuse the Jews of trying to burn them down. If a synagogue fire developed, wrote Popper, the Jews would have to fight the fire and might even be physically attacked by the angry non-Jews. To forestall such developments, it was far better that the Jews hire a non-Jew to extinguish the synagogue lights. Yet Rabbi Somekh told the Bombay congregation that Popper's ruling was currently inappropriate:

> In our times—thank God—Jewish life in exile has been sweetened, especially in the cities of Europe, and also in Turkey. And they will not cast libel upon us, if a fire happens to break out, and no-one will raise his voice to say, that Jews started the fire in order to harm Gentiles; for all have become almost as one people. In addition, when a fire breaks out, Jews are not required to personally extinguish it, for in such a case the firemen come quickly, with all their equipment, and it is them whose task it is to put out fires.
>
> (232)

Somekh relied on two modern developments in framing his decision: first, the new spirit of brotherhood between Jews and Gentiles lessened the probability of physical attack in the wake of fire, and, second, new forms of social organization—the professional corps of fire fighters—obviated the need for urban residents to participate in extinguishing fires. Although formally unconnected, both developments stem from the internal "logic" of modern, civil society: on the one hand, the move toward a political-territorial group identity that was not dependent on religious affiliation, and, on the other, the assumption by local and national government of an ever-widening range of social responsibilities that were fulfilled through a host of bureaucratic agencies. Both developments are favorable in Somekh's eyes, yet their halakhic implications led to greater stringency because what was permitted in the past—employment of a Shabbes goy to extinguish synagogue lights—would now be forbidden.

RECOGNITION OF A COMMON JEWISH-GENTILE RATIONALITY

Is the rationality characteristic of Jewish culture essentially the same as that of the intellectual elite of enlightened non-Jewish society? Several leading Sephardic rabbis of the modern period answered in the affirmative. For example, in the early twentieth century Egyptian law empowered the courts of each ethnic and religious community to deal with matters of personal status (marriage and divorce) for members of their community who were nationals of Egypt. As part of the official Egyptian court system, such *millet* courts allowed lawyers accredited within the system to represent any client whose case came before that court. Thus a Coptic Christian lawyer could represent a Jewish husband in a divorce hearing held in a Cairo rabbinic court. That lawyer or a Muslim lawyer or a Jewish lawyer uneducated in rabbinic law needed to know the substantive content of Jewish divorce law in order to represent his client. The heads of Egypt's Ministry of Justice also needed to know the law that Jewish judges—who were empowered by the state—were following and that state agencies were expected to recognize and enforce; however, at that time Jewish law was inaccessible to anyone not steeped in rabbinic texts.

In response to the widespread need for knowledge of Jewish law regarding personal status, Rabbi Masᶜoud Hai Ben-Shimᶜon (1869–1925), head of Cairo's rabbinic court, composed a major two-volume work, *Kitab al-Ahkam al-Shariᶜa fi al-Ahwal al-Shakhsiyya lil-Isra'iliyyin* (The Book of Religious Laws of the Jews in Matters of Personal Status, 1912, 1917). He presented in modern literary Arabic a complete survey of the halakhic norms that were followed by courts of the Jewish *millet.* His enterprise reflects an acknowledgment of the substantive accessibility of halakhah to non-Jews. In a letter of commendation and support to Ben-Shimᶜon, Rabbi Abraham Abikhezir of Alexandria (1866–1944) expressed an implicit recognition of a joint Jewish and non-Jewish universe of discourse:

> Your opus, work of a wise man and a thinker, is sui generis. No gold can equal its value, nor any silver pay its worth. You devoted days and nights, and banished sleep from your eyes, in order to retrieve pearls from the depth of the Sea of Talmud and Poskim [decisors of rabbinic law]. And from them you fashioned a necklace, inlaid with precious onyx and jasper, to adorn the members of your nation and to publicly sanctify The Name of Heaven. . . . And, so that it not be as a sealed book for a person who does not understand our pure and holy tongue, you toiled—and succeeded—to edit it in the language spoken here in Egypt, the harmonious and pleasant Arabic tongue. In doing so, you followed in the footsteps of our intellectual giants of old, Saᶜadiah Gaon and Maimonides, of blessed memory. Thereby, you fulfilled a keenly-felt lack. The people treading in darkness, who have

> never seen the light of Torah, will now see a great light, and happily rejoice. The lawmakers and the lawyers, of all peoples and tongues, will taste of this honey-comb and say: "Hurrah! we have become warmed and enlightened by just laws and regulations!"; they will thank and praise your name, for you will be to them a father and a teacher of justice. And they will sanctify the God of Jacob, and give adoration to the Laws of Israel, saying: "What great people has laws so just, as the laws of Torah which Moses set before the people of Israel?!" (28–29)

In other words, making halakhah accessible to a non-Jewish public in their own language will not only help non-Jews but will also openly sanctify God's name—a very high value on the Torah's scale. The final lines of Abikhezir's letter explain the matter by saying that such sanctification will occur as a result of the appreciation that Egyptian legalists will express for the content of Jewish marriage and divorce laws. Such a positive evaluation is meaningful only if one assumes that Jews and non-Jews share a world of rational discourse that enables mutual evaluation and critique.

AFFIRMATION OF MODERN POLITICAL VALUES

With the emergence of Jewish self-government at the beginning of the Palestine mandate, local rabbis also related to modern European political values, most notably the issue of women's suffrage. At that time the Jewish community (Yishuv) included four major constituencies:

1. The Old Ashkenazic Yishuv (i.e., Jews of European lineage)—they had decided to live in Palestine because it was the Holy Land, whose inhabitants achieved religious merit and some financial support from their Diaspora brethren. Leaders, as well as most members, of this group rejected Zionism. Most of this group had arrived in Palestine during the nineteenth century.
2. The Old Sephardic Yishuv: Jews of Sephardic Middle Eastern lineage, including some who had arrived in the nineteenth century and others whose families had been residents of Palestine for hundreds of years. Like the old Ashkenazic Yishuv, the Sephardim were traditionally religious; however, most had a positive regard for Zionism.
3. The new "bourgeois" Yishuv—Jews who had immigrated to Palestine since the 1880s with the intent of creating an economically viable and

productive Jewish national home in Palestine. Some were farmers, some town dwellers. Their social and economic views were generally conservative.
4. The new "socialist" Yishuv—several thousand Jews who had immigrated to Palestine since 1903 and whose vision included the establishment of a socialist Jewish national society in Palestine. Both sections of the new Yishuv were staunchly Zionist.

Toward the end of World War I representatives of these four groups began internal negotiations with the goal of electing an assembly that would evolve into an institution that would represent them vis-à-vis the local British authorities. Not surprisingly, the Old Ashkenazic Yishuv rejected women's suffrage. Surprisingly, they were supported by Rabbi Isaac ha-Cohen Kook, whose Zionist credentials were impeccable. Rabbis who rejected women's suffrage in the name of Jewish tradition argued that precedent supported their position—premodern Jewish communities had never regarded women as possessed of political rights. Rabbi Bernhard Ritter of Rotterdam asserted that women had been accorded no recognized status in the biblical definition of the Israelite polity and were not counted in the biblical census or included in Israel's genealogical lists. "So be it," responded Rabbi Ben-Zion Meir Hai Uzziel in his *Mishpetei Uzziel* (1935). "Let us grant that they are neither Kahal, nor Edah . . . nor anything. But are they not creatures, created in the Divine image and endowed with intelligence? And are they not connected to matters within the competence of the proposed assembly or of the committee it shall designate, whose directives they shall be required to obey?" Because women were "created in the Divine image and endowed with intelligence," and because they would be expected to obey the decisions of the Yishuv's elected leadership, Uzziel decided that, according to the Torah, women possess an inalienable right to vote. The conception that humans are created in the divine image is deeply biblical, yet the derivation of political rights from this conception was definitely modern, as was the notion that obedience to political authority is directly linked to one's right to vote. What Uzziel did was to affirm the halakhic validity not only of the biblical notion that each human being has been created in the divine image but also of the modern political implications that non-Jewish political theorists derived from that notion.

Not all religious leaders of Islamic lands held to the views and attitudes exemplified in this discussion. At various times and in various communities rabbinic figures and groups aggressively confronted specific aspects of modernity.

Rarely (as in Aleppo and Djerba, for example), such confrontation became a hallmark of rabbinic style. Yet this was not the dominant orientation.

Therefore we may sum up by stating that within Islamic lands, a synergetic interaction of economic and cultural factors led to the numerical contraction and social decline of the rabbinic class during the nineteenth and twentieth centuries. Nevertheless, an interesting and creative response to modernity may be found in the writings of leading Sephardic Middle Eastern rabbis of the times. Rejecting the schisms characteristic of European Jewry in modern times, these Sephardic rabbis expressed a distinctive religious-cultural attitude, well worthy of recognition and consideration by contemporary students and scholars alike.

REFERENCES

Ben-Shimᶜon, Masᶜoud Hai. *Kitab al-Ahkam al-Shariᶜa fi al-Akhwal al-Shakhsiyya lil-Isra'iliyyin.* Vol. 1. Cairo, 1912.

Ha-Levi, Hayyim David. "Al Gemishuta Shel Ha-Halakha." In *Shana B'Shana* (yearbook), pp. 182–86. Jerusalem: Heikhal Shlomo, 1989.

Hazan, Eliyahu. *Zikhron Yerushalayim.* Livorno, Italy: Ban Amozag, 1874.

Hazan, Israel Moshe. *Sh'erit ha-Nahalah.* Livorno, Italy: Ban Amozag, 1862.

Mesas, Yosef. *Ner Mitzvah.* Fez: Masᶜoud Sharvit and Amram Hazan, 1939.

——. *Otzar Ha-Mikhtavim.* Vol. 1. Jerusalem, 1968.

Somekh, Abdallah. *Zivhei Tsedek He-Hadashot.* Jerusalem, 1981.

Toledano, Yaᶜakov Moshe. *Yam Ha-Gudel* (responsa). Cairo: Moskowitz, 1929.

Uzziel, Ben-Zion Meir Hai. *Mishpetei Uzziel.* Vol. 1, 3. Tel Aviv. 1935, 1940.

RECOMMENDED READING

Angel, Marc D. *Loving Truth and Peace: The Grand Religious Worldview of Rabin Benzion Uziel.* Northvale, N.J.: Aronson, 1999.

——. *Voices in Exile: A Study in Sephardic Intellectual History.* Hoboken, N.J.: Ktav, 1991.

Stillman, Norman A. *Sephardi Religious Responses to Modernity.* Luxembourg: Harwood, 1995.

Zohar, Zvi. "Halakhic Responses of Syrian and Egyptian Rabbinical Authorities to Social and Technological Change." *Studies in Contemporary Jewry* 2 (1986): 18–51.

——. "Sephardic Halakhic Tradition on Galut and Political Zionism." In Yedida K. Stillman, ed., *From Iberia to Diaspora: Studies in Sephardic*

History and Culture, pp. 223–34. Leiden, The Netherlands: Brill, 1998.
——. "Traditional Flexibility and Modern Strictness: A Comparative Analysis of the Halakhic Positions of Rabbi Kook and Rabbi Uzziel on Women's Suffrage." In Harvey E. Goldberg, ed., *Sephardi and Middle Eastern Jewries: History and Culture*. Bloomington: Indiana University Press, 1996, pp. 119–33.

CHAPTER

6

Intellectual Life

AMMIEL ALCALAY

The intellectual life of Jews in the Middle East from 1800 to 1950 is a rich and complex field that has yet to be fully explored. The abrupt uprooting of ancient Middle Eastern Jewish communities in the 1950s meant that vast quantities of material (books, manuscripts, journals, newspapers, films, artwork, photographs, musical recordings, and personal documents) were left behind or survived only in fragments. The political and social circumstances of the transfer of these communities to Israel—along with the real ways in which the fates of Middle Eastern Jews and Palestinian Arabs become intertwined—bear the burden of a whole set of issues directly affecting the history of scholarship and general perceptions regarding the intellectual life of Middle Eastern Jews.

Middle Eastern Jews were typecast in the role of "primitive survivors" of an archaic past, and Israeli educational, social, and cultural institutions stigmatized them, reinforcing the boundaries of a class society based on ethnic, cultural, and linguistic background. Severed from their native space and cultures, a majority of these new immigrants found themselves in a vacuum. The very idea that these communities possessed densely textured and creative public and private intellectual lives ran against every stereotype embedded in the institutional structures and common rhetoric of the new state. In this context the intellectual life of these Middle Eastern Jewish communities—initiated at the dawn of the technical age and forged in the cauldron of colonialism and nationalism—was almost unimaginable. While mainstream Israeli discourse claimed to have saved these communities from backwardness and stagnation, it simply cut from the script the real and substantial participation of Middle Eastern Jews in crucial and transitional moments of modernity. Thus academic and rabbinic scholars, intellectuals, artists, and political and social activists, often working against great odds and deep prejudice, made enormous efforts simply to prove that such a history existed. The sheer quantity of surviving materials produced—in a vast array of forms, genres, and languages—is almost overwhelming. This has made the reclamation of modern Middle Eastern Jewish material, cultural, and spiritual existence quite daunting. Because of the geographic, generic, and linguistic range—and the circumstances involved in the demise of Middle Eastern Jewish communities—much of the scholarly research of the second half of the twentieth century went into simply recording what was produced where, when, and by whom, a vast undertaking that is not yet complete. This stage of scholarship has been descriptive rather than interpretative. As invaluable as such research is, it has left little room for the formulation of a wider, more general intellectual history of the period. The bulk of research on literature, for example, has simply used literary texts as sociological evidence to interpret the "status" of Jewish communities in decontextualized and uncritical ways. Attempts to use only the conventional terms of European aesthetic or literary history to discuss Middle Eastern Jewish intellectual production has preempted more useful and exploratory descriptions of the unique hybrid qualities that characterize it. No one has yet made a systematic attempt to look at all the available writing produced by Jews in the region during the period as diverse pieces of a larger picture.

To begin doing this we must look at the larger historical context. A towering intellectual figure of the period, Abraham Shalom Yahuda (1877–1951), wrote,

> During the years of their history with which we are fairly familiar, the people of Israel voluntarily or involuntarily led a wandering life; and indeed not as an uncivilized nomadic tribe, but as a people, seeking, creating and transmitting spiritual and material culture did they wander from nation to nation, from land to land. Through all the different periods of Jewish civilization, it was in the first place the language of the peoples among whom they dwelt that exerted the most extensive influence upon them. The Hebrews, with their staunch conservatism, preserved the Hebrew language throughout; this language, even at times when only in literary and scholarly use, did not by any means cease to live in their midst but was continually enriched by the adoption of new elements through close contact with many other peoples and the most varied cultural surroundings. In the development of the Hebrew language, one can even follow the very route of Israel's

> wanderings. In its expansion and enrichment, we can see reflected the fresh cultural values acquired in all periods. All the newly created conceptions, all the borrowed or imitated phrases and modes of speech, as well as the adopted, partly hebraized foreign words, are to be found embodied in the language and worked into its texture.
>
> (1933:XXVII)

Yahuda's own career attests to this: born in Jerusalem to a family originally from Baghdad, he studied under his older brother, Isaac Ezekiel Yahuda, author of a comprehensive collection of Arabic proverbs. Abraham Yahuda published his first book, *Arab Antiquities,* in 1895 when he was fifteen. He attended the First Zionist Congress in Basel, Switzerland, in 1897, then embarked upon an academic career that took him to Berlin (where he taught from 1905 to 1914), Madrid (where he taught from 1915 to 1922), and the New School for Social Research in New York. A polymath with profound knowledge in many fields, languages, and eras, one of Yahuda's most extraordinary encounters was with Sigmund Freud, whom he visited in Vienna; Yahuda's knowledge of Egyptian culture and the Egyptian language prompted him to write an extensive critique of Freud's *Moses and Monotheism.* In addition to works on ancient Near Eastern languages and literature (his 1933 *Language of the Pentateuch in Its Relation to Egyptian,* and the more popular version published a year later, *The Accuracy of the Bible,* sparked international discussion), pre-Islamic poetry, and medieval Judeo-Arabic texts, Yahuda published *Dr. Weizmann's Errors on Trial* (1952), a scathing attack on Zionist policies that Yahuda felt had irreparably damaged relations between Arabs and Jews. He was also an avid collector and left about fifteen hundred manuscripts to the Jewish National Library. They are mostly in Arabic, but several hundred are in Hebrew and other languages, including numerous rare illuminated manuscripts.

While Yahuda's claims about cultural and linguistic transformation hold true throughout Jewish history, most relevant to modern Middle Eastern Jewish intellectual life is the period that the great scholar of medieval Jewry S. D. Goitein called "the great bourgeois revolution" of the ninth century. During this period of rapid urbanization Jewish communities established many of the legal and communal parameters—as well as the cultural sensibilities—that would come to characterize them for the next millennium. Before the nation-state framework, despite the variable conditions they might find themselves in, Jewish communities maintained relatively high states of legal and communal autonomy. This concept of autonomy could also be translated into cultural terms. Much the way that biblical authors forged their own style within the context of other ancient Near Eastern literature, medieval Jewish poets used Arabic models to fashion an entirely new statement, filtered through a particular sensibility and experience. This sense of translatability was a primary fact of cultural expression, reaching far beyond the skills of translating texts from one language into another. Such modes of cultural practice led to an enormous diversity of expression in genre, language, and approach; this in turn was paralleled in the range of vocations, roles, and capacities available to Jews on the social and economic level. Thus the idea of mobility encompasses cultural practice, social possibility, and the actual physical movement by people between urban centers across a large geographic space.

Even before the advent of the technical age in 1800, a diverse range of artistic and intellectual property—from fashions to legal commentaries and new poems—traveled far and wide with remarkable rapidity. A poet like Israel Najara (ca. 1555–ca. 1625), for example, with firm roots in the classical poetics of Islamic Spain, tailored his verse to fit popular Turkish, Armenian, Spanish, and Greek melodies, a combination that made him popular not only throughout the Levant but as far as Aden, Calcutta, and Cochin. This kind of mobility, transfer of style, and ease of exchange remained very much a fundamental part of Middle Eastern Jewish intellectual life even after the actual dissolution of empires or political alliances that, in many cases, made such exchange possible. To take another example, this one from the 1940s, a master musician, the Moroccan rabbi David Buzaglio (1902–75), set Yehuda Halevi's twelfth-century poetry to popular contemporary *sharqi* (eastern) melodies from Egypt; at the same time he modified them modally and rhythmically to fit ears attuned to the West, that is, the Maghreb, with its cultural memory of Andalusia, inherited after the expulsion of Jews and Muslims from Spain during the Inquisition.

Such inherited and deeply ingrained cultural characteristics—defined here under the terms *autonomy, translatability, diversity,* and *mobility*—were exposed to a different set of possibilities and constraints from 1800 to 1950. While many of these possibilities and constraints were part and parcel of the particular effects of different forms of colonialism and nationalism, a more fundamental phenomenon must be taken into account to describe the context in which Middle Eastern Jewish communities redefined themselves. The great historian of Islamic society Marshall G. S. Hodgson has called this phenomenon "the great Western Transmutation" and the advent of the technical age. This "world event" marked a decisive break from the "relative evenness of historical development among all the societies" of the Old World since Sumer:

> The same generation that saw the Industrial and French Revolutions saw a third and almost equally unprecedented event: the establishment of European world hegemony. Only a limited part of the world's surface was actually occupied by European troops, at least at first. European hegemony did not mean direct European world rule. What mattered was that both occupied ("colonial" or "settled") areas and unoccupied ("independent") areas were fairly rapidly caught up in a world-wide political and commercial system, the rules of which were made by, and for the advantage of, the Europeans and their overseas settlers.
>
> (1974:177)

For the intellectual life of Middle Eastern Jews, the effects of this process of transmutation were extensive, ultimately transforming in a drastic way the nature and particular qualities of life within the ancient Jewish communities of the Old World. Despite the fragmenting effects of the Spanish Inquisition, the "old" Middle Eastern world still maintained a relatively holistic sense of the intellectual enterprise. That is, knowledge and the conventions of intellectual life were still deeply bound to rabbinic culture and the legal and liturgical life of the community. To a great extent this applied to vernacular forms and women's culture as well, even in cases where these forms of expression commented on or critiqued the implied or enforced norms of rabbinic culture. Integral elements of the "great transmutation" held deep implications for Jewish intellectual life. To begin with, according to Hodgson, the technical age brought with it "an expectation of continuous innovation" in which "the notion of 'progress' becomes the dominant theme of serious thinking about historical change." The result was that the goal of intellectual life was no longer "primarily to preserve old knowledge but to seek out new" (1974:193).

The speed of the new that characterized changes in how people spent their time and money in the technical age struck each community and each class within those communities at a different velocity. Foreign culture came along with the foreign capital and foreign-based financial institutions that widened the gaps between urban and rural populations and fueled the fires of popular resentment, particularly against minorities. French education came to the Middle East hand in hand with the kind of imperial ventures that disenfranchised native populations paid for with their blood. Clearly, the effect of this "civilizing mission" was to ally certain classes within Middle Eastern Jewish communities to the movement of European expansion and detach them from the concerns of the local populations with and among whom they lived. The breakup of the Ottoman Empire and the rise of British imperial interests only further marginalized these communities, particularly within the increasingly nationalist concerns of European and Eastern European Jewry as expressed through Zionism. As Eliyahu Eliachar (1899–1981), an important public intellectual figure during the period, noted: "During the days of the Ottoman Empire, leaders of the Zionist movement were accustomed to take counsel with Sephardic leaders in the Land of Israel. After the British occupation, this practice ceased. Apparently, their reasoning went like this: since authority has passed from Turkey to Britain then the authority of the Sephardic Jewish leadership has also passed on to Anglo-Saxon, Eastern European and Western European Jewry" (1975:23–24).

The institutionalization of this shift would have profound effects upon all aspects of Middle Eastern Jewish life, particularly intellectual life. The great Middle Eastern rabbinic intellects and leaders of the period still managed to temper their massive erudition with profound and practical knowledge of local and global conditions. In this, they attempted—often with great success—to integrate legal, communal, and spiritual concerns within newer secular structures and points of reference. Yet, as competing ideologies and political interests converged, the rabbis and other intellectual leaders did not have as much space in which to maneuver, and their positions were presented in communities less able to usefully apply, implement, or fully integrate such intellectual powers and practical concerns in a changing world. The whole question of advantages given to minorities by colonial powers can be seen in this light, creating a wedge between the Jewish community and the Arab population. The most extreme case of this would be the Crémieux Decree of 1870, which granted French citizenship to Jews, while the Arab population would have to endure ninety-two more years of colonial rule, until the independence of Algeria in 1962.

A useful rubric for the most widespread form of Middle Eastern Jewish intellectual activity is simply "writing." Within this broad category we can begin to sort out the various strands through which Middle Eastern Jews carried on inherited traditions and created new forms of literary and intellectual expression. Before looking at the kinds of writing involved or the changing role of intellectuals, we need to consider the materials themselves, that is, the raw elements, the actual languages that Middle Eastern Jews used. As in other periods in Jewish history, Jewish intellectuals worked at the crossroads of at least three traditions: the local language, the inherited body of known or useful works in other languages (primarily Hebrew but also Judeo-Spanish, Arabic, and other languages, each one also influenced by different local contexts), and contemporary developments in these ongoing traditions that were taking place in or arriving from other communities and intellectual centers.

Sections of the monumental *Me-am Lo^{c}ez,* the mideighteenth-century encyclopedia of Bible stories and folktales, were translated from Judeo-Spanish into Judeo-Arabic. Hebrew works of the European Jewish Enlightenment movement were translated into Modern Arabic, Judeo-Persian, Judeo-Arabic, and Judeo-Spanish, as were contemporary works from a variety of European languages, including French, Italian, German, and English. Avraham Mapu's novel *Love of Zion,* for instance, appeared in Judeo-Arabic, in Tunisia in 1890 and Calcutta in 1896, and in Judeo-Persian in 1908. Middle Eastern Jews also served as correspondents for Hebrew newspapers or journals in Warsaw, London, or other European centers, opening up another channel of linguistic and cultural influence. Nor did these channels travel only from east to west: Jews were involved locally, in local languages, in every facet and medium of cultural production, including print, broadcasting, recording, and film. As political, legal, and educational structures became institutionalized in new ways, certain kinds of knowledge had to be codified. Thus a major facet of intellectual life included the production of institutional and pedagogical materials: bureaucratic documents, civil legal codes, lexicons, dictionaries, textbooks, and the like. Again, Jews were involved at all levels. At the same time both older and newer forms of poetry could always count on finding new modes of transmission: Classical Persian poetry was transcribed into Hebrew characters and even inserted into prayer books, while contemporary Arabic lyrics from such popular musicians as Umm Kulthum or Mohammed Abdul Wahab were translated into Hebrew and then maneuvered into communal selections of liturgical poetry.

The primary languages of intellectual production were Hebrew, various forms of Arabic (modern literary Arabic, Judeo-Arabic, North African dialects), Judeo-Spanish, and French. We also find significant activity in a variety of other languages. Judeo-Persian and Farsi were used in what is now Iran, parts of Central Asia, and Afghanistan; Turkish, Greek, Macedonian, Serbian, and Bosnian were used in various parts of the Balkans during the Ottoman Empire and in countries, including Turkey, that formed after the empire's breakup; in India we can find works in Judeo-Arabic, English, Malayalam, and Marathi; in Kurdistan, Aramaic was used continuously; in other parts of Central Asia, such as Georgia or the Caucasus, Georgian, Tajik, Tatar, and Russian were used. In some cases Jews used these languages for translating classical Hebrew texts, often prompting the development of a literary language (such as in Tatar) in which they pursued more conventional genres such as poetry, short stories, drama, or the novel. In Georgian, for example, one could see within the same generation the translation of texts like the *Song of Songs* (by Nathan Eliashvili in 1925), along with the remarkable work of a writer like Herzl Bazov (1904–38). Bazov founded a nationalist Jewish paper, the *Maccabee,* in 1925 in then-Soviet Georgia and was the chairman of the dramaturgical section of the Georgian Writer's Union. A poet, novelist, and playwright, Bazov became one of Stalin's many victims, and it took years for his works to be "rehabilitated." Sometimes these languages engendered their own particular diasporas. Take the remarkable case of Tajik, in which a circle of roughly twenty Jewish intellectuals found themselves working intensively in Jerusalem at the turn of the nineteenth century when the group published approximately 125 volumes, including translations of Hebrew classics, as well as original dramas and short stories. New centers of activity displaced old ones as Jews maintained the same range of geographic mobility that had characterized Jewish life in the region for a millennium. Raphael Hayyim Ha-Cohen (1883–1954), for example, came to Jerusalem with his parents from Shiraz in 1890; in 1912 he founded a publishing house that printed many Judeo-Persian works. Another example is Bombay in the 1850s, where the transplanted Baghdadi community began publishing translations of the Bible, liturgical texts, popular literature, and newspapers in Judeo-Arabic. A wide range of works appeared, including popular versions of classics like *A Thousand and One Nights* in Judeo-Arabic (printed in Hebrew characters) in 1886. Another common practice in various languages involved the translation of diverse European texts from extant Hebrew translations.

None of these languages worked in isolation but rather in varied spheres of intersecting influence and contact, depending on geographical location, immigration patterns, trade routes, or colonial influence. A significant number of Jews in the cities of Syria, Palestine, and Egypt, for instance, were effectively trilingual and tricultural, at home in Arabic, Hebrew, and Judeo-Spanish. Turkish, French, or English were common additions to this mix. Such combinations tended to be the norm rather than the exception. In the case of Italian we can see a variety of cross-cultural movements and influences: Italian influence existed in Tunis even before the Italian occupation of Libya in 1911, because of the immigration of Jews from Livorno. Likewise, the community of Livorno was affected by Jews arriving from North Africa and other communities in the Middle East. A prominent example of this can be seen in the biography of one of Europe's most important rabbis and Jewish humanists, Eliyahu Benamozegh (1823–1900), whose parents came to settle in Livorno from Fez. The Italian influence on both Arabic and Hebrew in Libya is evident in the work of Mordechai Ha-Kohen (1856–1929). Ha-Kohen's *The Book of Mordechai,* published in English in 1980, is a detailed account of the history, customs, and institutions of Libyan Jewry that is based on firsthand observation, interviews with Muslim and Jewish elders, and an examination of sources in Hebrew, Arabic, and Italian.

In Iraq, English influenced both the Jewish community there and newly settled communities made up primarily of Iraqi Jews in Bombay, Calcutta, and Hong Kong. This can be seen in careers as varied as those of Shaul Abdallah Yosef (1849–1906) and Nissim Rejwan (ca. 1925–). In the Baghdad of the 1940s Rejwan was the manager of the al-Rabita Bookshop, a meetingplace for Iraqi writers and intellectuals, including such major figures as Bulund al-Haidari. The shop offered works by T. S. Eliot, Ezra Pound, W. H. Auden, James Joyce, Franz Kafka, Horace Mann, Arthur Koestler, George Orwell, and many others, as well as progressive journals from the United States and England, all of which would have great influence on the generation of Arab intellectuals then coming of age. A journalist and scholar, Rejwan began his career at the English-language *Iraq Times,* where he wrote film criticism as well as reviews of writers like James Joyce, Virginia Woolf, D. H. Lawrence, Saul Bellow, and Henry Miller. The career of Shaul Abdallah Yosef, on the other hand, took him from his birthplace of Baghdad to India and Hong Kong. Yosef was a profound scholar of Arabic and attended the David Sassoon School in Bombay in order to perfect his English. His writing features numerous English references, including the quote from Alfred Lord Tennyson that ends his major work. Although Yosef was a frequent contributor to the Warsaw-based Hebrew periodicals *Mevasser, Havatzelet,* and *Ha-Levanon,* his life's work is *Gibeath Shaul: Being a Commentary in Hebrew on the Poems of R. Judah Ha-Levi,* published posthumously in Vienna under the name of Saul Joseph in 1923. This line-by-line gloss and interpretation of Yehuda Halevi's poetry, tempered by profound knowledge of the full corpus of Arabic literature and its sources, remains one of the most consistently erudite and informed poetic readings of a medieval Hebrew poet available.

In Hebrew, liturgical poetry and rabbinic literature still formed the bedrock of literary activity, despite deep inroads made by journalism and new forms such as the novel. While recent scholarship has revealed a rich intellectual enterprise largely hidden until now because of the specialized knowledge required to read these texts, the rabbinic literature of the period also represents an opportunity for literary historians and critics to investigate questions with far-reaching implications for the study of writing itself. Important figures representative of this field of intellectual life include Hayyim Yosef David Azulai (1724–1806), a major figure who ends one era and begins another. Qualities that characterize Azulai's career—erudition, cultural knowledge, worldliness, and geographic mobility—carry over into the new age. We can see this in the careers of Shalom Hai Gagin (d. 1883) and Yaqob Shaul Elyashar (1817–1906). Gagin inherited a large library from his father, Hayyim Abraham Gagin, who had been chief rabbi of Jerusalem and the first to hold the title *hakham bashi.* As an emissary from Jerusalem, Shalom Hai Gagin visited Tripoli, Algeria, Tunis, and Rome; he wrote five volumes of commentaries and responsa as well as liturgical poetry. Yaqob Shaul Elyashar was a cultured scholar and fluent linguist who wrote thousands of responsa in answer to questions from both Ashkenazim and Sephardim from around the world; greatly respected by the authorities and the heads of other religious communities, he received orders of merit from the Turkish sultan Abdülhamid II in 1893 and Kaiser Wilhelm II of Germany in 1898. Like many rabbinic figures of the time, Elyashar served in different communities, including Smyrna, Damascus, Alexandria, and Livorno. His works span ten volumes of responsa, sermons, and homilies.

Other rabbinic figures, such as Yehuda Bibas (1780–1852) and Yehuda Hai Alkalai (1798–1878), played crucial roles in the revival of Jewish nationalism. Born in Gibraltar, Bibas studied in Livorno and was only one of the many rabbis deeply marked by the independence movements of peoples and nations within the Ottoman Empire. Bibas obtained a secular education in Italy and apparently received a doctoral degree from an Italian university. Between 1805 and 1832 he lived in Gibraltar, London, and Livorno. In 1832 he was appointed chief rabbi of Corfu, where he introduced reforms in the educational system. He traveled through Europe in 1839, visiting Turkey, the Balkans, Vienna, and Prague. In Zemun, Serbia, he met Yehuda Hai Alkalai, who also was deeply influenced by the independence movements in Greece and Serbia. After further service in Corfu and another stay in London, Bibas went to Palestine and settled in Hebron. Alkalai, on the other hand, was born in Sarajevo but brought up in Jerusalem. He wrote his first two books in

Judeo-Spanish and published thereafter in Hebrew. In terms of rabbinic thought, Alkalai is known for his interpretation of repentance as being in human hands; this meant that one did not have to wait for the coming of the messiah before embarking upon concrete political action. Many institutions and ideas that would come to characterize aspects of the Zionist movement found their articulation in Alkalai's writings and proposals.

Some rabbinic intellectuals, like Nathan Coronel (1810–90), moved from the West to the East. Born in Amsterdam, he settled in Palestine, first in Jerusalem and then Safed. He was a Talmudic scholar who gained great fame as a bibliographer. While in Vienna in 1872 he exchanged manuscripts with the Emperor Franz Joseph from whom he received a decoration. In addition to geographical movement, the rabbis strove to cross communal boundaries. Solomon Eleazer Alfandari (1825–1930), for example, was widely respected by both Sephardim and Ashkenazim, and the Hasidim of Munkacs dedicated a hymn to his praise after his death. Alfandari was born in Istanbul, and his rabbinic career took him to Damascus, where he served as chief rabbi, before he went on to Safed and Jerusalem. As liaisons to the governing authorities, rabbis also needed the respect, trust, and cooperation of other communal leaders. A case in point is Eliyahu Suleiman Mani (1818–99). A native of Baghdad, Mani went to Jerusalem in 1856 before settling in Hebron, even though he also went on missions (usually fund-raising for communal institutions in the Holy Land) to India, Egypt, and Iraq. His charitable and communal activities won him the admiration of all the Hebronites—both Jews and Muslims were said to have flocked to his funeral.

Far from being oblivious to the new currents around them, rabbis also ventured into new genres. Eliyahu Hazzan (1845–1908), the author of diverse rabbinic literature, also wrote *Neveh Shalom* (1894), which described the customs and life of the Jewish community in Alexandria. Another example of this can be seen through the work of Ya^cakov Moshe Toledano (1880–1960). Born, educated, and ordained in Tiberias, he wrote extensively for the Hebrew paper *Havatzelet* from 1899 to 1909. After he developed an interest in ancient manuscripts preserved in Middle Eastern libraries and seminaries, Toledano formulated a plan to establish a society to publish them and began corresponding with scholars in Western countries. He settled in the ancient upper Galilee community of Peqi^cin in 1903 where he worked on his masterpiece, *Ner Ha-Ma^carav* (Western Light, 1911), a text that remains a starting point for research on North African Jewry.

As the careers of these rabbis show, the rabbis gravitated to various centers of activity in a densely interconnected world. Of the hundreds of rabbinic figures from the period, we should at least mention Hayyim Palaggi (1788–1869); Raphael Asher Covo (1799–1874); Israel Moshe Hazzan (1807–63); Raphael Yishaq Yisrael (1809–1902); Abdallah Somekh (1813–89); Yishaq Abulafia (1824–1910); Yosef Hayyim (1834–1909); Rahamim Yosef Franco (1835–1901); Aharon Ben Shimon (1848–1929); Ben-Zion Meir Hai Uzziel (1880–1953); Shem Tob Gagin (1884–1953); and Yosef Mesas (1892–1974).

Works by rabbinic authorities on legal issues for audiences outside the Jewish community and in languages other than Hebrew were rare. However, one important text of this kind was the remarkable two-volume *Kitab al-Ahkam al-Shari*ʿ*a fi al-Ahwal al-Shakhsiyya lil-Isra'iliyyin* (The Book of Religious Laws of the Jews in Matters of Personal Status, 1912–19) by Rabbi Masʿoud Hai Ben-Shiʿmon, head of Cairo's rabbinic court. The rarity of this kind of work, however, does not mean that the rabbis were cut off from the cultures they lived in; references to contemporary events and particular phenomena (including linguistic designations of such specifics in the local languages) are abundant. Rabbi Yosef Hayyim, one of the most prominent Iraqi rabbis, explicitly used Arabic sources in popular sermons. Throughout the period both prominent and less prominent figures continued to write rabbinic literature in Hebrew and other languages (particularly Judeo-Arabic in North Africa); their works still need to be contextualized within a more general intellectual history. Rabbinic intellectual authorities were local, regional, and international, with a relatively fluid interchange between these levels. While much larger and more general shifts in the function of Jewish intellectuals in the Middle East were under way during this period, roles also began to change within rabbinic culture itself. Here it is important to differentiate between rabbis who were recognized for their intellectual achievements in the traditional rabbinic genres of textual commentary, responsa literature and legal interpretation, and those whose achievements lay elsewhere. Two prominent but equally distinctive examples of this are the diverse careers of Haim Nahoum (1872–1960) and Moise Ventura (1892–?), both of whom rose to high rabbinic positions, Nahoum as chief rabbi of the Ottoman Empire from 1909 to 1920 and Ventura as chief rabbi of Alexandria.

Rabbi Haim Nahoum was a member of the Egyptian senate and a founder of the Arabic Language Academy, appointed by a royal decree in 1933. Born in dire poverty in 1872 in Magnesia, Turkey, he was eight when his grandfather took him to a yeshiva in Tiberias, where he was introduced to the Talmud and learned Arabic. From there Haim Nahoum went to the college at Smyrna before studying Islamic jurisprudence at the faculty of law in Istanbul. After getting a degree, he went on to Paris where, in 1897, he was graduated from the rabbinical seminary as well as the Collège de France, where he specialized in Semitic languages. After directing the rabbinical seminary in Istanbul, he was appointed by the Ottoman government to be professor of languages at the Superior Academy of Artillery and Military Engineering. In 1907 the Alliance Israélite Universelle sent him to Abyssinia to study the early history, customs, and particular needs of Ethiopian Jews. In 1908 he was appointed chief rabbi of the Ottoman Empire, a post he held until 1918. In 1925 he became chief rabbi of Egypt and the Sudan, a post he held for many years. However varied and important Nahoum's political and communal career was, it was not distinguished by traditional rabbinic scholarship.

The career of Moise Ventura, on the other hand, is distinguished by scholarly and intellectual achievement but not in the traditional fields; his major works, written in French, include books on Saadia Gaon, the great Jewish thinker of tenth-century Baghdad; the logical terminology of Maimonides; medieval Arabic philosophy; a critical translation of Yehuda Halevi's *Khuzari* (twelfth century), as well as a variety of Hebrew textbooks, and a collection of articles and sermons called *Hopes and Aspirations: Echoes of the War, 1939–1945* (1948). Like many prominent Middle Eastern Jewish intellectuals of the period, Ventura expressed bitter disillusionment with Europe while still harboring hopes for a revitalized Middle East where Jews would continue to have a central role in an integrated society. In a New Year's sermon in 1942, Ventura said,

> After the lamentable failure of Western civilization, the Orient is again called upon to play an important part in the cultural life of Nations. The Orient means Egypt, Palestine, Syria, Iraq; more specifically, the Semites—Jews and Arabs—are again called upon together to play a vital role within the scene of history. Everyone whose mental capacities are in free working order must recognize that today the enemies of the Jews are as well the enemies of the Arabs—that is, the enemies of civilization.
>
> (1948:76)

In perhaps an even more remarkable sermon, given in 1945 and entitled "An Echo of the Atomic Bomb," Ventura tempered his profound knowledge of philosophy and experience of religion with an acute sense of the very real and terrifying developments of the age. When he declared that "the state of the discovery of the atomic bomb marks the historic moment of the most spectacular explosion of materialism, that world system founded on the principle of the eternity and indestructibility of matter" (1948:99), he projected a spark of spiritual and intellectual brilliance into the nuclear age by reaffirming the monotheistic concept of eternity, as delineated by both the classical Islamic and Jewish theologians and philosophers whose works he knew so well.

The rabbis were public intellectuals in the true sense, and their legacy as role models remained even after much of their authority had been qualified or diminished by the availability of newer outlets of expression. Some, such as Isaac Morali (1867–1952), managed to span different realms of intellectual activity: rabbi, scholar, and poet, Morali was born in Algeria where he lived and became director of the Ets Hayyim (Tree of Life), a religious school. In 1903 he withdrew from his business activities to devote himself to research and writing. He wrote for the Hebrew press and periodicals and researched Hebrew literature, particularly that written in Algeria. One of his books, published in Berlin in 1897, deals with early liturgical poetry by Algerian rabbis. Morali himself wrote poetry in French and Hebrew, as well as a book dealing with the French occupation that was published in Algeria in 1929.

As European dominance in the region grew, Middle Eastern Jewish intellectuals lacking a normative rabbinic education often attempted to assume the traditional public and communal role of rabbis through other means. This included providing moral and educational instruction to the public. As the governing powers of religious authority began to erode, the learned class (or those aspiring to it) branched out into a whole new assortment of endeavors. Alongside the kind of traditional rabbinic literature aimed at a wider audience and found in such works as *Me-am Lo*ᶜ*ez,* subcategories and genres exploded: tracts on Ottoman legislation; historical works; biographies; travel chronicles; scientific works dealing with zoology, medicine, and astronomy; and textbooks on a variety of subjects, including mathematics and Hebrew. The renowned Semitic philologist Joseph Halevy (1827–1917) taught at the Alliance in Turkey and promoted the establishment of a Hebrew academy while producing many students who spread enthusiasm for the language throughout the Ottoman Empire; in fact, Halevy, along with one of his prize students, Barukh Mitrani (1847–1919), and Nissim Behar (1848–1931), the founder of modern Hebrew education in Palestine, were all formidable figures in the revival of Modern Hebrew. Born in Jerusalem, Behar was graduated from the Alliance teachers' institute in Paris in 1869 and taught in Syria, Bulgaria, and Turkey, where he introduced the "Hebrew in Hebrew" (*ivrit be-ivrit*) teaching method.

While certain nonrabbinic genres persisted and even flourished (hundreds of original plays were written and performed in Judeo-Spanish before and between the two world wars, for example), those whose primary avenue of expression would have been through rabbinic discourse now began to explore new modes. For some the encounter with European dominance represented liberation from the fetters of an overtly repressive and coercive social structure. For others it meant a kind of estrangement from the local context and a loss of grounding in their own native space. Unquestionably, though, new areas of cultural space opened up. Intellectual and artistic life before the nineteenth century would have included forms of theater as well as modes of theatrical and musical entertainment, such as public recitation or performance. The entertainment industry emerged only in the latter part of the nineteenth century. Given the different attitudes among Jews, Christians, and Muslims regarding the public role of women, for example, I should note that even before the development of a full-fledged entertainment industry, Jewish (as well as Christian) actresses, particularly those from Syria, played a significant role in the development of the Arab theater from 1848 on.

Certainly, the most prominent figure in this regard is the Jewish playwright Yaq'ub Sanu^c or, as he was commonly called, Sheikh James Sanua Abou Naddara (1839–1912). The prolific author of thirty-two dramas in Arabic, as well as a number of others in Italian and French, Sanu^c is generally regarded as a major pioneer of the modern Arabic theater. He was an equally prolific journalist whose daring satires incited Egyptians to reject the old order as he coined the phrase "Egypt for Egyptians." Recently, the Iraqi-born Israeli novelist Shimon Ballas published a novel based on Sanu^c's life. Other important Egyptian Jews in this realm include the musician Daud Husni, whose 1919 *Cleopatra's Night* was the first full-length Egyptian opera; the singer and actor Laila Murad; the actor Lillian Cohen; and the film director and producer Togo Mizrahi, also known as Ahmed al-Mashriqi (1901–86). Mizrahi founded the Egyptian Film Society and directed and produced thirty-three films from 1930 to 1946. He was the first director to exclusively use the talents of Murad after she had been introduced to the cinema by Mohammed Abdul Wahab (1910?–91), the great Egyptian musician who also starred in many musicals. Several of Mizrahi's early films, including *Cocaine* (1931) and *Children of Egypt* (1933), are still considered landmarks of Arab cinema. Nor are such activities or figures peculiar to Egypt: wherever one looks, prominent Jewish figures emerge. In North Africa, for example, Abraham Daninos wrote a popular play in Algerian colloquial Arabic. This text, *Nazahat al-Mushtaq wa-Ghussat al-ᶜUshshaq fi Madinat Tiryaq fil-Iraq* (The Entertainment of the Enamored and the Agony of Lovers in the City of Tiryaq in Iraq), published in Algeria in 1847, is the first known Arabic play in print. We can find traces of a rich theatrical life in Jewish Iraq as well. Actors such as Kaduri Shahrabani, Eliyahu Samira, Naim Atzlan, Arie Elias, Salman Abdallah, and Yitzhaq Battat were prominent, some of them graduates of Baghdad's Institute of Fine Arts. Naim Atzlan was a renowned and popular entertainer who played Kish-Kish Bey, a character created by the great Egyptian playwright Najib al-Rihani (1891–1949), who was known as the Arab Molière. Atzlan apparently was also the author of about three hundred popular plays that he burned after he emigrated to Israel in 1951.

Because no comprehensive history of Jewish involvement in this aspect of contemporary Middle Eastern culture exists, we must begin to envision the milieu in which the kind of prominent figures we do know about must have operated. If we take the music industry as a case in point, there can be little doubt that prominent musicians I have already mentioned, such as David Buzaglio or Laila Murad, as well as others like Reinette and Zohra al-Fasiya in North Africa, Abraham Levy Hayat and Isaac Ben Solomon Algazi (1882–1964) in Turkey, or Morteza Ney-Davoud (1900–90) in Iran, did not work in a vacuum. More traditional musicians like Buzaglio, Levy Hayat, and Algazi maintained a deep relationship to the culture of which they were a part: all North African and Turkish musicians considered Buzaglio and Algazi to be musical authorities and performers par excellance. Levy Hayat, whose stage name was Misirli Ibrahim, was born in Aleppo and settled in Turkey at the end of the nineteenth century. There he studied with well-known dervish teachers such as Hodji Karami Effendi. Morteza Neydavood, on the other hand, an acknowledged master of the tar (long-necked lute), performed with the renowned unveiled singer Ghamar in the 1930s, a revolutionary event in the history of Iranian classical music; Neydavood also regularly performed live on Iranian National Radio. In the first Iraqi Radio Orchestra, founded in 1936, every musician except one was Jewish; they included such well-known figures as Daud and Salah Kuwaiti, Ibrahim Qazaz and Yaqub al-Amari. Other prominent Iraqi Jewish musicians, such as Ezra Aharon, Yehuda Shamash, and Salah Shmuel, were featured at the Congress of Arab Musicians in Cairo in 1932. The point here is that musicians like these—as well as actors, film directors, and producers—worked in a dense urban cultural milieu where Jewish participation was simply a given. This milieu naturally would have to include not only the consuming public but all the other occupations related to these artistic activities such as instrument makers, radio announcers, recording engineers, set designers, photographers, impresarios, and a host of other vocations.

Writing continued to inscribe and internalize all the issues dredged up by this new order and the new aspects of cultural expression that came with it. Older established printing centers like those of Livorno and Amsterdam, set up primarily to reprint classical texts, rabbinic works, and belles lettres, found themselves overwhelmed by the new publishing enterprises that began operating in the 1850s and were geared toward a much wider audience. Even so, many Arabic texts originating in North Africa were still published in Livorno. In 1885, for example, Eliezer Farhi from Tunis published a series of tales in Arabic, *Al-Malek Sayf al-Azal* (The King of the Eternal Sword), consisting of twenty volumes numbering more than two thousand pages. The emergence of a popular press that flourished throughout the Levant, the Balkans, and the Middle East in Hebrew, Arabic, Judeo-Spanish, French, Farsi, Italian, English, and a host of other languages became a great catalyst in shifting the pace at which news traveled as well as in affecting the type of information exchanged. Prominent newspapers in Iraq came out in Hebrew and Arabic and included *Dover Mesharim* (1863–71); *al-Misbah* (1924–29); *al-Hasid* (1929–37), and *al-Burhan* (1929–38). In Iran newspapers appeared in Hebrew, Farsi, and Judeo-Persian; in some cases Farsi papers were written in Hebrew characters, while others (*Israel, Alam-e-Yahud, Sina,* and *Nisan*) were bilingual, with both Farsi and Hebrew written in Persian and Hebrew characters. Papers in Judeo-Persian included *Shalom, Ha-Geulah,* and *He-Hayim.* Another journal, *Kavian,* was modeled on the format of *Life* and *Paris Match*; it began in 1949, published by Rabi Moshfeq-Hamadani, a well-known journalist who went on to become the head of the Iranian news agency Pars and editor of *Kayhan,* one of the two major Iranian dailies. The first of many North African Jewish journals in Judeo-Arabic and French appeared in Algiers in 1870; it gives us some idea of the scope that its journalism intended to encompass. Called *Adziri, Jurnal Bilyahud wa-Bilfransis* (*Algiers, A Journal in Jewish and French*), it billed itself as a "journal of commerce, industry, agriculture, maritime affairs, literature, science, law and news." The diversification of roles initiated by the press also affected gender roles: the writer and translator Esther Azhari Moyal, for example, edited *al-Alam al-Isra'ili* (*Jewish World Arabic Weekly*) in Beirut from 1929 to 1946.

Middle Eastern Jews coming of age in the late nineteenth and early twentieth centuries found themselves influenced by a variety of competing forces.

On the one hand, they felt the push and pull of competing Arab and Jewish nationalism; on the other hand, Jews were attracted to the universal messages imparted by progressive social movements such as communism. At the same time the social class of an individual could either contradict or corroborate the advantages of minority of preference within a colonial framework (such as in Algeria, where Jews were granted French citizenship). All these factors played themselves out within the context of ancient Jewish communal structures, institutions, and values struggling to either accommodate or resist rapid and significant change. In terms of intellectual discourse, these phenomena are inscribed within the very kinds of writing that Jews undertook; participation in the creation of new literary genres and national literatures marks a watershed in the shifting terms that constituted Jewish identity. In this process the legal, covenantal, and communal bases of Jewish existence gave way to the racial, the ethnic, and the national, something to which the new forms of written authority lent credence, often unintentionally.

Historical writing, for example, came to occupy a distinct place within Jewish communities in a significantly different way than it had in the past. This is evident in the work of such figures as Abraham Danon (1857–1925), Moise Franco (1864–1910), Solomon Rosanes (1862–1938), Abraham Galanté (1873–1961), Joseph Nehama (1880–1971), and Rosa Taudidyashvili (1886–1967). Although many who wrote in this mode can be viewed as typical products of the Enlightenment, their work needs to be seen not only in light of European influences but in the context of other genres, such as personal memoirs, local annals, and travelogues. Both Franco and Galanté were, in different contexts, extremely involved in Ottoman and Turkish society well beyond the confines of their interest in and scholarship on Balkan Jewry. Franco, for example, served as principal at several Jewish schools and founded schools in Safed. Along with his colleague Col. Rushdi Bey, he wrote the French readers that were officially introduced into Turkish schools. Abraham Galanté was both a politician in the Ottoman Empire and a scholar whose work concerned a variety of subjects and comprised about sixty books and pamphlets, as well as more than a hundred essays and articles. His writings ranged from works on the Hittites and the laws of Hammurabi to his important two-volume *History of Anatolian Jewry* (1939) and texts on subjects as varied as an Armenian poem on Shabbetai Zevi, the false messiah, or an examination of new documents relating to the life of Esther Kyra, who wielded great influence in the Ottoman courts during the reigns of sultans Murad III (1574–95) and Mehmed III (1595–1603). All were involved in the use of modern methodological approaches to historiography. During World War II Abraham Danon left Edirne for Paris, where he taught Hebrew at the Ecole Normale Israelite Orientale Alliance and edited a historical journal that came out in Hebrew and Judeo-Spanish. It was devoted to collating and publishing documentary materials on Eastern Jews. Solomon Rosanes had neither a conventional rabbinic nor academic career but was forced to combine scholarly pursuits with business in order to support his family. While on business trips he managed to pursue his research in libraries and archives. His works include a treatise on ancient Jewish coins; his best-known work is the six-volume *History of the Jews in Turkey and the East* (1930–45). Although she began as a writer of fables and children's stories, Rosa Taudidyashvili went on to produce a comprehensive ethnographic study of Georgian Jews that was published in 1941. The notion of historical writing also developed in Iran; in 1946 Parviz Rahbar wrote *The History of the Jews from the Babylonian Exile to the Present.* In 1956 a monumental work called *The History of the Jews of Iran* appeared, written by Habib Levy in three volumes. A French-educated dentist, Levy spent many years interviewing older members of the community and incorporated their recollections in his research.

To fully contextualize the work of such figures, we must also consider all kinds of other works. Thus a text like David Carasso's *Zikhron Teman o El Viage de Yemen* (Voyage to Yemen), published in Salonika in 1875, should be seen as forming one strand of a larger and more tangled web of interrelated texts that would include, on the one hand, the work of historians like Rosanes and Galanté and, on the other, specific and less widely disseminated chronicles like those of Hayyim Habshush (d. 1899) or the remarkable Mahalal ha-Adani (1883–1950). Habshush was a copper engraver in Yemen who served as Joseph Halevy's travel guide during his expeditions there to uncover Sabean inscriptions. Habshush is known for *The Travels of Habshush* (1893), as well as texts written about episodes in the history of Yemenite Jewry from 1668 to 1817. The three volumes of ha-Adani's twelve-hundred-page *Between Aden and Yemen* (1988–91) presented a panorama covering every aspect of life from a point of view that combines personal, communal, and political history with ethnography, folklore, sociology, and literature. The point I am making is that texts emerging from this period of drastic change and transition must be read through a critical vocabulary and perspective that is as sophisticated as the works themselves.

As in historical writing, the conventional literary genres of prose, poetry, and drama must be looked at not simply as newly discovered European inventions but rather as complex hybrid creations reaching back to a diverse range of more familiar forms and conventions. In modern literary Arabic the primary centers of Jewish activity were in Egypt and Iraq, where Jews played a significant role in the development of a number of genres and movements. In addition to Ya^c^qub Sanu^c^, whom I mentioned earlier, the career of Murad Faraj (1866–1956), a Karaite (member of a sect that rejected the authority of the Talmud) who was born and lived in Cairo, also stands out. Faraj was a prolific writer, publishing about forty books on a variety of topics: five volumes of poetry, including a four-volume collection of work; essays; translations; and philological and legal studies. In addition, Faraj wrote a rhymed verse translation of the Book of Job; a commentary on the Torah; Hebrew textbooks for Arabic speakers; a study of the Jewish poets of the *jahalliya* (pre-Islamic period); and an ambitious Hebrew-Arabic etymological dictionary. As the founder of a newspaper aimed at a Karaite audience, he worked toward reconciliation between the Karaite and rabbinate communities. In 1936 Faraj was chosen as a member of the Egyptian Academy for the Arabic Language.

Jewish writers played a prominent role in Iraq. To an even greater degree than in Egypt, the events and movements following World War I in Iraq fully reflect the dilemmas and options facing Jews in Arab modernity. Iraqi Jews were deeply involved in all aspects of Iraqi society, and we can see several generations of significant literary production in Arabic by Iraqi Jews. The first generation includes major figures like Anwar Shaul (1904–84) and Murad Michael (1906–86). Shaul was a lawyer by profession, and his versatility and range of activities is more typical of an era before the particularization and specialization of intellectual activities. A poet, prose writer, translator, and editor, Shaul published his first book of short stories in Baghdad in 1930. He was editor of the Jewish weekly *al-Misbah/Ha-Menora* and founder of the journal *al-Hattsad/Ha-Kotser*; he edited the latter from 1929 to 1938, writing under the pen name of the pre-Islamic Jewish poet Ibn al-Samawal. This choice reflected a theme that would become predominant in Shaul's work—his faithfulness to the Arabs. It is important to note that such sentiments were by no means unique: Nissim Yakob Melloul (1892–1959), in addition to his many translations from Hebrew into Arabic and his journalism in the nationalist Arab press, published a play in Baghdad in 1928 called *The Remarkable Qualities of the Arabs or: Samawal and Umr al-Kayis.*

Like so many other Middle Eastern Jewish writers during this period, Anwar Shaul translated widely from world literature, including stories by Oscar Wilde, Ivan Sergeyevich Turgenev, Shalom Ash, Fyodor Dostoevsky,

Anton Chekhov, and Maksim Gorky, as well as German and Italian writers. In addition, he wrote the screenplay for an important Iraqi film, *Aliya wa Atsam* (Aliya and Atsam), which came out in Baghdad in 1948. In 1945 he established a modern publishing house and remained its director until 1962. Shaul's contemporary, Murad Michael, is best known for "He Died for His Country, and She Died for Love," a short story published in 1922, and his 1931 volume of prose poems, *Desert Mirage.* Both are considered pioneering works of modern Iraqi literature. Influenced by figures like Rabindranath Tagore, Khalil Gibran, and Amin al-Rihani, the innovative work of a writer like Michael needs to be read within both a local and an international context.

Another Iraqi Jewish writer active between the two world wars was Mir Basri (b. 1912). He began publishing his work in 1928 in journals in Iraq, Egypt, Syria, and Lebanon. Basri was an economist by profession and wrote in Arabic, English, and French. Although he published four books of poetry and short stories in Iraq until 1950, much of his work remains uncollected. Shalom Darwish, also born in 1912, is considered a pioneer of realism. After the *Death of His Brother,* a play, was published in 1931, Darwish published several collections of short stories. Salman Darwish (1910–82), a physician, was one of a handful of prominent Iraqi Jewish intellectuals (along with Anwar Shaul and Mir Basri) who remained in Iraq after the 1950s. Darwish's play, *Faithfulness and Betrayal,* was published in 1927. It is interesting to note that another play, written by Aziz Ibrahim Sawdayee (b. 1913) and published in Basra, was performed in Palestinian Nablus in 1935.

Writers in the next generation came of age during a time of great conflict and change. As the struggle over Palestine intensified and anticolonial and antifascist movements arose, Jews found themselves indelibly marked by the events of the age. These events included the infamous Farhud of 1941, an outburst of brutality directed against the Jewish community of Baghdad. Many of these writers would find their lives split in two, part encompassed by Iraq and part anticipated by Israel. Notable figures of this generation who began publishing before 1950 include Ya^cqub Bulbul (b. 1920); his collection of stories called *The First Ember* appeared in Baghdad in 1938, while a collection of his sonnets that first appeared in the Baghdad press in 1942 came out as a book in Jerusalem only in 1979; Salim al-Katib, now known as Shalom Katav, began publishing prose poems in Iraq when he was sixteen. He published his first book, *Procession of Dearth,* in Beirut in 1949. Meir Mu^callem (1921–79) published a novel called *Silwa* in Baghdad in 1940 and continued to publish short stories in the Iraqi, Lebanese, and Egyptian press.

The poet Abraham Ovadiah (b. 1924) was widely admired and published four books in Baghdad and Cairo from 1945 to 1950. Maliha Suheik was born in Baghdad in 1925 and was one of several women who published widely in the press; these writers included Esterina Avraham, Esperance Cohen, and Miriam el-Mula. Suheik apparently is the only one of the group who published a book of her own work, *Reason Is My Guide,* which appeared in Beirut in 1948.

From the middle of the nineteenth century on, a wide range of writing in French appeared throughout North Africa, Egypt, and the Levant. The literary scene in Egypt is filled with figures who split their time between Paris and Cairo or Alexandria. Carlo Suarès (1892–1976) was born in Alexandria and lived between France and Egypt. An architect and artist, Suarès wrote more than twenty books on Jewish mysticism, the kabbalah, the relationship of Judaism and Christianity, and philosophy. Along with Elian Finbert, he published the journal *Le Message d'Orient.* Georges Cattaui (1896–1974) also lived between Egypt and France; in Cairo he was the founder, along with Finbert and Paul Benzaquen, of the literary journal *Revue Littéraire.* Cattaui published original poetry, critical works, art history, and historical studies, most significantly *Muhammad Ali and Europe* (1950), written with René Cattaui. Two of the most important and beloved figures in Egyptian Jewish literary life of this period were Albert Josipovici (1892–1932) and Albert Ades (1893–1921). Josipovici was born in Istanbul but moved with his family to Egypt. He was educated in France and, in addition to writing a novel that was published in 1928, collaborated with Adès on a number of works. Adès also left a novel, called *The King, Completely Naked,* published posthumously in 1922. The most important literary figure to emerge from this Franco-Egyptian milieu was Edmond Jabès. Born in Cairo in 1912, Jabès published his first six books in Cairo between 1930 and 1949. The work of Jabès, a hybrid of surrealism and postmodernism, in a curious way provides one of the most ambitious responses by any writer attempting to come to terms with the deep internal schism that occurred as ancient Middle Eastern Jewish communities found themselves cast adrift at the end of an era.

North Africa also was a center of literary activity in French, particularly in Tunisia and Algeria; if anything, it was characterized by a less eclectic and deeper indigenous tradition than French writing in Egypt. In addition, significant women writers were not uncommon; they include Elissa Rhais, Adelaide Azoubib-Benichou, Blanche Bendahan, and Berthe Aboulker-Benichou. Elissa Rhais was born in Blida, Algeria, and is a figure certainly deserving serious study. She published a dozen novels from 1919 until the

1930s, when traces of both her and her work disappear. Adelaide Azoubib-Benichou, a poet and prose writer, published her first book, *Meditations on the Holy Books,* in 1922. Blanche Bendahan, born in Wahran, Algeria, was a poet and novelist who received numerous literary awards for her work from the French government, the Union of African Peoples, and various French municipalities. *Sail Along the Water* came out in 1926 and *Poems in Shorts* in 1948. Berthe Aboulker-Benichou wrote poetry and plays published in Algiers in the 1930s; one of her best-known works is a play based on the life of the renowned seventh-century Berber queen Kahena.

Other important North African figures include Adelaide Azoubib-Benichou's son, Raymond Benichou (1890–1955). Born in Algeria, Benichou was a polymath whose scholarly degrees and concerns spanned many disciplines; his writings include works on history, linguistics, and philosophy. In addition, he wrote poetry in French. Another important figure was Vitalis Danon (1897–?). Born in Edirne, Turkey, he became a teacher in Sfax, Tunisia, after completing his studies in Paris under Nahum Slouschz (1872–1966), a European Orientalist who traveled widely; in addition to other works, Danon published six novels and short story collections in Tunis from 1929 until 1938, including his popular collaborations with two other authors, Ryvel and Vehel. Vehel, the pen name of Jacques Victor Levy, collaborated with Ryvel and Vitalis Danon; their best-known work is *The Ghetto Bestiary,* published in Tunis in 1934. Ryvel (1898–1972), whose given name was Raphael Levy, studied in Paris before coming back to teach in Sus, Casablanca, and Tunis where he published more than a dozen books of stories, poems, and plays, many of which were performed.

In keeping with the fluidity of borders that still constituted a fundamental parameter of Jewish intellectual life during this period, we can look at a figure like Avraham Navon (1864–1952). Born in Adrianople, Turkey, he finished his studies at the AIU in Paris and became a teacher with the following posts: Tunisia, Bulgaria, Tripoli, Jerusalem, Istanbul, and Constantine. Navon wrote several novels in French, one of which, *Joseph Peretz* (1925), was translated into Hebrew by the important intellectual Avraham Elmaleh (1885–1967). A journalist and writer, Elmaleh published extensively on a variety of subjects and was an important lexicographer who published Hebrew-French, French-Hebrew, Hebrew-Arabic, and Arabic-Hebrew dictionaries. Soleiman Haim was another important lexicographer who also wrote plays; his Persian-English dictionaries, published in 1933, remain in use to this day. Others, like the Tangier-born Joseph Benoliel (1888–1937), moved in a different direction: although he studied at the Alliance as well as rabbinical seminaries in Morocco and Palestine, Benoliel spent most of his mature life in Portugal, where he was a scholar, lexicographer, translator (from Hebrew and Arabic), and poet who wrote in French and Portuguese. Finally, of the many Judeo-Spanish writers whose works were published in Jerusalem, Cairo, Sarajevo, Izmir, Istanbul, and Salonika, I should also mention Aharon de Yosef Hazan (author of *El Chico Eliezer o el Muchacho Abandonado* (Young Eliazer or the Abandoned Kid), thought to be the first Judeo-Spanish novel and published in Smyrna in 1877), and Eliya Rafael Karmona (1870–1931).

During the latter part of the nineteenth and well into the middle of the twentieth century, we find important literary figures in different parts of the Mediterranean and Arab world who manage to preserve, memorialize, and transform cultural materials that were disappearing. These figures were of two types: one group actually still belonged to the community it was trying to depict, represent, or preserve; the other did not. An excellent example of the first type would be Yakov Yona (1847–1922). Born in Monastir, Yona already sensed the transient nature of his time, the precarious state of the five-hundred-year-old Judeo-Spanish tradition of poetry, song, and legend that still bound the community of his birth. Thus he spent the better part of his life attempting to collect, preserve, and transmit as much of that tradition as he could gather and record. It is interesting to note that while Yona spent most of his life in Salonika, his 1907 volume, *New Verses on Fate: Poems, Proverbs, and Impressions of Egypt,* was published in Cairo. Another example of this type of figure is Daniel Hagège. He was born in Tunis in 1892; by the time he was twelve, he had already begun working at the press of the writer Yakov Cohen. Hagège went on to become a writer and journalist himself, publishing many articles on a wide range of themes, as well as numerous short stories. Hagège's *Publications in Tunisian Judeo-Arabic Literature* appeared in 1939. This combination of biography and bibliography brings to life hundreds of writers and publications that could easily have vanished without a trace; his descriptions of various kinds of figures—from traditional rabbis with a literary bent, playwrights, and modern teachers to simple tailors, artists, and socialists—begin to make imaginable the ambience of the rich world that he so fully inhabited.

The second type of writer was no longer fully part of a community, like Yona was part of Judeo-Spanish popular culture or Hagège part of the modern North African tradition of print and journalism. We see, rather, figures who tend to look back, with a mix of nostalgia and regret, at a community that may no longer even exist. Often the writer has idealized or transformed the community left behind, recasting it through various assumptions that pit the old against the new, the modern against the archaic, the secular against the religious, Europe against the Orient. In many cases writers in this second category are fully aware of the precariousness of their position and interrogate these issues consciously, as can be seen in the work of a writer like Laura Bohoreta Papo (1891–1941), as well as through the intellectual milieu of which she was a part. Born in Bosnia, Papo lived in Istanbul from 1900 to 1908 before going to Paris to study French; she was killed in a concentration camp in Yugoslavia. With knowledge of Spanish, French, German, Turkish, Greek, and English, she wrote songs, poems, plays, short stories, and essays, one dealing with the position of women in Bosnian society. Her work must be placed within the range of writing available to her in any number of intersecting traditions, which would include the Western European literature she was familiar with; Turkish and Greek literature, then undergoing important developments; the work of writers in Judeo-Spanish that preceded her, like that of Avraham Kappon (1853–1930), a poet, playwright, and translator active in Turkey and the Balkans who wrote in Spanish and Hebrew; and the work of a scholar like Kalmi Barukh (1896–1945), a romance philologist who was killed at Bergen Belsen and who formed part of a generation of Sephardic intellectuals with an international standing. Finally, the influences on Papo would include the new national writing that was appearing in Bosnian, Croatian, and Serbian, among which were the prominent works of Jewish writers like the novelist and playwright Haim Davičo (1854–1918), the novelist and short-story writer Isak Samokovlija (1889–1955), and the surrealist poet Moni de Boully (1904–68). The best-known writer to emerge from this milieu is Elias Canetti, born in Ruschuk, Bulgaria, in 1905 and awarded the Nobel Prize for Literature in 1981. In many senses Canetti's work forms a Balkan parallel to the Levantine world of Edmond Jabès. While Canetti grew up in the old world of Judeo-Spanish, he ended up living in England and writing in German; he is buried in Zurich next to another famous exile, James Joyce.

Other writers who interrogate and negotiate the dissolution of community include Yitshaq Shami (1888–1949) and Shoshannah Shababo (1910–92). Born in Hebron, Shami received a traditional religious education before attending a new school, attached to the Talmud Torah, that was dedicated to introducing students to a wider range of orientalist studies. After this Shami shed his native garb and donned the clothes of the *franji,* the European, in order to go to Jerusalem and continue studying at the Ezra School, an institution paralleling the Alliance. There he began writing and publishing his first stories, along with poems and descriptions of the workshops of the potters, glassblowers, and other artisans of Hebron. In addition to the modern writers he encountered in school, part of Shami's immediate frame of reference would have included the work of a writer like Suleiman Menahem Mani (1850–1924), the chief rabbi of Hebron who also tried his hand at short fiction. Before completing his studies, Shami left Jerusalem to teach Arabic in other parts of Palestine, Syria, and Bulgaria. He returned to Hebron in 1919, eventually settling in Haifa in 1930 where he remained until his death. His collected works can be found in one slim volume of six short stories and the novella that he is most known for, *The Vengeance of the Fathers* (1929). While his work has often been categorized as naive or primitive, Shami's mastery of narrative form and style reaches a height of such highly self-conscious artistry as to make his achievement among the most significant in Modern Hebrew literature.

Recently rediscovered by scholars, Shoshannah Shababo was born in Zikhron Yakov and spent most of her life in Haifa. Her first novel, *Maria,* was published in 1932; this was followed by *Love in Safed* (1942). In addition to the novels, she published many short stories, including a remarkable collection of animal fables. Shababo's work displays an uncanny sense of colloquial language and contemporary usage, and she depicts a diverse society of Christians, Muslims, and Jews; a keen sense of dramatic detail and psychological insight also characterizes her work. Another important writer to be considered in this context is Yehuda Burla (1886–1969) who at one point was Shoshannah Shababo's teacher. He later went on to criticize her work in rather harsh terms. Of all the modern Middle Eastern Jewish writers I have mentioned, Burla was the most deeply committed to ideological, party-based Zionism, something that Eliyahu Eliachar harshly criticized him for. Burla served as an interpreter in the Turkish army in World War I; after the war he became director of the Hebrew schools in Damascus for several years before returning to Palestine. Among his many novels and collections of short stories is a three-volume historical novel based on the life of Yehuda Hai Alkalai, *On the Horizon,* published in 1943. Beyond the undeniable power on the surface of Burla's narratives, the internalization of conflicts within the narratives themselves is equally significant. The more deeply embedded and firmly bound ties to music and a collective, communal voice, seen in the unbroken tradition of liturgical poetry, begins to unravel and scatter in the work of a writer like Burla. The "Jewish" world depicted becomes just that, subject matter, and not the very material of a way of life that is simply practiced from within. From this point on the gap steadily widens between a more popular, indigenous Middle Eastern Jewish culture and the secular Hebrew culture of Zionism or one of the many versions of culture inherited by European colonialism.

Nevertheless, despite the diverse inroads made by new forms of expression, the production of liturgical poetry in Hebrew continued to flourish throughout the period, and it remains an astonishingly rich and neglected field of study, despite significant scholarship—primarily on North Africa—that appeared in the last decades of the twentieth century. While the major centers of activity were in North Africa, Yemen, Syria, Palestine, Iraq, Turkey, and the Balkans, poets were writing throughout the region, maintaining their role of communal voices serving as liaisons to spirits both within and above. All kinds of new cross-cultural phenomena take place as poets move from one center to another, bringing new melodies, methods, and traditions with them. In Jerusalem, for example, we can see poets arriving from Syria and settling in at synagogues comprised of Bukharian and Persian Jews. From this, new styles emerge through the work of poets and anthologizers like Mordekhai Abadi (1826–84), Raphael Antebbi (d. 1919), and Yaᶜqub Ades (1857–1925). A number of poets from Syria, like Moshe Ashqar (1877–1940) and Yaᶜqub Abboud, emigrated to the United States. Abboud returned to Jerusalem where he had an enormous effect on the influence of Syrian poetic and musical practices in all the Middle Eastern communities of the city. The publication of books of liturgical poetry also served as a source of influence: for example, one of the early editions of Mordekhai Abadi's important Syrian collection was printed by Eliyahu Benamozegh in Livorno in 1864. Livorno, of course, remained a direct reference point for North African communities that produced dozens of important poets during this period, including Raphael Berdugo (1747–1822), Josuè Bessis (1773–1860), Shmuel Ben Yehuda Elbaz (1790–1844), Joseph Borgel (1791–1857), Yaᶜqub Ben Shevet (d. 1858), Nathan Borgel (d. 1873), Yaqob Massoud Abuhatzera (1807–80), Raphael Moshe Elbaz (1823–96), Yitzhaq Hai Bokhobza (1853–1930), David Elkayyam (d. 1941), and David Buzaglio (1902–75).

The collective and individual experiences and encounters of these and other Middle Eastern Jewish intellectuals surveyed here open up vast new territories of inquiry applicable beyond the times and places under consideration in this study. The nature of both the encounters and the variety of responses proffered can be instructive in ways that we have barely begun to imagine. Now that maps have been drawn and the constituents identified, to begin filling in the contours and details of this rich and varied intellectual history will take the collective efforts of many.

REFERENCES

Eliachar, Elie. *Life Is with the Palestinians.* In Hebrew. Jerusalem: Council of Sephardic Communities, 1975.

Hodgson, Marshall G. S. *The Venture of Islam: Conscience and History in a World Civilization.* Vol. 3: *The Gunpowder Empires and Modern Times.* Chicago: University of Chicago Press, 1974.

Ventura, Moise. *Soupirs et espoirs: Echos de la guerre, 1939–45.* Paris: Librairie Durlacher, 1948.

Yahuda, A. S. *The Language of the Pentateuch in Its Relation to Egyptian.* London: Oxford University Press, 1933.

RECOMMENDED READING

Alcalay, Ammiel. *After Jews and Arabs: Remaking Levantine Culture.* Minneapolis: University of Minnesota Press, 1993.

——, ed. *Keys to the Garden: New Israeli Writing.* San Francisco: City Lights, 1993.

Bahloul, Joelle. *The Architecture of Memory.* Cambridge: Cambridge University Press, 1996.

Benamozegh, Eliyahu. *Israel and Humanity.* New York: Paulist Press, 1995.

Faur, José. *Golden Doves with Silver Dots: Semiotics and Textuality in Rabbinic Tradition.* Atlanta: Scholars Press, 1999.

CHAPTER

7

Jewish Languages Enter the Modern Era

David M. Bunis, Joseph Chetrit, and Haideh Sahim

Before their modernization, an outstanding characteristic of Jewish communities throughout the world was their use of a vernacular that differed in diverse respects from the vernacular(s) used by their non-Jewish neighbors. Such vernaculars tended to be "fusion" languages, containing components derived from several stock languages: elements drawn from Hebrew and to a lesser extent Aramaic (the earliest known "Jewish" languages); material preserved from other Jewish languages once spoken by the community (e.g., Medieval Judeo-Italian elements in Yiddish, Old Judeo-Greek elements in Judezmo); and the predominant component of the language, which consisted of elements selectively borrowed and/or adapted from the major language in use by the community's non-Jewish neighbors (e.g., regional German in Old Yiddish; Castilian in Old Judeo-Spanish, which came to be called Judezmo in the Ottoman Empire and Hakitia in North Africa). Some Jewish linguistic varieties of the Middle East (e.g., Judeo-Arabic in Baghdad) became significantly distinctive with respect to their non-Jewish correlates whenever the speech of neighboring Gentiles underwent changes not adopted by the Jews. Where other languages were used in a particular region (e.g., Turkish, Kurdish, and Persian in addition to Neo-Aramaic in Azerbaijan), or when speakers of a Jewish language migrated to an area where Gentiles spoke another variety of the same language (e.g., in Iran), or other languages (e.g., Slavic in the Yiddish speech regions of Eastern Europe; Turkish and Arabic in Judezmo and Hakitia speech regions in the Ottoman Empire and North Africa, respectively), these too made their contributions to the Jewish languages. Special, often highly hebraized, varieties of Jewish languages (known, for example, as Loshn Koydesh in Yiddish and Lotorai in Judeo-Persian) were used as secret jargons during trade or when Jews found themselves in potentially dangerous situations and they suspected that the non-Jews present understood their ordinary language or vernacular.

Another linguistic characteristic of Jewish communities during the same period was a situation of internal diglossia; they used everyday Jewish vernaculars for conversation and in writing of an essentially nonscholarly nature, whereas scholars used Hebrew and Aramaic in original, high-level rabbinic writing, and men in general used Hebrew and Aramaic in religious services (although many men who participated in the services had little understanding of the sacred texts that they recited). Throughout the Jewish world a major component in the elementary education of boys was their training in the translation of the Hebrew Bible and other sacred Hebrew texts into a highly literal, often archaized, variety of the vernacular spoken in their locales. (These vernaculars were known by such names as Taytsh in Yiddish, Ladino in Judezmo, and Sharh in Judeo-Arabic). Before modernization, writing was also generally taught within the context of religious studies, so the members of the different religions tended to write their everyday language in the alphabet that they knew from their sacred texts; thus Jews tended to write their distinctive vernaculars in the Hebrew alphabet. In several regions the languages that Jews and their non-Jewish neighbors spoke were constituted of entirely discrete entities; therefore, the identification of the Jews' language with the distinct ethnic group that spoke it led to its being called, by both Jews and Gentiles, "Jewish" or "the Jewish language" (e.g., Yiddish was called *Yidish*; *Judezmo,* or *Djidyó,* was the term for Judezmo; *Ebrí* was the word for Judeo-Persian; and the term for Judeo-Aramaic was *Lishna Yehudiya*).

Although all Jewish languages used before modernization shared certain general features, the Jewish vernacular languages of the Christian lands and those of the Islamic lands constituted two subgroups that diverged in several ways. First, speakers of Jewish languages living under Islamic rule (these included distinctive varieties of Arabic, Castilian, Neo-Aramaic, Persian, Greek, Georgian, Berber, Turkish, and others) were in direct or indirect contact with Islamic peoples and their languages, cultures, ways of life, and worldviews, and thus they were influenced by them. Although all Jews wrote their vernacular languages in the Hebrew alphabet, Jews in Islamic lands used styles of handwriting that reflected an Eastern aesthetic sense. The orthographic systems for Semitic languages were similar to those of the Arabic letter systems. The Jewish handwritings and orthographic systems in

European Christian regions tended to reflect those of Roman and Cyrillic scripts and writing styles. Then too, the pronunciation of Hebrew elements used by Jews under Islam often preserved distinctive characteristics of the original Semitic sound system, as encountered in Arabic and other languages of the region, whereas a more European-influenced sound system was reflected in Jewish languages spoken in Christian lands. To a certain extent the Jewish languages of the Islamic world shared a common fount of Hebraisms and often used them in the same sense, whereas in Christian lands those Hebraisms were used in a divergent sense, or other Hebraisms were used to denote those meanings. In the Islamic world such parallels sometimes reflected shared or related rabbinic and liturgical traditions, but they were distinct from those that were evolving at the same time in Christian lands.

The languages of Islam, especially Arabic, had a pervasive influence on the Jewish as well as non-Jewish languages of the Eastern region. Jewish men often were somewhat familiar with several languages of the region, which aided in the diffusion of features from one language to another. Thus the Jewish and the non-Jewish languages of the Islamic world shared much everyday vocabulary, modes of expression, and metaphorical imagery; speakers throughout the area were even united by some personal and family names. Jews and non-Jews of the Middle East were also bound by numerous elements of and attitudes toward oral tradition, including the importance assigned to proverbial sayings. These features of the shared Judeo-Islamic tradition were not part of the Jewish languages of the Christian West, which developed other shared linguistic and cultural traditions. Before modernization Eastern language features tended to be preserved, even when Jews under Islam relinquished one language for another, because the new language was also apt to be Islamic-influenced (e.g., when Judeo-Arabic speakers became Judezmo speakers in medieval Spain or Portugal). The Jews under Christianity had also preserved the Western features in their languages during migrations within Europe (e.g., when Judeo-Italian and Judeo-French speakers became Yiddish speakers in medieval Germany).

With the modernization of the Jewish communities under Islam, many of their distinctive traditional language features began to disappear, as, eventually, did the languages. For the Jews under Islam modernization primarily meant westernization and secularization. Both resulted from direct and indirect exposure to the cultures, lifestyles, and aesthetics of Western Europe. There was also an eventual accommodation to anticolonial, nationalist aspirations. Several channels diffused such influences through the Middle East and North Africa. For the Jews the major channels were the secular literature and press published by Jews in Western Europe and distributed in Islamic regions, as well as the parallel secular literature that developed in the local Jewish languages. From the midnineteenth century Jews and non-Jews from Western Europe introduced secular school systems; Jews also had direct contact with people from the West who visited or lived in Islamic cities, and Jews made trips to Western Europe. Dissatisfaction with the status quo made the young generally open to change, and the message transmitted in the new, Western-style schools—that the languages and cultures developed over the centuries by Jews under Islam were "inferior" to those of the West—led young people to view their own traditions with disdain. These schools taught their students, who now included girls, that their traditional vernaculars were not "Jewish languages" at all but corrupt jargons. Secular education in Western and local languages led pupils to attempt to modernize their communities' languages, which they now referred to as "Judeo-" dialects. The forms that this "modernization" assumed often included writing the languages in non-Hebrew alphabets, rejecting as antiquated and irrelevant the special translation varieties used in traditional Bible study and the rabbinic styles cultivated by local scholars, and transforming the lexical composition, sounds, grammar, and stylistic structures of the languages under the influence of Western and non-Jewish models. Ultimately, modern education in the Jewish communities under Islam led the younger generations to abandon their communities' traditional languages and cultural patterns in favor of Western and/or local non-Jewish languages and cultures.

This chapter analyzes how the processes of modernization affected three Jewish languages of the Middle East: Judezmo/Hakitia, Judeo-Arabic, and Judeo-Persian. —*David M. Bunis*

Modernization of Judezmo and Hakitia (Judeo-Spanish)

David M. Bunis

The Jewish language popularly known in the modern period as Judezmo in the Ottoman Empire and Hakitia in North Africa—also called Judeo-Spanish, Ladino, Spanyol, and others—began to take shape in medieval

Spain. I will refer to the language in all its varieties as Judezmo. The medieval variety of the language used in Spain, Old Judezmo, exhibited elements adapted primarily from Old Castilian and other varieties of Ibero-Romance, as well as from Hebrew-Aramaic and Jewish varieties of Greek and North African Arabic. When in 1492 a newly united Christian Spain expelled Spanish Jewry, its many speakers transported the language to the Ottoman Empire, North Africa, and the Middle East, as well as the Italian states and other parts of the Mediterranean region. There, Middle Judezmo began to develop, its Ibero-Romance component growing distant from the languages used in Iberia as a result of distinctive internal trends and innovations. Meanwhile, its Hebrew-Aramaic component was increasing quantitatively and evolving qualitatively, and its lexicon was becoming enriched through borrowings from local languages, especially Turkish in the Ottoman Empire and Arabic in North Africa and the Middle East. Toward the end of the eighteenth century the Modern Judezmo period began with the gradual westernization and secularization of the speakers in the Ottoman Empire and North Africa. More than 150,000 Sephardim, most of them elderly, in the former Ottoman regions, including Israel, as well as in immigrant communities in Western Europe, the Americas, Africa, and Australia, still speak Modern Judezmo today. This section focuses on the rise of Modern Judezmo, the historical and social factors leading to it, and some of its characteristic linguistic features. For the most part the discussion concerns the language as it developed in the Ottoman Empire; there, the more than one thousand books, periodicals, and manuscripts that were produced in Istanbul, Salonika, Izmir, Sofia, Belgrade, Jerusalem, and other former Ottoman cities from the sixteenth through the twentieth centuries document its evolution. There is little documentation of the language in North Africa before the twentieth century, and the analysis of the existing material from the Italian regions is still insufficient.

In the fifteenth and sixteenth centuries the Ottoman armies conquered the Balkans and parts of the Middle East and North Africa. Among the prestigious newcomers to the empire were Western Jews, mostly of Italian and Portuguese background and language, who were known among the Ottoman Jews as Francos, or Western Europeans. The popular Judezmo rabbinic literature that flourished in Istanbul and Salonika in the eighteenth century makes occasional allusions to the Francos. Though these texts never question the Francos' Jewishness, the rabbis nonetheless considered them a group apart from the Ottoman Jews of the eighteenth century, from whom the Francos diverged in their everyday habits, customs, costume, liturgical rites, and in other respects. However, the Ottoman Jews evidently recognized a strong similarity between the Romance languages (e.g., Italian, Portuguese, Castilian) that the foreign Western Jews used and their own, essentially Iberian-based, language. The similarities between the languages must have been particularly striking against the background of the other completely unrelated or only distantly related languages used in the empire, such as Turkish, Greek, Armenian, Arabic, Albanian, and South Slavic. The Ottoman Jews so identified their own variety of Romance (Judezmo) with the Romance languages of the Francos that as early as the sixteenth century Judezmo speakers began to use *Franko*—a term paralleled by the Turkish word *Frenkçe*—as a synonym for *Judezmo.* The eighteenth-century rabbi Avraham Asa of Istanbul, author of a Judezmo summary of the precepts of Judaism in rhymed verse, suggested, for example, that his couplets would be especially appealing to the average Sephardic reader because he wrote them "en Franko" rather than in Hebrew, a language hardly understood by the Ottoman Sephardic masses.

With the intensification of contacts between the residents of the Ottoman Empire and of Western Europe toward the late eighteenth century, the empire as a whole began to undergo a measure of westernization. The interaction of the Ottoman Jews with the Francos in the Ottoman Empire, and the experiences of those Jews who traveled to the West for business or pleasure, set the scene for the profound changes that occurred within Ottoman Jewish society: westernization, modernization, and considerable secularization. Hints of the beginnings of these processes appear in Judezmo works produced in the empire in the eighteenth century. Whereas until that period Judezmo publications were generally staid prose texts, with a religious content and a serious self-important tone, the first half of the eighteenth century saw a revival among the Ottoman Sephardim of a medieval Hispanic poetic tradition with a unique Ottoman Sephardic variant: rhymed *komplas,* or couplets, that were meant to be sung to Ottoman musical modes and revolved around Jewish themes such as holiday observance and morality. Some compositions, such as those in honor of the festival of Purim, were at times whimsically satirical, perhaps reflecting the liberalism and individualism of the European Enlightenment. Ottoman Sephardic commercial contacts with the Italian states and interaction with early Jewish settlers of Italian origin in the Ottoman Empire had led to the incorporation of Italianisms within Judezmo as early as the sixteenth century. In eighteenth-century Judezmo texts the frequency of such terms increased; most were connected with trade (e.g., *pédrita,* financial loss; *valuta,* monetary value) and medicine (e.g., *dotor,* physician; *malatia,* illness); the corresponding Italian words are *perdita, valuta, dottore,* and *malattia.*

Unique among the Judezmo works known from the eighteenth century was an educational manual entitled *La gwerta de oro* (The Gold Garden), published in Livorno in 1778 by Sarajevo-born David Attias, whose family had established itself in Livorno. Attias was perhaps the first Judezmo writer to recognize the vernacular of the Ottoman Sephardim as a distinct language, which he called "our Levantine Spanish language," the "Levantine language," or simply "our language." He was one of the earliest writers to suggest that its speakers could derive pleasure from reading a work that had the true taste of the authentic spoken language, but he also noted that his work was intended for those who could not understand "real Spanish," by which he meant contemporaneous Castilian—probably the first expression in Judezmo literature of the "enlightened" (i.e., essentially self-denigrating) attitude that the language of the Sephardim was both different and somehow less valid, less "true" than Castilian. It is probably no coincidence that the book, of an essentially secular nature, was published in Livorno, far from the reach of the conservative Ottoman rabbis whose approval Jews needed to publish within the empire. In his introduction Attias noted that previous works published by Ottoman Sephardim were all related to the Torah and mostly in Hebrew—which was the prestige language for serious rabbinic scholarship, not the Judezmo used primarily as an educational tool in popular texts meant for readers who could not cope with a work in Hebrew. Writing during the first period of the Jewish Enlightenment (Haskalah) in Western Europe, and only two years after the beginning of the American Revolution, Attias argued that the young Levantine Sephardim of his time were "of a new spirit," "wide awake," and did not all "incline toward the Torah." He bemoaned the complete absence of historical works, treatments of geography and other sciences, and commercial manuals in their everyday language. His own work was an innovation: a manual, of nonrabbinic orientation, offering information of diverse kinds, including a brief introduction to Italian, an essay criticizing Eastern fatalism, and advice for Sephardim in the East who intended to visit Western Europe. He wrote all this in a reasonably popular, light variety of Judezmo, which on the one hand incorporated Hebraisms in popular forms ordinarily absent from rabbinic works in Judezmo (e.g., *maymazí,* liquor, and *sevarodes,* opinions, words that came from Hebrew—*mayim azim,* mighty waters, and *sevarot,* opinions, combined with the Spanish plural-forming *-es*) as well as Turkisms (e.g., *shashareamyento,* bewilderment, and *konushear,* to converse, which come from the Turkish *şaşirmak* plus the Spanish noun-forming *-eamiento,* and *konuşmak* plus the Spanish verb-forming *-ear*).

Despite Attias's example and his call for what amounted to the modernization of Judezmo literature, both in language and content, Ottoman Sephardic writers in the late eighteenth and early nineteenth centuries continued to produce strictly Torah-related Judezmo works, such as translations of rabbinic classics (e.g., the wisdom book *Sefer Ben Sira* [Book of Ben Sira], published in Istanbul in 1823) and original rabbinic treatises (e.g., *Sefer Musar Mikre'e Kodesh* [Book of Holy Convocations] by Efrayim Hayot, published in Constantinople in 1828). The Jewish Enlightenment, however, was already having some effect in the Ottoman regions toward the end of the eighteenth century. With the increasing prestige and practical importance attributed to Western languages in the Ottoman Empire and its satellite communities in Western Europe (e.g., Vienna, Livorno), Levantine Sephardim made efforts to master them. In the eighteenth and early nineteenth centuries, such efforts took the form of private study or study abroad. The Ottoman rabbis continued to stress the primacy of Hebrew, the "holy tongue," and even late into the nineteenth century they chastised fathers who taught their sons Judezmo or other foreign languages rather than Hebrew.

In the Vienna of 1823, inspired by Haskalah writings in Hebrew and educational manuals in German that had been published in Austria, Belgrade-born Yisra'el Hayim (or Ben-Hayim) published his own multifaceted Judezmo work entitled *Otsar a-Hayim* (Treasury of Life), which offered instruction in basic German, as well as in the Ottoman Turkish writing system; it soon facilitated the study of foreign languages at home and in Sephardic elementary schools. The work also included an introduction to the Hebrew language and to daily prayers, a dictionary of biblical Hebrew, a survey of world geography, and a treatment of basic mathematics. Hayim, who may be called the father of Modern Judezmo, added to his work the earliest Judezmo primer; its texts—meant to be copied out for reading and writing practice—exhibited most of the distinctive characteristics of the modern language. In 1813 he had already published his own translation of the Bible in the arcane variety of Judezmo called Ladino.

Encouraged by or profiting from the Hebrew-language contributions of the Haskalah writers, other Judezmo writers of the early nineteenth century began to broach fields formerly ignored by Ottoman Sephardic writers, such as Hebrew grammar (e.g., Yehuda Hai Alkalay's *Darkhe No*ᶜ*am* [Paths of Pleasantness], published in Belgrade in 1839), astronomy (e.g., *Sefer ha-Berit* [Book of the Covenant], a translation of a work by P. E. ben Me'ir, published in

Salonika in 1847), Jewish history and world history and biography (e.g., Y. B. Amarachi's *Keter Shem Tov* [Crown of Good Name], an adaptation of biographical works by A. M. M. Mohr, together with a geographic treatise by Yehoseph Schwartz, published in Salonika around 1850), and geography (e.g., Y. B. Amarachi's translation of Samson Bloch's *Shevile Olam,* published in Salonika in 1853–57).

While the influence of the German-Jewish Haskalah indirectly resulted in the beginnings of something approaching scientific literature in Judezmo, it also had a deleterious effect on the way in which "enlightened" Sephardim began to perceive their native language. The Haskalah pioneer Moses Mendelssohn, who lived in Germany, had translated the Pentateuch into German using the Hebrew alphabet (1780–83) in order to wean Ashkenazim away from Yiddish—he maintained nothing but contempt for what *maskilim* (modernizers) came to call that "corrupt," "mixed" Ashkenazic "jargon." In the early nineteenth century, while Yisra'el Hayim and other Sephardic rabbis were continuing to produce educational works in Judezmo without overtly denigrating the nature of that language, westernized Ashkenazic onlookers were already casting Judezmo in maskilic terms—as *leshon Shpanien meᶜorav* (the mixed language of Spain). That was what Aharon Pollack called it in his introduction to the first volume of Hayim's Ladino Bible (Vienna, 1813). In the 1818 German preface to the Viennese publication of Hayim's Judezmo translation of *Hokhmat Yehoshuᶜa ben Sira* (The Wisdom of Joshua Ben Sira), the censor explained that the work had been "translated literally, in the mixed Spanish Turkish language in Hebrew letters, for the use of the Israelites living in Turkey." Written at a time when *maskilim* were infatuated with the notion of linguistic purity, such descriptions carried negative connotations.

By the 1840s a further if somewhat marginal linguistic factor was being brought to bear on the development of Judezmo in the Levant. Protestant missionaries had arrived from England and the United States with the task of converting the Ottoman Jews and others to Christianity. They sought to do so with the aid of beautifully printed, widely circulated educational and religious texts, composed in a novel synthesis of traditional Judezmo and Modern Castilian. These were printed in the Hebrew-letter rabbinic typeface known as "Rashi letters," which was customarily used in Judezmo texts throughout most of the history of that language. As a community, the Sephardim of the Ottoman Empire probably acquired their first taste of Modern Spanish through missionary publications issued in Istanbul, such as Alexander Thomson's Bible story collection, *Ele Toledot Bene Yisra'el* (Now

These Are the Generations of the Sons of Israel, 1854), William Gottlieb Schauffler's dictionary of Biblical Hebrew "in the Sephardic language" entitled *Otsar divre leshon hakodesh o diksyonaryo de la lingwa santa* (Treasury of the Words of the Holy Tongue or Dictionary of the Sacred Language, 1855), and the literary and scientific periodical *El manadero o la fwente de sensya* (The Source, or Fountain of Science, 1855). In addition to seeking the Jews' conversion to Christianity, the missionaries' publications attempted to convince the Ottoman Jews to abandon Judezmo in favor of Spanish.

The year 1845 was an especially significant one in the history of Judezmo language and literature: The editor Raffael Uziel published the earliest-documented Judezmo commercial, scientific, and news periodical, the biweekly *Shaᶜare Mizrah* (*Gates of the East*) in Izmir. Animated by the success of Jewish periodicals in Western Europe, Uziel saw his own newspaper as a potentially peerless tool for the education and enlightenment of the young people of the Judezmo-speaking world. In the early nineteenth century Haskalah-inspired publications explored fields of knowledge that preceding generations of Judezmo rabbinic writers had ignored. The authors were forced to confront the problem of technical terminology, and the treatment of topics that had not yet been addressed in Judezmo left them with the challenge of how to express new concepts. Writers with a rabbinic orientation, such as Alkalai and Amarachi, continued to cultivate the traditional rabbinic Judezmo of earlier religious treatises. That variety of the language featured a synthesis of popular and archaizing Ibero-Romance elements, a wealth of Hebrew-Aramaisms, and numerous Turkish-Balkanisms, yet Alkalai in his 1839 Hebrew grammar in Judezmo proudly stated that his book was written "belashon tsah sefaradi" [in the pure Sephardic, or Spanish, language]. The rabbinic writers saw little need to be introspective about the Judezmo language in general or its specific terminological shortcomings, because they attributed little importance to the language; for them it was a foreign tongue, a bitter reminder of the centuries of exile, whereas Hebrew was the sacred language of world Jewry and the symbol of Israel's ancient glory. When neologistic terminology appeared in the Ashkenazic Haskalah source texts, the rabbinic Judezmo translators just reproduced those terms, often of German or Yiddish origin, sometimes even preserving their Yiddish spellings.

The success of the Haskalah-oriented, secular Jewish press of Western Europe, with which Uziel was thoroughly familiar, was the direct inspiration for his decision to publish a newspaper in Judezmo. Probably to circumvent its being banned by the local rabbinate, Uziel did not publish his paper at a Jewish press but at the press of George Griffith, an Englishman in Izmir who also published Anglican missionary texts in Judezmo. In the totally new framework of the first secular-oriented Judezmo periodical, Uziel felt compelled to address directly, for the first time in an Ottoman Judezmo text, the broad questions of language composition and linguistic variation in his own community's language (a problem that had disconcerted the earlier Ashkenazic *maskilim* as well with respect to Yiddish). He also resolved the problem of insufficient (or maskilically undesirable) terminology in a manner distinct from that of his rabbinic predecessors.

On the cover page of Uziel's first issue of *Sha^care Mizrah,* he began his "composer's introduction" by apologizing for any errors of language or style that readers might find in his paper, which he attempted to write in the "dialect" of the language that he claimed most Jews in Turkey spoke. Uziel's remarks contained the first formulations by an Ottoman rabbi of criticisms against Judezmo; these would continue into our own times, leveled by those who considered themselves "enlightened" (assimilated to European or local national culture). Uziel argued that, following the expulsion from Spain, the Jews had forgotten and ruined the true Spanish, which he believed their ancestors had spoken in Spain (he failed to consider that all languages, including Castilian, change through time and that even before the expulsion, Jewish speech had diverged somewhat from that of coterritorial non-Jews); that present-day Judezmo was really a mix of assorted languages (which, of course, could also be said of more "respectable" languages, such as English or Turkish); that Judezmo varied from region to region (as, in fact, do most of the world's languages); that it was learned solely through oral transmission rather than through formal instruction (Uziel here ignored the existence of a written literature in the language, much of it of a didactic nature, from the Old Judezmo through Modern Judezmo periods); and that no one had paid attention to its grammar or lexicon (which really meant that the structure of the language exhibited a measure of free variation, of the kind typical in languages that have not attained official national status). Uziel argued that the tribulations suffered by the Sephardim after their expulsion from Spain had left them no time for observing linguistic niceties.

In his periodical Uziel laid the foundation for a new westernizing and secularizing variety of Modern Judezmo. That variety predominated in subsequent Judezmo secular periodicals, more than three hundred of which appeared in regions of the former Ottoman Empire and immigrant communities in Western Europe and the United States between 1845 and 2002. While preserving some linguistic characteristics of traditional rabbinic Judezmo in his *Sha^care Mizrah,* Uziel westernized, modernized, and secularized his language by reducing its Eastern elements—the centuries-old Hebrew-Aramaic and Turkish-Balkan components—to a bare minimum. He also introduced scores of replacement terms, supplementary vocabulary, and elements of grammar and syntax from what came to be considered the more "civilized" Western languages, such as Italian and French (e.g., *blu,* blue, from the Italian *blu* and/or the French *bleu,* replacing Turkish-origin *maví*). Uziel's writings include some of the earliest examples of the typically Modern Judezmo use of the plural possessive pronoun *sus* to denote *their,* even when preceding a singular noun (e.g., *sus aktivitad,* their action); it supplanted the earlier singular *su* in that context, apparently under the influence of the French *leur* and Italian *loro.* In a letter to the editor of *Shaᶜare Mizrah,* a Jewish French "well-wisher" advised the Ottoman Sephardim not to content themselves with Judezmo monolingualism but to study the language of their own country as well. Five years before, in 1840, after the inauguration of the Ottoman Tanzimat reforms, Chief Rabbi Moshe Hayim Fresco had informed the empire's Jews of Sultan Abdülmecid I's desire that they learn Turkish. But neither royal decree nor fraternal advice convinced most Jews of the empire to master Turkish until the proclamation of the Turkish Republic in 1923.

The Damascus Affair, an anti-Semitic outburst in 1840, had rocked the Jewish world and left its scattered communities feeling an urgent need for solidarity. In 1858 the Mortara case, which involved forced conversions in Italy, further strengthened the desire for unity and self-help. In 1860 the prominent Jewish community in France responded by founding the Alliance Israélite Universelle (AIU) in Paris. Its aims were primarily to work toward the emancipation and moral progress of the Jews and to assist Jews suffering from anti-Semitism, especially those in the Eastern communities. Shortly after its founding, the AIU began to establish a network of French-language schools of an essentially secular nature that Jewish pupils throughout the Balkans and the Middle East attended. In such schools, and in other foreign-language educational institutions opened in the Ottoman Empire, increasing numbers of young Ottoman Sephardim acquired proficiency in French, Italian, German, and other Western languages, and they learned to admire Western culture and civilization as well. Under the influence of their European-trained teachers, whose attitude toward the Ottoman Sephardic language and culture was overwhelmingly negative, those pupils also began to question the worth of their own cultural patrimony, especially the components of it that derived from Eastern sources, which their teachers considered to be of negligible value.

For the most part, the rabbinic Judezmo texts produced during this period and into the twentieth century by students trained solely in the old-fashioned religious schools tended to be linguistically conservative, preserving the traditional form of Judezmo that similar texts had used for centuries. Yet the first Judezmo play, *Pyesa di Yaakov Avinu kun sus ijus* (A Play About Our Forefather Abraham and His Children, published in Bucharest, 1862), by Moshe Shemuel Kofino, written for the pupils of a religious school in Giurgiu, Romania, already has some modern Western elements, such as borrowings from French and Italian.

The linguistic consequences of the modern westernized worldview acquired by pupils in secular schools are all the more obvious in the nonreligious Judezmo publications of the time—especially newspapers—from the second half of the nineteenth century into the twentieth century. The writers, who had received their educations in the foreign-language schools, used fewer and fewer elements of Hebrew-Aramaic and Turkish-Balkan origin; replacing them, and sometimes even supplanting elements of Medieval Spanish origin, were new borrowings from French, Italian, Modern Castilian, and other Western European languages. Many publications (often translations of French, Italian, German, or English works) were produced in the new westernized and secularized Judezmo, and from the 1870s their authors designated their language with such pseudoscientific terms as *Djudezmo Espanyol, Djudayko-Espanyol,* and later, overwhelmingly, *Judeo-Espanyol.* The latter was analogous to the term *Jüddisch-Deutsch,* already used for Yiddish in the 1820s by Leopold Zunz, founder of the maskilic Science of Judaism movement. The Ottoman rabbis spurned such translations and sought to compete with them by producing collections of religious stories translated from Hebrew. But the secular authors gained wide popularity among the gradually westernized and modernized Sephardic masses, whose Jewish education grew progressively thinner.

From the second half of the nineteenth century, enlightened Sephardim expressed increasing scorn for Judezmo and advocated its replacement by other languages. In 1868, inspired by German-language monographs on the glories of medieval Spanish Jewry by Haskalah historians, the editor of the Viennese Judezmo periodical *El nasyonal* proposed that Judezmo speakers abandon their traditional language and adopt Castilian, to be written not in the Jewish alphabet but in Latin letters. In a supplement to the Viennese Judezmo periodical *El koreo de Vyena* that was published in 1872, the Sephardic rabbi David Halevi of Bucharest characterized the language of the Sephardim as a "bitter souvenir" of their tragic Spanish past. To him it seemed a bizarre irony that in Turkey the descendants of Jews who had been exiled from Spain should consider the truest sign of a Jew to be speaking *el Judezmo,* "Jewish" ["In Turkia es il vidraderu sinyal di un djidyó, kwandu avla il djudezmu"]; to Halevi, the Jewish language was merely "defective Spanish." Halevi was perhaps the first to stress the problematic absence of modern technical terms in the language ["Il djudezmu ki avlamus es difiktozu. . . . Li faltan las palavras téhnikas"]. While praising the loftiness of Hebrew, he proposed that Judezmo speakers replace their language with a "broad, cultured and civilized language" such as those of Europe.

In the 1880s David Fresco, editor of the influential maskilic Judezmo periodical *El tyempo* of Istanbul, initiated a chain of controversial exchanges in the Judezmo press around the "language question" by publishing an article entitled "A Mute People." In it he accused the Ottoman Sephardim of being a people without a language—because for him Judeo-Spanish lacked any linguistic or literary merit—and he urged them to adopt one. He argued that the monolingual use of "Judeo Espanyol" by a large percentage of the Ottoman Sephardim had the effect of isolating the group and preventing its integration within Ottoman society. In a series of replies to Fresco published in the Judezmo periodical *La epoka* of Salonika at the turn of the nineteenth century, Sam Levy came to the defense of Judeo-Espanyol. While Levy was in favor of Ottoman Jews' learning other languages, especially Turkish, to demonstrate identification with the empire, and Western European languages to ensure success in commerce, he proposed that Judezmo be retained as the unifying communal language of the empire's Jews. Well aware of the campaigns being waged during this period on behalf of minority languages, including Yiddish among the Ashkenazim, Levy maintained that Judeo-Espanyol too could flower into a full-blown modern language, provided it underwent "reforms" and "refinement." He suggested, toward those ends, that the traditional Rashi-letter orthography be improved, though not abandoned, and that the literary language be based primarily on the spoken language. Levy's ideas were in turn criticized by Jacques Danon of Edirne, who contended that standardization might be impossible because of the diversity of the language's regional dialects, as well as internal variations in the grammar, syntax, and lexicon of the recently westernized literary language that was characteristic of the press and that had arisen primarily from the influence of French and Italian. Danon instead proposed that Judezmo be replaced by Castilian.

Just before World War I several Judezmo writers and journalists again advocated Judezmo as the national language of the Balkan Sephardim; some demonstrated their identification with the popular perception of the language as a "Jewish" tongue by consciously preferring to designate it by the traditional grassroots name *Judezmo* rather than by the maskilic *Judeo-Espanyol.* Support for Judezmo among writers of that period should be seen against the sociohistorical backdrop of the Young Turk uprising of 1908; the rise of independent, ethnicity-conscious nation-states that were being carved out of the former Ottoman Empire and the attention increasingly paid in them to the cultivation of their neglected ethnic languages, literatures, and cultures; and the advent of the socialist movement in the region, with its emphasis on the people and the public sector. The Balkan Sephardim were also well aware of the First Yiddish Language Conference, which had been held in Czernowitz in 1908 to promote Yiddish as a Jewish national language.

Still, Judezmo had its detractors: Hebraist Zionists inside and outside the Ottoman Empire attacked it as a factor contributing to the splintering of Jewish unity; Sephardic Castilianists who, under the wing of Iberian men of letters, denigrated it and proposed that the Levantine Sephardim adopt Modern Spanish, perceiving any Judezmo deviations from it as a sign of linguistic and cultural degradation; and the "cosmopolitans," who preferred more prestigious Western European languages, ridiculed Judezmo, and argued that it was of no consequence internationally and that its use severely limited self-expression. In addition, Judezmo was anathema to supporters of local nationalism, who agreed with much of the coterritorial non-Jewish population in regarding the use of Judezmo rather than the local national language as a demonstration of disloyalty to the state and stubborn separatism.

Time and again, proposals raised during the earliest stages of the "language question" resurfaced: that Judezmo be abandoned in favor of Hebrew or prestigious Western European languages or local national tongues; or that it be maintained as the Sephardic communal language but reformed in accordance with a variety of models of internal or foreign origin. These were repeated in a variety of forums but primarily in the Judezmo press and into our own times. Among present-day Judezmo speakers and writers, the controversies about the use of the language tend to revolve around the name of the language, the writing system, and the structure and lexicon of the language.

The Judezmo speech community is considerably smaller today than it was during the first half of the twentieth century because of the atrocities of World War II, the exodus of Judezmo speakers from the regions in which the language was traditionally spoken and their integration within new societies, and the increasing linguistic assimilation of those speakers who remain in the traditional Judezmo speech region. Entirely monolingual Judezmo speakers perhaps no longer exist. Yet the heated debates about controversial issues in the use of the language, which one continues to hear and read in Judezmo and in other languages, attest to the vitality of the remaining community of speakers and their passionate concern for the language and its propagation. So too do the popular collections of Judezmo folklore and original writings, which are published occasionally; the frequent international conferences and scholarly writings, periodicals, and radio programs devoted to Judezmo language and culture; and the Judezmo language, literature, and culture courses increasingly offered at universities, community centers, and synagogues in Israel, the United States, and countries in both Western and Eastern Europe. Through such efforts Modern Judezmo may well survive into the foreseeable future.

Judeo-Arabic

JOSEPH CHETRIT

Modern Judeo-Arabic includes the various spoken or written vernaculars of Arabic, ordinary or special, that Jewish communities of Arabic-speaking countries used since the 1500s for their daily interaction and/or for their literary or liturgical creation and life. These vernaculars were used in Yemen, Eretz Israel, Lebanon, Syria, Iraq, Egypt, Libya, Tunisia, Algeria, and Morocco. They represent hundreds of Judeo-Arabic communal dialects, and most were distinguishable from the contiguous Muslim Arabic vernaculars by their discursive, textual, and morphosyntactic structures. Here I describe these modern Judeo-Arabic varieties sociolinguistically in order to trace their late transformations and to appraise the efforts by local cultural leaders to promote or accelerate them.

Linguistically, Judeo-Arabic is composed of a vocabulary and grammar that is basically Arabic, enriched by Hebrew and Aramaic. Judeo-Arabic varies from place to place and was affected by geographical, economic, and historical circumstances. Nevertheless, this great diversity of communal linguistic traditions and the conditions that led to their transformations are balanced by a certain sociolinguistic homogeneity, one based on a profoundly similar rabbinic tradition throughout the region. Basically, Hebrew and Aramaic were used for Judaic liturgy, and the local or communal vernacular was used for daily life. The Judeo-Arabic–speaking communities regarded both Hebrew and Aramaic as sacred languages, because liturgical texts and rabbinic discourse had been written in them. Both were reserved for literary, intellectual, halakhic, and exegetic writing. As a local and principally spoken language, Judeo-Arabic was reserved for daily interaction and was regarded as common low-level dialect. Yet these distinctive language functions did not remain separated; instead, the knowledge and use of the two languages by the same Jewish speakers (and writers) contributed to various blended varieties of Judeo-Arabic. A high-level variety of Judeo-Arabic, generally called al-Sharh (al-Tafsir or al-Maqshiya in some communities), was traditionally used for the translation of holy texts for children and others not conversant in Hebrew. The Hebrew and Aramaic components of Judeo-Arabic in its varieties were important. One of these was the language that the rabbi used in his sermons, to transmit information and tradition to the people; so was the secret Jewish argot that was used in the presence of foreign or unknown people (principally Muslim Arabic speakers).

Other varieties of Judeo-Arabic were formed and developed through contact with nearby languages. These include Berber dialects in North Africa, Neo-Aramaic in Arab Kurdistan, and Turkic or Persian (Farsi) in Iraq. Until the new dispersion of the Jewish communities during the second half of twentieth century, Judeo-Arabic continued to be contiguous with Arabic dialects. Some Muslim texts were incorporated into Jewish folk culture, such as the folktales, folk songs, and proverbs that Jewish women adopted and principally used. Professional and semiprofessional Jewish singers and artists adopted and Judaized many other Muslim poetic texts on lyric and romantic themes, accompanied by melodies, and performed them during family and communal ceremonies. Until the end of the nineteenth century, rabbinic tradition and communal censure had limited the creation in Hebrew or Judeo-Arabic of these lyric and romantic materials, and that was the reason for the massive absorption of such Muslim texts in all the Judeo-Arabic–speaking communities. This borrowing was constant.

The arrival of the Sephardim, because of the expulsions from the Iberian Peninsula in 1492 and later, added a new linguistic dimension to Middle Eastern and North African Jewish dialects. In some communities great tensions sometimes accompanied the absorption of the newcomers, who spoke Spanish and/or Judeo-Spanish, Portuguese or Judeo-Portuguese, and who had different cultural and socioeconomic traditions from local ones. In some cases the restabilization of the émigré communities led to the creation of a new linguistic amalgam and in others to the retention of their own dialect. Daily contacts and the interaction of both communities led to the borrowing of new concepts and terms. Some *megorashim* (Spanish exiles) continued to speak pure Judeo-Spanish, while new communities founded in North Africa absorbed into the Judeo-Spanish matrix thousands of Arabic and Judeo-Arabic lexical items; other *megorashim* formed a new kind of blended language, usually called Hakitia. In the seventeenth and eighteenth centuries the Sephardim known as Grana arrived in Tunis from Livorno, where their grandfathers had found refuge after their expulsion from Spain and Portugal, and they continued to speak Italian and Judeo-Italian until the twentieth century. In Tunis and other communities of Tunisia and Libya, Judeo-Arabic was in this way enriched by numerous Italian words and phrases that dealt with material culture and leisure activities.

Modern educational systems and the spread of printing in the nineteenth century soon challenged the status of Judeo-Arabic. Subsequent contact with European languages and Modern Hebrew further enriched Judeo-Arabic, but at the same time these languages challenged its status as the official communal tongue. With colonialism and emerging Zionism, new communal elites tried to reform their Judeo-Arabic to meet the challenges of modern life, even generating new varieties, as in Tunisia. Modern developments hardly affected the rural dialects, however, or Judeo-Arabic as it was spoken in Yemen. In Oran, Algiers, and Tunis a new era began for Judeo-Arabic literature as a result of the introduction of the printing press with type in Hebrew characters. The first Hebrew printers in North Africa produced such new rabbinical works as *Shay La-Morah* (A Gift to Piety), by Rabbi Shelomo Zarqa and Rabbi Yehuda Darmon from Oran, and the Judeo-Arabic translation by Abraham Lasri in Algiers of sections of *Me-am Lo*ᶜ*ez,* the eighteenth-century anthology of Bible stories, homilies, and folktales.

Several Judeo-Arabic newspapers first appeared in the late nineteenth century, giving accounts of Jewish life in various countries, including North African communities, and introducing their readers to new kinds of literary and narrative texts in Judeo-Arabic adaptations. They also published translations of European, Arabic, and Hebrew works, serialized in several issues in the format called feuilleton, or entertainment magazine. Many were taken directly from newspapers printed in modern Hebrew.

In Algiers in the 1890s Chalom Bekhache used his Judeo-Arabic newspaper *Beth Israel* and the review *Or Ha-Lebana* to publish such Jewish narratives as the story of Bustenai (about Jewish exilarchs in Iraq before the geonic period), European novels such as *Robinson Crusoe,* and stories and reports on Eretz Israel, folkloric events, and scientific news and articles. His publishing ceased before the end of the century because he was losing Judeo-Arabic readers at a time when Algiers was adopting French as the communal and familial language.

Toward the end of the nineteenth century, the first *maskilim* in Tunis steadily read new Hebrew writings and newspapers, as well as European literary narratives and Arabic newspapers, and they transposed their readings to their Judeo-Arabic writings and their often ephemeral newspapers. Only one journal, *Al-Bustan* (the *Garden*), lasted for ten years. The pioneers of the Jewish Enlightenment were Eliezer Farhi, Chalom Flah, Jacob Chemla, Messod Maarek, Vita Sitruk, Semah Levi, and Jacob Cohen. They published dozens of semiclassical Arabic narratives in Hebrew characters, translated into Judeo-Arabic dozens of Hebrew books (including those of the Eastern European author Avraham Mapu), and wrote many poetic pieces on contemporary Tunisian Jewish communities. They also used serialization for improving the circulation of their newspapers, then published the entire narrative in a book or booklet. Among the new militant activities, *maskilim* supported ardently modern and democratic reforms in communal institutions and founded new committees for promoting their sociocultural goals.

Although this cultural production decreased slowly in Tunis after World War I because of the growth of French education and French culture among the new generations of readers, it was transferred to communities on the periphery, Sousse and Djerba. In Sousse the editor Makhlouf Nadjar published new editions of Judeo-Arabic poems and for seventeen years published a newspaper, *Al-Najma* (the Star), that continued after his death in 1938, surviving until 1959. In Djerba, where Jewish traditions were constantly safeguarded, several rabbinic authors and editors published hundreds of didactic and halakhic works, as well as commentaries in Hebrew and Judeo-Arabic; they were the last to maintain the Judeo-Arabic publishing tradition in North Africa.

In the late 1800s the Iraqi Jewish communities living in Calcutta and Bombay published their own Judeo-Arabic newspapers, some European and Hebrew works, as well as those in Iraqi Judeo-Arabic, and some traditional Jewish writings and Muslim Arabic narratives. Yet as their social integration into the English colonial society of India increased, their editorial and creative activities decreased. They ceased soon after the beginning of twentieth century.

In Morocco and Libya printing in Modern Hebrew arrived late, in the first decades of the twentieth century, but there too it produced Judeo-Arabic newspapers and the printing of new halakhic, didactic, and exegetic works. Their publication lasted until after World War II, until the dispersal of the Jewish communities after 1950. Before that the Hebrew works of Moroccan authors, as well as of those from other Mediterranean communities, had been printed principally in Livorno, London, and Vienna.

Tunisian *maskilim* were not enthusiastic about appreciating or maintaining Judeo-Arabic dialects. Tunisian authors had worked carefully at the beginning of their nineteenth-century cultural movement to distinguish the language of their literary writings by using a mixture of Judeo-Arabic grammar and words taken from formal Muslim literary texts, both written and oral. Their new literary language was in fact a genuine conversational Judeo-Arabic that became stabilized and was adopted in Tunisia and Libya in literary and journalistic Jewish writings for more than fifty years despite its clear Muslim roots. Nevertheless, in the last decade of the nineteenth century, this new kind of literary Judeo-Arabic precipitated a great linguistic dispute among the editors of Judeo-Arabic newspapers in Tunis concerning the journalistic language most desirable for Jewish readers. Jacob Chemla and his colleagues argued for an elitist language, similar to the one used in Jewish literary works and in the newspaper *Al-Nahla* (the *Bee*). His contemporary, Messod Maarek, opposed such Islamization of the Jewish language, and he founded a rival newspaper, *Al-Bustan,* in which he promised to present news to Jewish readers in their own language, not pure Arabic. Despite his efforts Maarek did not completely succeed in implementing his linguistic program, because no one Judeo-Arabic academy was founded to orient the writers and establish valuable linguistic norms.

In Tunis, Eliezer Farhi and Mordecai Hai Dayyan proposed that a new translation of the Bible was desirable, and they attempted not only to translate the Bible into Judeo-Arabic but to incorporate classic rabbinic commentaries. Their new translations showed that the authors did not succeed in extirpating numerous traditional linguistic structures of Sharh. In Morocco at the beginning of the nineteenth century, the famous *dayyan* (religious court judge) and scholar Rabbi Raphael Birdugo from Meknès had successfully initiated a similar but partial reform. He scrutinized fallacious literal translations in Sharh literature and corrected them for Talmud Torah (rabbinical school) teachers. His manuscript *Leshon Limudim* (The Pure Language) was transcribed many times in various Moroccan communities, where it became a normative work for teaching biblical texts. In an attempt to reach an increasingly secular community in Algeria, some rabbis published biblical commentaries in Judeo-Arabic. For example, in Oran in 1854 Rabbi Shelomo Zarqa and Rabbi Yehuda Darmon wrote in Judeo-Arabic their commentary on the book of Genesis, *Shay La-Morah.*

As for Judeo-Arabic poetry, it too underwent some transformations from the 1850s on, because of the growing acquaintance of Jewish writers with contemporary Arabic poetry and because of their new collaborative activities in performing Arabic music and songs. One was the *dayyan* and poet Rabbi Nathan Djian, who at the turn of the nineteenth century wrote numerous liturgical poems in Tlemcen dedicated to the description of the Exile, to his aspiration for redemption, and to messianic times. He used an Arabic similar to that used in the Andalusian poetry tradition of Muslims of Algeria. Then Jewish poets began to use contemporary Arabic poetry and songs not only for their melodies (for new Hebrew and Judeo-Arabic poems) but also in imitation of poetic forms, transposing some of their linguistic structures into their own Judeo-Arabic poems. In this way the popular and semiclassical genre called *qasida* was adopted by North African Judeo-Arabic poets as well by by Hebrew poets, such as Rabbi Raphael Moshe Elbaz in Sefrou (1826–96) or Nissim Elbaz (nineteenth century). The latter lived in several Moroccan and Algerian Jewish communities, and he wrote valuable songs and poems about life in the Jewish quarters and about his own experiences in a poeticized and personal Judeo-Arabic (based on Arabic items in one part and on Hebrew elements in another). This trend of Jewish poetry increased in the twentieth century, as Jewish singers and poets in the Middle East and North Africa wrote new Arabic songs incorporating Arabic modes for a Muslim and a Jewish audience.

The subsequent decline of Judeo-Arabic may be attributed to the introduction of modern and secular education, based on Western languages, and the emigration from Judeo-Arabic communities. Today, only elderly and monolingual Judeo-Arabic speakers continue to use their dialects. More and more, as with other Jewish languages, Judeo-Arabic has become more of an identity language than a living language. Henceforth, only scholars and students may maintain Judeo-Arabic into the next few generations—particularly through courses taught at the universities and through the study and publication of Judeo-Arabic texts.

Languages and Literature of the Jews of Iran and Afghanistan

HAIDEH SAHIM

What we know about the historical development of the Jewish dialects of Iran is limited to short passages recorded in Judeo-Persian texts and what modern scholars have preserved or recorded in interviews. By the 1940s the number of speakers of these languages had already started to decline, mostly because of migration, particularly to Tehran; the widespread use of radio and other media in Persian, the official language of Iran; and other social factors. It is rare to find people born after the 1950s who would claim any of these dialects as their mother tongue.

In the nineteenth and early twentieth century, the mother tongues of most Iranian Jews were dialects different from those spoken around them. Contrary to some claims—that Jews spoke only the particular dialect of their *mahalle* (neighborhood), evidence exists that Iranian Jews, particularly men, were multilingual, since there was a necessity to communicate with the speakers of Persian, Turkish, Armenian, and various other languages and dialects who lived around them. The Iranian Jews' universal usage of Persian, which is also the language of the bulk of Judeo-Persian literature, and their transcriptions of Persian literary masterpieces into Hebrew script demonstrate their knowledge, if not command, of Persian.

The dialects of the Jews of Iran can be divided into two main groups: Aramaic (Semitic) dialects and Iranian dialects. The Aramaic dialects, also known as Lishna Yahudia (Jewish tongue), were spoken mostly in the western parts of Iran, in the Kurdistan area and western Azerbaijan. These are among the Eastern Neo-Aramaic dialects and are related to the Old Aramaic dialects of the Jews that linguists refer to as Babylonian Talmudic. Jewish Aramaic dialects of Iran, spoken in some parts of Kurdistan, such as Sanandaj and Saqqiz, and by the Jews of Urmieh, are also related to the Assyrian and Chaldean dialects spoken there. It is not known why certain groups of Jews maintained a Semitic language while all other communities of Jews became speakers of Iranian languages. While the Jews of Kurdistan were culturally similar to the general population of the area, the Urmieh Jews maintained their own culture and traditions. These Judeo-Aramaic dialects contain, in addition to Hebrew and some Persian loan words, some words from local dialects as well.

The second group is Iranian dialects. Iranian languages are Indo-European, a group that includes Hindi, Persian, English, French, and other European languages. Judeo-Iranian dialects are divided into two groups of southwestern or Persian dialects, and Central dialects.

Before the founding of the Persian Empire by Cyrus the Great in the sixth century B.C.E., a large part of the Iranian plateau was under the rule of the Median Empire, whose language and dialects were dominant in most parts of the plateau. The language of ancient Persia, which was different from

Median, became dominant with the expansion of the Persian Empire, particularly in the cities. In other words, Persian was the intruder in these areas, and the Median dialects are native. However, people in remote areas and in small towns and villages continued to speak the local Median dialects. For example, people living in Isfahan, Kashan, and Hamadan must have spoken in Median dialects before they adopted Persian, as indicated by the Median dialects spoken in the villages around them. In the cities the local dialects either died out completely or only a few words remained. However, the Jews in cities continued conversing in the old dialects. That is why it has often been said that the Jews of Iran are the keepers of the ancient languages.

The dialects that fall into the Persian group of Judeo-Iranian dialects are those that are phonetically and grammatically related to Modern Persian. The dialects of the Jews of Shiraz and surrounding areas are among this group, as are the dialects of the Jews of the eastern part of Iran, the Jews of Afghanistan, and the Jews of Central Asia (Tajikistan and the Bukhara area).

The majority of the Jewish dialects of Iran belong to the Central or Median dialects, which occur in the central parts of the Iranian plateau in a geographical area approximately between Isfahan, Hamadan, and Kashan. The dialects of the Jews of Hamadan, Ray, Kashan, Isfahan, Natanz, Sedeh, Na'in, Borujerd, Khomein, Arak, Nahavand, Malayer, and many other cities in the area are in this group. The dialects of the Zoroastrians in Iran also belong to this group. The geographical area of the influence of these dialects is not limited to the geographical boundaries of present-day Iran. The Jewish dialects contain a number of loan words from other languages, including Hebrew, Persian, Turkish, and various local dialects.

In addition to the languages and dialects I have discussed thus far, Iranian Jews use a language known as Lotra'i (Lotorai), a corrupt form of the Hebrew *lo Tora*, "not the [language of] Torah." It is also defined as a secret language in classical Persian texts and a hybrid language by linguists. Used by Jews in the presence of "outsiders," it is a combination of Aramaic and Hebrew words and the local Jewish dialects, so there are local variations of Lotra'i. While nouns and verb stems are Aramaic or Hebrew, the prefixes, suffixes, pronouns, verb endings, and prepositions are in the local Jewish dialects.

Judeo-Persian Literature

Although the Jews spoke in a multitude of dialects, they mostly wrote in the Persian language, using the Hebrew script, which is the main reason that Judeo-Persian literature has remained largely unknown in its own land. To compensate for the extra ten letters that Persian has, writers used specific diacritical marks, different from the vowel marks, over or under the Hebrew letters. Aside from the Hebrew script in which they are written, there are linguistic traits that distinguish Judeo-Persian texts from the classic Persian works that were written using the Arabic script. The style of these texts is simple, with some colloquialism, and there are Hebrew loan words and occasional words of Judeo-Persian dialects in them. Religious texts, such as commentaries, however, were sometimes written in Hebrew.

During the Ilkhanid period (1256–1336), an era of greater tolerance, the Jews flourished in every respect and produced a large body of literature in this period and the next two centuries. The greatest Judeo-Persian poet, Shahin of Shiraz (active in the first half of the fourteenth century), whose works could be found in almost every Jewish home, is a product of this tolerance. Later poets, such as Emrani (active early in the sixteenth century), also benefited from this cultural prosperity, as did Khwaja of Bukhara (active around 1604). In the middle of the Safavid period, in 1656, Baba'i Lutf of Kashan related the miseries that befell the Jews at that time in a major book of history in verse. The work is quite valuable, because very few histories are known from the Jews of Iran. A similar book, written around 1729 by his grandson, Baba'i Farhad, is indicative of the cultural decline of the Jews during and after the Safavid period, a decline that continued until the twentieth century.

The works of poetry and prose that Persian Jews created from the thirteenth century through the end of the nineteenth century draw from both Islamic Persian and Jewish cultures. They used prose for commentaries and translations of Torah and other religious texts, dream interpretations, astrology, stories, medical books, philosophical discourses, dictionaries (Hebrew-Persian), sermons, and scientific and legal explanations.

Poetry was the major medium of the Judeo-Persian texts, but their subject matter does not vary much. The lack of development of Judeo-Persian poetry may be because Jewish poets were not connected to any amir or court and did not benefit from their patronage. Except for Shahin's poem praising Sultan Abu Said (1316–35), no panegyric poems are known to exist. Many works of major Iranian poets also have been transliterated into the Hebrew alphabet. Among them are the poetry of Nizami (who died ca. 1209), Ferdowsi (who died ca. 1020), Hafiz (d. 1389), Saᶜdi (d. 1292), Jalal al-Din Rumi (d. 1273), Omar Khayyam (d. 1131), and many others.

Very few significant Judeo-Persian literary works were produced in Iran between the seventeenth and the nineteenth centuries when the Jews went through a major social decline. The works of Binyamin b. Mishal, known as Amina (who lived from the late seventeenth to the early eighteenth centuries), Elisha b. Shamu'il, known as Raghib, and Yusuf b. Ishaq b. Musa are exceptions. The only Judeo-Persian works of significance produced in the nineteenth century are those of Simantob Melamed (Tubia), a poet and mystic. He was born in Yazd but later moved to Herat and then to Mashhad, where he died in 1828. Melamed's most important work is *Hayat al-Ruh* (The Life of the Soul), a didactic work of philosophy and religion of eight thousand verses and prose, based on *Hovot ha-Levavot* (The Duties of the Hearts) by Bahia ben Pekuda, the twelfth-century Judeo-Spanish scholar. *Hayat al-Ruh* shows evidence of influence of Persianized Islamic and Jewish mysticism (kabbalah), as well as neo-Platonic philosophy. Melamed wrote many *qazals* (lyrical poems), most of them mystical, and scattered verses in both Persian and Hebrew. The many surviving manuscripts demonstrate the popularity of his work.

In addition to Melamed's writings, a number of texts written by Bukharan Jews between the seventeenth and nineteenth centuries survive. They were published in Palestine by Shamᶜun Hakham, a Bukharan Jew, in the early part of the twentieth century.

The Twentieth Century

The opening of the Alliance Israélite Universelle schools in 1898, although a blessing in the lives of many Iranian Jews, brought with it a cultural challenge. As Jews gradually achieved higher status, a better command of Persian became a necessity. Thus their ancestral or home dialects and accents became liabilities and were forsaken for the educated, standard Persian. As Jews joined the mainstream of society, it gradually became difficult to distinguish between what was Judeo-Persian and what was not.

A revival of Jewish literary and intellectual activity did not occur in Iran until the early part of the twentieth century. At this time a very significant change occurred: Persian script replaced Hebrew in Jewish texts, thus reflecting the transition that the Iranian Jewish community was going through. Students at Alliance schools were taught Persian script, and they were employed by government offices; gradually, they became part of the mainstream Iranian community. By the beginning of World War I there already was a large circle of intellectual Jews, and the focus of power began to shift from the rabbis to the young secularized intelligentsia.

The literary activities of Iranian Jews in the twentieth century should be divided into before and after the Islamic Revolution.

The Pahlavi Era

The first known Jewish newspaper published in Iran was *Shalom,* which initially appeared on March 21, 1915, on the Iranian New Year (*Nowruz,* in Judeo-Persian). The publishers were two brothers, Mordechai and Asher ben Abram (d. 1964 and 1963, respectively), who worked at a Jewish printing shop in Tehran. The paper printed news about the Iranian Jewish community, as well as coverage of Jews around the world. *Shalom* was followed by *Ha-Geulah* and *He-Hayim,* also both in Judeo-Persian. Other papers that followed, *Israel, Alam-e Yahud, Sina,* and *Nisan,* were in both Hebrew and Persian scripts and, as time went by, the Persian sections increased in size. In subsequent years most Jewish publications proved unsuccessful, because Jews were reading the regular daily papers. The exception was a magazine called *Kavian,* first published in the fall of 1949 by Rabi[c] Moshfeq-Hamadani, a well-known journalist. *Kavian,* which was published for five years, followed the format of *Life* and *Paris Match* and was directed at the general population.

During most of the twentieth century, Jewish publications were aimed at an Iranian Jewish readership, with topics that were of interest almost exclusively to this community. They strictly avoided criticism of Muslims and, following government policy, did not contain editorials about political issues. Iranian Jews have found it difficult to freely express themselves on issues related to their community, as they always fear that such material may fall into wrong hands. Consequently, they have been self-censoring.

As the Iranian Jewish community gained some freedom in the twentieth century and as its members' level of education increased, interest in their heritage led to the production of several histories. The most famous is a monumental three-volume work, *Tarikh-i Yahud-i Iran* (History of the Jews of Iran) written by Habib Levy and published in 1956.

In 1933 Soleiman Haïm, a graduate of the American (Presbyterian) College in Tehran, published major Persian-English dictionaries that have yet to be surpassed. Haïm also wrote a number of plays, among them *Yusof va Zuleikha* (Joseph and Zuleikha), which have never been published.

The Islamic Republic

After the Islamic Revolution of 1979, and mostly outside Iran, we see a flourishing of Iranian Jewish writing that critically examines various issues of importance to the community. The United States has become the center of

Iranian Jewish literary activity because of the freedom and opportunities available. The Jews still in Iran, and those who now live in the United States, in particular, have produced a body of literature that deserves recognition, as it is a continuation of the same literary tradition.

After the revolution, a newspaper, *Tamuz,* edited by Parviz Yeshaya'i, was published in Tehran from 1978 to 1988. The paper contained translated and original articles of high standard. Anjoman-e Kalimian-e Tehran (the Tehran Jewish Society) continues to regularly publish a four-page newsletter. A new monthly magazine, *Bina,* started publication in March 1999, with diverse articles and even Hebrew lessons. The journalistic activity of Jews in Iran today is mainly limited to translations in periodicals. A kind of Jewish self-censoring still seems to be in existence.

In the United States, where there is a large Iranian Jewish community, a number of periodicals published in Persian are aimed at the Jewish community. Most of them make an effort to maintain a high literary level. Most of these periodicals are bilingual, with an English section, in an effort to reach out to the younger generation born here.

The younger generation's interest in its background and history has generated numerous books and articles on modern Iranian Jewish history, and two journals of Judeo-Persian studies are published mainly in Persian in the United States and dedicated to Iranian Jewish history and culture. Books and articles on various scholarly topics have been produce by Jewish authors in Iran, among them, Shirindokht Daghigian, a prolific scholar of philosophy.

Works of fiction, written by Iranian Jews inside and outside Iran, are not numerous. Fiction writing among the Jews in the Pahlavi period was almost nonexistent. Today, one writer in Iran, Elham Yaghoubian, publishes novels of popular literature. In the United States, Nurollah Kharrazi is one of the most prolific of Iranian Jewish writers of novels and short stories. His style is simple, with much colloquialism and English and many Judeo-Persian expressions.

Poetry, once the major medium of Judeo-Persian literature, became secondary to prose in the twentieth century. Among contemporary Iranian Jewish poets who write in the classical Persian tradition is Abdollah Tale^{c}. His poems, spanning more than five decades, also have been set to music. Tale also writes poems in his native Hamadani dialect. Mahin Amid is one of the foremost female Iranian Jewish poets, and she has been publishing for decades. Among the published poets active in Iran after the Islamic Revolution are Manuchehr Kohan and Mozhdeh Rufeh. Persian poetry writing also continues among the younger generation, educated mostly in the United States. Roya Hakkakian, a promising young poet who writes modern Persian poetry, is an example of the strength of the tradition and continuation of Judeo-Persian poetry. Her father, Haqnazar Hakkakian, is also a poet, who writes in both Persian and his Khwansari dialect.

Today, Jewish dialects, like many other dialects of Iran, are dying out, not because of political or religious pressure from outside but because of an inner desire to become part of a larger Persian entity. Meanwhile, Judeo-Persian literature, which was always a branch of Persian literature, has remained unknown in its homeland, while it flourishes in exile.

RECOMMENDED READING

Assmussen, Jes P. *Studies in Judeo-Persian Literature.* Studia Post-Biblica Series, ed. J. C. H. Lebram. Leiden: E. J. Brill, 1973.

Bar-Asher, Mosheh. *Traditions linguistiques des juifs d'Afrique du Nord.* Jerusalem: Mossad Bialik, 1998 (in Hebrew).

Bunis, David M. *A Lexicon of the Hebrew and Aramaic Elements in Modern Judezmo.* Jerusalem: Magnes Press, 1993.

——. "The Language of the Sephardim: A Historical Overview." In Haim Beinart, ed., *The Sephardi Legacy*. Jerusalem: Magnes Press, 1992, vol. 2, pp. 399–422.

——. *Voices from Jewish Saloniki.* Jerusalem: Misgav Yerushalayim Press, 1999.

Fischel, Walter J. "Israel in Iran (A Survey of Judeo-Persian Literature)." In Louis Finkelstein, ed., *The Jews: Their History, Culture, and Religion,* New York: Jewish Theological Seminary 1949, pp. 817–58.

Harris, Tracy K. *Death of a Language: The History of Judeo-Spanish.* Newark: University of Delaware, 1994.

Lazard, Gilbert. "Judaeo-Persian." In *Encylopaedia of Islam,* new ed. Leiden, The Netherlands: E. J. Brill, 1978, vol. 4, pp. 308–13.

Luria, Max A. *A Study of the Monastir Dialect of Judeo-Spanish Based on Oral Material Collected in Monastir, Yugoslavia.* New York: Instituto de las Españas, 1930.

Mansour, Jacob. *The Jewish Baghdadi Dialect.* Or-Yehuda, Israel: Merkaz Moreshet Babel, 1991.

Netzer, Amnon. "Persian Jewry and Literature: A Sociological View." In Harvey E. Goldberg, ed., *Sephardi and Middle Eastern Jewries: History and Culture in the Modern Era.* Bloomington: Indiana University Press/New York: Jewish Theological Seminary of America, 1996, pp. 240–55.

Sahim, Haideh. "The Dialect of the Jews of Hamadan." In Shaul Shaked and Amnon Netzer, eds., *Irano Judaica,* vol. 3: *Studies Relating to Jewish Contacts with Persian Culture Throughout the Ages.* Jerusalem: Ben Zvi Institute, 1994, pp. 171–81.

Stillman, Norman. *The Language and Culture of the Jews of Sefrou, Morocco: An Ethnolinguistic Study.* Manchester, U.K.: University of Manchester, 1988.

Yarshater, Ehsan. "The Jewish Communities of Persia and Their Dialects." In Philippe Gignoux and Ahmad Tafazzoli, eds., *Mémorial Jean de Menasce.* Fondation Culturelle Iranienne 185. Louvain, Belgium: Imprimerie Orientaliste, 1974, pp. 435–66.

——. "The Hybrid Language of the Jewish Communities of Persia." *Journal of the American Oriental Society* 97, no. 1 (January–March 1977): 1–8.

CHAPTER

8

Education

Rachel Simon

Education is the process of preparing a person to achieve certain goals, be they short term or long term, technical, physical, mental, or spiritual. Worldview, cultural and social order, economic conditions, and tradition strongly shape educational aims, contents, and methods. In the case of a minority—and its characteristics and relations with the majority—the tensions between isolation, assimilation, and different role models all have a role in shaping education.

For most of the last six hundred years, the roles of individuals in the Jewish communities of the Middle East and North Africa were gender based, as they were in the surrounding Muslim society. Men were in charge of spiritual and temporal communal affairs and provided for the family through work conducted mostly outside the home. Women were responsible for managing the home from the inside: maintaining the household; caring for the young, feeble, and old; and preparing food for all. Women also had an important role in forming the values of household members through proverbs, parables, and stories. The different roles played by men and by women required different educations. As a result traditional Jewish educations, especially until the midnineteenth century, were gender based, differing in place, content, methods, and teachers. Social, economic, and political changes in the region, as well as European involvement, influenced daily life, including the education of both the majority population and the Jews. Changes did not come simultaneously to the whole region or even to a whole community. Differing amounts of contact with the authorities and with the West, as well as socioeconomic status, age, and gender, all were factors that influenced the timing and scope of changes in education as part of overall lifestyle.

TRADITIONAL JEWISH EDUCATION

Jewish men had to be able to read the Hebrew alphabet to participate in the religious services of their synagogue, and they had to learn a profession to provide for their families. These requirements dictated the content and structure of their education, which was divided into academic and vocational parts. In the first phase, which usually lasted about three to four years, boys aged five and six learned the Hebrew alphabet and read some parts of the Holy Scriptures. They were later trained in a profession, usually by a family member.

Private tutors or schools provided the formal primary academic education for boys. The teachers were graduates of advanced Jewish religious schools who did not reach senior religious positions; they were usually not greatly respected. Private tutors often taught several family members; at times even the girls joined the boys. Yet most boys attended schools run by individual teachers or sponsored by the community. Accommodations in most schools were rarely satisfactory: rooms tended to be crowded, dark, and damp, and the children, who sat on the floor surrounding their teacher, lacked sufficient reading materials.

A school run by an individual was generally in the teacher's home, where usually only he taught, sometimes assisted by an advanced student. Parents had to pay these teachers weekly, toward the week's end, and often had to supply some food. Students started by learning the Hebrew alphabet, the vowels, then single words and whole sentences. They then read the Bible, usually limiting themselves to the Torah (the Five Books of Moses).

Schools established by the community were bigger than privately owned schools, were set in a public building (at first mostly in a synagogue but later also in separate buildings), and they employed several salaried teachers who taught according to a set curriculum that was wider than those of tutors or privately owned schools. Tuition was based on the ability of the parents to pay, and the communal council paid the teachers. Many communities, especially the larger ones, had two stages of community schools: the lower one was similar to the privately owned schools, while the upper one taught the Bible as a whole, as well as the Talmud and Jewish law.

Hebrew was the liturgical and scholarly language of the communities, whereas the spoken language was usually a Jewish dialect of the regional vernacular. For advanced Bible classes some schools added a classical Judeo-Arabic translation, which often was not very well understood because it differed from the local Jewish dialect. Thus most men could decipher the

Hebrew alphabet but did not really understand the Torah or prayers that they recited, nor could they write easily. Only scholars had a command of liturgical Hebrew.

The situation in Yemen was representative of traditional Jewish education throughout the region. Little boys learned some prayers and at times also the alphabet from their fathers, whom they accompanied to the synagogue. Once in school their main textbook was the Torah, and after learning the alphabet and combinations of letters and vowels, students read the whole text, regardless of content and difficulty. Books were rare, and children sat around the teacher and looked at the book, acquiring the ability to read from any angle. The emphasis was on teaching boys to pray and to read the Torah in public in the synagogue; it was not customary to have a special functionary for that purpose. Parents faced strong public pressure to bring their sons to that stage of learning, and most boys could read well. Because most Yemenite Jews were craftsmen, not traders, they did not regard the ability to write as necessary. The school day lasted from dawn until sunset for the youngest children, while the older ones stayed longer to prepare themselves for reading in public and to participate in some advanced studies, such as of the writings of Moses Maimonides (1135–1204). Because most schools had only one teacher and some student assistants, they had no overall teaching program. Children learned by rote, reciting in a loud voice and often not understanding what they read. They commonly were beaten for making mistakes and misbehaving.

The Jewish schools in Yemen were privately owned, and parents paid the teacher daily or weekly. Each boy brought the teacher a loaf of bread every day, and the teacher sold what his family did not need. In addition, teachers collected tuition from the parents each Friday. In many places it was customary for the teacher to eat lunch with the students' parents on a rotating basis. Because the fees paid by parents were low, some teachers also received monies from the communal welfare fund. Many had a second job, such as knitting or weaving, that they could carry on during school time. Because teaching was limited to study by rote, teachers did not need much education themselves. Although a teacher was addressed as *mari,* Aramaic for "master," teachers were not of high status. Teachers were often men who could not find other work, slightly older boys who started as teaching assistants, or older men who could no longer do other work. Boys, especially orphans, often taught in the numerous small rural Jewish communities of the hinterland.

Because girls were destined to run a household, their education was mainly conducted at home by older female relatives. This was an experience-based education in which girls were taught how to run a Jewish home properly; Jewish law regulated all the tasks. Thus their religious instruction included the Jewish laws that regulated everyday life, as well as various prayers, including those special for women, such as lighting Sabbath lights. Because women were not obliged to participate actively in synagogue services, the family and the community did not find it necessary to teach them to read. Consequently, most girls remained illiterate. Only a few received a formal academic education, usually as a by-product of their brothers' education, especially when tutored at home. Some traditional Jewish schools, mostly privately run, accepted girls, but girls attended for a shorter period than boys. Women's spiritual life was not poor, but it was very different from that of the men. Reciting poetry, singing, story telling, dancing, and handicrafts enabled women to enjoy the arts and develop their creativity and spirituality.

THE STATE AS AN AGENT OF CHANGE

Until the nineteenth century education in the Middle East and North Africa was segregated not only by gender but also by religion, so Jews rarely attended gentile educational institutions. Because the Muslim state as such did not provide social services, including education, each community took care of the needs of its members. This state policy changed in the nineteenth century because regional powers wanted to reform the way the state was run and started to import ideas, programs, and technology from Europe. The Ottoman Empire and Egypt were the first to invite European experts to help modernize their military, agriculture, and industry, and they sent some students abroad for a European education. This change in attitude gradually transformed the region's education, creating new systems, methods, syllabi, and opportunities. Modern professional schools were established at state expense in regional centers, at first for state functionaries but later for wider segments of the population. Although these schools were primarily for Muslim men, they later admitted non-Muslims, and then separate schools for women were established. These developments created a new educational environment, with significant implications for the education of Jews within and outside the community.

While few Jews took advantage of these state institutions in the nineteenth century, an increasing number did so during the twentieth century. This resulted from the Jews' cultural background and state policy. Most Ottoman Jews did not speak Turkish during the nineteenth century, and until the establishment of Mustafa Kemal Atatürk's secular Turkish republic in the 1920s, attempts to spread the Turkish language among the Jews had been unsuccessful. As a result few Jews could attend state schools even when they accepted non-Muslims. Jews, however, did attend those state schools where the language of instruction was not Turkish (e.g., the Galatasaray secondary school in Istanbul and the schools of medicine and law). Consequently, only a few hundred urban Jews received secondary and higher education in Turkish institutions during the Ottoman period. The Young Turk Revolution of 1908 affected the education of Jews throughout the empire, because the state wanted to Turkify the population; creating a welcoming environment for the minorities in state schools was a major tool toward this end. Ottoman attempts to incorporate Jews in state schools took advantage of communal developments, as in Sanᶜa, Yemen, where the Ottomans collaborated with the leader of a group known as *dardaᶜim (dor deᶜah*—generation of knowledge) that was against mysticism and in favor of introducing secular subjects, including foreign languages. State law notwithstanding, Jews could not attend state schools where the population at large rejected them—as was the case in Iran, where the 1906 revolution gave Jews equal rights, but the Muslim Shiite population regarded Jews as impure and refused to come in physical contact with them, even to sit next to them in school. This situation changed after the accession of Reza Shah Pahlavi to the throne in 1925. Thereafter Jews were permitted to study with Muslims in state schools.

The rise of nationalism and the establishment of independent states from the old Ottoman Empire affected the education of the Jews. A growing number of Jews attended state schools, and the curricula of Jewish schools gradually incorporated an increasing number of courses resembling those in state schools and were often taught by non-Jews (e.g., the local language and literature, history, and geography). This happened both because of state intervention in the running of private and religious schools and the wish of parents to prepare their children for careers through continued education in state educational institutions.

EUROPEAN AND AMERICAN SCHOOLS

In the nineteenth century, European and American schools had a growing influence on Jewish education in the Middle East and North Africa. Religious organizations (usually Christian missionaries) established many foreign schools, and private organizations founded schools as well; the goal of some of the latter was to advance the interests of their governments through cultural penetration of the Middle East and North Africa. Although most of these foreign schools were not run directly by foreign governments, the organizations that operated them were often supported by their governments. Christian missionary schools were allowed to exist in some cities for a long time, but their variety and numbers greatly increased in the nineteenth century. Whereas in the past missionary schools were mainly Roman Catholic, run by French and Italians, the nineteenth century witnessed an increase in the number of American and European—mainly British and German—Protestant groups (mainly Presbyterian and Episcopalian) that operated in the major provincial centers of the Middle East and North Africa. Because the Muslim governments had opposed Christian missionaries' proselytizing of Muslims, Western missionaries focused their efforts upon non-Muslim minorities, such as Eastern Christians and Jews. The Jewish leadership opposed the missionaries in principle, but some parents still took advantage of their educational offerings.

The number of foreign Christian schools grew from the midnineteenth century onward. At first they were intended for the small European urban mercantile communities. Missionary schools did not force students to convert, but some did target Jews by obliging them to take Christian religious studies and participate in ceremonies. To attract students many schools offered economic benefits: free tuition, textbooks, food, and clothing, and they provided vocational education. Training in modern professions was an important incentive because of the economic deterioration of many Jewish communities, so parents even agreed to send their daughters to female vocational workshops or schools that combined vocational and academic education. The missionary schools also taught secular subjects, mainly languages, literature, history, arithmetic, and sciences, often complemented by some Jewish components, such as Hebrew and the Bible. European languages were of special interest to merchant families that traded with Europe, as was the cultural background that the schools provided. The missionary schools also enabled students to continue with secondary and higher education, both within the region and abroad, often with financial aid. As a result Jews studied there even when doing so required that they desecrate the Sabbath, participate in Christian prayers, or pay tuition.

As a result of these attractions, the missionary schools competed not only with traditional education but even with modern Jewish schools once these were established (in part, to thwart non-Jewish education). Missionary schools did suffer some setbacks because of political developments. For example, after the gradual closing of religious schools in the Republic of

Turkey in the mid-1920s, fewer Jews could attend religious schools, their own or Christian, and had to attend state schools.

WESTERN JEWISH EDUCATIONAL ENTERPRISES

As early as the 1840s, philanthropists and scholars began Western Jewish educational enterprises in the Middle East and North Africa. In the 1860s these attempts were overshadowed by organizational activities in most of the region. The Westerners wanted to provide modern education within a Jewish environment, and they targeted those Jews who wanted their children to have a modern education but not be exposed either to Muslim state functionaries or Christian conversion attempts. Because these Westerners were Jews, their attempts to establish secular schools for Jews represented a potentially greater danger to local traditional Jewish education than the missionaries did: no one could accuse them of proselytizing students, although the education that they provided prepared the children with belief systems, lifestyles, behavior, and occupations that were different from those customary in the community and the society at large at the time.

The major turn in Jewish education in the Middle East and North Africa resulted from the 1860 establishment in Paris of the Alliance Israélite Universelle (AIU). Its goals were to protect persecuted Jews and to advance what it regarded as backward communities, taking French Jewry as its model. The main tool of the AIU was lobbying governments to improve the condition of the Jews and the provision of education for boys and girls (in separate schools). The educational aims of the AIU were to advance "primitive" Jews; to make them productive citizens in their own states; and to enhance and modernize their Jewishness. As a result the AIU educational program had three components: general secular studies, vocational training, and Jewish studies. The main emphasis was on general studies, which were taught in French and followed lycée standards for course time and quality of teaching. Some schools paid attention to local conditions and also taught the local language or European languages common in the area (e.g., English in Iraq).

After the establishment of its first school in Tetuán, Morocco, in 1862, the AIU network spread swiftly. Morocco became one of the AIU's major spheres of activity. Moroccan teachers counted for 10 percent of the network's teachers, with communal schools countrywide. The first AIU teachers were European Jews and were later drawn from the network's graduates, mainly from the Ottoman Empire and the Maghreb. They were trained in special AIU-run institutions in Paris, where the main AIU school was the Ecole

Table 8.1 AIU Educational Network, 1862–1999

YEAR	Number of Schools	Number of Students
1862	1	300
1865	3	680
1871	14	2,365
1880	43	5,190
1891	55	12,400
1901	109	29,000
1909	149	41,000
1913	183	43,700
1922	112	35,426
1931	126	43,708
1939	127	47,746
1946	116	40,955
1949	133	49,357
1956	143	50,977
1959	135	47,736
1969	68	21,310
1979	39	13,413
1989	48	21,228
1999	73	29,201

Source: Alliance Israélite Universelle.

Normale Israélite Orientale (ENIO). From 1869 to 1925 ENIO graduated 403 students (247 men and 156 women), about 40 percent of whom came from Turkey and about 10 percent each from Palestine, Bulgaria, and Morocco. These French-trained teachers were qualified to teach modern secular subjects but not Jewish subjects. This compelled the AIU to hire local teachers for the Jewish subjects. As a result the Jewish component of the AIU education was usually at the same level as the traditional education that the AIU had criticized or even lower, because less time was allocated to it and because of the higher regard for the secular component, which had better teachers and teaching materials. The communities and the AIU were often at odds over the deterioration of Hebrew and Jewish studies in the AIU curriculum.

Table 8.2 AIU Schools (Founded 1862–1935)

Area	Number of Schools	Date of Earliest School
Algeria	3	1900
Balkans (Bulgaria, Greece, Macedonia)	37	1865
Egypt	8	1896
Eretz Israel/Palestine	12	1868
Iran	16	1898
Iraq	15	1864
Lebanon	3	1869
Libya	2	1895
Morocco	46	1862
Syria	7	1864
Tunisia	8	1878
Turkey	40	1867

Source: Adapted from Aron Rodrigue, *Images of Sephardi and Eastern Jewries in Transition* (Seattle: University of Washington Press, 1993), table 2, pp. 15–21.

The AIU established schools when requested to do so by local residents. In the first stage indigenous Jews formed an AIU committee, which then tried to convince a substantial number of parents to support an AIU school financially and to send their children to it. The AIU agreed to establish schools only after such local support was guaranteed. Nonetheless, it often had difficulty collecting tuition because many Jews were poor and expected free education. Although the AIU was invited to establish schools in the region, important segments of the community, including major traditional leaders, opposed it for several reasons: the competition it posed to traditional education, the lower quality of its Jewish education, and the goals for which it aimed. Because the AIU took French Jewry as its model for shaping Jewish communities in the Middle East and North Africa while sustaining their loyalty to regional regimes, the organization soon faced growing competition from the Zionist movement—whose politics and cultural endeavors the AIU actively opposed.

The AIU schools used a comprehensive program to which local directors had to adhere. The AIU center in Paris had to approve any deviation, and directors and teachers were required to report to the Paris center regularly. The basic curriculum encompassed four years, but some towns added an additional grade. The AIU opposed what it regarded as too much education for its students; it tried not to tear them away from their community or attract them to higher education in Europe, which might result in their emigration. The only exceptions were those students trained in the AIU's Paris-based institutions who became teachers in its network or improved their vocational skills. The lack of AIU secondary schools became an impediment to its success in many places.

World War II was a watershed period for the AIU. The branches were cut off from the center, which in turn had to find refuge in the nonoccupied zone. After November 1942 the isolation was complete. After the war the AIU put more emphasis on the Hebrew language and developed a positive attitude toward Zionism. The destruction of most of European Jewry and the consequent growth of Zionism worldwide, including among Jews in the Middle East and North Africa, resulted in the AIU's new position.

The AIU's success was not universal; its network was limited in both Algeria and Egypt because of local preferences for state and other modern schools. It could never operate in Yemen. Its operations in Lebanon and in Syria suffered several setbacks from the competition of missionary schools and from rabbinical opposition. Growing nationalism and the establishment of independent states also curtailed the AIU's activities because it was a private foreign institution. In Turkey in 1928 the AIU closed or transferred ownership and management of its schools to local communities because the Jews had renounced their minority status in Atatürk's newly established secular republic. In Iraq a 1923 law prohibited the operation of foreign elementary schools. In 1961 Moroccan law nationalized a third of the AIU's network, and the state tried to integrate AIU teachers who were Moroccan nationals into its Ministry of Education. Even in those countries in which the AIU continued to operate, its programs had to change; courses were taught in the local language, and the state education ministries supervised the AIU schools.

Other European Jewish organizations became active in the region, but they were less extensive than the AIU. The Anglo-Jewish Association, established in London in 1870, often cooperated with the AIU in those countries where the teaching of English was important. The Hilfsverein der deutschen Juden, known as Ezra, was established in Berlin in 1901. It was active mainly in Turkey and Palestine, where it established kindergartens, schools, and the Technion, which became an important teaching and research facility. Ezra was active in teacher training but had to stop operating after World War I.

Its insistence on using German instead of Hebrew in its institutions brought about the 1912 "language war" between the Zionist advocates of the revival of Hebrew and the Ezra organization in Palestine.

The AIU can be credited with the first major comprehensive effort to modernize Jewish education in the region. With qualified teachers and an elaborate curriculum, it introduced secular studies in a Jewish environment and used modern equipment in appropriate teaching facilities. Still, the Jewish component of its curriculum was often of poor quality, and some parts of its secular program alienated children from their environment. Consequently, in many places AIU education served as a trigger for improving local traditional Jewish education and developing modern Jewish schools. Although the AIU's work was curtailed in several countries as the twentieth century progressed, its earlier work had already brought significant changes in regional Jewish education.

EDUCATION UNDER COLONIALISM

In the nineteenth century Europe had increased its involvement in the Middle East and North Africa, starting with cultural and economic programs. Soon European powers were involved politically and militarily as well, and some European powers dominated various countries, where they implemented European educational practices. The official attitude toward the Jews was shaped by European state policies toward the various segments of the indigenous population, as well as the status of the Jews in the European state in power.

Algeria was the first to come under direct European rule, occupied by France in 1830. Algerian Jews were incorporated in the state educational system in 1845, based on legislation that encouraged Jewish religious instruction as long as Jews regularly attended state schools. From then on, a growing number of Algerian Jews attended state schools, while their traditional education decreased. They soon had a strong tendency to assimilate. The other countries under colonial rule granted the Jews the right to attend state schools, some of which were especially organized to accommodate Jewish students, and many took advantage of this. Only in Morocco did the French try (from 1916 to 1924) to establish schools exclusively for Jews (Ecoles Franco-Israélites); there the French also tried to develop specially tailored school systems for Morocco's various other ethnic groups. Because many Jews preferred the semisecular AIU schools to the almost purely secular French Jewish schools, the protectorate government agreed to cede control to the AIU of most French Jewish schools, but the AIU had to be under its pedagogical supervision. The result of the new schooling in the region meant that a large number of urban Jews in countries under European rule were imbued with colonialist ideology and became comfortable using European languages.

VOCATIONAL EDUCATION

Vocational schools did not exist in the region until the midnineteenth century. Professional training was conducted within the family or in apprenticeship, and most boys continued in the family business. Western organizations aware of the economic hardships in the Middle East and North Africa tried to provide vocational training that attracted students to their educational networks, some of which were sponsored by Christian missionaries. Although many students felt the need to acquire qualifications for modern professions, Jewish students did not at first appreciate the necessity of the long, formal, institutional training. Nonetheless, many students received vocational training and through it were exposed to Western ideas.

Vocational training was an important element in AIU education—mainly for girls and especially in the early stages of its operation. The AIU tried to attract students by offering vocational training in its workshops or through apprenticeships that it arranged with local craftsmen and supplemented with evening courses. In most cases the craftsmen were unsuited to the teaching aspects of the job, and the population did not respect this initiative. The AIU also met with little success when it tried to send students to Europe to learn professions that were hitherto unknown in the region. The AIU was more successful in its agricultural school in Palestine, Mikveh Israel (established in 1870), which trained students from the entire network. Various attempts to establish formal vocational education in Iraq were short lived; the one exception was a school for the blind in Baghdad (from 1927), where the main subject was music. After Moroccan Jews demanded that the AIU train their youth in modern profitable professions in the 1920s, the organization increased its vocational training to include crafts and agriculture; by 1947 it had fifteen institutions for boys and eleven for girls.

After World War II, ORT (Organization for Rehabilitation through Training, originally established in Russia in 1880 to promote manual and agricultural work among the Jews) became important in Morocco, Palestine, and Iran. Its girls' vocational training was primarily in sewing and related fields, thus confining the girls' professional development within a traditional framework.

During the British administration of Palestine, vocational training became an important component of Zionist education, for both ideological and practical reasons. The schools of rural communities devoted some time to agriculture, which enabled the youth to assist in the daily work. Zionists considered farming and manual labor important, to be promoted as a significant element in the regeneration of Jewish life as it broke with Diaspora life. By the 1940s, with the establishment of the State of Israel imminent, the Halutz (Pioneer) movement, which had been established in 1904 in Europe, spread, and it emphasized the pioneering aspect of Zionism. The movement encouraged vocational training for two reasons: to promote an appreciation of physical, manual, and productive work in order to change the socioeconomic structure of Jewish life, and to achieve physical fitness. Of special ideological importance was agriculture, which combined manual work and self-sufficiency. The Halutz combined agricultural training with preparations for communal life, including self-defense, carpentry, electricity, shoemaking, and printing. The main vehicle of the Halutz for carrying out these goals was the *havat hakhsharah* (training camp), several of which were established in the Middle East and North Africa. Despite the Halutz attempt to give men and women equal roles, it too trained local women mainly in sewing. Nonetheless, lectures, discussions, and courses in Modern Hebrew were important to all Jews in most areas but especially to women, who were less exposed to formal education. Many Halutzim became teachers in Jewish schools, which they wanted to turn into Zionist schools.

ATTEMPTS AT MODERNIZING LOCAL EDUCATION

As a result of both state and foreign educational activities in the Middle East and North Africa, some of which primarily targeted Jews, Jewish students encountered a greater variety of educational systems that led toward different goals. These systems varied in content, teaching methods, language of instruction, and facilities, and for the first time girls had the option of formal academic and vocational education outside the home. These developments encouraged a growing number of Jewish parents to send their children to nontraditional, noncommunity schools. As a result the nontraditional goals that these students tried to attain were threatening to community teachers and functionaries. The modern educational systems had almost no use for veteran traditional educators, and once the attitude and character of the Jewish community changed, it required a different kind of leadership.

The traditional Jewish leadership took some time to acknowledge these developments and to reorganize its educational program to counter this competition. The first step was to warn parents not to send children to noncommunity schools, sometimes even threatening them with excommunication. Leaders also warned local teachers not to accept jobs in "external" educational systems. When the community leaders realized that these measures were not working and increasing numbers were sending their children to modern schools, they established local committees in many places to reform Jewish education. This was a particularly difficult assignment, because the leadership opposed secular nontraditional subjects, did not have appropriate teacher-training institutions, and lacked funding to establish and equip facilities to compete with those of most foreign and state educational institutions.

By 1900 most major cities in the Middle East and North Africa had reformed Jewish educational institutions, and they were run by trained traditional personnel who were teaching mainly Hebrew and Jewish studies and using facilities designed for this purpose. Many community schools, however, especially those in the countryside, did not change, so their traditional offerings were focused on boys well into the twentieth century. The modernization of traditional education was only the beginning of the transformation process. Gradually, a growing number of local Jewish schools taught fewer traditional subjects and more secular ones, as a result of the wishes of both parents and students and because of outside competition and state laws. Still, the community tried to provide students with the basic concepts of Judaism and the Hebrew language, employing mainly teachers who had been trained in Jewish schools.

Even in Yemen, where most Jews attended traditional schools (and Western schools did not exist), there were attempts to modernize Jewish education. The reestablishment of Ottoman rule in 1872 introduced some modern concepts of education, while contacts with the outside world increased. As a result Jewish scholars and emissaries visited Yemen and exposed some Yemenite Jews to new ideas. Furthermore, the large group of Jews that emigrated to Palestine in 1882 informed their relatives in Yemen about life there, including innovations in education. All this had some effect on educational developments among Yemenite Jews, although their education remained basically traditional until their mass emigration to Israel in the 1950s after the establishment of the Jewish state.

Conditions in Aden, which had been under British administration since 1839, were different from those in Yemen. In the nineteenth century Jews there attended state schools, and both boys and girls went to Christian missionary schools. During the twentieth century local Jews founded, and the state supported, modern Jewish schools for boys and girls in Aden. These schools were burned during the anti-Jewish riots of late 1947 and were then temporarily closed. With emigration to Israel the number of students decreased; by 1954 the Jewish school was coeducational. It was closed in 1967, when the rest of the community left for Israel and other destinations.

In Iraq the first modern community school was established in Baghdad in 1902. Following the Young Turk Revolution of 1908, a growing number of Jews became involved in political life, and this affected education: parents were pushing for a less Jewish and more secular curriculum. Modern Jewish schools used Iraqi state textbooks for most subjects, and Hebrew was taught first from the Bible and from 1906 also from special textbooks written in Baghdad or Palestine. In major cities outside Baghdad, Jews could study in community, private, AIU, or state elementary schools. For secondary education they had to attend state schools or go to Baghdad. Rural Jews, especially in Kurdistan, had to content themselves with small, privately run Jewish schools, which the great majority of girls did not attend.

In Lebanon an attempt to improve traditional Jewish education in Beirut took place as early as 1875 to 1904, when a local rabbi established a school where he taught several languages. The school attracted students from Damascus, Aleppo, Jaffa, Izmir, and Istanbul, because it was headed by a rabbi, provided Jewish studies, and had language instruction.

In Syria the Jewish community of Damascus had difficulty operating its few schools, which were twice turned over to the AIU, thus somewhat changing their curricula. By 1941 Damascus had no community-sponsored traditional religious education for Jews. Yet in Aleppo two community schools were active during the twentieth century. In 1939 Jewish leaders decided that these schools should follow the government's curriculum in addition to Jewish studies, which would enable students to continue in state secondary schools and acquire at least one foreign language.

In Ottoman Turkey the modernized Jewish community-based schools struggled against rabbinical opposition to the instruction of languages—they even excommunicated a school director in Istanbul. In addition, the poverty of many of Turkey's Jewish communities and their lack of experienced teachers, especially in modern studies, made it hard for them to compete with both the traditional Jewish system and the AIU. In 1902 in Turkey, Talmud Torah schools began to gradually merge with the AIU or to adopt a modern curriculum. As a result only two, in Istanbul and Izmir, even functioned on the eve of World War I, and none in 1949, after the founding of the State of Israel. Most privately operated Jewish schools in Turkey closed during World War I, and after the war their student numbers decreased. Many of Turkey's modern community schools had to close, and none remained in 1923 when the republic was established. The curricula of the communal schools, which were defined as Turkish schools, did not differ much from regular state schools: they did not teach Hebrew, and state-appointed teachers taught Jewish history as part of general history. Consequently, many Jews opted for regular state schools. In 1945 the prohibition against teaching Hebrew was lifted in Turkey, and in 1949 the special Turkish state supervision was lifted. By then most Turkish Jews did not know any Hebrew and had only a weak knowledge of Judaism.

Toward the middle of the twentieth century, foreign-based Jewish religious organizations started to operate throughout the Middle East and North Africa because of the weakness of local traditional bodies and the growing strength of secular education, which was supported by both foreign and state institutions. In 1944 the New York–based Otzar ha-Torah, an organization of Sephardic Jews for the religious education of Jews in the Middle East and North Africa, established schools in Iran to teach both modern and Jewish subjects, including Hebrew. In 1948 Otzar ha-Torah, with the financial support of the American Jewish Joint Distribution Committee, became active in Morocco. In the mid-1950s it operated directly or partially supported more than thirty religious institutions with nearly five thousand students in towns and villages and had almost seven thousand students in thirty-two institutions by 1960. Another organization that became active in the region in the 1950s was Ohole Yosef-Yitzhaq of the American Habad movement (a Hasidic sect known as the Lubavitchers that was founded in 1777 by Schneur Zalman of Lyady and advocated a combination of intellectuality and mysticism). The Lubavitchers entered Morocco in 1950 and established yeshivas and small schools countrywide. In Syria some revival of traditional education came with the opening of a school by Otzar ha-Torah in Damascus in the 1950s. With the establishment in 1948 of the State of Israel and the mass emigration there, the management of the schools in Aleppo was also transferred to Otzar ha-Torah in the 1950s.

ZIONISM

With the spread of political Zionism from the late nineteenth century on, a new element started to play an important role in Jewish education, at first mainly in Ottoman Palestine but gradually throughout the Middle East and

North Africa. The growing number of Zionists in Palestine had special educational needs: education had to be Jewish as well as Zionist, with Modern Hebrew and modern secular subjects. Moreover, ideology and local conditions required a vocational component, usually agricultural, based on the Zionist goal of self-sufficiency—a change in the traditional Jewish economic structure from one that was service oriented and mercantile to one that was productive. This meant an agricultural base, complemented by industry, engineering, and technology.

The Zionist movement regarded education as a major tool in its revolution, so much thought and planning went into it. Most Zionist teachers, especially in Ottoman Palestine, were European idealists, well educated, even intellectuals, and they tried to use modern pedagogical methods to implement new educational processes. They put a great emphasis on the usual secular subjects and on teaching Hebrew as a living language, using the Sephardic pronunciation (believing it was closer to the original usage and a break with Diaspora habits), although most Zionist settlers in Palestine had been Ashkenazim. Zionists taught Jewish history as it related to the Land of Israel and the Zionist movement and taught the Bible in relation to the Land of Israel as well, more as history and literature than as Holy Scripture. Geography also became localized, with the focus on the Land of Israel as it related to the Jews. Zionists promoted physical education with the notion of "a healthy soul in a healthy body." Consequently, the Zionist educational system in Palestine had to plan a new curriculum for all subjects and methods, because several of these subjects had never been taught before, and none had been taught in Hebrew.

At first the Zionists established only elementary schools in Palestine because of economic constraints and the view that farmers and laborers should content themselves with basic education. They soon established secondary schools in the major cities (Jerusalem, Tel Aviv, and Haifa) after they realized the need for well-educated citizens, both for nation building and for future state leadership. Despite ideology, parents and students often wanted or needed a more comprehensive education in local schools.

Zionist teachers of all levels—kindergarten, elementary, and secondary schools—had a strong commitment, and they regarded the building of a new nation as their mission. More women worked as teachers at the kindergarten and early elementary school levels, while men more often occupied the more prestigious positions of school directors and served as the specialized teachers of older students. The Zionist teachers in Palestine became unionized as early as 1903, and they had an extensive platform detailing their goals. Both genders were members of the teachers' association, but mostly men reached leadership positions in the organization and in the schools, despite the talk of gender equality.

Zionist influence started to affect Jewish education outside Palestine by the late nineteenth century. It was first manifested by individual teachers who taught Hebrew as a living language; these people often had a traditional educational background but taught themselves new methods and prepared special curricula. Many subscribed to the new Hebrew and Zionist periodicals that were published in Palestine and Europe. As time passed, they tried to stay in contact with teachers' groups and Zionist organizations abroad. During the early period these Hebrew teachers taught within the existing systems, or privately, and some Zionists even opened Hebrew schools (for example, in Damascus and Basra). During World War I a large number of non-Ottoman Jews, especially those of enemy nationalities (i.e., British, French, and Russian), had to leave Ottoman Palestine. Many were Zionists who then settled temporarily in Egypt, Syria, and Lebanon, but they did not want the education of their children to be disrupted. As a result exiled teachers established classes for these children and accepted local students. Many of these teachers became involved in local Jewish education, infusing it with new content and methods.

After World War I, with the breakup of the Ottoman Empire, Zionist activities in the region continued, as did the spread and study of Modern Hebrew and Hebrew literature, mainly on a voluntary ex-curricula basis. Hebrew courses, which became centers of Zionist activity, involved youth and adults of both genders; self-taught, slightly more advanced students taught these courses. By the 1930s, with the growth of the Hebrew educational system in British Mandatory Palestine, Hebrew courses in the region started to rely on the textbooks and programs developed in Palestine. Teachers from Palestine came to teach and direct these initiatives, training local staff to take over. Thus by the late 1930s most major towns in the Middle East and North Africa had a nucleus of Hebrew speakers, although they were not many. World War II interrupted these developments.

Rising Arab nationalism and the concomitant political pressures had already dealt setbacks to the revival of Hebrew. This was first felt in Iraq, where Zionism was outlawed after independence in 1932. There, the teaching of Hebrew was forbidden except as part of religious education. Similar situations developed in other Arab countries from the mid-1940s on. Nevertheless, during World War II Palestinian Jews in the British army in Egypt, Iraq, and Libya were instrumental in promoting the local study of Hebrew. These Zionist soldiers aided local Jewish communities by their devoted involvement in local education, at times even establishing a modern

Hebrew system. Zionist soldiers, surprised and excited to meet Hebrew speakers, regarded their participation in the war as both military and national—to help the region's Jewish communities, to make active Zionists out of them, and to convince them to emigrate to Palestine and settle in rural communal settlements, such as the kibbutzim. Consequently, the soldiers regarded their teaching and youth activities as an undertaking of the highest importance. Although many soldiers were not teachers, by 1943 they were deeply involved in developing new trends in local Jewish education in Libya, for example. The soldiers developed their own courses and obtained teaching materials from Palestine, while educators among them trained local youth to replace the soldiers who would leave the region with the Allied forces. The teachers and students of the former Ben-Yehuda voluntary society for Hebrew revival became the basis of the Modern Hebrew educational system in Tripoli and its surroundings. As a result most schoolage children in Tripoli attended that Hebrew school after the war; most of its male students also took courses in traditional schools.

LITERACY

During the twentieth century literacy increased among the Jews of the Middle East and North Africa, and in many urban communities it was high, especially among the youth, including women. Literacy lagged among the region's rural Jews and among women in Yemen, Iran, and Iraq. Jews were mostly literate in Hebrew or European languages and less literate in the local language, because most attended either Jewish or foreign schools, not state schools. The main exceptions were the Jews of Turkey, Iraq, and Egypt, where a large number attended the state schools. As a result Iraqi Jews were literate in Arabic, and some became prominent authors and journalists in Arabic. Because many Jews studied several languages simultaneously for a short period, they sometimes had only a low level of literary proficiency in any language. Still, for many, literacy in several languages and modern secular education brought about the transition from handicrafts and peddling to secretarial and financial jobs, as well as to the professions, with their improved economic conditions.

HIGHER EDUCATION

Jewish education in the region did not prepare students for higher education: Jewish secondary schools were rare, except in Palestine. Modern institutions of higher learning—colleges, universities, and professional schools—were slow to develop in the Middle East and North Africa, and Jews needed fluency in the local or European languages to attend them. Advanced education was first established in Turkey and Egypt in the nineteenth century, then in Iraq, with the opening of a law school in 1909. Many of Iraq's Jews who attended state schools received their higher education in Iraq or in Europe, especially in law, medicine, pharmacy, engineering, and economics; few were women. During the first half of the twentieth century, about a thousand Iraqi Jews were college graduates; the first women were graduated in 1941.

In Egypt the concentration of Jews in the two major cities, Cairo and Alexandria, their having studied in modern schools, enabled them to attend state and foreign institutions of higher education. In 1947 Egypt had 927 Jewish university graduates (126 were women). The number of Jewish university graduates from Lebanon and Syria was, however, small. In the 1960s more than 350 Iranian Jewish students enrolled annually in Iran, and a few dozen studied abroad in Europe and the United States.

Before the University of Algiers restricted the admission of Jewish students in the 1940s, they accounted for 13 percent of the student body. The highest number was in the medical school. Once admissions were restricted, many more Jewish students applied than were accepted.

In Palestine the increased Jewish population resulted in the need for higher education there, and new institutions were founded early in the twentieth century. The first, in 1906, was the Bezalel Academy of Arts and Crafts in Jerusalem, established by the sculptor Boris Schatz; the Technion, the Israel Institute of Technology, was established in Haifa in 1912 by the Jewish German organization Ezra; the Hebrew University of Jerusalem officially opened in 1925. Several teacher-training colleges were also established. All these institutions attracted not only local students and staff but students, scholars, and artists from abroad, and they were gradually able to incorporate locally trained faculty.

YESHIVAS

Only a few boys continued their studies in institutions of traditional Jewish higher education. Although Jewish seminaries functioned in Baghdad, Djerba, Gabès, Marrakesh, Meknès, Fez, Algiers, Tetuán, and Aleppo, poverty and the emphasis on modern secular studies led to a deterioration in local Jewish scholarship. As a result the publication of rabbinical literature decreased, whereas that of modern studies (written in Hebrew, local, and European languages) increased, as did the spread of daily newspapers and periodicals.

Most of the countries in the Middle East and North Africa suffered a deterioration in their Jewish educational offerings as a result of changes in educational trends in the community. State policies were also responsible for the deterioration, as was the case in Turkey, where the state strongly favored westernization and state-imposed Turkification, which resulted in a vast decrease in the number of Jews qualified to attend yeshivas. In 1945, following a relaxation in the antireligious policies of the Turkish government, a yeshiva reopened but soon closed because of low enrollment. In 1955 it reopened as a seven-year religious school, accepting elementary school graduates, and it prepared them for religious positions but not for the university.

A major exception to this regional trend was Palestine. Traditional Jewish education there continued to be strong, and yeshivas even increased in number after World War II, when survivors of destroyed European yeshivas reestablished them, mainly in Jerusalem and Bene Berak. In Morocco too, traditional education continued in many communities, and beginning in the 1940s numerous schools and yeshivas benefited from the support of the American organizations Otzar ha-Torah and Ohole Yosef-Yitzhaq.

TEACHERS

The overall level of teachers in regional Jewish schools was low. Most Middle Eastern and North African Jews turned to teaching only as a last resort and usually did not receive any special training. There were two main exceptions: the AIU teachers, who were better prepared in general studies from training at the Paris AIU institutions; and the teachers in modern schools in Palestine, who were trained either in Europe or in teacher-training colleges, which had been established in Palestine as early as 1904. In Iraq several attempts were made to improve the situation, and the academic level of the teachers rose, but pedagogical training was limited. In 1946 the AIU supported the establishment of a Hebrew teacher-training center in Casablanca, Morocco, the Ecole Normale Hébraïque (ENH). It was a four-year institution that led to the French *brévet* (high school diploma), and it offered a fifth year, in teacher training. The ENH then replaced traditional rabbi-teachers with qualified educators in ancient and Modern Hebrew language studies and studies in Jewish culture. The graduates of the ENH could acquire a special degree, called the Jerusalem Certificate (*ha-Te*ᶜ*udah ha-Yerushalmit*), which was administered by the Jewish Agency and recognized by Israeli universities. Thus Morocco, one of the few countries with a large Jewish community after the establishment of the State of Israel, had a continuous supply of qualified, well-trained teachers in Jewish studies.

TRANSFORMATION OF EDUCATIONAL GOALS IN CHANGED COMMUNITIES

Internal pressures and needs among the Jews changed their educational needs from mostly religion centered to mostly career oriented, especially in the large cities. If formal education once was primarily meant to prepare boys to participate in synagogue services and take part in community leadership, both parents and students gradually de-emphasized Jewish studies in order to prepare youth for careers, mainly in banking, trade, law, the civil service, and the natural sciences. Although a high proportion of Jews continued to study in Jewish institutions, the size and importance of the Jewish component of their education decreased. An increasing number of girls also received formal education—and in contrast to the boys', most of it was modern—but their social environment was slower to change. Consequently, women often had difficulty making use of their new qualifications and finding suitable employment.

In some countries government interference after World War I was a major factor in changing Jewish education. Thus the official policy in Algeria, Iraq, and Turkey was to provide unified education to the population at large, or at least to major segments of it, in order to limit the uniqueness of religious or minority education. Despite the changes in content, basic teaching methods did not change in most countries of the region, and study was often by rote, emphasizing the acquisition of data rather than understanding it and analyzing it. This was not unique to Jewish institutions, and the overall literacy among Jews was high, with Jewish students generally successful on state matriculation examinations and in higher education.

RECOMMENDED READING

Cohen, Hayyim J. *The Jews of the Middle East, 1860–1972.* New York: Halstead, 1973.

Laskier, Michael M. *The Alliance Israélite Universelle and the Jewish Communities of Morocco, 1862–1962.* Albany: State University of New York Press, 1983.

Rodrigue, Aron. *French Jews, Turkish Jews: The Alliance Israélite Universelle and the Politics of Jewish Schooling in Turkey, 1860–1925.* Bloomington: Indiana University Press, 1990.

——. *Images of Sephardi and Eastern Jewries in Transition: The Teachers of the Alliance Israélite Universelle, 1860–1939.* Seattle: University of Washington Press, 1993.

Sawdayee, Maurice M. *The Baghdad Connection.* Locust Valley, N.Y.: Author, 1991.

CHAPTER

9

Zionism

RACHEL SIMON

Political Zionism blends traditional religious "love of Zion" with modern nationalism. It grew out of the centuries-old yearning of Diaspora Jews to return to Zion (i.e., Eretz Yisrael, the Land of Israel), but it started in a social environment in which nationalism was a major political force. Political Zionism emerged in the late nineteenth century in Central and Western Europe, where an emerging nationalism was strong within states that had an active political life shared by Gentiles and Jews alike. Many founders of modern Zionism had a modern Western secular upbringing; they communicated in European languages and often did not use (or even know) Jewish languages (e.g., Hebrew, Yiddish, or Ladino). Those who were Labor Zionists wanted to get away from religion and create a "new Jew"—someone more earthy, active, and productive and less spiritual, less dreamy, less a luftmensch. Their major theme was the need to turn around the "upside-down pyramid," as the economic structure of the Jews was called, which emphasized study, services, finance, and commerce, whereas the productive elements (agriculture and industry) were lacking. During the European Enlightenment, Jews got involved in various aspects of gentile life—education, culture, economics, and politics—yet individuals and communities often felt estranged in the face of the growing local nationalisms and traditional anti-Semitism. These factors, together with a long-standing love and yearning for Zion, paved the way for modern political Zionism.

In the Middle East and North Africa, which were mostly under Muslim rule, the situation during the late nineteenth century was different. Although in most of the region Islamic law regarding Jews did not have political implications, both Jews and Christians were still considered second-class citizens and in some places, like Iran, even impure and untouchable. The Ottoman sultanic decrees of 1839 and 1856 stated the equality of all citizens before the law, but social patterns were slow to change, and Jewish life remained mainly one of community. National political life had not yet developed, so Jews' political activity was largely confined to the administration of their own communities and to contacts with the local authorities and foreign powers.

The growing involvement of the European powers in Middle Eastern and North African affairs gradually changed this situation and, with this, the sociopolitical position of the Jews and their behavior. Once European political penetration began, many Jews felt that they had much to gain from the change in regime; they hoped that the colonial powers would widen economic opportunities and political freedoms and would treat the Jews of the Middle East and North Arica as the European powers treated their Jewish citizens in Europe. Thus in Algeria as early as 1830 Jews were shifting their identity from Muslim state and society toward the colonial power. About a century later, after World War I, European governments ruled most of the region (except for Turkey, Iran, Saudi Arabia, and Yemen) in one way or another. The Muslim state plus colonialism began to have a strong influence on Jewish life, including the development of Zionism. A Middle Eastern Jew's level of traditionalism, religiosity, and exposure to political ideas, with the new existence of political life and the possibility of advancement and improvement, influenced the belated but growing political Zionism in the region.

The traditional "love of Zion" was constant among Middle Eastern and North African Jews, and most remained observant even after exposure to Western civilization. Two major components of Zionism had long been carried out in the region, without the mantle of Zionism and with no nationalist connotations—the study of Hebrew and the concept of aliyah (Jewish emigration to the Land of Israel). Much of the traditional education of Jewish boys—for the vast majority—consisted of learning the Hebrew alphabet and reading the Bible and commentaries in Hebrew. Most Jews, however, did not use Hebrew in daily exchanges but conversed mainly in local Jewish dialects. Jewish men knew and used the Hebrew alphabet, often not knowing a non-Jewish language or a non-Hebrew script.

The cultural unity of the Middle East and North Africa facilitated regional travel. Jews from Muslim lands went on pilgrimage to the Jewish holy places in Palestine but then returned home in the same way as their Muslim neighbors who made a pilgrimage to Mecca. Aliyah did occur, although it lacked nationalist connotations until the twentieth century. One large-scale attempt at return was initiated in the sixteenth century by Don Joseph Nasi and Doña Grácia Mendés, Sephardim who wanted to revive

Jewish life in Tiberias and the Galilee as a refuge for persecuted Jews. Until the Zionist movement, however, most immigration to Eretz Israel was for religious and personal reasons, usually by pious men who wanted to live close to the holy places, study in important yeshivas, and be buried in the Holy Land. Many moved for more earthly reasons, such as the large-scale moves from the Maghreb in the first half of the nineteenth century, mostly to Jerusalem, Jaffa, and Haifa; those of the 1860s from Kurdistan and Georgia; those from Yemen in 1882 and thereafter to Jerusalem and the new *moshavot* (agricultural communities); and those from Iran and Bukhara, mainly in the 1890s. Smaller numbers of Jews came from Baghdad, Damascus, Aleppo, and Urfa. These returns were not intended to change the basic socio-economic and cultural life of the immigrants, although in one aspect these people were similar to the later Zionist pioneers and different from the pious Ashkenazim of the Old Yishuv (before 1882): most lived on their own economic products. They did not rely on *halukkah* (charity), as did most Orthodox Ashkenazim who spent their lives in study, not in economic pursuits.

Because of the political differences among Jews in Europe, the Middle East, and North Africa, their ideological and organizational patterns also differed. Thus modern Zionism drew mostly from developments in Europe, but two Sephardic rabbis became known for their contributions to early Zionist thought. The first was Rabbi Judah Bibas (1780–1852), of a Moroccan rabbinical family, who advocated the return of Jews to the Holy Land and interpreted *teshuvah* not merely as "spiritual repentance" but as actual "return to Palestine." The second, Rabbi Yehuda Alkalai of Sarajevo (1798–1878), was known for his proto-Zionist ideas. He called for the return of the Jews to the Holy Land and wanted Western Jewish political figures to convene an international congress that would effect the resettlement of the Jews in Palestine. Alkalai viewed Jewish national revival as part of the nineteenth century's general political trends, and he stressed the importance of cultural revival in this process, including the revival of Hebrew as the unifying language of the Jews. Other rabbis also advocated the revival of the Hebrew language and wrote Hebrew grammars. Several North African rabbis were involved in the local Jewish Enlightenment movement (Haskalah) of the late nineteenth century, subscribed to Hebrew periodicals, and read books published in Hebrew from Europe and Palestine. During this early stage one characteristic of Zionism in the Middle East and North Africa was already evident: the rabbis were involved in the revival movement in all its aspects, cultural as well as political, and they continued to be involved in Zionism even as their communities became less and less observant.

Some rabbis, though, opposed Zionism on religious or political grounds. The opposition rabbis were mainly in leadership positions and therefore in direct contact with Muslim authorities. These rabbis thought Zionism would endanger their communities. This became even more obvious with the growth of twentieth-century Arab nationalism.

Information about the emergence of political Zionism in Europe reached Middle Eastern and North African Jews who had commercial, social, and educational contacts with Europe; they got information from the media (especially Jewish publications), through trade and mercantile relations, and from visitors. Shortly after the First Zionist Congress met in Basel, Switzerland, in 1897, Jews from numerous communities wrote to the World Zionist Organization (WZO), congratulated it on its foundation, and asked to establish local branches of the movement. They volunteered to head these branches, solicit membership, and collect the shekel (individual annual dues, which in 1897 equaled one deutsche mark, the basis on which regional representation was granted at the congress). The WZO often took quite some time to answer these letters, if indeed they were ever answered. A recurrent request was for information, but the WZO was at times insensitive to or unable to cope with language issues, sending publications in German and Yiddish, which were hardly known in the Middle East and North Africa. Thus much Zionist activity in the region received lukewarm support from the WZO and remained at the grassroots level.

Early Zionist activity in the region suffered from lack of political experience. Political life, based on parties and elections, was just emerging in a few countries of the Middle East and North Africa, and only male property owners older than a certain age could participate. Many Jews who were likely to be active Zionists were European nationals, so they could not participate in local political life. Leadership positions in the Jewish community were either religious or temporal, and leaders were appointed by local authorities (who sometimes based their choices on local recommendations) or by the community, following the decisions of religious scholars or the powerful families. Only at the end of the nineteenth century did some Jewish communities start to have elections for their administrative positions.

Zionist activity soon became a new venue of political life, although it lacked an operational tradition. Many Zionist societies were established at the beginning of the twentieth century, some by Europeans who settled in the Middle East and North Africa and who had some experience of Western, including Zionist, political life. Personal rivalries were often responsible for the proliferation of organizations, most of which were short lived and had small memberships. Much of their activity centered on the collection of the shekel, distribution of Zionist publications, and discussions of Zionist issues. Despite many requests, senior Zionist figures rarely visited the region. This, together with the scarcity of appropriate reading materials, resulted in feelings of neglect. Local Zionist activity also suffered from the negative attitude of state authorities toward separatism—mostly in the Ottoman Empire—and directed mainly at Armenian and Greek nationalists. The Zionists were therefore careful to emphasize their loyalty to the Ottoman state, and their plan to work within it, but emerging nationalisms were a threat to the integrity of the empire.

During most of that period the Alliance Israélite Universelle (AIU), whose Paris-based educational network began to spread across the region in 1860, opposed Zionism. It wanted to Westernize the region's Jews, based on the French model, and make them loyal citizens of their respective states. Because of the high number of AIU graduates, their roles in the communities, and the AIU's contacts with French authorities, the organization's opposition was a major force. Only after World War II did the attitude of the AIU change as a result of the Holocaust and the complicity of Vichy France with Nazi Germany during the war.

Zionism was greatly affected by World War I. During that conflict thousands of Jewish citizens of countries at war with the Ottoman Empire (mainly Russians) were expelled from Ottoman Palestine; they found refuge in Egypt and gave impetus to Zionism there. More important for the future of Zionism were agreements made between Zionist leaders and several European powers, culminating in Britain's 1917 Balfour Declaration, the declaration of the British foreign minister stating that "His Majesty's government view[s] with favour the establishment in Palestine of a National Home for the Jewish people." By 1922 the League of Nations had established the British mandate in Palestine, and its first high commissioner was Jewish. By that date the overall political structure of the region had changed. The victorious European powers had dismembered the Ottoman Empire and had apportioned most of it to their colonial rule. This had implications for Zionist activity, because of the varying policies of the colonial administrations regarding Zionism, the growth of local nationalism, and the characteristics of the Zionists.

In Europe the colonial powers did not oppose Zionism, but they did not want to encourage Zionism in the Middle East and North Africa, because growing nationalism would complicate their rule. Although the colonial powers had often used the policy of divide and rule, they did not want to be perceived as supporters of the small and hitherto despised element, the Jews, in their national aspirations while advocating a different policy toward the majority Muslim society. The policy of colonial powers should be viewed in the framework of growing Arab nationalism, which fed on the Europeans' inconsistency. European powers failed to fulfill promises they had made to Arab leaders during the war, yet they made an Arab leader king of a new country, Iraq. Some Arab nationalists then moved to Iraq, but others continued to work for Arab independence, mainly in Syria and Egypt, aiming to end colonial rule. In the new Republic of Turkey secular Turkish nationalism resulted in the decision of Turkish Jews to renounce their minority status, which consequently prevented public expressions of Jewish identity and religion, including support for Zionism, which was a competing nationalism.

Many early proponents of Zionism in the region were Westernized mercantile Jews, those who would surely benefit from colonial rule. They started to be somewhat detached from Judaism, although they observed tradition and were not antireligion, like some European Zionists. During the interwar period these characteristics had implications for local Zionist activity. While advocating aliyah as the ultimate goal of Zionism, Zionist societies did not usually require their members to carry out this goal. Zionist clubs were often a meetingplace for social and cultural activities related to Jewish history. Many towns had a Jewish sports club, often related to the Maccabi Zionist sports organization, that encouraged its members to be athletically active. While at the beginning most Maccabi clubs were for men, they gradually included activities for the whole family, spreading the idea of "muscular Judaism"—another Zionist innovation. Thus early in its development Zionism introduced new social, behavioral, and cultural concepts into Jewish life.

The revival and modernization of the Hebrew language became a major activity among Zionists. Jews who wanted to read foreign publications in Hebrew had to teach themselves the language. Although they could decipher the Hebrew script, it had not been a living language for them. Societies were established to spread Hebrew as a modern, spoken language among all levels of the community. Some places benefited from Hebrew teachers from Palestine, who combined teaching with Zionist activities, but most teachers were at first self-taught and were later joined by graduates of these courses. A growing number of the teaching materials came from the Hebrew education network in Palestine, so students became acquainted with notions and songs common among Zionists there. Another important resource was the international organization whose purpose was to revive the Hebrew language, Berit Ivrit Olamit (World Hebrew Union). As a result many young

Jews became fluent in Modern Hebrew while absorbing Zionist ideas from a young age. Moreover, the educational activities triggered by Zionism challenged traditional education and had modernizing effects on the region's Jewish communities. From World War II on, this facilitated the work of Jewish soldiers and emissaries from Palestine.

Zionism provided a forum in which lay members and rabbis cooperated for a nontraditional goal. It enabled those hitherto uninvolved in leadership to embark upon communal activity. It gradually changed the face of local Jewish political life by introducing new elements, including the principle of elections. Many Zionist activists were either young or lower middle-class professionals, teachers, and craftsmen who did not belong to either group of traditional community leaders, the wealthy and the religious scholars. The growing involvement of these new elements in Zionist affairs prompted some to aspire to more influence in communal politics; this caused much rivalry at times, owing to the traditional power sharing among the dominant families. Zionism also increased the involvement of women in public life, but they never gained a proportionate share in Zionist leadership.

During the interwar period Zionist societies increased in the Middle East and North Africa, though the membership remained small relative to the size of the communities. Modern Hebrew did spread among the youth, and many read Zionist publications and paid the shekel. Yet their participation in the Zionist congresses was limited, mainly because of small memberships, coupled with language differences and a lack of political experience. Few emigrated to Palestine because of the improved economic, social, and political conditions under colonialism. Then too, most local Zionists did not feel it urgent to emigrate, and in this respect they resembled Jews almost everywhere. In the 1940s World War II did not affect the Middle East and North Africa as it did Europe, but it did change Jewish life and attitudes. Under French and Italian colonial rule Jews suffered from "racial" legislation, incarceration, internal exile, and even expulsion to concentration camps in Europe, as well as discriminatory economic legislation in Turkey. They felt unsafe under the European administrations that they had once viewed as providing protection, progress, and freedom. Anticipating independent Arab rule, they also became worried about their safety because of the growing local nationalism, combined with long-held anti-Jewish feelings and a few violent riots.

Under these conditions local Jews viewed the Palestinian Jewish soldiers within the British forces as the true liberators from fascism and oppression. The "new Jews" (stationed in Egypt, Libya, and Iraq) soon began pointing to a way to compensate for the hardships of the Diaspora—self-fulfilling Zionism, namely, emigration to Palestine—to start a new national life there. Many Palestinian Jewish soldiers (and some Jews in the U.S. Army stationed in the Maghreb) felt obliged to help local Jews, and they got involved in their social and cultural activities. Serving as role models for local Jews, they managed to establish clubs and point education in a Hebrew-oriented Zionist direction. Only a few soldiers were educators, but their enthusiasm, knowledge of Hebrew, and the respect with which the communities viewed them enabled them to both introduce innovations and to train local Jews to carry on. The soldiers and the *shelihim* (emissaries sent by Zionist organizations in Palestine) who followed them succeeded because Zionism already existed in the region, so local Jews were ready to spread and strengthen it.

As World War II progressed and contacts with European Jewry became almost impossible, the Zionist leadership in Palestine became aware of the potential of Middle Eastern and North African Jews for Zionism. Then in 1943 the Jewish Agency for Palestine organized special training courses within Palestine for emissaries destined to operate in the region. Many trainees or their families were of local origin, so they were knowledgeable about customs and behavior patterns in the Middle East and North Africa. The emissaries from Palestine went to Middle Eastern and North African communities as individuals or in small groups, usually under a false identity, to act clandestinely—only a selected few in the host community knew their true identity. All together, various departments of the Jewish Agency sent about 150 emissaries in the 1940s, mostly during the war years, and mainly to Lebanon, Syria, Egypt, Iraq, Iran, and Turkey. The Palestine-based Mossad le-Aliya Bet (Organization for Illegal Immigration) directed many of these emissaries. After the war, from 1945 to 1948, the organization redirected most of its efforts to operations in Europe, but some emissaries continued to operate in Islamic countries, and they usually started their activities within existing Jewish, preferably Zionist, organizations. The emissaries from Palestine tried to disguise their operations to avoid conflict with the surrounding community. In acting clandestinely, they were well aware of the prevailing opposition of the authorities to Zionism. Consequently, although many emissaries were not religiously observant, they were careful not to be conspicuous about their lack of religiosity and daily behavior—or to openly advance party politics. Their mission included organizing the aliyah, sociocultural activities, and self-defense.

The major innovation introduced by the emissaries was the Zionist youth movement and the training camps (*hakhsharot*). The concept of a youth movement was quite revolutionary for local Jews. The youth clubs focused on nontraditional subjects, such as Modern Hebrew, Zionist ideology, song, and dance, aiming to create a new society. Although some organizations for youth had been in existence, they were religion-based or were offshoots of adult sports clubs. Until the 1940s no Zionist activities targeted local youth, except for the Hebrew study groups. The new youth movements reflected much of what existed in Palestine but without the link to Zionist political parties (because of the clandestine nature of the operation, the different political environment, and the small number of emissaries who had to cooperate despite their political differences). The youth movements wanted to instill among their members new cultural, social, and economic values—including gender equality, readiness for a communal-cooperative life, and appreciation of manual work, especially in agriculture. Participation in the youth movement was for both genders (although mostly in separate groups), and the activities resembled those conducted in Palestine, the source of the terminology, reading materials, and insignia. The emphasis in the youth movement was on *hagshamah atzmit* (self-fulfillment, by which the Zionists meant emigration to Palestine, preferably followed by settlement in a kibbutz). To prepare young people for communal agricultural life, a special organization, He-Halutz (Pioneer) was made available for young adults, usually people who had graduated from the youth movement. He-Halutz was a widespread European movement, originally established in 1904, that had prepared interwar Jews for settlement in Palestine. In addition to operations in several cities, He-Halutz established *hakhsharot,* most of which were agricultural, though some were urban-industrial. The *hakhsharot* were even more radical than the youth movements, because they brought urban youth to the countryside to be trained in agricultural work while living the communal life. Because of local social customs and family resistance the most difficult part was the inclusion of women in this enterprise—and few women joined. Although few in number, members of He-Halutz were often those who took leadership positions in self-defense and aliyah activities, and they served as role models for what the early emissaries expected local Jewish communities to become.

To secure a loyal secretive following within which they could operate safely, the emissaries selected trustworthy young men and women and swore them into the Haganah (Defense), the major prestate Jewish military organization in Palestine, established in 1920. The main purpose of local Haganah units was to protect Jews from Muslim rioters. The need for Jews to learn organized self-defense stemmed from some Arab anti-Jewish riots (for example, in Palestine in 1921, 1929, and 1936–39; Baghdad in 1941; Cairo and Tripoli [Libya] in 1945) during which the colonial powers were slow to intervene or ineffective and the Jews suffered injuries, death, and loss of property. Local Haganah units were small and compartmentalized, to minimize leakage of information; their preparations for self-defense were not easy because they had to acquire and store weapons and to conceal training. Nonetheless, they had some success in acquiring arms—through illegal arms dealers, smuggling, and military leftovers, the latter mostly where Jewish Palestinian soldiers had been stationed. In some places, mainly in Palestine, a clandestine arms industry developed. Training in defense could be concealed as part of the operation of the youth movements, during hikes and in camps in the countryside. Where self-contained *hakhsharot* communities were established, they also served as military training camps. Most Haganah units outside Palestine were established by emissaries, but later their leadership was mostly local. Although defense training outside Palestine was not widespread, it was important for self-confidence and for preventing the spread of riots. Haganah units were also used to protect clandestine aliyah operations.

From 1919 to 1948 about 12 percent of the Jewish immigrants to Palestine were from Asian and African countries, where about 6 to 8 percent of world Jewry lived. The proportion of immigrants from Muslim countries was higher than that from Europe and the Americas, with more coming from Asia than from Africa. As important as the religious attachments and the Zionist activities might have been in the decision to emigrate, the main motives of these Jews were political and economic. Thus when Jews felt politically oppressed and economically distressed, they tried to emigrate. The destination they chose was not necessarily Palestine; many emigrated to countries where they had contacts or where the economic prospects seemed favorable. From the 1930s on, restrictions on emigration to European and American countries and the proximity of Palestine often made the latter the only choice available. Consequently, regardless of the difficulties of entering British Mandatory Palestine or of leaving their own countries, numerous Jews, independently or in groups, found their way to Palestine. There, legal immigration depended on a fixed number of immigration certificates of several kinds. These were distributed annually by the Jewish Agency, which was often haunted by the dilemma of how to best distribute the few certificates. Regular certificates allowed a whole family to enter Palestine, so families often claimed additional children or a spouse. Special He-Halutz certificates went to the young and able-bodied, to engage in productive manual work. From 1919 to 1947 more than fifty-three thousand Middle Eastern and North African Jews emigrated to Palestine, mostly from Yemen and Syria, including about forty-five thousand who entered Palestine legally. Most immigration certificates were distributed in Europe, because of the urgency, especially from the 1930s on, in rescuing Jews endangered by Nazi Germany. To encourage participation in the Middle Eastern and North African youth movement and He-Halutz, the emissaries tried to reserve some immigration certificates for Halutzim, although this practice decreased the total number of legal immigrants (a Halutz certificate enabled only one person to enter Palestine, whereas more than one person could emigrate on a regular certificate). The British caught quite a few illegal immigrants and from mid-1946 to mid-1948 transferred them to holding camps on Cyprus; they eventually got to Israel after the British mandate ended.

Until the 1940s most Jews from the Middle East and North Africa emigrated to Palestine independently. Because so few could immigrate legally, Jews developed and used illegal methods. Palestinian Jews often initiated these operations, but local Zionists, many of them He-Halutz members, later took over. So long as Palestinian Jewish soldiers were stationed around the Middle East and North Africa, they helped local Jews get to Palestine by lending them their papers when they were due for home leave or to be demobilized. For example, soldiers going on home leave for Passover in 1946 smuggled as many as two hundred Egyptian Jews into Palestine. Some soldiers married local Jewish women to bring them to Palestine, with the understanding that they would be divorced upon arrival; nonetheless, some couples chose to remain married. Another means of emigration, mainly from 1945 to 1947, was Aliyah Dalet, in which Jews received tourist visas after leaving a deposit at the British consulate in Egypt to guarantee their return. This was financed by the Mossad le-Aliya Bet, which often got the deposits back anyway, after having the unaccompanied passports stamped with a return confirmation.

Border smugglers were always an option, and for hefty sums they helped Jews cross borders into countries from which emigration to Palestine was easier (for example, Jews moved from Libya to Tunisia and then to Palestine, or from Iraq to Iran, Jordan, or Syria, then to Palestine), or the smugglers helped to get Jews directly into Palestine (as from Lebanon, Syria, or Transjordan). These smuggling operations were dangerous, because border patrols were on guard against smuggling and infiltration, and because smugglers were not always reliable. The terrain was often difficult and the climate harsh. Among these operations was Aliyat ha-Elef (the Immigration of the

Thousand) in 1945, when emissaries convinced Jewish families in Syria to send unaccompanied children to Palestine. Communities with access to the sea tried to use that route, mostly crossing from North Africa to France or Italy by fishing boats and from there to Palestine; there were even attempts, mostly unsuccessful, to buy boats and navigate them without experienced seafarers. Some Jews even tried to get to Palestine by air; in 1947 U.S. pilots flew about one hundred Jews in two flights from Baghdad to Yavne'el (near Tiberias).

As the 1940s progressed, and World War II escalated, the struggle over Palestine intensified, and the situation of the Jews in the Middle East and North Africa became even more delicate. With the growth of nationalism and the strengthening of pan-Arab relations, regional support for the Palestinian Arabs increased, and being a Zionist became tantamount to supporting the enemy. Although Zionist activities continued in the region, in some countries, like Iraq, they were illegal, and in most countries they became dangerous and ever more clandestine. Even contacts with Jews in Palestine, whom Arabs considered the Zionist enemy, became risky. This was a difficult situation, because many Jews, even non-Zionists, had relatives and friends in Palestine.

The Palestine question soon increased Arab hostility toward local Jews, especially following the U.N. Security Council's resolution on the partition of Palestine (November 29, 1947) and the establishment of the State of Israel (May 15, 1948), when the British mandate was to end. Fund-raising in support of the Arabs in Palestine, and the mobilization of volunteers in various Arab states to help the Palestinians fight the Jews in Palestine, made the situation of the region's Jews even more risky. Jews living in Arab lands were expected to demonstrate their loyalty to their country by making donations and declarations in support of their country's pan-Arab cause. Nonetheless, the Muslim majority commonly believed that, contrary to outward appearance, the Jews in fact supported the Zionists in the struggle. This gave rise to anti-Jewish attacks (e.g., in Aden, Aleppo, and Tripoli), which grew more violent and widespread as Israeli victories in the Arab-Israeli War of 1948 became known. In addition, some Jews were imprisoned and even condemned to death (as in Iraq) after being accused of supporting Israel financially and militarily.

The growing anti-Jewish atmosphere in the region, and the abolition of restrictions for Jews to enter Israel once the state was established, made aliyah the favored choice, even during the Arab-Israeli War of 1948. The difficulty for awhile was that of emigration—the Arab states did not want their Jews to strengthen the Israel Defense Force against the Palestinians in the

Table 9.1 Emigration to Israel, 1948–1990

Year	Iran	Iraq	Syria and Lebanon	Turkey	Yemen and Aden	Egypt and Sudan	Libya	Tunisia	Algeria	Morocco
1948	43	15	5	4,362	270	31	1,065		←6,821→	
1949	1,780	1,709	1,570	26,306	38,062	7,268	14,357		←17,363→	
1950	10,561	32,462	1,014	2,491	9,043	6,675	8,965	4,852	457	4,371
1951	9,526	89,185	324	1,388	940	2,054	6,589	3,491	270	7,741
1952	4,236	2,104	275	433	147	1,217	1,195	2,709	95	4,872
1953	1,114	535	203	325	91	980	250	618	82	3,031
1954	488	295	136	184	629	960	199	2,646	267	8,291
1955	244	252	132	339	32	654	136	6,126	493	25,151
1956	673	147	179	1,710	32	865	110	6,543	1,009	36,401
1957	1,251	255	450	1,911	63	11,762	69	2,667	936	8,886
1958	5,736	134	555	845	63	523	58	1,326	160	1,902
1959	1,526	79	649	737	88	352	19	425	245	3,369
1960	531	188	137	387	25	208	43	509	246	4,260
1961	920	146	235	1,829	271	255	49	(0)	5,942	11,676
1962	2,197	145	560	968	279	393	56		3,413	35,839
1963	2,883	144	298	749	112	292	66	904	169	36,988
1964	2,889	106	208	1,247	42	293	147	816	156	15,851
1965–71	10,645	1,609	2,945	9,280	334	1,730	2,148	7,753	3,177	30,153
1972–79	9,550	939	1,406	3,118	51	535	219	2,148	2,137	7,780
1980–84	3,435	81	840	1,604	12	237	51	1,232	1,301	2,522
1985–89	5,052	30	334	484	11	115	16	710	529	1,287
1990		13	40	105	3	19	20	86	83	220
Subtotal	75,280	130,573	12,495	60,802	50,600	37,387	35,827	47,654	21,167	274,775
Total: 739,323										

Source: Central Bureau of Statistics, *Immigration to Israel 1948–1972* (Jerusalem: Central Bureau of Statistics, 1975), table 1; *Immigration to Israel, 1990* (Jerusalem: Central Bureau of Statistics, 1991), table 6.

Note: The data for Tunisia, Algeria, and Morocco for 1948 and 1949 are combined, with most of the immigrants coming from Morocco through Algeria. These data are included in the totals for Morocco.

war, and the British in Libya declared that they did not want to assist any of the belligerents. Once Israel prevailed and cease-fire agreements were signed between Israel and most Arab states, local conditions regarding aliyah changed. Then Israeli emissaries operated openly in Libya and Aden and in cooperation with state agencies to organize the emigration of Jews to Israel. Even where Israeli emissaries operated clandestinely (mainly in Egypt, Iraq, and Morocco), they were often known to the authorities, and state policies dictated the degree of toleration.

The periods of record emigration to Israel were from 1949 to 1950 from Libya and from Yemen (On Wings of Eagles), and 1950 to 1951 from Iraq (Operation Ezra and Nehemia). The emigration to Israel from Turkey (1949) and Iran (1950–51) was driven largely by religious and economic events. From 1948 to 1953 Jews from Asian and African countries (mostly from the Middle East and North Africa) were the majority of Israel's 722,443 immigrants: 35.3 percent came from Asia and 15.4 percent from Africa. That 50 percent came from Asia and Africa is especially impressive because the Jewish Diaspora was so spread out. Before the mass emigration, 3.8 percent of world Jewry lived in Asia and 6.5 percent in Africa; by 1953 only 1.5 percent remained in Asia and 5.5 percent in Africa. The percentage of Jews in Israel in 1948 from Asian and African countries increased from 12.5 percent and 2.6 percent, respectively, to 27.5 percent and 9.4 percent at the end of 1953.

Throughout the Jewish world the Hebrew language was being revived, and Israeli culture had some effect on new developments. The number of recognized Israeli musicians, artists, writers, poets, playwrights, and scholars was growing. Israel developed a new educational system that taught modern, secular, Jewish, and vocational subjects in Hebrew—and Zionists outside Israel followed that lead. Political life in Israel became increasingly lively, with wide-ranging parties. Defense organizations had developed and served as the foundation for the Israel Defense Force.

Following the mass emigration to Israel in the early 1950s, the Jewish communities of Yemen, Aden, Iraq, and Libya were almost completely depopulated. Large numbers of Jews still lived in French North Africa and in Egypt, Iran, and Turkey, so Zionist activities continued there clandestinely, mainly in Morocco and Egypt. The emigration of Jews resumed, much of it to Israel, as a result of independence in Morocco, Tunisia, and Algeria (but Algerian Jews went mainly to France) and following the Arab-Israeli wars of 1956 and 1967 (mainly from Egypt and Libya). Another wave of emigration, some of which reached Israel, followed the establishment of the Islamic republic in Iran in 1979. Within thirty years, then, most of the ancient Jewish communities of the Middle East and North Africa were depopulated, with sizable communities remaining only in Turkey, Iran, and Morocco. Large immigrant groups soon felt themselves to be in a new diaspora, although they were in Israel, following their evacuations from what had been their homelands for centuries. They found themselves anxiously trying to keep their uniqueness alive by practicing and reviving local traditions and customs.

RECOMMENDED READINGS

Gat, Moshe. *The Jewish Exodus from Iraq, 1948–1951.* Portland, Ore.: Frank Cass, 1997.

Krämer, Gudrun. *The Jews in Modern Egypt, 1914–1952.* Seattle: University of Washington Press, 1989.

Laskier, Michael M. *North African Jewry in the Twentieth Century: The Jews of Morocco, Tunisia, and Algeria.* New York: New York University Press, 1994.

——. *The Jews of Egypt, 1920–1970: In the Midst of Zionism, Anti-Semitism, and the Middle East Conflict.* New York: New York University Press, 1992.

Parfitt, Tudor. *The Road to Redemption: The Jews of the Yemen, 1900–1950.* New York: E. J. Brill, 1996.

Schechtman, Joseph B. *On Wings of Eagles: The Plight, Exodus, and Homecoming of Oriental Jewry.* New York: Thomas Yoseloff, 1961.

CHAPTER

10

Beliefs and Customs

Issachar Ben-Ami

The study of the daily life of the Jewish communities scattered throughout the Muslim world requires a thorough examination of the intricate web of customs and beliefs embedded in the lives of the Jews of those countries for hundreds and even thousands of years. Such a study is difficult, though, as it depends on global as well as regional factors. The period of existence for a Jewish community in a certain region, its exposure to the various local cultures, the competition with its gentile neighbors, as well as its relations with other centers of Judaism—including the Land of Israel—all play a dominant role in shaping the image of a Jewish community in a particular region.

After considering such obvious superficial contrasts as clothing, culinary habits, language, and physical appearance, the question remains of how to judge the uniformity or diversity of the popular customs and ways of life of the Middle Eastern and North African Jewish communities.

A society's ideological and religious system establishes and sets the pattern for most of its customs and beliefs, which then are influenced by changes in the ideological and social basis of the society. These rules apply to society in general, but the prolonged existence of the various Jewish communities in the Diaspora—in essence, as a threatened minority group—has led to the development of characteristics specific to the Jewish people. Environmental and other factors have had a direct influence on the life, customs, and beliefs of each community, causing an apparent blurring of the general criteria that characterize the Jews in the Diaspora, whose yearly and life cycles are based on rules, ideals, principles, and concepts that began as survival mechanisms and who are steeped in the customs and beliefs of their daily life.

THE LIFE CYCLE

Childbirth and the circumcision of male infants have always been important to Jewish society, on the one hand symbolizing religious tradition and, on the other, forming part of a complex structure of customs and beliefs patterned by popular tradition but dominated by folklore and mysticism. The condition of the Jews as a religious, ethnic, and national minority struggling for its physical existence, as well as for the preservation of its spiritual and cultural heritage, determined the character of many such customs.

Sterility was obviously a menace that threatened the very existence of the religious-ethnic minority and therefore not only constituted a problem for individuals but was a threat to the entire community. In Morocco, after the relatives of a barren woman had proved unsuccessful in their efforts to help her become pregnant, a group of old women would get together to try to solve the problem. They began by appeasing the spirits associated with the barren woman's house, by offering them a sacrifice of oil and couscous, dispersed in various corners of the house. Similarly, in Greece old women were always active in trying to treat sterility; the Jews of Salonika, for instance, believed that on Tu Be-Shvat (Arbor Day) the trees embraced and copulated. On that occasion the Jews would hang on the trees pitchers full of well water diluted with rosewater. In the morning the barren woman would drink this water; it was hoped that the reproductive powers of the trees would cure her sterility. In short, the large number, nature, and variety of formulas for the treatment of sterility clearly demonstrate that the barren woman would seize any opportunity, no matter how hopeless or ridiculous it might seem to us, in an attempt to remedy her situation.

In the case of the more fortunate, the announcement of a woman's first pregnancy has always been a most important event in the life of any family, heralded with great joy and accompanied by much celebration. The Jews of Amadiya, Kurdistan, would take the young pregnant woman to her father's house, where she would be joined by the women of the family and some elderly women. During this gathering an old woman would sew diapers, while musicians playing drums (*dola*) and trumpets (*zirne*) provided entertainment. The women would sing and dance, and the pregnant woman received much good advice from the experienced women. In the evening a festive meal was held at the husband's home. Holding this event also disseminated the news of her pregnancy to the community, and the notification was by no means accidental; it served to close the circle that was opened when the bride was given in marriage to the bridegroom. Because a woman's barrenness was considered a stain on her parents and her family, her pregnancy served as a proclamation to the community of the family's fertility. Such celebrations also aimed to strengthen the ties between the pregnant woman and her family. On the whole, the pregnant woman has always enjoyed a privileged position in Jewish family and society, enjoying special attention and care. However, in some communities a woman would conceal (Yemen) or disregard her pregnancy, and she was expected to carry on with her work as usual (Kurdistan).

The beginning of pregnancy signified the beginning of a new period in a woman's life, and she would enter into a system of interdictions, taboos, and rules dictated by popular traditions and customs, often rich in folkloristic rites. These increased in strength with the progression of the pregnancy and its culmination in childbirth, the week of the circumcision, and the *pidyon haben* (redemption of the first-born son) ceremony. One widespread belief was that ignoring a pregnant woman's cravings caused her to miscarry. According to other common theories and beliefs, if the expectant woman's desire to eat something remained unfulfilled, the baby would be born with a mark on its body the same color as the food for which its mother yearned; if she touched a particular part of her body while having a craving, the baby would bear a mark on the corresponding part of its body.

The Jewish women of Salonika used to open up everything in the house during a pregnancy—doors, cupboards, drawers, and so on. Many families kept the front door open during the entire nine-month period, even at night. Such customs were based on the folkloristic belief that this would encourage the smooth development of pregnancy and lead to an easy birth. For this same reason the pregnant woman in Morocco would unbuckle her belt, while her husband would buy the right to open the Heikhal (Holy Ark) on Shabbat at the synagogue.

There was always the constant fear of the many dangers that the pregnant woman faced. Prevention of the dreaded miscarriage was her, as well as her family's, responsibility. Moroccan Jews attributed miscarriage to a female ghost called *atab'a* (the persecutor). A woman wore a special amulet called *hizab tab'a* (the persecutor's amulet) to protect against the ghost's evil powers. Entire families have been known to leave their homes and even their towns in order to prevent an attack by the ghost. In Salonika women would take a linen thread and wrap it seven times around a famous rabbi's tomb, then wrap it around the pregnant woman's belly. This thread, called *detendor* (the holder), remained with the woman until the birth of her child. In Kurdistan women twisted five threads of different colors—red, green, yellow, white, and black—while uttering the names of some special spirits, then wrapped the twisted threads obliquely around the pregnant woman's body from shoulder to loin. The pregnant women of Iran were terrified of being given "the evil eye" by barren or bereaved women, and they were also afraid of ghosts and spirits. For protection they wore at their breast a jewel made up of an amulet rolled within a silver or gold cylinder that was decorated with precious stones. For the same purpose many women wore around their wrist or ankle a silver bracelet called *telsem,* made by a rabbi specializing in the kabbalah.

Many customs were associated with guessing the unborn child's gender. Tunisian Jews believed that marks on the pregnant woman's face signified a boy. In Algeria someone would offer a key to the woman, and if she held it by the rounded end, the child would be a girl; if she took the narrow end, the child would be a boy. The Jews of Kurdistan believed that if the pregnant woman's belly was long and narrow and her face became marked or dark with the mark of pregnancy, she would give birth to a son; if her belly was flat and she remained unmarked, she would have a girl. People often tried to influence what the child's gender would be. In Salonika the pregnant woman would address the fetus every Friday by a male name of her choice to ensure that the baby would be a boy.

When the woman reached her final month, she participated in many activities in preparation for the birth and the new baby's needs. In Fez, Morocco, the midwife would bless the pregnant woman and cut out pieces of cloth for the baby's layette before a group of mothers in a special ceremony called *teqqti' el-gwader* (the cutting out of the layette). This ceremony had folkloristic significance, intended to calm the future mother and strengthen her relationship with the midwife. In Salonika, at the beginning of the ninth month the pregnant woman and others would make a pilgrimage to the local cemetery, and they would pray at the tomb of a righteous person, or *zaddik.* At the same time they visited the graves of relatives to enlist their help in making sure that the delivery would go smoothly. Such visits occurred in a festive atmosphere with food and refreshments in abundance. Once back home the woman would immerse herself in a hot bath, because heat was a symbol of life, thus removing all trace of the coldness associated with the cemetery. Should the pregnant woman be unable to go to the cemetery, her family would bring her a tuft of grass from the ground near the *zaddik's* tomb, thus safeguarding her with his protection.

The birth of a child was, understandably, a special event—the pinnacle of a woman's life—anticipated with eagerness and excitement but also with anxiety and trepidation. New life was being created, but both mother and newborn were in mortal danger. According to popular belief, this was the moment when all the forces of evil would come together and try to overcome the two weak creatures. To ward off such forces of evil the community practiced various customs and followed various formulas at the birth. For example, people believed that the delivery room should be covered with holiness. They brought holy objects from the synagogue, spread dirt around the room that had been gathered from the grave of a famous righteous man, and offered prayers and recited psalms. Someone would tie one end of a thread to a Torah scroll in the synagogue and the other to the woman's bed, blow the shofar, place the key to the synagogue under the woman's bed, and so forth. Similar considerations led the Jews of Yemen to take precautions in a different fashion: when the woman felt labor pains, she retired secretly to a room seldom used by the family. As the pains increased, the family would call an elderly or experienced woman of the family or a neighbor. She would help the woman in her confinement, occasionally going out to report to the family, which would keep the matter a secret, making sure that nobody knew that the woman was giving birth. In Morocco upon the birth of a son the midwife would shout in Hebrew, "Barukh Habah!" [Blessed be he that comes], while a baby girl was received with the blessing in Judeo-Arabic "Mbarka mesᶜuda" [Blessed be she and happy].

It was generally believed that from the time of birth until the circumcision eight days later, the dreaded image of Lilith (Adam's legendary first wife before the creation of Eve) could appear, posing threats and dangers. The family took many measures to neutralize Lilith's evil as well as other dangers. The use of metal (charms, knives) against Lilith and other spirits stemmed from the principle of using a strong material against a weaker material. Another common measure was the use of the *Dapei Shemirah*—pages on which were inscribed Psalm 126, the names of the angels involved in the punishment of Lilith (Sini, Sinsini, and Samangalof), the names of Adam and Eve, the names of the patriarchs and the matriarchs, and a passage from Exodus: "Thou shalt not suffer a sorceress to live" (22:17). Many ceremonies, some of them repeated daily, escorted the male infant during his first week of life, which culminated in the Brit Milah (circumcision ceremony). For example, each night before the circumcision ceremony a proud father would hold his son in his arms, touching him, whispering the letters of the alphabet in his ear, blessing him with the benediction of the Torah, and kissing him. In addition, another ritual practiced by the Jews of Morocco, called *tahdid*, brought together relatives, friends, and neighbors every night at the house of the new mother to read portions of the Zohar (the book of Jewish mysticism) and to sing. Two women poets would compete in riddle and rhyme, making sharp comments to each other. At midnight the doors of the house were locked, and one man—the child's father, a Cohen, an old man, or one of the honorable guests—would take a sword and strike the walls of the house, making circles in the air to banish the spirits. At the end of the ceremony the man would place the sword under the mother's pillow. All the guests remained awake the whole night, while the woman's mother or an old woman professional chanted special songs.

Another group of customs, familiar to many communities, involved efforts to protect infants from death. To protect her newborn boy, a mother whose other sons had died at an early age would betroth him to a girl who had just been born. According to another custom, a newborn was "sold" to another family, and the Ladino name *Mercado* or *Mercada* (purchased), depending on the child's gender, was added to its name. Then the child would live because the family "bought" him or her. According to this superstition, something in the parents caused children to die, so selling the baby (like the betrothal at birth) was a way to remove the baby from its parents' domain.

The Jews of Iraq used to hold a small party for a baby girl on the sixth day (*lilt al-sitti*) after her birth, when she was given a name, but they held a big celebration for a baby boy. During the evening celebrating a boy's brith, the mother wore a special amulet to guard against the evil eye, and the midwife would draw seven lines on the mother's bed. Before this, a ceremony called *taqsim al-shasha* (distribution of popcorn) took place, whereupon children of the family, friends, and neighbors gathered in the new mother's house, and each received some popcorn, while musicians played. Sephardic Jews in Israel used to bring from the synagogue a candlestick called *tara* to light the new mother's room. In Iran each visitor to the woman's room would light a candle on a tray laid out for this purpose, thereby providing much heat and light, both of which are life affirming.

The night before the Brit Milah is known by different names throughout the Jewish Diaspora and has been the focus of special rituals and intense activity. A few days before the brith, one day at the latest, the chair of Elijah the Prophet is brought from the synagogue. In Iran the Jews used to cover it with a *parokhet* (the curtain over the Holy Ark in a synagogue) and decorate it with *rimonim* (bells for the Torah scroll) and with green branches. Iraqi Jews bound the chair with myrtle, and this night was called *lilt iqd a-liyas* (night of binding the myrtle). In Libya women would go at dusk to prepare perfumes from spices and dried flowers, while some, known to be good singers, would sit under Elijah's chair and sing holy songs in Arabic. These songs, called *ghna a-sefer* (songs of the Book, meaning the Torah) told of the Messiah, of Elijah the Prophet, of the patriarchs, of Moses and Aaron, of Joseph the Righteous One, of Eretz Israel, and more. Near the chair of Elijah the Prophet was a chair prepared for the *sandaq,* the child's godfather. On the eve of the circumcision the men would spend all night singing, praying, and reading the Zohar. The next morning, the day of the brith, both the father of the child and the godfather would go to have a ritual bath at dawn. The circumcision usually took place at home, but sometimes it was performed in the synagogue. In Morocco during the ceremony the women would pray to Elijah the Prophet and to the Angel of the Covenant for barren women to become pregnant and for the fertile to give birth to a boy. Sick people would place a glass of water under Elijah's chair and drink from it after the ceremony. The foreskin of the baby was sometimes cut up and swallowed by barren women or by women who had given birth only to girls.

Some families in Morocco used to pierce the earlobe (sometimes only of the right ear) of the baby boy in the first month of his life and insert a gold earring that he would wear for his whole life. During a period of forty days after the brith, the new mother was supposed to avoid meeting another new mother or a bride. This meeting, called *kabsa* by Iraqi Jews, was believed to be dangerous (from the folkloristic point of view) for both women, because the two were under the power of a special force.

When the child's first tooth appeared, the Jews of Kurdistan would proclaim: "Oh God, give us satisfaction and peace!" It was considered a special event, and the family prepared large quantities of porridge and distributed it to both friends and the poor. A small amount of the porridge was poured on the roof of the house so that the birds could share the family's enjoyment. Another rite of passage was the baby boy's first haircut—celebrated in Morocco when the baby reached the age of nine months but more often when he was twelve months old. The family, relatives, and friends would gather at the house or sometimes the synagogue, and they would drink tea and eat cakes while watching the barber cut the child's hair for the first time. Musicians played, and the atmosphere was festive and cheerful.

When the boy reached the age of five, his family would hold a birthday party for him. The boy wore a fine outfit, specially made for this occasion, called in Morocco *kaswa dal khams sninn* (suit of the five years), and was presented with a talisman of gold inscribed with the Hebrew word *Shaddai*

(God). To celebrate this important episode in a boy's life, some communities performed a "child marriage" on the evening of the Mimuna (the Moroccan festival on the day after Passover) or at Lag b'Omer.

THE BAR MITZVAH CEREMONY

According to the Mishnah (a collection of traditions that is part of the Talmud), when a boy reaches the age of thirteen he becomes bar mitzvah (son of the Commandment), attaining his religious maturity. In Yemen no celebration was involved: when the time came for the father to find his son responsible for his own actions, he would teach him to put on tefillin (phylacteries). He then took him to the synagogue for this purpose, and it might occur at any age, frequently when the boy was nine years old.

In Greece, Iran, Iraq, and Kurdistan and among the Sephardim of Israel, the boy would put on tefillin close to his thirteenth birthday. The following Saturday he was called up to read the Torah at the synagogue. There were no festivities, with the exception of the Sephardic families in Israel, who used to distribute candies in the synagogue and to invite relatives and friends to a small party at home. At the party the boy delivered his bar mitzvah speech, which was written by the local rabbi.

The custom in North Africa, particularly in Morocco, was different. The boys there became bar mitzvah at the age of ten or eleven, or even at eight or nine. In the 1930s Moroccan Jews began to celebrate the event close to the age of thirteen. Six months before the date of the bar mitzvah, the boy's parents would hold a party at home, when the tailor would cut and fashion a suit for the boy in the presence of many guests. On this occasion the boy read a small portion of his bar mitzvah speech in the presence of the rabbi who was preparing him for the celebration, and the guests would put on a tray a donation for the rabbi. On the same day the boy's colleagues at the heder (school) received cookies and candies. Later on the parents would order from a skilled embroiderer special bags for the tefillin and the tallith made of red or green velvet, on which various designs, featuring the boy's name and sometimes also the date, were embroidered in threads of silver or gold.

In many cases, during the morning of the day before the ceremony, the boy would go with his family to the barbershop to have his hair cut and from there to the *mikveh* (bathhouse) for a ritual bath. That evening the family would celebrate the ceremony of the henna, when henna (a red-brown plant pigment) was rubbed onto the hands of the boy and of the other participants. On this occasion the boy would give a speech prepared by the rabbi. In some villages of the Atlas Mountains region, the boy would be taken for a ride around the village on a white mule before dark. He was escorted by two boys, one on either side, while a crowd of others followed behind bearing branches. Many adults came behind them singing and offering *mahia* (an alcoholic beverage) to each person they met on their way. The next morning relatives helped the boy to put on his fine new clothes, and the rabbi would help him put on his tallith and tefillin.

In Libya the bar mitzvah boy would beg his mother's pardon for any misbehavior, and she would slowly pour water over his outstretched hands, a sign of her forgiveness. After the ceremony the boy, his parents, relatives, musicians, *paytanim* (singer of liturgical hymns), and friends would hold candles and set off in procession to the synagogue. There the boy prayed, sometimes conducting the entire service in place of the cantor, and he was given the honor of reading the Torah. Then he would give a sermon, while the women rained sugar, rice, almonds, dates, and candies on the congregation. After prayers the group would return in procession to the boy's house for a festive meal.

A Catholic priest who visited Morocco in the seventeenth century and was present at several bar mitzvah ceremonies, commented, "Nowhere in the world is a thirteen-year-old boy so learned in religious matters as a Jewish boy." Such testimony to bar mitzvah boys is valid in all Jewish communities around the world.

THE MARRIAGE CEREMONY

In the traditional Jewish society of the Diaspora the survival of the individual, the family, and the community has always been of utmost importance. Marriage not only ensures the continuation of the community but also reinforces its bonds, because each new couple is a symbol of the unity of the group and an affirmation of its durability. The customs and ceremonies described here are those of traditional marriage ceremonies, which, with the exception of a few groups, are fast disappearing because ways of life are constantly changing. Changes, even in Jewish customs, were linked to the passage from traditional to modern society, a process that began in the eighteenth century and culminated, to a large extent, in the creation of the State of Israel in 1948. Despite individual differences in the Jewish communities of the world, fundamental characteristics of the Jewish marriage ceremony can be identified as common to all.

A general overview of Jewish marriage ceremonies in the communities of the Middle East and North Africa reveals a number of special characteristics.

One is their duration, which could be two to three weeks and in some communities even two to three months; another is the great number of rituals characterized by a strong folkloristic flavor. These ceremonies can be followed in chronological order, culminating with the day of the wedding, the day of the Sheva Brachot (Seven Benedictions), as well as in synchronization, because some ceremonies took place simultaneously at both the bride's and groom's homes.

The ceremonies leading up to the wedding can be viewed as having a weekly structure, presumably inherited from biblical times, as in the seven-day banquet of Samson. In most communities each day was known by a special name, according to the particular ceremony, such as the Day of the Henna and the Saturday of the Swing. Another common characteristic was the involvement of the whole community, because properly carrying out the ceremony required the active participation of people with special skills, qualities, status, and spiritual power. This participation also helped the family to shoulder the tremendous financial burden imposed by the cost involved in celebrating a marriage. An old Jewish Yemenite proverb may be translated as "The marriage for two and the joy for thousands."

One characteristic trait of Jewish marriage was its timing early in life. Girls were married between the ages of five and fourteen; boys were thirteen to eighteen. According to a Jewish proverb of Yemen and Kurdistan, "When the girl receives her first menstrual period, the bread of her father's house is forbidden" to her. In other words, the girl should be married *before* that. In Kurdistan, however, Jews believed that the girl and her future sons would be in grave danger if she did not become engaged immediately *after* her first menstruation. As for the aims of such early marriage, it was hoped that the girl would "open her eyes" on her husband as soon as she became a woman and that she would never think of anyone else. Girls were never allowed to lose their virginity before marriage, which would dishonor their families. Youthful marriage, then, protected the girl from all sexual misbehavior and from its consequences. The economic factor was not an issue, however, because the young couple might live with the family of either side. The bride, still a child, was joined to her husband and educated beside him by her mother-in-law. The girl learned her husband's character, and those of the other members of his family, as well as respect for her parents-in-law. The ties between the husband and his wife, and those between the wife and her in-laws, were thus reinforced. Her education covered all aspects of life in the house, from the kitchen to decor. By the time the couple became independent, the change to their own home was harmonious and presented no apparent danger.

Fear of the girl's remaining "on the shelf"—sometimes she was considered a spinster at fifteen or sixteen—gave rise to a group of customs dedicated to the "acceleration" of the marriage, namely, rituals to ensure a girl's marriage. These formulas were current in all the regions of the Middle East and North Africa. In Kurdistan, for example, a mother would take her daughter out to the fields on Tu Be-Shvat and give her in marriage to a tree. After a few weeks she would return to the same place, and if the tree produced buds, it was a sign that the girl would soon marry. In Tunisia when the bride left the ritual bath, she would distribute her old clothes and some candies directly from her mouth to her unmarried friends. It was believed that each young woman receiving such candy or clothing would marry within the year, and the recipient of the bride's undergarments would be the first to marry.

In Kurdistan two weeks after the formulation of the terms of the marriage, the *kiddush erusin* (consecration of the betrothed) would take place. The women of the groom's family prepared rice and chicken, which they would send to the bride's home on a Tuesday. In Yemen where, as the proverb goes, "A man has nothing but his wedding day or the day of his death," intensive preparations would commence about two months before the wedding ceremony. In Marrakesh, Morocco, one month before the day of the wedding, on a Monday or a Thursday, in a ceremony called *fssala* (cutting of cloth), a piece of fabric sent by the groom's parents was cut in the presence of the women of the family, for preparing clothes for the bride. A similar ceremony was performed in Kurdistan. The women shouted cries of joy to bless the cutting of the cloth. That same day a *khamsa* (Arabic for hand, an amulet used to ward off evil spirits) was painted on the outer wall of the bride's house to announce the marriage. Its painter would also write a blessing and greetings of *mazal tov* (good luck), while neighbors and passersby gave him money and the women cried out in joy. Two weeks later a whole day was dedicated to preparing the young couple's mattress. The women sang and gave money to an upholsterer. They put a small bag with *harmel* (seed of *Peganum harmala*) and sugar inside the mattress. The *harmel* was for protection against spirits and the sugar to ensure that the bride would be sweet to her husband. The women danced and offered cookies and *mahia* to the guests.

One week before the wedding day, on a Thursday that Moroccan Jews called the "day of counting the seven days," the groom's mother would set off with her daughters, relatives, and other guests to visit the bride's family, bringing trays full of flour, henna, soap, shoes, dried fruits, and jewels as gifts. An amulet called the *srira,* containing *harmel,* was prepared that evening for the young couple and put around their wrists. From that day forward the bride and groom were not allowed to leave their houses except for certain ceremonies, during which they were never alone. On the following Saturday (called the Saturday of the Beginning in Morocco and Yemen), or *sebt erray,* the families prayed together in the synagogue and were invited for lunch by the bride's family. After the meal the friends of the bride, who was wearing her traditional *kiswah el-kebira* (the great wedding dress), would gather to admire her trousseau, which was displayed afterward to all the guests. The groom and his friends then arrived to visit the bride and her friends. In the evening the groom chose a group of five young men, called *islan,* or *zara,* to be his personal servants. The groom was raised to the status of sultan, and he appointed the vizier and other officials, the most important of whom was the treasurer. The groom, accompanied by the *islan,* would then return to the bride's house, where a big audience would await him to celebrate the ceremony called *asmomeg* (a word of unknown meaning). The groom's mother would present the bride's mother with a tray that held sugar, henna, a raw egg, some cloves, a mirror, and a piece of unbleached muslin, all covered with a scarf. In the presence of all the guests a young man (other than the groom) would take the egg and crack it over the bride's head while the women chanted. At this point a *tamezwara,* a happy mother of sons, would put the henna, the cloves, and the mirror on the bride's head, covering her hair with the muslin. The bride had to keep all this on her head until the next Tuesday night. In Salonika this night was called *almosama* (again, a term of unknown meaning).

The Jews of Kurdistan were known to celebrate the ceremony of *siney* on the Sunday before the wedding: the girls of both families would meet at the groom's house and prepare a large amount of rice while singing. Before dark they took trays with the rice and meat by procession to the bride's house, and bystanders along the way threw nuts and candies on the participants. An old woman standing on the roof of the house threw wheat on them upon their arrival while saying, "The evil eye shall split." The gifts were offered to the bride's mother, while the groom's parents danced before two young men bearing the gifts. Guests danced in the bride's room, after which the groom's and bride's mothers danced with mule saddles on their backs, holding cooking spoons (the meaning of this ceremony is unknown).

In Salonika the Sunday before the wedding was called the Day of the Ajuar (Day of the Dowry) or Day of the Preciadores (Day of the Evaluators). The bride's dowry was exhibited before many guests. Appraisers valued the beautiful objects, and this sum was included in the *ketubbah* (marriage contract), which was prepared on the *n'har shevua,* or Day of the Oath, which was the following Monday. Then the groom, his family, two scribes, and guests arrived at the bride's house to prepare the contract, and the rabbi extended a handkerchief to the couple, or, if they were still very young, it was held out to them by their fathers, who kept it taut at all four corners as a sign of obligation to uphold the terms of the *ketubbah*.

On Tuesday morning the groom's friends would adorn the room where the wedding ceremony was to take place and prepared the *talamon*, a raised platform with a kind of throne on which the couple would receive the marriage blessing on Wednesday. This day was also called Day of the Slaughter in Morocco, because a cow ready for slaughter was dressed in clothing resembling the bride's, with a handkerchief and jewels, and was paraded around the courtyard of the bride's house, while musicians played and the women cried out in happiness. The bride invited her friends for a meal, during which they lit incense and sprinkled the walls of the room with orange blossom water. Likewise, the groom would offer his friends a meal that day, or the next day, when he would give them each a small farewell gift.

On the Tuesday night, the eve of the wedding ceremony, the most auspicious ceremony of the entire marriage took place at the bride's house, the borrowed ceremony of the henna, which was the most purifying and prophylactic rite of Islamic marriage. During the ceremony the couple, along with members of their families and guests, were painted with designs in henna. Dressed in her beautiful wedding dress, called *keswa al-kbira* in Morocco, the bride would be seated on the *talamon* with her face covered. The groom's friends would escort him to her side, where he would be seated. The groom would then try to tread on the bride's toes as a sign of his dominance over the household. (Sometimes, she would tread on the groom's toes for the same reason.) The scene was dazzling: women adorned in their most beautiful finery and most expensive jewelry would shout joyfully while musicians played, interrupted only by the cries of the herald announcing the sums of money offered to the musicians by the guests. Late that night a family member painted the young couple's hands with henna, while the attendants sang. Guests also gladly extended their hands to be painted with henna.

Yemenite Jews on this day, or the previous one, celebrated the Day of the Adornment, which involved painting with henna and other pigments, as well as the adorning of the bride with splendid clothes and dazzling jewels. While the bride was being dressed, a woman serenaded her with love songs. This ceremony of adornment lasted for many hours and, if performed on a Monday, was continued on Tuesday. Recently wedded brides (within the previous six weeks) would attend the ceremony dressed in their own wedding dresses. After the ceremony of the henna, the young couple was taken before dawn to the *mikveh* for the ritual bath. The young bride was covered from head to toe with a sheet, so that no one would see her on the way to the *mikveh.* A group of women from both families accompanied the bride and cut her nails and shaved her body, according to tradition. Women from the groom's family brought *swaq* (walnut shells), henna, lapis lazuli, a comb, and a small mirror. They entered the bathhouse and placed lighted candles on the ground that were neither to be touched nor extinguished, as a protection against spirits. Before the bride was submerged in the bath, a woman would first throw into the room all the objects brought along by the group and then immerse herself. The bride was believed to be in great danger at that moment from the presence of her counterpart—*jinn* (a spirit born with the bride)—and the objects were offered to distract and appease such evil. After the bath the women had cakes and drinks and then accompanied the bride home, again without allowing anyone to see her en route. The groom took a similar bath in the company of his friends in the men's room and then immersed himself in the women's bath after the bride had left the building.

On Wednesday morning the women in the family and the bride's friends appeared at her house to dress and coif her while singing songs in her honor. The guests flocked to the house from the beginning of the afternoon. When the rabbi arrived, the couple would be waiting near the *talamon,* with two young men at their side holding candles. At a certain moment the bride and groom would try to be the first to sit on a chair placed on the *talamon.* Musicians had been playing incessantly since early morning. After reciting three blessings, the rabbi would take a glass of wine, drink from it, then give it to the young couple to drink. At the end of the ceremony the bride's and the groom's fathers and some honored guests guided the bride around the house seven times to keep spirits away. The men sang while the women sprinkled milk over the bride. The groom then returned to his parents' house accompanied by his friends. One hour later the bride arrived, carried on a chair or riding a mule. Her mother-in-law welcomed her with milk, sugar, and mint leaves. In certain regions the bride would also be given a raw egg, which she would break at the threshold of the house.

The Jews of Kurdistan accompanied the groom from the bathhouse to his home and then moved on in procession to the bride's home. In Zakho people would stand on the rooftops all along the way, crying out with joy. A man would head the procession and announce: "Women! None of you should sew or spin!" Then all the women stopped these activities, lest the groom be a failure and become impotent. As the procession passed by the houses of relatives and friends, the women would come outside and throw wheat on the groom's head and break a jug in front of him. In Amadiya men brandishing swords would dance in front of the procession, while a girl walking beside them burned incense, and several girls holding lighted candles circled the groom, chanting in his honor. The ceremony of the Seven Benedictions was usually held at the bride's house. When the rabbi read the *ketubbah*, the groom would put his right foot on the bride's left foot as a sign of his dominance over her. The rabbi asked the participants not to cast a particular spell on the couple, in a reference to a ritual (known in Morocco as *tqaf*) that was widespread in the Muslim world but also found in Europe; the spell was believed to "lock" the sexual organ of the bride, preventing her from having sexual intercourse and becoming pregnant, or of the groom, rendering him impotent. Many different formulas of *tqaf* were believed and feared by all. Moroccan Jews thought that if someone were to tie a knot or lock a cupboard or a box while pronouncing the name of the bride or groom, these actions would cast a dreaded spell on the young couple.

After the wedding ceremony the groom would be accompanied to his house, while the people sang, musicians played, and young men fired rifle shots into the air. The bride was then brought to him, riding on the back of an adorned mare. The procession did not go directly to the groom's house but passed through many streets, where women standing on rooftops would welcome the bride with cries of joy. Women of the families threw wheat and nuts over the bride and broke a glass in front of the mare. The mother-in-law would do the same when the bride finally arrived at her house and would then smear the bride's feet with honey to render her blessed and sweet. After a festive meal the groom would enter the wedding room, where the bride awaited him. He would ask her for a glass of water, and if she had not been warned by her parents not to hand the glass to him but to put it near him, he would let the glass fall as a sign of domination. The guests would then leave the room, and the groom would close the door, an act known as *el encierro* (the encirclement) among the Sephardic Jews of Salonika. If the bride was past the age of consent (past puberty), her mother had advised her about sex; the groom's friends instructed him on what he must do. After the first act of sexual intercourse, the groom would open the door so that all could see the sheet stained with blood, the proof of the bride's virginity. The women would then shout with joy; however, if no such signs of virginity appeared, the whole family would be dishonored. For seven days, or for longer periods in some communities, the couple was not allowed to leave the house.

The first Saturday after the wedding was known as the Saturday of the Groom. In Salonika it was called *el sabba de talamo.* That morning the young man was accompanied in procession to the synagogue, where he was given the honor of reading the Torah. He went outside to the courtyard of the temple while holding the Torah scroll and circled a cistern with it in order to influence the couple's fertility. On the eighth day after the wedding, a Wednesday called *el dia del pescado* (the day of the fish), the groom was permitted to leave the house for the first time. Accompanied by friends and musicians, he set off to market to buy fish. Then, still in procession, the group would visit the bride's parents, who would give the groom money, sugar, and a rug. Upon his return the newlyweds would hold a contest in the presence of guests. Each would be given a fish and a knife, and it was said that the one who successfully opened the fish first would be the dominant personality in the household. Moroccan Jews called the second Saturday after the wedding the Saturday of the Regret. The groom's friends gathered at his house and, in the presence of both families and many guests, criticized him for having married. His task was then to ardently defend the advantages of marriage over celibacy. In Yemen this Saturday was called *al-juliya,* and the bride's friends, women in the family, and other invited female guests arrived in the afternoon to dress her up in beautiful clothes provided by her in-laws.

The third Saturday after the wedding was known as the Saturday of the Swing by the Jews of Morocco, where the bride, her friends, and other invited women would gather in the yard. A swing was set up, and the bride would take the first turn, followed by the others. An elderly woman or the mother of the bride would praise the bride's beauty in song, referring to parts of her body. A similar melody would be sung by the Jews of Iraq. In Yemen this day was called the Saturday of the Visit, when the bride's family paid the young couple a visit. The fourth Saturday was called the Saturday of the Adornment, when the wedding ornaments of the bride, prepared on Friday, were used to adorn her on that Saturday afternoon. The fifth Saturday was known as the Last Saturday, when guests came to bid the young couple farewell. The last day of the marriage period, called *tornaboda* (return of the wedding) in Morocco, was the day when the bride would go for the first time to take a ritual bath.

MOURNING CUSTOMS AND RITES

Death, especially when it comes suddenly and tragically, has always been a startling and incomprehensible event in human life. Its mystery was even more puzzling to humans than the secret of fertility. Few cultures consider death to be the absolute end of life. The idea of life after death not only permits us to confront the frightening and absolute certainty that we will one day disappear but also provides a way for us to integrate a particular death into the social and cultural system in which it occurs. Jewish communities developed funeral rites partly from an intricate and ancient tradition—based on the Bible, the Talmud, and all the interpretations and commentaries that have enriched Jewish tradition—and partly from long-term exposure to surrounding cultures.

According to a Moroccan Jewish proverb, "Death within the family is a joy," which relates to a complex ritual practiced there by Sephardic and Middle Eastern Jews. This ritual, practiced only when death occurred at home, was deemed necessary for the eternal rest of the deceased and absorption into the next world and for a good relationship with the mourners. A dying person would make preparations—by washing his hands, putting on his prayer shawl, and reciting the *vidui* (confession) in the presence of a minyan (a group of ten Jewish men). The family would approach the death bed to receive a blessing from the sick relative. Candles were lit around the room to ward off spirits. Once death had occurred, the windows of the room were briefly opened to allow Providence to enter and lift the soul from the dead body. The corpse was sometimes left on the bed for nearly an hour with its face covered; the body was then laid on the floor, a piece of wood supporting the head, the feet pointed toward the door, and covered with a sheet. The Jews of Salonika would remove all water containers from the sick room during the agony of death and, after death, poured out all the water in the house and from the three neighboring houses. They believed that the Angel of Death used this water to rinse his sword.

In most communities the cleansing and washing (*taharah*) of the corpse would be taken care of by the Hevrah Kadishah (burial society), although sometimes, for example, in Yemen, there was no such society and this task could be performed by any person of the community. The body, still clothed, was first washed. This would be followed, in North Africa and other communities, by the ceremony of the Arba Mitot Bet Din (four forms of capital punishment—stoning, burning, beheading, and throttling), symbolic gestures performed to prevent the pious from undergoing such pain at the entrance to heaven. A member of the Hevrah Kadishah "stoned" the body with three or seven small stones; laid a candle on the deceased's back or burned the fingernails; passed a knife over the deceased, representing beheading; and staged throttling with a sheet. During each act of simulated punishment society members recited prayers and eulogies. Because they were forbidden to pronounce the divine name Adonai during the entire purification procedure, they used the term *ha-Shem* (the Name) instead. Then they wrapped the body in a white linen shroud sewn earlier by women members of the Hevrah Kadishah. In Morocco and other places sewing the shroud was a ceremony in its own right, accompanied by singing and dancing and ending in a festive meal held in an atmosphere of joy and celebration. In Libya, if the deceased's wife was pregnant, she would pass under the coffin in the presence of all the mourners before the coffin left the house.

Immediately before the funeral, a member of the Hevrah Kadishah would tear an outer garment of the mourners. This act, known as *keri*ᶜ*ah* (tearing), was accompanied by this blessing: "Blessed be Thou, O Lord, the righteous Judge," which all Jews still practice today.

Mourning was divided into three successive periods, the first, lasting seven days (shivah); the second, thirty days; and the third, eleven months. During the shivah the mourners were not allowed to leave their houses. In some communities the mourners were not permitted to do any cooking during the shivah, and visitors would bring them food. The women in mourning, especially the widow, and sometimes professional mourners, performed lamentations during the shivah; they sang dirges about the deceased and the misfortune of the family. The women in mourning cried and screamed their sorrow in a moving ceremony, sometimes scratching their faces, a practice known from the time of the Bible but forbidden to Jews. Today a common and widespread practice during the shivah is the veiling of the mirrors in the house of mourning or turning them against the wall. This is done in the belief that if the spirit of the deceased is allowed to look at itself, it will never leave the house.

At the end of each mourning period the deceased is commemorated in a ceremony of prayers and sermons, followed by a *se*ᶜ*udah* (meal) for the family and friends.

THE ANNUAL CYCLE OF HOLIDAYS AND COMMEMORATIONS

The passage of time in daily life is rhythmical, with the marking in the calendar of special days, as distinguished from normal days. These special days have been fixed by halakhah (Jewish law), as well as by the continuous and rich tradition of customs and beliefs related to the local environment. The yearly cycle of the Jews of North Africa and the Middle East therefore reflects the combination of general Jewish socioreligious concepts and deep-rooted links with an indigenous reality steeped in imagination and folklore. This annual calendar has religious, national, and mystic features; it expresses the general Jewish tradition in relationship to the reality that characterizes the group.

Many communities considered Purim a symbol of the miraculous salvation of the Jewish people. The Talmud teaches Jews to recite a special thanksgiving benediction when returning to the place where someone was miraculously saved from danger. A custom evolved whereby Jewish families and communities celebrated the anniversary of their salvation with a special Purim. This celebration had a ritual similar to that of Purim and included the reading of a scroll relating the story of the personal or communal salvation. Jewish communities of the Middle East and North Africa held more than one hundred special Purims; they were known by the term *Purim,* followed by the name of the community or special event.

The festival of Passover (Pesach) was, no doubt, a pivotal point of intense popular activity connected with Eretz Israel, as illustrated by several specific examples. In Iraq, Kurdistan, Greece, and North Africa a kind of theatrical play was presented to the family on the night of the seder. The father and/or youngsters (in Kurdistan) disguised themselves as nomads, wearing ragged clothes and carrying a stick, on the end of which was attached a matzo wrapped in a bundle. They knocked at the door, begging to be let inside. A dialogue would then ensue between the newcomers and the other guests:

GUESTS: Who are you and where do you come from?
BEGGARS: I am a Jew and I come from Egypt
GUESTS: Where are you going?
BEGGARS: To Jerusalem.

After the dialogue the father would recount the whole tale of the Exodus from Egypt.

Greek Jews made the symbolic food *haroset* from the five fruits—apples, nuts, figs, raisins and dates—mentioned in the Song of Songs, which is chanted at Passover. The intense need for exiled Jews to remember the Holy Land and to identify with its destiny led them to practice rituals that substantiated this link. For example, in Kurdistan at the fast of Tishah-b'Ab, youngsters played games involving dust and ashes, in remembrance of the destruction of the Temple in Jerusalem. In Morocco the meal served before and after the fast of Tishah-b'Ab consisted of lentils and hard-boiled eggs, similar to the menu served to mourners during the shivah. Some Moroccan Jews used to dip the hard-boiled egg in ash instead of salt. The lights in the synagogue remained unlit, the benches were upturned, and the congregants seated themselves on the ground. In addition, the *parokhet* was turned up, and a few ashes were thrown over the Torah scroll and over the heads of those praying. In the Jewish quarter old women would get together and move in procession through the streets, chanting dirges in memory of the destruction of the Temple.

An examination of the customs and beliefs of Middle Eastern Jews related to the holidays brings to light many ancient customs that have been preserved. In Djerba, for instance, on the day after Yom Kippur, called the Day of the Cohens' Joy, the *kohanim* of the island do not work and consider this day a holiday, in memory of the festive meal that the high priest offered on that day in Jerusalem.

An important and prominent characteristic of the Jewish holidays in the Middle East and North Africa concerned the practice of special rituals as an integral part of the traditional religious commemorations. In Libya, on the eve of Rosh Hodesh Nisan, called *leil al-bsisa,* the mother prepared a sweet porridge of wheat, barley, and other ingredients; the family would gather, and each member had to eat from the porridge. They practiced the same ritual when they entered a new house. Libyan Jews do not know the significance of this custom but say it will bring them good luck for the entire year. It is not known whether this ritual is related to a ceremony widespread among the Muslims in North Africa, when they present a newborn baby to the spirits of the house and offer them a meal called *bsisa.* The Muslims also carried out the same ritual on entering a new house. The Jews of Greece believed that the Passover *afikomen* had a special power to protect the house from attack by evil spirits. That is why they hung pieces of this special matzo in various places around the house. Before the eve of the next Passover, they burned the old *afikomen,* then substituted it with the new one, once it had served its ritual function at the seder. During the seder the water that the father poured into the bowl while reading about the ten plagues was called "water of the plagues" by the North African Jews. They considered this water highly dangerous and sometimes used it to thwart enemies by throwing it on the walls of an enemy's house.

Several commemorations are particularly characteristic of certain communities, such as the "sabbath Jethro" of the Tunisian Jews, the Sehrane of the Kurdish Jews, and the Mimuna of the Moroccan Jews. At Pesach in the spring and at Sukkoth in the fall, the Jews of Kurdistan, who were scattered in tiny communities in a mountainous region, used to get together to celebrate the Sehrane in a predetermined location. There they would spend some days in a pleasant atmosphere. In some places additional local Sehrane were performed by youngsters at Shavuot and Hanukkah. Moroccan Jews still celebrate the Mimuna on the day after Passover. In the evening before they prepare a feast at each house, the women wear their beautiful clothes and jewels, and guests go from house to house to taste the delicacies prepared for this day. The next day the families continue the holiday outside, in natural surroundings. This celebration, characterized by elements of hospitality, visits, costumes, songs, camping out, and the like, is an expression of a custom also celebrated by other communities, including the Sephardic people of Eretz Israel, who adorned their tables on the last day of Passover with greenery, prepared delicacies, lit oil lamps under which some silver coins were laid, and went to the meadow to pick green heads of barley. With these sheaves they would beat one another while saying a blessing: "May your year be green."

PILGRIMAGE AND *ZADDIK* VENERATION

Pilgrimage and *zaddik* veneration play an important role in the daily life of some Jews. Two types of activity characterize the veneration of *zaddikim* (the righteous) among the Jews in the countries of the Middle East and North Africa (excluding Eretz Israel). One focal point is the link to the *zaddikim* of the Holy Land as expressed by the pilgrimage to Eretz Israel and by the celebration of the *hillula* (festival to celebrate the anniversary of the death of a righteous person)—mainly those of Rabbi Shimon Bar-Yohai and of Rabbi Meir Baal Ha-Nes. Another focal point finds expression in the worship of local *zaddikim*, a phenomenon prominent in North Africa but also found in Iraq, Iran, and some other locations, although in a less conspicuous form.

In Iraq seventeen holy tombs are known; twelve are tombs of biblical figures, one is related to the Temple, two are from the Talmudic period, and two are of local popular *zaddikim*. In Morocco 656 *zaddikim* have been identified, twenty-five of whom are women. These figures have no parallel in any other Jewish center in the Diaspora. Again, North Africa has traditions linking the *zaddikim* to the Land of Israel; almost 20 percent of all male Jewish *zaddikim* known in Morocco are believed to have been originally from Eretz Israel.

In order to understand the continuity of the link of the different communities from the Mediterranean area to the *zaddikim* in Israel today, one must study the importance of particular phenomena within their countries of origin and examine the complex network of *zaddik* veneration and its influence on the flock of believers. It is clear that North Africa in general, and Morocco in particular, are areas in which the intensity and scope of *zaddik* veneration have no parallel in other countries. One of the most intriguing and fascinating questions in popular *zaddik* veneration relates to the emergence of *zaddikim*, in other words, to the process by which a *zaddik*, either while living or after death, is consecrated by the believers. It is worth pointing out that in North Africa most of the *zaddikim* became objects of veneration after their death, and only a small number were recognized as such during their lifetimes. The main process by which a *zaddik* comes into existence, either in life or after death, is the performance of "miracles" associated primarily with the curing of illness and the salvation of individuals or an entire community. Yet the supernatural power of the *zaddikim* may also manifest through other deeds. In addition, a *zaddik* may be recognized as such by exemplary personal behavior, exceptional erudition, revelation through a dream, or by an extraordinary event that occurs at the time of death or burial. For instance, intensive study of the Torah, above all with Elijah the Prophet, would be a distinguishing mark.

North African Jews had three types of *zaddikim*. Of them, the vast majority were local *zaddikim*, buried near a small village and known to and venerated only by the inhabitants of that village; their graves were visited frequently, usually every Friday, by a small number of villagers who also celebrated the *hillula* in their honor on the anniversaries of their death. The second type acquired the status of municipal or regional *zaddikim* and were venerated by Jews from several neighboring villages or a whole city, such as Rabbi Eliyahu in Casablanca or Rabbi Hananiah Ha-Cohen in Marrakesh. The third type, recognized as national *zaddikim*, were few but venerated by all Jews of the country, who would flock to their tombs throughout the year and particularly for the annual *hillula* in their honor.

The relationship between a *zaddik* and his followers is complex, sometimes ambivalent. Veneration, blind faith, respect, awe, fear, and total compliance are coupled with haggling, disagreement, and even menacing threats. Well aware of the sensitivities of the *zaddikim*, their disciples are careful not to offend them; followers believe that any offense, even if committed inadvertently, will be punished. A living *zaddik* may grant forgiveness upon receiving a contribution and a dead *zaddik* upon receiving offerings of olive oil, candles, or a ritual meal or after the ritual slaughter of an animal near his tomb. People particularly attached to a *zaddik*, usually after the *zaddik* has performed some special deed on their behalf, consider themselves as the *zaddik's* "slave," so the relationship may reach a personal status of exclusive servitude and loyalty.

In North Africa such elements of the natural world as trees, bushes, stones, rocks, boulders, springs, waterfalls, rivers, caves, and mountains are associated with both Jewish and Muslim *zaddikim* in one way or another. Dreams play an important role in the relationship between *zaddikim* and followers. A *zaddik* may appear in a dream to someone visiting the *zaddik's* shrine or sleeping at home.

The attachment of a Jewish family to a given *zaddik* is expressed in several ways: by calling its name in times of distress, lighting candles in its honor, visiting its grave regularly, or, if the grave is too far away, visiting a synagogue bearing its name or the grave of another *zaddik* in the vicinity. However, none of these rites and rituals can compare in intensity and significance with the *hillula,* usually held on the anniversary of the *zaddik's* death or, in the case of several national *zaddikim*, either on Lag b^cOmer or in the months of Elul and Tishri, toward the end of summer. The *hillula* is the climax of the sacred activities connected with *zaddik* worship and attracts thousands to the *zaddik's* shrine. After extensive preparations at home, the pilgrims start their journey to the *zaddik's* grave, often making brief stops to visit the tombs of other *zaddikim* along the way. Upon arrival at the holy place the visitors prepare themselves for a stay of a week or more. The most privileged live in rooms built especially for this purpose, and the others pitch tents with the assistance of the committee responsible for the arrangements at the holy site. After the initial preparations are completed, the pilgrims visit the shrine or tomb to pay homage. The mass celebration includes many rituals and ceremonies: people recite prayers, read Psalms, sing and dance near the grave, light candles, slaughter animals, and offer a festive *se^cudah* in the *zaddik's* honor. It is also customary to give a boy his first haircut at the *zaddik's* grave, and sometimes bar mitzvah ceremonies are held there.

Many practices at the *zaddik's* shrine are associated with folk medicine. People leave bottles of water or olive oil, jewels, coins, and other objects at the tomb overnight, to receive the *zaddik's* sanctity. Barren women leave a belt on the tomb for the same reason. Streamers, ribbons, threads, and hairs are hung on the branches of trees growing nearby the grave as votive offerings. The insane, blind, paralytics, and epileptics are roped or chained to the grave or to a nearby tree for the whole night, and young sick children are put to sleep on the tomb, in the hope of their being healed.

A most important ceremony held at the holy shrine is the dramatic ritual slaughter of chickens, lambs, goats, or cattle. Another is the public auction and sale of candles and glasses in the *zaddik's* name; a large number of pilgrims gather for the auction, and the highest bidder is accorded the great honor of purchasing the first candle or the first glass. The ceremony is accompanied by cries of joy, singing, and dancing. In these moments of intense prayer and ecstasy, the hope for an immediate miracle reaches its climax. Many signs are believed to indicate that the *zaddik* has accepted the worshipers' requests, including the appearance of the *zaddik* in person or in the form of an animal, usually a dove or snake; the appearance of the *zaddik's* image in the flames of the bonfire; water miraculously emanating from the tomb; a pillar of fire descending from the heavens; or the appearance of the *zaddik* in a dream to a worshiper sleeping near the grave.

Worshipers find the *hillula* an unforgettable experience; it includes the preparations in advance of the pilgrimage, participation with a large number of other pilgrims in the ceremonies at the holy place, the many prayers and praises to the *zaddik*, and the continuous recounting of miracles. All these contribute to an atmosphere imbued with holiness that leads to an almost physical contact with the *zaddik* and to the purification of the pilgrim's soul. The pilgrims then return home with their faith in the *zaddik* strengthened as a result of knowing that others share their faith and their awareness of the *zaddik's* greatness and protective power.

The weak and scattered Jewish minority in Morocco saw in its *zaddikim* an important safeguard against the strong and sometimes hostile Muslim majority. Through the *zaddikim* individual Jews as well as whole communities were protected from Muslim threats. The Jews' intensive veneration of *zaddikim* did not cease with their emigration to Israel; before leaving Morocco, many believers took pains to say farewell to the *zaddikim*. Some, mainly those who performed a role at the shrines, did not regard themselves as free to leave the country but waited and yearned for a sign from the *zaddikim*, most commonly in the form of a dream.

The detailed observation of the holidays and commemorations of any society calls for an examination of the concepts that concern the essence of human existence and the reality linked thereto. A society's worldview and perspective on the cosmos find expression in the yearly and life cycles of the group, with the social order and the cosmic order coming together in their own sense of perfection. "In each and every generation it is a man's duty to regard himself as though he went forth out of Egypt." This quotation from the Hagadah is intended not only to evoke the flight from Egypt but to create the continuous bond between the modern Passover and the original Passover of the days of Moses. This means that the deed of today has value as long as it can be linked to the original deed, which constituted a model for the future and thus represents proof of continuity, with its unquestioned strength.

The mode of practicing the holidays and festivals—the intense anticipation, the preparations, the enthusiasm and joy in the celebration of the holiday itself, and the complete identification with the values of Jewish tradition—clearly strengthened the Jews in their day-to-day battle with the environment. A Muslim proverb of Morocco says that the Christians spend their money in court, the Jews on their holidays, and the Muslims on weddings. The yearly and life cycles of the Jews in the Mediterranean area express the same valid approach, with regard to both written and oral tradition. This approach is carried through to completion by the interaction of each group with its surrounding culture. In each country Jewish popular tradition resulted from a blend of religious ideology, the influence of local customs, and mysticism, as well as the communal life shared with their local neighbors.

RECOMMENDED READING

Ben-Ami, Issachar. *Saint Veneration Among the Jews in Morocco.* Detroit: Wayne State University Press, 1998.

——, ed. *The Sephardi and Oriental Jewish Heritage.* Jerusalem: Magnes Press, 1982.

Goldberg, Harvey E. *Sephardi and Middle Eastern Jewries.* Bloomington: Indiana University Press, 1996.

Stillman, Yedida K. and Norman A. Stillman, eds., *From Iberia to Diaspora: Studies in Sephardic History and Culture.* Leiden, Netherlands: E. J. Brill, 1998.

CHAPTER

11

Material Culture

Esther Juhasz

The material culture of Jewish communities—their manufactured objects, from day-to-day utensils and ritual objects to architecture—provides ample evidence that they had an ongoing dialogue with the larger gentile community and various degrees of symbiosis with it. Jews adopted many elements of the local lifestyle. They lived in similar houses, used the same furniture, wore similar costumes, and ate similar food. And if one compares the material culture of different Jewish groups—whether Yemenites, Moroccans, Iraqis, or Libyans—one can fairly say that it is closer to the material culture of their country of residence than to that of other Jewish groups.

Two major factors act as unifying agents in Middle Eastern and North African communities in the nineteenth and twentieth centuries, creating some traits common to diverse local cultures: these Jewish communities lived within Islamic society and culture, where they were a protected minority, and the Jewish communities were affected by modernization. External circumstances as well as Jewish factors determined the diversity of Jewish local culture. External circumstances included the raw materials available, local technologies and artistic styles. In some societies Jews participated in the production of the local material culture, working as craftsmen or artisans, at times side by side with non-Jewish workers. For example, they produced metal inlay work in Damascus, metal thread, embroidery, and leather products in Morocco. Also, non-Muslims usually worked in gold and silver in Islamic societies because the Qur'an prohibited work with precious metals (with certain exceptions, by the Islamic Hadith tradition). As a result Yemen, Kurdistan, Persia, and Iraq had many Jewish and Christian goldsmiths and silversmiths.

In some places Jews were influential in shaping segments of the local material culture, because Jews were the main practitioners of some crafts. As they left in the mass emigration to Israel of the 1950s, these crafts were no longer practiced in the same manner. Such was the case of the Jewish jewelers of Yemen, who provided wares for both Jews and non-Jews, and the Jewish weavers in Kurdistan, who wove rugs and hangings, sometimes for the local district governors. Jews often bought items designed for general use and modified them so that they could be used in a Jewish context, such as decorated mirror covers used as Torah breastplates in Turkey (figure 34).

External factors that played a role in shaping Jewish lifestyle included the restrictions of *dhimmi* status. Laws and restrictions were designed to differentiate the Muslim population from nonbelievers, such as by dress; these go back to the Pact of Umar of the early centuries of Islam—the pact guaranteed the *dhimmi* security and protection, and they in turn promised the Muslim ruler, among other things, not to resemble the Muslims in any way with regard to dress. The laws also restricted the building of new synagogues. Internal Jewish factors that created differentiation from the surrounding culture were based on Jewish law, halakhah. Halakhic rules regulated everyday life, including matters connected to material culture, such as *sha^{c}atnez* (prohibition against mixing linen and wool) rules, kashruth (dietary laws), and the wearing of a fringed garment by men; as formulated in the standard code of Jewish law, the *Shulhan Arukh,* Orthodox Jews throughout the world adhere to these practices. The varying interpretations of the halakhah and its adaptation to local and temporal circumstances, created the custom (*minhag*)—the specific way in which each regulation is fulfilled. Therefore, practicing such customs in conjunction with local circumstances created a variety of material expressions of the same religious laws, and each material expression reflected its respective period and milieu.

In the Middle East and North Africa the wider customs encompass many communities and include the Sephardic tradition common to Jews whose ancestors arrived in the region after the expulsions from Spain in the fifteenth century and thereafter. Iberian customs therefore are found in North Africa, the Balkans, Turkey, Syria, and Egypt, alongside other broad traditions such as the Babylonian in Iraq. Many local Jewish traditions were practiced in isolated areas such as the Atlas Mountains in Morocco. For example, any Jewish wedding would have a *huppah* (bridal canopy), but custom and time-honored traditions determine its shape and the objects associated with it. The Sephardic *huppah* is a boothlike structure, with a seat for the bride and groom called *talamo* or *talamon,* made of lavish fabrics. Made from locally available textiles, it stood during the seven days of the marriage festivities, while the actual marriage ceremony, the *nissu'in,* was performed under a tallith held over the bride and groom. Another example is the marriage contract (*ketubbah*), an indispensable component of every Jewish wedding that is decorated in Sephardic and Middle Eastern communities. Each town often evolved its own tradition of decorating *ketubbahs*, even within a wider cultural tradition. In general, traditions reflect local artistic styles, but sometimes they preserve older iconographic or stylistic traits (see figure 21). For example, a horseshoe arch frames marriage contracts from both North Africa and the Ottoman Empire. In North Africa it reflected contemporary local architectural forms, whereas in the Ottoman Empire it was only an echo of the medieval Islamic culture in Spain preserved in memory and in art. Jewish local customs produced particular objects, such as the mezuzah cover prevalent in Morocco; according to halakhah, every Jewish house has a mezuzah affixed to the doorpost. Tiny parchment scrolls with the required Torah verses are enclosed in these small protective cases, which are often decorated. In Morocco mezuzahs have a flat cover that is either embroidered with metal threads or is made of cut metal. According to local Moroccan custom, in addition to the name of God, the mezuzah cover bears the name of the woman owner of the house, who usually brought it as a bride to her new home.

Throughout the nineteenth century various aspects of material culture expressed the process of modernization. Both non-Jews and Jews made selective changes in costume, interior decor, and the economic profile of the community. The material aspects of modernization were those immediately visible. In some cases they attested to deeper changes within the social norms, values, and mentalities; in other cases they were only superficial, an imitation of expected manners and forms. Modernization differed in pace and manner in the various communities. In some societies it became part of the entire surrounding culture; in others Jews were catalysts for modernization. In central urban communities modernization began in the second half of the nineteenth century or even earlier. In remote rural communities—as in Yemen, Kurdistan, parts of Libya, and the Atlas Mountains of Morocco—the Jews adhered to their traditional modes of life well into the twentieth century, many of them until their mass emigration to Israel.

Throughout the Ottoman Empire the government instigated modernization through the Tanzimat reforms of the nineteenth century. Westernization came in through many other channels as well. Trade with Europe had brought into the urban centers an increased flow of foreign goods. A class of Jewish merchants took part in these activities; major towns like Aleppo and Izmir had communities of foreign residents called Francos, who conducted trade with Europe and lived a European lifestyle, imitated by the local communities. A network of schools, especially those of the Alliance Israélite Universelle (AIU), was a major constituent in changing lifestyles, home decoration, costume, and norms of cleanliness. The schools also strove to change the economic profile of the communities, to eliminate traditional professions in favor of modern crafts that used modern tools and equipment. Although many believe that modernization brought a uniform lifestyle and eliminated differences, this is only partly true. For instance, the AIU schools introduced contemporary French culture, but other channels brought other versions of modernity. The casting off of traditional culture took many forms, and despite the uniform fashions in clothing, home textiles, and furniture that swept through the region, in every community or locale a variant of modernity emerged to accommodate the prevailing fashions. Sometimes an old custom disappeared together with the objects connected with it; in other cases a custom prevailed while the objects changed. For example, the custom of bringing a dowry and of displaying a bride's trousseau before the wedding, which was widespread in many communities, did not cease, whereas the contents of the trousseau changed with the new fashions in clothes and linen. Conversely, some objects continued to exist but changed their function.

Specific illustrations of material culture that demonstrate common traits and differentiation are costume, synagogue architecture and decoration, and ritual objects.

COSTUME

Costume in any society, traditional or modern, is an expression of social and personal norms and values. As a whole, traditional costume and its constituent parts transmit messages regarding the economic and social class of the wearer, as well as occupation, ethnoreligious affiliation, and marital status. Traditional society attributes great social significance to modes of dress; it is less a matter of personal taste and more a part of society's rules of etiquette regarding taste and modesty. Traditional wear is perceived as part of a venerated tradition that has to pass unchanged from one generation to the next, an external embodiment of religious, ethnic, and social rules. The essence of modern clothing is the introduction of novelties and the changing of fashion every season. Although it seems that traditional costume does not change, in the course of time changes infiltrate through various channels, and even a costume that seems to be unchanged for generations does change gradually.

In the Islamic world the Pact of Umar required that all non-Muslims had to be distinguished by their external appearance—by their clothing, the external manifestation of the lower legal status of "nonbelievers." This distinction had far-reaching legal and social implications, and it served as a tool for the continuation of legal and social hierarchies; it was the conceptual guideline to the restrictions imposed by rulers who had varied interests and power in various parts of the Muslim world. Government decrees and restrictions imposed the costume distinction on the population but did not dictate entire outfits; the decrees dealt mainly with colors, quality, and sometimes particular components of dress, such as headdress or shoes.

Nonbelievers were supposed to wear dark colors, such as black, dark blue, or dark brown; some places had specific colors for Christians and others for Jews. Green was reserved for Muslims because it is the holy color of Islam, and white turbans were the prerogative of Muslims. The nonbelievers had to restrict themselves to simpler and less expensive fabrics in their dress and had to wear smaller turbans and less ample gowns. These restrictions were by no means uniform in all Islamic countries, and they were imposed differently, depending on local circumstances and on the relationship of the minority community with the local ruler or with the surrounding population. Jews did not necessarily regard wearing a costume with distinguishing features as a humiliating discrimination, for it was also recommended by the rabbis, following the biblical injunction "nor shall you follow their laws" (Lev. 18:3).

Jewish communities issued sumptuary regulations that echoed the humility or modesty imposed by government authorities. Aimed mainly at women's attire, these regulations prohibited the wearing in public of luxurious clothes such as gold-embroidered gowns and opulent jewelry. Jews in non-Islamic lands also issued sumptuary regulations. Their purposes were twofold: to avoid arousing jealousy among non-Jews, and to avoid internal tensions between rich and poor within Jewish communities. Despite the importance attributed to visible distinction, identifying signs of the Jewish costume were in many cases expressed in a code recognized or understood only by the locals and nuanced in a way not noticed by outsiders. For example, in Yemen the embroidered leggings of women's trousers convey a whole array of messages, some known to the whole society and some only to a close circle of people; the embroidery communicates geographical and ethnoreligious affiliation, social status, marital status, and age group and the periodic ritual impurity of the woman in the time of her menses. Sometimes symbolic meanings were attributed to parts of dress, mainly as *zekher la-hurban* (remembrance of the destruction of the Temple), such as the black color of men's dress in Morocco. Although the authorities imposed this color, it gained an internal interpretation. Similarly, in Yemen the black pearls in the headdress of the Jewish bride of San^ca also evoked the destruction of the Temple, as did the deliberately incomplete hem of the men's dress. Parts of a costume or certain motifs in costume and jewelry were believed to have protective powers, some of which were shared by the surrounding population, such as the fish motif, but some were particular to Jews, such as Jewish symbols or inscriptions. In Turkey amulets embroidered on head scarves worn by Jewish women in childbirth were inscribed with names to protect the mother and the baby. In Iran, Bukhara, and Afghanistan Jewish women wore a sequin-embroidered tulle scarf bearing the Magen David (Star of David) for their marriage ceremony, or the scarf bore inscriptions such as the Hebrew *Mazal Tov* or the names of the bride and groom or the hand motif (the *khamsa*).

When Middle Eastern societies modernized, costume was one of the visible signs of this process. The change in costume was not merely a change in style, for it involved a change in attitude toward aesthetic norms, boundaries between groups, and religion. Some parts of the Jewish communities welcomed this change of costume from traditional to modern, but it aroused some opposition as well. Some saw modernization in dress as a manifestation of secularization, or at least some irreligious implications, and the opposition to it was mainly on religious grounds (though the opposition was much less fierce than that of some nineteenth-century Eastern European rabbis to that process). In certain Middle Eastern circles of traditional Jewish society opposed to modernization, the opinion prevailed that changing one's mode of dress was an act of apostasy. This feeling was expressed by the most prominent rabbi of Ottoman Izmir, Rabbi Hayyim Palaggi (1788–1868), who objected to the elimination of differences between Jews and non-Jews that was brought about by modernization of dress; he believed that Jews had to willingly distinguish themselves from non-Jews through dress, reasoning that if Jews dressed like non-Jews, in modern dress, they would imitate the ways of non-Jews or those of the Jews of the European Enlightenment.

In most Islamic countries traditional urban men's attire was rather uniform for Jews and non-Jews alike. It had several common components that were worn with certain variations in the whole region. Jews could sometimes be recognized by the colors or materials worn and sometimes by their beard and side locks of hair. The most significant part of the costume worn by both Muslims and Jews was a cap, usually with a turban wound around it.

The turbans varied in their materials, colors, the length of the fabric, the volume of the turban, and the way it was wound around the cap. Jews usually wore a small turban. In Yemen, Jewish men wore a checkered cloth over a small felt cap; in Bukhara only Muslims wore the turban, and Jews had to wear a fur hat.

In Turkey, Syria, Lebanon, Eretz Israel, Egypt, and Iraq the male urban costume consisted of an inner robe with a diagonally cut overlapping front part made of a variety of fabrics, such as a striped satin weave. Sometimes a man wore a matching waistcoat over it. The robe was held by a sash, or girdle, folded and wrapped around the man's waist; its fold held money, tobacco, or a pen case. The man wore an outer cloak, often of felted wool, atop the robe (figure 22). Ottoman rabbis wore a similar costume with a special wider cloak and a larger turban (see figure 25). Like functionaries from other religions, the *hakham bashi* (chief rabbi) appointed by the Ottoman government received with his written appointment a ceremonial mantle embroidered with metal thread. In Morocco, Jews had to wear cloaks in dark colors, the djellaba was black and made of material coarser than that worn by non-Jews. A law also regulated the quality and color of shoes. In the Ottoman Empire only Muslims could wear a certain kind of yellow boot, while Jews and Christians had to wear dark shoes. In some places in Morocco, Jews had to walk barefoot in the Muslim quarter or in front of the mosque.

In several nonurban regions of Morocco typical local attire prevailed, such as the hooded cloak, the burnoose (see figure 2). A type of burnoose was the *akhnif*, a richly decorated gown worn in a region of the Atlas Mountains. There, Jews were allowed to don this gown only inside out, the decorated part inside, but they would fold the hems over the shoulders so that some of the decoration could be seen. In Yemen the men wore a rectangular shawl over their clothes; Jewish men had four fringes attached to the corners of these shawls, thus adhering to the biblical injunction (Num. 15:38) to wear fringes on one's clothes. While in most Jewish communities the fringed garment (tallith) evolved into an independent ritual garment (and the *tallith katan* that was worn under the outer garment), in Yemen men wore the fringed garment as part of the outer costume, as inscribed in the Bible. In Kurdistan, Jewish men wore the typical Kurdish outfit—the wide trousers and short jacket (see figure 24)—with the heavy turban; they had no distinguishing signs on their clothing.

In areas under Ottoman rule modernization in men's costume was decreed through the Tanzimat reforms of the midnineteenth century, for example, the abolishment of the variety of turbans and the introduction of the fez as a replacement (see figure 22). The reforms of 1856 eliminated, theoretically, the need to distinguish between Muslims and others through clothing. Although opinions differ as to the degree of compliance with these decrees throughout the empire, in Istanbul European dress became an alternative mode of dress. The transition to European attire happened most quickly in the high merchant class, which had direct connections to Europe. It produced different mixes of traditional and Western costume, such as the baggy trousers (*shalvar*) or an oriental robe with a European jacket. The most common male outfit was the European suit worn with the fez (see figure 29; the fez was introduced at the beginning of the nineteenth century as an innovation, by the early twentieth century it was the symbol of Islam and, as such, abolished by Mustafa Kemal Atatürk when he founded the secular Turkish Republic). The European suit was also worn with local hats, such as the *sidara* in Iraq under the monarchy or the *shashia* in Morocco. In some cases men wore European clothes outdoors but traditional robes at home, especially on the Sabbath and for Jewish holidays.

Traditional women's costume in the Middle East was more varied than men's, with a rich variety of material, cut, form, and decoration. This variety was mainly found in the indoor attire; there was a marked distinction between indoor and street wear. When going out, in Muslim society all respectable women had to cover their bodies entirely with a wrap or cloak and veil their faces. This was a protective device to secure their virtue from strange men and was the custom in towns and in some rural and nomadic societies but not everywhere. Low-status women, such as servants and non-Muslim women, were not obliged to veil themselves. Veiling was considered the prerogative of Muslim women; the others were not considered worthy of its protection (see figure 28). Jewish women, as nonbelievers, were not required to veil their faces. Because the custom in Muslim society was for women to cover themselves when going outdoors, Jewish women also adhered to that norm when leaving the house or the Jewish quarter, so as not to place themselves in danger. In some places, such as Baghdad, Jewish women veiled their bodies and faces entirely well into the 1930s. In other places Jewish women lifted a part of their outer kerchief to cover their face while walking on the streets. In places such as Kurdistan, where non-Jewish women did not veil their faces, neither did Jewish women.

The Ottoman woman's outdoor outfit consisted of a long wrap or cloak worn over the clothing and covering her from head to toe. A large kerchief or scarf covered her headgear. In cities under Ottoman rule Jewish women wore the *ferace,* the customary cloak of dark color with a long back collar;

the collar decoration was specific to Jewish women (see figure 23). The head scarf was an embroidered shawl or a cashmere shawl. In Baghdad, Jewish women wore the *izar,* a sheetlike wrap made from two attached rectangular fabrics that was wrapped around the body and covered the head. The face was covered by a square black veil woven from horsehair; this was replaced in the 1920s by a more transparent black scarf. In modern times the Baghdadi Jewish woman's *izar* was made of pastel-colored patterned silk interwoven with metal threads. This type had been prevalent among Muslim women in earlier times, but in the early twentieth century, when they changed into the plain black wrap, the older fashion was considered a distinctively Jewish outfit. This process was typical of the evolution of Jewish costume in many places, when a whole outfit or one item of dress was kept and worn by Jews after the surrounding society abandoned it. After some time it is then considered exclusive to the Jews and even an identifying trait. Moreover, the Jews consider it to be part of their traditional heritage, to be followed and transmitted to the next generations. The wearing of the *izar* became the subject of dispute in Baghdad between Jewish traditionalists and the modernizers who wanted to discard it, to go unveiled in modern attire.

The indoor costume of the Jewish married women was customarily brought by a bride in her trousseau, in sets, to be worn during her married life. After the wedding the bride would be clad in these outfits, which signified her new social status. The most significant part of this costume was the headdress. According to halakhah, Jewish women are required to cover their hair, but the varied headgear had no one feature in common. Some head coverings were peculiar to Jews, and some were similar or identical to those of the surrounding society. Some were elaborate, consisting of several layers of caps and kerchiefs or incorporating jewelry work. In some places women wore the headgear all the time; in others, women wore a simple scarf at home and the headgear only on festive occasions.

As the norm in Islamic society was to cover the head, Jewish women were no exception. In some places they could be identified as Jews by the meticulous care they took in covering every bit of hair, such as with the *fotoz,* the voluminous headgear worn by the Jewish women of Istanbul and Bursa at the beginning of the nineteenth century. Jewish women wore it to conceal their hair, while Turkish women wore it with some parts of their hair showing. In several places in rural Morocco and in Bukhara, Jewish women's coifs incorporated false hair that served as partial wigs to conceal their own hair. A fine example is the *mahdur* headgear of the Jewish women of the Sus region on the southern coast of Morocco; this is an intricate work of silver wire interwoven with the hair of a horse's tail, two locks of which frame the woman's forehead, and is topped with parallel silver cylinders decorated with colorful cloisonné typical of the region's jewelry. Another interesting example of headgear is the *gargush* of the Yemenite women (see figure 27); this hoodlike headgear distinguished married Jewish women from Muslims. It prevailed in Sanᶜa and several other towns of Yemen, but it varied in material and decoration according to locality, marital status, and occasion. Both married women of child-bearing age and little girls wore it, with the *gargush* differing only in symbolic decoration. It was made of cotton, velvet, or brocade and was decorated with embroidery and delicate silver work. The most sumptuous *gargush* of the married women of Sanᶜa was the *gargush mizahhar mirassaf* (the full golden), which was decorated with delicate gilt-silver filigree (made by the Yemenite Jewish silversmiths) and with some gilt coins. Both formed part of the woman's dowry, which she received from her father, and they were her capital or cash reserve from which she could draw in time of need. A common practice in Islamic societies is that married women keep their own capital in the form of jewelry, on their bodies.

The great variety of indoor female attire ranged from the rural sheetlike wraps in the south of Morocco or Libya to the trouser sets in Tunis to the several layers of coat dresses in the core Ottoman region to embroidered dresses with leggings in Yemen.

An important category is festive or ceremonial dress. In many cases the most sumptuous garment worn by a woman was her wedding dress, which she wore afterward on other festive occasions. Western-style white wedding dresses were introduced with modernization, and they gradually replaced the local variety of wedding costume. The urban centers of Morocco, especially the communities of Spanish origin, had several variations of the "great costume" (*kiswah el-kebira*) as bridal and festive women's dress. It consisted of a wraparound skirt, a tight-fitting short-sleeved jacket cut low in the front, into which an embroidered plastron breast part was fitted. This outfit was made of dark red, green, blue, or purple velvet, embroidered with heavy metal thread or with gold braid attached. It was completed with wide flowing sleeves that began well above the elbow of the jacket, and a wide stiff brocade sash was wrapped around the waist. Strikingly different from the local Muslim costumes, it was reported by many travelers to Morocco in the eighteenth and nineteenth centuries. It strongly resembled the Spanish costume of the sixteenth century and preserved many of its traits in fabric cut and decoration. The Moroccan great costume is a rare example of the preservation of dress by an immigrant group for hundreds of years. Although it is probable that in Spain this outfit was worn only by Jews, in Morocco it was exclusive to them and one of the aspects of culture preserved by the Jews coming from Spain, thus attesting to the importance that they attached to upholding their distinctive heritage.

Another costume that testifies to the attachment to the Spanish heritage and tradition—still strong in the nineteenth and twentieth centuries—was the dress of the married Jewish woman in Salonika. This outfit, called *kofya* (see figure 26), still worn by Salonikan Jews well into the 1920s, was distinct and was recorded by travelers as a local curiosity. The costume, and especially its headgear, was considered to have been preserved from Spain, yet an analysis of its components reveals a combination of Ottoman attire and Greek folk costume; it only echoes some features of Spanish medieval costume. Its Spanish origin cannot be easily traced, stylistically and historically, as that of the great costume in Morocco, yet the *kofya*'s Spanish identity was strongly rooted in the consciousness of the Salonika Jews, corroborated partly by the Spanish names of some of its components. The Moroccan and Salonikan examples testify to the expression of ethnic or group identity and affiliation through attachment to material objects.

Two outstandingly elaborate outfits are those of the Jewish brides from San^{c}a, Yemen, and from Herat, Afghanistan (see figures 27, 30). The Yemenite bridal outfit is a complex ensemble, consisting of a large quantity of heavy jewelry that covers the bride with strings of large silver and gilt beads; her hands and ankles are covered with bracelets, anklets, and rings. A tall triangular headdress surrounded by flowers and embroidered with coral and pearls enframes her face with jewelry. Her embroidered leggings feature an exclusively Jewish motif, the six-pointed star. Muslim brides in San^{c}a wore a similar outfit, with only some differences in the details of the decorations. The bride did not own this ensemble; the parts were collected from several families, who loaned them to the bride for the wedding. The bride would borrow some parts from Muslim families. This outfit was worn only for the marriage ceremony; on the seven days of festivities that followed, the bride would wear and display in sequence all the other sets of clothes she brought in her dowry.

The Jewish bride from Herat wore a silk dress and trousers with braided trimmings, a decorated jacket, and several kerchiefs over her head. But the epitome of the bridal outfit was the colorful facial decoration, combined with a luxurious set of gold and enameled jewels. The facial decoration consisted of colored spangles stuck to the bride's forehead in concentric rhomboids. Golden foil wrapped her tresses. This decoration to the face and head was an amalgamation of elements from India, Central Asia, and Persia in a style unique to the Jews of Herat. The brides of San^c^a and Herat sat for long hours as they were prepared by women who specialized in wedding decoration. In a sense, these heavily decorated outfits had majestic connotations, making the bride a queen for one day; yet by restricting the bride's movements with heavy apparel, the outfit made the bride into a passive, beautifully decorated object.

The transition from traditional to modern clothing for women affected their identities as women as well as Jews. The decision to wear modern attire often involved changes in body image, social status, conduct, and attitude toward Jewish traditions regarding chastity and decency, such as covering the hair or arms. In many cases there were several transitional stages, starting with indoor clothing. Midnineteenth-century women's travelogues in particular reveal that some upper-class Muslim women wore combinations of fashionable Parisian clothing inside the house, but when they went out to the street, they would be covered. Jewish women in Baghdad were also wearing some modern clothing under the veil. Opposition came from the traditional rabbis who objected to women's modern attire on religious grounds, because it might lead the women to immoral behavior. Such opposition was pronounced by the influential rabbi of Baghdad, Rabbi Yosef Hayyim (1835–1909), and others. Modernization in women's dress came in stages, with imported fabrics first used to make traditional dresses. Then came some concessions to European trends, such as set-in sleeves and darts at the bustline. Then a type of mixed dress evolved as the transitional dress of the Jewish women of Iraq. But as one can observe in family photographs of several generations sitting before the camera, several styles also existed simultaneously, identified mainly with age groups (see figure 29). While older members of the family wore either traditional attire or modest European dress with a head cover, the younger women wore fashionable European outfits with no head cover. Sometimes items from the traditional outfit persisted, but their function changed. For example the *rozeta,* or hat pin, of the Jewish woman from Izmir, which at one time stated her status as a married woman or a widow, continued to as an accessory to European clothing long after women discarded traditional headgear.

SYNAGOGUES AND CEREMONIAL AND RITUAL OBJECTS

The construction of synagogues attested to different channels of communication and reciprocal influences between the Jewish and non-Jewish populations, as well as to distinctions in internal Jewish traditions. Following the restrictions of the Pact of Umar, Muslim law prohibited the erection of new synagogues and limited the renovation or repair of existing ones, controlling their location, size, height, and the materials from which they were built. The community requested permission to rebuild or repair burned or ruined synagogues, and the authorities granted permission in official documents that specified the manner of repair in detail. Nevertheless, because these laws were not enforced equally in all places and times, many synagogues were built under Muslim rule. Some synagogues that stand today date from early times. Although they occupy the same sites, the buildings often are more recent, and they have been subjected to repeated repairs and renovations, sometimes layer upon layer. Determining the form of the original building and the nature of the intermediate stages often is difficult. Some synagogues are associated with famous Jewish figures, such as the Synagogue of Ezra Hasopher or the Rambam Synagogue in Cairo. Some are considered holy sites of pilgrimage, such as the Griba synagogue on the island of Djerba in Tunisia.

The synagogues are found within the confines of the Jewish quarter, and they differ in size, structure, shape, and style of decoration. Small rural and remote communities boast a large variety of synagogues. There are monumental urban synagogues, as well as those belonging to a certain neighborhood, to a community adhering to a common rite of prayer, to the sharing of common ancestral origins, or belonging to a professional guild, such as the tailors. Some synagogues belonged to families of rabbis, such as the Beit Hillel synagogue in Izmir, which belonged to the Palaggi family. Some wealthy members of the community had their own private places of prayer. The synagogues, even the large or medium-size ones, were generally not conspicuous in their surroundings. In some places, such as Turkey, they were surrounded by walls and had no prominent facades. In modern times, after the reforms in the Ottoman Empire and the establishing of the French protectorate in Morocco in 1912, a new kind of large synagogue with a prominent facade emerged as Jews moved to new quarters. These synagogues were influenced by the trend in European communities. After the establishment of the Republic of Turkey in 1922, and the republic's separation of religion from state affairs, as well as the prohibition of public gatherings by religious groups, synagogues again become inconspicuous.

In many cases buildings of various types were converted into synagogues. Sometimes synagogues were located in private houses or in a room allocated as a synagogue. The synagogues ranged from opulent elaborate buildings to modest intimate rooms with only the Torah scroll. The synagogue compound often comprised a courtyard, with a small *beit midrash,* or study hall, and a place to build a sukkah, a ceremonial hut to celebrate the fall festival of Sukkoth. Synagogue interiors also varied, and the hall might be rectangular, a basilica-type with one or more rows of arches resting on pillars, a long room or a broad room, or some other shape. The inner structure and layout of the synagogue depended on the relationship between its two main parts: the ark and the reader's desk. The ark, a cabinet where the Torah scrolls are stored, is called the *heikhal* by Sephardic and Middle Eastern Jews. The reader's desk, called *bimah,* or *teva,* is where the Torah is read. The *heikhal* is located in the wall oriented toward Jerusalem. In many synagogues the ark is situated in a large niche in the wall; in many instances it is arched at the top, similar to the niches typical of Muslim houses, and closed with two fitted wooden doors or a curtain, or both, with the curtain drawn over the doors. A characteristic feature of many synagogues is several *heikhalot,* with three or more niches on that wall. Another type of *heikhal* is an ark generally made of wood that stands against the wall and is decorated in local style (see figure 33). The *bimah* is located on the same axis as the ark; it might be located on the opposite wall. It could be in the center of the room, standing within a structure of four pillars that form part of the architectural structure of the hall, or it might be a portable wooden structure (see figures 31, 32). The layout determines the seating arrangement; typically, the seats are arranged around the walls of the hall and around the central reader's desk but sometimes in rows on the axis between the reader's desk and the *heikhal,* facing one another. (Rows of seats facing the *heikhal* were introduced in the large European-style synagogues.) Only some Middle Eastern synagogues have a women's gallery. In some places it is a second-floor gallery in the back of the hall or around the sides. Sometimes it is a confined area on the same level as the men's sections, and sometimes the women would sit outside the synagogue because women are not required to attend services and their presence does not count toward the minyan needed to conduct a service. The decorative style of the synagogue usually reflects local style. For example, in Turkey some synagogues have painted ceilings with landscapes, in the monumental eighteenth-century style of Turkish architectural decoration (see figure 32). Some Moroccan synagogues have intricate colorful stucco decorations or the typical cut-tile mosaic called *zillij.* In many synagogues the dominant color is the turquoise blue characteristic of Mediterranean interiors, considered protective in Islamic culture.

Ceremonial objects in synagogues used for Jewish ritual include the Torah cases and decorations and ark curtains. Personal ceremonial items include Sabbath lamps, scrolls of the Book of Esther and Hanukkah lamps. Both public and private objects display great variety in form and style. Although it might be expected that Jewish ritual and ceremonial objects would be traditional and reflect few external influences, this is not the case. The diversity that exists in secular objects is also seen in religious objects. There may be detailed instructions concerning the writing of the Torah scroll but no instructions concerning the cases, wrappers, or ornaments. They therefore evolved through different traditions and customs. In some cases Jews made the ceremonial objects; in other cases they were made by non-Jews according to instructions or by copying models. In many cases the artisan is not known, because many Middle Eastern silver objects lack hallmarks. Today they can only be grouped according to stylistic affinities, information gleaned from dedicatory inscriptions, or contextual information.

A principal characteristic of Jewish ritual and ceremonial objects from the Islamic world is the intentional avoidance of figural art. As in Islam, they are not decorated with human figures, and, except for occasional birds and fish, animals are not common. One notable exception is two rampant lions with a personified sun behind their backs, a Persian imperial symbol that appears on Persian Jewish *ketubbahs.* The calligraphic, vegetal, and geometric decorations of Islamic art appear also on Jewish ceremonial objects in the corresponding styles. Some local prevailing architectural forms also appear as decorative motifs, for example, the horseshoe arch found on North African Hanukkah lamps and marriage contracts, and minaret-shaped Torah finials. Other motifs found on Jewish ceremonial objects include symbols associated with Islamic rule, such as the crescent and star (see figure 21), which became an official emblem in the Ottoman Empire in the nineteenth century. On many Jewish ceremonial objects the crescent and star appear as a tribute to the authorities or serve as identification with the host culture. Other motifs on Jewish ceremonial objects are borrowed from Muslim locales and some have magical connotations; among the most widespread is probably the hand motif, the *khamsa* that is popular on both Jewish ceremonial objects and secular objects. Typical Jewish symbols—the Magen David, Luhot ha-Berit (Tablets of the Law, which include the Ten Commandments), and the seven-branched menorah—appear mainly on semiamuletic plaques, such as the *shivviti,* or menorah plaques, hung in the synagogues. In many cases these are recent additions to the local repertoire of motifs, they were introduced through contact with Ashkenazim and the influence of ceremonial objects sent from Eretz Israel. Some were brought by the rabbinic emissaries sent to communities to collect funds for the Jews living on *halukkah* (donations) in the four holy cities of Jerusalem, Hebron, Safed, and Tiberias.

Although Jewish ritual function determines the form of the objects, Jews borrowed some objects from the surrounding culture and adapted them to Jewish ritual function. This involved either modification of the object or additions of Jewish inscriptions. For example, Torah finials were made from pieces of jewelry in Morocco or Afghanistan; cylindrical handles were added to pendants or to fibulae (clasps or pins from traditional women's draped dresses) to transform them into Torah finials. Sometimes no alterations were needed and the objects' functions were changed; in such cases only contextual information could identify them as being in Jewish use. Torah shields were made from repoussé mirror backs in Turkey (the mirror was removed, and the backs were hung on the Torah mantles as decorative shields, sometimes with an additional dedicatory inscription) (see figure 34). These adaptations are examples of a procedure common throughout the Jewish world and known as *ma^{c}alin bakodesh* (raising in sanctity), by which everyday objects are transformed into sacred articles and dedicated to the synagogue.

The reuse of textiles in the synagogue was common as well. For example, in the late nineteenth and early twentieth centuries, the main body of textiles in Sephardic synagogues, from the Balkans to Egypt, was in secondary use. In that period a certain type of metal thread embroidery was the most popular textile in Sephardic synagogues—a velvet or satin background embroidered with heavy metal thread; this style was typical of Turkish baroque, which was a mixture of baroque and rococo style elements and traditional Turkish elements. Embroidered textiles in different shapes and sizes fulfilled many ceremonial functions in the life of the urban population of all ethnic groups, including the Jews. They were used at home, especially in lifecycle festivities. A bride customarily brought such objects to her new home, including bridal dresses and sets of bedcovers, cushion covers, and wrappers. They were used to decorate the bridal bed and later to decorate the lying-in bed after a birth. Sephardic Jews appropriated the use of these embroidered textiles, sometimes adapting the custom along with the object. Sometimes they used these textiles for a specific Jewish ceremonial purpose, such as constructing the *huppah* for the wedding. Eventually, many of these textiles found their way to the synagogues, where they were used as ark curtains, reader's desk covers, and Torah mantles. We find ark curtains made of dresses or of bedcovers and mantles made of cushion covers or of wrappers. They were donated to the synagogues after they had fulfilled their ceremonial functions at home or in order to commemorate deceased members of the family. As modernization penetrated more domains of Middle Eastern life, the use of these embroideries went out of fashion in Turkish and Jewish society, and European textiles replaced them; thus the synagogue became the repository of these embroideries. They have become the hallmark of these Sephardic Ottoman synagogues.

One interesting example of a Jewish adaptation is an Islamic object, the prayer rug, used as an ark curtain or reader's desk cover (see figure 36). Muslims use small rugs with an arch motif as prayer rugs. This arch, which represents the mihrab, the niche in the mosque wall facing Mecca, is often accompanied by a hanging lamp, and it symbolizes the gate to paradise for the Muslim believer. The Muslim places the rug in the direction of Mecca and performs his five daily prayers on it. This rug creates a pure and sacred space for the believer, a substitute for the mosque (although prayer rugs are also used in mosques). Prayer rugs were, and still are, in common use throughout the Muslim world, and they are woven in many variations and styles. From textual testimony in the Jewish responsa literature, we know that Jews used these rugs in the synagogue, at least as early as the fourteenth century in Muslim Spain and in Egypt, and in the Ottoman Empire until the twentieth century. A famous responsum by Rabbi Asher ben Yehiel of Spain (early fourteenth century) forbids the use of these rugs next to the ark and not even as seat covers. This responsum is quoted several times later when the same question was brought to other rabbis, attesting that these rugs were in use in synagogues despite the prohibition.

Some rugs designed like prayer rugs and woven with Hebrew inscriptions were intended for Jewish use and probably were ordered by Jews. The inscriptions on these rugs, apart from personal dedications, include biblical verses containing the word *shaʿar* (gate), such as "This is the gate of the Lord into which the righteous shall enter" (Pss. 118:20). Thus a decidedly Muslim iconographic motif acquired a parallel Jewish iconographic meaning. This was how an Islamic religious object was adopted, with its symbolic meanings reinterpreted within a Jewish religious context, into the synagogue.

A good way to illustrate the diversity of Jewish internal synagogue traditions, in conjunction with influences from local styles, is the various traditions of covering the Torah. Generally, the Torah covers are of two main types: textile coverings, mainly mantles, and wooden or metal cases. Each type comprises a variety of shapes, styles, and colors. Each cover type entails different manners of holding the scroll when reading the Torah. The textile mantle is taken off and the scroll laid upon the reader's desk, while the scroll in a wooden or metal case is stood upright on the reader's desk to be read. For the most part textile mantles prevail in communities of Sephardic origin, while other communities, following other rites, used Torah cases (see figure 33), although this division is not clear-cut. Torah mantles are also associated with Ashkenazic rite, but in all the countries into which the Sephardic Jews arrived after the expulsion, they kept their Torah scrolls in mantles, from Holland and England through Italy to Morocco to Greece and Turkey. Textual and pictorial sources from Spain before the expulsion are not decisive but show that textile mantles as well as cases were in use. Because the mantle prevails in all the later Sephardic communities, they were probably more widespread. When wrapped in a mantle, the scroll is rolled around two staves, *atzei hayyim,* and held in place by a long textile strap binder; on top of the mantle a crown, *keter,* is set, into which two finials, *rimmonim* or *tappuhim,* fit on the staves. On the mantle in some cases hangs a Torah shield, *tas.* The Sephardi mantles are mainly cylindrical, with a wooden circular plaque with fabric attached at the top; these differ from the Ashkenazic mantle, which is rectangular and flat. They display a variety of fabric and decoration, although metal thread embroidery on velvet is common, and the style and motifs differ and reflect the local styles.

Torah cases are mainly of two types—one is cylindrical or faceted, with an onion-shaped crown (see figure 35). It is made in one piece, with two or more rods that stick out diagonally from the crown and bear the finials. Many of these cases are made of wood, often covered with silverplate that is decorated with rich repoussé work or sometimes covered in leather or fabric with metal decorations attached. The shape of these cases probably reflects architectural forms from the surrounding culture. When opened, the cases have decorated dedications in the inner halves of the crown. These cases are customarily decorated by women's silk scarves or other fine textiles that were donated. This type originated in Iraq and prevails in Iraq, Iran, Afghanistan, Kurdistan, and Syria. The second type is a cylindrical or faceted wooden box, with an open coronet on top. This type is made of wood; it is sometimes painted, sometimes has gesso decoration, or sometimes is covered with decorated silverplate. Some cases of this type are undecorated but covered by an outer textile. These cases are found in Egypt, Tunisia, and Libya, in some Kurdish communities, and among Romaniote communities in Greece (the Romaniotes were descended from Jews who had lived in the area under Eastern Roman, then Byzantine, rule).

Material culture creates the visual and tangible aspects of everyday life, those that form immediate sensual experiences and dominate daily routine, as well as those for festive events. The change of country, especially when abrupt, affects our feelings, which are manifested through the change in everyday habits to which people grow accustomed. Such an abrupt change was part of the life experience of many Jews who left their homelands in the Middle East and North Africa after the establishment of the State of Israel in 1948, whether they went to Israel, Europe, or the United States. These swift changes in the texture of life left people frustrated, full of nostalgia for the past, for the old country, and the old way of life, even if it had been modernized or was not a comfortable or easy life. These feelings of loss have been acknowledged, and ethnic revivals that incorporate music, rituals, food, and material objects represent an effort to link the younger generations to the older ones and to their ethnic heritage.

RECOMMENDED READING

Juhasz, Esther, ed. *Sephardi Jews in the Ottoman Empire: Aspects of Material Culture.* Jerusalem: Israel Museum, 1990.

Mann, Vivian B. "Jewish-Muslim Acculturation in the Ottoman Empire: The Evidence of Ceremonial Art." In Avigdor Levy, ed., *The Jews of the Ottoman Empire,* pp. 559–74. Princeton, N.J.: Darwin, 1994.

Rubens, Alfred. *A History of Jewish Costume.* London: Weidenfeld and Nicolson, 1967.

Sabar, Shalom. *Ketubbah: Jewish Marriage Contracts of the Hebrew Union College Skirball Museum and Klau Library.* Philadelphia: Jewish Publication Society, 1990.

Stillman, Yedida K. "The Costume of the Jewish Women in Morocco." In Frank Talmage, ed., *Studies in Jewish Folklore,* pp. 343–74. Cambridge, Mass.: Association for Jewish Studies 1980.

CHAPTER

12

Music

Mark Kligman

It is impractical, as some have suggested, to look at the music of Middle Eastern Jewry as if it were produced by a single community that has remained unchanged over time. Instead, reviewing the Jewish liturgical and paraliturgical (informal rituals of a religious nature) music reveals a range of influences both musical and cultural: Spanish, Andalusian, Arabic, Turkish, and Western. The music of Jews in the Mediterranean, like the music of Jews throughout the world, is as diverse as the music of the surrounding culture. Therefore, the music of Jews from Spain and Portugal shows a good amount of Spanish influence, and the music of Jews in the Levant shows a good amount of Arab influence. The music of Jews from Morocco and Turkey shares aspects of both Spanish and Arab influence but to differing degrees.

For Middle Eastern and North African Jews the musical influence of the surrounding culture took different forms: in some cases Jews adapted Spanish, Arab, Turkish, or European melodies with Hebrew lyrics; in other cases the music's aesthetic and style guided its use within liturgical and nonliturgical contexts. The innovative adaptation of music for new contexts provides a useful description of the music of Jews in the Middle East. Such song genres as Ladino (Judeo-Spanish) songs, *bakkashot* (supplications before prayers), and *piyyutim* (Hebrew poems) may have origins in or similarities to non-Jewish contexts, but these genres accompany Middle Eastern Jewish life and are important representations of Jewish life within the region.

Because of the diversity of music made by Jews in the Middle East, its study presents significant difficulties. The problem is compounded because the majority of Sephardic musical practices are still maintained orally; only a limited amount of the repertoire has been notated and collected in written form. In addition, Sephardic liturgical music has not received much study. Today, with recordings and computer-assisted data storage, there is hope for further research. The discussion that follows is based on the musical practices of Middle Eastern Jews during the modern period, with most of the focus on the twentieth century.

INFLUENCES FROM ARAB MUSIC AND POETRY

Jewish life in the medieval Iberian Peninsula was greatly influenced by the dominant Arab culture there. The most significant period was known as the golden age of Spain (eleventh to thirteenth centuries), wherein Jewish culture also flourished in an unprecedented way. Every dimension of Jewish religious and cultural life drew from free interaction with the host culture, which provided a fertile source for the adaptation of sociocultural elements.

Most notably, theoretical writings on the nature of music had a lasting influence on the manner in which music was viewed. Islamic scholars had followed the ancient Greeks in viewing musical phenomena as philosophy and science—through the study of acoustics and other abstract principles. In *Emunot ve-Deʿot,* written in 933 C.E., Saadiah Gaon discusses the way in which eight types of musical rhythms affect the human temperament and mood. Similar writings can be found even earlier, in the works of such Arab writers on music as Al-Kindi (died ca. 874 C.E.). Some Jewish writers applied Saadiah's ideas to such musical moral phenomena and biblical events as David's harp playing for Saul (1 Sam. 16:14–23). In this way, the theoretical discussion of the nature of music by Arab theorists was incorporated in Jewish musical concepts.

An area of innovation that significantly affected music was the creation of *piyyutim,* Hebrew religious poetry that was often incorporated in liturgy. At about the same time Arabic poetry increased in prominence through new rhyme schemes and a consistent use of meter; Hebrew poetry was influenced by that of Dunash Ibn Labrat (tenth century) and others. After the 1492 expulsion from Spain, inheritors of this rich tradition took it with them. One significant figure was the rabbi and poet Israel Najara (1550–1620) of Eretz Yisrael, who further developed the *piyyut.* He wrote hundreds of poems and often used Turkish, Arabic, Spanish, and Greek songs to create Jewish songs, replacing the original words with Hebrew. In this process of adaptation some sounds or assonance of the text were incorporated in his Hebrew poetry (a twentieth-century example of this process appears later in the chapter). Often the melody was also adapted to fit this new text. Thus the music of Middle Eastern Jews, both past and present, is composed through adaptation. The adaptation of thought in theoretical writings about music paralleled the adaptation of music and text found in the *piyyutim.*

Musical Influences and the Major Regional Styles

Several distinct musical styles can be used to classify Sephardic liturgical music within its geographic region. The four major regional styles are the Spanish and Portuguese, the Moroccan, the Middle Eastern, and the Yemenite. This discussion is based on the practices established during the twentieth century. Because historical sources are so few, this chapter takes a comparative approach to understanding the music of these traditions, through their similarities and differences. Similarities in two Jewish cultures separated by large geographic distances do not necessarily mean that their practices have a single origin. The liturgy of Jews from Spain and Morocco is more westernized than the other two styles. Spanish and Portuguese Jews who traveled to Western Europe, England, and Amsterdam, as well as the Americas, have also developed a more westernized tradition. These descendants of Spanish Jewry first took their tradition to these new locations, and it became adapted over time. Moroccan Jewry had received a large number of Spanish Jewish refugees during the fifteenth and sixteenth centuries, and Jewish musical traditions in Morocco have been continually influenced by regional Spanish traditions, such as Andalusian. The two other Jewish musical styles of the region, Middle Eastern and Yemenite, are marked by their influence by Arab music. Spanish elements within these two traditions are faint or nonexistent. Middle Eastern Jewry includes the Jews of Israel and the Levant—Lebanon, Syria, Iraq, Iran (Persia), Egypt, and neighboring locales—who incorporated the Arab modal system, known as *maqamat,* into their liturgy and Torah cantillation (see CD examples 1–7). The Yemenite tradition also makes use of local Arab musical practices. Turkish Jewish music, with its Ottoman flavor, has incorporated some Spanish and Arab elements. The Bukharan and Ethiopian musical traditions are in the early stages of study.

LITURGICAL CONTEXTS AND CHANTING OF PRAYER

Middle Eastern Jewish liturgy uses a range of musical styles: cantillating biblical texts; chanting of portions of liturgy by the hazan or by the entire congregation; and singing liturgical melodies initiated by the hazan and sung by the congregation. The chanting of prayers is done to known melodies as well as through improvisation. In the Spanish and Portuguese tradition the use of a chanting pattern occurs for the portions of the service where the hazan prays alone. The chanting pattern for the *amida* (silent prayer) in the Spanish and Portuguese tradition is similar to that of the Moroccan tradition. Many Middle Eastern communities adhere to the *maqamat* in some manner during their prayers. Some of these modes include notes that are a quarter-tone apart, which is unlike Western scales, which have one-half as the smallest distance.

The Syrian Aleppo tradition provides a useful example. Since the eighteenth century, and probably even earlier, Aleppo cantors have developed a system of associating the weekly biblical portion with a *maqam* (Arabic mode) for the reading. Within the Aleppo tradition, sad events in the biblical portion, such as the death of Sara the Matriarch or the building of the Golden Calf, would be associated with a *maqam* seen as having a sad effect; the *maqam* in this case is called *hijaz.* For happy biblical readings the *maqam* used is called *ajam.* The use of the *maqam* during prayers is a bit complicated. Every week the biblical reading is done in the same *maqam,* which is called *sikah,* and the association of a *maqam* with the biblical reading does not affect its intonation. Only the cantor's rendering of the *shaharit* (morning prayer) portion of the morning Sabbath service is affected by a musical mood. When the hazan recites certain portions of the liturgy, like the kaddish, he chooses the proper melody in the *maqam* associated with that particular day. When the reading about the building of the Golden Calf takes place, the hazan uses a melody in *maqam hijaz,* because that is the proper *maqam* for that biblical reading. *Maqam hijaz,* then, is used during the morning prayers. In the Aleppo tradition portions are sung with known melodies in the *maqam* of the day, but other liturgical portions are improvised melodically. Syrian cantors living in various locations throughout the world keep the practice alive. Jewish traditions from the Ottoman Empire are similar to the Aleppo tradition. This would include liturgical traditions in Turkey, Iraq, and neighboring regions, such as Morocco.

Liturgical Melodies

Examples 8 to 11 on the compact disk accompanying this book illustrate renditions of four Sephardic traditions. The liturgical text, *Nishmat Kol Hai* (The Soul of Every Living Thing), begins the cantor's prayers for the morning Sabbath service. The text states that all living things will bless God. The

Spanish and Portuguese rendition (CD example 8) and the Syrian rendition (CD example 11) are the most distinct. The former possesses a consistent rhythm throughout and is not melodically ornate; the latter is rhythmically freer, with more notes per word. The Moroccan example (CD example 9) is the same melody as the Spanish and Portuguese rendition but not as strict rhythmically and emphasizes different words in each phrase. The Turkish rendition (CD example 10) is stylistically between the Spanish and Portuguese, and the Syrian; the Turkish has a consistent rhythm and some slight embellishments throughout. All four renditions are similar, in that they repeat musical phrases. It is interesting to note that they are distinct as to when the musical material is repeated. Communities may render this, or any, liturgical text differently, so no single interpretation exists. Each may express a different nuance of the text.

Sephardic liturgical music makes use of the congregation's regular participation. The differences are based on where in the liturgy this occurs. In CD examples 8 to 11 only the Spanish and Portuguese tradition sings *Nishmat Kol Hai* congregationally, whereas in the Moroccan, Turkish, and Syrian traditions the cantor alone recites it. Since the Spanish and Portuguese rendition needs to facilitate group singing, the regular rhythm and simple stepwise musical line allow the congregation to sing together. In the Syrian, and even in the Moroccan, tradition the hazan begins with a known melody for this liturgical section and then improvises the text that follows. Group singing appears in all traditions, but they emphasize different parts of the liturgy. The kaddish and *kedusha* (holiness) are emphasized by congregational singing, yet each community may highlight liturgical passages between these phrases differently. Choral singing, two or more voices sung to composed music, appears only in the Sephardic traditions that were influenced by Western music in European locales, especially the Spanish and Portuguese tradition, which includes many nineteenth- and twentieth-century liturgical choral compositions in its repertoire. Choral singing is not practiced in Moroccan, Middle Eastern, and Yemenite traditions.

Liturgical Performance Practice

The practice of lively congregational singing describes Sephardic liturgy. While many portions are recited by the hazan as required by Jewish law, congregational participation is enthusiastic and joyful. Unlike the Ashkenazic practice, which intones the last two to three lines of a liturgical text, a Sephardic hazan recites the entire liturgical text. Congregants may join in the recitation, and some do so in an undertone. The uniqueness of the Sephardic tradition is displayed not only by the melodies used but also in the liturgical performance practice itself, which combines both active and passive participation from the congregation.

MUSIC IN PARALITURGICAL CONTEXTS

Holiday and Life-Cycle Celebrations

Many Sephardic liturgical melodies are adaptations of melodies used elsewhere within each tradition, and most often the melodies are adapted from *piyyutim*. The *piyyut* genre began in fifth-century Palestine and flourished in fourteenth-century Europe. Even today the venerable tradition of the sixteenth-century poet Israel Najara has been kept alive in the Jewish communities of Yemen, Morocco, Turkey, and Syria. Many of these musical traditions are unique developments and reflect local practices. Only since the 1960s have the musical practices of *piyyutim* been studied in earnest. Often liturgical melodies, following the practices of Najara, were taken from known non-Jewish melodies, but these tunes became so popular throughout the region that they are known in a variety of secular and religious contexts. In general, then, the distinctions between sacred and secular use are arbitrary, because many melodies are used in both contexts. CD example 12 demonstrates the practice of cultural interaction in this Judeo-Arabic text, which is sung to accompany a dance performed at the henna ceremony by a group of women from Habban, Yemen.

The main context of the singing of *piyyutim* is the celebration of a holiday or a life-cycle event. Specific texts are associated with particular holidays and are sung in the synagogue or at home during meals. Some recurring occasions make use of the singing of *piyyutim* as the main source for these rituals; these are paraliturgical occasions where the event is for religious enrichment and not a mandated or required service. One occasion is known as the *bakkashot* (or *nuba* in the Moroccan tradition), which is practiced in some Syrian and Moroccan communities. Participants go to the synagogue at midnight or early in the morning before sunrise and sing supplications before prayers, which is intended to elevate their spirits before the formal morning prayers.

Like the liturgy, the texts of *piyyutim* draw from biblical, rabbinic, and mystical texts. In many instances a *piyyut* expresses or even amplifies an idea taken from a midrash (interpretation of Scripture). This rich body of poetry also follows the model of the golden age of Spain when the *paytanim* (the poets) used the rhyme schemes and meter from non-Jewish poetry. Inspiration was often drawn from the popularity of a non-Jewish song. CD example 13 provides an illustration of a Moroccan *piyyut*; the song was taken from a melody popularized by the famous Arab singer Um Kulthum (1898–1975) in the 1930s and adapted to a new Hebrew text. Some well-known *piyyut* melodies are sung often and are best known within a community in the Jewish context rather than its original non-Jewish source (CD example 14).

The extent of Arab influence on Jewish music, and its limits, can be ascertained by studying a melodic example. The following example comes from the Syrian tradition, in which the typical progression of musical adaptation is as follows: a song in Arabic becomes a *pizmon* (paraliturgical song) through the creation of a newly composed Hebrew text; the melody of this song is then classified by *maqam* for use in the liturgy. For example, *Hawwid Min Hina* (Come, Stop Over; CD example 15) is an Arabic song composed and recorded by Zaki Murad (1880–1940) between 1915 and 1920. The genre of this composition is known as a *taqtuqah,* which typically consists of several verses and a short refrain. Its text, like the music, is simple and straightforward, in colloquial Arabic, on a light-hearted topic, and uses a simple rhythmic mode (*wazn*). *Hawwid Min Hina* and the *pizmon Bo'i Berinah* (CD examples 15–16) have a similar rhyme structure. Here is a line-by-line comparison of the transliteration of the Arabic song and the Hebrew *pizmon*). Locate the words *ya-allah indinah* at the end of the first line of *Bo'i Berinah*; this phrase follows the assonance of its Arabic song model with the words *ta^{c}ala indina,* which are underlined.

line 1	Hawwid min hina:	Hawwid min hina, ta^{c}aala indi**na**
	Bo'i be-rinah:	Bo'i be-rinah ya^{c}alah adi**nah**
line 2	Hawwid min hina:	Yalla ana win**ta** nihibbi ba^{c}di**na**
	Bo'i be-rinah:	Le-beiti a**tah** ve-imekh eshko**nah**
line 3	Hawwid min hina:	Gaana-l fa**rah** zaala-l ta**rah**
	Bo'i be-rinah:	Oivech ba**rakh** yish^{c}eikh pa**rakh**
line 4	Hawwid min hina:	Sadri-n sha**rah** imta nistila
	Bo'i berinah:	Orekh za**rakh** eit le-ennah

Hawwid Min Hina
Stop over, come to us.
Come on, let us love one another.

Joy is here, sorrow disappears.
My heart is enchanted. When shall me meet?

Bo'i Berinah
Come in Song, gentle graceful woman.
To my house now and with you I will dwell.
Your enemy fled your salvation blossomed.
Your light shined, time to be bestowed to her.

CD examples 15 to 17 illustrate the process of adaptation with Murad's recording of the Arabic song *Hawwid Min Hina* (CD example 15), Cantor Isaac Cabasso's singing of the *pizmon Bo'i Berinah* (CD example 16), and Cabasso's application of the melody to the liturgy *Shav'at Aniyyim* (CD example 17), a text that precedes the kaddish in the Sabbath morning prayers. Cabasso lives in Brooklyn and has been a practicing cantor for about fifty years. Note that the melodic line is maintained in each of the three versions with slight changes to accommodate textual accentuation. This process of melodic adaptation remains faithful to the original melody with only slight changes.

Judeo-Spanish Songs

Sephardic Jews of medieval Spanish ancestry have retained many aspects of Ladino culture. Ladino, their Judeo-Spanish dialect, represents more than a language; it represents the synthesis of Jewish and Spanish cultures. The rich traditions of this cultural interconnection from the golden age of Spain have continued, although the amount of preservation versus new influence has varied during the past five hundred years. The Spanish tradition has been ongoing for Jews in Morocco, whereas Jews in Turkey and Greece have adopted some local Middle Eastern influences. Some historians hold that the venerable musical forms of these Sephardic Jews, namely, the ballad and *romancero,* were time-honored traditions, untouched by new cultural influence and thus faithfully transmitted. Modern scholars, however, have been unable to validate this claim. Nevertheless, Judeo-Spanish music has deep historic roots and, like other forms of Jewish music, is both perpetuated and innovatively revitalized by modern performers.

Women have long conserved Judeo-Spanish music, and many of the lyrics of the *romancero* and ballad deal with women's experiences in life-cycle events, passionate or erotic courtly poetry, and epic tales or stories (CD example 18). Dirges related to the death of individuals in untimely and other circumstances are known as *endechas* (CD example 19). *Komplas* are short holiday songs (CD example 20). The wedding context has been a particularly rich source of music for Sephardic women (several short examples appear in CD example 21). The preparation of the bride for the *mikveh* (ritual bath) before the wedding, a bride's dowry, and her relationship with her mother-in-law are some subjects of the lyrics. Some Judeo-Spanish melodies are also incorporated into the liturgy (CD example 22).

Rituals of home include the singing of melodies on the Sabbath and on holidays. Examples include songs at the Passover seder from the *Haggadeh*. An example is the *Ekhad Mi Yode*ᶜ*a* poem sung after the meal in the Judeo-Persian tradition (CD example 26), which shows a melodic reading style; in the Judeo-Spanish tradition, the melody receives greater emphasis (CD example 27).

Each performer has personalized the Ladino repertoire because no standard forms exist. Musicologist Israel Katz has devoted his scholarly efforts to understanding Judeo-Spanish songs through their past and present manifestations. He sees a distinction between two musical types with respect to the ballad. The Ladino singing style of the western Mediterranean or Morocco includes regular phrases and rhythms with few embellishments (CD examples 20 to 21). Within this style many modern performers of Judeo-Spanish music incorporate the Spanish and Arab musical styles in their song renditions as well (CD example 23). The Judeo-Spanish singing style of the eastern Mediterranean, Turkey, and the Balkans includes more melodic embellishments in a freer and often less regular rhythm (CD examples 18 to 19). Over time, however, the eastern and western styles have merged. Katz has also postulated that a third style may exist in the ballad style of Greece (CD example 22).

The performance of Judeo-Spanish music grows steadily. Performers draw from a range of sources, which includes printed material (such as Isaac Levy's *Chants Judeo-Espagnols*, 1965–1973) and documentation from informants; these melodies are then adapted to a range of musical styles: medieval, Spanish, Arabic, Turkish, and Balkan. Some composers have adapted traditional songs into art songs, most notably Alberto Hemsi, Paul Ben Haim, and Yehezkiel Braun.

Israeli Mediterranean Music

In the first half of the twentieth century, European and Middle Eastern immigrants to the British mandate in Palestine brought with them and perpetuated the culture of their country of origin. These early immigrants, however, wanted to discover or invent a uniquely Jewish music. The music of Yemenite Jews was viewed as ancient, and it served as a model. Music in synagogues did not make use of instruments after the destruction of the Temple in the first century because a state of mourning was declared. This practice changed in the modern period, first in the nineteenth-century Reform movement in Germany. Music made for nonsynagogue purposes had no limitations other than the Sabbath restrictions. For Yemenite Jews the refusal to use musical instruments except for the rhythmic beating on oil cans and copper trays is the result of a Muslim prohibition in Yemen. They use a drum to accompany dance and singing (CD example 14). One performer of the prestatehood period, Bracha Zephira, gained wide popularity by singing Yemenite songs. She collaborated with composers and arrangers, such as Nachum Nardi and Paul Ben Haim, and adapted Yemenite music to folk and artistic styles. Several immigrant composers, such as Paul Ben Haim, Partos, and Marc Lavry, developed music in this direction, creating their own Mediterranean style. In the course of this westernization of Middle Eastern musical features, the indigenous Middle Eastern music became marginalized; however, this state of affairs changed dramatically in Israel from the late 1960s through the end of the twentieth century.

In Israel, Middle Eastern immigrants and their descendants were initially treated as second-class citizens by the European Jews who worked to found the modern state of Israel. The Ashkenazic hegemony then often delegitimized Sephardic and Middle Eastern culture. As efforts to integrate Ashkenazic and Sephardic/Middle Eastern culture gained priority with Israel's Likud government of the late 1970s through the early 1990s, non-Western cultural expression gained legitimacy. This led to an integrated musical style now known as Musika Yam Tikhonit Yisraelit, or Israeli Mediterranean music. It was first known as Musika Mizrachit, or eastern music, and Musikat Ha-Takhanah Ha-Merkazit, or Central Bus Station music, which refers to the place of purchase. The music is panethnic and integrates a variety of styles. Hebrew lyrics comingle with Arabic, Persian, Kurdish, and Turkish texts, while the Eastern European, Greek, Turkish, or Arabic tunes feature local aesthetic markers that draw in Egyptian, Jordanian, Lebanese, Syrian, and Palestinian listeners. A mix of Western and Middle Eastern instruments and musical styles provides a rich source of creative expression. Performers of note include Zohar Argov, Daklon, Ben Mosh, and Haim Moshe (CD examples 24, 25). Other artists, such as Ofra Haza, have tried to reach to broader audiences and have recorded songs in

Western languages. The core Musika Yam Tikhonit Yisraelit repertoire uses Hebrew for the text and is popular in Israel and throughout the Middle East.

A diversity of styles is found in the music of Middle Eastern Jews. The music reflects Jewish culture: it has synthesized influences that were adapted dynamically and grew through the perpetuation of tradition blended with innovative changes. Although once unfamiliar to non-Middle Eastern Jews, there are rich living genres of liturgical, paraliturgical, and popular music. Today, Middle Eastern music, and its connection to Jewish culture, persists amid the larger and more populous Ashkenazic religious authority and institutions in both the Americas and in Israel—even after undergoing significant relocation in the twentieth century. Middle Eastern music continues as a tradition that evolves while inspiring both religious and secular musical compositions.

RECOMMENDED READING

Hirshberg, Jehoash. *Music in the Jewish Community of Palestine, 1880–1948: A Social History.* Oxford: Oxford University Press, 1995.

Katz, Israel J. "A Judeo-Spanish Romancero." *Ethnomusicology* 12, no. 1 (1968): 72–85.

Seroussi, Edwin. "New Directions in the Music of the Sephardic Jews." In Ezra Mendelsohn, ed., *Modern Jews and Their Musical Agendas: Studies in Contemporary Jewry, an Annual,* vol. 9:61–77. London: Oxford University Press, 1993.

——. "Sephardic Music: A Bibliographic Guide with a Checklist of Notated Sources." *Jewish Folk and Ethnology Review* 15, no. 2 (1993): 56–61.

Shelemay, Kay Kaufman. *Let Jasmine Rain Down: Song and Remembrance Among Syrian Jews.* Chicago: University of Chicago Press, 1998.

Shiloah, Amon and Erik Cohen. "The Dynamics of Change in Jewish Oriental Music in Israel." *Ethnomusicology* 27, no. 2 (1983): 222–51.

CHAPTER

13

The World of Women

Sara Reguer

The world of women in traditional Islamic society existed for the most part alongside, yet separate from, the world of men. Islamic, Middle Eastern, and North African culture dictated almost total segregation of the genders, limiting the world of women to the family and the community of women, except in one important arena: economics. In discussing Jewish women in that region, therefore, we must look at the ever narrowing concentric circles of the larger Islamic society, the smaller circle of the Jews, and the even smaller circle of Jewish women.

The premodern, or traditional, Middle Eastern world was a complex one, yet in a general cultural sense it was united. The Ottoman Empire and Morocco of the eighteenth century were multiethnic, pluralistic, and diverse; the Persian Empire was less so. Jews, as *dhimmi,* were part of this milieu, with a strong religious identity. That does not mean that all Jews were the same, for they too identified themselves according to their differences in social class, economic status, gender, and specific customs. Jewish women were also members of many different social categories, but their lives were alike enough in the sum of their parts to permit generalization. The main exceptions to most generalizations were the women of Yemen, Kurdistan, and those living in tiny rural farming villages because the Jews were an urban group for the most part.

Middle Eastern society held it as a truism that men and women had different natures and capacities and so ought to play different roles. Male superiority was assumed, and all were brought up to accept the gender inequalities as part of the natural order, along with accepting one's place in society and one's deference to superiors. When a girl child was born into this premodern Jewish world, the celebration was more muted than had the child been a boy. Judaism had several rituals for boys, but for girls it had only the naming ceremony in the synagogue on the Shabbat after the birth. Girls were often named after living grandmothers or were given names in the local dialect instead of a Hebrew name. Thus acculturation was manifested early in this area of life. Prayers of thanksgiving were given both for the arrival of the new member of the family and for the mother's having survived childbirth, the major killer of women until modern times. To protect the newborn child, folk religion offered a variety of semimystical actions against the evil eye, including the placing of pictures or little turquoise eyeballs, or written talismans, near or under the child. The evil eye—a widespread belief that a look or stare might harm or bewitch—was a real presence to these communities, especially among the women, and they took no chances in protecting the infants as well as the new mothers.

Girlhood, as in other parts of the premodern world, was brief. The lower down the economic scale, the heavier the household burdens for the female family members. The poorest families lived in one or two rooms in a courtyard house, with rights to the inner yard and the well. The earliest tasks of the girls included supervising younger children and drawing the water from the courtyard well. The poorest of all had to go to the nearby public fountains and carry the water home in pails. Girls were quickly inducted into the laborious daily work of cleaning, washing, and, most important of all, food preparation. Food was purchased daily, usually by the men. The majority of the women brought their already milled flour to the bakery to be made into bread. Only in the countryside did women still bake their own breads; few still ground their own flour.

The higher up on the economic scale, the more elaborate was the food preparation, with the most elaborate foods prepared for the sabbath, holidays, and special celebrations. Local markets carried a wide variety of fresh vegetables, legumes, fruits, dairy products, nuts, cereals, and spices. Kosher meat was the most expensive item; the poor seldom ate it. The wealthiest homes had many female servants doing the food preparation, as well as the cleaning and washing, supervised by the woman head of the household. Even moderately comfortable households had a maidservant, usually a girl from a poor Jewish family. She usually started at the age of nine or ten, working mainly for her keep.

Girls received little, if any, formal education. Because they would not be active participants in prayer services, nor would they ever be called up in the synagogue to read from the Torah, they did not need to know how to read Hebrew. That did not mean that women did not pray or say blessings; they did—especially the weekly Shabbat lights ceremony in the home at sundown—but they memorized these prayers. As for a more general education, few boys received this, either. Books were scarce, and ordinary people had not yet cultivated the leisure practice of reading for enjoyment. Reading was limited to the scholars, rabbis, and the wealthy who could afford to build up private libraries. Girls learned what they needed to know for survival or to earn a living; therefore they probably understood calculating, weighing, and measuring. They gained their Jewish knowledge in the household, from their mothers, grandmothers, and the other adult women in charge; this oral transmission was effective and often accompanied by songs, stories, and sayings or proverbs as the women worked together in preparing foods or cleaning, especially for holidays. Only a select few females learned to read and write, taught by private tutors.

If a girl's mother or other female member of her extended family worked as a spinner, weaver, or embroiderer—three popular women's crafts—the girl's education was extended into this area as well. Women practiced these crafts as early as the eleventh century, at the time of the Geniza documents in Cairo, and they continued into the eighteenth century, in part because they could be done at home in keeping with female modesty. Most women knew the rudiments of these crafts, but Yemenite Jewish women were especially well trained in embroidery skills.

As a girl reached puberty, she prepared for marriage, the most celebrated and festive time of her life. Marriages—certainly first marriages—were arranged by the two fathers. The families arranged the match only after considerable inquiries and negotiations, most revolving around the *mohar,* or brideswealth, to be paid by the groom and his family to the bride's family. In most families the bride's father supplemented this sum with a gift to the young woman. These were practical ways of providing for the clothing, jewelry, bedding, and the rest of the trousseau that the young couple needed. The money paid by the groom's side was for her protection and security (to be repaid in case of divorce), but it also reflected her negotiated value and status. Then too, the lavishness of the wedding reflected family status.

The traditional women's world enfolded the bride-to-be with myriad local customs. She was beautified, coddled, hennaed, and entertained. Her trip to the ritual bath, or *mikveh,* on the eve of the wedding was a women's celebration. The Middle Eastern bride was the center of public female attention, in some cases with her future mother-in-law making sure that the bride was physically perfect. Women socializing at the *hammam,* or public bath, is a given in Middle Eastern society, and therefore the partying and celebration of a bride's first ritual immersion was a major event.

The wedding ceremonies varied according to local custom, but in general the bride was dressed in traditional embroidered finery, with heavy jewelry—mainly silver—on all parts of her body. In some communities the bride wore an ornate silver headdress so heavy that she could not stand. The ceremony's basic elements consisted of the groom's giving a coin to the bride as he sanctified her to himself; the reading of the *ketubbah,* or marriage contract; the seven blessings over the wine; the bride and groom's drinking of wine from the same cup; and the smashing of a glass, to symbolize the sadness, even in the midst of joy, that the Temple in Jerusalem had been destroyed. This was the core ceremony; how it was elaborated upon depended on the particular community.

The celebration lasted a week. The bloodied sheet to prove virginity played a role in only some communities. Everyone assumed that a young woman of approximately fourteen, brought up in a traditional Jewish home, and generally segregated among women, would be a virgin at her first marriage. Female chastity was also integral to family honor. The marriage price, to be paid upon divorce or the death of the husband, as specified in the marriage contract, was half that for a woman who was remarrying than for a virgin.

The bride moved into the realm of her husband's family, and often that meant under the rule of her mother-in-law, because the traditional Middle Eastern household was that of an extended family. The practice of universal and early marriage, as well as the tendency of single adults, especially women, to live with relatives, were factors that contributed to this family structure. The core family was parents and their children. Yet their level of wealth was a factor, for only the upper and middle classes could afford to help a young couple and have the room to house them. Among the lower classes separate nuclear families formed immediately. Another factor was that the members of the extended household shifted constantly, because of the early death of a parent or divorce or a remarriage that added new children from a previous union to the household. Polygyny was allowed but rarely practiced, except in Yemen. A man usually took a second wife only if the first was childless or never gave birth to a son and only if he could afford it, because cowives had to be treated on an equal economic basis.

The newly married woman found her niche in her new extended household and shared the work with the wives of her husband's brothers. She did not run a household until she and her husband moved away to set up their own nuclear household or until her mother-in-law died. To secure her status in the new household, as well as because it was expected of her, the new wife's goal was to become a mother as soon as possible. High fertility reflected many things, among them the value placed on children from the religious, cultural, and personal perspectives, as well as the insurance that some children would survive the dangers of childhood and be able to care for her in her old age. A woman's children were the focus of her love as well as her duty. Barrenness was a curse, and the woman would do everything in her power to alter this state. She could use a large variety of folk medicines and formulas, and a popular measure taken by many childless women was a pilgrimage to a holy place. She would sleep at this holy place—often the tomb of a *zaddik*; if she gave birth as a result of the visit, she would name the child after this person.

Family ties were complex, because they were based on Jewish values, Middle Eastern cultural traditions, and emotional bonds. Although married and removed to a new household at a young age, women remained emotionally tied to their parents and siblings; their brothers remained lifelong protectors, and their homes could serve as havens in case of divorce or widowhood. Nonetheless, a woman's first obligation was to her husband. The husband was responsible for providing his wife with food, clothing, and shelter, according to Jewish law. He was also obliged to satisfy her sexually, and rabbinic lore provided a guide for this. Middle Eastern patriarchal culture made the Jewish husband the protector of his wife. In return, she owed her husband obedience and respect and was duty bound to care for the home, food preparation, and children. For women chastity before marriage and faithfulness afterward were assumed, given the combination of the strict Jewish laws forbidding adultery and the realities of a segregated society.

Early death was a distinct possibility in the premodern world. Childbirth claimed the lives of many women; plagues, diseases, infections, and accidents could claim anyone. Remarriage was readily accessible, and the younger the widow, the more likely she would easily remarry. This held true for divorce as well. Death and divorce also redistributed property and wealth within a family, similar to what happened in marriage, so divorce was a considered an event and not automatic.

Some women did live into old age, and Jewish tradition gave them a respected place in society. They were valued for their wisdom and cared for by their sons, daughters-in-law, and grandchildren. They ruled their women's domain as long as they lived. No one questioned the hierarchy of power in traditional society. For an old woman to have no family to care for her was almost unheard of, unless all were lost in plague, warfare, or another catastrophe. If that happened, the Jewish community provided for her needs.

Many women participated in the economics of the community, not only as skilled workers or as menial servants but also as midwives, professional wailers, and as investors. Widows could not inherit from their husbands under Jewish law; however, they could run their minor children's inherited estates, and they could have brought some money into the marriage, which would have remained their own. In this way, women could invest in things, like manufacturing equipment, which would be rented out to artisans, or they could buy rental property or lend money at interest. Court records abound with cases that show how active women were as investors, how skilled they were, and how easily they had access to the courts to right perceived wrongs. They recorded everything, even loans to their husbands, "just in case." Yet, as I mentioned earlier, for the masses of Jewish women, just as for the masses of Muslim women, economic security was an impossibility, and life consisted of the constant pressure to make ends meet.

Most women had little leisure, but those who could made the weekly trip to the public bathhouse, one of the main times to socialize. The traditional woman went to the ritual bath only after her period and after childbirth. Considering the high fertility rate, this may have been only a once-a-year visit for many. The public bathhouse was not for ritual but for cleanliness and pleasure. There she could socialize with women outside her immediate family circle and perhaps even form friendships. Topics of discussion were the common experiences of the woman's world. In many towns and cities Jewish women could mix with Muslim and Christian women on the bathhouse ladies' day, but at some times and in some places *dhimmi* women could use the public bathhouses only when Muslim women were not there, lest the *dhimmi* ritually contaminate believing Muslims or have undue influence on them.

Women also socialized through household visits. These were Shabbat and holiday occupations, and tended to be segregated. During these visits, usually within the larger extended family, the women indulged their interest in clothing, among other things. The variety of fabrics, colors, headgear, jewelry, and cosmetics was wide. Periodically, the community enacted sumptuary laws to guard against overindulgence or to avoid arousing the envy of the Muslims, but these were aimed just as much at the men as at the women. In some towns Jewish families arranged and paid for visits to private gardens and orchards on the outskirts of town before Shabbat or a holiday, so they could have a break from the overcrowded houses and enjoy the shade of the trees. Socializing at the Middle Eastern synagogue was minimal, for women tended not to go. In contrast, the Geniza material of the High Middle Ages attests that Cairo women did attend, as they did in Spain; however, the majority of the Middle Eastern communities had small women's sections in the synagogues or none at all. Those who did attend generally could not read the Hebrew prayers, but they answered in loud "Amens" to every blessing, made wailing sounds, and gesticulated toward the Torah when it was held up in front of the congregation, kissing their fingers or hands as part of the gesticulations. Fasting was also a popular mode of expressing religious feelings.

The roles of women were private, their religious participation was oral lore, and their knowledge of kashruth (proper food preparation) and the laws of Passover was impeccable. Every ritual or ceremony concerning them, like challah, the *mikveh,* Shabbat lights (not only candles but wicks floating in special oil), kashruth, and preparing the dead for burial was handed down from one generation to the next, with a healthy admixture of folk religion. In many communities the duty of men to provide for and protect the women may have been behind the custom of not allowing the women to attend the actual burial. Women were prominent at the funerals, however, where they openly displaying their anguish, urged on by the professional wailing women. Society recognized that such emotional bereavement was therapeutic but barred women from the actual act of interment, perhaps in fear of hysteria, which fits the general approach toward the need to protect them, even from themselves.

As private as women were officially, they were also well aware of their immediate world, albeit a limited world for most. In keeping with Jewish values, women knew how to give charity. Their acts of charity were personal, unlike those of the men, whose communal taxes financed relief. Food distribution, especially on the eve of Shabbat and holidays, was the women's bailiwick, as were clothing distribution, visiting sick women or sending nourishing soups and herbal concoctions, taking in poor orphan girls as servants, and contributing to the celebration of a poor bride's wedding in the form of fabrics or henna or perfume. Independently wealthy women, however, voluntarily donated money the way men did, sometimes so generously that buildings or printed books or parts of the synagogue were dedicated to them. Yet this was more the exception than the rule.

As for politics and international trade, Jewish women's participation in these arenas were a thing of the past. There was no Doña Grácia Méndes or Esperanza Malkhi in the Middle East of the eighteenth century. Public life was a male province and a none-too-comfortable one for *dhimmis* in general on the eve of the new era of European colonialism and modernization. With modernization all aspects of life began to change, some faster than others. The arena of life that changed most slowly was that of the world of women. The multifaceted process of modernization, which first affected economics and public life, and then education and religion, moved last into the stronghold of the family that was the private domain of women.

Economics set off a chain reaction of modernization within the world of women but from two different angles. The poverty of the lower class—the majority of the Jews—resulted in families' allowing their girls and young women to work outside the home. Only the poorest had done so in Ottoman times, but with the arrival of the Western influences—the French, Italians, and British—more Jews allowed their women this type of work. Most of these women became maids in rich Jewish homes but soon in the homes of non-Jews as well, especially in the new European communities. They also began to work in the cigarette factories of Salonika and in the processing of ostrich feathers in Libya for the European fashion market. To protect these women from abuse the Jewish community reluctantly agreed to the next step toward modernization—providing vocational education for the Jewish poor. Economic necessity may have been the starting point, but education was the key to the new world. Economics was also the driving force behind the modernization of women from the middle class. In this case it was because of their fathers' exposure to the modern world. For their own prestige they sent their daughters to the new schools available to them. Educating daughters became a sign of status, and sending them to the colonial European schools meant that the daughters might even socialize with the daughters of the Europeans. Here too education would be the main modernizing force.

Illiteracy, common in the early nineteenth century, was gradually eliminated in most Middle Eastern countries; the number of graduates of secular elementary and then secondary schools would continually increase into the twentieth century. Girls had a slower start than boys, but this applied to them too. A parallel decline occurred in both the number of religious schools and the pupils attending them. The progress in education varied from one Middle Eastern country to the next because of the varied political, economic, and demographic conditions under which Jews lived. Egypt led the way, followed by Turkey, Iraq, Lebanon, and Syria; progress was slower in Iran but almost nil in Yemen, Afghanistan, and the Kurdish regions. In North Africa the degree of advancement was greatest where French influence was deepest and most prolonged. Therefore, northern Algeria led the way, followed by northern Tunisia. Urban Morocco started last but proceeded rapidly. By examining the educational material it is possible to infer the more elusive changes that applied in the laws concerning girls.

The focus of most schools—whether state, foreign, or Jewish—was on languages. Knowledge of languages enabled young Jewish men and women to expand their economic opportunities as civil service officials and bank and commercial company clerks; women could take jobs as secretaries, teachers, pharmacists, and nurses by the twentieth century. Vocational schools trained poorer Jewish girls, mainly in the needle trades, but some also entered foreign-owned factories, such as the Italian tobacco industry in Libya.

The first Jewish communities in the Middle East to receive a modern education were those of Algeria, Egypt, and Turkey. By 1858 seventeen hundred Jewish boys and girls were attending the new state schools—which included religious instruction—in Algiers, where the first modern school was opened in 1832. In 1860 a young Jewish woman took second place in the final schoolteachers' examination. Christian secular and missionary schools admitted Jewish boys and girls, and by 1883–84 about 40 percent of Jewish children of school age in Alexandria were in these schools. The majority of Jewish girls who attended school in Alexandria received all their education in these schools, probably because of parental indifference to religious education for girls.

The first modern Jewish schools were set up in Egypt in 1840, as a result of the activities of Adolphe Crémieux, a leading French Jew who had visited Egypt in connection with the Damascus blood libel, when Jews were accused of killing a missing Capuchin friar and using his blood to make matzo. But these schools failed. Not until the Alliance Israélite Universelle (AIU) expanded its activities into Egypt did Jewish schools succeed. In 1896 the AIU opened a school for boys in Cairo and soon after opened one for boys and girls in Alexandria. By 1902 two girls' schools were functioning in Cairo. Despite the resulting decline in girls' and women's illiteracy, not many continued beyond elementary school.

In Ottoman Turkey at the end of the nineteenth century, hundreds of Jewish girls were attending Catholic and Protestant mission schools in Istanbul and Izmir. Most attempts by private individuals to open Jewish schools in Turkey had failed because of the concerted opposition of the rabbis. Not until the AIU founded its schools was there success; the first, for boys, opened in 1867, and one opened for girls in 1875. AIU schools soon existed in a dozen Turkish cities, including Istanbul. Unlike Egypt, where the language of instruction was French, in Turkey it was Ladino and French, with the teaching of French beginning only in the higher grades. Most Alliance schools were trade schools, with the focus on dressmaking for the girls.

After World War I, however, and the sociopolitical changes brought to the new Republic of Turkey by its first president, Mustafa Kemal Atatürk, most Jewish children began to attend state schools. Turkey forbade the teaching of Hebrew until 1945, but Istanbul had one Jewish lycée for boys and girls that lasted into the 1950s. Girls also began to graduate from Turkish general secondary schools and enter universities after World War II.

In Iraq traditional education stood its ground as modern education was introduced, and few children attended missionary schools. Alliance schools opened there at the end of the nineteenth century, and modern Talmud Torahs opened after World War I. In 1890 a vocational school for girls opened in Baghdad, followed by a regular girls' school three years later, then more in other cities. Soon local communities responded by opening their own modern schools, which attracted much higher attendance than those of the Alliance. By the 1930s Iraqi Jewish girls were finishing secondary school. Only the Kurdish Jewish community in Iraq had continued widespread illiteracy among girls. The educational level in Iraq gradually improved as a larger proportion of teachers graduated from higher education programs. Jewish vocational education was introduced in Baghdad, with a half-dozen schools teaching dressmaking to girls. As the economic circumstances of Baghdadi Jews improved, the girls attended academic elementary and secondary schools.

In Lebanon the AIU was successful in its Beirut girls' school, which opened in 1878. The competition from the Christian school there caused the AIU school to raise its standards and add a secondary school. By the end of the 1920s the Alliance girls were able to pass the French *brevet* examinations. In Syria the AIU had mixed results because Jews in Aleppo preferred traditional education, or rich Jewish families preferred the Christian schools.

In Persia modern education in general, let alone for girls, had a late start—and it never reached Afghanistan. The AIU opened its first girls' school in Teheran in 1899, where Christian missionary schools were in stiff competition, so it was difficult to find competent personnel. With the overthrow of the old regime and the crowning of Reza Pahlavi as shah of Iran, the barriers to Jews began to fall, and Jewish children could attend secular state schools. At that time the AIU could also expand throughout the country, and it soon set up secondary schools. A network of the Otzar ha-Torah schools began in the 1940s and ORT (Organization for Rehabilitation through Training) schools in the 1950s. Illiteracy for girls, however, was not completely eradicated. Since the Iranian Revolution of 1979, about seven Jewish schools continue to function in Iran but under the close supervision of the Ministry of Education.

In Yemen illiteracy for Jewish girls remained almost total until the Yemenite Jewish community left for Israel in 1949. Before that the educational system continued along traditional lines, with only men learning to read Hebrew as a religious duty. The state schools were not open to Jews.

In North Africa the direct connection between modern education for Jewish girls and European activity is easier to see. In 1877 a modern Italian-style school opened for Jewish girls in Tripoli, run by Jewish women from Livorno. Two more opened in Benghazi and Homs. Because these schools charged tuition, most students were well-to-do, with Italian citizenship. By the 1890s the curriculum included Jewish subjects, the schools had hired Jewish teachers, and schooling was free. In Libya the AIU began opening schools in 1896 that appealed to the lower classes, for they provided vocational education for girls. The AIU general studies, taught in French, also attracted upwardly mobile middle-class Jews.

When Italy took over Libya in 1911, the new government introduced modern mandatory schooling. Jewish boys got a supplementary Jewish education, but the girls did not. Only when small Zionist schools opened to teach Hebrew did Jewish girls begin to attend, in segregated classes. During World War II and the British occupation, Palestinian Jewish soldiers encouraged local men and women to study and teach Hebrew. In Libya the British emphasis on higher-level teacher training helped the Jewish community, but the situation changed with independence in 1969, and the Jewish schools could place less emphasis on Jewish topics.

When Algerian Jews were granted French citizenship in 1870, they were educated in the secular French state schools. By 1941, when Vichy law was introduced, Algeria's primary and middle schools were educating nineteen thousand Jews, half of whom were girls. On the secondary level Jews accounted for 13 percent of all students, one-third of whom were girls. In the late 1800s the AIU had set up schools in Algiers, Constantine, and Oran in conjunction with community concerns about the assimilation of youth. Only a few girls attended these schools, but the AIU could not compete with the state schools, and secularization of Jewish students continued.

In Tunisia, unlike Algeria, private agencies set up the modern schools in the 1800s. Christian missions soon opened their doors to Jewish boys, but the new era really began in 1878 when the Alliance opened its first school for Jewish boys in Tunis, then one for the girls four years later. Jewish trade-apprentice schools opened in Tunis in 1881 for Jewish boys and in 1895 for girls. With the establishment of the French protectorate in 1882, Jews could attend the public schools, and the government subsidized the AIU schools. By 1945 more than fourteen thousand Jewish pupils were attending school in Tunisia; half were girls. Jewish education was more widespread in Tunisia than in Algeria—in part because of the difference in political structure, in part because of the AIU network's success, and in part because the legal jurisdiction of the rabbis was maintained, so traditional Hebrew schools were as well.

In Morocco, as in Tunisia, modern schooling for Jews was a private issue. In 1862 the AIU opened its first school in Tetuán, and by 1901 eight were operating, attended by twenty-five hundred boys and girls. By 1912, when the French officially arrived, attendance was up to forty-five hundred in twelve schools. By 1950 the AIU had nearly seventy schools, with a total of twenty-five thousand pupils. In addition, seven cities had dressmaking schools for Jewish girls. Thousands more attended modernized Talmud Torah schools, American-sponsored Otzar ha-Torah and Lubavitcher schools, as well as Morocco's public schools. Unfortunately, there had never been enough facilities for all Moroccan Jewish children, so it was not until the 1950s, on the eve of the mass emigration to Israel, that all were receiving an education.

It is difficult to generalize about the practice of Middle Eastern veiling. In some countries and in certain periods Muslims forbade Jewish and Christian women to veil themselves in public, in order to differentiate the *dhimmi*. In other countries traditional Jewish women veiled themselves in public to protect themselves from men, for the veil made the woman psychologically invisible. Like the Muslim women, some Jews even veiled themselves at home in the presence of men other than close relatives. Yet Jewish law and custom require only that a bride be veiled in the presence of her betrothed and at the marriage ceremony. The local customs that involved the veil were just that, local customs, based on accommodations to the dominant local Muslim cultures.

The key to the changes in the status of women was education, for this enabled them to change their occupation as household servants, which also involved changing their dress style. To be modern meant to discard the veil, if such had been the custom even for Jewish women in some traditional Muslim communities. It could mean Western dresses, shoes, hairstyles, and makeup, which did not automatically mean immodesty. The definition of Jewish modesty would vary, depending both on the country and the amount of urbanization, and it changed slightly with each generation. As Western countries in the twentieth century, one generation, for example, would consider showing an ankle or wrist as immodest; a later generation would consider showing the knee or the elbow immodest. The last realm of dress to modernize and imitate the West was the wedding outfit, namely, the adoption of the white gown and the headpiece.

Modernization also brought scientific approaches to health and hygiene. The more affluent and educated the women were, the faster they helped eradicate diseases and conditions endemic to the premodern world. The overcrowding of the North African Jewish sectors, for example, gave rise to a long list of illnesses and abuses, including alcoholism and obesity, which came about as a result of poor nutrition and total lack of exercise. Infant mortality, always high, also declined according to the level of modernization. The more modern a woman was, the more apt she was to give birth in clean conditions or in a hospital. Until the arrival of Western notions of pre- and postnatal care, most women relied on folk medicine and on midwives, whose lack of hygienic methods often caused both the early deaths of infants and the deaths of the mothers from infections and "childbed fever." The connection between housing conditions and health had been proved by, for example, the direct correlation between the move from the old Jewish quarters of Meknès and Fez and a lower incidence of infant mortality.

The rise in the age of marriage was also an indicator of modernization. Whereas in premodern Jewish life women would marry at puberty or certainly by age fourteen, with the exposure to modern ideas and styles the age of marriage rose to seventeen or eighteen. This enabled girls to complete a secondary education and even to work for a while before marriage; lower-class girls were working at a much earlier age, but the later marriage age also affected them. What did not change much was the extent of their freedom to have contact with the opposite sex. Traditional conservatism, both in the surrounding culture as well as within the Jewish world, still segregated the sexes. Even mixed schools had separate classes for boys and for girls, from the age of nine or ten. Young women might meet young men at work or at Jewish clubs, which became popular in the 1930s—such as the Zionist clubs or the Alliance alumni clubs—but rarely did young women choose their own husbands, and they never dated, Western style. Family gatherings, traditional festivities, and wedding celebrations continued to be the arena for young men and women to glance at each other and speculate. The parents and professional matchmakers continued to arrange the marriages, but in keeping with Jewish law, the young woman had to consent.

Brideswealth, or *mohar,* was still a factor in the marriage arrangements for many Middle Eastern Jews, as was dowry. The father of the young woman searched for a groom from a good family—often one known to him or one allied by business—who was a good person and who had a decent trade or profession. It helped if the groom's father was wealthy. The father of the young man searched for an attractive bride for his son, one well born and with as big a dowry as possible. Compatibility became an important question only late in the twentieth century, usually after Middle Eastern Jews left for Israel and other parts of the world. Even after the betrothal was arranged, the couple could not "go out"; they could meet in a family or family-approved home but always with an escort. Gradually, throughout the twentieth century the extended family structure began to give way to nuclear families; however, couples tended to live in near the man's parents and to spend Shabbat and holidays with them. The woman's main role continued to be that of wife and mother. She had learned early, through her own mother's example and advice, to honor and obey her husband and his parents. In some communities she served her husband his meals but did not eat at the same table with him. Traditionally, women learned how to run a Jewish home through the example of the older women and also songs, Bible verses, sayings, and tales that went along with the rhythm of the year and the cycle of life. With modernization women learned the music popular in the larger world at the time, as well as Zionist songs taught in their schools. Singing was always popular with women, and many performed in public, their modesty guarded by their brothers, who accompanied them to these performances.

Over the centuries, although Jewish law allowed divorce, many wealthier Jews began to consider it shameful. The woman usually did not want a divorce, for it had become difficult to remarry. If the wife was childless, the preferred solution continued to be polygyny; but in general, except among the Yemenites and Kurdish Jews, and Jews of rural areas, polygyny was not widespread.

Food preparation continued to be a focus of women's activities. Cooking in the Middle East in general is deeply traditional, although the precision and sophistication of Chinese cooking is lacking (as is the experimentation of American cooking). It has loyalty to custom and tradition, in its unwavering attachment to the dishes of the past. One of the only changes that came with modernization was the use of ovens. The traditional cooking style had been the long, slow procedure of simmering, sometimes even overnight, although communal ovens at the local bakery came to be used to bake dishes. Gathering at the bakers' ovens was part of the women's social life, and some sealed their pans with a paste of flour and water to ensure that no one introduced an unhealthy or prohibited ingredient out of spite. Some women sat by the ovens watching their food and directing how to move the pans around. Today families have ovens in their homes, but they still cook food slowly.

Middle Eastern foods are heavy on cooking fat, but Jews tended always to cook with oil—especially corn or nut oil—and olive oil for dishes to be eaten cold or for the deep frying of fish. Meats and vegetables are usually fried or sautéed before water is added to make stews. Middle Eastern cooking uses a large variety of spices, and each country has a favorite combination of spices and/or herbs. A favorite is ground coriander fried with crushed garlic; another is the "four spices"—cinnamon, nutmeg, cloves, and ginger. A combination of coriander and cumin is also popular. French coriander is used in salads and stews; dill is used in Turkey and Iran; mint is used everywhere, as are oregano, marjoram, and a variety of pungent seeds (fennel, mustard, dill, anise). Saffron is still highly prized, especially in Morocco and Iran.

Cooking ability is still rated highly among women's accomplishments. Cooking is still often done in company, and at all religious holidays and festivals the hostess can count on relatives and friends who come to help prepare food. Food marks all special events and ends all fast days, so many occasions are marked by a particular dish or delicacy. For example, Syrian Jews drink a special cold almond concoction for an engagement and eat almond cookies with the initials of the couple on them. Upon returning from a burial they eat hard-boiled eggs with round pita bread (similar to other round foods eaten by Jews around the world), as well as a cooked dish with brown lentils and rice. At the shivah, or seven-day mourning period, a guest giving condolences must be served something, usually Turkish coffee. A special food marks even the arrival of a first tooth, in this case a sweet dessert with wheat berries cooked with raisins and nuts.

The Middle Eastern code of etiquette for serving and presenting certain dishes still exists, reflecting subtle social distinctions. Which piece, of what, in what order shows one's status. The male head of the family is served first. The bride-to-be is ceremoniously served in her future husband's home, but her status drops to the bottom once she is married, to rise slowly as she becomes pregnant and the mother of a son.

Modernization brought a slight expansion of women's roles in Jewish public life. Their move into general public life was a factor of their jobs, which, for example, in Algeria, included teaching, as well as personal services like hairdressing, cosmetology, and manicuring; jobs in banking, commerce, transport, and the textile industries also were open to women. The sudden breaking of the old society, especially in North Africa, produced a mass of unfortunate Jews who lost their precarious jobs and trades. Reduced to beggary, many fathers looked the other way as their daughters turned not only to jobs outside the home but also to clandestine prostitution to help support the family. Prostitution was morally abhorrent to Jews but not punishable by death, as it was in Islam. This situation was so alien to Jewish tradition that although many will unofficially attest to it, it is difficult to document.

If public roles expanded for Jewish women, home life for most continued to be limited to the family circle and the world of women. Many women did begin to attend synagogue regularly, although most could still not read Hebrew, and their charities expanded as European models were introduced. For example, in Libya during Italian rule the Societá Ebraica Femminile was founded in 1912 to aid women, which included providing a sewing workshop, medical care, and education. A branch of the Associazione Donne Ebree d'Italia opened in Libya in the 1940s and then a branch of the Women's International Zionist Organization after World War II. Young women participated in small numbers in the youth movement, especially the Zionist organizations with a focus on Hebrew, but not in active leadership roles.

With the move into modern society and the lessening of religiosity among most Middle Eastern Jews, especially those with Western education, religion became not so much ideology and doctrine as a basis for the pattern of life. The stage on which this pattern of life was acted out was the family and the community. Modernization proceeded in public life, but the traditional Jewish rules on food and the proper conduct of men and women were reinvigorated as the focus of loyalty. In other words, the women's preparation of food for Shabbat and the holidays became acts that contributed to Jewish continuity; this gave new religious importance to domestic work and, by extension, to women's oral traditions.

The challenge that faces Jewish women of Middle Eastern origin today is the same as that which faces their men—how and what to retain of their customs in a world that is no longer Middle Eastern, because most now live in the Americas, Western Europe, or Israel.

RECOMMENDED READING

Goldberg, Harvey E. *Jewish Life in Muslim Libya: Rivals and Relatives.* Chicago: University of Chicago Press, 1990.

Marcus, Abraham. *The Middle East on the Eve of Modernity: Aleppo in the Eighteenth Century.* New York: Columbia University Press, 1989.

Rodrigue, Aron. *Images of Sephardi and Eastern Jewries in Transition: The Teachers of the Alliance Israélite Universelle, 1860–1939.* Seattle: University of Washington Press, 1993.

Simon, Rachel. *Change Within Tradition Among Jewish Women in Libya.* Seattle: University of Washington Press, 1992.

Figure 1.
The newly wed Douek-Sakkals in nineteenth-century Damascus.
Courtesy Yad Tabenkin Institute, Ramat Ef^{c}al, Israel.

Figure 2.
A Jewish shoemaker, Morocco, 1955.
From H. Z. Hirschberg, *Land of the Sunset* (in Hebrew). Jerusalem: Goldberg Press, 1957.

Figure 3.
Elementary school children at Talmud Torah, Morocco, 1955.
From H. Z. Hirschberg, *Land of the Sunset* (in Hebrew). Jerusalem: Goldberg Press, 1957.

Figure 4.
Scribe, Morocco, 1955.
From H. Z. Hirschberg, *Land of the Sunset* (in Hebrew). Jerusalem: Goldberg Press, 1957.

Figure 5.
The Maccabi Youth Group, Cairo, 1938.
Courtesy *Goshen Magazine,* Haifa.

Figure 6.
Ya^{c}akov Saadoun, the swimming champion of Sfax, Tunisia, during swim practice in Sfax in the 1940s.
Courtesy Haim Saadoun.

Figure 7.
A Hebrew class in Sfax, Tunisia, 1950.
From the Gaston Cohen-Solal Collection, courtesy Haim Saadoun.

Figure 8.
The mayor of Tunis and other officials aboard the Revisionist Zionist ship *Sara I* in Tunis in the 1930s. Courtesy Haim Saadoun.

Figure 9.
Voters wait at the AIU School on Malta Srira Street in Tunis before casting ballots in elections for the Tunis Community Council, 1934. Courtesy Haim Saadoun.

Figure 10.
A nineteenth-century Jewish Algerian wool spinner.
Courtesy David Cohen.

Figure 11.
Haim Partosh, a Jewish notable from Ghardaïa, capital of Mzab region in the Sahara (southern Algeria), 1962.
Courtesy David Cohen.

Figure 12.
The Jewish quarter of Constantine, Algeria, 1910.
Courtesy David Cohen.

Figure 13.
A postcard photo showing a Jewish family in Constantine, Algeria, in 1908.
Courtesy David Cohen.

Figure 14.
Algerian Jewish soldiers from Constantine in Lyon, France, during Passover 1916.
Courtesy David Cohen.

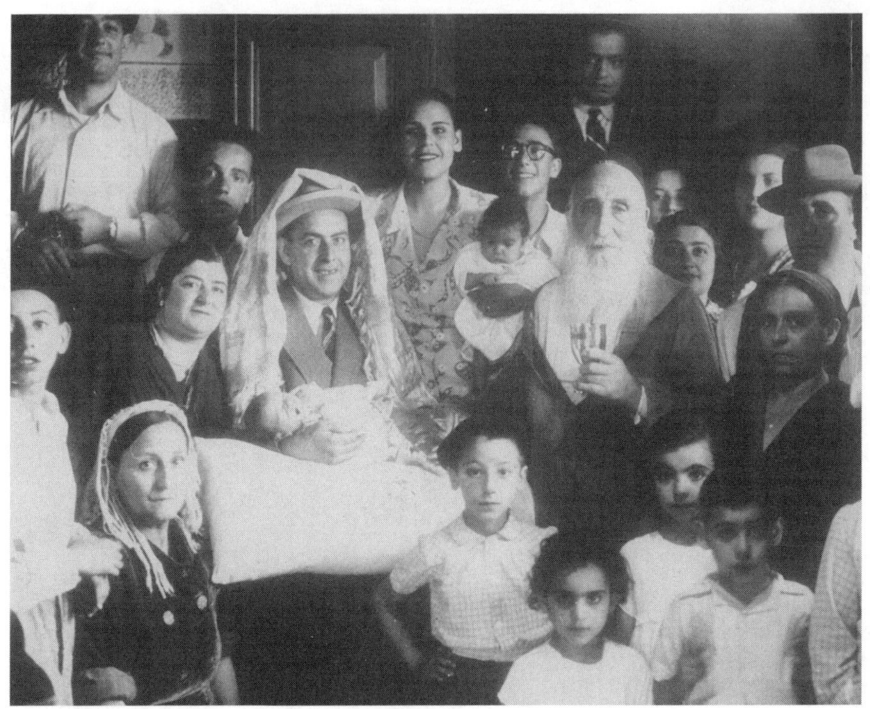

Figure 15.
Celebrating the Brith Milah in the *mellah* of Fez, Morocco, before 1948.
Courtesy American Friends of the Alliance Israélite Universelle, Inc.

Figure 16.
Typing class, Casablanca, Morocco.
Courtesy American Friends of the Alliance Israélite Universelle, Inc.

Figure 17.
Jewish high school class in halakhah (law), Ecole Normale Hébraïque de Casablanca, February 1952.
Courtesy American Friends of the Alliance Israélite Universelle, Inc.

Figure 18.
Hebrew class, Tunis, 1958.
Courtesy American Friends of the Alliance Israélite Universelle, Inc.

Figure 19.
Physical education class for girls, Alliance school in Iran, 1936.
Courtesy American Friends of the Alliance Israélite Universelle, Inc.

Figure 20.
Sukkoth play, Talmud Torah, Otzar ha-Torah, Hamadan, Iran.
Courtesy American Friends of the Alliance Israélite Universelle, Inc.

Figure 21.
Marriage contract (*ketubbah*), Alexandria, Egypt, 1835 (paper, watercolor, and ink). Courtesy of Israel Museum, Jerusalem.

Figure 22.
Rabbi Yehuda Albagli (1870–1937), Izmir, Turkey.
Courtesy Israel Museum, Jerusalem.

Figure 23.
Midnineteenth-century Jewish women of Turkey in outdoor costume wearing the *ferace* cloak and the voluminous *halebi* covered by a scarf (wood engraving).
Courtesy Israel Museum, Jerusalem.

Figure 24.
Jewish couple in traditional Kurdish attire, Kurdistan, 1950s.
Courtesy Israel Museum, Jerusalem.

Figure 25.
Rabbi Avraham Palaggi (1809–99), Izmir, Turkey. In official attire.
Courtesy Israel Museum, Jerusalem.

Figure 26.
A Jewish family, Salonika, Greece, early in the twentieth century. The seated woman is wearing the traditional *kofya,* with its echoes of Spanish tradition.
Courtesy Israel Museum, Jerusalem.

Figure 27.
Bride wearing traditional garb, with her bridesmaids, Sana^{c}a, Yemen, 1930s.
Courtesy Israel Museum, Jerusalem.

Figure 28.
Jewish woman spinning, Djerba, Tunisia.
Courtesy Israel Museum, Jerusalem.

Figure 29.
A Jewish family from Iraq in traditional and transitional attire.
Courtesy Israel Museum, Jerusalem.

Figure 30.
Models wear the traditional bridal attire of Herat, Afghanistan.
Courtesy Israel Museum, Jerusalem.

igure 31.
ummer *teva,* the platform from which prayers and Torah readings are conducted, in courtyard of the syna-
ogue, Aleppo, Syria.
ourtesy Israel Museum, Jerusalem.

Figure 32.
Yambol Synagogue, Istanbul, Turkey, 1983.
Courtesy Israel Museum, Jerusalem.

Figure 33.
Synagogue interior, Sanaʿa, Yemen, ca. 1907–9.
Courtesy Israel Museum, Jerusalem.

Figure 34.
Repoussé Torah shield made from the back of a mirror, Turkey, dedicated 1907.
Courtesy Israel Museum, Jerusalem.

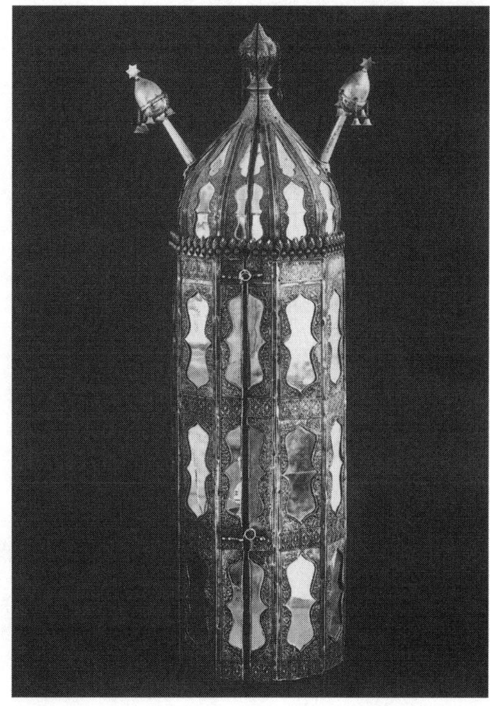

Figure 35.
Torah case, Iraq.
Courtesy Israel Museum, Jerusalem.

Figure 36.
Cover for reader's desk, originally a prayer rug, wool and cotton, Turkey, early nineteenth century. Courtesy Jewish Museum, New York/Art Resource, N.Y.

Part 2

COUNTRY-BY-COUNTRY SURVEY

CHAPTER

14

Ottoman Turkey

Jacob M. Landau

Turkey—that is, Anatolia—the hub of the Ottoman Empire, with Istanbul (formerly Constantinople) as the capital, was for centuries an important center of Jewish life and activity. Jews were one group among many in the Ottoman lands. Although the population ratios changed frequently because of internal and external migration, eastern Anatolia was inhabited chiefly by Turks, Kurds, and Armenians, while a sizable number of Greeks lived in the main towns of western Anatolia, in addition to Turks and Armenians. Members of many other groups, both European and Middle Eastern, entered the region (to trade or to settle there), a process that continued throughout the nineteenth century. Muslims were generally the majority, most of them Sunni, although Shiites inhabited parts of central and eastern Anatolia, especially among the Kurds. Jews lived mostly in the cities and towns of western and central Anatolia, with sizable communities in Istanbul and Izmir (Smyrna). In the eighteenth century the population of both cities became increasingly heterogeneous, and European newcomers became increasingly evident.

By the end of the eighteenth century the Ottoman Empire was in a state of destabilization. It had lost numerous wars with Europe and Russia and had retreated from several provinces, notably Hungary. In the last years of the century the French occupied Egypt. Even if that were to be temporary, it was symbolic of Ottoman military weakness; this was related to outdated technology, economic difficulties, administrative inefficiency, and the erosion of integrity among the political leadership.

In technology the Ottomans had fallen well behind the European powers. This was evident in the deterioration of their naval power and marine commerce, as well in their sea and land transport systems. External trade went increasingly to the European powers, which were gaining mastery of the seas. For this reason and others, the Ottoman currency was repeatedly devalued, agriculture and industry remained traditional and largely manual, and taxes were collected by using harsh measures. The public administration was corrupted by greed and nepotism and, from the sultan down, was often incapable of making reasonable decisions in the public interest.

From Istanbul and the nearby Anatolian region came many of the ideas and activities aimed at improving the crumbling empire. Various Ottoman intellectuals had earlier pointed out the need to acquire and use knowledge from the West. Yet the political establishment, long content with adopting only military innovations, began serious social change only in the last century of the empire. This modernization was essentially selective and defensive; it was not designed to alter the traditional system but to strengthen it against foreign pressures and dangers.

Called the Tanzimat, or Reforms, period, it began in the 1820s and 1830s and had periods of some success. Sultan Mahmud II (r. 1808–39) disbanded the janissary corps, a conservative military group, and Abdülmecid I (r. 1839–61) and Abdülaziz (r. 1861–76) contributed to some modernization in the fields of education, finance, public administration, and justice. Gradually, the Ottomans built roads, took measures to control epidemics, inaugurated regular postal services (1834), strung telegraph lines (since 1856), and built railroads later in the century. State schools (and private foreign schools) led to professional colleges for the training of doctors, dentists, veterinarians, engineers, and lawyers. The number of printing presses increased (in Istanbul alone, from nine to fifty-four between 1850 and 1883), the number of newspapers grew (from 1860 on), and many books were published (from 1876 to 1890, four thousand titles in Turkish).

Two imperial edicts, in 1839 and 1856, abolished certain state-imposed abuses and emphasized the full equality of all Ottoman subjects, irrespective of religion. The edicts were intended both to impress foreign powers and to recruit the support of the empire's entire population. While some reforms were carried out, at least in part, and prepared the ground for future modernization, the proposed full equality of Christians, Jews, and Muslims had only a limited effect. For example, the Ottomans appointed few non-Muslims to municipal or state councils, and by 1885 only ninety-nine Jews were reported to be employed in government service. It was, after all, a Muslim empire. The Turks were strongly conscious of the superiority of their religion; they had their own culture, literature, and traditions, all deeply infused with Islam. The minorities had their own economic, trade, and craft activities—in which they often proved quite successful—but even the nineteenth century was too early to talk practically of full social, legal, and political equality. In fact, the turn-of-the-century reign of Abdülhamid II (r. 1876–1909) was markedly authoritarian and overly influenced by the Islamic establishment. The Committee of Union and Progress (known as the Young Turks), which ruled Turkey between 1909 and 1918—the period that included Turkey's losing role in World War I—was inclined to base itself on the empire's Turkish elements. The Young Turks' policy of Turkification discouraged those who favored Ottomanization (the mobilization of all Ottoman subjects, irrespective of origin and religion) to save the empire. The Jews of Turkey, a relatively small community, had to live cautiously among those forces and tendencies.

JEWS IN OTTOMAN TURKEY

Even before the Ottomans came out of Central Asia, Jews had established communities in Anatolia, as well as in other regions of what became the Ottoman Empire. These communities grew in number and size from immigration, chiefly that of Jews expelled from Spain and Portugal at the end of the fifteenth century. In Anatolia the first new arrivals settled in the western parts (largely in Istanbul and nearby places) and later in the central region. The oppression of the Jews in several other Christian countries (France, the Italian states) soon increased Jewish emigration. While earlier emigrants had been mostly Eastern European Ashkenazim, those from the Iberian Peninsula and southern Europe were chiefly Sephardim. Istanbul, proclaimed the empire's capital upon its conquest from the Byzantines by Sultan Mehmed II in 1453, attracted many Jews for its economic potential. What attracted Jews and others to the Ottoman Empire was the relatively unhampered freedom of religious practice and education, as well as a relatively liberal policy of immigration. Thus Turkey's Jewish population is a mix of old-timers and waves of newcomers, of former Ottoman subjects and foreign ones (the latter prominent in Istanbul and Izmir), even as late as the twentieth century.

While there is some doubt about the figures, Istanbul had almost 52,000 Jews in 1911–12; Izmir, about 16,000 in 1891; Aydin, about 36,600 in 1912; Bursa, more than 2,000, in 1911–12. The total Jewish population of Anatolia (including Istanbul) was estimated at about 116,500 in 1911–12, and about 17,000 Jews were living in Edirne (Adrianople) in nearby Thrace. The numbers increased soon afterward with the arrival of Jews from Balkan territories lost to the Ottoman Empire in the Balkan Wars. Most of the

Anatolian Jews lived in provincial capitals and settled only in the rural areas of those provinces bordering on Iraq. During World War I (1914–18) and Turkey's War of Independence (1919–22) the number of Jews was considerably depleted through emigration.

Almost all Jewish townspeople lived in the same quarter (*mahalle*), or quarters, or sections thereof, ghettoizing themselves voluntarily. This was long-standing practice in the Ottoman Empire, and many Jews preferred it so that they could more easily observe their own rites and customs, be near their synagogues and schools, and avoid the temptations offered by close contact with members of other faiths. Living accommodations were limited, and fires were frequent and destructive. In Istanbul most Jews lived in the Balat and Hasköy districts, divided into wealthier and poorer streets, whose role shifted with time. In the nineteenth and twentieth centuries the better-off moved to the "European" districts of Galata and Beyoğlu, as well as to the suburbs of Kadiköy, Kuzguncuk, Ortaköy, and Arnavutköy, and to islands in the Sea of the Marmara. Jewish people started to settle in Izmir only in the late sixteenth century; increasing numbers of Sephardim moved there, with Converso families (false converts to Christianity) from Spain and Portugal remaining prominent into the early twentieth century.

JEWISH COMMUNITIES

During the nineteenth century the Jewish community was organized in a *millet* (a religious unit) whose main principles incorporated a form of autonomy; it was based not on geographical location but on religious affinity and was led by religious figures who had both religious and secular authority. The Ottoman authorities retained some control but left the *millet* to administer its own affairs, courts of justice, education, hospitals, philanthropic institutions, sanitation, and lighting. They expected the leaders of the *millet* to collect taxes and forward the required amount to the state. Certain economic activities were earmarked for Jewish merchant and craft guilds affiliated with the *millet*, and these frequently reflected the majority choices in occupation and artisanship.

The *millet* system continued until the end of World War I and the collapse of the empire. Its greatest advantages were that it allowed each *millet* to maintain and foster its own traditions and culture with minimal state interference, thus reducing social conflict with other *millet* communities. Its disadvantages were that it precluded modernization and did not ultimately prevent intercommunal conflict, because economic relations with other *millets* continued to exist, as did prejudices perhaps further nourished by pride, competition, and a lack of reciprocal acquaintance.

The communities that formed the Jewish *millet* were made up of various groups—with different heritages—in every large town and in some smaller ones as well. Many preserved their original traditions. Three distinct groups were prominent at the beginning of the *millet* system: Romaniotes, Ashkenazim, and Sephardim. The Romaniotes were descended from Jews who had lived in or come from the area under Eastern Roman, then Byzantine, rule; as they frequently spoke Greek, they were also known as Griegos. The Ashkenazim (from *Ashkenaz,* Hebrew for Germany) were descended from Jews who had emigrated from Central Europe during the Middle Ages or later, seeking a more congenial environment. In the eighteenth to nineteenth centuries they were joined by Ashkenazim escaping persecution in Eastern Europe; they spoke Yiddish or various European languages, and many were strictly observant in their religious practices. The third group was the Sephardim (from *Sepharad,* Hebrew for Spain), descended mostly from Jews expelled from Spain and Portugal in the 1490s; they spoke Judeo-Spanish (sometimes called Judezmo or Ladino) and, more rarely, Arabic, as they were joined in the Ottoman lands by North African and other Arabic-speaking Jews. In time the Romaniotes fused with the Sephardim, while the two other groups split into subgroups, generally by area of origin, such as the Italian Jews. The subgroups often differed from one another not only in language and liturgical traditions but also in food, drink, and behavior. Even greater differences existed between all the Jewish groups and the Karaites, a sect that accepted only the Bible as its authority. Another group was the *dönme,* descendants of the seventeenth-century messianic pretender Shabbetai Zevi and his followers, who converted to Islam in 1666 but who continued to be crypto-Jews.

Consequently, in Istanbul, Izmir, and other large cities (but also in some smaller ones) the Jewish community comprised many self-governing *kahals* (congregations), usually organized by common geographical origins; the *kahals* selected their own officiating rabbis and managed their own schools (Talmud Torah), synagogues, social services, bathhouse, slaughterhouse, hospital, pharmacy, cemetery, and charities. They donated food and clothing to the poor, provided dowries for indigent brides, visited and helped the sick, made loans to the needy, buried the poor, ransomed captives and slaves, and assisted needy pupils. The heads of the *kahal* maintained contact with the leadership of the Jewish community, the town authorities, and other Ottoman officials, such as the *qadi,* or Muslim judge, who regulated and registered property and commercial transactions, legal documents, and tax payments; the *muhtasib*, responsible for prices, measures, and weights in the marketplace; the guild leaders; and others. The *kahal* official who served as a go-between with the Ottoman leaders was called *kâhya* or *kethüda* in Turkish and *shtadlan* in Hebrew.

RABBIS AND OTHER COMMUNITY LEADERS

The rabbi was the Jewish community's highest official, a spiritual leader who had a say in many day-to-day secular matters as well. He led the services in the synagogue, as well as at weddings, circumcisions, and funerals; he chaired the meetings of the *bet-din* (religious court), issuing ordinances, signing contracts, and occasionally imposing fines and other penalties; he took responsibility for Jewish schools and was sometimes the teacher. The rabbi was assisted in the *bet-din* by the *dayyanim* (judges), and in his secular duties by the *parnasim* (lay representatives who sat in a council, the *ma^ca-mad*). From the eighteenth century on, with the general Ottoman economic decline the wealthier members of the *kahal* became increasingly influential in the decision making that had been the responsibility of the rabbis and other officials. Thus the rabbis had to contend with the sometimes officious intervention of the wealthier members, with fractious members within the *kahal*, and even with those who distanced themselves from the *kahal*.

The *parnasim* administered most of the lay affairs of the *kahal*, guided by the rabbi and in consultation with some of the more influential members. They frequently appointed the rabbi and schoolteachers; supervised prices and quality of products; and regulated community taxation, collecting more from the rich than from the poor. Also, they set social norms within their *kahal*: the order of precedence at ceremonies; the form of clothes, hairstyles, beards, conversation, and behavior; and the size of tombstones and the form of the inscriptions on them. Moreover, they often strove to settle disputes amicably. The *kahal* enforced the codes of law and behavior by surveillance and punishment, although the *kahal* had to appeal to the Muslim authorities for intervention in serious infractions and sometimes for enforcing the decisions of the *bet-din*.

While many Ottoman Jewish communities elected their own chief rabbi, in 1835 the Ottomans conferred the title of chief rabbi (*hakhambâshi*) on Rabbi Avraham Levi of Istanbul. The new position was in principle equal to the parallel appointments of the Orthodox and Armenian patriarchs. This made the chief rabbi a representative figure before the authorities and necessitated a special diploma of appointment (in Turkish, *berât*). The Jewish community of Istanbul, which preferred to select its own rabbi rather than accept the one imposed by the authorities, regarded this arrangement with some reserve. Only a generation later, in 1865, did the chief rabbi come to be accepted there, but power struggles between traditionalists and reformers continued. The *nizâmnâme* (constitution or charter) of that year, prepared by Rabbi Yakir Astruc Geron under state supervision, offered an Ottoman solution to some tensions within the Istanbul Jewish community—reorganizing it. This organic law for the Jews was modeled on somewhat similar ones for the Greeks (1860) and the Armenians (1862), which followed the sultan's edict on minorities of 1856. The *nizâmnâme* for the Jews contained five chapters. The first dealt with the appointment of the chief rabbi, who had to be an Ottoman subject aged thirty to seventy. The second set down the chief rabbi's duties and prerogatives: to act according to prevailing laws and remain in touch with the community councils. The third established a general council of eighty delegates from Istanbul and another forty from the Ottoman provinces; the Istanbul delegates, sixty public representatives and twenty rabbis, would carry out the day-to-day work. The fourth and fifth chapters provided that the general council would elect a spiritual council of seven rabbis, appointed for life, to safeguard religious practice, ensure conformity to Ottoman law, and impose penalties for infractions; and a lay council of nine members, appointed for two years to supervise the community's financial contributions to the government, protect the property of orphans, and, more generally, see that the *nizâmnâme* was obeyed.

In the first elections in Istanbul (carried out in the late 1860s), 5,141 Jewish men aged twenty or older participated, with almost half the voters coming from the Hasköy quarter. The bottom line was that this *nizâmnâme* curtailed the powers of the rabbis and increased those of the *parnasim*; however, the various bodies specified were not always fully active, and the members who favored reforms had to be careful during the absolute reign of Abdülhamid II. Moreover, for some time the chief rabbi of Istanbul was unable to impose his full authority on local rabbis, who also called themselves chief rabbis, in such other important towns as Izmir, Bursa, and Edirne. While in certain cases local chief rabbis and others consulted the chief rabbi of Istanbul, more usually they all led and served their own communities as they saw fit. The chief rabbi of Istanbul took part in official state ceremonies and was supposed to recommend to the government the appointment of local chief rabbis, but in practice these were duly elected by their own communities and merely confirmed in their jobs by the authorities.

The situation changed radically with the appointment of Haim Nahoum as chief rabbi of Istanbul in 1908. During the twelve years that he officiated, Nahoum showed himself to be a capable diplomat and probably the most political of all rabbis in the Ottoman Empire up to his time. He had studied in Izmir and Istanbul and then in Paris, where he established close relations with the Alliance Israélite Universelle (AIU), an association set up in 1860 to promote Jewish welfare and particularly Jewish education, and with several of the leaders of the Young Turks. When the latter organization seized power in 1908, Nahoum used the trust it had in him to gain nomination as chief rabbi, after he was duly elected by the Jewish community in Istanbul. His 1909 *berât* emphasized that Nahoum was chief rabbi not only of the Jews in Istanbul and its dependencies but of all Jews in the empire. He then traveled among the Jewish communities of the empire to persuade or pressure them to accept his mediation and leadership. Closely affiliated with the AIU and a Sephardi, a French speaker, and a reformer by reputation, Nahoum used all his talents and government support to have his leadership accepted. On his travels he moderated and resolved the perennial squabbles within numerous communities, between the strictly religious and the liberal minded, the Sephardim and Ashkenazim, the partisans of France or Germany, the supporters of the AIU or the Zionists, *kahals* based on different areas of migration, as well as individuals and groups competing merely for power. Moreover, he succeeded in increasing the revenues of the entire Jewish community. As the last chief rabbi of the Ottoman Empire, Nahoum, ally and companion of several of the Young Turks, shared their eventual defeat and left his position in 1920. He became the chief rabbi of Egypt in 1925, while the Jews soon had to contend with a new situation in what became the Turkish Republic, under the secular government of Mustafa Kemal Atatürk.

The knowledge of languages changed over time, partly due to internal and external mobility and partly the result of acculturation into Ottoman society and migration into the Jewish communities in Anatolia. A major factor in language loss, shift, and preservation was education. In the nineteenth and twentieth centuries the Ottoman Empire provided heterogeneous education.

EDUCATION

Anatolia, which had the large cities of Istanbul and Izmir, several medium-size ones, as well as rural areas—all with a mixed population, culturally and religiously, offers a good example of Ottoman education. Ottoman reformers of the nineteenth century, while not always discussing education specifically, were very much aware of its significance. In addition to the institutions for training military experts, they fostered a wide network of lower secondary schools (the *rüshdiye*) that they opened to non-Muslims in 1861. Eight years later they also opened the secular primary schools (the *iptidâis*) to non-Muslims and increased the size of both state networks. Separate religious schools for the minority groups continued to exist until World War I. Few Jews attended the state schools, preferring their own.

Throughout the nineteenth and early twentieth centuries, the emphasis in Jewish education continued to be on religious instruction. It started in the *meldar* (Judeo-Spanish for 'to read'), where boys traditionally learned to read the Bible in Hebrew and translate it into Judeo-Spanish. The Talmud Torah (sometimes synonymous with the *meldar*) frequently took study further, continuing into Bible commentaries and, in rarer cases, into the Talmud, often taught by an experienced rabbi. In the larger urban centers a yeshiva (college of religious studies) would prepare experts in Jewish law, up to and including rabbinate standard. In the nineteenth century the level in many Anatolian Talmud Torahs declined to a *meldar* level. The establishment of Christian missionary schools in Istanbul and Izmir heightened the need to modernize the Jewish schools so their programs could compete with the best missionary schools—which religious Jews suspected of intending to convert any non-Christian pupils (meaning Jews, because the Ottoman authorities forbade the conversion of Muslims). The Christian missionary schools attracted the upwardly mobile wealthy Jews interested in foreign-language instruction and poor Jews looking for free education and a hot meal.

The modernization of Jewish education in the larger cities and towns was a by-product of the modernizing and Westernizing trends in Ottoman society and became quite evident in the midnineteenth century. By then a small but articulate Jewish middle class lived and traded with Europeans and others in Istanbul and Izmir. Without renouncing their traditional outlook in matters of religion, they were well aware of the need for some European education, including a knowledge of languages, to cope with the demands of growing foreign trade. These Jews were also well aware that their main rivals in the European trade, the Greeks and Armenians, had already instituted school systems more practically suited to changes in commerce. Foreign Jews in Istanbul and Izmir, often called Francos, formed part of the international Jewish business class that worked in many Mediterranean cities, maintaining contacts with Italy and enjoying the protection of foreign states (which afforded them a certain freedom of action). The Francos and others helped to enlist the assistance of Western European Jewry in modernizing Jewish education in the Ottoman Empire—at a time when the Jews of Europe and the Americas were becoming more interested in modernizing their brethren in the Ottoman Empire.

The main effort took the form of investment by Jewish personalities and organizations in establishing modern schools, with the intention of propagating Western educational goals, curriculums, and methods of instruction. Albert Cohn, sent by the French branch of the Rothschilds, managed in 1854 to open such schools in Istanbul and Izmir (as well as in Jerusalem). The school in Istanbul, directed by a French teacher, started in the Hasköy quarter with seventy-six pupils; the one in Izmir closed down soon afterward. The main innovation was the teaching of secular subjects and French, Turkish, and Italian, in addition to Hebrew. Local rabbinical opposition to the teaching of French and secular matters started a conflict that was to be repeated time and again. A compromise, strengthening religious instruction, was respected only briefly. The conflict continued within Istanbul Jewry, based on differing worldviews and the fear of many rabbis that they might lose their modest teachers' fees. The *nizâmnâme* of 1865 increased the power of lay members in the Istanbul community over the rabbinical establishment in education and other domains, but the conflict continued in Istanbul, Izmir, and other Jewish centers. Traditionalist opposition brought about the closing of modernized schools in Izmir, Edirne, and Salonika, and limited their success in Istanbul. Committees of Francos in Istanbul, Salonika, and elsewhere contacted the AIU to solicit aid for reform-minded projects. While the school in the Hasköy quarter continued on its own until it closed in 1890, the AIU established new ones in Edirne, Izmir, and elsewhere. The AIU schools were segregated by gender and usually were established upon the request of local Jewish notables, who organized themselves as regional committees of the AIU and undertook to maintain those schools financially, at least for a while. Between 1875 and 1882 they founded eleven schools for boys or girls in Istanbul with the direct or indirect involvement of the AIU, with each major Jewish quarter getting one such school. The Judeo-Spanish press generally supported the establishment of these and other AIU schools, in Izmir and Edirne (as mentioned) and in Bursa in 1885. The number of pupils increased between 1879 and 1908 in Istanbul from 865 to 3,556 pupils; in Izmir, from 140 boys to 312, and from 100 girls to 351; in Edirne, from 216 boys to 1,106, and from 300 girls to 551. Education in French and vocational training was provided both in large cities and small urban centers such as Bursa, Aydin, Manisa, Tekirdağ, and others. This training and the vocational courses for girls had only limited attendance, perhaps because manual work was not perceived as prestigious enough by the Jews in Turkey and hardly suited their social aspirations. The general schools of the AIU had a profound influence on a large segment of the Ottoman Jewish population in the last half of the nineteenth century, chiefly in the direction of westernization and secularization, as well as in its bicultural orientation in Ladino and French. Through their schooling parts of the Jewish secular elite adopted a distant culture rather than that of their immediate vicinity, leading to a continuing erosion of traditionalism. By the turn of the twentieth century, a small group of students from throughout the empire attended Ottoman universities. Included in this group were at least two Jews from Palestine, David Ben-Gurion and Itzhak Ben-Zvi, who attended the law faculty in Istanbul during the years immediately before World War I.

THE STRUGGLE ABOUT MODERNIZATION

Defined strictly as westernization, modernization became the goal for only a segment of urban Jews in the late Ottoman Empire. Many traditional circles considered it anathema, and not a few religious Jews in Istanbul, Izmir, and elsewhere, clustered around their rabbis, had a vested interest in the continuation of the traditional ways of life; coupled with their religiosity, their opposition to modernization was all the more powerful. Much opposition focused on law and education: these circles were against bringing Jewish suits to any court but the *bet-din,* and they worked hard to discourage parents from enrolling their children in secular schools, arguing that these might induce conversion to Christianity. They even opposed Jewish enrollment in the new Military Medical School in Istanbul—even after a kosher kitchen had been installed there. Soon the number of local Jewish physicians decreased, although a Jewish hospital was founded in Izmir in 1874. A similar one was created in Istanbul only later, in 1897, due to lack of funds and physicians and to squabbles within the Jewish community there.

Not all rabbis, however, opposed modernization. The chief rabbi of Istanbul, Yakup Avigdor (1860–63), was inclined toward modernizing Jewish schools, but he ran into strong traditionalist opposition. He had more success in modernizing the community's administration, in altering the tax laws to raise revenues, and in organizing the Council of Notables and the Bet-Din ha-Gadol (superior court) to standardize the dispensation of justice. Socially, most signs of modernization were noticeable among the Francos, as well as among the wealthier Jews in the cities and towns, who had been moving away from the Jewish quarters and into European suburbs and neighborhoods. Gradual changes in headgear and clothing followed, religious bans against these innovations notwithstanding. For men the fez replaced the turban, later to give way to the hat; coats replaced cloaks and other robes; women's clothes changed more slowly, but women gradually adopted European fashions, with modifications for modesty's sake. These changes penetrated much more slowly into the poorer classes, who were still living and working in their accustomed quarters in Istanbul and Izmir, as well as in the smaller cities and towns of Anatolia.

These and other aspects of modernization were promoted by the founding of new organizations and associations, an innovative feature of socialization, compared to older conservative groupings of a traditional character, such as religiously inspired ones or professional guilds. Similar trends also occurred in non-Jewish Ottoman society at that time. Among the Jewish modernizing associations, the AIU had an important role. The local committees, set up in 1863 to initiate schools and then to support them, continued to function, and later in the century alumni of the AIU schools established new associations, in Izmir (1896), Salonika (1897), Edirne (1901), and Istanbul (1910). Although each had only a few hundred members, together they set the precedent for a new type of association whose influence reached beyond its size. The AIU associations initiated a varied program of theatrical and musical events, lectures, sports activities, and libraries for all AIU alumni. In Izmir and Edirne they established "workers' societies" for graduates of the AIU vocational schools, and these resulted in both professional and social advantages. Many groups were also active individually in spreading modernization via cultural initiatives.

THE ADVENT OF ZIONISM

One of the few avenues of political modernization for Ottoman Jews was Zionism. The AIU leadership was consistently non-Zionist and even anti-Zionist. During the reign of Abdülhamid II, Zionism was soon regarded with suspicion by the authorities, apprehensive as they were about all nationalist movements that endangered the territorial integrity of the empire. During the decade of Young Turk rule, which followed the same antinationalist policy, the Zionist movement sometimes could operate in the Ottoman Empire, albeit circumspectly. This it did, chiefly in Istanbul and Salonika, in the years immediately before and during World War I—despite government surveillance and the reluctance of many Jewish community leaders, who were apprehensive that their standing would be compromised. Chief Rabbi Nahoum at first supported Zionism but later became a strong opponent—probably because of his friendship with several leading Young Turks and the persistently anti-Zionist AIU.

Zionists from Palestine and elsewhere, activists such as Ze'ev Jabotinsky and Richard Lichtheim, came to Istanbul and tried to mobilize local Jews into clubs to form an influential group; their supporters came largely from the middle class or from economically underprivileged groups on the fringes of modernity. In this way these support groups acquired a feeling and a taste for political action. They were also given an opportunity to use their leisure time constructively, in athletic activities, learning Hebrew, and debating ideology. A Zionist Hebrew weekly, *Ha-Mevasser*, appeared from 1909 to 1911, and other Ottoman newspapers, occasionally financed by Zionists, sometimes published articles favorable to Zionism. In 1914 the Ottoman Zionist Organization was founded openly and was soon banned by the minister of the interior. Another organization, the Fédération Sioniste d'Orient, established in 1919, represented the various associations in Istanbul and spread to other cities later; its membership reached four thousand in 1920. The Zionists failed to take over the Jewish community in Istanbul, despite gaining some sympathizers; however, in the Zionist conflict with AIU personnel and others, the Istanbul sympathizers helped the Jews of Turkey toward political modernization.

POLITICS AND CULTURE

Only at the economic level did Jews make any real progress. The Jews of Turkey were mainly involved in the politics of their own community. The few who participated in more general politics, like the chief rabbi or prominent businessmen, did not involve the community. Even the Jews elected to the Ottoman parliaments, such as Nissim Matzliah, generally spoke as individuals. The few involved in the Young Turk movement had only minor roles and acted on their own. Conversely, the Ottoman authorities, wary of nationalist movements, were well aware that the Jews had no state to support any secessionist designs (unlike the Greeks). The authorities realized that even the ambitions of Zionism regarding Palestine held little danger to the empire until and unless one of the great European powers supported the Zionists.

For Jews social contact was often limited to family and to business relations, whether with other Jews or non-Jews. For the Ottoman period the Jews lived in their own city quarter; even those who later moved into more "mixed" neighborhoods, as in Istanbul, frequently continued to socialize with other Jews. Perhaps the wealthiest Francos associated with some Christians or Muslims of their own class. Toward the turn of the twentieth century associations of the liberal professions became common; this afforded some added opportunities for meeting socially with non-Jews. Culturally, however, Turkey's Jews remained apart. With their own libraries and printing presses, they frequently moved in several almost mutually exclusive cultural circles: the Hebraic, for the religious and some of the secular Jews (including some Zionists); the Judeo-Spanish, with its lively press and Sephardic traditions; and the European (chiefly French, Italian, or German), for the Francos or newly arrived immigrants. Relatively few Jews assimilated into the Ottoman or Turkish social environment: knowledge of Turkish was far from widespread among Jews and even less so among Jewish intellectuals. Throughout the period discussed, no Jewish writer was working in Turkish—whether poet, novelist, or playwright. A historian of Ottoman Jewry living in Istanbul, Moise Franco (1864–1905), wrote his *Essai sur l'histoire des Israélites de l'empire Ottoman depuis les origines jusqu'à nos jours* (Paris, 1897) in French, not in Turkish. An expert in Ottoman history like Abraham Galanté (1883–1959) or a scholar of Turkish nationalism like Moiz Kohen (1883–1961, alias Munis Tekinalp who moved from Salonika to Istanbul in 1912) is the rare exception—and even they wrote only a part of their studies in Turkish.

Contrast the rare Turkish periodical published by Jews, *Üstad* (1889), with the active Judeo-Spanish press. Izmir alone had the following publications: *La Buena Esperansa* (started in 1842), *La Puerta del Oriente* (1846), *Esperansa* (1871), and *La Verdad* (1884). In Istanbul the Judeo-Spanish press was headed by *El Tyempo*, which was edited from 1871 to 1930 by David Fresco, who also had a hand in *El Telegrafo* (1872–1930); *El Nouvelista* appeared there too, from 1890 to 1922. All three Jewish papers in Istanbul were remarkably long lived.

JEWS IN THE ECONOMY

The most important arena for Ottoman Jews was the economic, and their main relations with the authorities and with other communities were concentrated there. The nineteenth and early twentieth centuries were a time of serious economic decline in the empire, a sizable part of whose population became poorer, although a wealthy group continued to prosper (chiefly several families like the Camondos, philanthropists and supporters of the arts). Competition increased between the individuals and communities in commerce and manufacturing, particularly between the Jewish and Christian communities, because the Muslims had—and maintained—their own occupations. Only in the early twentieth century would a Turkish Muslim entrepreneurial class come into its own to rival those of the Jews and Christians. Jews, Greeks, and Armenians in Turkey were rivals in banking and the export-import business (they all had connections abroad), as well as in textile products (chiefly silk and wool) and such other manufactured goods as hardware, paper, books, and glassware. Some were intermediaries in the internal trade between Anatolia and Istanbul; a few Anatolian Jews took part in the production and trade in rugs. Most however, busied themselves with the more modest work of manufacturing and selling buttons and ribbons or of dyeing cloth. Others were reduced to working as peddlers and porters along the coasts. The Jews of Bursa (near the Sea of Marmara) were reported to be particularly impoverished.

Tensions caused by commercial competition affected other areas, sometimes expressed in anti-Semitism from Christians (but rarely from Muslims). This, when combined with Christian suspicions and superstitions, sometimes brought about entirely baseless blood libels (the claim that Jewish ritual used Christian blood) by Christians against Jews. In Izmir and elsewhere blood libel sometimes even led to pogroms. The delicate fabric of social and economic relations within and beyond the Jewish communities was increasingly strained in the last decades of the Ottoman Empire. In 1920, following the Ottoman defeat in World War I and the constitutional establishment in 1923 of the Jews in the new Republic of Turkey, the centuries-long chapter of Ottoman Anatolia ended.

RECOMMENDED READING

Benbassa, Esther. *A Sephardic Chief Rabbi in Politics, 1892–1923*. Tuscaloosa: University of Alabama Press, 1997.

Landau, Jacob M. *Jews, Arabs, Turks*. Jerusalem: Magnes Press, 1993.

Levy, Avigdor, ed. *The Jews of the Ottoman Empire*. Princeton, N.J.: Darwin, 1994.

Rodrigue, Aron. *French Jews, Turkish Jews: The Alliance Israélite Universelle and the Politics of Jewish Schooling in Turkey, 1860–1925*. Bloomington: Indiana University Press, 1990.

Shaw, Stanford J. *The Jews of the Ottoman Empire and the Turkish Republic*. New York: New York University Press, 1991.

Weiker, Walter E. *Ottomans, Turks, and the Jewish Polity: A History of the Jews of Turkey*. Lanham, Md.: University Press of America, 1992.

CHAPTER

15

The Ottoman Balkans

Aron Rodrigue

Jews lived for centuries as as a small but significant element within the various ethnic and religious groups that inhabited the valleys, coasts, and mountainous areas of the Ottoman Balkans, which marked the northwestern reaches of Ottoman rule. By the seventeenth century Sephardim originating from the Iberian Peninsula demographically outnumbered the local Greek-speaking Romaniote Jewish communities in this distinctive region of southeastern Europe. The Sephardim absorbed the Romaniote Jews and the small groups of Ashkenazim that arrived periodically from elsewhere in Europe. The new group beginning to emerge from this mix had Judeo-Spanish culture, customs, and rabbinical traditions that marked it as distinctive. The Jewish communities were located along the overland trade routes that went from Venice east to the Adriatic ports of Split (Spalato) and Dubrovnik (Ragusa), Sarajevo, Monastir (Bitola), and Skopje (Üsküb) and down the Aegean coast, either to Salonika or through Belgrade to Central Europe. Jewish communities were also located along another important artery of trade that linked Salonika through Thrace to the Danube River, with communities such as Plovdiv (Philippopolis), Sofia, and Ruse (Ruschuk) connecting the Ottoman Balkans to the Romanian principalities that paid tribute to the Ottomans but nevertheless remained autonomous, and to Hungary and the wider Habsburg Empire. One Jewish community—Salonika, which had fifteen thousand Jews by the early seventeenth century—dominated Balkan Jewry because of its size, economic activities, and cultural life.

Like the rest of the Jews of the Ottoman Empire, each Balkan Jewish community was relatively autonomous, with no juridical hierarchy and no legally recognized center. The chief rabbinate in Istanbul existed briefly as an institution in the fifteenth and sixteenth centuries and was revived in the nineteenth; nevertheless, it never really managed to establish authority over communities beyond Istanbul.

In the Balkan cities that housed many ethnic and religious groups—Turks, Greeks, Bulgarians, Armenians, Serbs, Albanians, and others—the Jews lived in their own city quarter, which also included members of other groups. In many cities, such as Sarajevo and Monastir, a specific type of Jewish dwelling emerged as early as the sixteenth century, a sort of compound in which many families lived around a large courtyard (giving the building complex its name, Il Kurtijo, from *courtyard* in Ladino). Jews had relations with other groups mostly in the realm of economic life, with considerable daily social interchange regarding food, music, clothing, and folk culture. The outside influences were eventually Judeo-Hispanicized through the Ladino language and through the all-encompassing rabbinical culture that set its stamp on all areas of social existence.

The successful years of Balkan Jewry were well over by the eighteenth century, with the general decline of the Ottoman Empire. The empire's central power became weakened, quasi-feudal overlords emerged in the provinces, and local rebellions took their toll. The economic lifeblood of the Balkan Jewish communities—commerce with Venice—went into serious decline with the growing presence of other Western European traders in the Mediterranean and Aegean port cities. Then too, the economic center of all Balkan Jewry, Salonika, was declining because its textile industry was seriously weakened by competition from European textiles in the Ottoman markets. In the sixteenth century work in Salonika's textile industry had provided jobs to thousands of Jews. Large-scale unemployment followed its eclipse in the seventeenth century. Fires, earthquakes, and disease added to the growing misery. Within this social context the Sabbatean messianic movement gained thousands of adherents in Salonika—many of whom would follow the "false messiah" Shabbetai Zevi (1626–76) into apostasy after his conversion to Islam in 1666. With the demoralization that set in after this debacle, the rabbinical culture that had flourished around the great sages of Salonika in the sixteenth century also underwent a serious loss of importance. The economic and social repercussions of these developments reverberated across the Jewish communities of the Balkans. While important families such as the Aries of Samakov in Bulgaria continued to play a significant economic role, the Balkan Jews lost much of their preeminence by the end of the eighteenth century.

The major changes of the nineteenth and early twentieth centuries irrevocably altered Jewish existence in the Balkans. The rise of nationalist movements among the non-Muslim peoples of the region, the overthrow of Ottoman rule and the rise of new nation-states, the introduction of Western industrial capitalist power into the area, and cultural and political westernization all left their marks on the Jewish communities. Whereas the Judeo-Spanish community had constituted itself as a distinctive cultural area under one Ottoman reality, from Belgrade and Sarajevo in the west to Istanbul and Asia Minor in the east (with offshoot communities such as the one in Jerusalem in the south), it soon became fragmented, with new countries establishing suzerainty over the different Jewish centers. The Sephardim of Belgrade were ruled by Serbia, which became independent de facto in 1830 (de jure in 1878). In Bosnia-Herzegovina, Sarajevo came under Habsburg rule in 1878. The state of Bulgaria came into existence in the same year and encompassed most of the Jewish communities of northern Thrace and those south of the Danube. Greece, independent from the Ottomans since 1830, had a relatively small Jewish population until it annexed Salonika during the Balkan Wars of 1912–13. The Macedonian communities of Monastir and Skopje (Üsküb) then became part of the Serbian state. Of all the Sephardic communities of the Balkans, only Edirne (Adrianople) and a few other small Jewish communities in Eastern Thrace remained under Turkish rule on the eve of World War I and would continue to do so with the establishment of the Turkish Republic after the war.

The Ottoman Empire had tried to put its house in order with a series of westernizing reforms that it launched, beginning with the Tanzimat in 1839, the Reform Decree of 1856, and the constitution of 1876 (which remained unimplemented under Abdülhamid II until it was reinstituted after the Young Turk Revolution of 1908). Centralization and state building were, however, the main impetus behind most of these developments. Nevertheless, largely at Western prodding, the Ottoman state improved the civil status of non-Muslims, eventually granting them equal rights in 1856 (they were not subject to compulsory conscription until 1909). The reforms, however, also eroded the autonomy of the non-Muslim *millets,* the members of which now began to be subject to the new Western-inspired secular courts of criminal and civil law. Still, the educational and cultural realms remained within the purview of each *millet,* with the Ottoman state acting episodically and rather weakly in creating a unified school system. Until the Balkan Wars and World War I the overwhelming majority of non-Muslims still attended their own educational institutions, and the Jews were no exception. While successive Ottoman governments were slowly moving toward creating a state-sponsored Ottoman Turkish educational system, a process that received an increased nationalist impetus after the Young Turk Revolution, the goal was far from being reached at the time of the empire's demise.

For Ottoman Jews, after the third quarter of the nineteenth century the educational institutions of the Alliance Israélite Universelle (AIU) came to provide mass Western-style schooling. Imbued with the message of the French Revolution, about citizenship and emancipation—and convinced that the transformation of French Jews in the modern period should be the norm for all Jews—this organization was founded in the 1860s and came to provide a vast network of schools in the Sephardic and Eastern Jewish Diasporas. The schools dispensed an essentially French instruction, with Jewish subjects taught according to the dictates of the ideas of modern Franco-Judaism. After initial struggles with some rabbis and traditionalists, AIU schools displaced much traditional Jewish education. They played a crucial role in the creation of a French-speaking Jewish bourgeoisie.

Nowhere was the work of the AIU more successful than in Salonika. It was supported and facilitated by the presence in the city of a significant group of Francos—Jewish merchant families from Italy, mostly from Livorno—who had begun to arrive in the early eighteenth century. Protégés first of France and then of Tuscany, these merchants were an important part of a trade network that linked the southern and eastern shores of the Mediterranean with much of Europe, mostly through Italy. By the nineteenth century families such as the Allatinis, Fernandezes, and Modianos were some of the most successful entrepreneurs in Salonika. In touch with developments in Western Europe, intermediaries for and partners of Jewish economic interests there, they were the first to realize the significance of the growing economic presence in the Ottoman Levant of modern European capitalism. The Anglo-Ottoman trade convention of 1838 had opened local markets to finished manufactured products of the rapidly industrializing West. Port cities in the eastern Mediterranean grew quickly in this period, which also saw the increased use of the steamboat after the Crimean War.

The ability to speak French, the lingua franca of trade and commerce, became an increasingly desirable skill, and the Francos spearheaded efforts to teach it through Western-style education. Franco notables, such as the bankers and industrialists Moïse Allatini and Salomon Fernandez, working closely with the modernizer Judah Nehama, opened new schools in Salonika even before the arrival of the AIU. The Kupat Hesed Olam (Mutual Welfare Fund), a society that taxed Jewish merchants on their transactions in order to reform community institutions, was founded in 1853 under the sponsorship of Moïse Allatini. In 1856 this body brought a young rabbi from

Strasbourg to reform the central educational institution in Salonika, the great Talmud Torah, and to give evening classes in foreign languages and arithmetic; this effort lasted for five years but ended in failure because of rabbinical opposition. Still, the seeds of change had been planted. The Francos opened an Italian school in 1862, and in the same period the AIU contacted Nehama about exploring the possibilities of opening schools in the city. Only after the election to the chief rabbinate of Salonika of the reform-minded Aaron Gattegno in 1874 was an AIU school established securely. The number of AIU establishments, and others that emulated them, increased rapidly, dispensing an education on all levels to both girls and boys. In 1908 Salonika had 2,132 students in AIU schools, 3,250 students in private institutions that used the AIU curriculum, 1,300 students in foreign schools, and only 1,849 students in rabbinical establishments—most of them in the great Talmud Torah, which had also been somewhat westernized. By 1912 AIU graduates counted among their ranks the majority of the principal Jewish merchants and financiers in Salonika, four hundred in all, as well as 120 teachers, 18 lawyers, 15 journalists, 30 lawyers, 450 artisans, and 4,500 skilled workers.

The increased Western cultural orientation of the Jewish community of Salonika went in tandem with its upward social mobility. The Jewish population constituted the largest ethnic group in the city, 50,000 of a total population of 90,000 in 1870 and 61,439 of 157,889, according to the first Greek census of 1913. Jews came to dominate Salonika's economy by the end of the nineteenth century. A major entrepôt for import and export, linked to Central Europe by a railway since 1880, Salonika had an extraordinary economic boom late in the nineteenth century. It became the third-largest port in the Ottoman Empire, and the volume of goods passing through it doubled, to two million tons, between 1880 and 1912. Until the 1870s the city still exported raw wool and cotton from its hinterland, but it subsequently began to develop an industrial infrastructure, with small factories supplying Macedonian and Ottoman markets with flannel, knitted goods, and wool and cotton products. Tobacco also became a lucrative crop. The main tobacco-growing center was in northern Greece, near Cavalla, but Salonika was the hub of the tobacco trade, as well as an important center for tobacco processing and cigarette manufacture, a business that employed thousands of Jews, especially young women.

Nowhere else in the Ottoman Empire except in Baghdad did the Jews control the economy of a major city as they did in Salonika. The old Franco elite, composed of families such as the Allatinis, Fernandezes, Morpurgos,

Modianos, Saiases, and Torreses, rose to new heights. The Allatinis gained particular renown in international trade and banking. With the Modianos they operated in the cereal trade and in flour production and built a modern flour mill in 1857. They extended their activities to the tobacco trade, built a modern brickyard, and opened the Bank of Salonika in association with foreign partners. The Jewish firm of Capandji, Jehiel, and Bensussan set up a cloth factory in 1911, and Modiano and Fernandez created the famous Olympos distillery. Thirty-eight large Jewish businesses operated in the city in this period, most them specializing in the import and export trade. Hundreds of smaller Jewish enterprises did business in every sector of the Salonikan economy, and Jewish and European firms employed thousands of Jewish white-collar workers. The expansion in Salonikan industry resulted in the formation of the only important working class in the Sephardic world. This group, numbering about ten thousand, was mainly concentrated in the tobacco industry, though it was also to be found in other areas, at the beginning of the twentieth century. The new class of factory workers coexisted alongside the old type of craftsmen and groups such as the Jewish porters, longshoremen, and fishermen who were still present in large numbers in the city.

The smaller Jewish communities of the Ottoman Balkans, such as Monastir and Skopje in Macedonia and Cavalla, Alexandroúpolis (Dede Agach), and Dimetoka in Western Thrace, all in the orbit of Salonika, benefited from its economic rise, which improved their economic positions. Significantly, by the Balkan Wars most of these smaller Jewish communities (which had a population of about a thousand each) had also opened AIU schools. Modern education was a requirement in the new marketplace.

In the second half of the nineteenth century, the Western economic and linguistic reorientation of the Sephardim of the Ottoman Balkans led to an overall Jewish cultural reorientation. French became the language of culture and of the elite, invading Ladino, which became increasingly peppered with French words. At the same time, and paradoxically, the spread of French gave an impetus to the growth of modern Ladino culture. While French had become the language of reference, the masses still continued to use Ladino in daily life, so a popular press and a popular literature were aimed at this audience. The first Ladino newspaper in Salonika, *El Lunar,* was the creation of Judah Nehama in 1865. This was followed by the long-lived *La Epoka* of Saadi Bezalel Halevy, whose son Sam Levy edited the major French newspaper of the city, *Le Journal de Salonique*. Scores of Jewish newspapers, most of them in Ladino, followed. They became an important conduit for the dissemination of new ideas, and they facilitated, as elsewhere in the Sephardic world, the rise of such new genres as novels and novellas, first published as feuilletons (serialized novels) in their pages. Salonika became one of the most important centers of Ladino publishing, one of the linchpins of modern secular Ladino culture.

Modern ideologies such as liberalism, nationalism, and socialism had not yet emerged among the Jewish communities of the Ottoman Balkans before most of this region passed into the control of the new nation-states by 1878. In continuation of their traditional stance, the Balkan Jewish communities remained outside the main political currents that swept this area in the nineteenth century. No Jews were among the nationalists who overthrew Ottoman power. In fact, the interest of the Jews had been well served by the Ottoman multiethnic and multireligious structure that had treated them at worst with benign neglect. In the new nation-states they were to meet for the first time the full force of the modern nationalist state, with its politics of homogenization and its systemic unease in the face of minorities.

In the Balkan lands that remained under Ottoman rule after 1878, namely, Thrace, and Salonika with its Macedonian hinterland, staying out of state politics remained the rule. Political involvement was not really an option under the despotic rule of Abdülhamid II. The commercial elite of Salonika's Jewry, increasingly westernized, controlled the community. Many of its members, as well as the new intellectual class, became active in the Freemasonry movement, which facilitated links with members of similar groups among non-Jews. Many Jews involved with Freemasonry were among the most ardent supporters of the Young Turks, after the revolution of 1908 introduced a brief period of liberalism into the empire. One Jewish deputy from Salonika, Emmanuel Carasso, played an important role in the parliament in Istanbul, and the Salonikan lawyer Emmanuel Salem acted as a constitutional adviser to the government in drafting laws.

As far as the Jewish masses were concerned, real politicization occurred at the communal level. Liberalization allowed the emergence of new political ideologies, and there too Salonika became the main center. Longstanding class resentments in the city fueled the rise of Zionism and socialism. The elite and much of the middle class remained firmly pro-AIU, convinced of the goal of the westernized liberal transformation of the Jews. Nevertheless, some among them, as well as many among the poor, proved to be receptive to Zionism, which emerged in the empire after 1908 when representatives of the World Zionist Organization were sent to Istanbul. They also began to propagandize in other Jewish centers such as Salonika. The terrain had already been prepared by earlier developments. Religious Zionist ideas about the return to Zion had found few followers in the Ottoman Balkans in the midnineteenth century. Growing familiarity with the Hebrew press had, however, contributed to growing knowledge about Zionism among the rabbinical class, as well as among the journalists and the modernizers. This trend was strengthened by the creation of the Society Kadimah (Forward) in 1889 for the propagation of a modern Hebrew language and by the arrival of the famous Hebrew educator Isaac Epstein, who began to teach Hebrew at the Talmud Torah as its director after 1908. Zionism had emerged as the dominant ideology among the Jews of Bulgaria who came to power in their communities during the first decade of the twentieth century, and they closed the AIU schools there. The influence of Bulgarian Zionists on nearby Salonika proved to be an important factor in the development of the movement. Major polemics between the Zionist newspaper *El Avenir* (edited by David Florentin) and *La Tribuna Libera,* and some non-Zionist publications occupied much of the public arena in the years before the Balkan Wars. Numerous Zionist clubs and associations, such as the Maccabi, became important sites of Zionist politicization, and they threatened the non-Zionist communal leadership. Five delegates represented Salonika at the Ninth Zionist Congress in 1909. Zionists in the Balkans became cautious in subsequent years as the Young Turks became increasingly hostile toward them. But by the outbreak of the Balkan Wars, Zionism had become an integral part of the political landscape of Salonika, and it would continue to be so under Greek rule as well.

Socialism was even more successful than Zionism among the Jewish masses. In 1909 a group of Sephardim, a few Bulgarians, and some Macedonians founded the Workers' Socialist Federation of Salonika. Its leader, Abraham Benaroya, was a native of Salonika who had become a socialist activist in Bulgaria. The federation was recognized by the Second International in the year that it was founded. The federation's membership included various non-Jewish elements, but the majority, recruited among the workers of the Tobacco Monopoly and various sectors of nascent industry—typographers, craftsmen, clerks, and dockers—were Jews. The organization involved seven to eight thousand people, and it played a leading role in Salonikan public life through its pamphlets and newspapers, such as the *Jurnal del Lavrador*, *Solidaridad Ovradera*, and *Avanti* (the latter had a print run of more than five thousand in 1912), and had a major influence on the laboring masses. Eleven of the twelve pamphlets published by the federation were in Ladino. Jewish circles were thus introduced to socialism and to its vicissitudes in the Western world via Ladino, while socialist newspapers and publications in other languages also spread the ideas of socialism among the non-Jewish working class.

The Balkan Wars of 1912–13 ended Ottoman rule in the region. Macedonia and Thrace were split between Greece and Serbia. The smaller Jewish communities, as well as Salonika, the jewel of eastern Sephardic Jewry, left the Ottoman orbit, of which they had been an integral part for more than four hundred years. Jews in Salonika saw this as nothing short of a catastrophe. The new borders cut Salonika away from the rich Macedonian hinterland, and they severed the links between it as a port and what was left of the Ottoman Empire. Much of the prosperity of the town, and of its Jewish community, had been linked to those trade routes. The Jews, who feared discrimination, could greet the arrival of rule by the Greeks—long the economic rivals of the Jews in the empire—only with foreboding. Salonika's Jewish leaders of all political persuasions appealed to international Jewish organizations and to leading Western powers for the city to remain under Turkish control or, if not, to make it an independent port city, to no avail. The city was left under Greek rule by the international treaties that followed the wars.

The Jews of the Ottoman Balkans had seen remarkable changes in their last century under Ottoman rule. The Judeo-Spanish world, of which they had been a major part, had begun to slowly fragment with the rise of new nation-states that chipped away at Ottoman power. The empire had instituted reforms that had altered the contours of the political and social existence of the Jews. Deep penetration of the empire's economy by Western powers had offered new challenges and new opportunities, inaugurating the rapid westernization of the communities that succeeded in using the help offered them by Western Jewry—mainly the schools of the Alliance Israélite Universelle. Last but not least, these changes had made the eastern Sephardic communities full-fledged participants in all the major political and cultural currents that swept the larger Jewish world. Paradoxically, while Ottoman rule was weakening, the center of Balkan Sephardic Jewry, Salonika, had experienced a second golden age, one as significant as the one in the sixteenth century. Industrialization, growing trade, and the opening of the empire to the West had led to unprecedented prosperity.

Much of the foreboding that Jews evinced when the Greeks arrived proved to be justified, albeit in ways that they could not have foreseen. All across the Balkans the new nation-states proved to be more difficult politically than the Ottoman Empire had been. These states made increased demands on all minorities while engaging in the politics of nation building—with predictably deleterious consequences for those whose distinctive communal and cultural specificity was eroded. The Balkan states nationalized the school systems of the Jews. Ladino declined, to be replaced increasingly by the "national" language of the country. Jewish communal structures came under the close supervision of zealous state bureaucrats who interfered in community life. In Salonika the fire of 1917 destroyed the several Jewish quarters, and while the Jews received some compensation, they were not allowed to return en masse to their long-time areas, leading to considerable social and economic dislocation. Thousands of Greek refugees from Asia Minor settled in the city after the Greek and Turkish population exchanges that followed the Greek war with Turkey in 1922. The Greek refugees became the Jews' main economic competitors and a source of anti-Semitism in the interwar years. Many Jews emigrated from Salonika to France, the Americas, and to Palestine.

Despite these developments, major anti-Semitic movements did not emerge in Bulgaria, Yugoslavia, and Greece. The Jews remained as a distinctive minority, with small elements among them beginning to acculturate. Significantly, in the interwar years politics for the Balkan Sephardim remained distinctively Jewish, with Zionism as a major presence in Bulgaria and in Salonika. While not yet integrated fully into the Balkan nation-states, the Sephardim had begun to reach a modus vivendi with their new masters.

During World War II the invading Nazis deported Salonika Jews and the smaller Jewish communities of Greece in 1943 and exterminated almost all of them. Most of Belgrade's and Sarajevo's Jews were killed in local camps. In areas newly occupied by Bulgaria, the Jewish communities in Macedonia and much of Western Thrace were deported en masse; the Bulgarians turned them over to the Germans, who then exterminated them. The Monastir (Bitola) and Skopje (Üsküb) communities met this end. Although Bulgaria, an ally of Nazi Germany's, moved its own Jews (those living within the borders of the country in 1939) to the provinces and confiscated much of their property, it did not hand them over. Internal politics, opposition from several quarters, and the wish to preserve some independence from Nazi Germany had led Bulgaria not to accede to German demands for the deportation of Bulgarian Jewry. But the community was traumatized and left en masse for Israel after 1948.

Of the Jews that had lived in the Islamic orbit for centuries, the Balkan Sephardic communities were the only ones—with the exception of those in Bulgaria proper—that were annihilated during World War II. Because of nationalistic politics and warfare, the end of the old Ottoman order had not proved felicitous to Sephardic life in the Balkans. It came to an end a mere three and a half decades after the Ottoman withdrawal.

RECOMMENDED READING

Benbassa, Esther and Aron Rodrigue. *Sephardi Jewry: A History of the Judeo-Spanish Community, Fourteenth–Twentieth Centuries.* Berkeley: University of California Press, 2000.

Tamir, Vicki. *Bulgaria and Her Jews: The History of a Dubious Symbiosis.* New York: Sepher Hermon Press, 1979.

CHAPTER

16

Turkey

George E. Gruen

After the defeat of the Ottoman Empire in World War I, Turkish nationalists under the dynamic leadership of Gen. Mustafa Kemal (later, Atatürk) created the modern Turkish Republic. The Allies had occupied the Ottoman capital of Istanbul and planned to divide the bulk of the sultan's remaining domains, with the British and French to rule the former Arab provinces under mandates from the League of Nations, while the Italians and Greeks were to receive significant portions of coastal Anatolia. The Treaty of Sèvres in August 1920 also provided for granting autonomy and eventual independence to the predominantly Armenian and Kurdish regions in the east.

The Treaty of Sèvres was never ratified. The Greek occupation of Izmir on May 15, 1919, under cover of Allied warships, was the act that helped Kemal galvanize Turkish popular resistance, resulting in the reconquest of Anatolia. That was completed in September 1922, with the recapture of Izmir (Smyrna). The Allies agreed to restoration of Turkish sovereignty in Istanbul, the strategic Turkish Straits, and Eastern Thrace. (The straits consist of the Bosporus, which connects the Black Sea and the Sea of Marmara in Istanbul, and the Dardanelles, which connect the Sea of Marmara and the Aegean. Until the construction of several bridges in recent decades, the straits separated European Turkey from Asiatic Turkey.) After months of difficult negotiations, a peace treaty was signed at Lausanne on July 23, 1923.

In 1934 the grateful Turkish parliament bestowed upon the victorious General Kemal the name Atatürk (Father Turk). Atatürk consciously distanced himself from the multiethnic and polyglot characteristics of the defeated Ottoman Empire. He sought instead to forge a new unified Turkish identity, drawing on the myths of the Turks' pre-Islamic Central Asian tribal roots, but was also dedicated to rapidly bringing his country into modern Western civilization. The predominantly Muslim Turkish population is of diverse ethnic origins. Some, such as the Kurdish- and Arabic-speaking minorities, have inhabited southeastern Anatolia since ancient times, and others, including the Turkish speakers, came to Anatolia from Central Asia in the eleventh century. Still others arrived later from the Balkans as each state achieved independence from Ottoman rule. Atatürk sought to unite all these elements under the banner of Turkish nationalism; he cemented national unity by imposing the Turkish language and stressing integration through assimilation.

Most Turkish Muslims (90 percent) are Sunni with various forms of affiliation. These range from the highly secularized, who rarely go to the mosque, to those who attend services regularly and seek to provide religious education to their children. The sultanate was abolished in 1922, the caliphate in 1924. The Shariᶜa (Islamic law) was replaced by a series of secular laws based on Western European civil, penal, and commercial codes.

About 10 percent of Turkey's Muslims are Shiite, known as Alevi in Turkish. Unlike the Shiites in Iran, the Alevis of Turkey have been politically liberal and staunch supporters of the Kemalist principle of separation of religion and state. A small religious minority, the *dönme* (secret Jews), descended from the followers of the false messiah Shabbetai Zevi (1626–76), who converted to Islam, maintained their own neighborhoods and married only among themselves. Another small sect in Turkey of Jewish origin is the Karaites. This group, first recognized in the eighth century, emphasized the biblical texts and rejected the Talmudic oral traditions of the rabbinate Jews. The Karaites flourished in the Ottoman Empire, with major centers in Edirne, Istanbul, and Izmit. As a result of emigration to Eastern Europe by the time of the Turkish Republic, only a few hundred Karaites remained in Istanbul in 1923.

Following the 1923 Treaty of Lausanne, Greece and Turkey concluded a population exchange, resulting in the gradual emigration of non-Muslims from Turkey and the continuing emigration of Muslims, including the *dönme,* from Salonika. All non-Muslims today, nearly eighty years later, total fewer than 100,000 and constitute far less than 1 percent of the country's population. Thus the Turkish Republic differs markedly from the multireligious character of the Ottoman Empire.

The government of the Turkish Republic, which undertook to assure full and complete protection of life, liberty, and freedom of religion for all, spelled out the rights of the non-Muslim minorities. The non-Muslim minorities would also enjoy full freedom of movement and emigration, and they were free to use their own charitable, religious, and social institutions at their own expense. Although Turkish, as the official language, was to be taught in all schools and used in courts and other official business, non-Turkish speakers would be allowed to speak in court and teach classes in minority-run and -supported schools in their own languages. They would also be excused from legal proceedings on their day of rest.

After considerable debate in February 1926 the Jewish community's leadership officially renounced the rights to special personal status that they would have been accorded under the Treaty of Lausanne. The Jews professed their loyalty to Turkey and expressed full confidence that Turkish law would protect them. Marriage and divorce became civil matters, and practicing Judaism was a private concern. Put on the spot by the patriotic initiative of the Jewish community, the leaders of the Christian minorities followed suit.

The decade of the 1930s was marked by some ambivalence in efforts by the government to emphasize that it respected the integrity and freedom of religion of the Jews and Turkey's intense political and cultural nationalism. The government resisted efforts by Nazi Germany and a small number of Turkish anti-Semites to adopt anti-Jewish measures; it also confiscated anti-Semitic publications. A sizable group of Turkish Jewish athletes was permitted to take part in the 1935 Maccabiah Games in Palestine. In 1908 Zionist youth in Istanbul renamed the Jewish Gymnastiques Society as Maccabee. Within two years it had grown to a membership of five thousand with eleven branches, including several in Istanbul, Izmir, Edirne, and also Tel Aviv—founded by young Turkish Jews who had made aliyah to Palestine. Officially, Turkey forbade membership in the Zionist movement under the republic's law barring affiliation with any international movement; the law was designed primarily to prevent the spread of communism and reactionary Islamic influence among the population. Yet indigenous Jewish sports and cultural movements, such as Ne'emanei Zion (the Faithful of Zion), founded in 1934 in the Balat district of Istanbul, promoted the study of modern Hebrew and agricultural techniques, and it prepared the youth for aliyah. In 1940 the group in Istanbul and a branch in Izmir helped raise money and organize relief for the Jewish refugees from Nazi-occupied Romania, Bulgaria, and Greece and aided their transit to Palestine. While the Izmir group was clandestine, the one in Istanbul operated openly under the umbrella of Ozer Dallim (Aid to the Poor), an agency of the chief rabbinate. Istanbul Jews also worked in secrecy with the representatives of the Jewish Agency for Palestine and of American Jewish relief organizations in Turkey.

Even before World War II the Turkish authorities had begun formal economic and political relations with the Jewish Agency, which was authorized in 1938 to display industrial and other products of the Yishuv in its own booth at the Izmir International Fair and display the Jewish national flag. Because Turkey remained officially neutral during World War II, the Jewish Agency's agents in Istanbul played a crucial role, as listening post and rescue center, for Jews fleeing Nazi-occupied Europe. These agents also coordinated the supply of food and other provisions sent by Istanbul's Jewish community to refugees on ships seeking to pass through the Turkish Straits to Palestine. One ill-fated ship was the *Struma,* which arrived in January 1942 with 770 refugees fleeing Romania. For weeks they were kept aboard by the Turkish authorities, while the ship was docked in Istanbul awaiting British permission to land in Palestine. After repeated urgent appeals to the authorities by Jewish community leaders, the Istanbul Jewish community was permitted to provide food and other supplies to the stranded passengers. When word of the British refusal arrived in February, the ship was sent back to the Black Sea, where it either struck a mine or was torpedoed. All but one of the passengers drowned. The only other survivors were a pregnant woman and her family who had been permitted to leave the ship before it sailed from Istanbul.

The Turkish government had earlier welcomed several thousand Jewish refugees from Nazi Germany, including more than one hundred professors who eventually played an important role in strengthening the academic level of the university in Istanbul and other Turkish universities. There are also documented cases of courageous and successful efforts by the Turkish consuls in Marseilles and Rhodes to save Turkish Jews from Nazi deportations. Yet some Turkish Jews were dismissed from government positions in the early years of the republic, ostensibly because they had not assimilated quickly enough and were being linguistically loyal to Judeo-Spanish. Also, a trend in the private sector was to replace members of the minorities with Muslim Turks. More serious were the antiminority outbursts in Thrace in the mid-1930s, including a pogrom in Edirne in 1934 that led to the virtual disappearance of old Jewish communities in that region. The Jews of Thrace resettled in Istanbul and Izmir or emigrated. Jewish confidence in the Turkish Republic was undermined in those years.

The Jewish community produced two intellectual leaders in the 1930s whom the Turkish elite regarded as emblematic of the movement to better integrate Jews into their modern secularist state. The first was Moise Cohen, who was born in Serres in 1883 but spent most of his life in Salonika and Istanbul. Educated in Alliance Israélite Universelle (AIU) schools, he later combined religious and secular studies, receiving both rabbinical ordination and a law degree. Active in the Young Turk movement in 1908, he was successively a pan-Ottomanist, a pan-Turanist, and later, under the republic, an ardent Turkish nationalist and Kemalist. Turkifying his last name to Tekinalp, he published seven books, including *Türk Ruhu* (The Turkish Spirit, 1944?), which has become a standard text on Atatürk's ideology (known as Kemalism), and more than 150 articles in Turkish, French, German, and Judeo-Spanish (Ladino) that were addressed to both Jews and Muslim Turks and stressed the need to modernize and westernize. He used his experience as a business manager for various Turkish companies to advocate the introduction of European economic and social practices. He urged the Jewish community to learn and speak modern Turkish, following the practice of Jews in other emancipated countries who spoke the national language. It actually took decades before a new generation of Jews was fluent in Turkish. Among Turkey's Jewish youth today, knowledge of Ladino is waning, and English is replacing French as the preferred foreign language.

The other outstanding scholar and politically active Jewish representative of this period was Abraham Galanté. An educator and prolific author, Galanté was born in Bodrum in 1873 into a family that traced its ancestry to Spain. After completing his Jewish and secular studies in Bodrum, Rhodes, and Izmir, he was successively the founder of an AIU school in Rhodes and a journalist in Izmir who reported on the Jewish communities of the empire. After four years as a correspondent in Egypt and three in England, he returned to Istanbul in 1914 as an instructor at Istanbul University and in 1928 was appointed professor of language and history. Galanté served as deputy from Nigde in the Grand National Assembly from 1943 to 1946, and he continued his research and writing in Turkish and French until his death in 1961. The nine volumes of his collected historical writings, recently reissued in French, remain a key source for the history of the Jews; he developed the theme of the mutuality of Turkish and Jewish interests, dating to first contacts in the Seljuk and early Ottoman times. He called on the Turkish authorities to provide full opportunities for Jews to demonstrate their talents in the building of the modern secular republic, and he urged the members of the Jewish community to modernize and take an active part in Turkish affairs.

Yet the path to full integration was not to be without serious obstacles. Many Jewish men served in the Turkish army during World War II, as they had earlier, but until the late 1940s they could not become officers, and most were placed in units that were not armed but were required to do menial work. The low point in Turkish-Jewish relations was reached with the Varlik Vergisi (capital levy) of November 1942; it was officially described as "designed to tax the previously untaxed commercial wealth in the Republic and to curb the inflationary spiral" by sopping up the excess profits that some merchants and large farmers had made because of the shortage of goods during the war.

In application the law was clearly discriminatory against the minorities. It was subsequently revealed that there were separate lists, M for Muslims and G for Gayrimuslim (non-Muslims). Owners of large farms could not be taxed more than 5 percent of their capital, and corporations were required to pay 50 to 75 percent of their net profits for 1941. For other taxpayers special commissions set the assessments "in accordance with their opinions." Under the Varlik the non-Muslim minorities were often assessed at confiscatory rates up to ten times the Muslim rate, there was no appeal from the local assessments, and those who did not pay up within a month were deported to work at forced labor during the harsh winter to break stones for a new road at Aşkale. The published lists of defaulters and those who were arrested and deported were almost entirely of Armenians, Greek Orthodox, and Jews.

In debates in the Grand National Assembly Turkish politicians made the point that the law presented an opportunity to regain Turkey's economic independence by ousting non-Turks (non-Muslims). The press, led by the pro-Axis *Cumhuriyet* newspaper, applauded the harsh measures against people of "alien blood," "Turks only in name," who deserved to be punished for their disloyalty and ingratitude. In fact, the Jews and other loyal non-Muslim citizens who had put their trust in the republic were punished, while those who had retained their foreign passports were able to get their assessments reduced to the Muslim level. Under public criticism from the United States, including a series of articles in the *New York Times,* and from other Allied powers as the tide of war was turning against the Axis powers, the republic stopped enforcing the tax. Subsequent government inquiries exposed the injustices that had been committed, but proposals to compensate the victims were never implemented.

Shortly after the Varlik was promulgated, two other categories were added: *E* for *ecnebi* (foreigners), who were to be taxed at the Muslim rate, and *D* for *dönme,* who were taxed at twice the Muslim rate. This was evidence that despite their growing assimilation and outward posture as Muslims, their neighbors knew at least who some of the secret Jews were and did not treat them as fully equal. Because the *dönme* have continued to keep their Jewish roots secret, however, some have risen to high positions in every field in Turkey.

Atatürk's successor and long-time aide, Ismet Inönü, a victorious general in the War of Independence and an adroit diplomat who had headed the Turkish delegation at Lausanne, had managed to keep Turkey out of World War II by skillfully balancing opposing Allied and Axis pressures. Eager to win U.S. support in the struggle with the Soviet Union, which had renewed its territorial demands upon Turkey, and to enable Turkey to join with the Western democracies that had defeated the Axis dictatorships, Inönü first permitted multiparty elections in 1946 and peacefully handed over power when the opposition won in 1950. A pragmatic leader, Inönü also had recognized the State of Israel in March 1949, and Ankara established diplomatic relations the following year, when it had become clear that the Jewish state had successfully repelled the Arab attack and was developing a modern Western democracy that enjoyed the backing for the United States. Inönü also permitted the free emigration of Turkish Jews to Israel. His successors eased the restrictions on Hebrew language instruction in the Jewish schools.

According to official census figures, the total Jewish population in the Turkish Republic in 1927 was 81,454 out of a total population of 13.6 million. In 1945 the number declined only slightly, to 76,965; but by 1955 the figure had declined to 45,995, because more than 35,000 Jews had emigrated to Israel since its founding in May 1948. The trickle of aliyah became a flood once the Arab-Israeli War ended in 1949. Even though the Jews' passports were initially marked "Not valid for Palestine," the Turkish authorities allowed the Jewish Agency representatives in Turkey to facilitate the aliyah of Turkish Jews.

Some Jews were motivated by strong Zionist and traditional religious feelings. Many were eager to end the insecurity of living as a minority, to seize the opportunity and live in an independent Jewish state; however, because the overwhelming majority of the emigrants came from the lower classes, economic motivation was clearly a major factor. The poor, especially those living in the smaller communities, had remained more closely tied to their Jewish roots and had become far less Turkified and integrated than the westernized and more secular members of the middle and upper classes. The egalitarian principles and social structure of the socialist-led Israeli state, with its communal agricultural settlements (kibbutzim), also played a role, because these factors enabled the disadvantaged to marry off their daughters without paying the substantial dowry then still prevalent in the Turkish Jewish community.

Another consequence of the mass emigration to Israel was the gradual dissolution of the Jewish communities of Anatolia, with those Jews who remained in Turkey moving to Istanbul and Izmir, where their children were exposed to cosmopolitan environments. Subsequently, emigration waxed and waned, depending on the changing economic and political climate in Turkey. During periods of stability and economic growth emigration to Israel fell to a few hundred annually. Following Israel's victory in the Six Day War of 1967, and for a few years thereafter, aliyah exceeded two thousand a year. Emigration was also fueled by growing political turmoil and economic crisis in Turkey in those years. It fell again to a couple of hundred per year until the urban violence and economic crisis of the late 1970s led to the 1980 temporary military takeover and raised emigration to Israel to more than eight hundred per year. By 1998 it had again fallen to fewer than one hundred. Young Turkish Jews continuously leave for advanced study in the United States and Western Europe; while most have returned to join family businesses, an unknown number have chosen to remain abroad.

The socioeconomic profiles of the emigrants has also changed. In the 1990s emigrants included entrepreneurs and professionals who saw opportunities to participate in Israel's booming high-tech economy, as well as in the burgeoning Turkish-Israeli economic cooperation. These range from industrial and agricultural ventures in southeast Anatolia and the Turkish-speaking republics of Central Asia to generally expanded commercial ties. Since the signing of the Turkish-Israeli Free Trade Agreement in 1996, bilateral trade has risen rapidly, reaching $728 million in 1998. About six hundred Israeli companies operate in Turkey.

Ironically, following the 1980 military coup in Turkey, the secularist generals introduced a required course in religious instruction in the state schools, in the belief that teaching the Qur'an and traditional Islamic values would inoculate the youth against the dangerous virus of communism and other radical leftist ideologies that had led to armed clashes between youth gangs supported by extremist parties of the right and the left. A delegation from the lay council of the chief rabbinate successfully appealed to the authorities to exempt non-Muslim children from attendance at the Qur'an courses in the schools. In May 1991 the Ministry of Education officially exempted all non-Muslim students from Islamic studies, and it has provided instructors in the other religions, with basic introductions to either Judaism or Christianity instead. Some restrictions on the repair of old synagogues and the construction of new ones have also been eased.

The predominantly urban Jewish communities that are today concentrated in Istanbul and Izmir have naturally been affected by the transformations that have taken place during the seventy-five years of life in the Turkish Republic. Under the Ottoman Empire they contributed to and borrowed liberally from Turkish culture in their cuisine, music, dress, and decorative arts. Still, they also retained the strong institutions of scholarship, religion, and communal organization that they brought from the flourishing culture of the Iberian Peninsula, from which they had been expelled; they also generally continued to live in their own distinct districts. Today, with the exception of the approximately two thousand Jews in Izmir, the roughly one hundred in Ankara, and the few dozen each in Bursa, Antalya, and Adana, Jewish life in Turkey is centered in the rapidly expanding Istanbul metropolitan region, whose Jewish population is estimated at eighteen to twenty-five thousand. Following the mass exodus to Israel, the remaining Jewish community has generally improved its economic position, moving out of the older, poorer, and distinctly Jewish neighborhoods of Balat, Hasköy, and Kuzguncuk to the more affluent modern European sections of the city. The first move was to the Péra district, the center of international commerce near the historic Galata Tower and, starting in the 1920s, to Taksim. In the 1950s the move was farther north to Şişli and Nişantaş, quarters of the Muslim elite where Salonikan Jews have lived since the beginning of the twentieth century. Since the 1980s the move has been toward the Bosporus, in fashionable new suburbs such as Ulus and Ortaköy along both the European and Asiatic coasts. A Jewish presence in the historically ancient urban neighborhoods is being maintained by Jewish community support for a home for the elderly in Hasköy, and major renovations have been undertaken at the century-old Jewish hospital in Balat to transform it into a modern geriatric health center.

As their economic and social position has improved, Jewish and Muslim members of the secularized upper and middle classes have tended to live and work in the same neighborhoods and to attend the same schools and colleges, although among the older generation of Jews social relations have continued primarily with other Jews. The social cohesiveness of the Jewish community has also been fostered by the large number of families that still choose to spend their summer vacations on islands in the Sea of Marmara, notably Büyükada, which has a summertime synagogue, Burgaz, and Caddebostan on the Asiatic shore.

For some in the younger generation the uniqueness and salience of their Jewish heritage is lessening. One illustration of this is the decline in the choice of distinctively Jewish first names for newborn children. According to a survey conducted among Istanbul Jews in 1990, 23 percent of women and 29 percent of men preferred to give their children Turkish names, 42 and 46 percent favored "other" names—such as French names or those of movie stars—while the remainder favored giving their children "two names side by side," presumably one Turkish and one Jewish. This is similar to the practice in other Western countries with well-integrated Jewish communities. Despite becoming less ritually observant, Turkish Jews try to perpetuate a Jewish identity and keep the High Holy Days of Rosh Hashanah and Yom Kippur, and they participate in a Passover seder.

The major personal life cycle events—circumcision of boys, marriages between Jewish partners, and funerals—are both individual and community social events. They continue to be under the control of communal institutions, particularly the chief rabbinate. This consists of a religious council of five rabbis, who assist Chief Rabbi David Asseo, who was elected in 1961, (d. 2002) and who serve as *dayyanim* [religious judges] and a lay council, which in 2001 was headed by Bensiyon Pinto, who succeeded Rifat Saban, a prominent attorney. The lay council consists of forty-five members who serve on various committees, including a fourteen-member executive committee. As of 2001, Nedim Karako had been chosen as vice president, and Linda Filiba and Moris Levi had been elected as executive vice presidents. The veteran community leader and historian Naim Güleryüz presided over the advisory Council of Representatives, consisting of delegates from the various synagogues, foundations, welfare associations, and youth clubs. The chief rabbi is elected by men of the Jewish community and certified by the Council of Ministers as the official representative of the country's Jewish community. In an effort to stem the rising tide of assimilation and intermarriage, the chief rabbinate has urged adherence to Jewish dietary laws and has had some success in specifying kosher meat and the prohibition of shellfish on the menu for receptions accompanying bar and bat mitzvah and wedding celebrations. Among the upper classes, some celebrations have been quite ostentatious, and Istanbul's major hotels are equipped to provide kosher catering facilities. By way of contrast, Istanbul has only one kosher restaurant, and its clientele is largely American and Israeli Jewish tourists.

A boost to Jewish pride and identity was also provided by the communal efforts connected with the celebration in 1992 of the five-hundredth anniversary of the welcome given by Sultan Bayezid II to the Jews exiled from Spain in 1492. Prominent and affluent figures in the Jewish community, the Turkish government, business and industry, and academicians established the Quincentennial Foundation. One of its projects was to restore the historic Ahrida synagogue in the old Balat section of the city. Because only a few families still reside in the Balat district, the Association for the Renovation and Continuation of the Synagogues recruits ten men as volunteers from the Istanbul Jewish community to take turns in providing the minyan for Shabbat services at the Ahrida and nearby Yambol synagogues, the only two of the six in the district still functioning. This is to forestall reversion of the properties to the state under an old law requiring every charitable foundation to have a functioning local community. The historic synagogue in the old section of Ankara was restored and reopened in the mid-1990s after many years of neglect. It is now open only for High Holy Day services, because the small Jewish community lacks the money to provide adequate security for regular Sabbath services. In 1999 Istanbul had sixteen functioning synagogues, while in Izmir only four of the city's numerous synagogues were still in regular use. At the festivities culminating the quincentennial celebrations, President Turgut Özal and then–prime minister Süleyman Demirel announced that a new era in Turkish-Israeli relations had begun. Turkey was prepared to cooperate with Israel in every field. In fact, Turkey's diplomatic relations with Israel had been raised to the ambassadorial level earlier in the year.

While the great majority of the Turkish political elite, including the powerful military establishment, was favorably disposed toward the Jewish community, which had always demonstrated its loyalty to the country, and welcomed the improvement of relations with Israel, this was not true of Arab and Islamist extremists. In 1986 two Arabic-speaking terrorists had carried out a suicide attack at Istanbul's Neve Shalom Synagogue, killing twenty-two Jews.

With regard to education, after the French-affiliated AIU schools were closed in 1925, Jewish families in Istanbul had to choose between the new Turkish state schools, including the once-prestigious Galatasaray Lycée; French and English schools administered by Christian clergy; or the Bene Berit Lycée, where instruction was conducted partly in Hebrew but also in French and Turkish. This continued the pattern of westernization and modernization within the Jewish community that Ottoman reformers had actively encouraged in the midnineteenth century. Although limited religious instruction in Hebrew is permitted in Jewish schools under the Turkish Republic, the teaching of Zionism and any formal affiliation with international Jewish organizations, even such fraternal groups as B'nai B'rith and the World Jewish Congress, was forbidden until the 1990s. The ban was lifted when Turkish authorities realized that encouraging contacts between the Turkish community and the Jews in the United States and Western Europe could help to promote a more favorable image for Turkey in those countries.

Reversing the tide of intermarriage was a major factor in the community's decision to build a modern, new Jewish day school in Ulus, which had 582 students in 1998–99 from kindergarten through high school. This is a small percentage of the estimated thirty-five hundred Jewish children of school age. The school succeeds in getting its graduates admitted to prestigious universities. As the community shrinks in size, it becomes increasingly difficult for it to fund its charitable obligations, including those to the poor families. Three Talmud Torahs continue to function in Şişli, Ortaköy, and Caddebostan, as do a variety of afternoon and Sunday educational programs for children and parents in Istanbul and Izmir. In another effort to keep the youth of Istanbul within the Jewish orbit, the community has undertaken to renovate a large building in Ortaköy to create a modern Jewish sports and cultural center.

In economics the Jewish community benefited from the economic reforms instituted in the 1980s by Turgut Özal, who had served at the World Bank, to transform and liberalize the state-dominated economy for successful competition in world markets. Prominent Turkish Jewish industrialists, such as Jak Kamhi, head of Profilo Holding, an industrial conglomerate with eleven thousand employees, and Dr. Üzeyir Garih and Ishak Alaton, founders of the ALARKO Group of Companies, major international contractors, were among those in the expanding private sector who supported and benefited from the new economic policies. Kamhi, who also heads Turkey's commission to the European Union, has been made minister-for-life by the Foreign Ministry. Many Turkish Jews in Istanbul and Izmir are involved in the production and export of textile goods and other manufactured products. Jeff Hakko, heir to a prominent Sephardic family, heads the Vakko House of Fashion, the country's largest and most chic apparel manufacturer. In addition to the export-import and manufacturing fields, many Jews are merchants, small shopkeepers, jewelers, and other artisans. Turkey has about one hundred Jewish doctors and smaller numbers of pharmacists, dentists, accountants, lawyers, and advertising executives. Sami Kohen, the foreign editor of the major liberal Istanbul daily *Milliyet*, is both locally and internationally acclaimed. Turkey has about a dozen Jewish university professors, as well as a handful of Jewish painters, poets, and photographers. The Jewish community publishes the weekly *Şalom*, mostly in Turkish, with one page on Jewish subjects in Ladino. The old cultural traditions are also being maintained by the musical ensembles Los Pasaros Sefardis and Erensa Sefaradi.

The election in 1995 of Jefi Kamhi, son of Jak Kamhi, as a parliamentary deputy from Istanbul of the then-ruling True Path Party, is a sign that some Jews are also taking an active part in the country's political life. Jefi Kamhi pointed out that, unlike the designated minority representatives of earlier years, he considered himself not a Jewish representative but a representative of all the people of Istanbul. Nevertheless, he cautiously abstained from a controversial no-confidence vote, and the Islamist Welfare Party criticized President Demirel for choosing Jefi Kamhi to accompany him on his official visit to Israel. The Welfare Party has been outlawed, and in 2001 the Turkish Republic was governed by a coalition of three secularist parties.

To sum up, on the whole, except for a few unfortunate lapses, the authorities in the Turkish Republic have generally rewarded the loyalty of the Jewish community by allowing its members to live their communal lives in freedom and security and to engage fully in the economic—and lately even the international—affairs of the country.

RECOMMENDED READING

Gruen, George E. "Dynamic Progress in Turkish-Israeli Relations." *Israel Affairs* 1, no. 4 (Summer 1995): 40–70.

Rodrigue, Aron, ed. *Ottoman and Turkish Jewry: Community and Leadership.* Bloomington, Ind.: Indiana University, 1992.

Weiker, Walter F. "The Blending of Jewish and Turkish Identity Among the Jews of Turkey." In Norman Stillman and Yedida Stillman, eds., *From Iberia to Diaspora,* pp. 3–18. Boston: Brill, 1999.

CHAPTER

17

Syria and Lebanon

Michael Menachem Laskier

Syria, situated on the eastern coast of the Mediterranean, is bounded by Turkey to the north and northeast, Iraq to the east and southeast, Jordan to the south, and Lebanon and Israel to the southwest. Although most of the population is Arab, Syria is home to a significant number of Kurds, Armenians, Turks, Circassians, and Assyrians. Sunni Muslims account for 75 percent of the Arabic-speaking Muslim population, with a smaller presence only in the south and the Latakia province of the north. Alawite Shiites form the next largest group; most live in Latakia or in the northern cities of Hama and Homs. The Druze, a sectarian group since the eleventh century, live in the area of Aleppo, Damascus, and Jabal al-Druze. Christians, about 10 percent of the population, are represented by various denominations, chief of which are the Greek Orthodox, Armenians, Greek Catholics, and the Maronites.

Lebanon, with the port of Beirut (called Berytus in ancient times and in the Ottoman Empire was known as Mount Lebanon), is located on the eastern shore of the Mediterranean to the north of Israel and to the south and west of Syria. Founded in September 1920, Lebanon is home to Maronites, Druze, and a diverse population of Sunni and Shiite Muslims, as well as people of various Christian denominations. Outside the major urban areas the economy is agricultural, based on the production of olives, tobacco, citrus, cotton, grain, and silk. A small number of Jews lived in both countries from antiquity until the establishment of the State of Israel.

HISTORY: GREATER SYRIA UNTIL THE 1920S AND MODERN SYRIA

Captured by the Arabs in the seventh century, Syria was dominated by various dynasties until the sixteenth century, when it came under Ottoman rule. Yet the administrative decentralization of the Ottoman Empire, beginning in the seventeenth century, weakened it and relegated real power to local functionaries. The semiautonomous Ottoman governors neglected public works while heavy taxation, extortion of funds, and economic decline aroused local animosities. The Egyptian occupation of 1831 to 1840 served as a catalyst for improving the status of the Christians, instituting new methods of taxation, and eradicating lawlessness. With the Tanzimat reforms of the empire in the midnineteenth century, Syria and Lebanon once again came under Ottoman authority.

The practical effects of the Tanzimat were not apparent in Syria before 1855. The removal of the *jizya* (head tax) and its replacement by a universal tax in lieu of military service (and reforms related to the military, administration, education, the economy, and the minorities) encountered opposition from the Muslim religious authorities and the majority population. This opposition among Muslims and Druze was partly responsible for the Druze massacre of Maronites (Eastern rite Christians) in 1860. In 1908 the universal tax was lifted for Jews and Christians, obligating them to serve in the Ottoman military; however, most young men in these groups opted to evade military duty. Despite judicial reforms, as late the mid-1850s the new secular courts discounted a non-Muslim's testimony and often referred the case to the old-style Islamic courts, where it was invalidated.

Despite a failure to achieve genuine equality for non-Muslims, the effects of the Tanzimat cannot be discounted. The reforms did become catalysts for change. Representatives of the European powers and the recently enfranchised French and British Jews soon focused on initiating modern education in the region. This development was best illustrated by the efforts of Christian missionary and consular schools (sponsored by European and other Western consulates and legations), as well as by the Alliance Israélite Universelle (AIU). These institutions infused Syrians of various backgrounds with notions of national consciousness, contributing to the rise of both Arab nationalism and Zionism.

When the Ottoman Empire entered World War I, the emerging Syrian Arab nationalist forces aligned with the Hashemites of Arabia to assist the British in the capture of Damascus. Because of the Sykes-Picot Agreement on dismembering the Ottoman Empire, negotiated in 1916 between the French and the British, with the assent of Russia, France gained control of Syria in 1920, including the Lebanon mountains, and expelled the Arab nationalist forces. At the San Remo Conference four years later France was granted Syria and Lebanon as mandated territories under what would become the Treaty of Sèvres.

Although modeled on the concept of the modern nation-state, the new Syria was subdivided in 1924 into a number of local autonomous units—one for the Alawites, one for the Druze, and one for the rest of Syria. France built roads, promoted urbanization, engendered agricultural reforms, and built the University of Damascus but postponed independence indefinitely, which inevitably caused nationalist political unrest. At the start of World War II Syria and Lebanon came under Vichy control. Though liberated by the Free French and British forces in 1941, Syria did not achieve full independence until 1946, when the Allied forces left.

Syria's setbacks in the Arab-Israeli War of 1948 and its inability to cope with strong social and ethnic cleavages led to three military coups d'état that replaced civilian leadership with military rule. In the 1950s a return to civilian rule and democratic elections were followed by a political struggle between the admirers of Egypt's Gamal Abdel Nasser and the Syrian Socialist Ba^{c}ath party, which led to the formation of the United Arab Republic (1958–61), the political union of Syria and Egypt. Following a coup, Syria declared itself independent of Egypt in 1961. In 1963 the Ba^{c}ath seized control and was replaced in 1966 by the Neo-Ba^{c}ath, dominated by the Alawite faction. Four years later Hafiz al-Assad emerged as president and remained in control for more than thirty years.

LEBANON AFTER 1920

This republic had a government based on a Maronite president, a Sunni premier, and a Shiite speaker of the parliament, as well as proportional representation. Until the early 1970s Lebanon was dominated by an elite of wealthy politicians, some of whom maintained private armies or militias that posed a challenge to the sectarian national army. Lebanon was the center for quality higher education in the Middle East, with its prestigious American University in Beirut and the Jesuits' Saint Joseph University, noted for spurring career and economic development. Until the mid-1970s Beirut's seaport and the nation's free economic and foreign exchange systems, favorable interest rates, and banking secrecy law contributed to its prosperity. Although the brief civil war in 1958 heightened tensions, the one that followed in 1975 turned out to be bloodier and more devastating, because its effects continue, with the Middle East peace process the only hope for resolution. The Palestine Liberation Organization's activities inside Lebanon since the 1960s, and Israel's military response, which included military infringement on Lebanese sovereignty, helped fuel the crisis. Since 1976 the armies of

Syria and Israel have occupied parts of Lebanon, with its diverse populations supporting either intruder or attempting to struggle against them.

JEWS IN GREATER SYRIA UNTIL 1920

Jews inhabited Syria in biblical times and have always viewed themselves as an extension of the Land of Israel. Located between Baghdad and the Mediterranean, cities such as Aleppo and Damascus were commercial conduits that attracted Jews from all over the region; other Syrian centers of Jewish life included Hama, Tripoli (Lebanon), Beirut, Sidon, and Baalbek. In the sixteenth and seventeenth centuries the arrival of Sephardic exiles from Spain and Portugal helped transform Aleppo into the most dynamic trade center of the Arab East. Syrian Jews spoke Judeo-Arabic. Since the mid-1870s Aleppan Jews have preferred to teach their youth foreign languages, which are useful in commercial transactions, while in Damascus Jews remained more Arabized.

Although some Syrian Jews were merchants before and during the nineteenth century, the majority engaged in crafts and peddling. The Jews of Damascus enjoyed a virtual monopoly of the metal crafts. As silversmiths, goldsmiths, and coppersmiths, they dominated the metal crafts even in the nineteenth and twentieth centuries. This appeared to be very much the case with the Mosseri family, whose members were highly reputed craftsmen, working with silver, gold, and copper. In the 1930s Zion Mosseri designed the doors of the Latin patriarchate of Damascus, and in 1940 he was sent to Italy as the representative of Syria's metal products. The works crafted by Jews before and during the French mandate era included traditional Islamic designs, as well as Qur'anic passages, decorative silver and gold trays, and gold vases.

Prominent family names in the modern era were diverse and included Sasson, Shammah, Kazin, Matlub, Douek, Sutton, Safra, Shammush, Abadi, Safdeye, Dahlab, Totah, Laniado, Hamra, Abbas, Costica, Nahmad, Shevah, Harari, and Jajati. Some of the leading rabbis in recent times included Nathanel Habuba, Yosef Dana, Yitshaq Assa, Moshe Harari, Avraham Douek Ha-Cohen, Ezra Hammoui, and Moshe Cohen-Tawil.

The houses of the Jews in Aleppo and Damascus were built close together. In Aleppo the old-style pre-Ottoman houses were interspersed in modern times with Turkish buildings. The Jews lived in those parts of the city contiguous to the ramparts, between the Dark Gate and St. George, in the neighborhood of Bashita. For all intents and purposes Bashita served as a Jewish quarter along with the Jamiliya section of the city. In Damascus the houses of Jews and the houses of non-Jews were similar, plastered over with a yellowish stucco or mud and showing no windows on the street—while inside they were noted for their beautiful Italian marble and carved arabesque patterns.

The Jewish family in Syria was patriarchal, the head of the family wielding much influence in the household. In the presence of strangers Jewish women were always veiled, but they were more free and negligent about veiling in public than were Muslim women. Jewish women did not eat with the men, except on holy days when no strangers were present.

Rabbinic leadership and religious traditions were firmly implanted in the communities. From the sixteenth century on contacts between Syrian and the Yishuv-based rabbis (of Palestine) were strengthened. The influence of the Safed Kabbalists—Jewish mystical leaders and teachers who urged people to communicate directly with God—was also important, notably in Damascus. Although the proponents of Sabbateanism, the largest and most momentous messianic movement in Jewish history since the destruction of the Temple, succeeded in winning adherents in Syria, rabbinic authority over many of the converts reasserted itself shortly after the sect's collapse in the eighteenth century. Because of the growing affluence of the Aleppo community before the nineteenth century in trade and commerce, financial support from the leading merchant families enabled rabbis and scholars to devote attention to religious study and maintain their community. It is noteworthy, however, that the rabbis' income was also derived from labor, not only from income and taxes on ritual slaughters, communal fines, Hevrah Kadishah (burial society), circumcision, bar mitzvahs, and the *arikha* (a personal tax levied annually on the estimated income of the community members that was assessed by a special committee and payable in advance). These communal sources of income were directed mostly to the community fund for other types of charitable services.

The literary dynamism of Aleppan rabbis reached its zenith toward the end of the nineteenth century, during the tenures of rabbis Yitshaq Abulafia and Hayyim Eskenazi of Damascus, who prepared halakhic commentaries on Ottoman laws that affected Jewish concerns, especially matters pertaining to Jewish land holding and real estate registration after the Ottoman Land Law of 1858. Then and subsequently, Syria's spiritual leaders, such as Rabbis Shlomo Elfendari and Ezra Terrab of Damascus, commented on modern issues of commercial credit and the increased problem of Jewish debts to European banks; the vast body of responsa literature at the end of the nineteenth century encompassed subjects that varied from commercial credit to permission to forward divorce certificates and other important Jewish data via the mail, as well as the use of the urban electric tramway on the Sabbath. Fearing that modernization and the introduction of Western-style leisure activities would lead the young astray or violate the Sabbath, rabbis opposed such activities as frequenting coffeehouses, walking in the park, and going to the movies. Even Sabbath strolls to vineyards and orchards came under rabbinic criticism in Aleppo as late as 1900, for the rabbis feared that this activity might entice the young to violate the Sabbath through immoral acts.

After World War I the rabbis of Aleppo and Damascus lost some of their prestige, whereas those of Beirut never wielded any real influence. The decline of Aleppan and Damascene prestige at the time is attributable to emigration to Egypt, Palestine, and the Americas. As many rabbis also left, the remaining spiritual elite lost the influence that they enjoyed locally and in other communities. In addition, the lure of secular education attracted young men, so they often ended their religious studies at the level of the Talmud Torah or even before. The Paris-based Alliance Israélite Universelle (AIU) opened a school for boys in Damascus in 1880 and one for girls in 1883. The AIU also opened schools in Aleppo later. In Beirut the organization opened a school for girls in 1878 and one for boys in 1880. These taught French and secular subjects, balanced to a degree with a religious curriculum. At the same time Christian missionary schools offering a modern curriculum also intensified their educational efforts among both well-to-do and poor Jews. The graduates of such schools in Beirut, some of whom pursued higher education at Saint Joseph or the American University, were instrumental in developing this seaport's economy. In 1910 a school opened in Damascus that had been inspired by the Yishuv, the Jewish community of Palestine; it offered Modern Hebrew, French, Arabic, and some general education. AIU-style schooling influenced the Jews culturally and socially; they adopted European first names, and young women married at a later age. Such modern attractions as department stores, movie theaters, cafes, and restaurants tempted segments of the youth to distance themselves from the traditional mold, even to the point of violating the Sabbath.

The traditional lay leadership that was responsible for collecting the *jizya* as well as community funds remained unscathed during Ottoman rule. Separate councils for each community characterized the nature of Syria's decentralized Jewish *millet* (autonomous religious community). This was to change after World War I in Syria and Lebanon, where the new business and professional elites produced members of the lay leadership. Their newly acquired educations and ties to the authorities strengthened their position vis-à-vis the spiritual leadership. They, not the rabbis, were the founders of new schools and clinics. Several of them, belonging to the distinguished Farhi, Nahmad, and Laniado families, served on the municipal councils. They succeeded in removing the rabbis who opposed reforms.

The significance of the B'nai B'rith movement in Syria, founded in 1914, cannot be underestimated. The Beirut and Damascus community councils were dominated by activists who wished to democratize the lay community councils. These groups adopted the ideals of humanism and philanthropy from the Freemasons but not their ritual and critical attitude toward religion. B'nai B'rith members defined themselves as community reformists, cultural revivalists, and defenders of Jewish interests—whose goals were to combat the influence of Christian missionary schools and to promote modern education for girls. Its membership was composed of professionals who preferred modern schools to traditional ones.

Of the three major Jewish communities of pre-1920 Greater Syria, the one in Damascus was not endowed with a wide leadership elite, as were those in Beirut and Aleppo. Many of the urban educated men who went to study at the universities in Beirut remained there. With local industries in Syria ruined by the importation of European goods, and with the opening of the Suez Canal, which reduced trade with Iran and the East via the Syrian Desert, numerous Syrian Jews emigrated to Egypt and the Americas. The resulting communal depopulation was more acute in Damascus than Aleppo, because the Aleppans were better organized and were successful in collecting money through the *arikha.* The money sent back to Syria by affluent emigrants to Brazil, the United States, and Egypt enabled the Aleppans to maintain themselves effectively, despite the commercial decline.

In Syria relations between Jews and non-Jews were quite complex. The work of Christian missionaries exacerbated the economic rivalry between Jews and Christians and competition for the position of *sarraf* (financial adviser). The nadir of these relations was the Damascus blood libel: in 1840 a Capuchin friar in Damascus, Father Tomas, disappeared. At the instigation of Ratti Menton, the French consul, the government blamed the Jews for the friar's disappearance and made a case for ritual murder that led to arrests and torture. News of the event reached Europe, leading to intervention by European Jewish leaders to halt the anti-Jewish drive. The 1840 blood libel case is significant because it opened the way for European Jews to lobby on behalf of Jews in the Muslim world.

SYRIA FROM THE FRENCH MANDATE TO INDEPENDENCE AND THE IMMEDIATE POST-1948 PERIOD

The inauguration of the French mandate after World War I raised hopes among the non-Muslims for new rights and measures of autonomy. They envisioned economic development that would lead to prosperity. Despite French modernizing initiatives, economic growth was actually evident only in the early 1940s. Thus the emigration of Syrians to neighboring countries or beyond resumed. The hardships resulting from World War I, the Syrian-Druze revolt of 1925–27, and the perpetual labor and political strikes of the 1930s that accompanied Syria's struggle for national independence all were factors that affected the economy and accelerated emigration. Fearing the nationalist fervor and the possibility that they would be harassed, Jews also began to make illegal aliyah to Palestine.

Urbanization continued under the French mandate, leading to a concentration of the Jewish population in Damascus and Aleppo. Qamishli was settled in the 1920s, when the French began to develop the rural Jazirah, bordering on Turkey and Iraq. The French wished to settle the area with minorities of Bedouins, Kurds, Turkomans, Jews, and the Nestorian Christians who had fled Iraq with the massacre of Assyrians in 1933. Only 40,000 of al-Jazirah's inhabitants in the 1930s were Sunni Muslim Arabs; the area also had 80,000 Kurds, 40,000 Christians, and about 2,000 Jews. The Jews were mostly, but not exclusively, émigrés from neighboring Turkish Nusaybin; they settled in Qamishli and the rural villages of al-Shukra, Tel-Sha'ir, and Awaija, importing and exporting textiles, tobacco, wool, wheat, rice, leather goods, and milk products. They were among the few Arabic-speaking communities where agriculture was part of daily Jewish life. Their relations with the Bedouins and Kurds were rather cordial. Like the Aleppo and Damascus Jewish families, al-Jazirah's Jews were more at odds with Christians than with Muslims. In general, the remoteness of al-Jazirah from Syria's urban centers, the large presence of minorities, and the reduced size of the Sunni Arab population spared them from the problems of Aleppo and Damascus during the 1930s that were related to Arab nationalism and the unrest in Palestine; these issues were marginal to everyday life. Among the affluent Jewish families of al-Jazirah who purchased land in the village of Awaija, pioneered in the use of mechanized agriculture in the region, and introduced wheat and leguminous crops were the Hodaidas, Shevahs, and Rahimas. Moshe Nahum Abdallah, president of Qamishli's community, was the leading entrepreneur in building the city's trade center.

Despite some major improvements in Jewish life under the French mandate, Aleppo and Damascus Jews confronted some hardships, including poverty among the underclass. In this period the number of merchants declined as they emigrated, and more Jews entered the craft occupations. In 1931 a large segment of Aleppo's Jewish workforce was comprised of bootblacks, shoemakers, bookbinders, hawkers and peddlers, grocers, small shop owners, fabric merchants, druggists, customs agents working for the French, contractors, and wholesale merchants. Several Jews were influential bankers. The economic decline under French control has been attributed to political changes embodied in the Treaty of Lausanne (1923), the final treaty ending World War I. Until the collapse of the Ottoman Empire the Jews of Aleppo continued to benefit to some degree from Aleppo's location; they maintained commercial links with Cilicia, Iraq, and Iran, although the Lausanne treaty created customs barriers between Cilicia and Syria and between Iraq and Syria. The xenophobia of the post-Ottoman Turks and of the Iraqis—who were on the verge of obtaining independence from Britain—hindered economic ties between Aleppan Jews and the regions to the east and north. In Damascus the situation was no better in the 1920s and 1930s. French observers noted in the 1930s that the Jews of Damascus adapted well to French language and culture, whereas the Arabs barely mastered French. Nevertheless, major economic opportunities hardly existed.

After World War II the political and economic instability affecting Syria accelerated Jewish emigration to England, Lebanon, Israel, Egypt, and the United States for many affluent or middle-class people. Thus the absolute number of poor Syrian Jews increased. Anti-Jewish riots occurred in Aleppo in 1947, due to tensions in Palestine. The Arab-Israeli War of 1948–49 and the plight of the Palestinian refugees made matters worse for the rest of Syria's Jews. Although measures restricting the freedom of Jews to travel within Syria or to emigrate were enforced only after Syrian independence in 1946, the formation of the State of Israel and the war that followed served as an incentive for Syria to issue laws that made it illegal for Jews to sell property and that froze Jewish bank accounts. Many Jews who left anyway had their properties confiscated by the government, and the Palestinian refugees who made their way to Syria were housed in dwellings vacated in the Jewish neighborhoods of Aleppo and Damascus.

Syria's aid to the Palestinian refugees was part of the "politics of symmetry" embraced in connection with the Palestine catastrophe. From Syria's vantage point, Arab-Jewish relations in post-1948 Syria would parallel Arab-Jewish relations in Israel—connected to the plight of the refugees who fled to Syria and other Arab countries. Some Arab Israelis lived under Israel's military authorities, which meant that until December 1966 they were subjected to restrictive regulations that limited their freedom of movement, access to civil courts, and individual ownership of land; they were considered security risks. Syrian Jews were to suffer similar, even harsher, restrictions. Syria confiscated Jewish properties and scrutinized the Jews' movement inside the country, from one city to the next; the government required Jews to carry identification cards marked on both sides in bold red letters *musawi* (religion of Moses).

Jews in post-1948 Syria were deprived of employment in government agencies and parts of the private sector. By the time Hafiz al-Assad seized power in 1970, the main occupations in the Damascus Jewish community were in medicine, architecture, and handicrafts; however, hardly any of the architects or artisans were employed in non-Jewish firms, though Jewish physicians could care for non-Jewish patients.

Demographically, the Syrian Jewish communities reached their zenith from 1911 to 1913, when about 28,500 Jews lived in Greater Syria (excluding Palestine)—with more than 11,000 in Damascus, nearly 12,000 in Aleppo, approximately 5,000 in Beirut, and 500 in Sidon (Beirut was part of Greater Syria until Lebanon was formed in September 1920). The Syrian census of 1943 showed 29,770 Jews in the country, about 17,000 of whom lived in Aleppo and 11,000 in Damascus, with no specific data available for al-Jazirah. These figures are doubtless inflated. In 1947 the number of Jews was only 15,000, following emigration to the Americas, Lebanon, and the illegal aliyah to Palestine.

The Jewish populations of Damascus and Aleppo steadily declined from 1948 to 1958. Despite the difficulties in leaving Syria, the population was reduced in 1959 to 6,500, with 3,500 in Damascus, 2,000 in Aleppo, and fewer than 1,000 in al-Jazirah. In 1992, of the remaining 4,000 Jews, the majority lived in Damascus; in 1994, by virtue of the regime's liberal policies, most had left, and only 150 Jews remained.

In education the AIU became the main source of schooling among the Jews. The Yishuv-inspired Hebrew school in Damascus (directed by Jews from Palestine who had been expelled in the final days of Ottoman rule) that taught Modern Hebrew survived only into the early 1920s. It closed because of the absence of subsidies from the French, who regarded such schools as centers of British and Zionist influence, and the inability of Jewish communities to maintain them. In the 1950s local community schools expanded, and a Talmud Torah opened in Damascus, sponsored by the American Otzar ha-Torah.

It was natural for Zionism, as a modern current in Jewish life, to gain momentum in the Syrian and Lebanese communities. For one thing, unlike many other communities of the Muslim world, they were on the threshold of Palestine. For another, the influence of the Yishuv's exiles in Damascus proved to be enormous. They directed the Hebrew schools and wielded considerable influence in daily communal affairs. Moreover, while the AIU embedded in its educational philosophy the notion that Jews should become loyal and productive citizens in their country of birth while regarding France as their adopted homeland, graduates did not necessarily follow this thinking. As some AIU teachers themselves became converts to Zionism and other ideological currents, they imparted a mélange of principles, some of which contradicted the AIU's raison d'être and promoted Zionist causes.

Unlike the Maghreb or Egypt, where Zionist federations and associations abounded during the interwar and immediate post–World War II eras, most functioning legally or semilegally, Syrian Zionism, like its counterpart in Iraq, was somehow tolerated into the 1930s but was restricted thereafter. Jews were pressured to pledge loyalty to nationalist aspirations and to avoid supporting the Yishuv. Damascus emerged as the main center of Arab nationalism and an active arena of anti-Zionist sentiments, encouraged by the mufti of Jerusalem, Hajj Amin al-Husayni, and other Palestinian nationalists. Besides, the French regarded Zionism as an instrument for bolstering British political influence in the region. The anti-Zionist feelings discouraged the activists from publishing journals promoting the Yishuv. Beirut's Jewish newspaper, *al-Alam al-Isra'ili* (*Jewish World*), in fact called for Arab unity and studiously avoided extolling Zionism, while North African and Egyptian Jewish communities were served by journals emphasizing Zionist ideas.

Increased pro-German and pro-Italian fascist propaganda, directed in no small measure against the Jews of the Middle East, plus the effect on the Syrian public of the Arab Revolt of 1936–39 in Palestine, placed Zionist efforts in a more precarious situation. In times of crisis the Zionist activists went underground. Unable to maintain a federation of associations and organizations, Syrian Zionism revolved around pioneer youth movements: Ha-Poᶜel, He-Halutz, Ha-Tekhiya, and Ha-Tiqva. Syrian Zionism was also defined by the cooperation of certain local Jews and the Political Department of the Jewish Agency for Palestine on three fronts: serving as discreet intermediaries between the Yishuv's Zionist leadership and the more moderate leaders of the Syrian nationalist movement; gathering intelligence on political trends; and caring for European Jewish refugees passing through on their way to Palestine. The aliyah of refugees and local Jews, often the initiative of the emigrants, was conducted overland, across the Syria-Palestine border, with the use of a "tourist visa," or along the seashores via Beirut and Sidon, occasionally in conjunction with professional smugglers. During the 1930s several hundred young adults were involved with the diverse pioneer movements; taking risks, those activists assisted the Yishuv during the Arab Revolt, sending weapons and money to Palestine. The Mossad le-Aliya Bet (Organization for Illegal Immigration) also became a factor locally in stimulating emigration.

Whether as an initiative of the pioneer movements or as an independent undertaking by local Jews, the Syrian aliyah was unique. Large-scale movement to Israel from North Africa, Iraq, Egypt, Iran, Afghanistan, and Turkey became significant only in the late 1940s or soon thereafter. Before the 1940s only two communities, Yemen and Syria, made substantial aliyah. Between 1919 and 1948, 10,292 Syrian Jews settled in Palestine to escape harsh economic conditions and the rising tides of Arab nationalism. World War II and France's Vichy government sped their departure, although Syrian Jews were spared the racial laws that affected the Jews of North Africa. During the war forty-five hundred Syrian Jews reached Palestine, thanks to the efforts of Zionists, individuals, and the Mossad le-Aliya Bet. In short, the departure of the Syrian Jewish community gained strength after World War I, despite obstruction by the authorities of independent Syria (initially in collaboration with the British mandate in Palestine) and later by strict measures to prevent emigration, such as border patrols and the canceling of tourist visas. Large-scale Syrian aliyah—by both local Jews and refugees in transit—and emigration to other lands ended at about the time that this process was beginning in other parts of the region.

FROM THE EARLY 1950S TO THE HAFIZ AL-ASSAD ERA

With the exception of short periods in 1949, 1958–59, and 1961–62, Jews were unable to leave Syria freely to go to other countries, certainly not whole families, and aliyah was strictly forbidden. They could leave only if they paid ransom money, taxes, fines, and fees for travel documents. The affluent managed to leave on the pretext of seeking medical care or transacting business in the West; they deposited substantial funds with the authorities that were refundable only upon their return. Few Jews could afford to buy their way out, and often even bribes and other payments failed to achieve the desired results. Determined to escape, Jews tried to sneak out on their own or with the help of smugglers, who sometimes robbed or murdered the escapees.

Because the Mossad le-Aliya Bet was no longer able to operate inside Syria after 1948, it recruited Shula Kishik-Cohen, a Beirut shopkeeper's wife who had used considerable ingenuity in sending to the Mossad information that she had overheard. The agency wanted her to head a network that was linked to Israeli intelligence units. With the help of Hayyim Kovo and Albert Abdallah Alia, leaders of the Beirut community, Kishik-Cohen was instrumental in organizing and overseeing overland and maritime aliyah from Syria via Lebanon. They bribed officials of the Syrian and Lebanese Ministries of the Interior, at times with money from the Jewish Agency, to facilitate departures. Kishik-Cohen, connected with Lebanon's Deuxième Bureau (security services), obtained Lebanese permits for Syrian Jews who reached Beirut and sought to leave. A special arrangement was worked out in the mid- or late 1950s with Lufthansa, the German airline, to transport Syrian Jews to Israel from Beirut via Istanbul. The Lebanese authorities arrested Kishik-Cohen and exposed her work in 1961; during her long imprisonment Albert Alia, secretary general of the Beirut Jewish community, took up her efforts of working closely with the Israeli aliyah authorities in Europe, Turkey, and Jerusalem.

From 1949 on, overland emigration from Qamishli and Aleppo, usually via Nusaybin and Alexandretta in Turkey, emerged as another avenue for departure. It was assisted by a clandestine aliyah committee operating out of Aleppo, Aleppo-born Jews operating out of Alexandretta, Syrian Kurdish and Bedouin smugglers from al-Jazirah, and Turkish smugglers in Nusaybin. Upon arriving in Turkey, escapees who either left Syria on their own initiative or with the aid of local aliyah operatives were assisted by the Jewish Agency's Immigration Department, the Israeli legation in Ankara, and the Israeli consulate general in Istanbul—all with the cooperation of the Turkish authorities, who enjoyed a special diplomatic and intelligence relationship with Israel. When Syrian Jews in Israel asked to be reunited with families they had left behind, the Jewish Agency on various occasions actively stimulated the families' emigration rather than wait for people to leave Syria of their own accord. This was possible because of operatives inside Syria and their counterparts in Turkey.

The reliance on smugglers, particularly for the overland departure to Turkey from northern Syria, became essential in the 1950s. Using Turkish smugglers or contacts provided by Jewish aliyah activists within Turkey, the Jewish Agency helped Syrian Jews to reunite with family members living in

Israel. Upon arrival in Turkey emigrants boarded ships to Haifa or were booked on flights from Istanbul to Lydda.

The deteriorating financial situation of the communities as a result of the emigration necessitated outside support—all the more essential because of the further deprivation of Jews in the postwar Syrian economy and nationalization of private enterprise in the the 1960s. The confiscation of assets, and the smuggling by affluent Jews of their capital to other countries, greatly reduced the local funds available for community projects. Therefore the communities depended on assistance from the American Jewish Joint Distribution Committee and wealthy Syrian Jews living abroad. The support data for 1984–85 suggest that the Committee disbursed $300,000 for the Damascus community. The funds were transferred to Beirut and then went via courier to Syria. Before the community could put the money to good use, the police, security services, and the Commission for Palestinian Refugees deducted their share.

Since 1963 growing Syrian-Israeli tensions have adversely influenced the remaining Jewish communities. In March 1964 the Syrian government issued a decree that prohibited Jews in Syria from traveling more than three miles beyond the limits of their hometowns. Their identification cards were no longer the only document to bear the word *musawi*; the term now appeared on bank accounts, medical guild memberships, and driver's licenses. The Syrian secret police and the Ministry of the Interior regulated these policies. The exposure and execution in 1965 of Elie Cohen, the Israeli spy who had infiltrated the Syrian political hierarchy, and the 1967 war exacerbated an already perilous situation. However, Syrian Jews arrested at the outbreak of the war were not treated as badly as those in Egypt and Iraq. As in earlier wars, Egypt sent Jews to internment camps or prisons for extended periods. Iraq executed Jews after the 1948 and 1967 wars on charges of spying for Israel. Syria apparently did not adopt those measures against its Jews (rumors of the internment of Jews in Qamishli never have been corroborated).

In 1967 Muslim-Jewish hostilities in Damascus neither originated nor predominated among ordinary Syrians—but were promoted by local Palestinians who were supported by local Syrians. The police in Damascus and Aleppo protected the Jews as much as possible by posting guards in these cities' Jewish quarters. Jews were allowed to leave their homes to make essential purchases but only for a few hours a day. When leaving their homes they were subjected to petty harassment, including insults, shoving, and spitting. They found it impossible to open their shops or pursue their business ventures because the larger community was boycotting their products. The protection afforded by the authorities was less from compassion and more from an effort to be in control and avert anarchy.

Syrian Jews Under Hafiz al-Assad

The restrictions in Syria continued under the rule of Hafiz al-Assad, who came to power in 1970. The High Commission for Jewish Affairs, consisting of representatives from the Ministry of the Interior and the Muhbarat, the secret police and internal security services, kept tabs on Jewish daily life, making arrests and conducting investigations. The plight of Syrians Jews caught the attention of major Jewish organizations more than they had in the past. What distinguished Syrian Jews under Assad from those who lived under earlier regimes was not merely that knowledge about their plight was monitored in the West more effectively than ever before but that Syrian Jews had become unwilling to remain silent. In 1972 Damascus Jews protested by staging a public demonstration, an unprecedented and bold event that received little media coverage. The next demonstration occurred in March 1974, after four women were killed as they attempted to flee Syria via Lebanon. One thousand Damascene Jews participated in a demonstration, carrying a symbolic coffin in the city's streets. This event surprised Syrians, who could not believe the degree of courage that the small Jewish minority demonstrated. Nevertheless, the secret police continued to patrol the Jewish neighborhoods, monitor Jews' telephone conversations, and tamper with their mail.

During this period Syrian authorities planned a televised interview with the leaders of the Damascus Jewish community. They handpicked the leaders and offered them a printed text that described the situation of the Jews in glowing terms. When this became known to others in the Jewish community, they decided to prevent the telecast by not allowing the Jewish leaders to leave their homes. They did so in the full knowledge that their actions would warrant arrest. The arrests and interrogations followed, but the televised interview was canceled. At the same time in Aleppo, Jewish demonstrators took to the streets to protest the arbitrary arrest of parents whose children had fled Syria. There too both Muslims and Christians expressed astonishment at this activism.

In 1977–78 the Syrian regime briefly considered easing restrictions. However, by 1979 Jewish sources in the West had reported that restrictions on freedom of movement remained unchanged. Although free emigration was prohibited, by the mid-1980s Chief Rabbi Avraham Hamra was permitted to travel abroad on community business and meet Jewish leaders in the

West. At that time Jews in the West also suggested that Jews who could afford to move out of the Damascus Jewish quarter could buy homes in the more fashionable districts.

An outstanding example of individual dedication in assisting Syrian Jewry is Judy Feld-Carr, a Canadian, also known as "Mrs. Judy." Feld-Carr contacted Hamra, who asked that she supply badly needed prayer books and ritual objects. These objects as well as money were smuggled into Syria from North America, to be used in appropriate ways by the community. Hamra and Feld-Carr corresponded; reliable Syrian Jewish businessmen who were able to leave and enter the country carried important information sewn inside their coat linings—letters, detailed lists, and confirmation that Jews had received the money.

In 1977 many Jews were able to leave Syria because of Feld-Carr's efforts. A good example of what she did is the assistance rendered to Rabbi Eliahu Dahlab of Aleppo, who in the mid-1970s was dying of cancer. Feld-Carr personally arranged for Dahlab to obtain a plane ticket, fly indirectly to Israel, and reunite with his family. His unmarried daughter also managed to leave, again through the efforts of Feld-Carr. Every step required connections with Syrian officials—judges, attorneys, and police captains—who, for the right amount of money, procured travel documents and overlooked illegalities.

The turning point came in the spring of 1992, when Assad met with representatives of the Damascus Jewish community and informed them that Syria would regard the Jews as equal citizens. No limitations on the sale or purchase of property would be enforced thereafter, and Jews would no longer be barred from traveling within the country or abroad for vacations and business purposes. In behind-the-scenes talks Syrian and U.S. officials agreed that freedom of movement included emigration. To create a cordial atmosphere Assad agreed to release from prison the Soued brothers, who had been arrested several years earlier for attempting to leave the country illegally. All this followed the collapse of the Soviet Union in the summer of 1991, with Assad's patrons in Moscow burdened by internal problems and unable to sustain the Syrian military and its budget. Damascus then sought to improve ties with the United States, hoping to have Syria removed from the list of countries supporting terrorism and thus obtain generous U.S. economic and military assistance. By first demonstrating flexibility about emigration, Assad aimed to translate his hopes into reality.

Between April and October 1992 twenty-six hundred of the four thousand Jews remaining in Syria left the country. After a brief hiatus in emigration, ordered by Assad ostensibly because of the press attention, the exodus resumed. In October 1994 the Israeli press and Syrian Jews in the United States reported that all Jews except 150 to 180 who preferred to remain there had left Syria. Some settled in the Americas, and others chose Israel as their destination.

LEBANON UNDER THE FRENCH MANDATE TO THE PRESENT

The small Lebanese Jewish community was estimated in 1923 at 3,300. The 1932 census registered 3,588 Jews, with 3,060 in Beirut and the rest mainly in Sidon and Tripoli. Sidon, the second most important Jewish community, never had more than four hundred to five hundred Jewish residents in the twentieth century. Because most of Sidon's Jews were poor and vulnerable to physical attacks by the non-Jewish majority, they began to emigrate to Beirut or Palestine in the 1930s. Lebanon's total population in 1939 was about 934,000, of whom 7,000 were Jews. The sharp rise in the Jewish population since the 1920s, mainly in Beirut—where the Jewish population climbed to 10,000 in 1958—was caused by an influx of Syrian Jews. Lebanon was perhaps the only Arab country in which the Jewish population increased after 1948. After 1958, when Lebanon was engulfed in a civil war and the Syrian-Jewish influx came to a standstill, the Lebanese Jewish community declined through ongoing emigration.

No central leadership apparatus characterized the Jewish community's structure. Only Beirut's had well-organized and financially sound institutions. The Jewish community council in Beirut represented all the Jewish communities throughout the country in dealings with the authorities, and it offered the communities philanthropic and welfare assistance. The most impressive building of Lebanon's Jews was the Magen Avraham synagogue in Beirut, which housed as the main community center, the office of the rabbinate, a Talmud Torah, Bikkur Holim (community assistance to the sick and elderly), and a communal library. It was built in 1927 with a donation by Moshe Ben-Avraham Sasson of Calcutta in memory of his father, Avraham Sasson, who had lived in Beirut. More than the Jewish communities of Syria, the Beirut Jewish community shouldered the main responsibility during the French mandate for Jewish refugees from Europe, who either settled there or were in transit to Palestine. In the late 1940s, 90 percent of Lebanese Jews engaged in commerce, 5 percent were in the liberal professions (lawyers, educators, administrators, bankers, and the like), and the remaining 5 percent practiced various artisanal trades. Numerous Beiruti Jews lived in the fashionable districts among members of other religions. The economically disadvantaged lived in Wadi Abu Jamil, the old Jewish quarter.

Jews of Sidon and Tripoli attended tuition-free government schools, foreign schools, at one time even Yishuv-inspired Modern Hebrew classes, or the local religious school. In Beirut the majority enrolled at the AIU schools, leading to the primary school certificate and the *brevet* at the junior high school level. The foreign schools provided the bridge to full secondary education leading to a diploma. A significant number of Jews pursued higher education at Beirut's American and French institutions. The comprehensive education that they received, including instruction in Arabic, enabled young Jews to compete effectively in the Lebanese economy. The AIU schools' student body provides the best yardstick of the general Jewish demographic decline. In 1947, 968 youths were enrolled at the AIU schools; they had 1,510 students in 1956 and 1,443 in 1959. In 1964, as the Jewish population declined, AIU enrollment in Beirut was only 562.

The Yishuv exiles and Hebrew school directors advocated Zionism. In 1919, when the U.S.-sponsored King-Crane Commission arrived in Lebanon to survey local opinion about the postwar settlement of the territories, Jewish delegations from Beirut and Sidon recommended a separate Lebanon under a French mandate and publicly endorsed the establishment of a Jewish national home in Palestine. They made this bold recommendation despite pressure from Arab nationalist circles to do otherwise. Fund-raising for the Jewish National Fund and the Jewish Foundation Fund was intensive in the interwar period because of the relative affluence of the Beirut Jewish community. The rise in anti-Zionism in the 1930s induced community leaders and Pioneer youth movements to periodically become less visible, lest their activities arouse the hostility of the French and Lebanese authorities. Lebanese Jewry did not face the multiple negative challenges posed to Jews in neighboring areas. The exceptions were the anti-Zionist mood of the 1930s and 1940s, which unleashed sporadic violence against Jewish people and their property. World War II and France's Vichy government also had little effect on their status because Vichy domination in Lebanon ended in 1941.

The civil war in 1958 precipitated the emigration of Jews, but no harm came to them. They were usually free to leave the country, and since the 1950s the majority had opted for resettlement in Europe or the Americas rather than Israel. Despite the pro-Zionist position of Lebanon's Jewish leadership before 1948, only Sidon's Jews went to Israel. Until the Six-Day War of 1967, when the Palestine Liberation Organization (PLO) was not yet a pivotal force in Lebanese politics, and religious rivalries did not affect the Jews, those who chose to remain were still an active group in the economy. They did not wield any influence in the political system, however. The political structure rested on the principle of proportional representation of the Muslims and Christians in the Chamber of Deputies. Ministerial posts too were distributed by proportional representation. Given the small number of Jews, the system could not offer them even a minimal share in the body politic. After 1967, as Muslims came to identify Jews with privilege and to dislike Maronite Christians, Muslims viewed the Israel-Maronite nexus as a conspiracy against them, and in light of the rise of the PLO, prospects for Jewish continuity were reduced. Although Lebanon had five thousand Jews in 1960, only one thousand Jews lived there in 1970. Then the 1975 civil war ended it all. Schools and synagogues became beggars' lairs or served as barracks for the Amal movement (a Shiite political and military organization), the PLO, or the Syrian military, which was sent in by Assad. By 1998 only several dozen Jews remained.

RECOMMENDED READING

Khoury, Philip S. *Syria and the French Mandate: The Politics of Arab Nationalism, 1920–1945*. Princeton, N.J.: Princeton University Press, 1987.

Maᶜoz, Moshe. *Ottoman Reform in Syria and Palestine*. Oxford: Oxford University Press, 1968.

Marcus, Abraham. *The Middle East on the Eve of Modernity: Aleppo in the Eighteenth Century*. New York: Columbia University Press, 1989.

Menachem, Nahum. *Syrian and Lebanese Jewry in the Crossfire of Arab Nationalism and the Zionist Movement*. Jerusalem: Hebrew University, 1990.

CHAPTER

18

Eretz Israel/Palestine, 1800–1948

RUTH KARK AND JOSEPH B. GLASS

Eretz Israel, the Land of Israel, consists of four geographical regions: the Negev in the south, the coastal plain in the west, the hill regions, and the Jordan Rift Valley in the east. The coastal plain along the Mediterranean Sea, sparsely populated in the early nineteenth century, became the focus of new Jewish settlement activity of the twentieth century. The hill regions were the most densely populated areas in the nineteenth century. The climate is Mediterranean, distinguished by cool rainy winters and dry hot summers.

Ottoman rule, which began in 1517, divided Palestine longitudinally, between the *vilayets* (provinces) of Damascus and Sidon (later the *vilayet* of Beirut). In 1864 the Ottomans created a new autonomous administrative unit, the *mutasariflik* of Jerusalem, and a few years later ruled it directly from Istanbul. After World War I and the demise of the Ottoman Empire, the whole of Palestine was placed under a single administrative unit by the League of Nations, and in 1920 the Conference of San Remo conferred the mandate over Palestine on Great Britain. The British divided the territory, creating the protectorate of Transjordan in 1923, which became the kingdom of Jordan in 1946. When the British mandate ended in May 1948, the State of Israel was established and recognized by the United Nations.

PEOPLES

Until the British conducted a census in 1922, information about the size and composition of Palestine's population was incomplete. In 1800 the region had 250,000 to 300,000 inhabitants (including 5,500 Jews). In the early 1870s the total population was estimated at about 350,000 (including 18,000 Jews), with an additional 25,000 Bedouins; a conflicting estimate placed the population at 470,000 inhabitants in 1882 (including 24,000 Jews). In 1914 the population was about 800,000 (with 85,000 Jews). The predominant population was rural Sunni Muslim Arabs. In the nineteenth century the population increased through slow natural growth and the migration of small groups of Muslims from other parts of the Ottoman Empire (Egypt, Algeria, Libya, Syria, Lebanon, Bosnia, Turkestan, and the Caucasus). Other small minorities included the Druze, Samaritans, Karaites, Bahais, and Ahmedis. The Christian minority, mostly Arab, was comprised of a number of communities: Greek Orthodox, Armenian, Roman Catholic, Maronite, Syrian Orthodox (or Jacobite), Coptic, and Ethiopian. The Ottoman regime recognized only the Greek Orthodox, Armenians, and Jews as separate *millets* (religious communities organized around the political-religious authority of its spiritual leader). Protestants began to be active only in the early nineteenth century. Some were missionaries to Christians and Jews; their activities included setting up schools, hospitals, and orphanages for these communities. The German Templers established agricultural settlements and urban neighborhoods.

World War I (1914–18) had a negative effect on Palestine's population. The Ottoman regime had some elements expelled or conscripted. Others died in epidemics and from famine. Health services and economic conditions improved after the war, and Muslim immigration continued from adjoining countries—Egypt, Syria, Lebanon, and Transjordan—mainly in pursuit of economic opportunity. The population of Palestine increased by 923,000 from 1922 to 1943, with 62 percent from natural increase (births minus deaths) and 38 percent from immigration. In 1931 the Bedouins numbered 66,553, with more than two-thirds in the Negev. In 1922 only 35 percent of the population was urban, but by 1945 Palestine's population was 49 percent urban; 30 percent of Muslims, 80 percent of Christians, and 74 percent of Jews lived in Palestine's cities in 1945. As a result of the 1948 Arab-Israel War, half the Arab population was displaced, some fleeing and others forced out. In 1949, 140,000 Arabs became a minority under Israel's rule.

HISTORY OF THE HOST SOCIETY

With Napoleon's invasion of Palestine in 1799, the area became of great interest to the European powers. The Ottoman Empire ruled Palestine through strong local governors in the early nineteenth century. After a brief Egyptian occupation (1831–40), the Tanzimat reforms marked the return of Ottoman authority. The rights of foreign nationals, including Jews, to own land throughout the empire were revised after 1867, and Sultan Abdülhamid II attempted from 1876 on to integrate the empire under a centralized rule. Edicts restricting Jewish immigration and land purchase in Palestine were issued in 1882, when the "Lovers of Zion"—organizations established since 1881 to foster Jewish settlement in Eretz Israel—began their emigration from Eastern Europe. The immigration edicts were more strictly enforced after 1897, the year of the founding of the Zionist movement.

British rule began with military occupation in 1917, and along with it a rise in Arab nationalism, a reaction in part to the Balfour Declaration (1917), a letter of intent from the British government regarding the establishment of a Jewish homeland in Palestine. The British mandate (1922–48) began with appeasement, was followed by rising Arab nationalism—peaking in 1936–39 with the Arab Revolt, general strikes, and armed attacks against British authority and the Jews—and ended in 1948. During World War II Jewish pressure mounted for increased immigration and territorial control. It ended with the establishment of the State of Israel and Egyptian and Jordanian occupation of the remaining territories.

POPULATION: CHARACTERISTICS, COMPOSITION, AND SPATIAL DISTRIBUTION

From 1800 to 1948 the Jews of Palestine fell into three main groupings based on ethnic, cultural, and linguistic origins: Sephardim (speaking Ladino), Middle Eastern, and North African, including a small group of Palestinian Jews who spoke the local languages and Ashkenazim who spoke Yiddish. Over the years migration to Palestine led to greater diversity of Middle Eastern and North African Jews, and they divided into smaller communities, such as Moroccans, Yemenites, Syrians, Lebanese, Iraqis, Persians, Kurds, Turks, Bukharans, Georgians, Dagestanis, Afghans, Indians, and Ethiopians.

In 1800 the Jewish population did not exceed six thousand, with the majority indigenous—Sephardim and Middle Eastern Jews, with some Ashkenazic Hasidim and Perushim (followers of the Vilna Gaon). They were traditional, religious, and mostly economically unproductive, dependent on *halukkah* (money collected for support of needy Jews in Eretz Israel). In the 1820s, during the Greek War of Independence, scholars and traders came from the Balkans and Istanbul, including the families of Raphael Figotto from Aleppo and Joseph Amzalak from Gibraltar. From the 1830s on immigrants from Morocco, Algeria, and Tunisia settled in Galilee and in the coastal towns of Acre and Jaffa, then later in Haifa and Gaza; in Safed and

Tiberias these North Africans became the majority, and such families as the Abus, Shoshanas, Simhons, Sithons, Chelouches, and Bahluls joined the leadership beside families of Turkish origin (e.g., the Abulafias). Some were entrepreneurial and instrumental in the development of those cities and their surroundings. From 1854 to 1914 the number of Jews in Jerusalem from North Africa grew from about ten families to about twenty-five hundred people.

The Sephardic and Middle Eastern Jewish majority and their central role in the Old Yishuv eroded after 1882. About twenty-five thousand Ashkenazim arrived during the First Aliyah (1882–1903) fleeing from the pogroms in Russia. Eastern Europeans established *moshavot* (farming communities) in Eretz Israel at the time of the "Yemenite First Aliyah" of 1881, motivated in part by political and economic changes in Yemen and in part by messianic aspirations. By 1914 about five thousand, or one-tenth, of Yemen's Jews had emigrated to Palestine, settling mainly in Jerusalem and Jaffa. From the early twentieth century, Yemenite immigrants were integrated into the *moshavot* as manual laborers, and they played an important role in the idealization of Hebrew labor. Jews from Persia and the Caucasus (Georgia, Dagestan) also settled in Palestine at this time, while Bukharan emigration had begun in 1868, and Bukharan Jews built a spacious neighborhood in Jerusalem in 1891. The Second Aliyah (1904–14) brought about forty thousand immigrants, mainly from Eastern Europe, which changed the ethnic composition of the Yishuv, creating an Ashkenazic majority in Palestine for the first time.

In the first half of the nineteenth century, Jews had lived mostly in the four holy cities of Safed, Tiberias, Jerusalem, and Hebron. After the devastating earthquake of 1837, the center of of Jewish activity shifted from the Galilee to Jerusalem. There the various ethnic groups, mostly urban, kept to their unique lifestyles, and they preserved a pattern of segregation by choice in their distinct residential areas; each group concentrated in separate subquarters and courtyard complexes in the old cities or the neighborhoods outside the city walls. In the Old City of Jerusalem's Jewish quarter, Sephardic residences and their spiritual and social activity focused on the Four Sephardic Synagogues. Most houses in Jerusalem were owned by Muslims who rented them to Jews through a Jewish agent. Philanthropists who settled in Jerusalem, such as Shlomo Yehuda (1855), and other Iraqi Jews from Baghdad or those from India donated money to build Sephardic and Ashkenazic synagogues and yeshivas. North African Jews were concentrated around their two synagogues, yeshiva, and almshouses in the Jewish quarter and in the late 1860s began construction of Mahaneh Israel, the first neighborhood built by local Jews outside the Old City. The Jerusalem-born Joseph

Navon, a Sephardi entrepreneur, led the efforts to build commercial neighborhoods with reasonably priced housing. The Baghdadi scholar Rabbi Eliyahu Mani settled in Hebron and became the leader of its Jewish population.

Jaffa, which developed from a small walled town in 1800 to one of the major eastern Mediterranean ports in 1914, had no Jewish community until the 1830s. With the settlement there of Jews from North Africa, Rabbi Yehuda Ben Menachem Halevi of Ragusa began his fifty years of service. Jaffa's Jewish community grew from 122 in 1839 to 5,000 in 1905; 55 percent were Ashkenazim. After 1882 Jaffa became the center of the New Yishuv. Its Sephardic and Middle Eastern residents came from Bulgaria, the Balkans, Yemen, Persia, India, Morocco, Georgia, and Bukhara. The Yemenites chose to concentrate in their own neighborhoods. By 1914 Jaffa was the second largest city in Palestine, after Jerusalem; it had a population of 50,000 including 15,000 Jews, whereas Jerusalem had 75,000 people, including 53,800 Jews. Sephardic, Middle Eastern, and Ashkenazic investors developed new neighborhoods around Jaffa, including the Ahuzzat Bayit garden neighborhood (1909), which became the nucleus of Tel Aviv and grew rapidly, to 46,301 by 1931. Other urban communities with Sephardic, North African, and Turkish Jewish majorities were Acre and Haifa (3,000 in 1914, mostly Turkish and North Africans). The few Sephardim (62 in 1866) who lived in Nablus left the city during the late nineteenth century. Some North African Jews settled in Gaza in the early 1900s.

After World War I natural increase and immigration resulted in a rapid growth of the Yishuv. From 1922 to 1945 the average natural increase for the entire Jewish community was 2 percent annually (but it was much higher in Middle Eastern communities). Almost 400,000 Jews went to Palestine between 1919 and 1945 (85.9 percent Ashkenazim, 6.9 percent Sephardim, 4.1 percent Yemenites, and 3.1 percent others). After World War II Jews displaced (*she'erit ha-pleitah*) from Europe tried to emigrate to Palestine, including Sephardim from Greece and Bulgaria. Despite British quotas and restrictions for Jews to enter postwar Palestine, 120,000 Jews managed to get in between 1945 and 1948.

COMMUNITY: LEGAL STATUS, ORGANIZATION, AND LEADERSHIP

In the nineteenth century the Sephardim of Palestine perceived themselves as an elite group with a spiritual mission—a deeply religious and ideological identity—within the Ottoman Empire. Supported by endowments or philanthropists, they studied halakhah and kabbalah in yeshivas. The control of Istanbul officials over the internal affairs of Jerusalem's Sephardic community diminished from the beginning of the nineteenth century. Under Ottoman rule the *millet* system gave non-Muslim communities autonomy, but Jews were second-class citizens, with either the authorities or the Muslims sometimes oppressing, extorting, and punishing the Jews for blood libels, the claim that Jews used the blood of Gentiles to make matzo. For this reason many Jewish immigrants to Palestine kept their original nationality (non-Ottoman), thus gaining privileges and security of body and property under the Ottoman capitulation agreements with Western powers.

Despite his low status, a Damascus-born Jew named Haim Farhi exercised great power; he was a minister under the pashas of Sidon and Acre, and his position enabled him to be the patron of the Jews until he lost favor and was executed in 1819. As a result of the Tanzimat reforms (1841–76), *hahkam bashis* (chief rabbis) were nominated in the empire's districts. In Jerusalem the Ottoman authorities recognized only the Sephardim. From 1841 on, three Sephardic chief rabbis were nominated to the post: Avraham Gagin, Rafael Meir Panizel, and Yaakov Shaul Elyashar. With the elite of the Sephardic community, they played an important role in leading the Yishuv.

The Sephardic *kollel* (community group) was an important financial institution, controlling large funds and owning real estate. Prominent Sephardim and rabbis—among them, Haim Moshe Israel Shirizli, Izhak Israel Shirizli, Eliyahu Navon, Yaakov Shaul Elyashar, and Haim Aharon Valero—sat on the Jerusalem district council. With the growth of the Ashkenazic community, Ashkenazic rabbis eventually dominated the Old Yishuv. The Sephardic community vied with Ashkenazic groups for the *halukkah* (donations), but the power of the Sephardic leadership was eroded by a fragmentation of the Jewish community into *kolelim,* each with its own set of organizations for rabbinical courts, burials, the slaughter of animals, raising money abroad, real estate, and segregated residential neighborhoods. The first to withdraw from the Sephardic *kolel* was the North African community of Rabbi David Ben Simon of Rabat, who had settled in Jerusalem in 1854. In his capacity as community leader, he succeeded in establishing an independent North African *kolel* in Jerusalem in 1860. The community gained autonomy in running all spiritual and material affairs and in the collection and allocation of funds. The Bukharans and Georgians soon followed. The Yemenites, who felt relegated to the periphery and deprived in the allocation of funds, created independent organizational frameworks in 1908, forming their *bet-din* (rabbinic council) and cemetery and hiring ritual slaughterers. Other expressions of Yemenite organization included the 1922 formation of the Yemenite Federation, a Zionist body; Tel Aviv also had a unified community, with a rabbi and Talmud Torah and an association to buy land to settle Yemenite farmers.

A further blow to the chief rabbi's control occurred when Jaffa emerged as the administrative and cultural center of Zionism, with the establishment of schools, a library, and a theater and publishers of Zionist books and newspapers. Members of Sephardic and Middle Eastern communities supported many Zionist and Lovers of Zion activities. In 1882 Rabat-born Avraham Moyal was nominated to head the executive committee of the Lovers of Zion in Palestine. His knowledge of local conditions and languages and his familiarity with officials facilitated agricultural land purchases and assistance to new immigrants.

In 1903 a not very successful attempt was made to create the General Federation of the Jews of Eretz Israel, which had representatives from the Sephardi, Yemenite, and Persian communities. Rivalry with international Jewish organizations did not help. As the years passed, the process of secularization grew among Jews, many of whom went to Palestine from Europe. Ideological tensions and conflicts thus grew between the Old and New Yishuvs. The Sephardic and Middle Eastern communities were in the precarious position of identifying with certain of the values and ideologies of each of these groups, but they were unable to back either one. Important public figures, educators, and heads of the Alliance Israélite Universelle, such as Nissim Behar and Albert Antebi, became intermediaries with the Ottoman authorities and Palestinian Arabs for the Yishuv, the *moshavim*, and the Zionist organizations. In 1908 the prominent Sephardim in Jaffa—Amzalak, Chelouche, Malul, and Moyal—established the Magen Association to improve relationships between Jews and Arabs and Jews and the government, as well as to combat the negative attitudes toward Jews in Arab and Turkish newspapers. Before World War I it ran quite an extensive operation. Dr. Shimon Moyal of Jaffa worked to encourage Jewish and Arab cultural cooperation; he welcomed to his home Muslims of the Egyptian Masonic Lodge of Jaffa.

The British mandate perpetuated the Ottoman *millet* system, extending it to include Muslims. In 1920 Jews elected an assembly to run the affairs of the whole Yishuv. Women could vote, despite objections from Ashkenazic Orthodox elements. Of the 314 people elected, only 71 were non-Ashkenazic, their numbers decreasing through the years as Zionism grew. The assembly administered outside funding and guided various absorption policies, settlement projects, and negotiations with the British authorities. (Two of the Sephardic members were Eliyahu Hai Sasson, who headed the Arab Department of the Jewish Agency from 1933–48, and Dr. Eliyahu Elyashar, who worked for the mandate government, served as member and later president of the Jerusalem Sephardic Committee, and was elected as a deputy to the Zionist Congress in 1946.) Although several organizations were active among the Sephardic and Middle Eastern communities during the British mandate, the status of the Sephardic elite and its influence on the decision-making process in the Yishuv became diminished. Personal conflicts—mainly among the Jerusalem traditional elite, with the Elyashars at the top; the younger elite in Tel Aviv, as represented by Tiberias-born Judge Bechor Chetrit; and Istanbul-born Shabbetai Levi, who was mayor of Haifa—led to difficulties in creating a unified Sephardic front.

LANGUAGE, EDUCATION, AND NEWSPAPERS

In the nineteenth century members of each Palestinian Jewish community spoke in the language of their country of origin. Hebrew was then in use as a means of communication among the leaders of the different communities but was not used much in daily life. The Sephardim contributed to the revival of Hebrew as a modern language and helped reform Hebrew education in Palestine. The role of three Sephardic scholars—Joseph Halevi, Barukh Mitrani, and Nissim Behar—preceded and influenced the work of the better-known Eliezer Ben-Yehuda in those fields.

In the nineteenth century Jewish education consisted of religious schools (heders or *kuttabs*) for boys as well as yeshivas for their higher education. Most girls were illiterate, and their mothers and the other women of the household prepared them for life at home. The first attempt to open a modern school for boys in Jerusalem, the Eliza von Laemel School (1856), was met with fierce opposition from the conservative and pious Ashkenazim. Sephardim found no harm in sending their children to this school and to the Rothschild and Montefiore girls' schools, but only the wealthy took advantage of higher education. Poor boys usually attended school until the age of twelve and then entered the labor force. Most Sephardic girls lacked formal education. In 1906 Boris Schatz established the Bezalel School of Arts and Crafts; in 1911 a Bezalel community of Yemenite artisans was established at Ben Shemen. After World War I the Zionist Commission to Palestine established the Department of Education for Palestine, a system to provide an elementary education in Hebrew to all children.

In 1863 two pioneering Hebrew newspapers began publication in Jerusalem: *Ha-Levanon* and *Habazeleth*. The publishers were Ashkenazim. For short time *Habazeleth* published a supplement in Ladino for Sephardic readers, but the paper considered Sephardic news marginal. Moshe A. Azriel and Shlomo Israel Shirizli opened two printing houses in Jerusalem to fill the demand for Ladino publications in Palestine and abroad. In 1909, to counterbalance the political views of Eliezer Ben-Yehuda's newspapers, *Ha-Zevi* and *Ha-Or*, several Sephardic activists (including Antebi, Azriel, Haim Ben-Atar, and Avraham Elmaleh) established *Ha-Herut*, a Jewish nationalist newspaper for Sephardim. From a Ladino weekly it was soon a Hebrew daily, with a circulation of two thousand in the Yishuv and other Mediterranean Jewish communities. Its editorials supported Jewish colonization in Palestine, Hebrew and national education, and Arab-Jewish rapprochement. Dr. Shimon Moyal conceived the idea of an Arabic-Hebrew newspaper, *Saut al-Uthmaniyya* (the *Ottoman Voice*), which appeared in Jaffa from 1913 to 1914. In 1932 Elmaleh and Meir Laniado, a lawyer, tried to renew the publication of *Ha-Herut*, but it was short lived. In 1919 Elmaleh, a prolific scholar and writer, had initiated the publication of *Mizrah u-Maᶜarav* (*Orient and Occident*). He viewed it as a nonpolitical scientific, historic, and literary journal that would present the great heritage, history, customs, and rabbinical and literary writing of the Sephardic and Middle Eastern communities. It closed after a year and reopened in 1928 as a monthly, supported by the World Federation of Sephardic Jews.

In 1942 a new mouthpiece of the Sephardim—*Ha-Mizrah* (the *Orient*), renamed *Heid Ha-Mizrah* (*Echo of the Orient*)—was started in Jerusalem. Its first editor was Eliyahu Elyashar. This organ aspired to express the life, opinions, wishes, and demands of the Sephardic and Middle Eastern communities in Palestine, which then constituted a third of the Yishuv. It ceased publication in 1951.

CULTURE AND LIFESTYLE

Characteristic of the Sephardic and Middle Eastern Jews was a traditional lifestyle, expressed through housing, food, dress, daily customs, festivals, and rituals. These distinguished one community from another, and made each community unique. Among the Sephardic and Middle Eastern communities, the extended family was important, characterized by a feeling of unity, religious tradition, respect for parents and the elderly, and the desire to betroth or marry their children at early ages. (Among the Yemenites, marrying several wives was still common.) Marriage between communities was not frequent. The women ran the household. Family life was concentrated in the central courtyards. Cooking, washing, cleaning, and sometimes eating took place there. Shared by several families, the courtyard was also a focus of social life, and it enabled mutual aid. Sephardic and Middle Eastern women mostly stayed at home. Their men went to school, to work, and to the market. The meals were simple. Meat and fish were served only on the Sabbath and for holidays. Lag b^{c}Omer at Meron is a Sephardic festival day, as is the pilgrimage to the Tomb of Simon the Righteous in Jerusalem. Yet modern Tel Aviv–Jaffa influenced all youth, including Yemenites, with its theaters, movies, and concerts, so the Sephardic lifestyle became less traditional in the years before the founding of the State of Israel.

ECONOMIC ACTIVITIES AND AGRICULTURAL SETTLEMENT

Around 1800 the economic activities of the Sephardic and Middle Eastern communities followed the traditional patterns of commerce, crafts, and peddling throughout the countryside. Money sent by Jews living outside Eretz Israel and by organizations provided the main income. The Sephardim used the money for community needs (taxes, institutions, salaries, etc.) and for support of scholars and the poor. In 1839, of Jerusalem's 1,751 Jewish breadwinners, only 229 Sephardim and 28 Ashkenazim earned a livelihood from physical labor and crafts.

Changes in the economic structure began when Sephardic and North African families (e.g., Amzalaks, Moyals, and Chelouches) established themselves in the coastal towns of Jaffa and Haifa. They engaged in modern commerce, banking, rural and urban real estate development, and transportation and later in small-scale industry. Before 1914 they dominated Jewish-owned banking. The Turkish Valero family owned the largest bank, and Dr. Itzhak Levi, a prominent Sephardic leader of Turkish origin, managed the Anglo-Palestine Company in Jerusalem (it became the Anglo-Palestine Bank in 1925). Joseph Navon Bey received the concession in 1888 to construct the first railroad line in Palestine. Their entrepreneurial activities were facilitated by a familiarity with the Arab population. The entrepreneurs served as mediators to further European business interests. In Haifa, for example, Abraham Udiz and Abraham Ben-Aharon Cohen developed partnerships with Arabs. Sephardic and Middle Eastern Jews in the employ of foreign governments, such as Haim Amzalak and Joseph Moyal, the British and Spanish vice consuls at Jaffa, and Meir Abu, the French consular agent at Safed, used their status to further business and political influence. Before the formation of the New Yishuv, this group, together with Christian settlers and the Arab elite, privately fostered productivity in Palestine with modern technologies. Such Sephardic and Middle Eastern families continued as the economic elite during the British mandate, focusing on private enterprise but sometimes employing economic means to secure national objectives of fostering Jewish settlement in Palestine and the eventual establishment of a Jewish state. Hundreds of Jews from Salonika, experts in various vocations connected to port facilities, settled in Haifa. An important force in the growing economy of Jewish Palestine was the Histadrut (the General Federation of Jewish Labor, established in 1920), which functioned as a trade union and developed economic enterprises during the British mandate. Although Middle Eastern Jews and Sephardim were among its members, they wielded little power.

Between 1800 and 1882 the Sephardic and Middle Eastern Jews founded most of the experimental agricultural settlements. At first a small number were engaged in agriculture in the villages of the Galilee. In midcentury some invested in citrus groves and later served as intermediaries for citrus exporters. The Sephardic and Middle Eastern Jews engaged in agriculture as a business enterprise. Among those pioneers were Baghdad-born Binyamin Yehezkiel Yehuda, who in 1860 bought agricultural land in Kolonia (Motza) near Jerusalem, Morocco-born Yaakov Hai Abu, and the Mizrahi brothers from Safed, who established a short-lived Jewish agricultural colony in the Hula Valley in 1874. These preceded the failed attempts by the Ashkenazic Old Yishuv members in the Sharon Plain and in the Galilee, and the first four farming villages (*moshavot*)—Rishon Le-Zion, Rosh Pinna, Zichron Yaakov, and Petah Tikvah—set up by pioneers of the first aliyah. Sephardic and Middle Eastern Jews who facilitated some of these *moshavot* land purchases included Haim Amzalak at Rishon Le-Zion and Yaakov Hai Abu at Mishmar Ha-Yarden.

Three schools of technocrats and settlement engineers (French, German, and Eastern European) attempted to transplant European social and agrarian policies to Middle Eastern soil. Sephardic and Middle Eastern Jews connected mainly to French institutions, such as Albert Antebi, and Joseph Niego, an agronomist of Turkish origin and the director of the Mikveh Israel agricultural school from 1891 to 1904, played important roles in purchasing land for Jewish agricultural settlement. By 1904 twenty-eight Jewish settlements had been established, with approximately fifty-five hundred residents. Only a few of those were settled by Sephardic and Middle Eastern Jews. In

1895 some Yemenites tried unsuccessfully to establish an agricultural settlement in Ramma (Nebi Samuel) near Jerusalem. In 1896 Sephardim from Bulgaria founded the *moshava* called Hartuv. In 1907 farmers from the Caucasus founded the *moshava* Beer Yaakov. Few Sephardic and Middle Eastern Jews belonged to the kibbutzim (communal settlements) founded by the World Zionist Organization. The mixed Sephardic and Middle Eastern *moshav* called Kfar Baruch was founded in 1926 in the Jezreel Valley. Bulgarian Jews established the *moshav* of Beit Hanan in 1930—and the first *moshav shitufi* in Israel—Kfar Hitim in 1936. Stonecutters from Kurdistan built the *moshav* of Kfar Uriya in 1944. Because Yemenites constituted an important sector in their labor forces, Yemenite neighborhoods emerged near many *moshavot* (e.g., Yavneel, Kinneret, Beer Yaakov, Zichron Yaakov, Petah Tikvah, Rehovot, and Hadera). Concentrations of Yemenites were also to be found at Mahaneh Yehuda (1912), Kfar Marmorek (1931), Tirat Shalom (1932), and Elyashiv (1933).

The progress of agricultural settlements in Palestine was striking. From a few villages of 500 people in 1885, 153,000 lived in 266 villages by 1945. While in 1890 only 6 Jews out of every 100 lived in villages, by 1945 the ratio was 25 in 100. The Sephardic and Middle Eastern Jews comprised 16 percent of the rural population in 1941–42. This was a lower rate of participation in agriculture than their Ashkenazi counterparts. Sephardic and Middle Eastern Jews were 22 percent of the Jewish population in 1945.

RECOMMENDED READING

Ben-Zvi, Izhak. "Eretz Israel Under Ottoman Rule, 1517–1917." In Louis Finkelstein, ed., *The Jews, their History, Culture, and Religion*. New York: Jewish Theological Seminary, 1960, pp. 664–73.

Glass, Joseph B. and Ruth Kark. *Sephardi Entrepreneurs in Eretz Israel: The Amzalak Family, 1816–1918*. Jerusalem: Magnes Press, 1991.

——. "The Jews in Eretz-Israel/Palestine: from Traditional Peripherality to Modern Centrality," *Israel Affairs* 5/4 (Summer 1999), pp. 73–109.

Kark, Ruth. ed. *The Land That Became Israel: Studies in Historical Geography*. New Haven, Conn.: Yale University Press, 1990.

Ma^coz, Moshe, ed. *Studies on Palestine During the Ottoman Period*. Jerusalem: Magnes Press, 1975.

CHAPTER

19

Iraq

Reeva Spector Simon

The country known today as Iraq was created after the dissolution of the Ottoman Empire, as a result of World War I, from three former Ottoman provinces: Baghdad, Basra, and Mosul. Through most of its history it has been a battleground between empires. Iraq is bordered on the west by the Syrian Desert, which stretches east almost to the city of Baghdad; in the north it is bordered by the Kurdish mountains of southeastern Turkey, and by Iran, whose mountains are in the north. In the east the Shatt-al-Arab extension of the Tigris and Euphrates Rivers borders Iran and leads to the Persian Gulf; in the southwest the marsh areas and extensive date plantations near the city of Basra and the Arabian Desert are located near Saudi Arabia and Kuwait.

POPULATION AND DEMOGRAPHIC CHANGE

For the most part rural, the population of Iraq consists of a Shiite Muslim majority in the south but a Sunni Arab minority living in Baghdad that has dominated modern political life. Iraq has small communities of Eastern Rites Christians, heterodox Yazidis, and in the north the Kurds, a tribal people who are Sunni Muslims but not Arab and who consider their homeland to be in the region around Mosul. They dream of an independent Kurdistan.

Although some Jewish farmers in northern Iraq lived in villages—some entirely Jewish—that had patron-client relationships with the Kurdish tribes of the area, most Iraqi Jews were urban. The majority lived in Baghdad, while smaller communities were located in the major cities of Mosul and Basra. They lived in Kirkuk, Irbil, and Sulaimaniya in the north and to the south of

Baghdad in the towns of Hilla and Amara. Jews even lived in the Shiite holy cities of al-Najaf and Karbala for short periods, although, according to Shiite doctrine, Jews were impure and tainted the bread that they touched.

More than 120,000 Iraqi Jews, mostly from Baghdad, arrived in Israel during the mass exodus of Iraqi Jewry in 1950 and 1951; they constituted just over 2.6 percent of Iraq's population of 4.5 million. A century earlier travelers reported that Baghdad had only three thousand Jewish families, and Mosul had but 450 families. The process of modernization that Iraq underwent beginning in the midnineteenth century and the opening of trade through the southern city of Basra accounted for the demographic changes; these resulted in the internal migration of Jews from northern Iraq to more southern cities, the immigration of Jews from neighboring communities to Iraq, and significant natural increase. According to the Iraqi census of 1947, of the 118,000 Iraqi Jews, more than 83 percent were urban; the Baghdad community consisted of 77,542 Jews, and 10,537 lived in Basra, with 10,345 in Mosul. The Baghdad Jewish community was dominant in Iraq and provides the most data.

HISTORY OF IRAQ AND ITS RELATIONS WITH THE JEWISH COMMUNITY

Historically part of the Babylonian, Assyrian, and Persian empires, Iraq was conquered by the armies of Islam in the seventh century. One hundred years later, under the Abbasid dynasty, Baghdad, situated on the major trade routes, became the cultural capital of the Muslim community and the center of Diaspora Jewry.

Decline set in after the Mongol invasions of the thirteenth century, the shift in the trade routes that marginalized the Middle Eastern land routes, the almost constant wars between the Sunni Turks in the west and the Shiite Persians in the east, and the natural disasters of plague and flood that seemed to hit the region frequently. Although Iraq came under Ottoman rule in 1517, the Turks were not able to establish a centralized administration in the area until the midnineteenth century, during the period of Ottoman reform. For Iraq the Tanzimat reforms meant direct Ottoman administration, suppression of tribal brigandage, the institution of educational and health facilities, and the physical modernization of the city of Baghdad. Although from 1831 until 1908 Baghdad had forty-two provincial governors, the most significant changes occurred during the administration of Midhat Pasha, who governed Iraq from 1869 to 1872.

Midhat repaired the damaged irrigation works, paved city streets, and put in streetlights, a public park, a modern water system, and a tramway with carriages from England. His administration set up quarantine measures and a hospital, as well as factories for the production of cotton and wool. He was also responsible for the first official newspaper in Arabic that used a modern printing press; Western-style schools; and a vocational school. He encouraged trade, and when commercial routes shifted once again, this time because of the opening of the Suez Canal in 1869, Midhat promoted steamship navigation on the Tigris and Euphrates Rivers. The reactivation of the Syria-Baghdad land route and the completion of the rail connection from Baghdad to Anatolia and Syria linked Iraq to the western part of the Ottoman Empire. As demand increased for such Iraqi commodities as wheat, dates, and livestock products, the area once again became connected to world markets.

With the Ottoman Empire's Young Turk Revolution in 1908, Muslim clerics opposed the urban support for the secularism of the regime. Iraq sent representatives to the Ottoman parliament, but when a period of overt Turkification set in, a number of Iraqis, especially young military officers, began to lobby for Arabization of the Arab provinces; some advocated a separate Iraqi identity altogether. These discussions were put on hold during World War I, when Iraq once again became a battleground, this time between the Ottoman army and the British forces that marched north from India to take Basra in 1914 and Baghdad in 1917.

The British, whose imperial goal was not only to control the trade routes to India but also the oil that had recently been discovered in Persia and in Iraq, were awarded Iraq as a mandate by the League of Nations. The British imported a king, Faisal ibn Hussein, a respected pro-British ally during the war and a leader of the Arab nationalist cause, and they set up a parliamentary democracy in conformity with League of Nations guidelines. The rights of all citizens were ensured, and minorities were included in the government and granted freedom of religious worship.

A year after independence in 1932, Faisal I died. His son and successor, Ghazi (r. 1933–39), was an advocate of Arab nationalism whose rule was marked by political instability involving intense political maneuvering by a small group of pan-Arab Sunni politicians. These politicians saw Iraq as the leader of the Arab world as well as the advocate of the Palestinian Arabs in their struggle against the Zionist Yishuv and the British mandate. Independence from Britain and France by the rest of the former Arab Ottoman provinces and Arab unity were the goals envisioned by this ideology of Arab nationalism. These goals were transmitted through the schools by Palestinian and Syrian teachers hired to teach in Iraq and by the creation of a strong military, which, after a political coup in 1936, played a direct role in Iraqi politics. These views were augmented and embellished in the 1930s by German diplomats, who were active in disseminating anti-Semitic National Socialist propaganda.

Ghazi's suspicious death in a car crash in 1939 left a child, Faisal II, on the throne, with power in the hands of his uncle the regent, Abd al-Ilah, and a split in the government between pro-British and pro-Axis politicians. When the government refused to declare war on the Axis powers in 1939 and came under the direct control of pro-Axis military officers in the winter of 1941, the regent and his pro-British prime minister, Nuri al-Saᶜid, fled the country. Then, as Germany achieved military success in North Africa in the spring, Iraqi politicians led by Rashid Ali al-Kaylani, backed by the Arab nationalist army officers and the anti-British, pro-Axis Jerusalem mufti al-Hajj Amin al-Husayni, who had fled to Baghdad in 1939, went to war against Britain in May–June, 1941. After they were soundly defeated by the British, however, demobilized soldiers and tribesmen vented their frustration by attacking the Jewish community in June 1941.

The pogrom, or Farhud, was a turning point in the history of Iraqi Jews. The Arab nationalist–inspired attack on the Jewish community, after years of anti-Zionist and Nazi propaganda promulgated in the schools and in the media, resulted in the deaths of about 130 men, women, and children. Several hundred more people were injured, and property losses amounted to several hundred thousand pounds sterling (a pound was then worth $4.03). The regent and pro-British politicians, who had fled Iraq while the country was controlled by Rashid Ali and the nationalist military officers, remained with British troops on the outskirts of the capital during the Farhud—lest it be construed that they were returning to Iraq in anti-nationalist triumph. This policy weighed heavily on the Jewish community, whose relations with the government were forever changed after 1941.

The reassertion of British control over Iraq during the rest of World War II and Iraq's support of pro-British politicians endured until the revolution of July 1958. Before that, growing resentment toward British policy in Palestine, and the subsequent defeat of the Palestine Arabs and Iraqi troops sent to support them in the Arab-Israel War of 1948, exacerbated popular discontent over rising prices, unemployment, the lack of oil revenue (because the Iraqi government had turned off the Iraqi-Haifa pipeline), and the British connection with the regent and his political supporters. The opposition organized the Communist Party in Iraq and instigated a series of riots (Wathbah) against the government in 1948 in reaction to the renewal of the Iraqi treaty with Britain. Accusations against and executions of Jews as Zionist collaborators, as well as anti-Jewish legislation, led to the denationalization and emigration of virtually the entire Iraqi Jewish community to Israel in 1951 and 1952.

The economic void left by the mass emigration of Iraqi Jewry was filled by an emerging Sunni and Shiite middle class educated in government schools and by a shift to an oil economy during the 1950s. For the six thousand or so Jews who remained in Iraq, living for the most part in Baghdad and Basra, the revolution of 1958 and the regime of Abd al-Karim Qassem initially eased their situation. Then, with Kurdish revolts and the accession to power in 1963 of Abd al-Salam Arif and Abd al-Rahman Arif, Arab nationalist rule returned, and Jews were once again denied passports. Still more Jews left the country. The Arab defeat in the 1967 Arab-Israeli War resulted in a takeover by the Baᶜath Party, which reinstituted anti-Jewish violence when more than fifty Jews were killed and nine Jews were hanged in Baghdad's central square on January 27, 1969. The Baᶜath regime placed the Jewish community under the surveillance of the secret police. Jews were often denied higher education and economic opportunity. Virtually all the Jews who had remained in Iraq after the mass emigration left during the 1970s. Despite the invitation to return extended to Iraqi Jews by Saddam Hussein during the Iraq-Iran War of the 1980s, hardly any did. In 1999 fewer than thirty elderly Jews remained in Baghdad.

THE JEWISH COMMUNITY

Large numbers of Jews arrived in Babylonia after the destruction of the first Temple in Jerusalem by Nebuchadnezzar in 586 B.C.E. and their exile. Tradition in Mosul has it that Jews of the northern regions of Iraq trace their lineage back even earlier, to the exile of the ten northern tribes of Israel by Shalmeneser V of Assyria in 722 B.C.E. Population figures vary over time; despite natural disasters, war, and the exigencies of politics, Iraq had a continuous Jewish presence until the mass emigration of 1951–52.

Sura and Pumbedita in southern Iraq were the intellectual centers of Jewish culture when the Babylonian Talmud was codified. During the geonic period (the Middle Ages), which coincided with the Arab cultural efflorescence under the Islamic Abbasid Empire, the focus of Jewish life was transferred to Baghdad, where numerous religious luminaries such as Saadiah Gaon lived and wrote. By the eleventh century Diaspora Jewry was already looking to Spain for direction, and two centuries later the Mongols occupied Baghdad. After a short period of prosperity many Jews were forced to convert to Islam. The decline that set in was intensified by the conquest of the region and the decimation of the Jewish population by Tamerlane in 1353, who also destroyed all the synagogues in Basra. Many survivors took refuge to the north, in the Kurdish mountains. Although Mosul emerged as an important Jewish intellectual center at that time, and the Baghdad community reestablished itself at the beginning of the sixteenth century, the region once again became a battleground, this time between the Ottomans and the Persians, and it suffered a series of natural disasters. By the end of the eighteenth century, a notable Jewish community lived in Basra and engaged in commerce with India. It is said that the Jewish *sarraf* (financial adviser) of Basra, Yaᶜqub Gabbai, was instrumental in raising the money for the city's defense against the Persians in 1774–75. With the Ottoman victory the Jewish community declared a Yom ha-Nes (Day of the Miracle) and recited special prayers commemorating the miracle.

Jews began to emigrate to Baghdad from Kurdistan, Persia, and Aleppo, and they soon revivified life in the city. Apparently, the Spanish community of Jewish exiles had not settled in Baghdad as they had in the western part of the Ottoman Empire. Baghdadi Jews looked to Aleppo and Safed for religious leadership and, at that time, adopted the Sephardic prayer book then used in Safed. They also accepted Joseph Caro's codification of Jewish law, the *Shulhan Arukh.* Holiday visits—on Shavuot, Hanukkah, and on the eve of the new month of Tevet—to the tombs of Ezra the Scribe near Basra, the Prophet Ezekiel in al-Kifl near Hilla in southern Iraq (ancient Babylonia or Bavel), and Joshua ben Jehozadak the High Priest, buried at Karkh on the outskirts of Baghdad, became popular festive communal gatherings by Jews from the entire region.

The Tanzimat reforms that the Ottomans implemented in the midnineteenth century brought the empire and its Jewish subjects into the modern world. It was not only a matter of change of dress but the acquisition of Western languages and business skills through the educational auspices of the Paris-based Alliance Israélite Universelle (AIU) that enabled the Jews to play a key role in modern Iraq. Jews served as secretaries and legal counselors to the governors and as translators and physicians, in addition to their dominant role as merchants in the economic sector. For example, Abraham Haim Muᶜallem Nissim, secretary to the Ottoman governor in 1910, later represented Iraq in the League of Nations. Jews were appointed to the Baghdad municipal councils in 1873 and 1888 and to the Ottoman parliaments in 1877 and 1908. Menahem Daniel and Sasson Hesqail were the Jewish representatives. Daniel, a wealthy landowner and leader of the Jewish community, was later appointed a senator in the Iraqi parliament and served until 1940. Hesqail, a graduate of the AIU school in Baghdad and the University of Vienna, also held posts as undersecretary at the Ministry of Agriculture and the Ministry of Commerce, and served as director of the Ottoman Steamboat Company. He was one of the Iraqi delegates to the Cairo Conference in 1921 and served as minister of finance of Iraq from 1920 to 1925. As Iraqi negotiator with the British regarding oil royalties, he was responsible for their payment to Iraq in gold instead of pounds sterling.

Jews attended the Baghdad Law College, and some even volunteered to join the military, although Jews by and large were not happy about the imposition of compulsory military service under the Young Turks in 1909. Opposition to the new regime by Muslim conservatives was manifested by attacks on the Jews in Baghdad in 1908; in Mosul the Kurds were the victims. Nonetheless, the new regime spelled prosperity for many, and the wealthy began to leave the old Jewish quarters of Baghdad for new neighborhoods in the suburbs.

When World War I broke out in 1914, the British occupied Basra and many Jews fled south. Eligible for conscription, Jews were drafted and hundreds were sent to Turkish units in the Caucasus, never to return. Jewish physicians assisted the Ottoman forces, and some acted as translators for the Turks when they captured British prisoners of war as the British pushed north after they occupied Basra in 1914. For most Jews, however, the war meant disaster. Accused of hoarding money and not participating adequately in the war effort, some were executed by the Turkish authorities, and much of the community's assets were confiscated. When the British arrived in Baghdad in 1917 and the Turks retreated, the British victory was treated as a second Yom ha-Nes, with special prayers recited annually.

The British victory brought inflated hopes for the Jewish minority, which was prepared to fill the jobs in the banks and civil service that the British occupation provided. Jews were also represented in the municipal councils set up in 1918 in Baghdad and in Basra. When the war ended and rumors abounded that the British advocated an Arab government for Iraq, Jews requested British citizenship but were refused. Once the British-backed King Faisal I arrived, however, the Jewish leadership supported the new Iraqi regime.

Jews warmly greeted Faisal's overture to the minority populations in Iraq to participate as citizens in the new Iraq. Jewish poets sang the king's praises, and Faisal's regime was seen as a new golden age of Baghdad Jewry. Jews served in the top echelons of the ministries of justice, finance, labor, railways, post, telegraph, and telephones. They were secretaries of the chamber of commerce. Some Jews were involved in the military and defense, and although they taught in Iraqi schools, Jews were not represented in the higher posts of the Ministry of Education. Defense and education were bastions of Arab nationalist ideologues.

With the promulgation of the Iraqi constitution in 1925, Jewish representation in Parliament came through the community and not the political system. Only two Jews, Sasson Hesqail and Naᶜim Zilkha, sought election through political parties as candidates in an open system. The four to six seats allocated to Jews in Parliament and the one Senate appointment designated as Jewish were not contingent upon party affiliation or elections. The community leadership filled these posts by nomination.

Officially apolitical with regard to events in Palestine, and evincing little to no support for political Zionism, the Jewish community had to walk a fine line following anti-Jewish riots in 1929 and after Faisal's death in 1933, which ushered in a period of vociferous anti-Zionist sentiment. They accommodated themselves to the adverse political situation by closing schools when demonstrations were expected to occur and by conforming precisely to government regulations. As Iraqi Muslims became eligible for civil service positions, they began to replace Jews in government employment. Layoffs of Jewish civil servants in the Ministry of Economics began in 1934; Jews found jobs in the private sector.

By 1940 a younger generation of secularly educated Jews became affiliated with Iraqi (as opposed to Arab) political parties, and they joined groups involved in oppositional politics. This was partly because in the 1930s, as more Jews began to attend government schools than Jewish schools, some Iraqis of the Jewish faith became attracted to liberal and radical political groups and found kindred spirits in the small emerging Muslim liberal intelligentsia. Jews joined the progressive socialist Ahali group in the 1930s, but, surprisingly, unlike other Middle Eastern countries, no Jews were among the founding members of the Iraqi Communist Party, even though many Jewish workers joined the party in the late 1940s. For these Jews and their younger Muslim counterparts, the political issue that engaged them was British colonialism. It was only after the Farhud that Jews became attracted to the Communist Party and a revivified Zionist movement in Iraq. After World War II Jews worked for the National Democratic Party, wrote for its newspaper, and supported it financially; although it was open to all Iraqis and advocated reform, like all political parties in Iraq it opposed the establishment of a Jewish state in Palestine. Distinctions between Iraqis of the Jewish faith and Zionists soon blurred, as Iraq became involved in the Arab-Israeli conflict.

TYPES OF JEWS

Iraqi Jews were Arabized. Their language was Arabic, and they shared similar superstitions, cuisine, and dress. There is little evidence of either a Sephardic or an Ashkenazi migration to Iraq on a large scale. A few Ashkenazim settled in Baghdad when the area was opened to international trade in the nineteenth century but nowhere near the numbers that arrived in Egypt. Travelers who passed through during the mid- to late nineteenth century noted their impressions of the community for their European compatriots. These travelers included Joseph Israel Benjamin (called Benjamin II) and teachers from the Alliance Israélite Universelle. The Jews of Kurdistan whom they encountered in the 180 or so villages of Iraq, Turkey, and Syria were peasant farmers with a patron-client relationship to the Kurdish tribal chief (*agha*) who protected them, or they were craftsmen and peddlers who sold goods purchased in Baghdad to the Kurdish nomads in northern Iraq. Gradually, in the twentieth century Kurdish Jews moved to the cities of Iraq, and the entire community emigrated to Israel in the 1950s.

NAMES

Traditionally, Jewish first names were biblical or Talmudic, with Ezra, Ezekiel, Joshua, and Daniel common names for Iraqi males because the tombs of Ezekiel, Daniel, and Joshua the High Priest were located in Iraq. With the immigration to Iraq of people from Persia, Kurdistan, and Syria, other names appear, and the Syrian names are Arabized. English names, such as Victoria, became popular under the British mandate, as did Arab names.

As in most areas of the Middle East, Iraqis did not take family names until the eighteenth century. Once they did, their family names often denoted the name of an important member of the family, whose name was carried on as the family name, sometimes with the title of pasha, *nasi* (lay leader), or sheikh. Names also denoted occupations such as *dallal* (middleman) and *darzi* (tailor). The Arabic terms *abu* (father of) and *al* (the) were used as prefixes, as was *al-hajji* (one who made the pilgrimage). But in the case of Jews, the pilgrimage was to Jerusalem. Later generations often dropped these terms. Holders of public office such as *al-hakham* (rabbi), *gabbai* (beadle), *shamash* (sexton), and *shohet* (ritual slaughterer) are common. Nicknames appear, as do names that signify place of origin, such as al-Arbili (from Arbil in Kurdistan), al-[c]Ajimi (the Persian), al-Halabi (from Aleppo), or Hillawy (from the town of Hilla in southern Iraq).

COMMUNITY STRUCTURE

From the period of the Babylonian Exile, the Jewish community lived an autonomous existence ruled by a member of the House of David, the exilarch, whose authority was eclipsed by the religious authority (*gaon*). By the seventeenth century the actual descent of the Davidic family seems to have ended, and the lay leader (*nasi*) was usually a man of wealth who was also the *sarraf* to the local ruler; he was responsible for the collection of taxes from the Jewish community, served as liaison with the ruler, and provided the ruler with loans and securities. The *nasi* was appointed by the local governor, and his position rose and fell on whim. He hosted dignitaries, had his own synagogue (most of the synagogues in Baghdad were community owned), and provided feasts on festivals. Because there was no independent body of sages in Baghdad before the early nineteenth century, the *nasi* in Baghdad, unlike in other Middle Eastern Jewish communities, often intervened in religious issues.

By the midnineteenth century, as the Baghdad community recovered from its scholarly doldrums, the role of the *nasi* declined as rabbinic luminaries emerged. Their high status in the community was maintained and enhanced even as the social composition of Baghdadi society was changing because of the implementation of the Ottoman Tanzimat and the creation by the Ottoman authorities of the post of *hakham bashi* (chief rabbi) for every major city throughout the empire.

The *hakham bashi* was an Ottoman bureaucrat whose appointment was ratified by the sultan after the *hakham bashi* was elected in Baghdad by a council of Jewish notables from wealthy banking and landowning families. He was responsible for the collection of taxes due the government, and as far as the authorities were concerned, he was the head of the Jewish community and the chief religious figure. Serving alongside him were a religious council of seven rabbis who were to be elected every two years but in reality were appointed and replaced when necessary. Their authority was limited to matters relating to birth, death, marriage, divorce, and inheritance. Similarly, a lay council, initially composed of eight members drawn from the wealthy elite, were to be elected every two years and were concerned with education, health, charities, religious endowments, and financial affairs. Because the head of the community had become an Ottoman bureaucratic post, sages who belonged to notable and wealthy families avoided the position in order to remain apart from community politics.

Community dissension arose toward the end of the nineteenth century because of personality conflicts and issues that divided the community until its dissolution in the early 1950s. Questions of equitable division of the tax load due the government, education for women, and the establishment of modern schools preoccupied the community at the turn of the nineteenth century. In the 1920s members of the newly emergent professional class challenged the older generation of merchants and bankers for leadership. In the 1930s and 1940s the issue was Zionism, which involved the controversial rabbi Sasson Kadoorie, who held the post of chief rabbi from 1933 until 1949 and then from 1953 until his death in 1971. Heskel Shemtob served as the head of the community in the interim. To his supporters Kadoorie was an astute politician and a man of charm who was a suitable representative of the Jewish community to the government. His detractors resented his high income and standard of living and his neutral-to-anti-Zionist position in the late 1940s. Because he served during the years of anti-Semitic sloganeering, serialized publication of Adolph Hitler's book *Mein Kampf* in the Arab press, riots against Jews, and bombs thrown at Jewish establishments, Kadoorie walked a fine line in reassuring the Iraqi government that the Jews were loyal citizens.

In Iraq under the British mandate and after independence, Jews were citizens of the state with minority status. According to the Jewish Community Law of 1931, the communal structure remained virtually as it was under Ottoman rule, and the chief rabbi was still recognized as head of the Jewish community, even though Jews served in the parliament and entered the professions; individuals of means interceded with the government when necessary via time-honored methods of suasion. The Jews of Iraq saw King Faisal as a benevolent monarch who was called in on occasion to resolve communal disputes.

The Jewish community raised money for the support of the many Jewish institutions through taxes imposed on the sale of kosher meat (the gabelle) and on dowries, and from school fees. Local Jews and those from abroad supported schools, health services, and other community institutions. Some money came from leasing houses, shops, and land donated to the community and held in trust. Jews funded a hospital, a nursing home for expectant mothers, pharmacies, and surgical and eye clinics that provided care for approximately 70 percent of their Jewish and Muslim patients without charge. The money supported societies for aid to the blind, poor women, and the general poor, as well as a burial society and slaughterhouse.

The philanthropic societies and social clubs provided places for the Jewish social elite to meet and hold social fund-raisers for charity. Attire was Western. Younger men dressed in European suits; they shed their turbans first for the Ottoman fez and later the Iraqi *sidara* (a man's hat popular during the reign of King Faisal I) or they went bareheaded. Women of the younger generation eschewed the veil and favored shorter hemlines instead of the traditional *izar* (*burqa*), which enveloped the body from head to toe, and removed the *pooshee,* or face veil.

By the 1930s observers noted a laxity in Jewish religious practice. Although Jewish businesses and offices were closed on the Sabbath and holidays, many Jewish government employees went to work. As Iraqis became more Western, and with technological modernization such as the electrification of the city, which ushered in a more secular nightlife, daily routine changed. Jewish men went to the movies and to social clubs and less to synagogue. Respect for parents remained strong, however, and although adherence to tradition outside the home was weakened, no complete break with religion occurred. Hardly any Jews converted to Islam.

The Jewish community supported a network of educational facilities and more than forty synagogues, including the Great Synagogue. According to tradition, its building stood where the last king of Judah had built his synagogue using ashes of the destroyed First Temple in Jerusalem. Rebuilt several times, most recently in 1855, it was in the form of a square supported by seventy pillars over a partly uncovered courtyard.

Housing in Baghdad's old city was in the traditional style. The wealthy lived in multistoried dwellings that included a deep pool in the basement and a courtyard at ground level surrounded by upper stories capped with a flat roof, where the family slept in the summer. As the middle class and wealthy Jews moved to the new suburbs, Western-style villas with gardens replaced the "oriental" style. Jews lived in mixed neighborhoods and established their own residential suburbs beyond the South Gate of the city and along the Tigris. Walks along the river on the Sabbath, swimming in the river in summer, and meeting in coffeehouses were popular excursions.

LANGUAGES

At home Iraqi Jews spoke a dialect of Judeo-Arabic that was distinct from both the Muslim Arabic and the Christian dialects. In contrast to Muslim

Arabic, which was heavily influenced by Bedouin tribal Arabic, the Jewish dialect preserved elements of the old Arabic vernacular, albeit with a heavy infusion of Hebrew, Aramaic, and some Persian words. The Jews of Kurdistan spoke neo-Aramaic, which was Targum infused with Kurdish, Turkish, Arabic, Old Aramaic, and Hebrew expressions—a language that was never written down.

By the midtwentieth century Baghdadi Jews had adopted literary Arabic as a language of research and writing and had become renowned for their literary contributions. They also learned Modern Hebrew at AIU schools.

EDUCATION AND MODERNIZATION

The general decline of the Iraqi Jewish community reached its nadir after a plague in 1743 killed most of its scholars and notables. Appeals to the community of Aleppo were answered with the arrival of Sadqa b. Saadiah Hussin, who served as rabbi of Baghdad until his death in 1773. In 1832 the community founded a midrash Talmud Torah, a school for religious primary education, and eight years later opened a yeshiva, Beit Zilkha, which was headed by Rabbi Abdallah Somekh.

In this period Iraqi religious life reached a height it had not enjoyed since the period of the *geonim*. Two rabbinic luminaries stand out: Somekh (1813–89), who is renowned for his commentary on the Talmud and responsa on issues of modernization, and Rabbi Yosef Hayyim (the Ben Ish Hai, 1835–1909), known as "the Rambam [Maimonides] of the East." He wrote works on halakhah (religious law) in Hebrew and published an anecdotal work for women in Judeo-Arabic, *Qanun al-Nisa* (Law of Women).

For generations most boys and even girls who had any schooling at all attended a private *stadh* (religious elementary school), where they learned to read Hebrew. In 1868 the Baghdad community began to organize religious education in a more formal manner when it set up the Shomrei Mitzvah society to coordinate charitable organizations and to oversee religious education. By 1880 a number of private and public religious schools were already educating one thousand to twelve hundred students aged six to twelve. In 1908 a second yeshiva opened, this despite the decreasing enrollment of yeshiva students, probably as a result of the attractiveness of secular education.

Modern Jewish day schools, which provided a secular education as well as Jewish studies, had the greatest influence on the economic, social, and intellectual development of the Jewish community of Iraq. The Jewish schools, especially in Baghdad, were run under the auspices of the Alliance

Israélite Universelle (AIU) and later the Anglo-Jewish Association and took the lead in preparing future generations of Iraqi Jews for modern life.

By 1864 the community had established the first modern school and asked that the AIU send a headmaster. The Alliance School for Boys (the Albert Sassoon School) was followed by a school for girls (the Laura Kadoorie School) in 1893. These schools provided the Jewish community with a head start in their assimilation of Western languages, with a preference for English, mathematics, science, hygiene, history, and literature, as well as Turkish. Arabic was added later. An apprenticeship program for aspiring artisans was initiated, training poorer Jewish youth to be tailors, boot makers, weavers, and carpenters, more lucrative occupations than the traditional goldsmithing, silversmithing, and coppersmithing. The community's initial opposition to the school gradually ended. Hakham Somekh supported the work of the Alliance and sent his son to the school; one of his grandsons taught in Cairo. However, when the community leaders and the AIU disagreed about curriculum and language instruction, the community established its own schools where instruction was in Turkish before World War I. Another school brought in teachers from Palestine, Syria, and Europe to teach in Hebrew.

Few Jews attended the secular schools that the Ottomans set up in Iraq, but a number went on to attend the military academy and law school in Istanbul, as well as the Baghdad Law College. Steadily, Jews began to acquire a Western-style education; by the 1920s they were ready to fill the civil service and management jobs suddenly available under the British mandate.

By 1930 the Jewish community of Baghdad supported a network of schools that included religious schools with elementary studies in Arabic; the AIU schools for boys and girls whose graduates often went off to foreign professional schools; Jewish schools that followed the government syllabus; and the Shamash School, sponsored by the Anglo-Jewish Association, which taught the English curriculum geared for the British matriculation examination. The Jewish schools opened by the community followed the government curriculum as instituted by the Iraqi Ministry of Education, provided some religious instruction, and prepared students for the standardized entrance examinations to government secondary schools and for university matriculation examinations, and they helped to stem the flow of Jews to completely secular government schools.

More Jews began to attend government schools, however, because the schools were free. Working students could attend because both day and evening classes were available. A high school diploma from a government school was the ticket to a job in the civil service or a teaching position that guaranteed economic security. As long as the government needed Jews to fill civil service posts, Jews attended and completed secondary school in numbers far exceeding their proportion of the population. Graduation also meant the possibility of study at the Baghdad Law College or admission to the American University of Beirut and exemption from military conscription, which was enacted into law in 1935.

Jews taught in both public and private schools in Iraq and, until 1940, when the Public Education Law was passed, schools had merely to submit the names of teachers to the government. In keeping with the new Arab nationalist legislation, the Ministry of Education had to approve who taught "national" subjects—history, geography, the Arabic language, and literature—and how they taught these subjects in nongovernment schools. For example, in 1940 Murad Michael of the Shamash School was the only Jew to teach Arabic. Other teachers of history and Arabic were non-Jewish Iraqis or Arabs from Syria or Palestine hired by the ministry but paid by the Jewish community.

Most unfair to the Jewish students, who had to conform to government regulations, was the ban on teaching Jewish history in the Jewish schools, while government-appointed teachers and required texts emphasized a pan-Arab interpretation of Arab history, with no place for a "Jewish Arabism." The required texts also had sections that were derogatory of Jewish settlement in Palestine. Jews rarely protested government injunctions regarding the curriculum, except in the case of a memorandum that required the teaching of the Bible in Arabic.

Because the secondary schools sent their graduates on for higher education, Iraqi Jews took advantage of college and university education in Iraq and studied in Britain, Europe, the United States, Lebanon, Turkey, India, Syria, and Egypt. From 1900 to 1915 fifteen Iraqi Jews completed their university education. They attended the Iraqi Royal College of Medicine from the date of its inception in 1928, when the first class graduated ten students, among them six Jews. From 1940 to 1950 approximately 550 Iraqi Jews completed college. Of these, sixty were women. They came primarily from Baghdad and Basra and studied law, engineering, economics, education, and the humanities. Among the Jews who emigrated to Israel in the 1950s were more than two hundred physicians, including seventeen women; more than 175 pharmacists, nine of whom were women; and 154 engineers. At the time of the Iraqi emigration Jewish literacy had bumped the general literacy level to 50 percent of the population, whereas the overall literacy rate of the Arab population was 15 percent.

The liberal trends portended by the British mandate and Iraqi independence led to a strong association of Iraqi Jews with Arab culture. Their literary output was in Arabic, not Hebrew. These Iraqis were among the first Jewish poets to write in Arabic, and they produced a number of novels and short story collections. They used realism and local color and set their works in contemporary Iraq. Among the most notable were Mir Basri, Anwar Sha'ul, Murad Michael, Yaᶜaqub Balbul, Salim Darwish, Salman Darwish, Ibrahim Yaᶜqub Obadiah, and Naim Kattan. Jewish newspapers included *al-Haris* (1920), *al-Misbah* (1924–29), *al-Hasid* (1929–37), *al-Bustan* (1929–38), and *al-Barid al-Yawmi* (1948). Jews performed in Arabic in the nascent Iraqi theater and were among the most prominent Iraqi musicians, singers, composers, and players of traditional instruments.

ECONOMICS

Jews were financial advisers (*sarraf*), money changers, and sources of loans for the local governors. They collected customs duties, and some were even tax farmers (collected taxes on produce of the land for the government). Jews worked in metals as goldsmiths and silversmiths and were peddlers to rural areas. When trade by sea became less hazardous than by overland caravan from Baghdad to Syria, Jews in Basra became involved in the Persian Gulf trade as brokers for Indian rulers in the pearl-fishing industry. Merchants from Iraq, Persia, and India established a colony on the islands of Bahrain where a number of Jewish families still reside. By the midnineteenth century, however, the Basra community had suffered a severe plague that cut the population from three thousand families to fifty, and the city never regained its former stature within Iraqi Jewry, even with the influx of Jews from the north during World War I.

The plague and floods of 1831 that claimed more than fifteen thousand people and destroyed two-thirds of the city of Baghdad, coupled with the ruined harvest and war with the Ottoman forces, also left the Arab traders in ruin. As the Ottomans granted capitulations (legal rights) to foreign merchants, Europeans entered the Iraqi trade and used non-Muslims as their agents and middlemen. By the 1840s the British were able to protect the Jews from the high duties imposed by the government in Baghdad and that were set on goods transported by steamboat on the Tigris and Euphrates in 1859. The Suez Canal opened ten years later, bringing new opportunities.

The economic environment that enabled Jewish businessmen to forge ahead at the end of the nineteenth century, when *sarrafs* became bankers, continued well into the twentieth century. With family connections in Persia, Syria, and other countries and their monopoly of the position of *sarraf* in Baghdad, these Jewish bankers were able to accumulate enough capital so that some could import goods directly from India (bypassing the British), open firms in India and later in England, and establish private merchant banks in Baghdad. Among them were the Zilkha, Kradiyah, Edward Aboodi, and Kharith banks, which financed commerce, handled government transactions, provided credit and small business loans, and employed the burgeoning class of Jewish clerks educated at the AIU and other Jewish schools.

Although in 1910 the Jewish community was described as more than 60 percent poor, 30 percent middle class, and 5 percent wealthy merchants, the economic and social disparities all but disappeared from the lowest classes by the 1940s. By 1919 goods from England accounted for almost two-thirds of Iraq's total imports, and most of this trade was in the hands of Jewish merchants. Jews traded in groceries, drugs, iron, coffee, tin, loaf sugar, soft sugar, and copper; they were the dealers in precious stones and in jewelry. Growing urbanization caused demand for U.S. and British automobiles, foodstuffs, machine-made textiles, and manufactured household goods for the owners of the suburban homes in the new Jewish, Muslim, and mixed neighborhoods outside the old city of Baghdad.

By the mid 1930s Jews were among the wealthiest in Iraq. Almost half the members of the Baghdad Chamber of Commerce were Jews, who were the most important mercantile group in the city. Such families as the Adases, Rajwans, Sassoons, Nathaniels, Zilkhas, Lawis, Shammashes, and Aboodies dealt in insurance, tea, travel, and transport. Jews owned the new movie theaters and were the agents for foreign automobile companies. By 1948–50, 86 percent of the Jews of Baghdad were employed in commerce, government, and municipal services; 50 percent of the importers, retailers, and wholesalers of imported goods were Jewish, and Jews financed small businesses and internal trade.

With their education and linguistic skills Jews entered the civil service jobs created by the mandatory authorities. They were the senior clerks for the British advisers and were heavily represented in the departments of the treasury, banks, foreign companies, railways, and the port of Basra. It was only when enough Muslims had been graduated and other minorities began to compete for jobs that more and more Jews turned to running their own businesses. Even then, when many Jews were dismissed from government positions after World War II, many remained in the ministries of finance and commerce.

ZIONISM

The Baghdad Jewish community did not wholeheartedly embrace political Zionism. Through the centuries Iraqi Jews had maintained religious connections with Jerusalem, Hebron, and Safed, making pilgrimages to the Holy Land and studying in and supporting yeshivas. Some emigrated to Eretz Israel for religious reasons. Others purchased burial plots there. Many donated money expressly for the establishment of religious schools for Iraqi students.

Support for the Zionist movement in the 1920s amounted to financial contributions to the Jewish National Fund and cultural activities such as reading Hebrew newspapers and periodicals. As early as 1922, however, Jewish leaders warned of the precarious position that the Jews held in Iraqi society, despite their dominant position in the civil service and in the economy and despite the existence of an official Zionist organization during the 1920s, when Faisal was king. In Palestine the Labor Zionist leadership dismissed the Iraqi Jews as poor Zionist material because of their lack of interest in agriculture. In the 1930s the focus of the Labor Zionists was on Europe.

By the mid-1930s Zionist activity was officially banned in Iraq, and in the intensifying climate of Arab nationalism the Iraqi government also forbade the teaching of Jewish history and the use of Hebrew in Jewish schools. The shock of the Farhud resulted in some interest in emigration to Palestine, but British restrictions on immigration into Palestine prevented whole families from leaving Iraq. Some individuals entered Palestine clandestinely, but many went to Iran and later returned to Baghdad. After the return of the regent and the pro-British politicians during the summer of 1941, Zionist emissaries from Palestine, including Enzo Sereni, Shmaryahu Guttman, and Ezra Kadoorie, were sent in 1942 to train Iraqi Jews in self-defense, provide Zionist education, and to set up illegal emigration. Jewish Iraqi youth, embarrassed at the defenselessness of their community during the Farhud, were interested in learning self-defense so they could protect themselves in the future, but not necessarily to emigrate. The Zionist emissaries worked alongside Palestinian Jews sent to Iraq who were members of the British army or signed on as transport and construction workers for the Egged bus company or Solel Boneh, a Jewish Palestinian construction firm working for the British. From these positions they transmitted mail and smuggled weapons into Iraq and smuggled Jews from Iraq to Palestine. Until the end of World War II, when the British troops left Iraq, Zionism made little headway because few Iraqi Jews were interested in the socialist ideal of manual labor in Palestine. But the youth movement He-Halutz was revived in Iraq in 1946 as an underground network and attracted about fifteen hundred members. Though the Jewish leadership and the majority of Iraqi Jews were apolitical, the establishment of the State of Israel, coupled with stresses on the Iraqi domestic scene, began to have a direct effect on the Jewish community. People began to leave.

The government responded to the defeat of Iraqi troops sent to fight in the Arab-Israeli War of 1948 by placing Iraq under martial law in order to prevent violence. At the same time the regime imposed repressive measures against the Jewish community. The penalty for engaging in Zionist activity became imprisonment and heavy fines. Wealthy Jews were detained, Jewish government employees were dismissed, and quotas were placed on the numbers of Jews allowed to enter the universities or obtain entry-level civil service positions. Jews were prevented from leaving the country legally.

When Shafik Ades, a wealthy businessman in Basra with close ties to the royal family and a contributor to the Iraqi National Democratic Party, was arrested and later executed in September 1948 for allegedly selling military surplus to Israel, the Jewish community was once again in shock. The realization that Jews could never really integrate into Iraqi society began to grow, despite the government's attempt to ease the pressure on the community. Then, as more Jews began to leave the country illegally through the offices of the Zionist underground, which by that time had members all over Iraq, the government began to intensify efforts to root out the organization. The arrest of leaders and hundreds of He-Halutz and Haganah members in October 1949 exacerbated the tension between the underground and the Jewish leadership, which saw the Zionists as a threat to community security. There was pressure from younger people to remove Sasson Kadoorie as leader of the community because of rumors that he cooperated with the Iraqi government. Demonstrations by Jews and their subsequent arrest, whether they were activists or not, shook the community's confidence.

When martial law was lifted in December 1949, Jews began to leave the country in unexpected numbers. They moved to Basra and left Iraq clandestinely at rates of about one thousand per month. In order to stem the flow of people and assets from the country, the government passed the Denaturalization Law in March 1950, which allowed Jews to leave but revoked the Iraqi citizenship of those who did and froze their assets. The government thought that approximately ten thousand people would leave the country. Meanwhile, it continued to make arrests; almost two hundred Jews languished in Iraqi jails. By the end of the year, with more than sixty thousand Jews registering to leave, and facing continuing arrests and dismissals from their jobs, pressure to emigrate intensified and accelerated after a bomb exploded in January 1951 at the Mas'uda Shemtov Synagogue, the main registration center in Baghdad and point of departure for the airport.

By March negotiations between the governments of Israel and Iraq were underway, resulting in Operation Ezra and Nehemia, a plan to airlift more than 105,000 people to Israel; they left behind frozen assets and property worth in the tens of millions of U.S. dollars. By the end of 1952 almost the entire Iraqi Jewish community had left the country they had called home for more than two thousand years.

RECOMMENDED READING

Brauer, Erich. *The Jews of Kurdistan.* Detroit: Wayne State University Press, 1993.

Cohen, Hayyim J. "University Education Among Iraqi-Born Jews." *Jewish Journal of Sociology* 11 (1969): 59–66.

Gat, Moshe. *The Jewish Exodus from Iraq, 1948–1951.* Portland, Ore.: Frank Cass, 1997.

Rejwan, Nissim. *The Jews of Iraq: 3000 Years of History and Culture.* Boulder, Colo.: Westview, 1985.

Simon, Reeva S. *Iraq Between the Two World Wars: The Creation and Implementation of a Nationalist Ideology.* New York: Columbia University Press, 1986.

CHAPTER

20

Iran and Afghanistan

Haideh Sahim

Iran and Afghanistan have had a common history and cultural ties since ancient times. From the period of the Great Persian Empire of the Achaemenids (550–330 B.C.E.) until the middle of the eighteenth century, they were often parts of the same polity. After the Safavid period (sixteenth to eighteenth century), when Iran (referred to as Persia in the West until 1935) became a predominantly Shiite Muslim country, the region now known as Afghanistan maintained its Sunni majority.

Both countries are ethnically, linguistically, and religiously diverse. Iran is believed to consist mainly of Persian speakers, with Turkish speakers second. The major tribes of Bakhtiaris, Lurs, Baluchis, and Kurds are all speakers of Iranian languages, while the Turkmans, Shahsevens, and Qashqais are Turkic speaking. Some small tribes and people in areas in the south of Iran speak Arabic. Afghanistan too has many tribes, among them, the Turkmans, Baluchis, and Pashtuns. The official languages of Afghanistan are Dari Persian and Pashto.

Iran has a large minority of Sunni Muslims and small numbers of Zoroastrians (followers of the ancient religion of Iran), Jews, Christians (mostly Armenians), Bahais (an offshoot of Shiite Islam, considered heretical), and Mandaeans. Afghanistan is mainly Sunni, with about one-fifth Shiites. A number of Hindus also live there. Afghanistan once had a number of Jewish communities, but in 2002 only two Jews were said to be living in that country.

JEWS OF IRAN

Iranian Jews, numbering twenty-six to forty thousand, are almost exclusively of eastern heritage (non-Ashkenazi), with small groups from Iraq. They are concentrated in Tehran, Shiraz, Kermanshah, and Isfahan, with small numbers in other major cities.

The Jewish community of Iran is one of the oldest outside the Holy Land. Historical documents relate a Jewish presence in Iran in 721 B.C.E., when Sargon II (Shalmanasser in 2 Kings 17:6), the king of Assyria, settled the Jews in "the land of the Medes" (western and central Iran). Life flourished under Persian rule after the establishment of the Achaemenid Empire of Cyrus the Great in 550 B.C.E. Under the Sasanian dynasty, which ruled from the third century C.E. to the Islamic invasion in the seventh century, Zoroastrianism became the state religion and, as the power of its clergy grew, so did religious intolerance.

Jews were tolerated as *dhimmis* under Islamic rule, and some humiliating regulations, such as distinguishing patches, were imposed on them. During the period of Mongol rule (thirteenth to fourteenth centuries), Jewish life improved, but it took a turn for the worse in the sixteenth century, when the Safavid dynasty initiated the process of conversion of the population to Shiite Islam. From that point on the issue of *najis* (ritually unclean) affected the way the non-Muslims, including Jews, were treated in Iran. In the neighboring Sunni Ottoman Empire, however, the minorities were given self-governing status as separate *millets* (non-Muslim communities).

With the Safavids began one of the darkest periods in the history of the Jews of Iran. The persecutions there, which started during the reign of Shah Abbas I (1588–1629 C.E.) and continued until the end of the dynasty in the early eighteenth century, sometimes included horrendous acts of torture. By the end of this period the Jewish population had dropped significantly, as a result of forced conversion, death, and emigration, and never reached its pre-Safavid level. Whereas almost all cities in Iran once had Jewish communities, and many big cities had large sections called *yahudiyya* (Jewish towns), now many cities were empty of Jews.

The Qajar dynasty (1779–1925) began the slow process of modernization in Iran. The nineteenth century was a time of arbitrary rule, a low standard of living, and poor facilities for education and health care. It was also a period of decentralization and competition between Russia and Britain for control of Iran. Until the end of the nineteenth century the Iranian Jews had no protectors, unlike the Armenians, who were protected by the Europeans, and the Zoroastrians, who sometimes benefited from the influence of the Indian Parsis with the British. The morale of the Jews was low, and their numbers had been drastically reduced by emigration and forced conversions to Islam. Jews became the scapegoats and targets of persecution and mistreatment. By this time they had lost the right to own land or property in Iran. Also, they were not allowed to have shops and were prevented from practicing many professions. They were mostly apothecaries, goldsmiths and silversmiths, peddlers, musicians, entertainers, and wine sellers. Few managed to become merchants, and only a small percentage of them became prosperous. Surprisingly, the Jewish peddler was trusted inside houses to sell his wares. Physicians were among the few who enjoyed respect. As a rule, after each serious attack on the Jews, those who had the means would move to other areas, and those who remained were the unskilled and the less wealthy.

Around 1830 a blood libel—the accusation that Jews used the blood of a Muslim child in making matzo—in Tabriz in northeastern Iran, where Jews were successful in trade and quite prosperous, resulted in the deaths of about seven thousand Jews and the total depopulation of the Jews from that city. In 1839 in Mashhad in the eastern part of Iran, the accusation by a Muslim that the Jews had deliberately insulted the Muslims created an uproar in the city. The leading imam (Islamic cleric) issued a fatwa ordering the killing of all the Jews in the city. Mobs destroyed the synagogue, attacked and looted Jewish houses, and killed thirty-six Jews. Twenty-seven Jewish men went to the *imam jumᶜa* (leader of the Friday prayer), converted to Islam, and asked him to stop the massacre. In return, they promised to convert all the Jews. Incredibly, the entire Jewish population of that city converted in one day. The imam pacified the crowd and then married four converted Jewish girls himself.

From that moment on the Jews of Mashhad led a double life. Outwardly, they became devout Muslims, but they kept their faith at home, dangerous as it was if discovered. They went to the mosque, prayed, and followed the Muslim rites in every way, but they also secretly observed all Jewish traditions at home. They would open their stores on Saturday but would make excuses not to sell. They would buy meat from Muslim butchers but would dispose of it quietly. Jewish women of Mashhad were particularly tenacious in preserving Jewish life; until a Jewish butcher was established who could secretly provide kosher meat, they refused to touch meat. Mashhadi Jews even took Muslim names. They sent their children to the mosque for Muslim religious studies and held secret Talmud Torah classes. Couples went through two marriage ceremonies, one presided over by the Muslim clergy and one by the secret rabbi. To ensure that they could secretly gather for prayers or meetings, they lived close to one another, with their houses connected through the basements. More than a century of such life—they gradually left in the 1950s—has left its mark and made the Mashhadi community today a close-knit and rather insular group. They rarely marry outside the community and are usually distrustful of outsiders.

Unfortunately, conversion did not stop the Muslim community from harassing the Mashhadi Jews in an effort to reveal their true religious conviction, and their lives were in constant turmoil. Some Mashhadi Jews moved to other cities in the region, like Bukhara, Samarkand, or cities in present-day Afghanistan, where they established Jewish communities. A large group moved to Herat, where the majority of Muslims were Sunni and more tolerant of the Jews than the Shiites were.

Contacts with Europe toward the end of the nineteenth century led to the beginning of modernization for Iran. During his European trips the king, Nasir al-Din Shah (1848–96), became impressed with the economic and social achievements of European Jews. His meetings with their representatives and with the Alliance Israélite Universelle (AIU) eventually led to the opening of the first Alliance school in Tehran in 1898, followed by schools in other cities.

In 1878 the affairs of the Jews were entrusted to the Ministry of Foreign Affairs. Two years later the shah decreed that Muslims had no right to claim the inheritance of their Jewish relatives. However, the influence of the clergy was strong. In 1892, following the kidnapping and conversion of a Jewish girl in Hamadan at the instigation of an *akhund* (clergyman), Mulla Abd-Allah, on the eve of Yom Kippur, the Muslims attacked the Jews, who ran out of synagogues and barricaded themselves in their houses. Some converted out of fear. The *akhund* had gained such notoriety that neither the governor nor an army sent to Hamadan for his arrest could contain him. He imposed nineteen humiliating rules on the Jews; the most significant was the requirement that they wear a red patch. Finally, he was brought to Tehran by an invitation from a major *mujtahid* (high-ranking clergyman). Henceforth the name of Mulla Abd-Allah was anathema to Hamadani Jews. Following his example, six years later another mulla, Seyyed Rayhan-Allah, followed by mullas in other cities instigated a similar case of persecution in Tehran.

CHRISTIANS, BAHAIS, AND CONVERSION

In the nineteenth century Christian missionary groups started systematic proselytization in Iran. The Jews soon became the main target of these European and American missionaries. British and American missionaries placed great emphasis on the conversion of Jews. Through education and medical work and by means of Bible classes, they managed to convert a number of them. The missionaries published Judeo-Persian Bibles and other religious texts for this purpose. The main contributions of the missionaries in Iran were improving the lives of women and providing modern education. They even offered medical training to their outstanding converted students. Almost half the missionaries were women. They discouraged early marriages for girls and encouraged families to send their daughters to school, where in addition to traditional courses the missionaries offered classes in sewing, cooking, health, hygiene, and childrearing. Rabbis, fearing conversion of their people, bitterly complained to the government and asked for its intervention to restrain the missionaries. Mission activities among the Jews were greatly curtailed after the arrival of Alliance Israélite Universelle in Iran.

Babism, a popular messianic movement that was an offshoot of Shiite Islam in Iran, attracted Jews who were in spiritual and cultural decline. Without any support internationally or domestically, Jews responded to the Babi (and later Bahai) and Christian call of equality and unity. In a country where Jews were considered unclean, a "Muslim" Bahai's offer to share a cup was a heartwarming gesture because it showed that the person considered Jews to be clean and equal. With the constant mistreatment by the larger society, it was easy for the Jews to embrace warm treatment by and accept the religion of foreign missionaries. A number of converted Jews, however, later returned to their old faith.

Although a handful of Jews had managed to open stores in the bazaar by the end of the nineteenth century, they were still restricted in their business; their testimony was not valid in court; punishment for murdering a Jew was only a minimal fine; a new convert to Islam could claim the inheritance of all his relatives; Jews were not allowed to ride horses; and they were forbidden to walk ahead of Muslims on the street. Jews visiting in the house of a Muslim were not allowed to touch anything, lest they defile it; they were not allowed to touch fruits and vegetables when shopping (a custom that continued into the twentieth century), so shopkeepers took advantage and sold them their rotten goods. A Jewish woman had to reveal her face or wear a two-colored chador instead of the customary black; a Jewish man was not allowed to wear socks or matching shoes. Jews had to wear an identifying red patch. The door of a Jewish house had to be low, and Jews were not allowed to build nice houses or new synagogues. They were not allowed to enter the city after sundown. A Jew's voice should not be heard during prayer. The enforcement of any or all of these rules depended at any given time on the local ruler or mulla and the decency of the individuals in power. The struggle for respect and dignity was a daily effort. By the end of the nineteenth century, only physicians commanded respect. Iranian Jews were still struggling with injustices and persecutions instigated by mullas and not prevented by the weak shah.

Jews appealed to Jewish organizations outside Iran. Finally, the Alliance Israélite Universelle, which had for many years indicated a desire to open schools in Iran, sent Joseph Cazès in 1898 to set up the first AIU school in Tehran. He was received positively, and the shah donated some money to the school. Cazès demanded the abolishment of the distinguishing patch, but when Seyyed Rayhan-Allah refused, Cazès negotiated to replace it for his students with small pins with the AIU emblem. The students' clean European uniforms and the absence of the red "Jewish" patch helped to gradually change the attitude of the population toward all the Jews.

During the revolution that led to the establishment of a constitutional monarchy in 1906, the Jews, who hoped for some kind of equality, were once again caught in the middle and used by both sides. The intellectual movements that had started with the Constitutional Revolution affected the Jews as well. The first Iranian Jewish newspaper, *Shalom,* was published in Tehran at this time. The sociopolitical struggle that led to the Russian Revolution exported many social and democratic ideas to Iran. Among those were equality for women and democracy. There was also an effort to reduce prejudice against Zoroastrians, Armenians, and Jews.

Iran's new constitution allowed each of the major religious minorities to have a representative of their choice in the new Majlis (parliament). The first Jewish representative, Azizollah Simani, met with such hostility that he could not be effective and soon resigned. The Armenian representative followed suit, and they were both replaced by an influential Muslim clergyman. The Zoroastrians did not give in and maintained their representative. Not until the second Majlis in 1909 was Dr. Loqman Nehorai, a French-educated doctor, elected as the Jewish representative; he remained in office for several sessions.

The fervor of the numerous organizations and interest in self-help stirred the young Jews as well, and they created an organization dedicated to ridding the Jewish community of some of the restrictions.

PAHLAVI PERIOD

Reza Khan, a soldier who had climbed the ranks in the military very quickly, took power in a bloodless coup in 1921; in October 1925, after the

Qajar dynasty was deposed, he was proclaimed king by the Majlis. Influenced by Mustafa Kemal Atatürk in Turkey, Reza Shah (1925–41), though autocratic, was an innovator who pushed Iran into the twentieth century. He showed contempt for the clergy and the power and influence that they exercised. By removing the clerics' hold on law and education, he greatly reduced their influence, and the country became secular in practice. He abolished the turban and ordered all men to wear European clothing and a hat similar to the French kepi, now known in Iran as the "Pahlavi hat." In 1936 he banned the veil for women.

From the early years of Reza Shah's reign, the life of the Jews changed significantly, and the emancipated Jews finally advanced in a number of areas. They gradually left the Jewish quarters and moved to the better areas of their cities, sent their children to new secular public or private schools, and, after a university was established in 1935, could enter the university based on merit. The government officially protected minorities. Although sporadic attacks on Jews still occurred, Jews' association with Muslims in schools, enforced Western-style clothing, and compulsory military service for all Iranian males began to reduce the antiminority sentiments among Iranians. Jews were now free to open businesses of their choice. Young Jewish men were hired by foreign companies and embassies and by government and private offices, because their language skills proved valuable. Nevertheless, the economic condition of the Jews in the 1920s was so depressed that more than 90 percent lived in poverty. The *jizya,* a head tax imposed on minorities, was still in effect at the time of Reza Shah and was abrogated only after an appeal to him by Jewish, Armenian, and Zoroastrian delegates to the Majlis.

Under Reza Shah a formal national registry system became fully operational, and it became obligatory for Iranians to choose family names in the European fashion and to get identity cards. Jewish authorities encouraged Jews to select Jewish (Hebraic) last names, advice that some followed while many others chose Persian names. Although it was never required, in some localities administrative workers added the word *kalimi* (Jew) to the last name of some. Religious minorities had to appeal to the Ministry of Justice to get the shah's approval for having marriages and divorces performed by their own religious authorities, rather than at the official registry offices, which were run by Muslims.

Although Reza Shah did not have any particularly positive feeling toward Jews, he did not harbor anti-Jewish feelings, either. During the 1930s and World War II anti-Semitism increased as a result of German propaganda both within and outside Iran. Such propaganda emphasized the Aryan roots of the Iranians, which accorded with glorifications of the Iranian past that were popular at that time. Two Persian journals published in Germany, *Iranshahr* and *Farangestan,* and a Persian radio program broadcast from Berlin during the war promoted such sentiments and regularly attacked the Jews. Anti-Semitic sentiments became popular with the intelligentsia in Iran as well. Domestically, German influence increased so much that many Jewish teachers were laid off, and Jews could not work for some government offices or the railroad, which was controlled by German engineers.

With the attack of Germany on Russia in 1941, anti-Semitism in Iran increased. Although Muslim zealots prepared to massacre the Jews and seize their property and even Jewish women in anticipation of Germany's victory, the Iranian government was one of the few that gave visas to Jews fleeing European countries, making it a safe haven for refugees of war. Thus in 1941 during the Farhud about ten thousand Iraqi Jews escaped to Iran, where they were received by their coreligionists and joined the small community of Iraqi Jews who had immigrated to Iran two decades earlier and had become a part of the social fabric of Iranian Jewish society. They established their own synagogue and a school, which later adopted the Iranian curriculum. Most continued on to Palestine and the United States.

In 1941–42 a large group of Polish Jews, including 871 children, escaped via the Soviet Union and arrived in Iran. In Bandar-e Pahlavi (now Anzali) representatives of the Jewish Agency met these children and brought them to Tehran, where camps were set up for them. Known as *yaldei Tehran,* the Children of Tehran, the children (and adult Jews) were supported and cared for by the local Jewish community at a time when Iranian Jews were themselves in crisis. The Tehran community also assumed responsibility for their religious education.

In September 1941, when the Allied powers forced Reza Shah to abdicate, his twenty-one-year-old son, Mohammad Reza, was sworn in as the second Pahlavi king. The first decade of his reign was marked by an unprecedented period of freedom. More than twenty political parties and seventy daily newspapers appeared. Among them were several Jewish papers. The activities of the Jewish Agency and the American Jewish Joint Distribution Committee were made possible because of the shah's sympathetic attitude. Recognizing that they could not rely upon the forces of the United States, Britain, France, and the Soviet Union, Iranian Jews cultivated ties with the court and government circles. Their political activities, however, led to some antagonism among domestic rightists and religious newspapers, which accused the Jews of being a foreign group in the country and urged that they be eliminated. With the withdrawal of the Allied forces from Iran in 1946, anti-Jewish riots broke out in many cities. The worst was in Mashhad, where some *jadids* (Jewish converts) were killed and their houses looted. As a result all Mashhadi Jews left for Tehran, Israel, and other countries. At the time of the establishment of the State of Israel in 1948, about thirty-thousand Iranian Jews lived there.

The revolutionary movement in 1978–79 caused much concern among the Jews, because of the initial anti-Jewish remarks of Ayatollah Khomeini that later became anti-Israeli. The Jewish community saw that its fate was in the hand of just one person, the shah, and regarded his downfall as its own destruction. By the beginning of the summer of 1978, when demonstrations became widespread, a crisis committee consisting of about five young professionals and older Jewish leaders met to address concerns of the Jewish community. Initially, most members were not much concerned, but by November they recognized that a change of government was a real possibility. In view of the Jewish community's past experiences, and with the followers of Ayatollah Khomeini gaining power, the fate of the Jews in a clergy-run country seemed bleak, and some protective measures were necessary. The Jewish Intellectual Society was formed as an alternative to the Tehran Jewish Society, the central governing body of the Jews of Iran, so that the community would be protected with either turn of events. The Jewish Intellectual Society encouraged Jews to participate in pro-Khomeini demonstrations under its banner. Despite their unease with the turn of events, about seven thousand Jews participated in a demonstration that attracted about a million people on Ashura, a major Shiite mourning day (December 11, 1978). By this time Jews had become so much a part of the society that it seemed only natural to participate in an event alongside other Iranians. For those Jews, this was more a demonstration of how much they felt a part of the nation than a sign of their political support for Khomeini.

The contentment of the Jews with the Pahlavi rulers is little understood by many non-Jews in Iran, particularly the left and the liberals. It should be noted the expectation of this suppressed society in search of revival was not democracy in the form of political freedom but equality in social rights, a relative freedom in economic activities, and above all an end to oppression and imposed limitations. The secularization of the society, which was favored by the Pahlavi regime, reduced the power of the clergy. Subsequently, some religious issues, such as the issue of *najis,* lost some of their significance, at least among a majority of urbanites. The other factor was that for the first and only time the government took seriously its responsibility of protecting its people. The Pahlavi period proved to be the most tranquil for the Jews in several centuries.

ZIONISM

A love for Eretz Israel (the Land of Israel) always existed, though European Zionist ideologies were foreign to Iranians, and Zionism existed only in a religious sense. Organized Zionism began in Iran after 1912, when the Iranian Jewish Youth Cultural Society was created in Tehran, along with another society promoting the advancement of Hebrew. These organizations fostered some innovations, although they did not formulate an effective response to the conversions of Jews to Bahaism and Christianity that were then occurring. Only after a number of Jews had already converted did these organizations put an end to the Bahai gatherings that had sprung up in every part of most Jewish quarters. With their efforts to prevent injustices to the Jews, these organizations also brought some hope. Later they were known as Ha-Histadrut ha-Siyonit be-Faras (Zionist Federation in Persia), and they published a weekly newspaper, *Ha-Geulah.*

With the news of the Balfour Declaration in 1917, groups of Jews throughout Iran opted to leave Iran for Palestine. Some of the Jews who emigrated there during the 1920s returned because of lack of support there. The Jewish community, which viewed this as the start of freedom from exile, founded the Zionist Organization of Iran (Tashkilat-e siunit-e Iran). Its first action was to correspond with Zionist organizations in Russia and England, requesting aid, books, and newspapers. Being in touch with Jews throughout Iran and in Palestine and Europe had positive results. The community learned how to organize and began educational activities. About ten plays were produced, and hundreds of lectures on Jewish history and culture were sponsored. Although Reza Shah prohibited all organized political or party activities connected to foreign organizations, he did not strictly enforce the ban on Zionism. In the 1940s the Center for Iranian Jewish Youth (Kanun-e Javanan-e Yahud-e Iran) was founded by Dr. Ruhollah Sapir, who was instrumental in helping the Polish refugees.

In the United Nations, Iran voted against the independence of the State of Israel in 1948. Nevertheless, from the start the two countries developed a good working relationship. Mohammad Reza Shah was strongly criticized for his good relationship with Israel, for having his secret police, SAVAK, trained by the Israelis, and for neglecting the Palestinians, although his government was officially pro-Palestinian, and Zionist activities were formally banned.

From the end of World War II until 1978 the Jews of Iran enjoyed affluence and economic freedom. Young Jews there did not relate to Israel in a religious sense any longer. Because Israel had absorbed the poor and needy Iranian Jews, it had become a reminder of the hardship and struggles that Iranian Jews had strived to put behind them. Only in the late 1960s and 1970s did they readily learn Modern Hebrew and go to Israel to study, because they no longer saw it as a country for the poor. In Iran the economic prosperity of the Jews, their improved living conditions, and professional opportunities resulted in better relations with the Muslims. The persecutions of the past were replaced with some degree of prejudice and discrimination, but untoward incidents were rare. As Jews became more comfortable in Iranian society, they neglected their Judeo-Persian culture. Young Jews did not become assimilated, but they did become acculturated. In 1974 the Center for the Cultural and Social Advancement of the Jews of Iran was established to promote awareness of Jewish and Iranian culture among the Jews and to promote awareness of Jewish culture among other Iranians. The center had many innovative programs, including open lectures by both Jewish and non-Jewish speakers and summer camps for teenagers, which was one of its most successful programs.

POSTREVOLUTIONARY IRAN

After the return of Khomeini in 1979 the monarchy was replaced by an Islamic republic. The instability of the situation, Ayatollah Khomeini's early anti-Jewish remarks, and the advent of a religious government frightened many Jews; they fled in large numbers for Israel, the United States, and Europe, some leaving behind vast amounts of property. Khomeini soon changed his position from anti-Jewish to strongly anti-Israel. In the early days after the revolution, when Habib Elghanian, a prominent Jewish businessman and philanthropist, was executed on charges of Zionism and spying for Israel, more Jews left, despite government assurances of their safety.

Since the revolution the treatment of Jews has varied over time. They are permitted to consume wine and alcoholic beverages, but all non-Muslim food stores must display a sign saying they are not Muslim. For a period of time Jews were refused exit visas. Many hoped that the new president, Mohammad Khatami, who took office in 1997, would bring some moderation to the highly restricted life of all Iranians. Anti-Jewish sentiments abound, and official publications make regular use of anti-Semitic propaganda, such as the spurious *The Protocols of the Elders of Zion* and Holocaust denial material. Government statements assure the safety of Jews, but there are fears that they could become pawns to use against possible attacks by Israel. Jews who have remained in Iran live in a sensitive and unpredictable situation that requires constant vigilance. More Jews have been going to synagogues, which now serve as places for meeting and socializing. In 1998 Tehran had twenty-three synagogues, and there were fifty in other cities. The community has grown closer, as it always has in difficult times, and, despite all restrictions, it is managing. Kosher food has become expensive and difficult to obtain. The government wants to demolish the Jewish cemetery south of Tehran for a housing project. In 1999 the Jewish cemetery in Mashhad was asphalted over in the middle of the night to build a road. Iran has adopted a strong anti-Israel policy, and the media attack Zionism daily.

The fate of the Jews of Iran is unclear. A new wave of anti-Semitism started in 1998, with various newspapers and magazines publishing many anti-Jewish articles; some criticized the Jews for openly practicing Judaism. In December 1998 five Jews were arrested in Isfahan. On the eve of Passover 1999 eight more Jews were arrested in Shiraz. These Jews, among them a sixteen-year-old boy and a rabbi, were all very religious and openly wearing yarmulkas. At first no charges were brought against them, and the Iranian Jewish authorities tried to gain their release through quiet diplomacy. But when the story leaked to the press in June 1999, governments around the world strongly objected and demanded their release. The Iranian government then accused these Jews of spying for Israel, a crime punishable by death. (Since the revolution about thirteen Jews have been executed on similar charges, and more than five have died under suspicious circumstances.) The Jews arrested in Shiraz and Isfahan were detained under strict conditions; only after eighteen months in solitary confinement were they able to visit with their families, and then for only five minutes each week. They were refused access to legal counsel until they were provided with court-appointed lawyers before their trial. The only evidence against them seems to be their confessions to spying for Israel, but it is not known under what conditions these were extracted. International intervention on behalf of the Jews was not effective, yet the Iranian government insists that their trial was fair. The Jewish community in Iran, especially in Shiraz and Isfahan, is devastated, and morale is low. Jewish children are ostracized in schools, and one Jewish store has been firebombed. Jews are afraid to discuss the issue with outsiders, which makes helping them more difficult. President Khatami has repeatedly stated that all citizens of Iran are treated equally by law. At the time of the trial the names of four Muslims were announced as co-conspirators, but their faces were never shown, whereas all ten Jews (three were released after the trial) were paraded in front of the cameras. They received sentences of two to nine years. Two were recently released.

It has often been asked why the Jewish community of Iran has not left en masse. Many outsiders view the existence of Jews in Iran as a sign of a fairly comfortable life and lack of pressure. Many have stayed because of financial difficulty, old age, or language barriers that they would face in a new environment. Others have remained by choice, because they feel more comfortable in their own land than they would in another country, even Israel. This group thinks that they are financially better off in Iran, their moral values better realized there, and they would like to continue living in the land of their ancestors.

COMMUNITY LIFE

In Iran Jews traditionally lived in special quarters called *mahalles*; the only exception was the Jews of Hamadan, who were dispersed throughout the city. The *mahalles,* unlike the European ghettos, were not usually walled but were neighborhoods within the city walls and boundaries. They were often not very clean, as the Jews were not allowed to dispose of their garbage outside the area, lest they defile the Muslims. The only relief for the *mahalles* was that farmers would periodically collect the refuse for fertilizer.

Within the *mahalle* the most coveted houses were the ones at the ends of narrow streets and alleys, as they were the least accessible in attacks. Also, houses had low doors (in some cities this was mandatory for Jews so that they would have to bend and bow constantly) that opened to a long corridor that ended in a courtyard. The low entrances were easier to barricade and gave the residents a few extra moments to flee. The houses in the *mahalle* stood next to each other; their roofs were connected. In Mashhad Jewish houses were connected by doors in the basements that allowed residents to flee when they were attacked or to gather in secret for religious ceremonies.

Respect for tradition was and is quite pronounced among the Jews; that is why they have preserved the ancient dialects of Iran. Religious observance was also pronounced until the midtwentieth century. Family ties have always been strong, and it was normal even in the early twentieth century for three generations to live together. Despite restrictions that have kept Iranian Jews separate from the larger society, they have adopted many Iranian traditions over the centuries. For example, it is customary in Iran to visit friends and relatives for the Iranian New Year, Nowruz, which is on the first day of spring. Also, it is customary to sprout some wheat or other grain as a symbol of prosperity and the regeneration of vegetation at this time. Iranian Jews visit friends during Passover, which is shortly after Nowruz, and they sprout grains for this holiday. When Passover ends, Jews go out for a picnic, just as other Iranians do on the thirteenth day of the new year. Many other similarities of this kind exist. Since the 1950s Jews have celebrated Nowruz as a national holiday as well.

ORGANIZATIONS

In Iran, as elsewhere, the synagogues were the center of community life. Jews discussed and resolved their social and communal problems there. Women attended services on High Holy Days and occasionally the Shabbat, but their participation in prayers was almost nonexistent because they rarely learned any Hebrew before the twentieth century. This has changed somewhat in recent years, but because the Jewish community remains traditional, the role of women in the segregated synagogues is still minor. The synagogues do not require formal membership, and people are free to attend any one. Some have schools that teach Hebrew and Judaism. Their expenses are underwritten by donations and pledges, made particularly on the High Holy Days, when certain privileges (e.g., carrying the Torah scrolls or opening the ark) are auctioned to the highest bidder. Women are not barred from bidding on such privileges for male members of their family. Religious studies and observance diminished during the latter part of the Pahlavi period, as Jewish society conformed to Iran's secular atmosphere. Today, because of the dominant religious atmosphere in Iran, religious observance and attention to religious studies have actually increased, although the study of Hebrew is looked upon with suspicion.

For Iranian Jews religious leadership was neither continuous nor unified. With the death of Mulla Abraham ben Mulla Aqa Baba in 1910, the position of exilarch of Iran ended. He was one of the few people in Iran who was well versed in the Talmud and who had studied in the religious centers of Baghdad and Jerusalem. Mulla Abraham (mulla was also a title given to the learned), said to have been very charismatic with a holy countenance, was highly respected and influential in the Jewish community. All legal and religious affairs were referred to him, and cases rarely went to government authorities. He held the community together in good times and bad. Religious duties and laws were observed in his time. His eldest son, who succeeded him, lacked his father's influence and personality and became the last to hold the position. Some believe that after Mulla Abraham died, the Jewish community of Iran declined in religiosity.

In the past the affairs of the Jewish communities were managed by the *hevrah* (society), which consisted of prominent and trusted men and religious leaders of each city. The *hevrah* was in charge of such matters as kosher meat, baths, schools, and the distribution of Passover matzo, and it served as a council for arbitration and family counseling. It was later transformed into the Tehran Jewish Society (Anjoman-e Kalimian-e Tehran). Many of the society's organizational and internal problems were solved after all synagogues and Jewish properties were transferred to it. Similar organizations with like responsibilities were set up in other cities. The Jews soon determined that they needed a more effective financial organization and founded Sandoq-e Melli (the National Fund) (it has since folded) to collect donations and disburse funds to the needy and to other organizations. One organization took care of the affairs of the *mahalle.* Kanun-e Kheyr-khah (the Benevolence Center), one of the most active and respected Jewish organizations, was established by Ruhollah Sapir during World War II and had a clinic for the needy, which was later converted into a small, well-equipped hospital. During the Islamic Revolution this hospital, which was named for Sapir, accepted and treated many injured members of the opposition. The hospital is still active in Tehran and has modern equipment, but today only a quarter of its personnel and 5 percent of its patients are Jewish. The center also is in charge of two day-care centers and an old-age home.

In 1947 ten Tehrani Jewish women founded the Jewish Ladies Organization of Iran, which became one of the most active Jewish organizations in Iran. It established many classes, including sewing, literacy, English, and Hebrew, and was involved in many charitable works. It founded two day-care centers in Tehran, the first ones in Iran, and four in other cities, along with training classes for the teachers. It also established a nursing school that was later transferred to the Sapir Hospital. This organization was active in appealing for modification of inheritance laws for women. It is still active today.

EDUCATION

Traditionally, education in Iran was at Islamic *maktabs* (traditional schools), where a teacher (whose competence varied from semiliterate to well educated) conducted classes in rudimentary reading, writing, some arithmetic, and *siaq,* a system of writing numbers based on characters similar to the alphabet. Jewish children were excluded from these and went to Jewish *maktabs,* where they learned elements of Hebrew through studying the Torah, prayers, and some Persian literature, which they read and wrote in Hebrew characters. Few learned Persian script. Girls were rarely taught to read and write, because this was deemed unnecessary.

Modern institutions of learning were not established in Iran until the Dar al-Funun, a high school based on European models, was opened in 1851 with a secular curriculum and well-educated foreign and Iranian teachers. But Jews were not allowed in these schools, and it would be many years before non-Muslims would be admitted.

The opening of the first Alliance school in Tehran in 1898 was a turning point in the education of Jewish youth. The language of instruction was French, with Persian taught as a separate subject. French language, literature, history, geography, mathematics, sciences, Persian, Jewish history, and some religious studies were part of the curriculum. Students wore uniforms and were given lunch; most paid minimal or no tuition. Hebrew and religious studies were secondary to modern sciences, and this caused concern that the students might abandon their religion or convert, especially since the Christian missionaries and Bahais were actively proselytizing among Jews. Some refused to send their children to the school. Until Hebrew was added to the curriculum, students had to take instruction elsewhere. Many believe that the secular beliefs of the founders of the Alliance schools were instrumental in the secularization of Iran's Jewry. The Alliance has also been criticized for stripping the Iranian Jews of much of their native culture. Indeed, it encouraged a Francophilia that superseded their interest in their Persian heritage.

Still, the Alliance opened many doors for the Jews. Some Muslims also sent their children to Alliance schools, because they were often the only place to get a modern education and learn a Western language. This change of attitude was instrumental in the improvement of Jewish-Muslim relations. A major innovation of the Alliance was establishing schools for girls, which was unprecedented outside Tehran and the few cities where the missionaries had schools for girls. Jewish girls became among the first in Iran to receive a modern education. Soon, a few other modern Jewish schools were opened with stronger religious studies programs. Eventually, as they followed the official state curriculum, the schools placed more emphasis on Persian.

Under Reza Shah foreign and missionary schools came under the control of the Ministry of Education, which enforced a unified curriculum. The ministry limited the cultural and political influence that these schools once exerted; now all they provided was better foreign-language instruction and extracurricular activities, conducted with a minimal foreign staff. The Alliance also lost its special status but continued functioning as Iranian schools called Ettehad, with a strong French program. Yet the leadership that the foreign schools had fostered continued. The government continued to send students to Europe and United States for higher education, and a few Jews were among them.

Today the Jews of Iran try to maintain their organizations, although they have lost many privileges. The Islamization of Iran has brought about strict control over Jewish educational institutions. Before the Islamic Revolution, Iran had twenty Jewish schools throughout the country. In recent years most have closed, some for lack of pupils, and the ORT school (Organization of Rehabilitation through Training), a successful vocational school, has been transferred to the government. In the remaining schools Muslims have replaced the Jewish principals. Also, religious education in schools is now under the supervision of the Ministry of Education, and the government publishes Jewish religious textbooks in collaboration with Jewish organizations. Tehran still has about seven schools in which Jewish pupils constitute a majority or the entire student body. Such schools follow the official curriculum and teach the Torah in Persian, not Hebrew. On Fridays the Jewish organization holds special extracurricular Hebrew and religion classes taught by Hebrew teachers that it has appointed. The election of President Khatami and his administration has so far failed to bring about the expected reforms.

CULTURE

When the government invited foreign experts to Iran in the early part of the twentieth century, the need for people with good language skills increased. Among those who were qualified to fill such positions were the graduates of Alliance Israélite Universelle schools. By the time of Mohammad Reza Shah, AIU graduates had managed to achieve high-level positions in the country. For example, Rabi^c Moshfegh-Hamadani became the head of the Iranian news agency, Pars, and later the editor of *Kayhan,* one of the two major daily newspapers in Iran. Several Jews became university professors, and Dr. Iraj Lalezari was appointed the dean of the Faculty of Pharmacology at the University of Tehran, the only Jew to be promoted to such an academic position. Jews did not, however, reach high military or government positions. One exception was Fereydoon Nosrati, deputy director of the Plan

Organization (the government planning agency), whose position was equal to that of a deputy minister.

Despite a rich literary heritage, the literary achievements of Iranian Jews were insignificant in the nineteenth century; they resumed some activity in the twentieth century. Today a number of Jewish writers and poets inside and outside Iran have achieved fame. Among those in Iran are Shirindokht Daghighian, a prolific writer on philosophy and religion; Mozhdeh Sionit, a novelist; and Goel Kohan, a research scholar.

One of the most famous Jewish scholars in Iran was Soleiman Haïm (1888–1969). Born in Tehran and educated at the American College there, he compiled one of the first Persian-English/English-Persian dictionaries, which remains unsurpassed to this day. Dr. Habib Levy (1896–1984), a dentist educated at an Alliance school and in France, wrote a three-volume work on the history of the Jews of Iran, the most comprehensive ever written. Two prestigious publishing houses in Tehran, Brukhim and Safi Ali Shah, were Jewish enterprises. Shamsi Hekmat, one of the founders of the Jewish Ladies Organization of Iran, became the only Jewish woman to join the board of directors of the Women's Organization of Iran, which was headed by Princess Ashraf, the twin sister of Mohammad Reza Shah. Hekmat was its treasurer for a number of years; she represented Iranian women at many international gatherings.

Music was one domain that had always been open to the Jews. A number of Iranian folk entertainers have become famous, although folk music was traditionally considered low class. In classical Persian music Jews' achievements are on a par with the best masters of Iranian music. A well-known traditional classical singer of the twentieth century, Shokrollah Dardashti, was Jewish; so was one of the greatest masters of classical Iranian music, Morteza Ney-Davoud (1900–87), a master of the *tar* (a six-stringed instrument) who trained many other master musicians.

In the six decades of the Pahlavi dynasty Jews managed to overcome centuries of hardship and flourished in business. They made up for in commerce the advancement that they were denied in the army or the government. From the late nineteenth century until after World War II, the textile imports of Iran, particularly of British goods, were in the hands of Jewish merchants of Hamadan. Elghanian, who owned the biggest plastics factory in Iran, Plasco, was the best-known Jewish industrialist. The Aryehs were also major industrialists and among the economically successful. A few Jews were factory owners and industrialists, but almost none went into agriculture. The number of Jewish doctors in Iran was also high.

POLITICAL PARTIES AND JEWS

The years between the fall of Reza Shah in 1941 and the end of the government of Prime Minister Mohammad Musaddeq in 1953 brought unprecedented political freedom. During that time Jews published a number of newspapers and magazines, including *Alam-i Yahud* (the *World of Judaism*), *Sina, Yisrael* (an intellectual and political publication), the leftist political journal, *Bani Adam* (*Mankind*), with a circulation of three thousand, and *Nisan,* a newspaper with a circulation of ten thousand. In 1948, when most political papers were banned, *Nisan* became popular, even among non-Jews.

During World War II Jews became attracted to antifascist movements. Between 1941 and 1943 Jews were especially interested in the communist Tudeh party and its affiliated organizations, which raised their voices against all pro-German elements and for the rights of national, ethnic, and other minorities. Most Jews in the Tudeh party were from the middle and lower middle classes. Yet a few religious Jews were reported among their ranks. Both the Jews in the Tudeh party and later those in the National Front believed that coexistence with the larger Iranian community was the only way to make progress and that communication, through commercial transactions, friendship in the office, and a common political experience could extinguish the hatred of anti-Semitism. In fact, the Tudeh had an important role in reducing anti-Semitic feelings through its publications, particularly during the World War II years. No Jew, however, was elected to the central committee of the Tudeh, although a few advanced to higher offices. *Nisan* was pro-Tudeh. In 1948 the party was declared illegal, and the Jews turned toward Zionism.

The ideas of Musaddeq, who served as prime minister from 1951 to 1953 and promoted a democratic society and parliamentary monarchy, appealed to many Iranian Jews. However, despite the many Jewish intellectuals and writers who were among his followers, Iranian Jews were apprehensive about Musaddiq's following of religious Muslim groups and some old fascist elements. When the shah returned to power in 1953 and banned all political activities, the only group that was permitted to remain active was the Muslim clergy. They played on the theme of anti-Semitism and anti-Bahaism, and their main objection became the shah's ties to Israel. The new anti-Semitism that they created led to the beginning of the emigration of tens of thousands of Jews, mainly to Israel and the United States, in the 1950s.

Jewish Iranians played a prominent leadership role in the Confederation of Iranian Students, an outlawed organization of students abroad, which in the 1970s had an estimated five thousand members and twenty thousand sympathizers. The number of Jews in the confederation was a large percentage of the total population of Iranian students abroad, and their motive was combating anti-Semitism in Iranian society. The acceptance of the rights of different ethnic groups and the fundamentally nonreligious nature of the confederation made it appealing to the Jewish students. At the same time the problem of Palestine and traditional anti-Semitism was a constant dilemma for the Jews in the confederation. The organization was disbanded after the 1979 revolution.

The lot of Iranian Jews has been a difficult one, but they are resilient and patient. They were and are, outside or in the country, a close-knit community. Despite their disagreements and occasional internal conflicts, they have taken care of each other when necessary. Helping a stranded Jew is an unquestioned moral and religious duty, as was helping the Polish Jews without taking credit for it. Iranian Jews have managed to maintain their dignity and culture regardless of their treatment.

Many have criticized them for adopting a position of acceptance and humility and not fighting back as, for example, the Armenians have. However, the Jews fought back when and in any way they could. The case of the Mashhadi Jews is a good example. Jews in Iran have maintained a strong sense of family and community and an identity as Iranian that has enabled them to persist, if not thrive, for nearly three millennia, even as other Jewish communities in the Middle East have all but disappeared.

JEWS OF AFGHANISTAN

Because of its distance from the centers of Judaism, Afghanistan has been peripheral in the history of Jews. Balkh, Maymana, and other major cities of Afghanistan are known to have had large Jewish communities until they were dispersed by the Mongol invasion in the thirteenth century. Very little is found about them in histories until the nineteenth century, when Mashhadi Jews, impressed by greater tolerance there, established new communities in major Afghan cities and helped enrich the Jewish cultural life there. Although, compared to Iran, their life was relatively better in Afghanistan, it was not without any incidents stemming from prejudice. Traditionally, religious minorities had to pay *jizya,* which was abolished in 1919, when King Amanullah declared all Afghan citizens equal.

In the twentieth century Afghani Jews were concentrated in Kabul, Balkh, and Herat; they were banished from the other cities after the assassination of Nadir Shah Durrani, who ruled Afghanistan from 1929 to 1933. After 1952 the Jews were excluded from military service but had to pay the tax, *harbiyya*. As late as 1971, military service for Jewish men meant only cleanup duties and no training with weapons.

Economically, the Jews' situation in the twentieth century was not favorable. They worked as tailors and shoemakers and were engaged in commerce and handicrafts. They were officially banned from the import and export trade; however, they found means to get around this and traded with Central Asia and India.

No Zionist activity was permitted, and no emissaries from Israel or representatives of European organizations, including the Alliance Israélite Universelle, reached Afghani Jews. None of the Iranian reforms touched the Jews of Afghanistan, but the Jews themselves took some steps to improve their lives. During a famine in 1944 about one thousand left Afghanistan for British India in an attempt to go to Palestine. They were stranded in India when the British government refused them emigration permits. Many committed suicide out of desperation. In 1947 the newly established independent government of India ordered them deported, but U.S. and European organizations intervened, and the Jews were permitted to remain in Delhi and Bombay, from where they left for Israel by 1949. In 1950 Jews were finally allowed to leave Afghanistan, and most emigrated to Israel via Iran.

Traditionally, schools in Afghanistan were closed to Jews, so the Jews set up their own education system at their traditional schools, called midrash, taught by teachers referred to as mulla, or *khalifeh*. In the twentieth century in Herat, most Jewish children were educated privately because their parents, fearing assimilation, did not send their children to school. By midcentury Jewish education was, in effect, nonexistent. The older generation had learned enough Hebrew in their youth to converse. In Kabul children did attend government schools but could not attend Sabbath services because the schools were in session. They attended services in winter, however, when schools were on vacation, so Jewish education was seasonal and sporadic. Because of the various restrictions, standards for both religious studies and modern education were low.

The three cities of Kabul, Herat, and Balkh, where Jews lived, each had a *hevrah* (Jewish society), composed of the heads of families, led by the *kalantar* (leader of the community). In addition to care for the poor and attending to such needs as burial, the *hevrah* attended to legal matters. When two Jews were engaged in a dispute, a committee of ten or fifteen men would hear both sides, impose rulings, and mete out punishments, including excommunication. The *kalantar* represented the community to the Afghan government and was responsible for payment of taxes and official matters, including passports and military service. As of 2002, only two Jews were reported to still be living in Kabul, Afghanistan.

RECOMMENDED READING

Bar^{c}am-Ben Yossef, No^{c}am, ed. *Brides and Betrothals: Jewish Wedding Rituals in Afghanistan.* Jerusalem: Israel Museum, 1998.

Levy, Habib. *A Comprehensive History of the Jews of Iran: The Outset of Diaspora.* Edited and abridged by Hooshang Ebrami, translation by George W. Maschki. Costa Mesa, Calif.: Mazda, 1999.

Loeb, Laurence D. *Outcast: Jewish Life in Southern Iran.* New York: Gordon and Breach, ca. 1977.

Moreen, Vera Basch. *Iranian Jewry's Hour of Peril and Heroism,* Texts and Studies VI. New York: American Academy for Jewish Research, 1987.

Netzer, Amnon. "Islamic Lands: Iran." In Moshe David, ed., *Zionism in Transition*, pp. 225–32. New York: Herzl, 1980.

——. "Persian Jewry and Literature: A Sociological View." In Harvey E. Goldberg, ed., *Sephardi and Middle Eastern Jewries: History and Culture in the Modern Era,* pp. 240–55. Bloomington: Indiana University Press/New York:Jewish Theological Seminary of America, 1996.

Patai, Raphael. *Jadid al-Islam: The Jewish "New Muslims" of Meshhed.* Detroit: Wayne State University Press, 1997.

Shwartz Be'eri, Ora. *The Jews of Kurdistan: Daily Life, Customs, Arts, and Crafts.* Jerusalem: Israel Museum, 2000.

CHAPTER

21

Yemen

Bat-Zion Eraqi-Klorman

Yemen is in the southwest corner of the Arabian Peninsula, bordered on the west by the Red Sea, on the north by Saudi Arabia, and on the south by the former Aden Protectorates, where the majority of the Jewish population lived. (Aden was occupied by the British in 1839, became a crown colony in 1937, and in 1967 became the state of South Yemen, merging in 1990 with what was then called North Yemen. This discussion relates only to North Yemen.) Yemen has three distinct geographical regions: the hot coastal strip; the interior highlands, which are characterized by numerous narrow fertile valleys and rugged peaks that form natural boundaries separating parts of the population from one another and from any effective central control; and the arid eastern foothills, which lead to the Rub' al-Khali desert of the central Arabian Peninsula.

The Jews were Yemen's only non-Muslim minority, and they lived among a population almost evenly divided between the Shafiʿi Sunnis, members of mainstream Islam, and the Zaydis, members of one branch of the Shiites whose adherents believe that as the descendants of Ali, the cousin and son-in-law of the prophet Muhammad, they have the sole prerogative to lead the Muslim community. Unlike other Shiite sects, religious differences between the Sunnis and the Zaydis in matters of doctrine and law are relatively insignificant. Yemen has been under Zaydi domination since the sixteenth century, headed by Zaydi imams who were acknowledged as political and religious leaders.

During the nineteenth century internal instability characterized Yemen. In addition, because of its strategic location international interest in the affairs of the country was growing: Yemen had long been an essential link in the land-and-seagoing trade network of the Mediterranean, the Red Sea and its coastal land routes, the Persian Gulf, and the Indian Ocean. This factor, plus increasing political rivalry among world powers in the nineteenth century, ensured the involvement of Yemen in world affairs. In 1839 the British, motivated by their desire to secure communications with India, conquered the Yemeni port of Aden. In 1849 the Ottoman Empire dispatched an expeditionary force that occupied parts of the coast, including the port town of Hudayda. After the opening of the Suez Canal in 1869, Yemen's importance as a strategic stronghold on the Red Sea en route to the Indian Ocean encouraged the Ottomans to remain. During this period some leading citizens, mainly from the capital of Sanᶜa, desperate to return law and order to Yemen, asked the Ottoman pasha of Hudayda to help pacify the country. In 1872 the Ottomans occupied Sanᶜa and the central highlands around it and remained there until the end of 1918, when the Ottoman Empire collapsed as a result of its defeat in World War I. Throughout the Ottoman occupation the Zaydi tribes in the northern provinces resented the foreign regime, successfully defied all attempts to impose a central government on the region, and allied themselves with the opposition. Imam Yahya al-Mutawakkil, who had ascended to power in 1904, led the opposition forces until he entered Sanᶜa in 1918 as the temporal and spiritual ruler of an independent Yemen. Upon his death in 1948 his son Imam Ahmad replaced him on the throne and governed until 1962; soon after his death, revolutionary forces abolished the imamate, and Yemen became a republic.

There are no accurate statistical data for Yemen before 1975. Based on available evidence, toward the end of the nineteenth century the Jewish population of Yemen was sixty to eighty thousand, with nearly 85 percent living in the rural provinces. The Jews' demographic pattern was similar to that of the Muslim population, and Jews were scattered in more than eleven hundred settlements, sometimes consisting of only a few families and usually in the predominant Zaydi areas, alongside their villages and towns. The largest Jewish community was in Sanᶜa, where it generally constituted about 20 percent of the population.

THE LEGAL STATUS OF THE JEWS

Under the imams the Jews were *dhimmis.* The Zaydi state was strictly regulated by religious law and was careful not to impose any permanent taxes other than the *jizya* (head tax) on the Jews. Whenever a question arose, especially when the government wished to tax Jewish land formerly owned by Muslims and that had yielded taxes under Muslim ownership, Muslim religious scholars strongly opposed the idea. This does not mean that Jews were completely exempt from other forms of taxation. In times of need the imams would impose fines on urban Jews and/or one-time levies upon Jews or other segments of the population.

Because religious law remained the foundation of the Yemeni legal system well into the twentieth century, some restrictions imposed on non-Muslim subjects, which had gradually been lifted in other Muslim lands, were still in effect there, even after the last major Jewish exodus in 1950. Jews were prohibited, for example, from riding horses, riding on a donkey except sideways, living in houses taller than those of Muslims, or wearing colorful clothes. These discriminatory restrictions were more strictly maintained in the areas under direct imami rule—in the cities and in central Yemen—while in the territories dominated by the tribal sheikhs, where the majority of the Jews lived, they were not meticulously enforced. The Yemeni tribes usually resisted the imposition of any restriction that differed from their old practices and customary laws. Thus, for example, while Jewish houses in the Jewish quarter of San^{c}a were lower than Muslim houses, in the rural districts farther from the capital the heights of Jewish and Muslim houses were the same. Written and oral histories from the twentieth century also reveal that in central Yemen, whenever a Jew who was riding a donkey met a Muslim on his route, he had to descend and ask permission to continue his journey. Such incidents were unknown in the tribal territories, and usually the greater the distance from San^{c}a, the less these usages and restrictions were enforced. In the northern and northeastern parts of the country, Jews, like the tribal people, were even permitted to carry weapons, such as a jambiyah dagger or a rifle, and their Muslim neighbors were proud of the Jews' ability to use them.

JEWISH-MUSLIM RELATIONS

In the rural areas the safety of the Jews was further enhanced by the traditional tribal customary laws, under which they enjoyed the protection of the sheikhs and other members of the tribes in a sort of client-patron relationship. Like any other newcomer to a tribal territory, a Jew—or even an urban Muslim merchant—who wished to live within the boundary of a certain tribe had to first receive formal permission and guarantees of protection. Without these he would be in danger of physical assault and loss of property. The maxim "Whoever hurts the Jew in water, we shall defend him in blood," announced the protection relationship and defined it as a blood pact; the tribes perceived hurting "a tribe's Jew" as a provocation and an offense directed at the tribe. More than once a Yemeni tribe set out for war against another tribe whose members had offended a protected Jew.

In addition to the general tribal commitment to protect their Jews from any outside insults, each Jew had special ties with a *jar,* a Muslim tribesman who acted as his patron. The Jew would give him gifts and ask the *jar*'s formal permission to carry out important acts, such as purchasing or selling property or marrying off a daughter. When in need, the Jew turned to his *jar* for help.

The two communities depended on each other for medical care. Jews sought the help of famous tribal doctors and experienced midwives, and Muslims were treated by Jewish doctors who prescribed drugs or amulets. Because of the Jews' high literacy rate, they were especially trusted to write the appropriate charm for a remedy or for protection from evil and threatening forces.

Yet one aspect in the relationship between Jews and Muslims in Yemen put the Jews in a position of almost constant defense. This was the Zaydi statute known in Jewish sources as the Orphans Decree. This statute, anchored in eighteenth-century Zaydi legal interpretations and enforced at the end of that century, has no equivalent in other countries. It obligated the Zaydi state to take under its protection and to educate in Islamic ways any *dhimmi* child whose parents, usually both father and mother, had died when he was a minor.

The Orphans Decree was ignored during Ottoman rule (1872–1918), but it was renewed during the period of Imam Yahya (1918–48). In the first half of the twentieth century, Yemeni society continued to suffer from natural disasters, such as drought with famine and death in its wake, and epidemics that caused numerous deaths. Therefore both Muslims and Jews had the problem of orphaned children. The Muslim state saw itself as responsible for the support and education of Muslim orphans, and the Orphans Decree appears to have been intended to alleviate the severe plight of orphaned and deserted Jewish children, although it greatly dismayed the Jewish community.

The implementation of the Orphans Decree reflected the internal political struggle between the central government's attempt to control and the semi-independent nature of the Yemeni tribes, and it was contingent on the government's ability to impose its policies. The Orphans Decree was therefore known primarily in central Yemen; in settlements far from the cities—especially in the rural districts in the north, east, and south of the country—customary tribal laws continued to determine the nature of the relations between Jews and Muslims. In such places implementation of the Orphans Decree was almost unknown.

During the 1920s and 1930s, in the areas where the imam reigned supreme, the rules in the struggle over the orphans were formulated. It was clear to both sides that while the Muslims were obligated to carry out the commandment of their religion and to convert the minor orphans, the Jews were obligated to protect their people and to rescue them from Islamization. The Jews protected their minor orphans by marrying them off even when very young (girls as young as seven or eight and boys as young as eleven or twelve), thus "proving" their maturity, or by smuggling them to hiding places in other settlements within Yemen or to Aden, which was under British hegemony. So long as the Jewish community kept minor orphans from being seen in public (and the communities were so small that everyone knew who they were), the authorities generally closed their eyes and did not pursue the children. In contrast, the presence of Jewish orphans in public places, especially when they were neglected by the Jewish community and driven to begging, offended Muslim sensitivities—Zaydi Muslims saw this as intolerable, a situation that exposed orphans to conversion. (Some Jewish communities were so small and poor that in times of disaster they could not care for the weak. For the Jews it was preferable that the orphans remain in the community, even if they had to beg to survive.) Despite the maneuvers that the Jews had to take to evade the Orphans Decree, they generally continued to feel that their position in Yemeni society, among their Muslim neighbors, was secure.

THE JEWS IN THE ECONOMY

Yemen's economy was based on agriculture. If rain falls regularly, the land can produce nearly every vegetable, cereal, and fruit. Yet two crops are especially important: coffee and qat. For centuries coffee has been Yemen's most important and well-known cash crop. Exported from the Red Sea port of Mukha, Yemen's coffee reached world markets, became a popular beverage, and earned the country substantial foreign exchange, until Latin American coffee replaced it in the nineteenth century and especially in the twentieth century. Qat production is directed at the local market and is replacing coffee as the most profitable crop. Chewing the small young leaves of the qat, a medium-size bush, and swallowing the juice produces a mild narcotic effect.

Although some Jews owned agricultural land, especially in the southern, southwestern, and northern regions of the country, they leased it to

Muslims; in fact, Jewish earnings from farming constituted only a small addition to their income from their other, major, occupations.

The Jews of Yemen had expertise in a wide range of trades usually avoided by Zaydi Muslims. They were silversmiths, blacksmiths, experts in repairing weapons and tools, weavers, potters, masons, carpenters, shoemakers, tailors, and more. Usually, a skill passed from one generation to the next within a family, although sometimes a young apprentice, a son in a family whose vocational expertise was different, was accepted to work with another artisan, thus enabling a measure of professional and social mobility. One of the most widespread and lucrative arts from which many Jews made their living was silversmithing. Silver jewelry was ordinary daily attire for Muslim and Jewish women—and during religious holidays they added ornaments. Jewelry served not only as decoration but also as a means to preserve the family's property, which was invested in the precious metal and thereby guarded by women. Muslim men also regularly patronized the Jewish silversmiths. They decorated the Muslims' weapons, the sheath of the jambiyah or the handle of the gun, and ornamented the saddles of Muslims' riding animals as well as their nargilehs (water pipes). The amount and quality of jewelry that a Yemeni could afford announced his socioeconomic status.

This division of labor created a sort of covenant, based on mutual economic and social dependency, between the Zaydi Muslim population and the Jews of Yemen: the Muslims produced and supplied food, and the Jews supplied all manufactured products and services that the Yemeni farmers needed. The actual economic foundation of Jewish life in rural areas was the *umla,* the permanent liaison between a Jewish artisan and a number of Muslim farmers, each called *amil.* Throughout the year the artisan provided the farmer with all the services and goods he needed for his farm and household; at harvest time the farmer paid his debt in field crops, butter, honey, and the like. Each party could engage in a number of *umla* agreements, the Jewish artisan with several Muslim families in his village, in other villages, or even with a whole village, and the Muslim farmer with different artisans according to their expertise. In addition to its economic advantages the *umla* relationship contributed to the social solidarity between Jewish and Muslim members of Yemeni society, creating strong, almost magical, bonds of fidelity between the two parties. An *umla* relationship usually came into effect following a symbolic ceremony of some sort, such as the Jew's hammering a nail into the door frame of a Muslim house. Thereafter the Muslim would never replace his Jewish artisan with another, and the Jew would always be ready to give his services to his *amil.*

DOMESTIC AND INTERNATIONAL TRADE

As in other nonindustrial countries lacking modern infrastructures for transportation and communication, a major part of Yemeni commerce, at least until the beginning of the twentieth century, was based on barter. This was conducted in goods for goods, labor for goods, or services in credit in the *umla* system. Transactions in cash were more frequent only in the towns.

Commercial dealings, in which Jews were regular participants, were negotiated mainly in Yemen's town and village markets. San^{c}a, for example, was an important commercial center that supplied its many inhabitants, as well as those living in the towns and villages in its vicinity, with all their necessities. Commerce was concentrated in twenty-odd different markets, each usually named after its main commodity. Jewish merchants engaged mainly in retail selling; only a few were large wholesale traders. In the markets of both San^{c}a and other towns, Jews maintained shops in which they both made and sold their own products, such as gunpowder, soap, tobacco powder, saddles, sandals, shoes, pottery, ironware products, and silver jewelry.

Outside the towns most of the commercial activity took place on the weekly market days. In every district a special site near a number of settlements—and preferably near a water fountain—was designated as the market site, and one day a week an open market came to life there. The markets attracted many people who came to exchange their goods for other commodities or to sell them for money. Farmers displayed their agricultural products, some Muslim traders offered consumer goods brought from distant locations, and Jewish artisans sold their crafts and sometimes other merchandise. At the end of the day the marketplace emptied and was deserted until the next week. Some traders and artisans took part in a few day markets during the week.

The market functioned not only as an essential business center for the benefit of the regional population but also as a meetingplace for social encounters, cultivating acquaintances, and transmitting information. This social function was important for Jews and Muslims separately as well as for their intercommunity relationships.

Some Jews in Yemen made their living from peddling, carrying their merchandise or tools on their shoulders. They traveled throughout the week, or even for a few weeks or months, from one village to another, seeking their livelihood among the Muslim villagers. Only for the Sabbath or Jewish holidays did they return to their families, bringing their earnings—some grain, honey, and maybe a few coins.

During the Ottoman regime Jews' involvement in almost all commercial activities became more visible. In all the towns where Ottoman administrative and military personnel were stationed, Jews answered the numerous needs of government machinery as it developed. Jews took advantage of the new business opportunities; a considerable number engaged in large-scale trade and made substantial profits. They supplied the Ottoman officials and their families with meat, bread, coffee, clothes, and shoes and such luxury items as silk garments and precious stones, which were imported through Aden. Even after the Ottoman withdrawal in 1918, many Jews continued to earn their living from large-scale commerce in grain, raisins, tobacco, coffee, and textiles.

Yemen's strategic location at the junction of trade routes to the Far East, the Red Sea, Africa, and the Middle East resulted in an important share of the international trade until late medieval times. This resumed after the British occupation of Aden in the first half of the nineteenth century. Aden became an important harbor and commercial center, where Jews were suppliers of various products and commodities to the British army and administration; some of these Jews became large-scale international traders.

COMMUNITY LIFE

One outstanding characteristic of Jewish communal life in Yemen, which reflected the country's geography, demography, and political decentralization, was the absence of any meaningful central organization, except for the religious authority of the San^ca *bet-din.* Jewish unity was also based on the awareness that all Jews under formal imami rule shared the same cultural tradition and spiritual values. This awareness was intensified through marital bonds and the frequent migration of Jews within Yemen, which unified the people of distant regions, especially because there was almost no Jewish immigration from other countries.

POLITICAL LEADERSHIP

Jewish leadership comprised two types of authority, secular and spiritual. The secular leaders were known by several titles: *nasi* (president), *ra'is al-Yahud* (head of the Jews), sheikh, or *aqil* (a south Arabian term for sheikh). In the towns and villages the title of *aqil* was most common, borrowed from the terminology of the Muslim Yemeni administration. It was given to the head of a residential quarter in the capital city of San^ca, the head of the merchants in a certain market, and so forth. In the countryside the sheikh who was responsible for all the administrative aspects of his tribe appointed *aqils* to assist him; each *aqil* headed a village or a number of villages.

In the towns, and especially in Sanᶜa, the authorities appointed the *nasi.* This appointee was acceptable to the community and was usually from a rich family that had commercial or other ties to the imam's court. This position was indispensable to the government because it conducted all its dealings with the Jews through the *nasi.* He was responsible for all matters of taxation, primarily the *jizya* but also for other occasional levies or fines. He was in charge of determining the tax rate (which was progressive), according to which each male Jew aged thirteen to sixty paid the *jizya,* and of collecting the sums and turning them over to the imam. The imams sometimes provided guards to assist the *nasi* in the exercise of his authority.

The *jizya* was paid to the imams or to the tribal sheikhs, and to the Ottomans during their occupation. In the rural tribal districts the *jizya* payments often took the form of participation in some kind of public work, such as the building of a public project. In places under direct imami rule the *jizya* was usually collected in the Yemeni coin, the riyal. During the first half of the twentieth century, a Jew who was defined as rich had to pay approximately three to four riyals per year, the average earner paid two riyals, and the poor Jew paid one riyal. During the 1940s the yearly payment was estimated to equal the income from a few working days.

THE SECULAR LEADERSHIP OF SANᶜA

The head of the Jews of Sanᶜa held the most important and influential position of its kind. Yet in conformity with the nature of the Jewish Yemeni communal organization, his authority did not generally extend beyond the boundaries of his town, and he rarely represented Jews from other parts of the country. Only in the middle of the eighteenth century, during the leadership, consecutively, of two members of the Eraqi family, Aharon and Shalom, did the institution of the *nasi* exert its influence elsewhere in Yemen. This is not surprising because during this period Yemeni imams succeeded in establishing their strong domination over nearly all of Yemen, and the Jewish leadership followed suit. Both Eraqi *nasis* were wealthy merchants who traded in the local Yemeni market as well as with the Far East. Shalom Eraqi also acted as a general tax collector for two imams and was in charge of the imami mint, where he employed many Jewish silversmiths from Sanᶜa and other settlements. After he took office around 1733, the responsibility for operating the state's mint remained in Jewish hands. Because of their wealth and close connections to the court, these *nasis* could benefit the Jewish communities in San^ca and elsewhere. They built new synagogues, repaired old ones, constructed other public buildings, and contributed greatly to charity.

The strong standing of the Eraqis allowed them to interfere in religious matters that were totally outside their authority. Thus, for example, it is said that Shalom Eraqi used his influence in favor of the Sephardi siddur (prayer book) in a dispute about which version was more desirable. Yemenite Jews had been accustomed to pray in the *baladi* (local) tradition, which basically followed Maimonides. During the late seventeenth century and the eighteenth century, envoys and merchants from Palestine brought to Yemen new and inexpensive typeset books, among them prayer books in the Shami, the Sephardic prayer version, which differed from the local siddur both in the text and the order of prayers. The rabbinic leadership resisted the new version, which threatened to force out the old tradition. Nevertheless, the new prayer books were widely accepted. This issue remains unresolved.

The end of the Eraqis' leadership (circa 1760) coincided with the deterioration of the imami government, which by then could effectively dominate only San^ca and its environs. From then on the San^ca *nasi* was restricted to leading the Jews of his town. The political instability that prevailed during the nineteenth century resulted both in a lack of security and in economic stagnation for central Yemen. Many San^ca inhabitants, among them Jews, left the capital for distant settlements, mainly in central Yemen, in order to secure their safety and to find a way to earn a livelihood. On the eve of the Ottoman occupation in 1872, the town's population was estimated at twenty-three thousand, whereas it had been fifty thousand until the mideighteenth century.

In Yemen the Ottomans attempted to apply their administrative system in all governmental affairs, including those affecting the Jewish community. As in their provinces elsewhere, the Ottomans appointed a *hakham bashi* (chief rabbi) as the head of all Jews under their rule. In actuality, the Yemenite *hakham bashi* was primarily the head of the Jews of San^ca and fulfilled the functions that the *nasi* had and generally was not involved in religious matters. With the return of the imami regime at the end of 1918, the old institution of the head of the Jews, nominated by the Zaydi imam, prevailed once again.

In the smaller settlements the *aqil* was generally selected from the largest or wealthiest families and was responsible for determining the amount of the *jizya* and collecting it, acting as an arbitrator, and mediating disputes in his community and sometimes for the Muslim population. Sometimes he was the rabbi of his town or a member of the district court that met in the nearby town; in that event, his position combined secular and religious duties. He represented his community in joint matters of Jews and Muslims in the life of the village, such as joint public prayer for rain, chasing away locusts and regulating the distribution of water. The *aqil* worked to protect Jewish legal rights and to safeguard the Jewish neighborhood or village, its cemetery, and its water sources.

SPIRITUAL LEADERSHIP

The spiritual leader, the *mori* (rabbi), was recognized by the community because of his prominent scholarship and expertise in the Torah. He was completely independent in managing the religious life of his community and was not subordinate to any other authority. He did not need the consent of the Muslim rulers and had no responsibility for activities on their behalf, except when the same person was the *mori* and the *aqil.*

Because nearly all the spiritual life, and to a large extent men's social life, revolved around the synagogue, the *mori* stood at the center of Jewish communal life. He conducted the prayers and headed the regular learning sessions in the synagogue, which included the study and deliberation of the Torah and religious law, commentary and exegetic literature, and kabbalah (Jewish mysticism). The *mori* was often the judge who settled religious and civil cases, acted as mediator in personal disputes, performed marriages and granted divorces, and even led public singing at the meals at religious celebrations.

JUDICIAL INSTITUTIONS

The San^ca *bet-din,* though recognized by all as the appellate court, derived its power solely from its moral authority. It did not appoint the judges in the Jewish district courts or other religious functionaries, but local courts approached the *bet-din* when they needed to clarify a point of law or by tradition or when litigants wanted to appeal the ruling of the local court.

The most important religious personality was the *av-bet-din* (head of the court). With him sat two other judges, both of whom had been nominated with the consent of San^ca rabbis. Occasionally, the nomination of the *av-bet-din* was followed by an act of acknowledgment from the government, which always assumed that it had authority over the Jews. Because the *bet-din* did not have a permanent place for its sessions, it convened on Mondays and Thursdays at the home of the *av-bet-din* or in his synagogue.

Members of the *bet-din,* as well as the judges and *moris* in the smaller settlements, did not receive any regular payment for their judicial and other religious duties. They all continued to support themselves and their families from their professions, usually as artisans or tradesmen.

THE YESHIVA

The yeshiva of San^{c}a was not a school for higher learning. It was a judicial association that focused on the clarification and explanation of the law as well as on judgment. In fact, it was the final arbiter of the law, superior even to the San^{c}a *bet-din.* The yeshiva examined court decisions to prevent injustice and ensure that rulings would not contradict the public opinion of San^{c}a rabbis. The yeshiva had no set number of members, did not assemble on a regular basis, and accepted a rabbi as a new member when the public recognized his outstanding scholarship. In addition, the yeshiva or the *bet-din* was responsible for sending inspectors to settlements in central Yemen in order to authorize new slaughterers and to give permission to authorized *moris* to perform marriages and grant divorces.

EDUCATION

Because the primary purpose of education was to prepare a boy to participate as an adult in communal and religious life, he learned to read the Torah and a chapter from the Prophets (the *haftarah*) in the synagogue as well as their translation into Aramaic (*Targum*) and Arabic (*Tafsir*), to join in public prayer, to take part in daily religious study guided by the *mori* of the synagogue, and to possess and profess desirable communal manners and conduct.

A boy received his basic skills from the children's *mori,* a man versed in the Torah who could not make a living from any other trade and took it upon himself to teach young children. The school was usually located in a room donated and maintained by a member of the community on the ground floor of his house. Boys aged three to twelve or thirteen were divided into study groups, and all learned in the same room. The *mori* taught the reading and memorization of the weekly Torah portion, including the Yonatan Aramaic translation of the Bible (*Targum*). The older children were taught the *haftarah* and Rabbi Saadia Gaon's translation into Arabic and chapters from the Mishnah. The *mori*'s main role was to teach the correct reading in accordance with the rules of vocalization and biblical tonal notation (*ta*ᶜ*me ha-Miqra*) and not to explain the text. The assumption behind this educational approach was that after mastering accurate reading, the student could easily gain understanding at a later stage of study. On Saturdays the children took turns and read the translation of the Torah and *haftarah* in front of the congregation, thus preparing themselves for adulthood when they would read these biblical passages in Hebrew.

The education of a Yemenite Jewish boy did not consist only of the knowledge he gained from the *mori*. The other complementary educational task was his father's responsibility. In the evening or while the father was engaged in his trade, the boy read to him or to his grandfather and uncles what he had learned that morning while the father examined his understanding and explained the text. The child also sat with his father in the synagogue where they read together and studied portions of the Mishnah and commentaries. Even after the child had completed his formal studies, he continued to study with his father.

At about age twelve a boy usually learned his father's trade, but sometimes a boy was sent to learn a new trade with an artisan, at whose workshop he worked as an apprentice for a year without pay. In the second year he received a small weekly payment. Later, when his skills were perfected, he could become an independent artisan.

As in similar traditional societies, the men's society, which controlled Jewish communal life, legally, socially, and culturally discriminated against women. All that was expected from a girl was that she learn to run a Jewish household and be prepared for marital life. Girls had no religious studies, and women did not attend the synagogue. In 1943 a short-lived attempt in Sanᶜa, inspired by Yosef ben David, a messenger sent to Aden by the Jewish Agency for Palestine, was made to provide some formal education to girls. The "school" assembled for two hours a day in several private homes. The curriculum included Hebrew, arithmetic, and Hebrew songs from Palestine. After a year and a half the community's objections that the school had no women teachers ended the experiment.

Girls learned from their mothers and female relatives how to run a Jewish household and follow all strict religious precepts and laws. They usually knew and could recite the tales of the Bible and whole passages from the weekly Torah and also possessed a treasury of stories, legends, fables, and poems. The Yemenite women's society developed a unique genre of poetry and songs that centered on diverse aspects of women's life. These poems, which reflect an intimate familiarity with Yemeni popular culture, were actually a common enterprise of Jewish and Muslim women, who were not hampered from socializing by their religious or ethnic differences. These poems and stories, recited or sung in the common Arabic language, were transmitted orally, thus providing an additional link between Jews and the surrounding Muslim society.

ELEMENTS OF MODERNIZATION

As a result of Yemen's geographic and political isolation, the country remained a backwater until 1862. Although the British colonization of neighboring Aden in 1839 and the Ottoman occupation of central Yemen in 1872 served to introduce a measure of modernization to the life of the Jews and the rest of the population, until the middle of the twentieth century highland Yemen remained largely free of both foreign ideology and technology.

During the second half of the nineteenth century, Aden became the main channel for the movement of people and goods and ideas to and from interior Yemen. Following the British occupation, Aden became an important port town and commercial center. The new economic opportunities attracted Jews and Arabs, mainly from the southern regions of Yemen, to settle under British domination. Some stayed in Aden for only a few months or so, saved money, and returned to Yemen. Another channel for modernization was the direct contact with the Ottoman officials and troops who had invaded in 1872 and set up a telegraphic network and postal service. The effects of modernization were felt mostly in Sanᶜa and its environs and other major towns.

The modernization that began in the late nineteenth century left its imprint mainly in the technological and economic fields, gradually pushing the Yemeni economy closer to the Western system. A negative side-effect of the relative prosperity and development of commerce brought about by the Ottoman occupation was the damage caused to some Jewish artisans. Yemen received industrial goods that could compete in their variety, quality, and price with those produced by the traditional Jewish artisans. This development, which was felt mainly in central Yemen, was slowed by World War I and the return of the imami government. However, although Imam Yahya tried to restrain the process of modernization, he could not entirely halt the importation of industrial goods and new technologies or the infiltration of Western ideas. Thus, for instance, in 1928 the Soviet Union began to send diverse industrial products at highly subsidized prices into Yemen. Neighboring Aden was a closer source of inexpensive goods, produced in numerous workshops that used advanced technologies not familiar in Yemen. Many workshops relied on inexpensive Yemeni migrant laborers who sought their livelihood in Aden. Consequently, under Imam Yahya's government as well, Jewish craftsmen faced increasing competition.

Between the two world wars Jewish businessmen, like their Muslim counterparts, suffered from Imam Yahya's centralized economic policy and the nationalization of a significant number of commercial and industrial enterprises. In addition, the government entered new industrial fields, such as textiles and soap, that had formerly been controlled by Jews. Along with these economic steps Jewish artisans from Sanᶜa were forced to teach their trades to Muslims. Thus by the middle of the 1930s the only trade that remained exclusively Jewish in central Yemen was the production of alcoholic beverages. Though the imam did not intend to drive the Jews out of their occupations but rather to introduce Muslims to new economic activities, the inevitable result was that Jews' livelihood was crippled.

Some Jews from the capital tried to counter the imam's policy by using new technologies and improving productivity. In 1933–34 they imported modern machines from Germany and Italy for soap production and established flour mills and mills to grind coffee. These enterprises operated successfully until the government realized the business potential and built competing plants. Even a motorized moving company set up by Jews in the mid-1930s could not survive after the government entered this field. These developments may have been among the factors that made Jews willing to leave Yemen and emigrate to Palestine.

The opening of Yemen led to an intellectual excitement in the form of a dispute over the kabbalah between the *dor deᶜa* (generation of reason) and the *iqshim* (the stubborn). It is impossible to speak of an enlightenment movement as in Europe. Yemenite Jews knew and accepted their *dhimmi* status in society. As long as the parties followed the recognized rules, which by and large they did, a viable cultural and social coexistence between them continued as before.

Toward the end of the nineteenth century, however, new ideas reached Yemenite Jews and began to have some effect. The Ottoman Turks, for example, tried and gave up, because of a strong Zaydi opposition, to abolish the *jizya* and grant equal rights to the Jews. Hebrew newspapers began to arrive, and relations developed with Sephardic Jews, who came to Yemen from various Ottoman provinces to trade with army and government officials. As increasing numbers of Christian and Jewish tourists and travelers visited the country, two Jewish travelers, Joseph Halevy, a French-trained Jewish orientalist, and Edward Glaser, an Austrian-Jewish astronomer, influenced a group of young Yemenite Jews from Sanᶜa, of whom Rabbi Yahya Qafih was the most outstanding.

As a result of his acquaintance with Halevy and Glaser, and with the literature of the Jewish Enlightenment, Qafih introduced modern content to the educational system. The Ottomans had already established government schools. In Sanᶜa in 1905 Qafih opened a new school and, in addition to the traditional subjects, introduced arithmetic, Hebrew and Arabic, and the grammar of both languages. This school paved the way for the opening in 1910 of a Jewish school by the Ottomans, under Qafih's direction. The curriculum included subjects such as natural sciences, physics, arithmetic, history, geography, astronomy, sports, Hebrew, Arabic, and Turkish. At first the majority of the Sanᶜa community and rabbinic leadership perceived the Turkish-sponsored school as a great achievement and wished to establish a modern secondary school as well. However, as a result of the *dor deᶜa* and *iqshim* dispute, the school closed only five years after it opened and before the educational system could develop a reserve of young people who had been exposed to the ideas of the Jewish Enlightenment and who might have generated some modern changes in the life of the community.

The *dor deᶜa* and *iqshim* dispute about the kabbalah literature broke out in 1913, inflamed Sanᶜa's Jewish community, and split it into two rival groups that maintained separate communal institutions until the late 1940s. The dispute even spread to a number of other settlements. Rabbi Qafih and his friends were the leaders of *dor deᶜa,* which opposed the kabbalah and presented it as an irrational and alien current inconsistent with the true, reasonable nature of Judaism. They considered the engrossment of recent generations in kabbalah literature and the following of customs based on kabbalistic meaning to be in contradiction to the old authentic Yemenite Jewish tradition, which relied on Maimonides, the rational philosopher. As Qafih himself acknowledged, his attitude toward kabbalah was greatly influenced by the enlightenment ideas of Joseph Halevy, who rejected kabbalist ideas because of their irrational elements. In 1913, when it seemed that Qafih, then headmaster of the new Jewish school and working closely with the Ottoman authorities, enjoyed sufficient political support, the *dor deᶜa* faction made its views public and tried to impose them on the general Jewish public. The rest of the community rejected the *dor deᶜa* concepts. The opposition, the *iqshim,* headed by Rabbi Yahya Yishaq, the *hakham bashi,* refused to deviate from the accepted customs and the study of Jewish mysticism. One of the *iqshim*'s targets in the fight against Qafih was the modern Turkish-Jewish school, which made its closing inevitable.

WAVES OF EMIGRATION

The Emigrations of 1881–1914

Emigration from Yemen to Palestine began in 1881 and continued almost without interruption until 1914; during this period about 10 percent of Yemenite Jews left. Though Zionist organizations were never active in Yemen, political developments of the late nineteenth century were instrumental in advancing the migration because citizens of the Ottoman Empire could freely move from one place to another. In 1869 travel was greatly facilitated by the opening of the Suez Canal, which shortened the voyage from Yemen to Palestine. With news of Jewish life in Palestine readily available, Yemenite Jews knew that *moshavot,* the new Jewish agricultural colonies, were being established.

These developments fed into their religious and ideological readiness for a dramatic transformation in their lives, which continued to revolve around religion. Yemenites were especially inclined toward messianic hopes and speculations, and in the second half of the nineteenth century alone three consecutive messianic contenders appeared in Yemen, where they greatly influenced Jewish public life and drew substantial numbers of followers. Yemenite Jews who were not seriously influenced by Zionism could express their desire for a Jewish homeland through the only political theory known to them, messianic ideology. Consequently, each emigration wave disclosed some messianic motifs as part of the emigrants' attempt to clarify for themselves and for others their urge to leave for Palestine. They interpreted the recent political changes and the new developments in the Holy Land as heavenly signs that the time of redemption was at hand. By emigrating and settling the Land of Israel, they were taking part in actions that they believed could precipitate the anticipated messianic era.

From 1881 to 1882 a few hundred Jews left Sanᶜa and several neighboring settlements. This first wave was followed by other Jews from central Yemen who continued to flow to Palestine until 1914, most to Jerusalem and some to Jaffa.

The other notable wave of emigration before World War I originated in 1906 in north Yemen and continued until 1914. As described earlier, the life of the Jew in northern Yemen was generally prosperous and secure. But after receiving news about Yemenite Jews in Jerusalem and the *moshavot,* and when they became certain that living in the Holy Land was a realistic possibility, Yemenite Jews decided to emigrate. Hundreds of North Yemenite Jews headed to Palestine and chose to settle in the *moshavot*, where many made their living as agricultural workers.

Their arrival in the *moshavot* coincided with the formulation of a concept, termed the "conquest of labor," by Jewish workers' parties, the World Zionist Organization, and the WZO's office in Palestine, established in Jaffa in 1908. According to this concept, Jewish consolidation in Palestine would be achieved not only by purchasing land but also by its being cultivated by Jewish hands, that is, Jews should replace the Palestinian Arab workers with Jewish ones. When it became apparent that the Eastern European Jewish workers were incapable of this task, Zionist workers' parties decided that the "conquest of labor" could be accomplished by "natural workers," Jews accustomed to hard work, to inferior living conditions, and able to compete in productivity and payment with the Arab workers. Yemenite Jews, although never accustomed to hard labor but generally accustomed to spacious living conditions, seemed to be suitable "natural workers" and thus instrumental in the struggle to "conquer labor."

This was the background for the decision by the Palestinian branch of the WZO to send an emissary, Shmuel Yavne'eli, to Yemen to encourage Jews to emigrate to Palestine. Yavne'eli reached Yemen at the beginning of 1911 and returned to Palestine in April 1912. Despite his impression that the economic and living conditions in all the Jewish settlements he visited were healthier and better than those in the Jewish settlements in Palestine or in Eastern Europe, he urged the Jews to leave Yemen. As a result of Yavne'eli's efforts during this one year, about one thousand Jews, mainly from central and southern Yemen, left for Palestine, with a few hundred more arriving before 1914.

The Emigration of 1920–50

Until World War I the movement of people from Yemen to Palestine was free of political considerations and depended almost entirely on the emigrants' desire and capability to finance and organize for the long trip. After the war new factors determined the pace and fate of the emigration movement: Imam Yahya's attitude toward Jewish emigration to Palestine; the policy of the British, who were mandated to govern Palestine after the war, toward Jewish immigration; and the number of immigration certificates allocated to Yemenite Jews by the Jewish Agency. In response to Palestinian Arab demands, Imam Yahya issued an edict in 1924 that prohibited Jews from leaving Yemen, and he threatened to confiscate the houses and shops of those who violated this edict. Despite the prohibition, Jewish emigration from Yemen did not cease. In most cases government officials closed their eyes and allowed the Jews to make their way across the border to the Aden Protectorate, from where they continued to Palestine. The authorities were more strict, however, regarding confiscation of property. Migrating Jews, especially from San^{c}a and nearby settlements, were not permitted to sell their property, a great obstacle because the sale of their property usually financed their travel expenses.

Because the Red Sea port of Hudayda was under the full control of the imam, the major and nearly sole point of departure to Palestine was the port of Aden. In 1928 the Jewish Agency established an office in Aden that handled all matters related to facilitating immigration, such as the distribution of immigration certificates, health examinations, and the purchase of boat tickets, which the immigrants paid for. But during the 1920s the British authorities decided to limit Jewish immigration to Palestine by reducing the number of immigration certificates issued. These certificates were then allocated by the Jewish Agency according to various considerations. Therefore, Jews who reached Aden often had to stay there, sometimes for years, until they received immigrant certificates. During this wait many lost most of their resources; some managed to find low-paying jobs in Aden, while others had to rely on charity; almost all lived in unbearable conditions. The rate of the Yemenite emigration was completely dependent on the number of certificates allocated, which never answered the demand. Between the two world wars about eight thousand Yemenite Jews reached Palestine.

During the first years of World War II, emigration from Yemen continued at about the same pace as before the war. In 1943, however, Yemen received more certificates because European Jews could not use them. The news about available certificates, combined with a deterioration of the Yemeni economy after several consecutive years of drought, and permission to exit granted by Imam Yahya, caused thousands of Jews to pour into the Aden Protectorate. About four thousand left for Palestine, while a similar number could not obtain certificates and had to stay behind in a transit camp that was set up near Aden by the Jewish Agency. Between the end of the war in 1945 and 1948, Holocaust survivors had priority; immigration of Yemenite Jews practically stopped and the transition camp in Aden continued to shelter its inmates.

The establishment of the State of Israel expedited the emigration of all the Jews waiting in Aden, in an operation known as "On Eagles' Wings." An official edict published in May 1949 by Imam Ahmad, who succeeded his father, Imam Yahya in 1948, permitted all Jews to sell their property and leave the country. To the imam's surprise this decision, and the Jews' knowledge that the State of Israel was behind the recent movement of people from Aden, caused almost the entire Jewish population to leave Yemen. They flowed to Aden by the thousands and when On Eagles' Wings was completed, close to fifty thousand Yemenite Jews had been flown to Israel.

After this great exodus only a few thousand Jews remained in Yemen. Several hundred emigrated to Israel between 1951 and 1962, when the republican revolution of 1962 halted the exit of Jews from the country. Since political changes of early 1990s that hinted at a movement toward reconciliation between Israel and the Palestinians, a few hundred Jews were permitted to leave Yemen, and they chose to go to Israel. Others, probably, a few hundred, have chosen to remain in Yemen.

SUGGESTED READING

Eraqi Klorman, Bat-Zion. "The Forced Conversion of Jewish Orphans in Yemen." *International Journal of Middle East Studies* 33 (November 2001): 23–47.

——. *The Jews of Yemen in the Nineteenth Century: A Portrait of a Messianic Community.* New York: E. J. Brill, 1993.

Goitein, S. D. "Jewish Education in Yemen as an Archetype of Traditional Jewish Education." In Carl Frankenstein, ed., *Between Past and Future: Essays and Studies on Aspects of Immigrant Absorption in Israel.* Jerusalem: Henrietta Szold Foundation for Child and Youth Welfare, 1953, pp. 109–46.

Parfitt, Tudor. *The Road to Redemption: The Jews of the Yemen, 1900–1950.* New York: E. J. Brill, 1996.

CHAPTER

22

Egypt and the Sudan

Jean-Marc Ran Oppenheim

Egypt and the Sudan lie in the northeast corner of Africa. Separated from southwest Asia by the Sinai Peninsula and the Suez Canal, Egypt is on the southern littoral of the Mediterranean Sea. The Red Sea forms the east coast of Egypt, and its western and southern frontiers are contiguous with Libya and the Sudan, respectively. About 95 percent of Egypt's surface is desert; the remaining 5 percent is the Nile river valley and the Nile delta. The Sudan shares a border with Egypt to the north; the Red Sea and Ethiopia are to the east, Uganda and Congo to the south, and Libya, Chad, and the Central African Republic to the west.

The Nile River, which runs from the Sudan through Egypt, has been pivotal to the agricultural economies of both countries since the beginning of settled society in neolithic times; it united them during the rise of the great civilization of ancient times. Most of Egypt's cities and towns are located in the Nile river valley and delta, home to about 98 percent of the population. Similarly, more than 50 percent of the Sudanese population is settled in an area known as el-Gezira, an area north of the confluence of the Blue and White Niles in the Sudan's middle latitudes.

PEOPLES

Of Egypt's more than sixty-five million people, 93 percent are Sunni Muslim and about 6 percent are Coptic Christian. Ethnically, much of Egypt's northern population is Arab, while its southern inhabitants are mostly Nubians—closer in ethnicity to their sub-Saharan African neighbors than to the Arabs. Until the 1950s Egypt hosted Italians, Greeks, Maltese, Armenians, Syro-Lebanese, and Jews who had arrived in the nineteenth century at the same time as the colonizing British and French. The non-Jewish foreigners were Roman Catholic, Protestant, Eastern Orthodox, or members of the diverse Levantine churches, both Catholic and Orthodox. The vast majority of Jews living in Egypt in the modern period were either of Sephardic or Middle East origin; few were of Ashkenazic origin. Egypt also had a small number of Karaites.

The Sudan's population of more than thirty-one million is about 70 percent Sunni Muslim, concentrated in the center and the north; 25 percent of the Sudanese follow traditional African and animist practices; the other 5 percent are Christians—Roman Catholics, small pockets of Protestants, and Copts. The Sudan's Christian population is almost entirely the result of nineteenth- and twentieth-century Western missionary activity.

Like Egypt, during the first part of the twentieth century the Sudan also attracted a small number of foreign-resident minorities, including about one thousand Jews who lived and worked there, mostly in the capital, Khartoum. Initially, they arrived through Egypt after 1898, but they continued to emigrate from the eastern Mediterranean and Egypt until the 1950s. By the beginning of the 1960s, however, Sudanese and regional politics had forced Jews to leave the country.

HISTORY

Napoleon Bonaparte's landing in Alexandria with his troops and some scholars in July 1798 catapulted Egypt onto the stage of modern Western history. In 1801 the French army was expelled, however, and Egypt was restored to the Ottoman Empire. The Ottoman commander, Muhammad Ali Pasha, remained in Egypt as the governor appointed by Istanbul, but he soon consolidated his reign and established a dynasty, which ruled until 1952.

In 1820 Muhammad Ali Pasha invaded the Sudan to obtain slaves and conscripts for his army. Except for a brief period from 1885 to 1898, the Sudan remained a dominion of Egypt until 1954. From 1885 to 1898, during the period known as the Mahdiyya, the Sudan was ruled by the Mahdi, a self-proclaimed Muslim messianic leader who expelled the Turko-Egyptians, imposed his brand of revivalist Islam on all who lived in the Sudan, including Jews and Christians, and defeated Anglo-Egyptian efforts to depose him. The British reconquered the Sudan in 1898 and, through the Anglo-Egyptian Condominium Agreement of 1899, governed it officially in partnership with Egypt—but in reality, the British ruled unilaterally, until they proffered independence to the Sudan in January 1956.

In the 1860s the American Civil War propelled Egypt once again onto the international stage; the Union blockade of the Confederacy cut Britain and France off from their customary supplies of cotton from the American South, so Egypt became a major exporter of cotton to the West. This wealth generated the rapid urbanization of Cairo and the port city of Alexandria as well as the construction of the Suez Canal, which was completed in 1869. It also attracted foreign entrepreneurs, including Jews, to Egypt. The pace of this modernization ultimately led to the near bankruptcy of the Egyptian economy. A nationalist revolt in 1882 protested intrusive Anglo-French controls of Egypt's finances. Britain landed troops and restored order to safeguard the European residents and to oversee the repayment of Egypt's creditors, of which Britain was the largest. The British occupation lasted until 1954 and had a seismic effect on Egyptian politics and society until the revolution of 1952.

In 1914 the British declared Egypt a protectorate in order to safeguard the Suez Canal. The Egyptians revolted in 1919, in their frustration to achieve independence, forcing Britain to grant Egypt its nominal independence while keeping for itself four areas of direct control: British imperial communications; the defense of Egyptian territory; the status of minorities; and direct supervision over the Sudan, which had been part of Egypt since its conquest by Muhammad Ali in 1821. The third point is of significance for the country's Jewish population, because the British used it to protect the civil rights of local resident minorities, including Jews.

Hampered by British manipulation, palace intrigue, and myopic self-interest, Egypt's emerging political parties never succeeded in ousting the British or establishing a tradition of democratic politics. This failure was partly responsible for a momentous development: the formation of an Islamist movement in the 1920s known as the Society of the Muslim Brothers, whose goal was the eventual establishment of Islamic law for governing the nation. Another momentous development for the Jews of Egypt was the passage in 1947 of the Company Law, which stipulated that henceforth the majority of the board members of Egyptian joint stock companies were to be Egyptian nationals—implying Muslims and Copts rather than any of the minorities with Egyptian nationality. After World War II four events led to the demise of Egypt's Jewish community: the defeat of the Egyptian army in the 1948 Arab-Israeli War, the revolution of 1952, the nationalization of the Suez Canal in July 1956, with the ensuing Suez War in October 1956, and the thorough Egyptianization of the hitherto foreign-dominated economy. All led to a modern-day exodus.

The post–World War II period in the Sudan also marked the beginning of the end of British rule there. In 1948 the British began the "Sudanization" of the higher civil service, promoted the integration of the south with the north, and allowed the election of a legislative assembly. The Sudan became independent in January 1956. In 1958 a military coup d'état destroyed the constitutional structure, and the Sudan aligned itself with pan-Arabist and anti-Israel regional positions. These developments led to the departure of the country's Jewish community.

THE JEWS OF EGYPT AND THE SUDAN

After the Exodus under Moses and Aaron, some Jews returned to live in Egypt in the Hellenistic period (third century B.C.E.). Jewish communities of various sizes existed in Egypt during Byzantine rule, the Arab conquest of 641 C.E., and the subsequent medieval Islamic dynasties. The rich intellectual and vibrant community life, as described in the Geniza material of the eleventh century C.E., deteriorated after the onset of Mamluk and Ottoman rule.

In the middle of the nineteenth century the Jewish community of Egypt numbered 6,000 to 7,000 and had lived there for centuries. By 1897 it had grown to 25,000 and in the aftermath of World War I had reached more than 60,000. Although interwar figures of the Egyptian census place the number of Jews in Egypt at more than 63,000, reliable estimates place the actual number at 75,000 to 80,000, the peak of Jewish population in Egypt. By the interwar years approximately 30 percent of the community held Egyptian passports, 25 percent were foreign nationals or foreign protected, and the remaining 45 to 50 percent were stateless and thus unprotected by the capitulations, the legal and fiscal privileges that the Ottomans extended to foreign merchants in the sixteenth century.

The Sephardic migration to Egypt from Italy, southern Europe, the Ottoman Empire, and Corfu had begun in the early nineteenth century and continued until the 1920s; most settled primarily in the cities. Sephardic and North African Jews arrived in Egypt mostly between the 1890s and 1907, when the Egyptian stock market crashed; they settled mostly in Cairo and in the larger delta towns. Jews from Yemen and Aden on their way to Palestine between 1900 and 1914 could get no farther than Egypt because they ran out of money; they eventually settled along the towns of the Suez Canal and in Cairo. Ashkenazic Jews from Russia, Romania, and Poland arrived in the late nineteenth and early twentieth centuries and settled primarily in Cairo. During 1914 and 1915 more than eleven thousand

Ashkenazim expelled from Palestine by the Ottoman authorities arrived in Alexandria, Cairo, and the Canal Zone. Most returned to Palestine or Eastern Europe when World War I concluded, although many stayed in Egypt and became active in the local Zionist movement.

The nucleus of the Jewish community in the Sudan was formed in the early 1880s, when eight Jewish families moved south from Egypt. Seeking to expand the trade of gum arabic, then the Sudan's primary commodity, through Egypt to Europe and Arabia, the Jews settled in Omdurman and in Port Sudan on the Red Sea. At its peak in the interwar period the Jewish community numbered approximately one thousand, representing countries of the Mediterranean littoral, Syria, and Iraq; almost all had come through Egypt. Most were Sephardim, but Ashkenazim formed about 10 percent of the community and migrated from Egypt to the Sudan in the 1920s.

THE HETEROGENEITY OF EGYPTIAN AND SUDANESE JEWRY

Most Jews in Egypt maintained the strong cultural identities of their geographic and historical origins. They included, in addition to indigenous Jews, those from Italy, Greece, North Africa, Iraq, Syria, Turkey, and Yemen. The indigenous Jews were about 15 percent of the community and lived mostly in the Cairo Jewish quarter and in the smaller towns of the delta and Upper Egypt. They were at the lower end of the socioeconomic ladder, usually eking out a living in small trade, traditional crafts, or begging. The poorest depended on the charity of the community or the wealthy. Because of a high degree of assimilation to Egyptian culture in daily life, dress, customs, and eating habits, they spoke Egyptian Arabic rather than any specific Judeo-Arabic.

Jews in Egypt from Yemen, North Africa, and, with some exceptions, the Arab parts of the Ottoman Empire shared the low status of the indigenous Egyptian Jews. They lived in the poorer sections of Alexandria, Suez, or Port Said, engaging in petty trade and crafts. They retained their traditions, customs, and dialects—often for generations. Not all Jews were poor, however; some families from North Africa, Syria, and Iraq brought with them experience in regional and often international trade, language skills, and capital. They settled in Cairo and Alexandria, as well as in the smaller cities along the Canal, and by the second or third generation they had adopted the cultural ethos of the cosmopolitan middle and upper classes. They also abandoned the Arabic language and culture.

Iberian Jews began arriving in Egypt in 1492 and 1497 in the wake of their expulsion from Spain and Portugal. Among the Jews attracted to Egypt by British rule were entrepreneurs from the Mediterranean littoral, especially from North Africa, Salonika, Italy, Turkey, Syria, and Iraq. Because they benefited from a superior education, international business connections, and in some cases wealth, they quickly assimilated into the established middle class and gained influence within the community. Almost all spoke French, Italian, and Greek in addition to Judeo-Spanish or Judeo-Arabic.

The Italian Jews were a distinctive group. Primarily settled in Alexandria, they were prominent in both its Jewish and Italian colonies. Not all Italian Jews had come from Italy; many had come from other parts of the Mediterranean and only later acquired Italian nationality. All, however, identified with Italy, its language, culture, and politics—even when it was under fascist rule from 1922 to 1944.

While the subgroups of Sephardim represented diverse origins and layers of socioeconomic identities, they coalesced into the official Cairo or Alexandria Jewish community. Nonetheless, they maintained a sense of separate identity, based on regional origin—as reflected in synagogue rituals and in numerous associations such as the Società Israelitico-Corsirese di Mutuo Soccorso, founded in 1913; the Association des Juifs Orientaux, formed in 1916; the Cercle de la Jeunesse, established in 1920; and the Union des Juifs Hellènes, opened in 1934.

Ashkenazic Jews had arrived in Egypt in the sixteenth and seventeenth centuries in small numbers. In 1865 they tried to form their own community, but this effort foundered because of local resistance to institutional separatism. Their community increased substantially from 1880 to 1914, as Jews left the pogroms in Eastern Europe and especially at the beginning of World War I, when the Ottoman authorities expelled eleven thousand Jews from Palestine. Ashkenazim formed a distinctive subgroup within Egyptian Jewry, with their own rabbi, president, and council in Cairo. They cooperated with the larger community on questions of education and health, as well as in areas of concern to all Jews living in Egypt regardless of their rite and origin. The Ashkenazic community was divided along lines of geographic origin, language, and customs. The largest group came from Eastern Europe; 90 percent spoke Yiddish as their native language and the rest Russian. The use of their own languages and a cultivated European-style insularity maintained a gulf between Ashkenazim and Sephardim; however, signs of tension disappeared by the third generation.

The Karaites, whose numbers in the interwar years ranged from four to six thousand, formed a distinctly different group within Egyptian Jewry, and a greater percentage of Karaites than other Jews had Egyptian nationality. Seeking to underline their separateness from the Rabbanites (traditional Jews), the Karaites in Cairo had their own chief rabbi and community president. However, the Egyptian government did not officially recognize the Karaites as a separate community, preferring instead to have the Rabbanite community act as the sole representative for all Egyptian Jewry. Like the Ashkenazim, the Karaites had a middle class by the end of World War I.

In contrast to the socioeconomic heterogeneity of Egypt's Jewry, the Jews of the Sudan were a fairly homogeneous group because of the timing of the community's founding, its slow expansion, and the relatively focused economic opportunities requiring capital, experience in commerce, and connections to established export markets. The Sudan had no indigent Jews; they assimilated effortlessly into the established economic elite of foreign residents—Greeks, Italians, Armenians, Syrians, and Britons. While the Ashkenazim formed a tenth of the community, intercommunity marriage with Middle Eastern Jewry was extensive, thus eliminating the ritual and cultural dichotomies that were so evident in Egypt. Moreover, the Sudan had no Karaites.

NEIGHBORHOODS AND SPATIAL STRUCTURE

While the vast majority of Egyptian Jewry lived in Cairo and Alexandria, Jewish communities also existed in cities and towns throughout the delta and along the Suez Canal. Most of the Jews living in these provincial cities and towns relocated to Cairo and Alexandria after World War I, when these two cities became the commercial and cultural magnets of the country. Unlike Cairo, Alexandria never had a Jewish quarter; its Jewish community, as in most of Egypt's cities, shared neighborhoods along socioeconomic and occupational, rather than ethnic or religious, axes with members of the city's other foreign communities.

Cairo had adjacent Rabbanite and Karaite quarters. By the 1860s the two quarters' notable families had left to settle in newly developed Western-style suburbs such as Shubra, Abbasiya, and Tawfikiya. When these areas lost their exclusive character in the years before World War I and became middle-class neighborhoods, members of the upper classes, Jews included, moved again, to such newly developed areas along the Nile as Zamalek, Garden City, and

Giza and were still to be found there in the 1950s. The Ashkenazic community had originally formed its own neighborhood, bordering on the Jewish quarter, which continued to exhibit the characteristics of a traditional Eastern European shtetl as late as the 1940s. Even there, however, only members of the lower class remained in the area, because Ashkenazim who had achieved middle- and upper middle-class status had moved to neighborhoods favored by the city's other bourgeoisies.

Jews of the Sudan lived mostly in Khartoum and Omdurman, site of the first Jewish community. While the Sudan had no Jewish quarter, Omdurman had a quarter for converts to Islam. Unlike the Cairo Jewish quarter, which was home to the indigents of the Jewish community, the Omdurman quarter was an urban concentration of all those who had been forced to convert to Islam during the Mahdiyya. After the reconquest of the Sudan by the British in 1898, those Jews and Christians who had lived in the quarter of Islamic converts remained and were later joined by well-to-do Sudanese Muslims. A number of Jewish families also settled in Wad Medani, capital of the Blue Nile Province and center of the cotton plantations, located 175 miles south of Khartoum. Those Jews who were involved in maritime commerce continued to live in Port Sudan. Almost no Jews lived in the rural areas of northern Sudan and none in the southern part of the country.

THE EDUCATION AND MODERNIZATION OF EGYPTIAN JEWRY

Education within the Egyptian Jewish communities determined much more than just intellectual and professional trajectories. It was also a barometer of socioeconomic and cultural hierarchies that were represented by Jewish schools, schools of the Alliance Israélite Universelle (AIU), and non-Jewish schools that comprised foreign private secular, as well as Christian missionary, schools.

Until the middle of the nineteenth century, the Jews of Egypt had little formal education. When community schools were introduced, the emphasis on secular and religious subjects was equal. As the nineteenth century progressed, the more successful Jewish families left the Cairo Jewish quarter and sent their sons and daughters to the foreign schools that charged tuition; during the twentieth century only the indigent patronized the free Jewish community schools, which were maintained by the community or by wealthy individuals. Indigent Jews throughout the country relied on community schools.

Ironically, traditional rabbinic education was chronically weak in Egypt. By the interwar years only five or six yeshivas, three of which were in Cairo, existed in Egypt, with the result that all of Egypt's rabbis came from abroad. Only a few in the community knew Hebrew, because French was the main language of instruction in the community's schools.

After the 1860s Jewish education was transformed from a traditional system of religious schools into a modern one following European, especially French, standards. Between the end of the nineteenth century and the end of World War I, the widespread influence of French secular education and culture within the community owed to the influence of the AIU. This influence was still paramount in the interwar period in the cities and towns of the delta. After World War I the Alliance lost ground to the tuition-charging private and missionary schools favored by the community's well-to-do, and only the poorer members of the community continued to send their children to community schools. Nonetheless, until 1947 Jewish educational standards, whether in community or AIU schools, equaled those of other foreign minorities and were far superior to Coptic and Muslim standards.

Within the subgroups of the Egyptian Jewish community, distinct patterns emerged as alternate sources of education became available. The children of Karaites attended Egyptian or British rather than Jewish or French schools before entering the professions, commerce, or banking. Ashkenazim of the second and third generation sent their children to the same schools, whether community schools for the poor or the French lycées of the bourgeoisie. Although both used French as the language of instruction, the foreign secular and missionary schools undoubtedly had a substantial influence on the Egyptian Jewish community. From the last third of the nineteenth century on, both Cairo and Alexandria boasted a large number of such schools. Each ethnic community had its complement of schools teaching in its native tongue, and while children of the Jewish bourgeoisie patronized primarily English and French schools, Jewish students also attended Italian, Greek, and German schools. The European education and language skills thus acquired afforded Jews access to positions of leadership in business, the professions, and government administration. The resulting multilingualism and contacts with non-Jews who shared a similar education added to the assimilation of Jews into a well-to-do cosmopolitan class whose ethos mirrored the values of socioeconomic peers rather than that of their poorer coreligionists. This diversity of education within the Egyptian Jewish community generated differences in language, culture, residence, lifestyle, status and, ultimately, identity.

The Sudan's Jewish community had two choices for schooling: abroad or in-country. Boys and girls of primary school age attended the Sisters' School in Khartoum, Omdurman, or Wad Medani. Boys of secondary school age then attended Comboni College in Khartoum, while the girls remained at the Sisters' School. Both were Canadian Catholic missionary institutions that used English as the language of instruction. For most girls of the Jewish community formal education ended there. Occasionally, boys would be sent to boarding school at elite institutions in Egypt or Britain before attending university either in Khartoum or Britain. Formal Jewish education was disseminated to boys either privately in the community or at Comboni College, where a teacher of Hebrew and biblical studies, paid by the community, would lead classes while gentile boys attended classes in catechism. Jewish Bible classes at Comboni were conducted in Arabic, with occasional use of Hebrew terms.

THE LANGUAGES OF EGYPTIAN AND SUDANESE JEWRY

In Egypt geographic origin and education determined the languages spoken by Jews. While indigenous Jews and the Karaites spoke Egyptian Arabic, and a number were literate in Modern Standard Arabic, Jews from other Arab countries were usually conversant in the dialects of their regions: Iraqi, Syrian, Yemeni, and Tunisian Arabic. Although the Iberian Jews spoke Judeo-Spanish, they often knew French, Italian, Turkish, or Arabic. Greek Jews spoke Greek, Italian Jews conversed in Italian, and the Ashkenazim spoke Yiddish in addition to their native German, Polish, Russian, or Romanian. Until the end of the nineteenth century almost all the aforementioned groups limited their languages of origin to the family circle and their compatriots. Upper- and middle-class Jews used one of the dominant European languages among themselves and with the rest of non-Arab society. Until the 1870s Italian was the lingua franca of Alexandria and to a significant extent Cairo as well. By the turn of the twentieth century French had replaced Italian as the language of the elites, despite the British occupation and administration of Egypt. English was indeed spoken by well-to-do Jews in some, although not all, business and official circles. Privately, and especially socially, French was the dominant language. In fact, all the Jewish communities of Egypt held their business meetings in French.

In the middle of the nineteenth century the indigenous community rarely used Hebrew or Arabic except in liturgy. By the twentieth century the French-speaking schools of the Jewish community taught Hebrew, while in foreign schools it had achieved the dubious rank of a classical language, along with ancient Greek and Latin. Although the religious schools, the yeshivas, offered Hebrew courses, their focus was liturgical rather than vernacular. Only the Kevutsa Bar Kochba, a small Zionist group, used Modern Hebrew as the language of communication. Other Zionist groups used French primarily and Arabic secondarily.

Arabic, the language of the country (imported in the seventh century by the Islamic conquest), was for the vast majority of Egyptian Jews a foreign tongue. Although Arabic had been the language of communication and business of the established Jewish merchants, financiers, and artisans until the midnineteenth century, by the interwar years it was spoken primarily by poor Jews of Cairo's Jewish quarter, the Karaite community, and by Jews living in the delta and Suez Canal Zone towns. Most of the remainder of the community used Arabic primarily to communicate with those Egyptian shopkeepers who did not know a European language, domestics, and the indigenous lower classes on the streets of Cairo and Alexandria. In 1920 the Zionist movement initially published an Arabic edition of its newspaper *Israel,* but it suspended its publication in 1933 from lack of readership. Another newspaper published in Arabic by the Jewish community, *Al-Shams,* had a limited readership. Jewish commercial middlemen knew Arabic well, as did those employed in the agricultural sectors, primarily as cotton graders, because business took them to the hinterland.

The linguistic cosmopolitanism of Egyptian Jewry did not apply to the Jews of the Sudan. Most members of the Sudan's Jewish community spoke Arabic and English interchangeably, because English was the universal language of business in the Sudan, especially among the managerial and entrepreneurial classes. It was also the language used in the higher levels of the civil administration. Retailers spoke Arabic and/or English to their clientele. The language spoken at home was based on the origin of the parents: Egyptian Jews in the Sudan used mostly French, whereas others spoke Arabic, English, or a combination of all three. Unlike most Jews in Egypt, those of the Sudan knew Arabic, and most men could read and write it. Thus formal and informal conversation with indigenous Sudanese took place in Arabic.

JEWS IN THE ECONOMIES OF EGYPT AND THE SUDAN

Until the midnineteenth century Egypt's Jews, concentrated in Cairo's Jewish quarter, were involved in finance as money lenders, money changers, and pawnbrokers. They traded precious metals and stones, fruit, tobacco, silk, cotton, and cloth. They were tailors, silk weavers, and cigarette rollers. Because of cotton and sugarcane cultivation, a few Jewish families (the Tilches, Aghions, and Addas) benefited from the trade with Europe and became wealthy. The subsequent expansion of the Egyptian economy attracted entrepreneurs from around the Mediterranean, Jews included. Using their relatively high educations, their language skills, and their international networks of family and kinship ties, the Jews of Egypt contributed to the pivotal aspects of this economic boom—the banking and credit sectors.

The experience and reputation of established money lenders in the Cairo Jewish quarter—Sephardic families like the Cattaouis, Mosseris, de Menasces, Suareses, and Rolos, who had arrived in Egypt via Italy by the end of the eighteenth century—meant that they were able to make a rapid and smooth transition into international trade and modern banking. Diversification soon followed in real estate and land investment, infrastructure, and construction. Moreover, these families often formed financial and commercial alliances that lasted for generations through business partnerships and marriages. Their international contacts served to channel significant French and British capital into such major Egyptian projects as the founding of the National Bank of Egypt in 1898; the construction of the first Aswan Dam, completed in 1902; and the establishment in the 1890s of the Sugar Company of Egypt, which became a monopoly employing more than twenty thousand workers by the 1920s. The wealth and influence of such merchant princes allowed them to acquire substantial interests in the public transportation systems and waterworks of Cairo, Alexandria, and cities throughout the delta. Moreover, these Egyptian Jewish financiers had links to such prestigious international banking dynasties as the Rothschilds and Lazar Frères. The leaders of the Jewish communities of Cairo and Alexandria were elected from these financial dynasties. The Cattaoui family monopolized the presidency of the Cairo community until 1948, while the vice presidency was the preserve of the Mosseri clan. In Alexandria the de Menasces led the community until World War I, when their Austro-Hungarian title and nationality forced their replacement by the Aghion and the Rolo families, all British subjects.

While Sephardim who had been in the country before the 1800s held the monopoly on finance, land development, and infrastructure, the field of domestic commerce became almost the exclusive preserve of those Middle Eastern Jewish immigrants who arrived after the 1860s. Primarily engaged in importing European manufactured goods and exporting Egyptian cotton, and having weathered the Egyptian stock market crash of 1907, this second tier of notables made its mark on the Egyptian economy by establishing highly visible commercial enterprises, such as department stores, manufacturing concerns, and urban development schemes. The Hannaux, Cicurel, and Chemla families established large department stores that were the Egyptian versions of, say, Bloomingdale's or Macy's. Joseph Smouha, who emigrated from Iraq before World War I, bought a sizable swamp outside Alexandria, drained it, and built Smouha City, which offered Bauhaus-style villas on individual plots and featured a sporting club with a horse-racing track and a championship golf course. A Cicurel and a Cattaoui were among the founders of the Bank Misr in 1920, a consortium of financial and investment services aimed at weaning Egyptian dependence from foreign capital for industrial growth. Their involvement emphasized Jewish interest in the development of local economic projects.

Jews were also well represented in the professions, due partly to their high standards of education and partly to their widespread knowledge of European languages, which were vital in the practice of law, medicine, engineering, architecture, and so on. In the interwar years 14 percent of the lawyers who were registered with Egypt's Mixed Courts were Jews. The Mixed Courts, whose legal code was based on the Napoleonic Code, adjudicated in French all cases involving foreign nationals. Most Jewish physicians practicing in Egypt were immigrants, with many Ashkenazim among them. In fact, in contrast to the Sephardim, whose leadership was monopolized by merchant princes and financiers, leadership of the Ashkenazim was held from early on by professionals. Jews in Egypt also figured prominently in the higher levels of business administration; in 1943 they held 15 percent of the directorships and 16 percent of the management positions in joint stock companies. In the 1930s and 1940s Jews made up 75 to 90 percent of the registered Cairo and Alexandria stockbrokers.

Despite their successes, the vast majority of Egyptian Jews, regardless of origin, belonged to the middle, lower middle, and lower classes. Whether self-employed shop owners, brokers, or commercial agents, members of the middle class were especially prone to financial insecurity. Jewish members of the lower middle class swelled the rank-and-file of clerks in firms, retail shops, and government departments. The artisans included the Karaite working class and worked mostly in textiles, gold- and silversmithing, and precious stone cutting. Until World War I the cigarette and tobacco industries employed large numbers of Jewish workers.

At the bottom of the socioeconomic scale were those Jews who were either irregularly or never employed. Chronic poverty was a fact of life in the provincial towns of the delta and the Suez Canal Zone. Even Cairo and Alexandria were not immune to large numbers of poor Jews. In 1937 nearly one-third of the male population of the Cairo Jewish quarter was unemployed; the statistic for 1947 was not much better. Many at the bottom of the socioeconomic ladder depended on the charitable institutions of the community for their survival—institutions fueled by the wealth of well-to-do Egyptian Jews. Despite this philanthropic tradition, the Jewish press constantly chronicled what it perceived as a blight on the community: high unemployment, begging, and illiteracy among the Jewish poor, and the moral and material abandonment of the community's less fortunate.

Thus the Egyptian Jewish economic community has always contained a small but extremely affluent and influential upper and upper middle class, 5 to 10 percent of the community. Anecdotal chroniclers and contemporary memoirists writing nearly half a century after the exodus of 1948–56 tend to focus on these people, giving the impression of pervasive wealth and cosmopolitanism while overlooking the Jewish lower classes, which comprised as much as 25 percent of the Jewish population in Cairo and Alexandria and undoubtedly a higher proportion in the provincial cities and towns of the delta and the Suez Canal Zone.

Jews of the Sudan also participated in commerce, finance, and the professions throughout their tenure in that country. The original Jewish families who came to the Sudan from Egypt in the 1880s were traders who, both before and during the Mahdiyya, exported through Egypt goatskins and sheepskins, ivory, and ostrich feathers, then highly valued for ladies' hats. They also exported gum arabic, the Sudan's most important cash crop until 1925, when it was replaced by cotton. Gum arabic is a water-soluble gum obtained from acacia trees and used in the manufacture of inks, adhesives, pharmaceuticals, and confections. Sudanese Jews also imported textiles, soaps, and other manufactured products into the Sudan.

Not until 1898, when railway links with Egypt were established, did more Jews move to the Sudan. By 1916, when the railroad had reached Khartoum, Jewish merchants were retailing cotton and silk piece goods, textiles, and haberdashery. A few settled in the Blue Nile Province where, as in Egypt, they worked as cotton graders and classifiers, crop purchasers, and in other aspects of cotton agriculture. The largest number of Jews settling in the Sudan chose Omdurman, located across the Nile from Khartoum, to do business. Such major Cairo Jewish wholesale import firms as B. Nathan and Company and Giulio Padova and Company opened branches in Omdurman. Other prominent families included the Benous, who specialized in gum arabic; the Serousis, who exported animal hides and whose descendants continue the trade with branches in Nigeria and New York; and the Dweks, who imported textiles and had originally arrived from Aleppo in Syria via Cairo. Other prominent merchant families whose names reflect their geographic origin included the Pintos from Italy, the Safadis from Iran, the Feinsteins from Central Europe, and the Castros from Turkey.

Jews of the Sudan did not begin to enter the professions until the second generation acquired the education and training necessary, either in the Sudan or more often abroad. Unlike Egyptian Jews, however, they did not come to dominate any professional sector out of proportion to their numbers in the population. That was a British privilege. The one sector in which the Sudan's Jews did have a significant role was cotton brokering. Most of the Sudan's cotton companies had Egyptian origins, and they financed the cultivation of the crop through venture capital. Sudanese Jews also classified or graded and purchased the product of the various plantations.

In the Sudan business also had a social aspect. The Jews of the Sudan mainly married within their community rather than with Jews from other Middle Eastern countries; thus commercial dynasties were formed and partnerships established. Also, as in Egypt, the Sudan's various ethnocultural groups of foreign residents who lived through the period of the Condominium, the British-dominated Anglo-Egyptian Sudan (1899–1954), adjusted to one another through a sociability whose ethos was rooted in business.

Because business was at the heart and substance of the Jewish community of the Sudan, the vast majority of the community could be classified as middle class. No indigent Jews lived in the Sudan.

DOMESTIC POLITICS, ZIONISM, AND THE JEWS OF EGYPT AND THE SUDAN

Given the role of Jews in Egypt's economy, it is not surprising that a number were also involved in Egyptian politics. One of the first advocates of territorial nationalism in the late nineteenth century was Yaᶜqub Sanuᶜ, an Egyptian Jew and prolific propagandist known by his Arabic pen name, Abu Nadara (he who wears glasses). With the end of World War I and the formation of liberal political parties, prominent Jews joined the movement for Egyptian independence. Felix Benzakein, Vita Sonsino, and David Hazan joined the Wafd Party at its inception. In 1923 Hazan was condemned to death in absentia by the British because of his political activities.

Other Jews joined either the Wafd or competing political parties. Leon Castro, a lawyer and personal friend of Saad Zaghlul, the founder of the Wafd and the grand old man of Egyptian politics, directed Wafdist propaganda in Europe. Joseph Cattaoui joined the Liberal Constitutionalist Party in 1922. When Zaghlul returned to Alexandria from a British-imposed exile, Joseph de Picciotto, an Italian Jew, organized an immense reception in his honor. Also deeply involved in movements for Egyptian independence were three Jewish lawyers: Moise Dichy, Isidore Feldman, and Zaki Orebi. In the interwar years the Association de la Jeunesse Juive Egyptienne demonstrated on behalf of the Wafd. Through the 1920s and 1930s the discourse of Egyptian politics focused on independence from Britain and a concept of national identity that was essentially secular. As long as the Egyptian Jewish community embraced these aspects of Egyptian national aspirations, they were made to feel welcome by the liberal political parties of the interwar period. Until the 1950s Jews served as representatives in the Egyptian parliament. In addition to the aforementioned de Picciotto, a number of Cattaouis and Haim Nahoum, the chief rabbi of Egypt (1925–60), were senators, while Felix Benzakein and another Cattaoui were parliamentary deputies.

The communist movement was another area in which Egyptian Jews expressed their political priorities. Begun in 1905 in Cairo by Ashkenazic immigrants who were members of the Jewish Bund, a socialist movement, the communist movement was strengthened by Joseph Rosenthal, a Russian Jew who was born in Beirut and who moved to Alexandria in the 1890s. In 1921 he and a few Muslims founded the Egyptian Socialist Party, which changed its name to the Egyptian Communist Party upon joining the Third International the following year. By the 1930s a number of groups comprised mostly of Jews, members of other minorities, and leftist Egyptian intellectuals published numerous journals advocating a Marxist approach to Egyptian social and political problems. Marcel Israel, Henri Curiel, Hillel Schwartz, Raymond Aghion, and Ezra Harari were the most prominent Jewish activists in the Egyptian communist movement of the 1940s and 1950s. Along with proletarianization, it debated the issues of Arabism and Palestine.

The German antipathy toward the Jews in Europe first introduced political friction between Jews and Egyptians. Adolf Hitler's rise to power in 1933, and Egyptian Jews' awareness of his programs, caused significant concerns in the community. Nazis with the German community in Egypt undertook a campaign of anti-Jewish propaganda that only served to coalesce a significant portion of the Jewish community into an anti-Nazi movement. In April 1933 the Cairo B'nai B'rith formed the League Against German Anti-Semitism, an umbrella association of all Jewish institutions in Egypt, and the International Students League Against Anti-Semitism. Urging a boycott of trade with Germany—which was Egypt's third-largest trade partner in the early 1930s—the Jewish efforts at isolating and denouncing German anti-Semitism in Egypt had only limited effect. These efforts would soon be overtaken by the development of an equally momentous, and potentially far more destructive, movement for Egyptian Jewry: the formation of indigenous fascist and Islamist groups.

By the end of the 1930s, in tandem with the 1936 Arab Revolt in Palestine, Egyptian ultranationalist and Islamist groups were publishing blacklists of Jewish merchants. They placed bombs—which did not do much damage—in a Cairo synagogue and in private Jewish homes in the delta. The Wafd condemned those attacks, stating that Egyptian Jews were also sons of Egypt, but the Zionist genie had been let out of the bottle. As during the Palestine disturbances of 1929, leaders of the Egyptian Jewish community used their contacts in high political and diplomatic circles to try to put a lid on anti-Zionist and anti-Jewish propaganda. Their approach to the burgeoning problem was to try to remain inconspicuous—and thus avoid drawing attention to the existence of a Jewish minority in Egypt.

The outbreak of World War II in 1939 and the German advance across North Africa greatly alarmed the Jewish population of Egypt. Indeed, Alexandrian Jews fled by the thousands to Cairo as Gen. Erwin Rommel's Afrika Corps sped toward Egypt. Although most Italian Jews in the community had strong patriotic feelings for Italy, in 1940 they formed antifascist committees to counter a continuing and palpable fascist influence; nonetheless, a few prominent individuals remained loyal to fascist Italy. Egyptian Jews who held British, French, or Greek passports fought in British, French, or Greek units for the duration of the war. Wealthy Jews gave large sums of money to the British war effort in Egypt and were active in such aspects of its civilian structure as civil defense units and the formation of clubs, hospitals, and convalescent homes for officers and soldiers stationed in Egypt.

By the end of the war in 1945, the focus of community concerns had returned to the increasingly strident Islamists and their anti-Zionist rhetoric. In late 1945 Cairo police reported significant anti-Jewish feelings in the capital. On November 2, 1945, Balfour Day, a massive demonstration called by various Islamist and nationalist groups to protest British policy in Palestine turned violent and ended in arson that destroyed the Ashkenazic synagogue near the Cairo Jewish quarter, as well as in the looting of shops in the quarter itself. Shortly after, Chief Rabbi Nahoum, under pressure from the community leadership, wrote a note to the Egyptian prime minister, al-Nuqrashi Pasha, in which he essentially repudiated Zionist claims to Palestine.

The Zionist movement in Egypt was, from its inception, a reflection of local conditions and priorities. Sephardic-Ashkenazic tensions, linguistic diversity, and broad socioeconomic differences among Egyptian Jewry all served to chart a fluctuating course for Zionist activity in Egypt. Initially, a phenomenon limited mainly to lower- and lower middle-class Ashkenazim but including Sephardim, Zionism had established a few barely functioning outposts in Cairo, Alexandria, and a few towns in the delta by World War I. The war, with its Ashkenazic refugees from Ottoman Palestine, provided the movement in Egypt with an impetus for a few mass rallies to greet the Balfour Declaration and the visit to Egypt of the Zionist leader Chaim Weizman in 1918. The Zionist Federation of Egypt had been created in 1917. Prominent local Jews sat on its committees, and it published an official organ. Yet these efforts and the Zionists' subsequent momentum were deceiving, because the vast majority of Egyptian Jewry had no interest in Zionism. Even the Zionist movement was riddled by internal tensions that mirrored intracommunity dynamics and concerns.

To be sure, most Jews in Egypt and the Sudan were concerned about Palestine, the Yishuv, and the welfare of Jews in the British mandate, which would become official in 1922. The wives of the well-to-do periodically undertook fund-raising drives, and Jewish delegations went to or arrived from the Yishuv. Yet few Egyptian or Sudanese Jews elected to leave for Palestine. This reluctance to relocate reflected the most important of a number of factors in Egyptian Jewish apathy to Zionism: the comfortable and secure standard of living enjoyed by middle- and upper-class Jews in Egypt and the Sudan and the relative absence of anti-Jewish or anti-Semitic feelings in both countries. In addition to these two basic conditions antithetical to Zionist activity, the Egyptian Jewish elite viewed Zionism as a lower middle-class European issue that was unrelated to local conditions; it even posed a threat to their privileged position by drawing unnecessary attention to their communities. Thus the Ashkenazic essence of the movement, combined with its socialist and atheist aspects, rendered it highly suspicious to the Sephardim and the religiously traditional Jews of Egypt and the Sudan.

The rise of Yishuv-Arab tensions within Palestine—especially after the 1929 Western Wall riots and during the Arab Revolt of 1936–39—led to a number of measures by the community leadership vis-à-vis Zionism. In

1930 Nahoum imposed a total ban on fund-raising for the Yishuv, and although this continued clandestinely, Zionist activity ceased, and Zionist organizations went underground. During the more serious troubles of 1936–39, when radical nationalists and Islamists accused Egyptian Jews of being fifth columnists (spies) for the Zionists, community leaders used their influence and money to enlist the support of the authorities, the press, and the British in combating anti-Jewish manifestations. As in 1929, they also suspended all Zionist activities and fund-raising, although the latter resumed secretly.

With World War II Zionist activity in Egypt revived, thanks to the presence of thousands of Jewish soldiers in the Allied armies and the arrival of Jews from the Yishuv, including Zionist organizers. Focusing on the youth of the community, four major organizations, functioning independently of one another, were established: He-Halutz Ha-Tsaᶜir, Ha-Ivri Ha-Tsaᶜir, Bene Akiva, and the Egyptian branch of the revisionist New Zionist Organization. In 1944 the Zionist Federation was established in Cairo as the Egyptian office of the Jewish Agency for Palestine. Until November 1947 the youth movements and the Zionist Federation functioned legally, albeit discreetly, under the gaze of both the Egyptian and the British authorities. The British even provided arms to self-defense units in the Cairo Jewish quarter in the aftermath of anti-Jewish riots in early November 1945. Moreover, conditions were such during the war that Yishuv leaders traveled to Egypt to advise local Zionist leaders, and Egyptian delegates went to the World Zionist Congress in 1946 and 1947.

Despite these achievements, however, the community leadership increased its opposition to Zionist activities in Egypt. The presidents of the Cairo and Alexandria communities, along with the chief rabbi of Egypt, issued statements condemning such activities, demanding their suspension, and threatening to enlist the intervention of the Egyptian authorities if their calls were not heeded. They were motivated by apprehensions of increased anti-Jewish tensions and reprisals at the hands of nationalists and Islamists, who were incensed at the turn of events in Palestine and, especially by the United Nations decision in favor of partition of the British mandate territory into Jewish and Arab states. By May 1948 all openly Zionist activity in Egypt had ceased, and the movement went underground. After the Arab-Israeli War, the underground began to transfer Egyptian Jews to Israel in 1949 with the guidance of officials from Mossad Le-Aliya Bet (Organization for Illegal Immigration) who had been sent to Egypt and with the discreet financial support of some community leaders.

The 1952 revolution in Egypt, which toppled the monarchy, did not affect the Jewish community in any specific way. In fact, the leader of the new regime, Gen. Muhammad Naguib, went out of his way to stress the equality of all religions in Egypt and to reassure the Egyptian Jewish community. Nonetheless, in 1954 a group of young Egyptian Jews was arrested, and all were convicted of espionage on behalf of Israel. Known as "the mishap of 1954," the affair did not seem to adversely affect the rest of the Jewish community, although two members of the group were hanged and the rest imprisoned despite international appeals.

Because of the Sudan's special constitutional status as an Anglo-Egyptian Condominium until 1954, Jews did not participate directly in the political life of the country. No provisions were made for their involvement in the nascent parliamentary institutions that were to begin in 1954 with independence. Thus the participation of Jews in Sudanese political life was practically nil outside community affairs. Only during the Italo-Ethiopian War and during World War II were Sudanese Jews, along with other members of the foreign resident community, formed into auxiliary units, such as ambulance and logistics, to help the British war effort.

EMIGRATION

As early as 1947, when Egypt enacted the Company Law setting nationality quotas for employment, the dynamics that had seemed to presage a continued Jewish presence in the economy began to change. The Arab-Israeli War of 1948–49 had a significant effect on the Egyptian Jewish community. The Egyptian authorities interned more than one thousand Jews for Zionist activity, seized the assets of numerous Jewish concerns, forbade Jewish gatherings, and obtained lists of names and addresses of members of Jewish community associations. Moreover, homes in Cairo's Jewish quarter were firebombed and looted, and some of Cairo's largest Jewish-owned department stores also were firebombed. In the aftermath of the war, either through expulsion by the Egyptian authorities or through the efforts of Mossad Le-Aliya Bet, twenty thousand Jews left Egypt for Israel or Europe. This extensive rate of emigration slowed to a trickle in the aftermath of the Officers' Coup of July 1952 that toppled King Farouk. Then the Suez Crisis of October–November 1956 put an end to the illusions of a continued Jewish presence in Egypt; as in 1948, individuals were interned and properties were seized. Moreover, for the first time the regime passed a series of laws and regulations specifically aimed at encouraging Jews to leave the country. Fines were imposed on seized properties, promoting the idea of confiscation rather than mere custodial management for the duration of hostilities. More ominously, in addition to expelling Jews who held British or French passports, the authorities encouraged the emigration of Jews who were stateless, held foreign passports other than British or French, or who even had Egyptian citizenship. By June 1957 more than twenty thousand Jews had left Egypt. Coupled with the figures for Jewish emigration during and shortly after the 1948 war, this was more than 50 percent of the community.

Economic regulations implemented in the late 1950s accomplished what measures during the Suez Crisis did not. The authorities increased the percentage of "real" Egyptians to be employed by all corporations. Indigenous Egyptians needed permits to seek employment "with foreigners," and the government introduced the use of a work card listing the employee's religion along with his name. All import-export firms, as well as agents of foreign firms, had to register with the authorities, who did not provide work cards to Jews. Then, in accordance with a socialist economic policy, between 1960 and 1964 the regime of Gamal Abdel Nasser implemented a series of nationalization measures aimed at such sectors as banking and insurance in which Jews were strongly represented. The cumulative effect of these various economic policies was to drive home the point that Jews were no longer welcome to stay and work in Egypt. The subsequent departure of the Egyptian Jewish community was complicated because most of those who remained could not afford to emigrate. International Jewish and non-Jewish organizations assisted and subsidized their departure. Nevertheless, in 2001 approximately three dozen Jews too old or too sick to travel remained in Egypt; they were supported mostly by the American Jewish Joint Distribution Committee.

For the Jews of the Sudan the Arab-Israeli conflict initially had far milder consequences than for those in Egypt. In 1948 the government required Jewish-owned businesses to obtain an export license in order to do business; this was to disrupt any commercial trade with Israel. Also in 1948 unofficial Sudanese organizations attempted to impose a tax on the Jewish community on behalf of Arab Palestinians. Because of its official nature, and the presence of British authorities, the Jewish community refused to pay the tax—although Jews in the retail trade did pay it to avoid the type of boycott likely to affect their businesses. With the Sudan's independence in 1956, approximately nine months after the departure of the British, an increasing number of anti-Zionist pronouncements appeared in the press or aired on radio. Although relations between individual Jews and Sudanese remained correct, a malaise began to be manifested within the Jewish community. Most likely this resulted from the anti-Jewish measures implemented in Egypt, because much of the Jewish community in the Sudan was closely involved in trade with Egypt and represented Egyptian firms there.

The idea of emigration, already planted in the wake of the Suez Crisis, increased in Sudan after the introduction of Egypt's 1960 nationalization decrees. Many Jewish firms began to liquidate their assets while the atmosphere was still favorable, and Jewish families began to emigrate. The advent to power of Ga^{c}afar al-Numeiri in 1969, however, accelerated the pace of departures, especially because he introduced socialist economic policies and the Shari^{c}a (Islamic law).

SUGGESTED READING

Beinin, Joel. *The Dispersion of Egyptian Jewry: Culture, Politics, and the Formation of a Modern Diaspora*. Berkeley: University of California Press, 1998.

Krämer, Gudrun. *The Jews in Modern Egypt, 1914–1952*. Seattle: University of Washington Press, 1989.

Landau, Jacob M. *Jews in Nineteenth-Century Egypt*. New York: New York University Press, 1969.

Laskier, Michael M. *The Jews of Egypt, 1920–1970: In the Midst of Zionism, Anti-Semitism, and the Middle East Conflict*. New York: New York University Press, 1992.

Malka, Eli S. *Jacob's Children in the Land of the Mahdi: Jews of the Sudan*. Syracuse, N.Y.: Syracuse University Press, 1997.

CHAPTER

23

Libya

HARVEY E. GOLDBERG

Libya is the most eastern of the Maghreb countries, bounded by Tunisia and Algeria on the west, Egypt on the east, and the Sudan, Chad, and Niger on the south. Its area is 685,000 square miles, and it is made up of three regions that were loosely connected in the past. Tripolitania, in the northwest, was part of the Arab "West," while Cyrenaica in the northeast was linked to Egypt. These are separated by the northern extension of the Sahara Desert, which reaches the Mediterranean at the Gulf of Sidra. To the south of Tripolitania is the Fezzan, a region that was linked to sub-Saharan Africa and also had commercial ties to the north. There is no record of permanent Jewish settlement in the Fezzan, although Jewish merchants in Tripoli trafficked in goods arriving from the south.

The majority of Libyans are Sunni Muslims who follow the Maliki school of law. The Sanusi religious movement influenced Cyrenaica in modern times. A small concentration of Ibadi Muslims lives in the mountainous Nefusa region, southwest of Tripoli, which is also the enclave of a Berber language. Other pockets of Berber speakers exist in the far south. Some southerners have migrated to northern towns over the centuries.

Early nineteenth-century Tripoli featured Turkish speakers within the ruling class, an Arab majority (of various social ranks), Africans, Jews, Maltese, and such Europeans as consuls or representatives of religious orders. Toward the end of that century, Italian settlement in Libya grew and was reinforced by agricultural colonization in the twentieth century, under Italian colonial rule. Most of Libya's Jews emigrated between 1949 and 1951, on the eve of Libyan independence. Those remaining left in 1970, when the new government of Libya confiscated Jewish property and expelled thirty thousand Italians.

HISTORY

In ancient times the territory that is now Libya was occupied by Carthage and Rome before it fell to Islam in the Arab conquest of the seventh century. From 1551 until 1911 Tripolitania and areas of Cyrenaica were partially under the control of the Ottoman Empire. From 1711 to 1835 Tripolitania was ruled by the Qaramanli dynasty, which had emerged from within the Ottoman military ranks. The Qaramanlis retained nominal allegiance to the Sublime Porte (the Ottoman court in Istanbul) but made wars and concluded peace on their own. In 1835 the Ottomans, reacting both to Muhammad Ali's rise to power in Egypt and the French takeover of Algeria, recaptured Tripoli, placing it under direct rule. From the middle of the nineteenth century, the Ottoman Tanzimat reforms began to reshape the administration of the province.

Italy ousted the Ottomans from Tripolitania and Cyrenaica in 1911. Italians' involvement in World War I, however, kept them from controlling Libya's interior until later. Resistance to colonial rule continued in Tripolitania through 1923 and in Cyrenaica through 1931, but most Jews did not have direct exposure to the Italian political presence until the 1920s. The harsh treatment of Libyan Arabs by the colonial regime, which tried to win their loyalty while using the country for its own economic and international purposes, created a complex situation for the Jews. It became even more difficult as fascist Italy forged ties with Nazi Germany in the 1930s. Early in World War II, Libya was the scene of the Axis advance against Egypt and was one of the main battlegrounds; later it was conquered by the British Eighth Army. The British military continued to administer Libya until the early 1950s, while the future of Libya was debated in various forums and eventually placed before the United Nations. In 1951 it became the United Kingdom of Libya, under King Idris I, by international agreement the first independent Maghreb country. In 1969 the coup led by Col. Muʿammar Qadhafi resulted in an anti-Western regime.

JEWISH PRESENCE AND POPULATION

Jews lived in Cyrenaica and Tripolitania in antiquity, but no connection exists between those communities and the recent population of Jews. Tripolitanian Jews appear in the Cairo Geniza, and tombstone inscriptions point to communities in the Tripolitanian interior. Most Jews fled Tripoli in the early sixteenth century when the city was captured by Spain, and the reconstitution of Jewish life was linked to the expansion of Ottoman power in the region at midcentury. In that period some Jews moved to Benghazi while continuing to maintain links to Tripoli. The religious revival of Jewish life in Tripoli at that time is ascribed to Rabbi Shimᶜon Lavi, a Spanish exile and kabbalist, who decided to establish residence there rather than continue on to the Land of Israel. The Jewish population grew to several thousand, consisting mostly of local Jews along with some who had been expelled from Spain and Portugal in the late fifteenth and early sixteenth centuries. The latter included Jews from Livorno (Italy), who did not constitute a separate community. They were distinctive however, as they prayed in a synagogue identified with the Francos (the general term for local Jews of European origin).

The Jewish population of Tripolitania grew from the midnineteenth through the midtwentieth centuries, with growth more rapid in the city than in the hinterland. About 1,000 Jewish families lived in Tripoli in 1853; by 1914 the community numbered about 10,500 people and grew to about 19,000 people by 1943. Throughout that time Jews constituted one-fifth to one-third of the population of Tripoli. At the same time the total Jewish population of the hinterland communities rose from about 730 families to about 11,000 people in 1943. In the late 1940s about 6,000 Jews lived in Cyrenaica, including 4,000 in Benghazi. Jews in Tripoli lived in two adjacent areas in the western quadrant of the city. To the northeast lived the Christians, within whose area were several European consulates. To the southwest of the Jews were Muslim residential areas. At the beginning of the twentieth century Jews began to move into other parts of the city. Many established residence in the New City built by the Italians, but this involved less than one-fourth of the Jewish population.

Most Jews continued to live in or adjacent to the Jewish quarters. These neighborhoods were mainly residential but included many grocery stores, green grocers, butcher shops, restaurants, and street vendors. Some Jewish retailers who resided there could find clientele within the limits of the Jewish quarter. Procuring supplies, however, took them outside the quarter. Craftsmen, by contrast, plied their trades outside the quarter while continuing to live within it. Shoemakers, carpenters, builders, and silversmiths had shops in the southeastern end of the city, in the interlaced network of market streets, some of which were named for craft specialties.

LANGUAGE, CULTURE, AND EDUCATION

In Libya, Jews spoke a dialect of Maghrebi Arabic. It was comprehensible to Muslims but distinct in several features, especially the borrowings from

Hebrew. Another language that some merchants knew was a sort of "pidgin Romance," with influences from Italian, French, and Spanish. Wealthy merchants provided private instruction to their children in European languages. Some families who came to Libya from Italian cities may have spoken Italian at home, but in the nineteenth century most Jews did not know a European language.

Every Jewish male was expected to learn Hebrew so he could recite prayers and follow the Torah reading in the synagogue. The actual level of literacy, however, was not high. Learning to read stressed rote repetition. Boys learned to write using characters similar to standard printed letters so that they could copy books of hymns by hand. Some students learned a cursive script that might be relevant for religious purposes, such as writing a marriage contract, but could also be used in business letters, which were in Judeo-Arabic, employing the Hebrew alphabet.

The introduction of European languages beyond the circle of the wealthy merchants began toward the end of the nineteenth century and met with some resistance. Rabbi Eliahu Hazzan sought to reform the local education system and have Italian taught to all boys by a Jewish teacher. But among his opponents were merchant families that then enjoyed a monopoly of the knowledge of foreign languages. Some Libyan Jewish families from Italy invited teachers from that country to open schools, a move that provided the beginning of public education for girls. The Alliance Israélite Universelle also opened a school in 1890, stressing French, but its expansion was curtailed by the Italian takeover. A Turkish school attracted some Jews, while Italian became part of the standard education of most Libyan Jewish children in the 1920s. Girls attended the Italian schools as well, but their first formal exposure to Hebrew took place in the 1930s, under the auspices of the new and Zionist-oriented Ben-Yehudah organization. Hebrew culture of the Eastern European Haskalah (Enlightenment) reached Tripoli in the late nineteenth century, as seen in the historical writing of Mordecai Ha-Cohen, but it had a limited influence on educational practices.

Jews did not learn literary Arabic in schools, but most urban Jews and all rural Jews continued to speak Judeo-Arabic. Only a few in the small Italian upper class could not use the local language. Time-honored patterns of daily interaction with Muslims continued in the countryside, even as the formal situation of the Jews changed under first Ottoman, then Young Turk, and then Italian rule. In the hinterland during the nineteenth and twentieth centuries, Jews continued to wear traditional dress, including the old legislated marks of their Jewishness (like a black turban). They maintained forms of interaction derived from Islamic civilization, whereby they would dismount from a donkey when passing a Muslim or greet a Muslim with the term *sidi* (my lord). In Tripoli and Benghazi such practices waned, particularly among well-off Jews. Middle-class Jews in the New City adopted Italian dress and were in contact with Italian neighbors. These changes were gradual; older and new patterns coexisted. At the same time the new freedoms of daily life accorded to the Jews (and that were imposed on the Libyans by the Italians) laid the groundwork for ethnic and religious competition.

OTTOMAN REFORMS AND THE JEWS

The changing place of Jews in Muslim society did not begin with Italian rule; it had started under the Ottoman regime. Before 1835 the Jewish community enjoyed dependent autonomy, implied in its *dhimmi* status. The pasha of Tripoli appointed a Jewish *qa'id* (leader), who was responsible for the collection of taxes from the community. Internal affairs were guided by local ordinances that reflected both rabbinic tradition and local practice. The Ottoman reforms began to modify the principles and practice of the various Jewish communities.

The Ottoman governor of Tripoli, Mehmed Emin Pasha (r. 1842–47), appointed Rabbi Ya^{c}aqov Mimun to be head of the Jewish community and assigned him a seat on the local court. Under Mahmud Nedim Pasha (r. 1860–67) the court was reorganized in accordance with the Ottoman Provincial Reform Law. Separate courts—criminal, penal, and commercial—were established. Jewish magistrates were appointed to each and salaried by the government. The pasha no longer sat on the court, as had been the practice during the Qaramanli period. The separation of executive from judicial power represented a step in the demarcation of civil law, as distinct from family and personal status law. With regard to the latter, each religious community (*millet*) was governed by its own laws and officials. These new arrangements both limited the sphere in which rabbinic rulings could be made, with government backing, and formalized the newly circumscribed religious authority in the new regime. In the civic sphere the new rules also required that local councils established in regions with a Jewish community had to have a Jewish member.

In other realms as well Ottoman governors often found that their interests coincided with those of the local Jews. A new gate was opened in the western wall of Tripoli in 1865, to facilitate traffic between the countryside and the city. This was important to Jews, who contributed to the costs of the project, as it enabled them to carry their dead directly to the Jewish cemetery. Previously, their funeral processions had followed a route through Muslim quarters, where they were subject to verbal abuse and physical harassment. In the same period a steamship company established in 1860 began to provide mail service between Tripoli and Europe, which was especially important to Jewish merchants. Jews could also find common cause with local Muslims against Ottoman initiatives, such as the new law that made the state the trustee of an estate if orphaned children were younger than twenty. Muslims feared that the government was trying to expropriate the land of those who died without children, to keep it from devolving upon other heirs. Officials began registering the estates of the local inhabitants upon their death, despite popular opposition—and Jews organized in protest against these steps. Istanbul decided that the local council should decide the matter; it rejected the new laws.

Another case of the mutual intertwining of local interests concerned conscription into the army, which the Ottomans sought to apply to local Muslims and Jews. At one point they pressured the Jews first, based on the assumption that if Jews acquiesced to service in the military, Muslims would have no choice but to agree as well. Again, organized opposition by the Jews stymied the administrative reform. Eventually, some Jews were conscripted from 1908 to 1911, under the Young Turk regime. The case of conscription highlights the limits of the innovating reforms of the pashas. Despite real improvements in the situation of the Jews, the wider Muslim population made little basic cultural revaluation of the Jews' place in society.

CHANGES UNDER THE ITALIANS

At the beginning of the Italian era Jews in Tripoli constituted a well-defined religious and ethnic group, with an important economic role. Most of their leaders had a pragmatic approach to modernization; this orientation, however, was not part of a systematic ideology. The internal structure of the Jewish community was legally formalized by the Italians in 1916. At first they attempted to create leadership based on elections, and a Zionist group, led by Elia Nahaisi, challenged the traditional elite. The ensuing community conflict was never resolved. Later, under fascist rule in 1929, the colonial administration sought a modus vivendi with Libyan Muslims, and an Italian (non-Jewish) official took charge of administering the Jewish community. At the time of the Italian takeover in 1911 Italians thought that Jews in Libya would quickly become like contemporary Italian Jews; some colonial officials began to insist that the Libyan Jews were, in fact, similar to (or even "below") the indigenous Libyan Arabs. Throughout the Italian period, however, the receptiveness of Jews to European culture continued to grow, which resulted in some alienation between the "modern" section of community and those economically less well off, who were seen as "traditional." This division was less prominent in Benghazi, where a large percentage of the community consisted of middle-class merchants. Then throughout the country the developments of the 1930s, including attempts to quicken the pace of "civilizing" the Jews by enforcing the opening of shops and school attendance on the Sabbath, ensured that even "advanced" members of the community realized and retained a clear sense of Jewish identity and attachment to tradition.

During the Italian period almost all the Jewish boys got some elementary schooling, but the situation is less clear with regard to girls. Typically, education for boys involved a combination of traditional instruction and attendance at an Italian government school. In some instances boys—even those aged four and five—were sent to a traditional Jewish school, with the notion that they should get a basic religious education *before* attending the Italian school at age seven or eight. Most Jewish students were in state elementary schools where all the other pupils were Jewish, but Libya had no permanent state Jewish high schools. The relatively few Jewish teenagers who attended high school came from New City families, and they studied with Italian students in state schools.

The Italianization of the Jews did not proceed simply in other spheres, either. New forms of leisure appeared, such as movie going (which the poor could not afford) or walking on the boardwalk, where Jews mixed with Italians. While some middle-class Jews assumed the tastes and lifestyle of Italians, they were not necessarily accepted. The establishment of the Maccabi social and sports club, with a general Zionist but nonideological orientation, may have been the Jewish answer to the exclusive clubs formed by Italians. Zionism, in the form of the Ben-Yehudah organization, which focused on teaching Modern Hebrew, resulted from the influence of an Italian education on members of the "traditional" community from the Old City. During the Italian period synagogue life, the Sabbath, and festivals continued with vitality and changed only gradually. One of the few new prayer houses to be built outside the Old City was the synagogue of the Haddad family. Moshe Haddad, later a resident of Israel, painted pictures of life in Tripoli, including a portrait of his family's synagogue. Prominent in the picture is the mixture of men in European hats and those in red fezzes. Jewish merchants from outside Tripoli would dress in Italian style in the city but would don traditional barracans (hooded cloaks) at home on the Sabbath. The dress of women underwent change as well, but the Sabbath and festivals were for parading traditional wardrobes.

Some Italianized members of the community neglected careful prayer observance three times a day, but prayer remained part of daily routine for many of Tripoli's Jews. No one challenged the centrality of the synagogue as a religious and social institution, nor were "reformed" styles of worship suggested. Many who moved to the New City also prayed regularly. Only a few synagogues were built in these neighborhoods, while many New City residents organized casual synagogues in existing facilities. It was common for well-to-do families to attend the synagogues of the Jewish quarter for festivals, when prayers were longer and more elaborate. Festivals thus reunited members of the community who were growing apart in other ways. On these occasions economically successful families gave expression to their new social standing by exhibiting their dress or by making generous contributions that earned them prestigious portions of the worship or Torah-reading service. The poorer Jews of the *hara* (Jewish quarter) still constituted a relevant audience for the accomplishments of the wealthy.

The traditionalism of Tripoli's Jews—even while ostensibly moving in "modern" directions—was apparent not only in synagogue customs but also in deeply ingrained conceptions of social life. They made only surface accommodation to Italian forms. In the 1930s and 1940s even some Italianized Jews still practiced polygyny—which was permissible according to local rabbinic tradition, despite the disapproval of westernized members of the society and Italian officials. The westernization of the Jews of Libya did not follow the path to westernization taken by European Jewry in an earlier era. Several interrelated processes constituted the Libyan experience of westernization.

In fact, differences in the basic orientations of the "modernizing" and "traditional" sectors of the community were not wide. The differences in wealth and social class were clear, but most members of the community accepted the importance of receiving a modern Italian education. The different orientations of the traditional and modern well-to-do segments of the community were not perceived as antagonistic, even though they might seem so to an outside observer. Participation in Italian culture was not seen as inimical to Zionism—or Jewish tradition generally. Much of the involvement in Italian culture, even on the part of the elite, was important but did not involve a basic shift in Jewish identity. The Jews of modern Italy did not provide an ideological model for the Jews of Libya even though the ideal of their becoming like the Jews of Italy informed colonial policy and the activities of Italian Jews working to improve the situation of Libyan Jewry. Well-to-do Jews in Libya could turn to traditional modes of behavior if the situation demanded. Contact with non-Jewish Italians provided a model for some Jews, but imitating their lifestyle served as an example of upward mobility within the framework of the Jewish community. The type of ideological and cultural splits that characterized Europe did not correspond to the historical experience of the Jews of Libya.

POLITICAL DEVELOPMENTS TOWARD MIDCENTURY

The slow developments within the Jewish community were overtaken by political events, beginning in the 1930s, that originated outside Libya. Italo Balbo, who became governor of Libya in 1934, launched an energetic program of developing the colony, including the "progress" of the local Jewish community, modeled after modernized Italian Jewry. The ideology of fascist rule allowed respect for Jewish religious sensibilities only insofar as they did not hamper state-promoted modernization. In 1936, when Balbo was confronted with the issue of keeping open on the Sabbath stores that were owned by Jews in the New City, he pursued his policy of modernization. Two Jews who closed their shops were publicly flogged.

By the late 1930s Italy's alliance with Nazi Germany was affecting the Jewish community in Libya. Balbo, however, pointed to the importance of the Jews to the local economy to convince Benito Mussolini not to demand immediate application to Libya's Jews of the racial laws passed in Italy. Anti-Jewish policies, nevertheless, did impinge upon Jewish life. Beginning in 1938, Jews were not allowed to study with Italians in secondary schools, and attempts by the Jewish community to organize their own secondary education succeeded only briefly.

During 1941 German troops entered Libya to reinforce the Italians there. This brought further hardship to the Jewish community. Economic restrictions were imposed, and Jews holding foreign passports were deported. Those of French nationality were sent to Tunisia, then under the Vichy government. British nationals were shipped to Italy and eventually to the death camps of Bergen-Belsen and Ravensbruck. Ultimately, some were exchanged for German prisoners of war held by the British. During the war the welcome shown British forces by the Benghazi Jews led Mussolini to transfer most of them to a concentration camp in Tripolitania after Benghazi was temporarily retaken by the Italians. In mid-1942 male Jews in Libya became subject to civilian mobilization, and about one thousand were sent to a camp 150 miles east of Tripoli; from there some were sent to work behind the front in Cyrenaica. Because of the war many of the restrictive economic laws did not have a direct effect, and they became void with the fall of Tripoli to the British in January 1943.

The war itself, particularly the bombings of Tripoli by the Allies that began in 1940, led to Jewish-Muslim cooperation. Many Tripolitanian Jews sought refuge outside the city, renting rooms in Arab villages in the area. The Jewish community also made an organized effort to provide rooms in Arab homes for the poor. Some Jews who had commercial connections obtained black market supplies for their Muslim hosts. Many Jews remember this period as an era of life together, in contrast to the subsequent tension and tragedy of the 1945 riots. Perhaps the legislation and partial enforcement of racial laws by the Italians led some Jews to consider their ties to the Muslims more carefully.

Overall, Muslims did not applaud the special plight of the Jews at the end of the Italian regime. Some more politically conscious Arabs did consider that similar racial measures might eventually discriminate against them too. Jews and Muslims alike initially perceived the British victory as their liberation. In the Muslim view the British ended Italian rule, resulting in the departure of many colonists. As for the Jews, the British forces included the Palestine Brigade, soldiers who had enlisted so that there would be Jewish participation in the war. Members of the brigade succeeded in establishing contact with Jewish communities freed from Axis control. Their presence in Libya stimulated Zionist sentiment and helped reactivate work that had begun in the 1930s.

The period immediately after the war seemed to entail a settling down and even a sense of euphoria. In Tripoli some Jews joined the police and patrolled alongside Muslims. Many Jews, expecting an improved situation, moved into apartments in the New City, renting them at low prices from Italians who had returned to their homeland. As the euphoria declined, and postwar economic dislocation set in, everyday life resumed a sense of normality. With the conclusion of World War II, however, the question of the political future of Libya arose, a matter that created a perplexing situation for the Jews.

The uncertainty of the Jews' situation was suddenly and brutally demonstrated by riots that began on the evening of November 4, 1945. Disturbances broke out simultaneously at various places in Tripoli. The next morning Muslims from neighboring villages converged on the city. A Jewish leader, Zachino Habib, approached the police and requested military intervention because the police force, which included many local Muslims, would be unable to handle the situation. A colonel promised to look into the situation, but no effective measures were taken until the evening of November 6. The rioting involved looting, arson, and physical attacks. In Tripoli, Jews outside the Jewish quarters suffered most, while the majority of the population was able to protect itself in the old Jewish section. The participants were mostly poorer Muslims of all ages; some wealthier notables stood by and watched; women took part by cheering on the rioters. Individual Muslims helped Jews to safety. The British succeeded in stopping the riot only on the morning of November 7. During this period thirty-eight Jews and one Muslim were killed in Tripoli.

The disturbances spread from Tripoli to other towns in Libya, sometimes a few days later. In several cases the Jews were forewarned, but appeals to the police and to local Muslim leaders were not always effective. The toll in lives in the villages reached ninety-seven, all Jews. In at least one town a forced conversion to Islam took place. Throughout the province nine synagogues were burned and thirty-five Torah scrolls ruined. There were many injuries and a massive loss of Jewish property from looting and burning.

Many explanations for the riots have been proffered. There is evidence that they were organized, perhaps by nationalists seeking to push out all foreigners. Nationalism was not a widespread sentiment at the time, however; local Tripolitanian patriotism was more prominent than any pan-Libyan identity. The slogans that stirred the rioters drew upon religion more than political ideas, except for the basic desire to eliminate the rule of Europeans. Attacking Jews may have been a call to restore the correct order of things in a Muslim polity. The conflict between the Jews and the Arabs in Palestine was not in the minds of most Tripolitanians at the time, as it was when another riot broke out in June 1948. Nonetheless, the riots undermined the Jews' basic sense of security in a land where they had resided for centuries. The option of leaving Libya, however, did not arise until after the establishment of the State of Israel in 1948.

THE CONTEXTS OF EMIGRATION

In January 1949 the British government decided to allow Jews to emigrate from Libya, and the Jewish Agency for Palestine was empowered to organize emigration to Israel. The first ships sailed in early April. There was popular pressure to increase the number of Jewish emigrants, because of the uncertain future for the Jewish community in independent Libya, the creation of which was being considered in international circles. The Jewish Agency decided to bring the Jews of Cyrenaica and the Tripolitanian hinterland to Tripoli to await emigration. The American Jewish Joint Distribution Committee and the Jewish Health Organization provided food, clothing, and medical services to these migrants. From July through November Jews left the interior of Tripolitania.

Observers depicted the mood among Jews in Libya at that time as one of messianic enthusiasm. Immigration to Israel was imbued with religious meaning by applying elements of synagogue ritual to the events in the emigration process. After Jews obtained permission to leave for Israel, they auctioned the privilege of gaining the first visa, like a ritual honor in the synagogue. When the head of the Jewish Agency's Immigration Department appeared publicly, many threw rosewater at him, as they might at a bridegroom or bar mitzvah celebrant. Jews from the rural communities organized processions and presented the Jewish Agency official or other people representing Israel with Torah scrolls from their former villages. As the Israel-bound ships sailed from the harbor at Tripoli, immigrants sang Moses' song of redemption at the sea (Exod. 15). Immigration continued until the end of 1951. The pace of emigration slowed toward the end of this period, because the timetable for Libyan independence had been set, and Israeli leaders had to deal with other, more problematic "rescue" operations.

At Libyan independence in January 1952, about four thousand Jews remained in the country. Many were middle class, even wealthy, and were unsure that they would be able to maintain their position and wealth in the difficult economic and social conditions of Israel at the time. Italy, which was then going through postwar reconstruction, was not a major attraction, either. The constitution of the new United Kingdom of Libya, forged under U.N. supervision, guaranteed the rights of minorities. King Idris, with his base in Cyrenaica, was oriented to the West, and Jews believed that he was committed to their protection. But these factors did not make the place of the Jews secure. While some Libyans became wealthy as their country began to sell oil in the late 1950s, their legal and political positions were undermined. The Jews' ability to travel abroad became limited, and a special mark was inserted in their passports. Libya then joined the Arab League, and the ideology of pan-Arabism, as promoted by Egypt's leader, Gamal Abdel Nasser, had a growing effect on the country. Some Jews left as the opportunity arose, but the June 1967 Arab-Israeli War marked a turning point. During the war a number of Libyan Jews were murdered, in some instances by government officials. Most Jews in Libya were moved to protected barracks or camps outside Tripoli and Benghazi. After the war the king agreed that the Jews could leave the country. The majority took this opportunity, but they left under conditions that were economically disadvantageous. Most relocated to Italy. Two years later the revolution led by Muʿammar Qadhafi turned out to be the coup de grâce to Jewish life in Libya, culminating in the confiscation of Jewish property and in the exodus of all but a few Jews.

Of the approximately four thousand Jews who moved to Italy in the late 1960s, about half, mostly the oldest members of the community, later moved to Israel. Small numbers, from the final exodus and earlier migrations, reached other countries. The number of Israelis of Libyan Jewish descent was about 100,000 as of 1999, but the extent to which a "Libyan" identity and heritage continue to be important in their lives varies greatly among them.

SUGGESTED READING

De Felice, Renzo. *Jews in an Arab Land: Libya, 1835–1970.* Trans. Judith Roumani. Austin: University of Texas Press, 1985.

Goldberg, Harvey E. *Jewish Life in Muslim Libya: Rivals and Relatives.* Chicago: University of Chicago Press, 1990.

Ha-Cohen, Mordecai. *The Book of Mordechai: A Study of the Jews of Libya.* Translated, edited, and annotated by H. E. Goldberg. London: Darf, 1993.

Simon, Rachel. *Change Within Tradition Among Jewish Women in Libya.* Seattle: University of Washington Press, 1992.

CHAPTER

24

Tunisia

Haim Saadoun

The smallest country in North Africa, Tunisia is bordered by Algeria on the west, the Mediterranean on the north and east, and Libya on the southeast. It includes the Kerkenna Islands off the east coast and the island of Djerba in the southeast. The north and the Sahel are the most urbanized and most densely populated regions of the country. Tunis is the largest city, a port, and the national capital. Other important cities include Sfax, Kairouan, Sousse, Djerba, and Bizerte. Tunisia's ethnic population base is a mix of Sunni Muslim Arab-Berber or Arabized Berber, who speak Arabic. A few Berber speakers remain in isolated regions of the south; Berbers were the indigenous North African people of the country. A Jewish minority exists, consisting of the Touansa (Jews who settled in Tunisia long before the seventh-century Islamic conquest) and émigrés from Livorno (Italy) in the late 1600s and early 1700s. In the early 1950s Jews numbered about 100,000 in a population of three million that included more than 250,000 European settlers.

Tunisia was ruled by the Romans and Byzantines in the pre-Islamic period. Since the seventh-century Islamic conquest, the area has been ruled by various Arab-Berber dynasties. Although Tunisia became an Ottoman province in the sixteenth century, in effect, it was autonomous under the Husaynid dynasty. This dynasty, consisting of Mamluk and Turkish officials known as beys, controlled Tunisia beginning in 1705 and pledged allegiance to the Ottoman sultan. The Husaynids became an integral part of Tunisian society through intermarriage and acculturation.

In 1881 the French protectorate was imposed on Tunisia, ending any Ottoman controls; it lasted until 1956. The country became dominated by French colonial forces that functioned alongside the surviving the Husaynid dynasty. Serious anti-French nationalist reactions began in the 1930s and 1940s under the banner of the Neo-Destour movement, led by Habib Bourguiba. In the 1950s the violent anticolonial struggle forced the French to grant Tunisia internal autonomy in 1954 and full independence two years later. In 1956 the country was ruled by the Neo-Destour (which in 1964 became the Socialist Neo-Destour) Party, with Bourguiba as president from 1957 (after the Husaynid beylic was removed and Tunisia became a republic) to 1987, when he was overthrown by Zayn al-Abidine Ben Ali in 1987.

THE JEWISH COMMUNITY

According to Tunisian Jewish tradition, Jews first arrived in Tunisia after the destruction of the First Temple in 586 B.C.E. In the Middle Ages the Jewish community of Tunisia, especially of Kairouan, was famous because of the important role it played as a mediator between the Jewish community of Spain and the *geonim* of Babylon. This was the golden age of the community; it was the flourishing epoch of Isaac Israeli (Yitzhak Ben Shlomo), the governor's physician; Dunash Ben Tamim, a doctor, linguist, astronomer, and mathematician; the rabbis of the Shahin (or Shahoun) family; and Rabenu Hananel, whose interpretation of the Talmud is famous. This population increased after 1492 with the arrival of Sephardic exiles from Spain who adapted to local Jewish customs.

From the Islamic conquest onward, the legal status of the Tunisian Jews was that of *dhimmi.* This continued into the nineteenth century, when Jews were still obliged to wear special clothes to distinguish them from other ethnic groups. They were not permitted to wear the *chechia* (red hat) and the white turbans that Muslims wore but were forced to wear a black cap enveloped with a black or blue turban. They paid the *jizya* (head tax) to the bey, lived in separate quarters in every big town, especially in Tunis, and were not permitted to acquire properties in towns and villages.

As Tunisia was, albeit nominally, a part of the Ottoman Empire, the Tanzimat reforms of 1839 pressured the bey to improve the Jews' living conditions and legal status. On September 10, 1857, the bey enacted the Pact Fondamental, which along with the constitutions that followed, afforded the Jews more security in Tunisia than they had had before and abolished of some of the restrictions of the Pact of Umar. The Tunisians did not accept the Pacte Fondamental, because it required that they pay more taxes. Thus economic instability and the consequences of the Pacte Fondamental were the background for the 1864 rebellion against the rulers of Tunisia. The reforms in Tunisia came as a result of pressure from the Great Powers, which reflected the increasing intervention of Europe in Tunisian affairs. These reforms were just the first step that led to occupation by France in 1881.

Jews enjoyed full autonomy in the organization of their religious life. At the head of the Jewish community was the *qa'id,* who was nominated by the bey. The *qa'id* was in charge of organizing Jewish community life, from collecting the *jizya* to nominating the principal community functionaries. Some *qa'ids* even were in charge of the Tunisian treasury and paid the salaries of the mercenary army of the bey. During the second half of the nineteenth century, the Samama family performed that function.

In the late seventeenth and early eighteenth centuries, a group of Italian Jews, many from the seaport of Livorno, arrived in Tunisia, which created two communities—the indigenous Jews, called the Touansa, and the immigrants, called the Grana. The Italian Jews of Sephardic origin tried to preserve their political and cultural ties to Livorno. According to an agreement signed in 1710, the Grana had almost full autonomy as a Jewish community, but they did not have a *qa'id* of their own. The Grana had synagogues and a parcel of land in the Jewish cemetery, where a wall separated Grana and Touansa graves. The Grana lived in the European quarters, not in the Jewish quarter (Harat al-Yahud), and when possible sent their children to be educated in Italy. In Tunisia they enjoyed preferred legal status, for they remained Italian citizens with special rights, while the Touansa were still *dhimmi.* As a result of this, the Grana dressed in European style and were not obliged to wear all the humiliating signs of Judaism that the Touansa wore. The Grana spoke Italian and Arabic, but they kept their account books in Portuguese.

The intervention of France and Great Britain in Tunisia's internal affairs and the relations between the Grana and Italy were not the only examples of the involvement of external elements in Tunisian and Tunisian-Jewish affairs. The opening of Tunisia's first Alliance Israélite Universelle (AIU) school in 1878 was an important factor in Jewish life. The bey did his best to avoid the founding of the first school, but he could not resist French pressure. Those AIU schools were not only a framework for learning but also a challenge to the Jewish community, because they offered instruction in French, a secular curriculum, and new opportunities for social and economic improvement. Representatives of the Jewish community and the first AIU committee in Tunisia signed an agreement that ensured that Jewish cultural and religious material would be part of the school curriculum.

Another change at the end of the nineteenth century was the activity of Jewish scholars (*maskilim*). This activity was mainly intellectual, for they wrote letters and reports to the international Jewish newspapers of the time, such as *Ha-Magid* (Prussia), *Ha-Tzfira* (Warsaw), and *Ha-Levanon* (Jerusalem). The main objective of the *maskilim* was to arouse the awareness of Jewish leaders in Europe, encourage them to become involved in Tunisian affairs, and to help improve Jewish life there. The *maskilim* published their own newspapers and translated books of the European Enlightenment into Judeo-Arabic. Until World War I the tension between Judeo-Arabic scholars and the French-language bent of the AIU would be one of the main sources of conflict. At that time the AIU school was a cornerstone of French education and influence.

With the occupation of Tunisia by France in 1881, the French molded the development of modern Tunisia, both in theory and practice. They provided freedom from the restrictions of traditional society, new opportunities for the improvement of the economy, new modes of expression and activity—and all these became possible for Jews through French acculturation, as part of the modernization process.

The main problem for the Jews in this colonial society was that they were living within a Muslim society that had set patterns for Jewish existence. In the past a Jew had been obliged to be part of an autonomous Jewish community, living side by side with, yet in the shadow of, Islam. The new colonial society gave Jews the freedom, within certain limitations, to choose how to live or identify themselves. French culture presented the Jews with a challenge that was irresistible. French rule was both the source of the Jews' security and their means of release from the degradation of Islam. Consciously, then, but not necessarily by overt choice, the Jews tied their fate to that of French colonial rule, which eventually distanced them even more from the Muslim majority in Tunisia.

The Jewish population of Tunisia in 1881 was about twenty-five thousand, mostly in Tunis. As a result of the modernization process, Jews left the small villages and emigrated to bigger centers. Before mass emigration of Tunisian Jews in the 1950s, the Jewish population was estimated to be approximately 105,000, which means that in seventy-five years the Jewish population had increased more than fourfold.

Changes emerged in Jewish occupations, for with colonialism Jews were no longer restricted in their choices and could enter the liberal professions and midlevel colonial French administrative jobs. As workers, they also became active in unionization. The working Jewish population increased, with women workers more common than in the past, and soon children rarely worked. In the peripheral and provincial towns and villages, such changes were not as great as in the capital. Jews began to represent firms from France and to import steel, machines, and electrical appliances. They also began to open shops and groceries, where they offered European goods; they worked as salespersons, cashiers, and bookkeepers. A small business elite emerged from both the Grana and Touansa groups. Moreover, the number of Jews in all the liberal professions increased with the years.

One issue concerning the Jewish community was the question of French citizenship. Mardochee Smadja, leader of the radical La Justice group, prodded the French to grant Tunisian Jews the same rights as those that France had granted Algerian Jews under colonialism. Smadja also represented the group at the colonial congress held in Marseilles (1906) and organized a mass demonstration in Tunis in 1910. His efforts were not in vain, for the French authorities in Tunisia decided to naturalize the Tunisian Jews on an individual and selective basis. Thus all Jews who wanted to acquire French citizenship were asked to demand it personally and to prove that they met all criteria, such as special service to France, knowledge of the French language, and the right level of French education. At the beginning of the French protectorate in 1881, only a few Jews could be naturalized, but as a result of Jewish pressure the French resident general agreed to facilitate the conditions of naturalization. In the 1920s and 1930s Jews acquired French citizenship in large numbers. For example, 1,222 became French citizens in 1926 and 747 in 1929; however, the 1930s saw a decrease in the naturalization of Tunisian Jews because of French anti-Semitism stoked by Germany.

The consequence of that naturalization policy was that Tunisia's Jewish population was divided into three main categories: French citizens, Tunisian subjects, and Italians. Moreover, the second group, which constituted the majority of the Jewish population, was subdivided according to its degree of French acculturation. In Djerba, the most religious town of Tunisia, Jews did not want to have any connection with French culture; in Tunis most Jews were assimilated to French culture even if they were not French citizens. The struggle for French naturalization had proved that the French resident general would agree to change his policy under pressure, so Tunisian Jews became active and politically involved in order to achieve social change.

COMMUNITY ORGANIZATION

The function of the *qa'id* was gradually abolished. At the beginning of its protectorate in 1881, France created a new institution, L'Assemblée des Notables. The Touansa and the Grana each had a president and a chief rabbi paid by the French treasury. More important and permanent was the creation of the Caisse de Secours de Bienfaisance, which consisted of nine men nominated by the French and replaced all the traditional functions of the Jewish community. In order to meet all the needs of Tunisia's Jewish society, more than ten voluntary organizations were created under the patronage of Jewish notables.

The most important change occurred in 1921, when the French decided to create the Conseil de la Communauté Israélite, which was elected democratically every four years but only by men who had paid their taxes to the community. Each part of the Jewish community held separate elections. The electoral campaign was the stage for debates that emphasized the struggle between the political parties. The Zionists tried to ensure the Zionization of the council's activities, while the La Justice Party hoped to use the power of that institution to persuade France to exert French cultural influence over the Jewish community. The combat for the character of the Jewish council furthered the political and social awareness of the Jewish community.

INTELLECTUAL LIFE AND SPIRITUAL ACTIVITY

Expressions of Jewish political and social awareness can be found in the enormous number and the variety of newspapers and periodicals that were published by Jews in Tunisia; they published about 160 periodicals, newspapers, and yearbooks between 1878 and 1962. Seventy-eight were written in Judeo-Arabic, sixty-five in French, and sixteen in Hebrew; most of the latter were published in Djerba. Most of the newspapers in Judeo-Arabic were published during the first generation of the French occupation. During the second generation the domination of the French language was considerable, an expression of the community's assimilation to French culture. Of the 130 periodicals published in French between the world wars, 46 could be characterized as informative, 30 were Zionist newspapers, 15 were political, 12 were rabbinical, and 27 were literary. The Zionist newspapers included *La Justice*, *L'Egalité*, *Le Réveil Juif*, *La Gazette d'Israël*, and *El-Najma*. Those newspapers, as well as the community elections, set the stage for the political, social, and intellectual struggle within Jewish society, as well as for the relations of the Jews with the Muslims and the French. Under colonialism French newspapers employed Jews as reporters, editors, and publishers. Jewish scholars translated hundreds of Jewish books, mainly from Eastern Europe, into Judeo-Arabic, and the rabbinical literature in Djerba and the capital ran to thousands of volumes of religious commentaries and interpretations.

Beginning in the late 1920s Jews published a body of literature that they had written in French. Raphael Levy (Ryvel) (1898–1972) and Vitalis Danon (1897–1969) published novels and stories about Tunisian Jewish life. *L'enfant de l'Oukala,* by Ryvel, won the important Prix de Carthage in 1931. In 1929 Danon and Levy together published the famous "La Hara conte" (a story of the Hara, the Jewish quarter). In 1953 Albert Memmi—writer, philosopher, and essayist—won the Prix de Carthage for his autobiography, *La statue de sel* (Pillar of Salt, 1953). Later he published books such as *Agar* (1955), and *Portrait du colonisé* (Portrait of the Colonized, 1957). After the mass emigration of the 1950s, Tunisian Jews who moved to France and published memoirs included Nine Moati, Marco Koskas, and Claude Kayat. Tunisian Jews also had important roles in the arts, such as music and painting. In sports they had a strong soccer team and played on important all-Tunisian teams.

JEWISH-ARAB RELATIONS

French domination in Tunisia slowly changed the pattern of Jewish-Muslim coexistence. The Jews' assimilation to French culture gradually detached them from the Muslim society within which they had lived for hundreds of years. From the beginning of the French protectorate, a new ethnic element—French settlers—was added to Muslim-Jewish relations. Those three groups had different, and occasionally contradictory, interests. With the increasing Tunisian nationalist struggle, tensions between the French and the Muslims became obvious and understandable.

In the reported collective memory of Tunisia's Jews, Muslim-Jewish coexistence was both practical and tranquil. This is not an idyllic, nostalgic point of view. Most Tunisian Jews do not remember any violent outbreaks in Tunisia, apart from the three-day violence of August 1917; Jewish newspapers did carry bits of information about violent incidents in the early 1920s. At the end of the nineteenth century a short outbreak of French anti-Semitism had influenced French-Jewish relations. It resurfaced in the 1930s quite aggressively. Within this relatively good atmosphere, events in British Palestine emerged as a new factor in the relations among Tunisia's three ethnic groups.

In society at large tensions developed during the 1930s between the Tunisian national movement, the Neo-Destour, and the Zionists. The Neo-Destour took advantage of French sensitivity to public order to prevent the Zionists from expressing themselves publicly. For example, the Neo-Destour prevented Vladimir Jabotinsky, the Revisionist Zionist leader, from appearing in Tunisia in 1932 and banned the film *The Promised Land.* In 1937 the

Neo-Destour also sabotaged the visit of the *Sarah A*, a study ship run by Betar, the youth organization of the Zionist Revisionist Party, and condemned the Zionists at every opportunity. A close examination of the relations between the Zionists and the Neo-Destour shows that, despite the attitude of the Neo-Destour toward Zionism, the Zionists were not significantly harmed. The reason for this is simple. The Tunisian national movement's struggle was primarily directed against French rule, and it used Zionism only as a means by which to attack the French. For example, the Neo-Destour's denunciation of British colonialism in Palestine could be taken as a condemnation of French colonialism but only indirectly. The damage done to Zionism was an indirect indication of the level of relations between the French administration and the leaders of the Tunisian nationalists. In this manner the Muslims learned how far they could strain relations with the French without significantly harming themselves. Moreover, such activity allowed them to test their ability to organize the Muslim crowds, to consolidate movement cells, and to prepare movement leadership. Despite attacks on Zionism by the Neo-Destour, both were nationalist movements, which prevented the Neo-Destour from condemning the right of free speech and self-determination for the Zionists. A negation of such rights would have been self-defeating.

As far as is known, the relationship between Jews and Muslims did not deteriorate in the 1940s. During the Vichy government and the German occupation of Tunisia in World War II, Muslims did not turn the situation to their advantage. While violent anti-Jewish manifestations occurred in most of the Arab world, Tunisia saw nothing more than attacks in the newspapers or some public demonstrations.

ZIONISM AND POLITICAL ACTIVITY

Zionism was one response or reaction of Tunisian Jews to French colonialism and the modernization processes that affected them. Zionism could also be considered an expression of modernity. Its influence only increased with the years. The internal dynamics of the French colonial situation and the possibility that Zionism would realize its goal of a Jewish homeland were principal factors in the development of Zionism in Tunisia. Tunisian Zionists saw in their movement a means to achieve political and social expression, adapted to the spirit of the times.

Expressions of Zionism first appeared in Tunisia at the end of the nineteenth century. Organized Zionism began only in 1910, with the foundation of the first Zionist society, Agudat Zion (Society of Zion). French authorities legalized Zionism but restricted it to cultural activities. Agudat Zion published a Zionist newspaper, *Kol Zion,* collected Zionist contributions (the shekel for Eretz Israel), sent a representative to the tenth World Zionist Congress in 1911, contributed to Keren Kayemet (the Jewish National Fund), and held Zionist propaganda meetings. World War I virtually stopped Zionist activity until the end of the war. By 1914 other Jewish organizations had also been founded in all the major cities of Tunisia. The "formative years" of Zionism in Tunisia were 1918 to 1926. The Tunisian Zionist Federation was established in October 1920 as an organizational framework for all Zionist activities, but it did not succeed in rising above its internal problems and was unable to lead Tunisian Zionism. The weakness of the federation stemmed from its inability to enforce its authority, its lack of a fixed budget, and its disregard and neglect by the World Zionist Organization. In addition, opposition to Zionist activities by various sections of the Jewish community increased the difficulties.

By actively participating in all aspects of Jewish community life, the Zionists tolerated other Jewish social trends by publicly recognizing their importance in Jewish society. In addition to their struggles within Tunisian Jewish society, such as that with the Alliance Israélite Universelle (AIU), Zionists tried to make a place for themselves among the other political and social movements of the time, particularly with regard to the Communist Party and the socialist movement, both of which greatly attracted Jewish youth. These struggles, however, were general and ideological in character, and because of this their effect on Zionism was minimal.

Two major changes occurred from 1926 to 1939 in Tunisia. One was the creation of the Zionist youth movements—on the left, the Eclaireurs Israélites de France (EIF), the Union Universelle de la Jeunesse Juive (UUJJ), and Ha-Shomer Ha-Tsaᶜir; and Betar on the right. The youth movements brought an element of vitality to the full range of Zionist activity; they also lowered the average age of Zionist activists. The frameworks for activity were more rigid in the new youth movements than in the older Zionist organizations. In addition, youth movements made it possible for girls to participate in Zionist activity, which had been impossible for women, for both historical and cultural reasons.

Another change in Tunisian Zionism during this period was the penetration by world Zionist political parties: the Revisionists, accompanied by the Betar youth movement, and the socialist Ha-Shomer Ha-Tsaᶜir. Bitter struggles took place between the two ideological approaches to Zionism: the integrationist Zionist program of the Revisionists versus the Marxist

Zionism of Ha-Shomer Ha-Tsaᶜir. The struggle culminated when the Revisionists accused the Marxists of atheism, destroying family life, a bias toward communism, and aspirations that might be fulfilled only in a kibbutz setting. Ha-Shomer Ha-Tsaᶜir was forced to defend itself against these harsh attacks and retaliated by accusing the Revisionists of fascism and Hitlerism. This contest continued in public demonstrations, as well as in newspapers, and was also reflected in information passed on to the police by informers. Pressure from parents and rabbis forced Ha-Shomer Ha-Tsaᶜir to disband in Tunisia in 1935. The Revisionists' victory there resulted from a strong newspaper, a simple ideological ethic, being well-suited to a society in transition, and effective coordination of the party and its youth movement.

The greatest importance of Tunisian Zionism during this period was its primary position in the struggle against all anti-Semitic manifestations in the country, both those of the French colonists and also those of the Italians, who were trying to reestablish themselves in North Africa. The Zionists called for public demonstrations against German anti-Semitic outbreaks. In this way both Zionist groups made a place for themselves within Tunisian Jewish society, taking a stand on behalf of the Jewish community.

World War II in Tunisia (1939–43) totally changed the character of local Zionism. Until the war the importance of Zionism was within Jewish society. Zionism made possible a modern mode of expression and activity for Jews who had not received French citizenship yet wished to express their aspirations for the future without violating the Jewish character of their society. After World War II, Zionists understood that without aliyah (going to Israel), Zionism had no meaning, so they began to prepare for this move. Modern Hebrew became significant, and a Zionist was required to invest time in learning to speak the language. No less important for the Zionists were the attempts to establish preparatory camps in Tunisia and elsewhere; however, the number of Zionists who succeeded in completing this preparation was small. During this period Tunisian Jews began to emigrate to Israel. Many wanted to emigrate, yet doing so legally was nearly impossible in 1947 and 1948; this forced the Zionists to turn to illegal immigration. Tunisian Zionists were among the planners and implementers of the illegal immigration movement. Only about three hundred Jews left Tunisia illegally during this period, but their role was far more significant than their numbers because a sizable percentage were Zionists who not only ranked among the Zionist elite in Tunisia but contributed to Israeli nation building upon their arrival in Israel.

The postwar years in Tunisia were characterized by an increase in the number of ideological parties, particularly those connected to world movements. The Revisionists still enjoyed Zionist hegemony there, as exemplified by the results of the elections to the World Zionist Congress in 1946, and by its strong Zionist and Revisionist newspaper. Among the other various movements, which combined socialism and Zionism, were Tse^cirei Zion, which was aligned with the Kibbutz Ha-Meuchad, and Ha-Shomer Ha-Tsa^cir, which renewed its Tunisian activities in 1946. The religious Zionist movement had two branches. One was aligned with Torah ve-Avoda and the Mizrachi Party, and the other was Ateret Zion in Djerba, which had no affiliation. Other groups remained politically neutral.

WORLD WAR II

Tunisian Jewry was influenced during World War II by developments in Nazi-occupied France. French colonies, including Tunisia, were under Vichy government rule, and all its anti-Jewish legislation applied to the colonies.

The laws and decrees published by the Vichy government in Tunisia concerned three main areas: the legal status of the Jews, the quotas in education, and the measures that were taken against the Jews' economic influence. Published in Tunisia on November 30, 1940, the anti-Jewish laws were only partially implemented because of the small number of French Jews, their importance in the economy, the positive attitude of the French resident general, Admiral Esteva toward Tunisian Jews, and the involvement of the Italian government's representative in Tunisia. In Tunisia the representative of fascist Italy strongly opposed all French attempts to Aryanize Jewish property; this was part of Italy's policy to protect its colony in Tunisia.

During the six months between November 1942 and May 1943, the situation of Tunisian Jewry steadily deteriorated as a result of the German occupation, which was Rommel's defensive move against the imminent attack by the Americans' "Operation Torch" and the British military campaign from Libya. The Jews suffered from the aerial bombardment by the Allied forces, as well those of the German forces. As far as is known, most Jews who died during the German occupation were killed by these bombings. The Germans created a new Jewish community committee, whose most important task was to supply forced labor for military purposes—airfields, encampments, and fortifications that the Allies bombed relentlessly. It is estimated that five thousand young Jewish men were sent to forced labor. Jewish recruitment was carried out by the special Comité de Recrutement de la Main d'Oeuvre, which was headed by Paul Ghez, a famous lawyer who abused his power by enlisting the poorer Jews. The Jewish workers were interned at about thirty military camps along the battlefields. The dissatisfaction with the work of this committee was understandable, because the Tunis Jewish community had to pay for all the workers' necessities, such as food, clothes, and transportation. The Germans confiscated Jewish property—houses, cars, blankets, radios, and public buildings (such as the AIU school)—for their own purposes. They also imposed a fine of 53 million francs ($1.1 million) on the Jewish community. Admiral Esteva did not, and probably could not, help the Jewish leaders to protest the German demands. Thus Jewish feelings of isolation, abandonment, and disappointment with France as a protector were understandable, although France was also an occupied country. As far as is known, the Tunisian Muslims did not hurt the Jews during that tragic period; no incidents occurred between Jews and Arabs. On the contrary, many Arabs offered shelter to Jews in their villages until the German threat passed. On May 7, 1943, the Allied forces liberated Tunisia from Nazi occupation.

The Vichy government and the German occupation of Tunisia was a turning point for Tunisian Jews because it showed that assimilating to French culture was impossible. France not only failed to protect the Jews against harsh attacks but also initiated anti-Semitic activity. The process of decolonialization, disappointment with France, and the rise of Tunisian national aspirations for independence were among the major factors in the changed Jewish attitude toward France. Jews lost confidence that France could or would help them. The alternatives to living under a French protectorate were Zionism and emigration to Israel, communism, or awaiting further developments. Tunisian Jews also were disappointed with the leaders of the Jewish community, whom they blamed for cooperating with the Germans. The Jewish leaders had to resign, and the community then established a provisionary committee. Because the war had destroyed the European economy, France was unable to give any economic assistance to Tunisia after the war.

The creation of the State of Israel in 1948 lured more than four thousand Tunisian emigrants in 1951 and twenty-five hundred in 1952. Yet the following year was marked by a strong decrease in emigrants, about six hundred. Emigration again reached twenty-six hundred in 1954, because the political autonomy granted to Tunisia by the French and the advent of independence convinced many Jews to leave the country. In 1955 more than six thousand Jews emigrated to Israel, followed by sixty-five hundred in 1956, the year that Tunisia gained independence. The aliyah was organized by the Jewish Agency, which sent emissaries to Tunisia. The Mossad's Misgeret, Israel's Zionist-inspired underground, was also active in Tunisia, in the area of training young Jews in self-defense, beginning in the mid-1950s. In this period Tunisian Jewish leaders lost their standing in the community to Israel's emissaries and the Israeli political party representatives. As Jews left for Israel, Tunisia's Jewish newspapers started to fold.

JEWS IN INDEPENDENT TUNISIA, 1956–67

Independence came to Tunisia in 1956. Independent Tunisia's policy toward its Jews favored their full integration into the new Tunisian society. Thus, for example, all Tunisians were given the franchise in elections for the Constituent Assembly; ten Jewish judges were appointed to the country's courts, to judge cases dealing with Jewish litigants; and although the rabbinical courts were abolished, Tunisia established special courts dealing with matters of personal status that were open to Jews just as they were to all other Tunisians. The Jewish community council was disbanded and replaced by the Interim Committee for the Management of the Affairs of the Jewish Community until "associations for religious matters" were established. President Bourguiba wanted the Jewish communities to be reorganized and totally Tunisian, and he signed a law to that effect on July 11, 1958.

The authorities took two steps in developing the capital city of Tunis that proved detrimental to the Jewish community: the transfer of the old Jewish cemetery to another site and the razing of the Jewish quarter. These were carried out as part of an urban renewal plan that also saw the Muslim cemetery removed to a new location. Aware of the Jews' sensitivity, Bourguiba personally supervised all work related to the transfer of the Jewish cemetery, during which the Tunisians displayed a reasonable degree of consideration for Jewish feelings.

From 1956 to 1961 the tension between those Jews who remained in the country and the authorities decreased markedly. Jews were appointed to some positions vacated by the French, and Yom Kippur was proclaimed an official holiday, enabling Jews to absent themselves from work on the holiest day of the Jewish year. The Jews' sense of security and the degree of their identification with Tunisia were exemplified in the role they played in the "Campaign for the Dinar" (which called upon all Tunisians to shore up the declining value of the Tunisian dinar). The extent of emigration to Israel in those years also reflects the general climate of opinion in Tunisia. In 1957, the year after independence, Jewish emigration dropped to about twenty-six hundred and was even lower until 1961.

In early 1961 Bourguiba demanded that France evacuate the French naval bases at Bizerte, on the northern coast. The situation deteriorated into full-scale fighting, with the small Jewish community of Bizerte caught in the crossfire. Although rescued by the Misgeret's activists and the Jewish Agency, Jews were in doubt about their future in Tunisia. The French military presence, limited as it was, had been a sort of life preserver for them and made them feel more secure. This security was gone. During the next four years the condition of Tunisia's Jewish community deteriorated. After a plot to assassinate Bourguiba was uncovered in 1962, many Jewish families closed down their businesses and emigrated to France.

Gradually, Tunisia forbade the mailing of letters and parcels to Israel and cut off direct telephone communication between the two countries. Only Jews bearing French citizenship were allowed to leave with their belongings and this only if they were able to present proof of their citizenship and an affidavit certifying their destination as France. Jews holding Tunisian citizenship could leave the country without their property and were permitted to take with them only 30 dinars (a small amount of money) and some clothes. Thirty-five Jews from Djerba were arrested on suspicion of trying to smuggle gold from Tunisia to Libya; they were imprisoned, tortured, tried in court, convicted, and heavily fined. Only intervention by the Jewish community's leadership managed to alleviate their condition somewhat. Then, during the Six-Day War of 1967, Jewish retail establishments in Tunis suffered heavy damage. In 1966 only twenty-three thousand Jews still lived in Tunisia; two years later the Jewish population was estimated at ten thousand. From 1965 to 1984 most of the rest of the Jews left—11,133—for Israel and France. Then the Lebanese War of 1982 and the ensuing transfer of the Palestine Liberation Organization's headquarters to Tunis, joined by the Arab League's headquarters in 1979, along with the rise of fundamentalist Islamist activities encouraged by the Islamic Revolution in Iran, pushed Tunisia's remaining Jews to leave. Only fifteen hundred Jews continue to live there today, most of them in Djerba and Tunis.

SUGGESTED READING

Abitbol, Michel. *The Jews of North Africa During World War II.* Detroit, Mich.: Wayne State University Press, 1989.

Laskier, Michael. "From Hafsia to Bizerte: Tunisia's Nationalist Struggle and Tunisian Jewry, 1952–61." *Mediterranean Historical Review* 2 (1987): 188–222.

——. *North African Jewry in the Twentieth Century: The Jews of Morocco, Tunisia, and Algeria.* New York: New York University Press, 1994.

CHAPTER

25

Algeria

David Cohen

Algeria is bordered by Morocco and Mauritania in the west, the Mediterranean Sea to the north, and Tunisia and Libya in the east. It stretches south to the Atlas Mountains, the Sahara Desert, Mauritania, Mali, and Niger. Major cities include the capital, Algiers, and Oran, Constantine, and Annaba (Bone). Along the Mediterranean Algeria is relatively humid and mountainous. Algeria's population consists of Arabs and Berbers and, until 1962, had a Jewish community of approximately 140,000 people, as well as European settlers who arrived after the French conquest of the country in 1830. The Arabs of Algeria are descendants of the early Arab invaders of the seventh and eighth centuries; like the Islamized Berbers, who comprise 20 to 30 percent of the population, they are Sunni Muslims.

A Phoenician colony, Algeria was ruled by Rome until it was conquered by the Arabs at the beginning of the eighth century and rapidly Islamized. In 1520 the country passed under the rule of the Ottoman Turks. The Turkish governors, deys, dominated the Mediterranean coast of Algeria in conjunction with the Corsairs, local pirates who seized European ships, their cargo, and crews. In Algiers the Corsairs came to control the Ottoman Empire's political systems. With the French conquest of Algeria in 1830, real wealth and power lay in the hands of the European settlers called *colons*; both the powerful and rich and the small and poor (*pieds noirs*) formed, in effect, a superior class that dominated the indigenous population. The *colons* feared that any political concession to the indigenous people could only lead to the eventual disruption of the control structure that the French were imposing as France made Algeria its base of power in North Africa. As Europeans (French, Italians, Spaniards) settled Algeria in great numbers on land confiscated from both the Muslim Berbers and the Arabs, the Berbers revolted during the nineteenth century. From the 1930s on Algerian nationalists opposed French colonial rule. French rule remained stable until 1954, when the Front de Libération Nationale (FLN) emerged as the umbrella organization for different nationalist factions, both inside Algeria and those in exile, that were struggling for independence. Algeria was finally granted independence in 1962. The FLN ruled until 1992, and it was subsequently beset by civil war between Islamists and secularist forces.

THE ORIGINS OF ALGERIAN JEWS

During the Phoenician period (500 B.C.E.) Jews lived in the main towns on the Algerian coast. Later, when Carthage was at its peak, Jews lived there as well. The Romans under Titus (70–80 C.E.) sent Jews from Palestine to resettle Carthage, which the Romans had conquered and destroyed. From there the Jews spread into Algeria, where they established contacts with the Berber tribes. Jews also came from Arabia, which had exiled its Jews after the rise of Islam and the first conquests of Muhammad (630 C.E.). Some groups of Jews arrived via the Saharan trade routes and settled in the oases. They gradually moved north from the desert, settling near the Mediterranean coast. Legend has it that some Berber tribes may have converted to Judaism. Most of Algeria's Jews are, however, claim descent from the Sephardim who were expelled in the fifteenth century and later from Spain or Italy, who lived as *dhimmis* under Ottoman rule.

When France conquered Algeria in 1830, Jews were confronted with a new situation. Now they were under the domination of a European power, after centuries of being subjected to Ottoman rule and the particular status of the Jews in the Islamic world. The French authorities gradually gave Jews and Muslims the same rights and reduced the powers of the traditional Jewish leadership. Around 1840 the French government decided to confer the status of colony on Algeria and began to heed the pressure of French Jewry to protect Algerian Jews. In 1842 the French authorities sent to Algeria a delegation of two leading Sephardic members of the Jewish community in Marseilles, Jacques-Isaac Altaras and Joseph Cohen, to conduct a sociological survey and to recommend the most suitable ways to regulate the structure of the Jewish communities. In their report, known as the Altaras-Cohen Report (1843), they recommended canceling the functions of the *muqaddem* (head of the Jewish community) and the *bet-din* (the rabbinical court), bringing Algerian Jews under the French civil code, and conferring French citizenship on Algerian Jews. The community would be directed by a *consistoire* (committee) with a president originating from France to guide Algerian Jews in their assimilation to French civilization. The *consistoire* would pay salaries to the rabbis and the employees of Jewish institutions.

On the basis of the Altaras-Cohen Report, the French government adopted a range of decisions concerning Algerian Jewry. In November 1845 a royal order organized a central *consistoire* in Algiers; two provincial ones were organized in Oran (June 1847) and Constantine (December 1847). Some years later a chief rabbi of Algeria, originating from France, was appointed to serve Algiers, Oran, and Constantine. The Frenchifying of Algerian Jewry had begun.

During the Second Empire (1852–70) numerous organizations and elected representatives in Algeria sought the naturalization of Algerian Jews. In 1860 Adolphe Crémieux, a leader of the Alliance Israélite Universelle, advocated French citizenship for Algerian Jews; the goals of the Alliance were to improve the juridical, political, and social status of the Jews of the Muslim lands. According to Crémieux, conferring French citizenship on Algerian Jews would not pose a problem—because Algeria was a colony, the Algerian Jews were automatically French subjects. But Napoleon III refused to grant to Algerian Jews French citizenship. Only after the collapse of the Second Empire, when the Third Republic was proclaimed and a provisional government of national defense was formed on September 4, 1870, did the idea advance. Crémieux was appointed France's minister of justice, and on October 24, 1870, he proposed eight decrees that reorganized Algeria completely. The provisional government adopted them immediately. One of these decrees conferred French citizenship collectively on Algerian Jews.

The Crémieux Decree, as it was known, turned the life of Algerian Jews upside down from both a religious and social point of view. This was the beginning of their assimilation to French culture and civilization. They had to attend French public schools, serve in the French army, and answer to French civil courts. Yet Jews felt discrimination on the social level, for the arrival of the French in 1830 had completely changed the social structure of Algerian society. At the top of the social hierarchy were the French *colons* who never wanted to give Algerian Jews French citizenship. Below them were the Jews who had served in the French army. Foreign Europeans, established in Algeria since the 1860s, came next. They included the Italians, the Maltese, and the Spaniards, who did not look favorably on the higher status of Jews in Algerian society. Finally, at the bottom of the social ladder were the Arabs, who did not understand how Jews, who were *dhimmi,* could attain a social status higher than theirs. Ironically, this meant that Jewish success led to political, administrative, and economic anti-Semitism.

EDUCATION

Until the arrival of the French in 1830, Algerian Jews were strongly religious. They had produced such famous theologians and scholars as Rabbi Isaac Bar Sheshet (Ribash, 1326–1408) and Rabbi Shimon Ben Zemah (Rashbatz, 1361–1442), both originally from Spain, as well as such local scholars as Rabbi Saadia Chouraqui (1604–1704) and Rabbi Yehuda Ayache (1700–61), as well as Ayache's son Yakov Moshe Ayache, *hakham bashi* (chief rabbi) of Eretz Israel from 1806 to 1817. Other rabbis included Yosef Bouchara, Neorai Azoubib, Abraham Tobiana, Yaakov Morali, Itshak Aboulkheir, David Moatti and, more recently, Haim Beliah (1832–1919).

Algerian education was a traditional one for Jewish boys, who were entrusted to rabbis or to the *melamed* (a teachers in a Jewish religious elementary school), who taught in the heder (*kuttab*). After Algerian Jews became French citizens in 1870, French law compelled all children to learn in French public schools, so Jewish education declined rapidly, inducing the Paris-based AIU to open Talmud Torahs in almost each town beginning in 1900. They functioned two days a week, Thursday and Sunday, which were the days off from the French public primary schools. The children were taught Hebrew, some passages of the Bible, basic prayers, and ancient Jewish history. At the beginning the teachers were rabbis or people well educated in Jewish matters. They translated the texts of the biblical section of the week, which was read in the synagogue in Judeo-Arabic, but the AIU was strongly against this practice, and by 1930 all the translations in the Talmud Torahs (traditional Jewish religious school), despite the reluctance of rabbis and local teachers, were into French. In the 1880s a yeshiva called Etz Haim was founded in Algiers. It trained youngsters to become cantors but not rabbis. By 1925 the shortage of Hebrew teachers impelled the AIU to train Hebrew teachers in the Etz Haim schools in Oran and Algiers. In 1954–55 a rabbinical seminary was created in Algiers, but it functioned only until 1960.

Algerian Jews flocked to the French schools. In the secondary schools of Constantine alone, the Jews, who represented 12.89 percent of the total population there, accounted for 29.67 percent of the pupils. The 1941 census revealed that the Jews, who represented only 2 percent of the Algerian population, made up 37 percent of medical students, 24.4 percent of law students, 16.8 percent of science students, and 10 percent of art students.

POPULAR RELIGION AND CUSTOMS

As with every religious group, Algerian Jews have their popular religious customs. For example, they celebrated "Purim of Oran" on the sixth of the Jewish month of Av to mark the day in 1830 that the Jews of Oran escaped a massacre. On the sixth of Av every synagogue in Oran recited a Hebrew hymn entitled "Mi Kamokha," composed in 1838 by Rabbi Messaoud Darmon. In the M'zab (a region of five towns at the southern edge of the Sahara) the Jews of Ghardaïa would gather to recite *piyyutim* and *bakkashot* (hymns and supplications). In Bone the Griba synagogue, which contained a famous Torah scroll venerated by Muslims as well as Jews because of miracles connected with it, became a center of pilgrimage.

Other important Jewish landmarks included the tombs of Rabbi Isaac Drai of Sétif and Rabbi Sidi Fredj Halimi in Constantine, and the tombs of Rabbi Yeoshua El Kaim and Rabbi Sion Sion in Medea. The most venerated *zaddik* in Algeria is Rabbi Efraim Nkaoua (Rab) of fourteenth-century Tlemcen. Born in Toledo, Spain, Nkaoua, who was also a physician, came to Tlemcen in 1393, where he saved the life of the sultan's daughter. As a reward, the sovereign allowed the Jews of Tlemcen, who had been living outside the town, to reside in the city. After Nkaoua's death in 1442, his grave and its spring became the tomb of the Rab, and each year on the holiday of Lag bᶜOmer it is the object of *hillulot* (pilgrimages) of Algerian Jews; it is also venerated by Muslims.

JEWS IN ALGERIAN SOCIETY

With the exception of some merchant families such as the Bacris and the Busnachs, most Jews were craftsmen. Later, under the French they were employed in trade or government service, comprising more than 50 percent of the working population. The flamboyant role of the house of Bacri-Busnach in breaking the monopoly of Marseilles merchants in French trade at the beginning of the nineteenth century, and the family's extravagant lifestyle, led to its downfall and the departure of other wealthy Jewish families.

Algerian Jews began to take an interest in politics chiefly after World War I. A number, essentially from liberal professions, were elected to the local assemblies and took an active part in political debates between 1920 and 1962. Algeria also had numerous Jewish authors and instructors of higher education (law, medicine, and the humanities). Despite the tendency of Jews to assimilate, the number of mixed marriages was relatively low, except in Algiers.

Typical family names of Algerian Jews include Allouche, Amsellem, Atlan, Bacri, Benguigui, Benichou, Boccara, Boumendil, Chouraqui, Dadoun, Lelouche, Touati, and Zerbib.

ANTI-SEMITISM IN ALGERIA (1880–1943)

The collective naturalization of Jews by the Crémieux Decree led to an outbreak of Algerian anti-Semitism. It was largely manifested among the French and European settlers (Italians, Maltese, and Spanish), who had brought their anti-Semitism with them when they arrived in Algerian towns in great numbers after 1850 (anti-Semitism did not erupt among the Muslims, who were not opposed to the decree). Because the Jews were concentrated in the towns, where they sometimes represented 30 to 40 percent of the voters, candidates competed for their vote.

Anti-Jewish riots occurred in Oran in 1884. Riots in Algiers in 1897 and 1898, where two Jews were killed and one hundred severely wounded, coincided with the Dreyfus Affair in France (where a Jewish army officer was unfairly tried for treason and convicted), but this anti-Semitism was purely European Algerian. The first anti-Jewish league had been founded in July 1871 in Miliana, during the parliamentary elections, with the objective of turning the new Jewish voters away from the polls. It predated the first anti-Semitic league founded in France in 1889 and thus can be viewed as the founder of institutionalized French anti-Semitism.

With the outbreak of World War I in 1914, anti-Semitism again appeared in Algeria, but this time Algerian Jews organized and succeeded in foiling the attempts of the anti-Semites to interfere with their civil rights. Founded in Algiers in 1915, Le Comité Juif Algérien d'Etudes Sociales (CJAES) was supported by intellectuals, notables, traders, and merchants of the Algerian Jewish middle class and was headed by Professor Henri Aboulker. First, the committee decided to provide statistics about Algerian Jewish soldiers who had participated in World War I on French soil, how many had been killed and wounded, and how many had been decorated for bravery, in order to prove the patriotism of Algerian Jews toward France. Second, the committee wanted to grant material and moral assistance to the families of the Jewish soldiers who had served in the French army. Third, the committee wanted to investigate the social origins of anti-Semitism in Algeria. Aboulker concluded that the Algerian colonial civil service was the culprit, for through laws and decrees it had gradually made the Crémieux Decree meaningless. Algerian Jews were in fact second-class citizens, and he urged them to correct this injustice. His organization was a private one, for all recognized the powerlessness of the consistory system that had been instituted by the French colonial administration.

After 1923 the CJAES became inactive; it was revived after the Constantine riots of August 1934 when twenty-five Jews were killed by Muslims influenced by Nazi propaganda. Until the outbreak of World War II, CJAES faced a series of anti-Semitic incidents. The most serious occurred in Sidi-Bel-Abbes, near Oran, in 1938, where the mayor, an anti-Semite, struck the names of three hundred Jews from the list of voters. After a long juridical struggle, in May 1939 the CJAES won the cancellation of this illegal and arbitrary decision.

With the German occupation of France in 1940, the Vichy government adopted anti-Semitic statutes regarding the Jews and imposed them on France and its territories. Thus state policy merged with the anti-Semitic feeling of many Algerians. The first step against the Jews was the abrogation of the Crémieux Decree on October 7, 1940; this canceled the French citizenship of Algerian Jews and made them French subjects, like the Muslims. They could not return to their earlier juridical autonomy, that is, of the *bet-din* of the Ottoman period. In 1940 and 1941 the Vichy government promulgated a series of anti-Semitic laws that affected all spheres of Jewish life. In an atmosphere of intense Axis propaganda these regulations "Aryanized" Jewish real estate and industrial goods through confiscation by "Aryans." These laws also set quotas for Jewish civil servants, professionals, and students in public schools.

The Algerian Jews understood quickly that they had to rely on themselves. First, they reorganized their economy and education; then they undertook secret political activity. Some Jewish figures who had belonged to the CJAES, which was dissolved at the beginning of the war, founded a new organization, the Association d'Etude d'Aide et d'Assistance, known later as the Comité d'Aide et d'Assistance (CAA). The CAA helped the fired Jewish teachers and civil servants and suggested the establishment of a network of Jewish private schools to accommodate the Jewish children who were expelled from the French public schools. The organization and administration of this Jewish private education was entrusted to Professor Robert Brunschvig. At the end of 1942 seventy primary schools functioned in Algeria, and the main towns had several several secondary schools. Annual contributions and grants by more fortunate Jews ensured that they had operating funds. By the end of 1943 the American Jewish Joint Distribution Committee (AJDC) was providing material and financial support.

In politics several young Jewish officers, who had been demobilized in France after the German occupation, came back to Algeria and decided to join the political struggle because they did not accept the Nazi conquest, the discrimination, and the loss of their civil rights in 1940–41. They founded a secret organization, the Geo-Gras Group, headed by Dr. Raphael Aboulker, Emile Atlan, Charles Bouchara, and André Temime. Under the supervision of a non-Jewish instructor, Geo Gras, the mostly Jewish group, which had about 150 members, opened a sports facility in Algiers where they trained themselves to fight. At the beginning of 1941 two young Jews—Professor Henri Aboulker's son Jose, who had been a lieutenant in the French army, and Roger Carcassonne from Oran—joined the Geo-Gras Group. The two contacted the Algerian resistance army, composed of field officers of the French army and politicians of nationalist leaning who did not recognize the 1940 surrender of France to Germany. The aim of both Jews and non-Jews was to provoke an uprising against Vichy forces in Algeria whenever U.S. and British forces landed in French North Africa. Jose Aboulker and Roger Carcassonne were deeply involved in preparing for the landing of troops. They worked with the U.S. delegate in Algeria, Robert Murphy, and with U.S. Gen. Mark Clark, and as well as with British officers. Dwight D. Eisenhower, commander of U.S. and British forces for the landing in North Africa, and President Franklin D. Roosevelt were aware of these contacts. When the U.S. and British forces landed in Algiers on November 8, 1942, as a part of "Operation Torch," Jose Aboulker succeeded in paralyzing the main civil and military security services in Algiers for several crucial hours. His efforts helped U.S. and British forces to take control. After the landing of the Allies, anti-Jewish legislation was gradually abolished in North Africa but not without difficulty because Vichy administrators continued to hold responsible positions. U.S. and British officials were not even aware of this delicate situation. Thanks to a series of stories in the U.S. press, however, the anti-Semitic measures were abrogated and the Crémieux Decree restored in November 1943.

JEWISH PRESS IN ALGERIA

Jews published several small newspapers in Algeria from 1880 to 1900, some in Judeo-Arabic and some in French. Two later newspapers deserve particular attention. The first, *Bulletin de la Fédération des Sociétés Juives d'Algérie,* founded by Elie Gozlan (1876–1964), who would become the most active member of the CAA, appeared between 1934 and 1947 as a monthly political magazine; until 1947 it was the only newspaper of the Algerian Jewish community. In 1934, after the terrible Constantine riots, the *Bulletin* strongly recommended Jewish-Arab reconciliation and regularly took a stand on important events in Muslim Algerian life. The *Bulletin* also published information about the Jewish colonies in British Palestine and about anti-Semitism in the colonial administration.

During World War II, when the Vichy government forbade the publication of Jewish newspapers in Algeria, Tunisia, and Morocco, the *Bulletin* was exempted; we can assume that it was widely read during that period in Algeria and also in its two neighboring countries. Gozlan and the *Bulletin* courageously faced Vichy censorship and for that reason played an important role not only in providing information but also in holding the Jewish community together during one of the most difficult times in its history. The *Bulletin* was a popular newspaper because it was open to all opinions within the Jewish community—the religious, the assimilationist, and the Zionist—and fought anti-Semitism while preaching tolerance and harmony with Muslims.

The second Jewish newspaper, *L'Information Juive,* was founded by Jacques Lazarus, who had fought in the Resistance during World War II and arrived in Algiers in 1947 to open an ORT (Organization of Rehabilitation through Training) vocational school. Lazarus played an important part in Algerian Jewish community life, for he immediately became an active member of the CJAES. He also represented the World Jewish Congress in North Africa. *L'Information Juive* quickly became an indispensable coordinator of these two institutions with the Jewish community. The pages of *L'Information Juive* carried news about Algerian Jewry as well as Tunisian, Moroccan, and French Jewry and the Jewish world in general. The newspaper was Zionist, and from 1954 through 1962 *L'Information Juive* was the organ of the Algerian Jewish community in its relations with the three Algerian political groups—the government of Algeria, which represented the government of metropolitan France; the far right, which was represented from 1961 by the Organisation de l'Armée Secrète (OAS); and the Front de Libération Nationale (FLN), which represented the Algerian Muslim nationalists. Thus *L'Information Juive* was influential in Algerian public opinion because it was read with great interest not only by Algerian Jews but also by the main political groups of Algerian society.

THE DILEMMA OF 1930–60

Over the centuries the Algerian Jews were profoundly influenced by Arab civilization in all aspects of life. The French influence was important too but not as profound. As Algerian nationalist demands became more specific after 1930, Algerian Jews were faced with a political dilemma. Until 1962, the date of their mass exodus to France, the Algerian Jews were tormented by the painful choice of staying or leaving. They wanted to continue to live in Algeria, their native land, and in 1936 they joined a new body, L'Union des Croyants Monotheistes, which worked for rapprochement among the followers of the three monotheistic religions. This organization of liberal Jews included the writer and philosopher Raymond Benichou, and it supported the demands of moderate Algerian nationalists such as Ferhat Abbas, who asked for a gradual integration of Muslims into the political life of Algeria. That year the French government, headed by the socialist Leon Blum (who was of Jewish origin), became aware of the rise of Arab nationalism in Algeria, and made the Blum-Viollette proposal. Its goal was to give a few Algerian Muslims full French citizenship. But right-wing settlers wrecked the project, even asking for the abrogation of the Crémieux Decree.

The dilemma arose again with the outbreak of World War II in 1939. Algerian Jews were badly affected by French anti-Semitic policies. Although they had supported France during World War I and in 1939 and 1940 against the Nazi regime, the Vichy government's policy showed that the Algerian Muslim population was indifferent to the Jewish situation, or worse. Some Muslims were delighted at the thought that they could take advantage of the new situation. Others, especially the religious leaders, like Sheikh El Oqbi and the political leader Ferhat Abbas, went against the Vichy laws. When the war ended in 1945, the Vichy French were replaced by new military and civil authorities.

Civil war began in 1954 when the Algerian nationalists, led by the FLN, revolted against the French colonialists. During the first two or three years of the civil war, Jews remained neutral. Some were sensitive to injustice toward Muslims, wanted reforms, and supported the FLN, but some supported a French Algeria and worked with the *pieds noirs.*

Daniel Timsit, a member of the French Communist Party, worked for the FLN and was arrested in 1958. On the other side, although Jews were very much in demand by the extremists of the Front National Français and the Front de l'Algérie Française, at first they did not join the ranks of the followers of Algérie Française. When in December 1960 the Jewish cemetery in Oran was desecrated, the entire Jewish community of Oran sided with the European extremists, represented from then on by the Organisation de l'Armée Secrète (OAS). Jews joined the OAS's commandos and took an active part in murderous attacks against French liberals and Muslims;

twenty-one OAS members were arrested and sentenced to jail, among them, Elie Azoulay, Henri Azoulay, Henri Tordjman, and Albert Darmon. Darmon was called "the killer" and drew a salary from the OAS.

Jews faced a difficult situation. When they wanted to remain neutral, the FLN called them traitors, and supporters of Algérie Française did not hide their anti-Semitism. Algerian Jews were aware of the status of Jews in the newly independent neighboring Arab countries of Tunisia and Morocco, and as well as of the continuation of the Israeli-Arab conflict, and understood that life for a Jewish community in a Muslim country in the 1960s would be precarious at best. Thus the French solution took shape. Although the FLN's militants promised Algerian Jews that they would be treated as Algerian citizens, with the same rights as all other inhabitants, Algerian Jews opted by an overwhelming majority to move to France. The first departures occurred in 1957 and gradually increased as it became obvious that Algeria would soon be independent—that the French were leaving. About 100,000 Jews moved to France in 1962 and 1963. They left behind numerous properties, cemeteries, and synagogues.

MOSSAD ACTIVITY IN ALGERIA

In 1954–55 Israel's Mossad created a unit in North Africa called Misgeret (framework). Whereas in Morocco its activity concerned illegal emigration and self-defense, in Tunisia and Algeria it was concerned only with self-defense. The first operation of the Misgeret in Algeria took place in May 1956, a month after the first nationalist attack on Jews during the civil war. A Mossad agent arrived in Constantine, got in touch with interested local Jewish young people, particularly with the scouts belonging to Eclaireurs Israélites de France, and within a few weeks he had recruited, trained, and armed a hundred young people. Some were sent to Israel to participate in crash military training courses. When the attacks against Jews increased, the Jewish community warned that the situation in Constantine in 1956 was different from that in 1934, when the Constantine riots occurred. This time Jews would fight back if they were attacked. Still, the Misgeret leader in Constantine did not leave anything to chance and set up patrols in anticipation of the Muslim feast day of Id al-Fitr, which marked the end of Ramadan, which fell on May 12. When FLN members threw a grenade into a Jewish cafe, killing one and wounding thirteen, Misgeret men managed to kill about twenty Muslim attackers and to wound ten more before police arrived. The FLN immediately stopped its attacks against Jews and Jewish institutions.

ZIONISM AND ALGERIAN JUDAISM

Zionism attracted Algerian Jews from the start. In August 1897, when the First Zionist Congress met, only one person represented Jews from the Muslim countries, namely, Edouard Attali from Constantine. In 1920 a Zionist association called L'Union Sioniste Algérienne was founded in Algiers and led by Lucien Smadja. Its activities were confined to helping the Jewish National Fund, whose emissaries came to Algeria to collect money. That situation went on until World War II. During the Vichy era Zionist activity came to a halt, to be revived after the war. The Holocaust and its terrible consequences induced Zionist officials to take an interest in North Africa Jewry, with its half-million Jews. The Jewish Agency for Palestine and the Mossad le-Aliya Bet (Organization for Illegal Immigration) understood quickly that they needed to recruit in Algeria, where Zionist activity was not forbidden, as it was Morocco and Tunisia. Thus they developed such local Zionist leaders as Benjamin Heler, Andre Narboni, Elie Gozlan, and Eizer Cherki. From 1944 to 1948 they built the framework for underground emigration, and from 1948 to 1958 they assisted in the emigration from Tunisia and Morocco to Israel. Soon Algeria became the hub of emigration to Israel from North Africa.

In the 1950s emissaries from Israeli kibbutzim started small Zionist youth movements. Among them were Dror and especially Ihud Habonim, which in 1959 helped to found a *gar^{c}in* (group preparing to found a kibbutz) in Algiers. After a period of training, the members of the *gar^{c}in* emigrated to Israel and helped found the kibbutz Hanita near the Lebanese border. Zionism was not overly successful in Algeria, probably because Algerian Jews had acquired French citizenship in 1870 and inevitably became assimilated into French society. And as anti-Semitism became a dominant feature of Algerian Jewish life, keeping their civil rights became the priority of Algeria Jews.

THE EMIGRATION OF ALGERIAN JEWS TO ISRAEL

Few Jews from Algeria settled in Israel. Small groups—probably Zionist militants or members of youth Zionist movements—emigrated to Israel between 1943 and 1948, and they joined kibbutzim. In all fifteen thousand Algerian Jews settled in Israel between 1943 and 1963. In contrast, more than 100,000 of the 140,000 Algerian Jews counted in the census of 1950 arrived in France from 1962 to 1963. This occurred through a well-organized emigration; unlike emigration from other Middle Eastern countries, it was not an escape.

In January 1963 fewer than five thousand Jews still lived in Algeria. Various organizations went to work on their behalf. The main one was the Comité d'Action Sociale Israélite d'Alger, established in 1962. It was affiliated with the Algiers consistory and had a permanent working relationship with the French consulates across the country. It distributed cash relief to needy families, assisted the homeless, and supported the Maimonides religious school.

One reason that emigration continued after 1964 was the institutionalization of a socialist economy during the regime of Ahmed Ben Bella (1963–65) and after 1965 under Houari Boumedienne, Ben Bella's successor as president of the republic. Jewish communities assumed that with the liberal economy in Algeria withering away, their only alternative was to leave.

In 1966 only three thousand Jews lived in Algeria. About fifteen hundred lived in Algiers, one thousand in Oran, and only five hundred in Constantine and the south. Some were merchants and small businessmen; others were members of the professions, namely, physicians, pharmacists, lawyers. Many were aged and dependent on the AJDC, or they were well-to-do pensioners, seeking to live the rest of their lives in Algeria.

The Six-Day War of 1967 did not seem to bother them, despite the violence and some of the official anti-Israeli pronouncements. No anti-Jewish rioting took place in the country. The few acts of harassment included insults, the mistreatment of Chief Rabbi Simon Zini of Oran, and the expulsion by the authorities of six Jews.

By March 1970 fewer than one thousand Jews remained in Algeria—350 in Oran, about 300 in Algiers, and several dozen each in Constantine, Bone, Blida, Tlemcen, and Mostaganem. They were largely elderly people, but one Talmud Torah remained in Oran. Rabbi Simon Zini, who lived in Oran, traveled to perform circumcisions and other religious duties upon the request of several communities. Organized Jewish life in Algeria ended during the 1970s.

SUGGESTED READING

Abitbol, Michel. *North African Jewry in World War II.* Detroit, Mich.: Wayne State University Press, 1989.

Laskier, Michael M. *North African Jewry in Twentieth Century: The Jews of Morocco, Tunisia, and Algeria.* New York: New York University Press, 1994.

——. "The Regeneration of French Jewry: The Influx and Integration of North African Jews into France, 1955–1965." *Jewish Political Studies Review* 10, nos. 1–2 (Spring 1998): 37–72.

CHAPTER

26

Morocco

*Michael Menachem Laskier
and Eliezer Bashan*

Morocco, an area of 177,117 square miles, lies in the northwestern corner of Africa. It borders Algeria to the east and south and the western Sahara to the south; its northern border is defined by the Mediterranean and its western border by the Atlantic. The population in 2000 was about twenty-seven million. Morocco also shares a border with Spain's two urban enclaves, Ceuta and Melilla. Morocco's ethnic groups are Arabs, arabized Berbers, Berbers, and Jews. About 40 percent of the population is Berber; more than 5.6 million Moroccans speak one of the three primary Berber dialects, Tarrifit, Tamazight, and Tachelhit. The Berbers, the original inhabitants, live primarily in the south within the valleys of the Atlas Mountains but also in the north, around the Rif mountains. The Arab majority, including the Moors expelled from Spain in the 1400s as well as the Berbers, are Sunni Muslim. Jews claim to have lived in Morocco since the destruction of the Temple in 586 B.C.E. Their ranks were swelled by a wave of immigration following the destruction of the Second Temple in 70 C.E. and by the influx of Sephardim expelled from Spain. In addition, a few Christians lived in Morocco before colonialism. These were essentially European merchants. Like other urbanites, including Jews, they could be found in Essaouira (Mogador), Mazagan (Al-Jadida), Casablanca, and Rabat, as well as other Atlantic coastal seaports; they also lived in Fez, Marrakesh, Meknès, and Sefrou in the inland areas of central and southern Morocco, and in Tangier and such other northern towns as Tetuán, Larache, Alcazarquibir, Arsila, and Nador.

Morocco's national language is Arabic, but even today French serves as a language of commerce, education, and diplomacy. Economically, Morocco, then and now, relies on agriculture. About 40 percent of the labor force works in this sector, which contributes 20 percent of the gross domestic product. Manufacturing is geared to phosphate production, while tourism has been growing as a vital source of employment and hard currency.

Politically and dynastically, since the advent of Islam in the seventh century, the area has been dominated by, among others, the Idrisids, Almohades, Sa'adis, and sharifian Alawites (the latter from the seventeenth century to the present). The Alawite sharif sultans traced their descent from the prophet Muhammad. The sultans lived in the capital cities, Fez in the north and Marrakesh in the south. Fez, founded in 789 by Idris I ibn Abdallah, was the religious and cultural center. Until the nineteenth century, the *ulama* (Islamic religious elite) of Fez comprised the highest religious and political authority, to be rivaled in later years by the Marrakeshi *ulama*. In the last quarter of the nineteenth century, the *ulama*'s influence lessened, and some *ulama* became administrators in the sharifian *makhzan* (government).

During the reign of Sulayman II ibn Muhammad (1792–1822) and his heir, Abd al-Rahman II (1822–59), European intervention in Morocco's affairs grew significantly because of the Napoleonic Wars. In 1828 Britain blockaded Tangier, and the following year the Austrian fleet bombarded Rabat, Larache, and Tetuán in retaliation for the plunder of Austrian ships by Moroccan pirates. After Algeria's conquest by the French in 1830, tensions between Morocco and France grew. Morocco supported Abd al-Qadir, the Algerian Berber warrior who rebelled against France, and granted him refuge. In 1844 war broke out between Morocco and France, resulting in the bombardment of Tangier and Essaouira by the French fleet. The French defeated the sultan's army, and Moroccans signed a treaty in which they promised neither to help the rebels nor give refuge to al-Qadir and his men.

Under Muhammad IV's sultanate (1859–73) Spain declared war on Morocco, in response to attacks by Rifian Berbers on Ceuta (1860), and occupied Tetuán. Fearing Spain's strength, Britain mediated a Spanish-Moroccan agreement (1861) by which Tetuán was returned to Morocco in exchange for 20 million douros—the equivalent then of 5 million pounds sterling, or US$27.8 million. Britain lent the payment to the sultan in order to deepen his dependency. At that time agreements with European nations expanded trade activity. By 1865 Morocco had signed commercial treaties with most of Europe, which competed with the United States for influence in Morocco. Upon Muhammad IV's death his eldest son, Hassan I, succeeded him and reigned from 1873 to 1894; he demonstrated firm leadership and determination to instill stability. During Hassan I's sultanate the *makhzan* resorted to military action against Arab Berber tribes and strove, albeit with limited success, to eradicate bureaucratic corruption. Aided by French and British instructors, Morocco systematically reorganized its army. Hassan I's death in 1894 led to the succession of his fourteen-year-old son, Abd al-Aziz IV. Under the new leadership economic and political instability prevailed throughout the country. It was manifested by intertribal warfare and warring between rebel tribes and the sultan's army. The widespread anarchy and imperialistic goals brought the intervention of European powers, particularly France, which pressured the *makhzan* to secure the return of loans made to Morocco. In 1900 inhabitants of the Atlas Mountains declared war against France. The treaty of 1904 between Britain and France (the Entente Cordiale) and the Algeciras Conference of 1906 paved the way for the French protectorate. In 1907 French forces seized Oujda, a border town near Algeria, Casablanca, and Rabat, in response to the murder of French nationals. Anti-European incidents increased, and the *ulama* demanded that the sultan declare war against them. Abd al-Aziz's refusal to cooperate with the *ulama* made him vulnerable to accusations of collaborating with the infidels. Abd al-Hafiz, his brother, was acclaimed ruler in his place in August 1908.

A Franco-Moroccan treaty, drawn up in Fez on March 30, 1912, brought Morocco under a French protectorate. In November a Franco-Spanish treaty was signed dividing the protectorate between the two countries. France gained the major part of the territory, including the Atlas Mountains and the cities and regions of Casablanca, Marrakesh, Oujda, Fez, Meknès, Rabat, Salé, Sefrou Mazagan, Essaouira, and Agadir. France then embarked on a military pacification campaign to ensure the stability of the *makhzan,* which survived alongside the colonial apparatus, and to consolidate the economic and strategic status of Spain's newly acquired influence. Areas formerly under the partial or full influence of tribal groups were subordinated to both the traditional *qa'ids* (rural governors) and a French military administration (bureaux des affaires indigènes). In the cities the *makhzan*'s governors were supplemented and at times superseded by top-level French officials. The resident general in Rabat signed all royal *zahirs* (royal edict) in the name of the sharifian government. Henceforth Marshal Louis-Hubert-Gonzalve Lyautey, the first resident general of French Morocco, and his successors were able to influence, even dictate, the contents of the decrees. The *makhzan* granted them full police and military power for the restoration of public order and for Morocco's air and land defenses.

Spain, on the other hand, got parts of northern Morocco that included the cities of Tetuán, Larache, Alcazarquibir, Arsila, Xauen, Nador, and the Rif mountains. The Spaniards appointed a *khalifa* (viceroy), chosen from the royal family, as nominal head of state, providing him with a puppet Moroccan government. They also created European-staffed departments or regions that were administered by *interventores,* as the Spanish colonial supervisors or inspectors were known. In December 1923 representatives of France, Spain, and Britain established a separate international zone in Tangier. While Tangier remained part of the sharifian empire, it enjoyed a special status. A legislative assembly and the sultan's representative, the *mandub,* who was actually appointed by the French, governed it.

Unlike their violent takeover of Algeria, in establishing their protectorate in Morocco the French drew on the expertise they had gained in forming the Tunisian protectorate. In Morocco, Marshall Lyautey, an aristocratic soldier who possessed a deep aesthetic appreciation of the qualities of Moroccan civilization, carried further the concept that the French had applied in Tunisia: that they would preserve autonomous institutions while simultaneously imposing a parallel European administration designed to serve the interests of European settlers (whose numbers in the late 1940s exceeded 400,000).

The challenge to colonialism emerged after 1930. Young urban intellectuals protested by organizing the Bloc d'Action Nationale, then the Parti Nationale, and, finally in 1944, Istiqlal (the Party of Independence). In 1953, after the French exiled the popular sultan Sidi Muhammad ben Yusuf (who became known as King Muhammad V in 1957), the quest for national independence resulted in the protracted anticolonial struggle of 1953–55. In March 1956 Morocco achieved independence. Between 1956 and 2000 Morocco was dominated by the monarchy and political parties that participated in government coalitions. The parties included Istiqlal, Union Nationale des Forces Populaires, Union Socialiste des Forces Populaires, and Parti Démocratique d'Indépendance.

SOCIOECONOMIC AND CULTURAL FACTORS IN PRECOLONIAL JEWISH SOCIETY

Before the twentieth century the majority of Morocco's Jews lived under the protection of the sultans in the urban areas. Tribal chiefs ensured the well-being of Jews living among rural Berbers. Those earliest Jewish settlers, called *toshavim* by the Spanish Sephardic exiles, resembled Muslims in their language and customs. The Jews expelled from Spain, called *megorashim,* were better educated than the *toshavim,* and they soon enjoyed a higher socioeconomic status and dominated the life and customs of the Jewish community. In Morocco's southern region they preserved old customs into modern times. In the nineteenth century a tiny nucleus of Ashkenazim settled in Morocco, seeking refuge from the pogroms in Russia. Yet in contrast to the separatist nature of the Ashkenazic Egyptian community in Cairo, there is no evidence in Morocco of a separate community or the establishment of a synagogue of their own.

There were Jewish communities across Morocco in the early twentieth century. Groups of Jews who lived in the towns on the Mediterranean coast, like Melilla, Tetuán, and Tangier, and along the Atlantic coast at Larache, Salé, Rabat, Casablanca, Azemmour, Al-Jadida, Safi, Essaouira, and Agadir were merchants who traded with Europe. Jews living in these centers sometimes enjoyed better conditions than their counterparts in the inland towns of Fez, Sefrou, Meknès, and Marrakesh. The influence of the outside world reached these inland towns later. In the nineteenth century Jewish families migrated from small communities (including the Atlas Mountains) to the central inland and coastal towns, because the economic opportunities of the larger areas were greater and the physical security more apparent. Emigration increased, with Moroccan Jews setting out for Latin America, West Africa, and the United States.

Regarding language, the Jews who lived among the Berbers spoke Berber dialects but also Judeo-Arabic, the language spoken by most Moroccan Jews. In northern Morocco the descendants of the *megorashim* spoke Judeo-Spanish, a version of Spanish that Moroccans call Hakitia. The most common family names among Moroccan Jews were Souissa, Elmaleh, Lugassy, Ohana, Asseraf, Dahan, Chetrit, Bohbot, Wanono, Waknin, Bensimhon, Azoulay, Dery, Benharrosh, Edry, Asoulin, Amar, Zagouri, Zafrani, Abotbol, Assayag, Turdjman, Ben-Tulila, Bitton, Dadon, Danino, Abisrur, Amsallem, Abu-Hatseira, Bensoussan, Bouskila, Haliwa, and Khalfon. Noted family names of the Sephardic intellectual and affluent elites included Corcos, Hatchwell, Bengio, Mouyal, Nahon, Pariente, Afriat, Azancot, Benatar, Bibasse, Benasseraf, Benzaquen, and Amzallag. Different estimates have been made of the number of Jews living in Morocco in the latter half of the nineteenth century. Tourists, diplomats, and European Jewish organizations that maintained ties with Moroccan Jewry provide contradictory estimates, ranging from 60,000 to 500,000.

Doubtless, the latter figure is exaggerated. According to the French army officer Charles de Foucauld, who toured the country in 1883–84 disguised as a rabbi, 7,190 Jewish families, or about forty-thousand Jews, were living throughout Morocco. Another Frenchman who visited in 1902 estimated the group's size at 100,000. Data gathered by the Alliance Israélite Universelle (AIU) for 1904 point to 103,000. Further, the estimates of the general population of Morocco at the time (ranging from 5 to 10 million) are also exaggerated. According to the 1921 census, Morocco had 3.4 million people. Data for 1909 estimated the coastal cities' population at 189,000. The largest Jewish communities in 1912 were in Fez, Marrakesh, and Essaouira, with about ten thousand in each of those cities during the 1870s and 1880s. In some areas the majority of the population was Jewish. This was the case in Debdou in the northeast, where fifteen hundred of the two thousand residents were Jewish. In Tangier, Essaouira, and Sefrou, Jews accounted for as much as one-third of the population. Smaller communities of several hundred Jews could be found mainly in the mountains and valleys of the Atlas range.

European travelers regarded Moroccan Jewry as productive. Rather than compete with the Muslims, the Jews preferred occupations that the Muslims considered inferior or that were forbidden by Islam, such as the manufacture of alcoholic beverages. Therefore, the lowest socioeconomic group of Jews were petty traders and artisans; many crafts were passed on from father to son. The Jews' main sources of livelihood were food production and farming—making wine and *mahia* (an alcoholic beverage from fruit), extracting oil from seeds and olives, cultivating vineyards, and raising sheep and cattle. They were also in metalwork (silversmithing, goldsmithing, coin minting, smelting, blacksmithing, coopering, and tin engraving, the manufacture of pots and pans, and buckle and harness making); textiles (weaving, embroidering, and tailoring—essentially by young girls and women); leather works (tanning, shoemaking, and bookbinding); carpentry; the manufacture of soap, wax, and perfume; construction; pharmacy; and various services (sailing, portering, muleteering, music, house painting, watchmaking, barbering, butchering, cooking, and baking). Some artisans lived among the Berbers, repairing plows and farming tools. Among the petty traders, peddlers were active in selling their wares in the villages. Artisans like the silversmiths, goldsmiths, and coin minters of Fez were organized in guildlike associations.

The number of affluent Jews was small compared to the number of poor and low income, but their influence was significant. They dealt in international trade, some as agents or brokers for foreign trade firms. Others were independent merchants or commercial intermediaries for European and Muslim merchants, and yet others acted as translators or consular agents for European powers. Prominent among them was Yoseph ben Aharon Elmaleh (1809–86), appointed rabbi-judge in Essaouira. He ranked among the more affluent local merchants and served as consular agent for Austria; his son succeeded him in this function. These and other Jewish merchants enjoyed intimate ties with the ruling circles. They were known as *tujjar al-sultan* (the sultan's merchants), and they leased government monopolies, even the rights to port customs. These Jews were highly influential, especially in the seaport of Essaouira. In the 1820s most of the British trade in Essaouira was concentrated in the hands of four Jewish families; in the 1850s twenty-four of the thirty-nine *tujjar al-sultan* in Essaouira were Jewish. They belonged to the Pinto, Coriat, Aflalo, and Corcos families. During the early 1880s thirty of the fifty trade firms active in Essaouira were Jewish. Among the wealthy families in Tangier who amassed fortunes in trade, services, and banking, and by sending beef to Gibraltar, were the Hassans, Parientes, and Nahons. The monopolies and wealth were passed through the generations. Some affluent Jews spent time in Europe and acquired foreign nationality, then returned with a different status than their brethren, who remained subordinate to the *makhzan*'s jurisdiction.

Jewish society was patriarchal. The eldest man was the head of the family, and his word was law. Strong ties went beyond the nuclear family, with the extended family usually living together. The drive to ensure the continuity and survival of the family, and the fear of losing that continuity because of high infant mortality, sickness, and epidemics, were central factors in the struggle for survival. Continuity involved the continuation of marital customs such as child marriages. According to this custom, girls were betrothed at early childhood and married at puberty (twelve or thirteen, sometimes younger); boys married at fifteen to eighteen. Girls' marriages rested on the assumption that beginning family life early would be advantageous, because it would ensure their support and avert the danger of being abducted and converted to Islam.

Most communities were led by the *hakhamim* (rabbis) together with the distinguished lay leaders. At the head was the *nagid* (president), also called the sheikh, usually a wealthy member of the community who enjoyed cordial ties with the authorities. The *nagid* was elected and could be recalled by the community. On the one hand, he represented the community vis-à-vis the administration. On the other, his tasks included looking after the *makhzan*'s interests, collecting the *jizya* (head tax) and exercising responsibility for enforcing restrictions imposed on the Jews. The *nagid* became involved in enforcing the decisions of the rabbinic law courts, including punishing those who deviated from such decisions. Among the sentences handed down were excommunication, fines, flogging, and imprisonment. The community collected the taxes demanded by the authorities, which were progressive taxes (they depended on the individual's income). The income assessment often stirred disputes, particularly when it came to exemptions. Rabbinic scholars customarily were exempted from payment. The Jewish leadership allocated money to pay the guards of the *mellah* (Jewish residential quarter), to provide gifts to the sultan on Islamic holidays, and to support the needy. The communal charitable services were operated by such organizations as the *hevrah kadishah* (burial society), mutual loan funds, assistance to poor brides, ransom of prisoners, and donations to the Yishuv in Palestine.

For generations Moroccan Jewry had strong communal and religious commitments. The community was organized according to the rules of the Spanish communities before the 1492 expulsion. The regulations enforced until the mid-1700s in Fez were compiled by Rabbi Avraham Anqaoua from Salé and printed in 1871 at Livorno, Italy. Another compilation of regulations is derived from the Meknès community. The regulations cover all aspects of public and private life. They deal with the relations of Jews and non-Jews, including the prohibition of wine sales to non-Jews and personal status (marriage, divorce, inheritance, education, and donations to the poor and to the Palestine Yishuv). There were restrictions on luxurious feasts, as well as against ostentation in dress—done to prevent embarrassment to those who could not afford the expense, as well as to avoid antagonizing Muslims.

Education figured prominently in daily life. Traditional Jewish education meant training youth for daily ritual and for synagogue culture, and neither prepared them for economic advancement or for the practical side of life. The *kuttab* (or heder) was a private initiative, primary schooling in Judaism. Classes were frequently held in rented rooms rather than in permanent school buildings. In small communities the classes were held in the synagogues. Parents paid the teachers, and the community covered tuition for the disadvantaged or orphans. Boys began their learning experience from age three or four. They learned to read the Hebrew letters and words and the weekly portion of the Torah. Classrooms might be cramped or poorly ventilated, and some boys frequented the classes only intermittently. These schools had a general lack of discipline, compulsory community-inspired educational policies, and irregular attendance (from the need to work to help support families).

A wealthy or dedicated elite pursued studies beyond age thirteen. During the nineteenth century wealthy benefactors founded yeshivas, striving to train rabbinic scholars, rabbi-judges, ritual slaughterers, scribes, cantors, and circumcisers. These functions were passed from father to son for generations. There emerged rabbinic families whose sons had held the post of rabbi from the time of the Spanish expulsion: the Messas, Toledanos, Berdugos, Abensurs, Monsonegos, Serreros, and Ibn Danans were prominent. They performed multiple functions. They were court judges, gave sermons on the Sabbath and at festivals, spoke at family events, and solved problems encountered by local communities and beyond. When Jews suffered from persecution, the religious elite interceded before the authorities on their behalf.

Fez and Meknès were the key Jewish spiritual centers in Morocco before 1912, and the other communities turned to their rabbis for legal advice. Moroccan rabbis are known to have held posts in other places, like Gibraltar, where the community was composed of Tetuanese. Some prominent rabbis earned their living in other trades, either because they did not procure posts as clergy or refused them. They engaged in charitable deeds and healing and a not insignificant number were *zaddikim*, venerated in their lifetime, while after death their tombs became pilgrimage sites to be visited by the masses.

In addition to their contribution to Jewish law, the rabbis evinced interest in mystical studies: in kabbalah, mainly in the *Zohar* (The Book of Splendor, the central work in the literature of the kabbalah), and in Lurianic mysticism. They plunged into a wide variety of religious writing, ranging from interpretation of the Scriptures and the Talmud to ethics and philosophy to halakhic monographs on specific rulings to responsa, legal decisions, sermons, and liturgy. They wrote some books in Hebrew, which were translated into Judeo-Arabic.

The Hebrew press flourished in sixteenth-century Fez and, after a long pause, from the early 1890s, when publishers in Tangier, Fez, and Casablanca printed books in Hebrew. Books written by Moroccan rabbis appeared in Livorno, Amsterdam, and Jerusalem. A large number of works were never printed and remained in manuscript form.

Several distinguished rabbis collected manuscripts and printed books that were lost in riots. The private library of Rabbi Raphael Yehoshua Zion Serrero of Fez (1843–1902), which contained twenty-five hundred books, was burned down during an anti-Jewish uprising in April 1912. Another important collector was Rabbi Yoseph ben Naim of Fez (1882–1961), who wrote forty-seven works, only a few of which were printed. Tales written by Eastern European rabbis and Hasidic leaders captivated the interest of Moroccan Jews when they were disseminated in the local communities. The Jews felt affinity with Ashkenazic Jews, as stories of the Ba^{c}al Shem Tov (1698–1760, founder of Hasidism and a miracle healer) were translated into Judeo-Arabic by Rabbi Yosef Knafo of Essaouira. Halakhic decisions (on

Jewish law) by Ashkenazic rabbis influenced Moroccan Jewry. Yiddish terms like *yahrzeit* (annual memorial of a death) appeared in the writings of local rabbis in the nineteenth century.

PRECOLONIAL JEWISH LEGAL, POLITICAL, AND EDUCATIONAL STATUS

Before the twentieth century the legal and social status of the Jews in Morocco was based on the interpretation of the Qur'an and the Pact of Umar. In addition to paying the *jizya* and coping with other restrictions, the Moroccan-Jewish *dhimmis* were obliged to wear black clothing and a hairstyle different from that of a Muslim, in order to be distinguishable in public. Jews could neither ride horses nor bear arms; they were prevented from learning classical Arabic or erecting new synagogues; they were not allowed to bathe in a Muslim bathhouse or build houses higher than those of Muslims. Their evidence could not be accepted in Muslim courts. Compensating for the restrictions was that the Muslim authorities protected Jewish lives and property and granted the Jews freedom of worship and community autonomy.

Economic and political instability, popular rebellions, the death of a sultan, or even the rumor of such a death, rendered the Jews more vulnerable than the Muslims. Muslims often expressed their feelings toward Jews in epigraphs: "The Jew contaminates the sea"; "If a Jew can cheat a Muslim, his day is made"; "If a Jew laughs with a Muslim, he's up to no good." Yet on a personal basis relations between the two groups usually were good and commercial transactions fair. Furthermore, Muslims would ask Jewish leaders to pray for rain, and Muslims believed in the power of the *zaddikim* to perform miracles. Interestingly, Jewish attitudes toward the Muslims were not devoid of similar complexities. A local Jewish saying goes: "Whoever does an Arab a favor is like someone who sprinkles water on the sand." The Jews portrayed Muslims as attackers and scoundrels but also defenders who came to the rescue of Jews and as miracle workers. Just as Muslims tended to venerate *zaddikim* and visit their tomb sites, so did segments of Moroccan Jewry believe in the magic powers of the Muslim marabout, a dervish with supernatural power.

Before 1912 most Jews lived in the *mellah,* a walled quarter whose gates were locked at nightfall, on the Sabbath, and for festival days. The gates were opened on weekday mornings, when the Jews went about their business. The first *mellah* in Morocco—after Jews were compelled to move out of their homes among Muslims—was created in 1438 at Fez. Other cities followed: Marrakesh (1557), Meknès (1682), Tetuán, Salé, Rabat, and Essaouira (1808). The *mellah* area was limited and did not take into account the natural increase in population. The crowding and lack of reasonable sanitary conditions caused sickness and epidemics. Data on the *mellah* at Essaouira in 1875 give an average population density of 4.5 people per room. Some houses had as many as eighteen to twenty people living in one room. A report about Fez from 1882 mentions thirty people per room. In the 1870s the Jews of Essaouira and Marrakesh asked for additional land for the *mellahs.* In 1888 Sultan Hassan I provided land adjoining the Fez *mellah* for five hundred huts to be built for the homeless; most of the structures burned down in 1896.

The *mellah* was more than a degrading mechanism of segregation—the walled Jewish quarter served as a line of defense against attacks. Jews preferred to live close to one another and as near as possible to religious, educational, and other community institutions. Affluent Jews lived outside the *mellah,* notably in the neighborhoods of European merchants. In Essaouira they lived in the Casbah (the native section of city). In 1873 eight hundred to one thousand Jews lived in the Casbah and seven thousand in the *mellah.* Tangier, El-Jadida, and Safi had no *mellahs,* and the Jews lived among the Muslims.

In the nineteenth and twentieth centuries, as earlier, Jews faced conversion to Islam in parts of Morocco. In 1910 the twelve-year-old grandson of Rabbi Raphael Abensur was abducted from Fez and converted by the *qadi* (a Muslim judge). The rabbi called on his congregation to work for the boy's return. A delegation approached the government's chief minister, who turned a deaf ear to their protests. The *qadi* claimed the boy had converted of his own volition and would be adopted by a Muslim family. Delegates then approached the sultan, who also evaded their plea. Only the intervention of European diplomats led to the release of the boy. The "Suleika affair" is another instance: in 1834 a high-ranking official apparently was pressuring Suleika, a woman from Tangier, to marry him and convert to Islam. Suleika refused to comply and withstood all financial temptations. Although rabbis tried to persuade her that conversion would be preferable to her death, she steadfastly refused to convert and was executed in Fez. In several other instances whole families went into hiding to avoid conversion. Religious conviction appears not to have been the impetus for voluntary acts of conversion but rather the avoidance of attacks in times of crisis, gaining the pardon of someone convicted of a crime, or gaining the release of a debtor. During droughts the sultan distributed food only to Muslims—an additional incentive for conversion.

Christian missionaries were also active in nineteenth-century Morocco. Ten British Protestant missions extended their work to the area during this period. The British Society for the Propagation of the Gospel Amongst Jews became the first Anglican group to focus attention on the Jewish communities of Morocco. Assisted by Jewish converts, they worked in Essaouira, Casablanca, Salé, Rabat, Tangier, and Tetuán. Apostate members of the London Society for Promoting Christianity Amongst the Jews, which began its activity in Morocco in 1843, emerged as the most active group. Despite their relentless efforts, these groups succeeded in attracting only a few Jews. Similar initiatives by Franciscan missionaries were no more successful.

During the Franco-Moroccan war of 1844, the Jews of Tangier and Essaouira suffered from destruction as well as the bombardment. Local populations also attacked the Jews, accusing them of supporting the enemy. These conditions triggered the first intervention by European Jewry on behalf of Moroccan Jewry, a phenomenon that continued regularly in later years. Word of the Jews' plight in Essaouira reached London. The president of the Board of Deputies of British Jews, Sir Moses Montefiore, contacted the sultan and requested that he proclaim a *zahir* for the protection of the Jews. A committee headed by Montefiore founded the Morocco Relief Fund to aid Jews in distress. It collected donations for the needy and assisted Jewish refugees who fled the fighting between Spain and Morocco in 1859–60. About five thousand Jews from Tangier and Tetuán found refuge in Gibraltar and Algeciras. When the fighting subsided, most returned to their communities. Muslims accused Jews who had remained in Tetuán under Spanish occupation of colluding with the enemy. The sultan's military debacle in the Moroccan War served as a stimulus for unrest, some of which affected the Jews.

In 1860 the Board of Deputies of British Jews sent M. H. Picciotto to Morocco to report on the Jews and to recommend ways of ameliorating their status. His report detailed the difficulties of Moroccan Jewry and advocated the promotion of modern education among the youth as an avenue for social mobility. Upon these recommendations French Jewry's Alliance Israélite Universelle (AIU) and the London-based Anglo-Jewish Association (AJA) plunged into the education systems of Moroccan communities. These associations, which also functioned as lobbying forces on behalf of distressed Jews worldwide, fought for the economic and legal status of Moroccan Jewry. When they received complaints of persecution, the AIU and AJA appealed to the French and British governments, consuls, and ambassadors to demand that the sultan punish the offenders. They demanded compensation for the victim—or the family if a Jew had been murdered—as well as an official government pledge that such offenses would not be repeated.

However, these associations made their greatest contribution in education. The AIU set up modern schools, where pupils were taught foreign languages—first and foremost French—and vocational trades to help them more easily become part of Moroccan economic life or to prepare for emigration. The AIU encouraged emigration to Europe and the Americas where Jews had more opportunities. The Alliance opened its first schools in the coastal cities and subsequently in the inland communities. The first AIU school was opened in Tetuán (1862), followed by Tangier (1864), Essaouira (1867), Safi (1868), Larache (1875), Fez (1882), and Casablanca (1897). By 1912, on the eve of the colonial era, most urban communities had AIU boys' and girls' schools that subsequently extended their educational network into newly founded communities and the Atlas Mountains. Some schools received support from the AJA, the Board of Deputies of British Jews, and the Morocco Relief Fund. The Alliance also taught English and Spanish, essential languages in the coastal areas, and some Arabic. Several communities participated in the financing of the schools, and parents who could afford to pay tuition did so.

In the coastal towns parents and rabbis encouraged secular education and foreign-language training, whereas the inland communities were more conservative. There the rabbis objected to secular education, fearing that the youth would be led astray; however, gradually, the rabbis of the inland areas rallied around the AIU, particularly when religious instruction received proper attention in the curriculum. Part of the rabbinic support for the Alliance stemmed from the threat of the mission schools, such as those operated by the Franciscan Brothers in Tangier, and the need for an effective educational counterweight to their proselytizing efforts. Some middle-class Christian and Muslim pupils also attended AIU schools in Tangier, Tetuán, Larache, Alcazarquibir, Safi, Essaouira, and Casablanca.

Before 1860 few girls of any group received formal education. Girls could neither read nor write, and in many places girls and women never visited the synagogue. When women went to the synagogue on the Sabbath or for festival days, they said prayers that they had memorized and kissed the Torah from a distance. A girl helped her mother at home until she married. Mothers and grandmothers taught girls the religious laws pertaining to women and the home, which prepared them for the role of wife and mother.

Some wealthy Jews employed private tutors for their daughters, but this was an exception.

The AIU broke through by promising parents and rabbis that girls would learn skills helpful for supporting the family. The Alliance opened girls' schools in Tetuán (1860s), Tangier (1865), and Fez (1899) and in other communities at a later stage. After 1918 the AIU increased the enrollment of girls, but fewer girls than boys attended as late as 1912, when enrollment for girls was 1,822, compared to 3,214 for boys. As the number of girls at the Alliance schools grew steadily, the chief goal of their education became the prevention of child marriages, and teachers urged the rabbis to join them in the struggle against the practice. Yet the rabbis themselves married off their children at a tender age, so they foiled early efforts at reform. In time, and with the support of community lay leaders who had been educated in the West, the AIU's consistent pressure produced long-term results. In 1948 the rabbinic council of Morocco set the minimum marriage age for a girl at fifteen.

The influence of the AIU varied. Until 1912 most pupils came from the Jewish elite, though youth from humble socioeconomic backgrounds began to attend the schools in several inland and coastal communities. Modern education soon widened the gap between Jews and Muslims and increased the latter's antagonism. The schools enabled many Jews to integrate into the modern world and foster ties with their coreligionists in Europe and the United States. Their traditional lifestyles became somewhat less conservative, and a gradual, albeit noticeable, secularization process occurred in the coastal cities where contact with Christians increased. Rabbinic writings criticized the educated for not observing the Sabbath and opening their businesses on that day.

An important feature of modernization was the role played by Tangier's Jews in the Jewish and non-Jewish press. For example, Pinhas Assayag was a political reporter for a Madrid newspaper in the 1880s and, according to one report from June 1889, received the title of Knight of Isabella the Catholic. Levi A. Cohen was the owner and publisher of the French-language weekly *Réveil du Maroc,* founded in Tangier in 1883. He was a British citizen who had been born in Essaouira, and he arrived in Tangier first as a reporter for the London *Jewish Chronicle.* When he died in 1888, the *Réveil du Maroc* passed into the hands of the Benchimols, a Jewish banking family, and was edited by Abraham Pimienta until it closed in 1903. In 1894–95 the Jewish weekly *Mevasser Tov* (*Good News*) appeared, and in 1903 *Le Moghrebi,* devoted to matters of Jewish interest, was published in Judeo-Arabic and French. These represented the first efforts at journalism by Jews in Morocco, and the Jewish press there became more vibrant in the years after the protectorate era began.

The Jewish press chronicled the deterioration of Jewish-Muslim relations since the 1860s that was partly the result of the growing French and British interest in Moroccan domestic affairs—and the increasing intervention of European Jews on behalf of Moroccan Jewish communities. In February 1864 Moses Montefiore met with Sultan Muhammad IV in Marrakesh. The central reason for the journey was a letter from the Gibraltar community, dated October 1863, that warned of the dangers faced by Moroccan Jews. At the time the Jews of Safi were falsely accused of poisoning a Spanish tax collector, and four had been arrested. The Spanish vice consul demanded that the sultan execute them; in the aftermath of Morocco's military defeat by Spain, the sultan succumbed to pressure and executed two of the four. The other two were saved, thanks to Montefiore, who also presented the sultan with a petition highlighting abuses attributed to government officials—such as forced labor and violation of property rights. The sultan decreed that such humiliating practices were forbidden. Although the abuses continued, Montefiore's achievements set in motion the diplomatic lobbying efforts of British and French Jews on behalf of local Jews—the press brought abuses to the attention of European politicians, consuls, and the general public. This journalism encouraged Moroccan Jewish leaders to report abuses and placed government officials on the defensive.

According to agreements between European governments and Morocco that were signed as early as 1767, European diplomats could grant certificates of protection to subjects of the sultan. This exempted those known as protégés from paying the *jizya,* serving in the military, and being subjected to Moroccan judicial authority. In other words, protégés and their families enjoyed the benefits of aliens residing in Morocco, although they did not possess foreign nationality. Although non-Jews also benefited from this status, the Jewish elite figured prominently among the protégés. They were employed as vice consuls, consular agents, interpreters, and representatives of European businesses in Morocco during the latter half of the nineteenth century. As the number of protégés increased, and along with it European economic and political interests, Sultan Hassan I understood that the cause of the government's loss of authority at home and abroad was in part due to an abusive system that granted protection to a privileged elite. To curb the abuses he called on the major European powers to convene a conference, held in 1880 at Madrid. The conference reviewed the protégés' status, mostly that of *simsars* (commercial agents) and consular representatives, but did little to alter the status quo.

An opponent of this system was John Drummond Hay, the British ambassador to Morocco, who argued that granting protection to Jews only increased local enmity against them. Jews who held protection certificates acted boldly when faced with attacks, some bearing arms and injuring Muslims. The Muslims, unaccustomed to such behavior by minorities, even as an act of self-defense, soon escalated their attacks against Jews—both protégés and the less privileged majority who had no European protection. Moreover, the protection system aggravated the economic position of less fortunate Jews who, unable to obtain tax exemptions, shouldered the burden of increased taxation.

During the reign of Morocco's Sultan Abd al-Aziz IV, Jews, along with the rest of the population, suffered from economic hardships. At the Algeciras Conference of 1906, which debated the future of Morocco, representatives of the United States drew attention to the status of the Jews, particularly in Morocco's inland regions, demanding that they be protected. The Moroccan delegation affirmed that Abd al-Aziz would continue to protect them. Yet the abuses continued. An attack on Jews before the protectorate began, occurred in the Fez *mellah* on April 17, 1912, with a death toll of sixty. It was sparked by the army's objection to the Franco-Moroccan treaty governing the implementation of the protectorate.

JEWISH LIFE IN MOROCCO AFTER 1912

The military pacification policies of the protectorates enabled Muslims, Jews, and European urban and rural dwellers to lead more stable lives. The Jewish community of Morocco underwent major demographic transformations between 1912 and the mid-1950s. In 1912 no more than 110,000 Jews lived in Morocco; by 1952 their numbers had reached 240,000 in all three colonial zones. The sharp rise in population was the result of an increase in natural birthrates and a partial improvement in sanitary conditions. The majority of Jews were concentrated in French Morocco (about 210,000), 30 percent of whom lived in the villages and small towns in and around the Atlas Mountains, especially in Beni-Mellal, Demnat, Taroudant, Midelt, Kasr al-Suq, Amizmiz, Sidi Rahal, and Ben-Ahmed. The number of rural Jews was gradually reduced with the continuous internal migration from villages and hamlets to the major cities. Though this process long predated the protectorate era, it gained momentum after World War I.

In 1952 urban Jews lived mainly in Casablanca (75,000), Marrakesh (18,500), Fez (16,000), Meknès (15,000), Essaouira (6,500), Rabat (13,000), Tangier (12,000), Safi (4,500), and Salé (3,300). Until the 1920s Marrakesh had the largest Jewish concentration, followed by Fez and Meknès; after 1920 Casablanca became the main center of Jewish life. Rabat, which had several thousand Jews in 1939, doubled its Jewish population by 1952, becoming another important center. In Spanish Morocco the Jewish population distribution was much the same as on the eve of the colonial period. Tetuán's community stood at its precolonial 6,000, as did Alcazarquibir at 1,600 and Nador at several hundred; Larache's community dwindled from 2,000 in 1912 to 1,300 in 1952. The population at Nador remained the same, several hundred, while the Xauen community disappeared through migrations to French Morocco caused by Spain's civil war in the Spanish zone. The lack of growth, even decline, of Spanish Morocco's Jewish population is attributed to internal migration to Tangier and the French zone or to emigration to the Americas. Tangier's Jewish population grew slightly, from 10,000 in 1912 to 12,000 in 1952, mainly because of refugees from the Dodecanese Islands and Central Europe.

In a relatively short period the French built roads, established a modern rail system, and created other new transportation facilities that enabled Jews to extend their economic activities. Although the accessibility of transportation in the inland areas enabled Muslim itinerant merchants to cut into the business of their Jewish counterparts, as late 1945 many Jews continued to engage in this type of activity, in addition to other forms of petty trade, the traditional crafts, and some large-scale commerce. The elite of the sultan's merchants in French Morocco had declined long before the protectorate era. The modern large-scale merchants, graduates of the AIU and foreign schools who in the past had enjoyed European consular protection, lost their influence to non-Jewish European settlers.

Jewish banking and commerce continued to thrive in the international zone of Tangier. Jewish-owned banks, especially Banque Hassan and Banque Pariente, increasingly hired as managers and clerks graduates of schools run by the Alliance and other Europeans. Branches of the prestigious French Crédit Foncier placed Jews in key positions. However, Jewish financial banking and credit establishments suffered setbacks during the Great Depression of the 1930s; they recuperated only afterward. The Jews of Tangier controlled exports to England and the United States of leather goods, eggs, and tanned skins as well as the imports of wholesale and retail manufactured products from the Spanish protectorate—textiles, automobiles, furniture, flour, and spices. The few Jews who worked in agriculture were in the villages of the Atlas Mountains. A modern middle class of Jewish entrepreneurs emerged in all colonial zones, as well as those in modern urban trades.

Since 1918 one group of Jews had been relatively well represented in the public administration of the French protectorate though they competed fiercely for positions with Europeans, whose population in Morocco increased, and with the emerging Muslim educated elite. The Jews were employed in the French administration as minor clerks and officials and as senior functionaries. Whereas by 1952 more Muslims than the Jews had jobs with the French protectorate administrative agencies in absolute numbers, and eventually acquired representation in the liberal professions, the Jews were better represented proportionally. Of the 460,465 urban Muslims who were employed, 18,000, or 3.9 percent, had government jobs or worked in the liberal professions. In 1952, of the 53,685 Jews who had jobs in the cities, 4,143 men and women, or 7.72 percent, worked either for the government or business. In 1960, four years after Morocco's independence, Jews accounted for 13.2 percent of the employed urban male population and 23.8 percent of urban female employees. The growing number of Jewish women in the liberal professions, administration, and teaching, both before and after Morocco's independence, is an important phenomenon. As late as 1960 the Moroccan government employed educated Jews to keep them from emigrating and to replace departing colonial personnel. In Tangier during the colonial period Jews were better represented than Muslims in the international zone, but few were so employed in the Spanish zone.

Although Jews now had a stake in government as well as the professions, many had moved from the *mellahs* to European sections of the cities built by the colonial authorities, and the government and the American Jewish Joint Distribution Committee (AJDC) were subsidizing the schools, the struggle for greater social mobility was far from over. The main beneficiaries were the small but growing elites; many Jews were still poor or belonged to the lower middle class, engaging in traditional economic activities. Numerous *mellah* Jews still operated tiny stalls, often merely spots on the pavement, where they sold various wares—eggs, soap, or fruits. The intensity of modernization was mainly in the big communities: Casablanca, Rabat, Essaouira, Agadir, Fez, Marrakesh, Meknès, and Tangier. It was far less evident in the villages of the Atlas Mountains, the northern Rif mountains, and Spanish Morocco's communities of Nador, Arsila, and Larache. Seeking to improve their lot, rural and Spanish Moroccan Jews soon opted for permanent settlement in French Morocco's cities. Others became transients, awaiting aliyah or immigration to Europe and the Americas. Their presence in the major cities caused overcrowded conditions. Of the 75,000 Jews living in Casablanca in 1952, more than thirty thousand were crowded in the *mellah,* which was described as a place with crumbling houses lining narrow passageways.

The AJDC's role in combating poverty, disbursing funds to train American-style social workers, and subsidizing the AIU, Otzar ha-Torah, and Lubavitcher schools, as well as clinics run by ORT (Organization for Rehabilitation through Training) and the European-based Oeuvre de Secours aux Enfants, did alleviate conditions as the protectorate era drew to an end. These organizations collaborated in the 1950s with the Jewish Agency for Palestine and Mossad le-Aliya Bet (Organization for Illegal Immigration) to prepare Jews for Israel. The AIU benefited the most, for it received generous subsidies from both the AJDC and France. Because the French administration discouraged all but the most affluent Muslims and Jews from attending its schools for European settlers (*écoles européennes*), and opened just a few colonial-sponsored schools for Jews (*écoles franco-israélites*), the AIU monopolized modern Jewish education in the French zone. Although the authorities in Tangier and Spanish Morocco enabled Jews of all socioeconomic levels to attend most schools for Europeans with little opposition, and operated Hebrea-Español schools (schools for Jewish children with instruction in Spanish) in the Spanish zone, the AIU stood at the forefront of modern education in these areas too. Alliance schools in the Spanish zone, unlike those in French Morocco, placed great emphasis on French and Spanish language and culture; both Spanish and English were an integral part of the AIU curriculum in Tangier, the international zone.

Between 1945 and 1965 the AIU diversified and augmented its educational activities, not only in the number of schools and types of pupils but also in scope. In conjunction with the AJDC and with the approval of the rabbinic elite, the Alliance set out to renovate the outmoded rabbinic schools and compelled community leaders to close down elementary schools that failed to offer a modernized curriculum that combined religious and general education. In 1946 the Alliance opened a special institution in Casablanca to train teachers of Hebrew and Judaic studies for its North African schools. Named the Ecole Normale Hébraïque (ENH), the school produced teachers to replace the outmoded instructors who taught Jewish subjects at the Alliance schools. The ENH placed some emphasis on Modern Hebrew, Hebrew literature, and religious studies. In the 1960s the ENH became a modern high school that offered both Hebrew studies and general education leading to the French diploma, and it graduated numerous teachers and secondary students. Many ENH graduates became teachers in Morocco, Tunisia, Algeria, Western Europe, and North America.

In 1949 the Alliance also established special schools for pupils afflicted with trachoma, an eye disease, and enlarged its postelementary educational programs—the Cours Complémentaires—thus educating pupils with five or six years of schooling and providing them with education until the ninth or tenth grade. By then many saw in the postelementary classes a bridge to high school and higher education. Because Morocco, unlike Algeria and Egypt, did not have universities before the 1960s, in 1960 alone 239 Jewish university students studied abroad. The cumulative effect of the AIU, Otzar ha-Torah, and the Lubavitcher religious schools and yeshivas was not merely to challenge the outmoded rabbinic schools but to gradually eliminate the policy of sending children to the modern AIU school and the school run by the rabbis at the same time. The multiplicity of modern and semimodern schools served to spread spoken European languages and reduce illiteracy.

Educational and other features of modernization since 1912 also affected the rabbinic elite. Rabbi Raphael Baruch Toledano of Meknès (1892–1971), a member of a dynasty of spiritual leaders in a city whose streets bear their names to this day, served from the 1940s to the 1960s as the head of the local *bet-din*. He founded yeshivas and is renowned for writing a summary of the complete *Shulhan Arukh* and a number of poems. He sent his grandchildren to study at the ENH because he recognized that they needed to learn secular subjects alongside the Torah and Mishnah. In Meknès he helped modernize the Talmud Torah to meet the educational needs of modern times. Rabbi Raphael Encaoua (1865–1935) of Rabat and Salé, perhaps the most renowned Moroccan rabbi, was a staunch supporter of modern education; he established a special fund to enable AIU vocational school graduates to be placed in apprenticeship programs.

Two other rabbis, David Ovadia and Aharon Monsonego, have wielded considerable influence since the 1930s. Rabbi Ovadia (1914—) was the last spiritual leader of a generation of rabbis in Sefrou. In 1942 he became Sefrou's chief rabbi and ten years later was appointed by the authorities as chief *dayyan* in Rabat. In the 1950s the French appointed him to the post of supervisor general of Jewish education. That was when Ovadia, the AIU, and the AJDC collaborated to modernize religious education, obtained suitable school buildings, and improved sanitary conditions in the classes. Ovadia fortified the influence of a modern religious school network known as Em Habanim. In 1959 he was appointed to the Consultative Assembly, but five years later he settled in Israel, where he served as a member of the Council of the Chief Rabbinate. Like other members of the Fez rabbinic families, among them the Serreros and Aben Danans, Rabbi Aharon Monsonego was a scion of a rabbinic family of Spain that settled in that city after the expulsion. He had received his rabbinic training in a yeshiva at Aix-les-Bains. Since the 1960s Monsonego has directed the Otzar ha-Torah network and recently became Morocco's chief rabbi. He reconciled the differences between the Torah and modern education, transforming the Otzar ha-Torah schools into first-rate institutions that teach French and general subjects as well as religious studies.

The protectorates did not bring with them the notion of civil rights. Rather, a slow process of political evolution began, leading to partial reforms. In time the French protectorate did away with the protégé system, although it remained in Tangier. The French also distinguished between the secular jurisdiction of the government and the Islamic religious courts. Consequently, cases involving all Moroccans now came under the jurisdiction of the secular *makhzan* courts, created and supervised by the French. In theory the Jews were regarded as equals before the law, and their *dhimmi* status was formally eliminated. In the new system Jews were not defined by Muslim law, but they often had to appear before Muslim courts in addition to the secular courts. France granted the rabbinic courts autonomy in civil, personal, and commercial cases; yet in reality their authority was reduced to personal litigation.

Almost every large Jewish community in the French zone had a central council whose functions were defined by the *zahir* of May 7, 1945, as "assistance to the indigents and management of religious institutions." It also had to take "care of the administration of the cult and to present views and suggestions on all questions pertaining to the [Jewish] community." The councils supported themselves by levying taxes on the sale of bread, wine, and meat and donations from the better-off members of the community. The authorities also budgeted money for the councils.

Officially, the government entrusted the community leadership with these aspects of running the Jewish community. In reality, leaders needed the permission of Maurice Botbol, the French-appointed Jewish "supervisor" of the communities, to make any expenditure. Even when the communities succeeded in raising private donations from Jews living abroad, they could not spend the money without the supervisor's permission. After World War II the French helped the communities to create an umbrella organization, the Central Council of Jewish Communities (CCJC), whose headquarters was in Rabat. It never became an all-embracing and efficient centralized body and failed to form a united front of Jewish leadership associations. Whether it enjoyed full legal status remains unclear.

Thanks to the intervention of the AIU in France, six representatives of the CCJC were appointed in the late 1940s to serve on the French protectorate's consultative council. This body was authorized to advise the French on Moroccan Jewish affairs. The effectiveness of these representatives was debatable. Some critics argue that given the subservience of the CCJC to the protectorate, they hardly effected any change. Others observe that their representation constituted an avenue for the community's political progress. It does appear, however, that the representation of Jewish leaders in CCJC did little to ameliorate the lot of the Jews. In Spanish Morocco the old-style Jewish rabbinic and lay elite preserved the precolonial community structure and retained their authority. Community organizations in Tangier underwent certain reforms that were encouraged by the international zone. The lay council received full legal status, while Jewish leaders enjoyed influence before the international zone's legislative assembly. Jews served in the assembly, and that body disbursed money to the Jewish communities.

POLITICAL DEVELOPMENTS IN THE COLONIAL PERIOD

Throughout the French protectorate period, when some educated Jews sought French citizenship, they encountered stiff opposition from the resident general. Whereas in Spanish Morocco and Tangier segments of the affluent elite succeeded in gaining Spanish and other European citizenship status, the French avoided anything that might unnecessarily antagonize the Muslims. When Jewish leaders and AIU school principals, among others, lobbied the resident general, the response was that a decree along the lines of the Crémieux Decree, which granted French citizenship to the Jews of Algeria, or even individual naturalization ran counter to the will of the Moroccan government. Moreover, it would result in intercommunity tensions between Jews and non-Jews. Lyautey argued that individual or large-scale naturalization that would free Jews from Moroccan judicial jurisdiction would stir animosity among Muslims, which was what happened in Algeria. He feared that once the Jews of Morocco were politically equal to the European settlers, active anti-Semitism would increase. The French contended that Morocco was not a part of metropolitan France, like Algeria, but a protectorate; therefore, they lacked the authority to promote naturalization. Also, they were reluctant to challenge the rabbis over judicial matters.

Modern anti-Semitic tendencies, though prevalent among the European settlers, were practically nonexistent among Moroccan Muslims before the 1930s. The situation changed after 1933, when German and Italian fascist propaganda became widespread. European anti-Semitic elements in Morocco seized upon the Palestinian Arab Revolt of 1936–39. They presented "international Jewry" negatively before Muslims whose solidarity with the Palestinian Arabs was unquestioned. Furthermore, the Moroccan nationalists were then unhappy with local Jewry's lack of enthusiasm for their cause. Some nationalists were moderates, but others identified with aspects of European fascism. Muslim-Jewish tensions emerged in several inland French Moroccan cities as a result of this atmosphere. In the Spanish zone anti-Jewish nationalist declarations disturbed Jews. When the secretary of the grand mufti of Jerusalem, Haj Amin al-Husayni, visited the zone in July 1939 to raise money, nationalists held conferences where they yelled, "Death to the Jews" and "Death to the British." The Spaniards did nothing to contain the unrest. Yet the outbreak of the Spanish Civil War in 1936 prompted the Spaniards to restrain profascist youth gangs that harassed Jews.

The outbreak of World War II in 1939, the German occupation of France in 1940, and the establishment of the Vichy government rendered the Jews of French Morocco powerless. On October 3, 1940, the Vichy government enacted its first anti-Jewish law in France. Article 9 concerning the status of the Jews was introduced in the French zone by the *zahir* of October 31, 1940. It applied to all Jews by "race," which was defined as three Jewish grandparents, as well as all members of the Jewish faith. The law expressly authorized the exercise of rabbinic jurisdiction and allowed Jews to continue teaching at institutions intended solely for Jews. The Vichy law of June 2, 1941, increased the hardships inflicted by the law of October 3, 1940. It was implemented by the *zahirs* of August 5, 1941, which were issued separately for Moroccan Jews and the European Jews living in the zone.

The decrees that followed were designed to deprive Jews from working in a wide array of professions, including real estate, moneylending, banking, non-Jewish journalism, and radio broadcasting. Jews were allowed to engage in the crafts and wholesale trading. At the same time Vichy policy allowed only 2 percent of the total number of lawyers and physicians to be Jews. The Vichy law of July 22, 1941, concerning the "Aryanization" of the economy, was implemented in Algeria but was not introduced into French Morocco. In education the policy of limiting the number of Jews in the protectorate's schools to 10 percent was enforced harshly though perhaps not completely. The French continued to subsidize the AIU because they did not wish to see Jewish children developing an aversion to French culture. The landing of Allied forces in French Morocco on November 8, 1942, and its liberation did not result in the immediate obliteration of Vichy influence. This occurred in the summer of 1943 when French general Charles de Gaulle's supporters replaced the pro-Vichy elements.

While it is premature to assess the extent of the implementation of Vichy laws in French Morocco (most French archives remain closed to researchers), not a single discriminatory law was issued against the Jews in the Spanish zone after Gen. Francisco Franco came to power in Spain. Spanish and local government officials foiled the efforts of German agents in the zone to foment anti-Jewish feelings. Jews in Tangier, however, faced certain problems, some related to immigration. During 1942–43 Tangier had fifteen hundred to two thousand Jewish refugees, many of whom had arrived before the war. Approximately half were Sephardim originating from the Dodecanese Islands (then under Italian occupation); some had left Rhodes for Italy and France even before Italy introduced anti-Jewish laws in 1938. The Central Europeans had come mainly from Hungary and Poland via Italy. As long as Tangier remained an international zone, refugees were admitted without difficulty. After the fall of France and Spain's temporary occupation of Tangier in 1940, these people were deprived of various rights, including work.

The indigenous Jewish elites of Tangier were far better off than their counterparts in French Morocco before and during the Spanish occupation. The small businessmen and lower middle class, however, were heavily taxed, and they could not renew their import-export licenses. Politically, the Spanish occupiers dissolved the zone's legislative assembly, while the *zahir* of February 15, 1925, legalizing the Jewish community council, was abrogated. All community activity came under Spanish supervision. The Jewish community lost the subsidies that the government had hitherto allocated generously, as well as the right to elect a slate of community leaders from which the Spaniards would select appointees. All these restrictions were lifted with Spain's withdrawal in 1945 and the restoration of the international zone.

COLONIAL AND POSTCOLONIAL JEWISH POLITICAL ACTIVISM

In the years before the formation of the French and Spanish protectorates, Zionist sentiments imbued with modern notions of Jewish nationalism had gained some prominence among the elites; it was yet another manifestation of modernization, along with the development of European education and ideas. In the past the attachment to the Land of Israel and the Yishuv expressed itself in prayers, liturgy, poems, customs, and donations. Delegates from Palestine visited the communities to solicit donations. Elderly women would donate their life savings. Sources mention Jews who arrived in Palestine for visits or permanent settlement. The reasons for the small-scale aliyah before the nineteenth century involved the insecurity of the maritime routes separating Morocco and Palestine, and involved life in the Yishuv. When the security situation improved in the 1830s, coinciding with the promulgation of the Tanzimat reforms of the Ottomans, Moroccan Jews settled in Jaffa, Haifa, Jerusalem, Safed, Tiberias, and Hebron. From 1866 to 1868 the Moroccan rabbi David ben Shimon purchased land in Jerusalem for the new Mahaneh Israel neighborhood—the second community built outside the walls of the Old City after Mishkenot Sha'ananim—and he built two synagogues near the Western Wall. In 1891 the number of North African Jewish families living in Palestine was almost twenty-three hundred.

Political Zionism made inroads in twentieth-century Morocco, as it did in other communities of the Mediterranean basin. One characteristic of Zionist activity was its rabbinical support; the rabbis saw Zionism as a continuation of the longing to return to Zion. In contrast to the European rabbis, who thought a return before the coming of the Messiah was wrong, in Morocco Zionism neither caused desertion of religion nor a nationalism that replaced religion as an expression of Jewish identity. As reported in the London *Jewish Chronicle* on November 26, 1897, Morocco's rabbis discussed the First Zionist Congress in Basel, Switzerland, and identified with Zionism, as did the Jewish masses of Morocco—despite the fear of seeming disloyal to the Moroccan government. In 1900 Moroccan Jews made their first contact with the World Zionist Organization (WZO). In Tetuán they founded an association called Shivat Tsiyon (Return to Zion). A letter to the WZO in September 1900 requests books and newspapers and states its aims as being the propagation of Zionism and the Hebrew language. In the same year a similar association emerged in Essaouira, the Shaᶜarei Tsiyon (Gates of Zion), which accepted the WZO's rules and distributed the proceeds from the shekel, members' annual dues. Inspired by the newspapers *Ha-Melitz* and *Ha-Yehudi,* an association was formed in Safi known as Ahavat Tsiyon (Love of Zion).

After the death of Theodor Herzl, the founder of political Zionism, in 1904, there was a pause in Zionist activity in Morocco; it resumed in 1909 on the initiative of young middle-class Jews from Fez, Sefrou, and Meknès. Members of the Hibbat Tsiyon association of Fez corresponded with WZO president David Wolffsohn, apprising him of their ties to Zionists in other communities. Encouraged by their initiative, Wolffsohn wrote to welcome them into the Zionist fold, where Sephardi and Ashkenazi Jews could work together to revive the Land of Israel.

Nevertheless, Zionist activity before the 1930s was essentially philanthropic in orientation. It did not officially embrace the notion of large-scale aliyah, concentrating instead on the dissemination of newspapers to attract adherents to Zionism (*L'Avenir Illustré* in French Morocco and *Renacimiento de Israel* in the Spanish zone). Zionist federations, or "unions," emerged in Tangier and Spanish Morocco, where the authorities were inclined to tolerate them. In French Morocco a Zionist federation, headquartered in Casablanca, had emerged in the 1920s but encountered opposition from the resident general. It could operate as a section of the Zionist Federation of France (Section du Maroc of the Fédération Sioniste de France). While some leading activists were indigenous Moroccan Jews holding local or foreign nationalities, others were Ashkenazic settlers or Sephardim from Palestine. Whereas the AIU schools' graduates were imbued with the idea of regarding France as their adopted country, and the AIU itself was neutral in regard to Zionism, if not anti-Zionist before 1939, not all "Alliancistes" evinced ambivalence toward Zionism. In fact, AIU alumni associations became centers for Zionist activism in the 1930s. They collaborated with the envoys of the Jewish National Fund and the Jewish Foundation Fund in raising money for Jewish colonization and absorption of Central and European refugees in Palestine.

Although Morocco saw the proliferation of Zionist associations that were not always subordinate to the Zionist federation, prewar Moroccan Zionist activism still had a limited effect on the Jews as a whole. Nonetheless, it constituted a framework for post-1939 expansion, which came in the wake of Morocco's liberation for several reasons. First, the failure by the French to enact legislation to detach the Jews from the Moroccan government's jurisdiction disillusioned some of those who had obtained a French education at the elementary and postelementary levels and encouraged them to seek alternatives to European-style emancipation. Their Vichy experience, however brief, added to the disillusionment and had positive consequences for Moroccan Zionism. Second, political trends in the Yishuv encouraged segments of Moroccan Jewry, including those whose brand of Zionism was apolitical and traditional, to become more involved in supporting Zionist enterprises. Identifying with the Yishuv, Moroccan Zionists reproached the British Mandate because it had restricted immigration and had given in to Arab claims, playing Arab against Jew. Last, poverty was still rampant in the parts of Morocco where the Alliance and the French as well as the Spanish protectorate failed to extend their influence or where, despite their efforts, the level of destitution remained high. Poverty eventually became a weapon in the hands of the emissaries of the Mossad le-Aliya Bet and the Jewish Agency, for they could play on the frustrations of the poor, who sought alternatives to ameliorate their status.

Beginning in 1943 secular and religious Zionist emissaries arrived in French Morocco from British Palestine; they were affiliated with the Yishuv's Haganah (the major prestate Jewish military organization in Palestine), Mossad le-Aliya Bet, and the Jewish Agency. Their encounter with Zionist-oriented youths was to have long-range consequences. Operating illegally, the emissaries became involved in Morocco with the young adult movement of the influential Zionist Charles Netter. The leaders of Netter's movement and the emissaries infused Moroccan Jewish youth with the idea of aliyah instead of philanthropic Zionism. Given French policy until 1949 of opposing aliyah while overlooking other aspects of Zionism, the authorities watched these activists. The emissaries handpicked the more disciplined of the youths, trained them in self-defense, and saw them swear allegiance to the Haganah. Subsequently, branches of Haganah emerged throughout the French zone and received tacit support from the local Zionist federation.

Toward the end of 1947 more organizing was under way. Because many Jews in the French zone wanted to go to Israel, the leadership of the Mossad le-Aliya Bet organized their emigration illegally. Despite French disenchantment with Zionist endeavors in 1948 and 1949, Zionism in Morocco—youth organizations, a federation, and political movements—was like a microcosm of the Yishuv. In the 1950s Zionist or Israeli political parties and youth Pioneer movements, from Po^{c}alei Tsiyon and Habonim to Mapam, Ha-Po^{c}el ha-Mizrachi, Dror, and Ha-No^{c}ar ha-Tsiyoni, were represented. In 1955 the Zionist federation in French Morocco had an estimated membership of two thousand; however, the only newspaper that the Zionists had at the time was the French-language *No^{c}ar,* the organ of the Charles Netter group. In fact, with the exception of *L'Union Marocaine* in the 1930s and, among a few others, *La Voix des Communautés* (published intermittently as the CCJC's journal), the serious community newspapers were usually the Zionist-oriented ones.

As for the emigration to Israel in 1947 and 1948, the process was organized clandestinely inside Morocco by the local Zionist underground. Most emigrants reached transit camps in Algeria via Morocco's northeastern land border in Oujda City. In Algeria the Yishuv's emissaries escorted emigrants to ships whose destination was Palestine. The initial efforts were mostly unsuccessful, because the British seized the first two ships, and the emigrants were then transferred to camps in Cyprus; the third ship reached

Palestine toward the end of 1947 with only forty-four Jews. From that point on Jews continued to flee clandestinely to Israel via Oujda, Algeria, and Marseilles, either with the help of the underground or through other initiatives. In mid-1948 the exodus became large scale; from May 1947 to June 1948 fewer than two thousand escaped; the number of refugees who passed through Algeria from the summer of 1948 until spring 1949 exceeded ten thousand. Jewish enthusiasm for the State of Israel and the military success of the Arab-Israeli War, coupled with increased poverty in Morocco and the outbreak of a pogrom against Jews in Oujda and nearby Djerada, increased the number of emigrants.

After the political obstinacy revealed by the French in Morocco, the French Algerian authorities decided to soften their anti-aliyah stance in September 1948. They now allowed the great number of Moroccan Jews stranded in Algiers and Oran to legally depart for Marseilles' official Jewish Agency transit camps. In December 1948 the French administration in Morocco realized that the exodus could not be curtailed and sought an "orderly" aliyah. Because of the effective intervention of the Zionist Federation in France before the resident general in Rabat in the name of the Jewish Agency, and the decision of France to grant Israel de facto recognition (January 24, 1949), a suitable formula for semilegal aliyah was found. The resident general agreed that disorganized emigration would end and that the Jewish Agency would establish monthly quotas. The Jewish Agency could then open an emigration bureau in Casablanca that functioned under the guise of a social welfare agency to process emigrants. The semilegal emigration apparatus called Cadima (Forward) opened in July 1949 and its lifespan extended into 1956, several months after Morocco became independent. More than ninety thousand Jews emigrated through this operation. An emigration office affiliated with Cadima also functioned in Tangier. It catered to the relatively small number of emigrants from the international and Spanish zones. Whereas until 1952 the Mossad le-Aliya Bet processed the aliyah, the Israeli emissaries of the Jewish Agency's Immigration Department took charge afterward. The French then agreed to grant Moroccan Jews passports and visas to France, while the ships of a French maritime company transferred the emigrants to camps in Marseilles. From there they went on to Israel.

Cadima's emissaries also worked in the Atlas Mountains in the early 1950s, because some would-be emigrants were transients from the Atlas and other remote communities. The apparatus included physicians representing the Israel Ministry of Health and a social screening–selection team. To grapple with serious absorption difficulties, Israel enforced a policy of emigrant selection for North Africa.

Despite the expansion of Israeli activity inside Morocco on a semilegal basis, including the work of Jewish Agency departments such as Torah Education and Youth Pioneer, aliyah declined precipitously from 1952 to 1954. Most of those who wanted to emigrate were poor, and reduced emigration reflected their frustration with the harsh screening–selection process that split up families by sending the healthy to Israel and leaving behind those who did not qualify. During this time more than two thousand discontented Moroccan Jews returned from Israel to Morocco, complaining of discrimination and absorption problems—but there were other reasons. The United States had by then built military bases and other installations in Morocco's French zone, and the Americans were recruiting many Jews to assist in the undertaking and giving them excellent salaries and benefits. As far as these Moroccan Jews were concerned, aliyah could wait.

After August 1954 the escalation of the violent struggle for independence, especially in French Morocco, renewed Jewish avidity for a move to Israel. Moroccan nationalists pressured France to allow Sultan Sidi Muhammad ben Yusuf to return from his forced exile and to grant the country sovereignty. Following a 1954 pogrom in Petitjean and the violence that ensued, by 1955 an increasing number of middle-class Jews, not merely the poor, were seeking to liquidate their assets and emigrate. Consequently, the Jewish Agency accelerated aliyah from the urban areas and evacuated as many Jews as possible from remote villages in the Atlas Mountains. When the French protectorate authorities attempted to reduce emigration from two thousand per month to seven hundred, Israel intervened diplomatically in France to help override this policy. Protectorate officials feared that the departure of so many to Israel at the height of the Moroccan independence struggle could only demonstrate to the nationalists, and the world, that France was no longer in control. Ultimately, the French waived the restrictions, if only because of the close ties that Israel then enjoyed with France.

After negotiations with the nationalists to allow the return of the exiled sultan to Morocco, and after the country gained independence, Cadima was dissolved late in 1956, and semilegal emigration of Jews on a large scale ended; thereafter, only small groups or individuals managed to obtain passports. Upon joining the Arab League in 1958 and openly siding with the Middle Eastern Arab states against Israel, Morocco prohibited even individual emigration from Morocco via France. The new Morocco and King Muhammad V preferred not to alienate Egypt and Syria. They did not look favorably on young Moroccan Jews' settling in Israel to enter the Israeli army and the labor force and thus strengthen Israel from within.

While Moroccan authorities tightened restrictions on emigration, the remaining Jewish elite still held some privileges. In fact, the post-1956 elite was divided into three currents. The first, influenced by French and European schooling, emphasized the central importance of European culture. In general, the members of this group were not attracted to Zionism, and they eventually settled in France. The second group included those who, despite the education that they received at the AIU schools, were still influenced by Zionism. The third group, which favored a Judeo-Muslim entente,emerged during the mid- and late 1950s and was by no means homogeneous. This group included about four hundred activists with strong leftist tendencies and about five hundred communists, as well as moderate leftists and conservatives. One leading communist was Abraham Sarfati, an engineer and key opposition leader, who in 1974 was imprisoned for plotting to undermine the monarchy and then exiled.

Several activists in the third group advocated Jewish-Muslim integration, with Jews frequenting the same clubs as Muslims and attending the same schools, in order to bridge the political and intellectual gap between the two peoples. Others were more cautious, arguing that rapprochement should not compel Moroccan Jews to sever their ties with Israel or to embrace Arabic language and literature at the expense of French culture. In order to achieve national unity and engender reforms within the Jewish community, the leftist integrationists affiliated with the Istiqlal Party, and in 1956 the Union Marocaine de Travail, the Moroccan labor union, founded a pro-entente movement known as al-Wifaq (Agreement). During the late 1950s leaders sharing their political orientation gained some prominence within the community councils and CCJC, although eventually they either moderated their stance and remained in positions of authority or more moderate elements prevailed.

Morocco's first independent government included Dr. Leon Benzaquen, who served as minister of post and telegraph, while several Jewish integrationists were recruited into high officialdom, including consular duties in several Moroccan embassies in Europe and the United States, and into the new Consultative Assembly. The majority of Moroccan Jews, however, were neither elite nor elitist—and the granting of Moroccan citizenship through the Constitution of 1962 hardly reduced their determination to depart. They shunned all political parties, whether leftist or conservative; then too the nation's political forces did not appear eager to enlist their support.

Outwardly neutral in the Moroccan national struggle for independence, the Jewish community never identified with it, hoping colonial domination would linger on.

Three groups were determined to leave Morocco. In the first group were about sixty thousand Jews who passed the selection criteria in 1955 and 1956 but were prevented from leaving after Cadima was disbanded. The two other groups were Atlas Mountain Jews who had stayed behind and the urbanites from Fez, Meknès, Casablanca, and Marrakesh who sought to escape from economic marginalization and poverty.

In 1955 Israel had formed a Moroccan Zionist underground. The Mossad, Israel's secret service agency, created the Misgeret (Framework), which organized self-defense training for all of North Africa. Misgeret's operational headquarters were in Paris; Casablanca became its center in Morocco. Misgeret's Israeli emissaries arrived in North Africa between August 1955 and early 1956. In Algeria and Tunisia they engaged mostly in self-defense training, but in Morocco they had five units in the urban centers: Gonen (self-defense), Ballet (recruiters of activists), Oref Tsiburi (the channel for communicating with leaders of the CCJC and community councils), Modiᶜin (intelligence gathering for missions), and Makhela (illegal aliyah).

The need to organize illegal immigration and to create the Makhela unit stemmed from the Moroccan decision to dissolve Cadima; Mossad understood that the Jewish Agency had erred in not evacuating more Jews when the opportunity existed. Between the end of 1956 and mid-1961 Misgeret smuggled many of the eighteen thousand Jews who then left Morocco, using various land and sea routes. Many Misgeret operations were successful because of services rendered by Spanish and Moroccan smugglers, who assisted Misgeret in evacuating Jews without travel documents, falsifying passports, and bribing Moroccan officials. Equally important was the cooperation of officials in seaports, in the Spanish enclaves of Ceuta and Melilla, of British officials at Gibraltar, and of the French who still controlled Algeria. The Moroccan government failed to destroy the underground, although many activists were arrested.

In January 1961, on the occasion of Egyptian President Nasser's visit to Casablanca, Jews were beaten and jailed. Several days later the *Egoz,* one of Misgeret's smuggling ships, foundered at sea, and forty-two Jewish emigrants drowned. The repercussions of these events prompted local Jewish leaders, Israel, and international Jewish organizations to pressure Morocco to liberalize emigration. King Muhammad V promised to tolerate emigration and instructed his minister of the interior to grant passports to all Jews who wanted to leave. But the king died in February 1961 and was succeeded by King Hassan II; these events prevented the policy from being implemented immediately. The intercession of two influential Jews close to the palace enabled Israel to enter into discreet negotiations with the Moroccans through a series of meetings held in Europe; the result of the negotiations between the Misgeret's top envoy in Morocco and a representative of King Hassan II was a plan. HIAS (Hebrew Immigrant Aid Society) would open offices in Morocco, and under its auspices Israel could organize more semi-legal departures; Morocco would then receive "indemnities" for the loss of the Jews. Known as "Operation Yakhin," between November 1961 and spring 1964 about eighty thousand Jews left for Israel by chartered planes and ships from Casablanca and Tangier via France and Italy.

POSTSCRIPT ON CONTEMPORARY MOROCCAN JEWRY

In the 1960s improved relations between Morocco and Israel through intelligence contacts facilitated emigration. From 1964 to 1966 aliyah diminished in favor of emigration to France and Canada; it regained some vigor following the Arab-Israeli War of June 1967 but declined once again in 1970. In all, between 1948 and 1970, 230,000 Moroccan Jews reached Israel. After 1970 Moroccan Jewry was indeed moving slowly but definitely toward its self-liquidation. The school population was perhaps the best yardstick. Jewish day schools saw their enrollment drop by about 15 percent between October 1972 and October 1973, and they have seen subsequent drops of about 5 percent every year since. Yet the Arab-Israeli War of 1973 and subsequent Middle East conflicts did not result in the end of Morocco's Jewish communities. Those who remained weathered the crises and expressed confidence in the monarchy's ability to safeguard their well-being.

The Jews who stayed behind faced changing economic patterns. When Morocco won independence, European personnel left, and French-educated Jews tended to replace them in public administration, causing some resentment. Since the 1960s, however, the areas of competition and therefore conflict have been reduced. As Morocco Arabized its government, Jews found it increasingly difficult to compete, except in private enterprise.

Several communities of Jews delayed their complete departure in the 1980s and 1990s partly because they owned large pieces of communal property valued at many millions of dollars. These properties were registered with the Ministry of Interior and could not be sold without the ministry's permission, while the proceeds of the sales had to be kept in cash in a bank or reinvested in other property. Although Jews were leaving, the government attempted to repatriate Moroccan Jews who had settled in Israel, France, and the Americas. In 1975, when twenty-two thousand Jews still lived in the country, the monarchy urged Jews who were "victims of population uprooting to return to the country that is reserved to all Moroccan citizens of the Jewish faith." Only a few returned. Upon their arrival they were given board and lodging at government expense and assistance in finding jobs. Others merely visited, but their numbers since the 1980s have reached tens of thousands, contributing significantly to Morocco's tourist industry. Unlike other Arab countries, Morocco now allows Moroccan-born Jews to visit, even with official Israeli stamps in their passports. Those who have visited Morocco since the 1970s have noticed that Jews and Muslims are now integrated in what were once separate neighborhoods.

In 2000, six thousand Jews remained in Morocco, the majority in Casablanca. Influential Jewish leaders—among them, David Amar, a business partner of King Hassan II's; Robert Assaraf, a noted intellectual and one of the most affluent Jews in Morocco; and Serge Berdugo, who served as a minister of tourism in the 1990s—have wielded influence since the 1960s, playing a cardinal role in local politics. Their intimate ties to both the monarchy and opposition parties enabled them to promote diverse Morocco-Israel connections. While Berdugo was minister of tourism, Israeli-Moroccan tourist exchange gained considerable momentum. In October 1994 André Azoulay, one of King Hassan's Jewish confidants, was the driving force behind the first Middle East Economic Summit in Casablanca. The intermediary role played by King Hassan in bringing Israel and the Arab states closer together, leading to the Egyptian-Israeli peace initiative back in 1977, also contributed to Muslim-Jewish coexistence at home.

After King Hassan's death on July 23, 1999, his son, Muhammad VI, ascended the throne. In sharp contrast to his father's aspirations of involving Morocco in regional and international politics, Muhammad VI seems to concentrate on domestic social reforms, greater equality for women, and democratizing the nation's political institutions. Thus far he also has demonstrated a belief in peaceful Muslim-Jewish coexistence. He retained Azoulay as the monarchy's chief adviser and facilitated the return from France of Abraham Sarfati, the exiled communist activist, whom the king appointed as his chief expert on sources of energy.

SUGGESTED READING

Deshen, Shlomo. *The Mellah Society: Jewish Community Life in Sharifian Morocco.* Chicago: University of Chicago Press, 1989.

Laskier, Michael M. *North African Jewry in the Twentieth Century.* New York: New York University Press, 1994.

——. *The Alliance Israélite Universelle and the Jewish Communities of Morocco: 1862–1962.* Albany: State University of New York Press, 1983.

Schroeter, Daniel J. *Merchants of Essaouira: Urban Society and Imperialism in Southwestern Morocco, 1844–1886.* Cambridge, U.K.: Cambridge University Press, 1988.

Schroeter, Daniel J. and Joseph Chetrit. "The Transformation of the Jewish Community of Essaouira in the Nineteenth and Twentieth Centuries." In Harvey E. Goldberg, ed., *Sephardi and Middle Eastern Jewries,* pp. 99–116. Bloomington: Indiana University Press, 1996.

Stillman, Norman A. *The Jews of Arab Lands in Modern Times.* Philadelphia: Jewish Publication Society of America, 1991.

APPENDIX

Middle East and North African Jewry CD

CANTILLATION OF *BERESHIT BARA ELOKIM*

1. Spanish and Portuguese
2. Khalkis, Greece
3. Djerba, Tunisia
4. Egypt
5. Bagdad, Iraq
6. Shiraz, Persia
7. Yemen

Liturgical Example *Nishmat Kol Hai*:

8. Spanish and Portuguese
9. Meknes, Morocco
10. Turkey
11. Aleppo, Syria

Adaptation

12. *Yequl Abu Salim*, Judeo-Arabic in Yemen
13. *Ashir Lakh Eretz Khamdah*, Emile Zrihan and Orchestre Andalour D'Israel

Piyyut

14. *Levavi yakhsheka ʿofrah*, Yemen

Music in the liturgy in Aleppo

15. *Hawwid min hina*
16. *Bo'i Be-Rinah*
17. *Shav'at Aniyyim*

Judeo-Spanish

18. *La Muerte Del Duque de Gandia*, Cannakale, Turkey
19. *Irme quero madre a Yerushalaim*, Cannakale, Turkey
20. *Copla de Purim*, Casablanca
21. Wedding songs, Tangier, Morocco
22. *Las Ventanas Altas* and *Adon Olom*, Salonika, Greece
23. *Cuando El Rey Nimrod*, Voice of the Turtle

Modern Examples

24. *Shabbekhi Yerushalayim*, Avihu Medina
25. *Haperakh begani*, Avihu Medina

Ekhad Mi Yode[c]a

26. *Ekhad Mi Yode[c]a*, Judeo-Persian, Isaac Jahanfard
27. *Ken supiese y entendiense*, Judeo-Spanish, Voice of the Turtle

CANTILLATION OF *BERESHIT BARA ELOKIM* (GENESIS 1:1–5) [#1–#7]

ב ר א ש י ת

פרק א׳ פסוקים א׳ - ה׳

א) בְּרֵאשִׁית בָּרָא אֱלֹהִים אֵת הַשָּׁמַיִם וְאֵת הָאָרֶץ׃

ב) וְהָאָרֶץ הָיְתָה תֹהוּ וָבֹהוּ וְחֹשֶׁךְ עַל-פְּנֵי תְהוֹם וְרוּחַ
אֱלֹהִים מְרַחֶפֶת עַל-פְּנֵי הַמָּיִם׃

ג) וַיֹּאמֶר אֱלֹהִים יְהִי-אוֹר וַיְהִי-אוֹר׃
ד) וַיַּרְא אֱלֹהִים אֶת-הָאוֹר כִּי-טוֹב וַיַּבְדֵּל אֱלֹהִים בֵּין
הָאוֹר וּבֵין הַחֹשֶׁךְ׃
ה) וַיִּקְרָא אֱלֹהִים לָאוֹר יוֹם וְלַחֹשֶׁךְ קָרָא לָיְלָה וַיְהִי-עֶרֶב
וַיְהִי-בֹקֶר יוֹם אֶחָד׃

1. Bereshit bara Elokim et hashamayim ve-et ha-aretz:
2. Ve-ha-aretz hayta tohu va-vohu ve-khoshekh ᶜal-pene tehom ve-ruakh Elokim merakhefet ᶜal-pene hamayim:
3. Va-yomer Elokim yehi or va-yehi or:
4. Vayar Elokim et ha-or ki tov va-yavdel Elokim ben ha-or u-ven hakhoshekh:
5. Vayikra Elokim la-or yom ve-lakhoshekh kara layela va-yehi erev vayehi voker yom ekhad:

1. When God began to create heaven and earth:
2. The earth being unformed and void, with darkness over the surface of the deep and the wind from God sweeping over the water:
3. God said, "Let there be light": and there was light:
4. God saw that the light was good, and God separated the light from the darkness:
5. God called the light Day, and darkness He called Night. And there was evening and there was morning, first day.

Source: #1–#7, from National Sound Archives, Jerusalem from the fieldwork recordings of: #1, Avigdor Herzog YC2452/40; #2, Amnon Shiloah YC277; #3-6 Johanna Spector from "Johanna Spector Tape Collection" #3, Y47/13; #4, Y73/3; #5, Y61/2; #6, Y78/2; #7, Israel Adler Y272/9. Text Translation: *Tanakh: A New Translation of the Holy Scriptures According to the Traditional Hebrew Text* (Philadelphia: The Jewish Publication Society, 1985), p. 3.

NISHMAT KOL HAI [#8–#11]

נִשְׁמַת כָּל-חַ-י. תְּבָרֵךְ אֶת-שִׁמְךָ יְיָ אֱלֹהֵינוּ. וְרוּחַ
כָּל-בָּשָׂר תְּפָאֵר וּתְרוֹמֵם זִכְרְךָ מַלְכֵּנוּ תָּמִיד: מִן-
הָעוֹלָם וְעַד-הָעוֹלָם אַתָּה אֵל. וּמִבַּלְעָדֶיךָ אֵין לָנוּ
מֶלֶךְ גּוֹאֵל וּמוֹשִׁיעַ. פּוֹדֶה וּמַצִּיל. וְעוֹנֶה וּמְרַחֵם. בְּכָל-
עֵת צָרָה וְצוּקָה. אֵין לָנוּ מֶלֶךְ עוֹזֵר וְסוֹמֵךְ. אֶלָּא אָתָּה:
אֱלֹהֵי הָרִאשׁוֹנִים וְהָאַחֲרוֹנִים. אֱלוֹהַּ כָּל-בְּרִיּוֹת. אֲדוֹן
כָּל-תּוֹלָדוֹת. הַמְהֻלָּל בְּכָל-הַתִּשְׁבָּחוֹת. הַמְנַהֵג עוֹלָמוֹ
בְּחֶסֶד. וּבְרִיּוֹתָיו בְּרַחֲמִים: וַיְיָ עֵר לֹא-יָנוּם וְלֹא-יִישָׁן.
הַמְעוֹרֵר יְשֵׁנִים. וְהַמֵּקִיץ נִרְדָּמִים. מְחַיֵּה מֵתִים. וְרוֹפֵא
חוֹלִים. פּוֹקֵחַ עִוְרִים. וְזוֹקֵף כְּפוּפִים. הַמֵּשִׂיחַ אִלְּמִים.
וְהַמְפַעֲנֵחַ נֶעֱלָמִים. וּלְךָ לְבַדְּךָ אֲנַחְנוּ מוֹדִים:

Nishmat kol khai. Tevarekh et shimkha Adoshem Elokeinu. Veruakh kol bassar tefa'er utromem zikhrekha malkeinu tamid: Min ha[c]olam ve-ad ha-olam atta Kel. Umibal[c]adekha ein lanu melekh go'el umoshi[c]a. Podeh umatzil. Ve-one u-merakhem. Bekhol et tzara ve-tzuka. Ein lanu melekh ozer ve-somekh. Ella atta: Elokei ha-rishonim ve-ha-akharonim. Eloha kol beriot. Adon kol toladot. Hamehulal bekhol ha-tishbakhot. Hamnaheg olamo bekhesed. Uvriyotav berakhamim: Va-Adoshem er lo yanum ve-lo yishan. Ha-me'orer yeshenim. Ve-hamekitz nirdamim. Mekhayei metim. Ve-rofei kholim. Pokeiakh ivrim. Ve-zokef kefufim. Ha-mesiakh ilmim. Ve-hamefa'aneiach ne'e'elamim. Ulekha levadkha anakhnu modim:

Lord our God, the soul of all living shall bless Thee,
The spirit of all flesh ever praise and extol Thee, our King.
From eternity to eternity Thou art God.
Besides Thee we have no King and Deliverer,
Savior, Redeemer, Rescuer who answers us
with loving succor
At every time of sorrow and distress,
No king to help and stay us have we but Thee.
God of the beginning, God of the end,
God of all that exists, Lord of all that has birth,
Thou art extolled in all songs of praise.

With love Thou guidest Thy world,
With tender love those whom Thou hast created.
O Lord, in Thy watchful care
Thou dost not slumber nor sleep;
Thou awakenest those who sleep,
Stirring them from deep sleep.
Thou healest the sick, Thou quickenest the dead.
Thou openest blind eyes,
Thou makest the bowed walk upright.
Thou causest the dumb to speak,
Giving utterance to lips that are sealed.
Therefore Thee, Thee alone, do we thank and praise.

Source: #8 from LP recording *Music of Congregation Shearith Israel in the City of New York, the Spanish and Portuguese Synagogue*, vol. II "Songs for the Sabbath" (1959); #9 from National Sound Archives, Jerusalem fieldwork recordings of Avigdor Herzog YC417/12; #10 CD recording, *The Liturgy of Ezra Bessaroth*, recorded by Isaac Azose, Hazzan Emeritus of Congregation Ezra Bessaroth in Seattle, Washington; #11 Hazzan David Shiro, Archives of Milken Family Foundation. Text Translation: *Book of Prayers: According to the Custom of the Spanish and Portuguese Jews*, 2nd edition, David De Sola Pool editor and translator (New York: Union of Sephardic Congregations, 1997), p. 183.

YEQUL ABU SALIM [#12]

Source: National Sound Archives, Jerusalem fieldwork recordings of Yael Shai Y5873.

ASHIR LAKH ERETZ KHAMDAH [#13]

אשיר לך ארץ חמדה בלב חשוק
את ארץ נבחרה
את משוש תבל כי בורא דוק
את לנו תפארה

תמיד עיני צופיה עפרך אני שוקק
ובתוכך שוכן י-ה שופט בצדק
למה רועה נאמן בך חשק
ולראותך לו נתן רק ממרחק

ובתוכך לא נטמן   כך אל חקק

פזמון: אשיר לך...

דורך בך ארבע אמות   ארץ צבי
סולח לו אשמות   צור משגבי
יתמו המלחמות   מסביבי
יוצר כל הנשמות   גואל תביא

פזמון: אשיר לך ...

Ashir lakh eretz khemdah   belev khashuk
et eretz nivkhara
et masos tevel   ki bore davek
at lanu tif'ara

Tamid einei tzofia   efrakh ani shokek
u-vetokhekh shokhen Kah   shofet betzedek
lama ro'e ne'eman bakh khashek.
Ve-lirotakh lo natan   rak mimerkhak
u-vetokhekh lo nitman   kakh kel khakak
Pizmon: Ashir lakh

Dorekh bakh arba amot   eretz tzvi
soleyakh lo ashamot   tsur misgavi
yitamu ha-milkhamot   misevivi
yotzer kol ha-neshamot   go'el tavi.

I sing to you dear   land with a heart full of desire
you are the chosen land
you are the joy of the world   the creator of heaven
to us you are glory.

My eyes always look to you   for your dust I yearn
in you G-d resides   the righteous judge.
Why was loyal shepherd (Moses)   who was enamored of you
And you only allowed him   only from a distance

And he was not buried in your midst so G-d decreed.
Chorus: I sing to you . . .

Your beloved is 4 cubits ensconced land of Israel
forgive him his sins rock my fortress.
Let the wars end around me
O creator of all souls bring the redemer.

Source: CD recording *Jerusalem* Orchestre Andalou D'Israel, Emile Zrihan soloist (Magda MGD007, track 2). Text by Rabbi David Buzaglo. Translation Howie Sherman and Stanley Nash.

LEVAVI YAKHSHEKA OFRAH [#14]

לבבי יחשקה עפרה

לְבָבִי יַחְשְׁקָה עָפְרָה לְשִׂכְלִי הַחֲלִי
וְאָשִׁיר שִׁיר וְקוֹל זִמְרָה בְּנִגּוּן מַמְלְלִי
וּבָאוּ כָּל בְּנֵי חֶבְרָה וְעֹפֶר בָּבְלִי
פְּרִידַת אַהֲבָה קָשָׁה
כְּאֵשׁ חֶרֶב מְלֻטָּשָׁה
יְדִידִי בָא וְלֹא נָשָׁה
וְהֵאִיר אָהֳלִי:

יְלוּד יוֹסֵף אֲשֶׁר נֶעְזָר בְּאֵל חַי פּוֹעֲלוֹ
וְהוּא גוֹלֶה בְּאַדְמַת זָר מְצַפֶּה גוֹאֲלוֹ
יְקַבֵּץ עָם אֲשֶׁר נִפְזָר וְיָסִיר סֻבֳּלוֹ
זְקֵנַי בַּקְּשׁוּ עָלַי
בְּחֵן אָשׁוּב לְאוֹהָלַי
וְשָׁלוֹם עַל בְּנֵי גִילַי
וּמַקְשִׁיב מַמְלְלִי
לְצוּר קוֹנִי, אֲנִי אֶקְרָא יְרַפֵּא מַחֲלִי:
וְהַלְלוּיָה

Levavi yakhsheka ofra lesikhli hakhali
ve-ashir shir ve-kol zimra beniggun mamleli
u-va'u kol bnei khevra ve-ofer bavli
peridat ahava kasha
ke'esh kherev meluttasha
yedidi va ve-lo nasha
ve-he'ir ohali:

yelud yosef asher ne[c]ezar be-el khai po[c]alo
ve-hu gole be-admat zar metzappe go'alo
yekabbetz am asher nifzar ve-yasir subbalo
zkenai bakkshu alai
bekhen ashuv le-ohalai
ve-shalom al bnei gilai
umakshiv mamleli
letzur koni, ani ekra yerappe makhali
ve-haleluya

My heart longs for the
gazelle [the (Divine) beloved] [Oh] ease my mental anguish
And I will sing in poetry and melody With my words set to music
And all our kinsmen will come [Along with] the gazelle [the (Divine) lover] from Bavel
The separation of love is as excruciating
As the flame of a sharpened sword
My [Divine] Friend is come and
has not forgotten (or forsaken)
And he will brighten my dwelling

The One born of Joseph
(mashiach ben Yosef) Whose actions are done through the Living god
And he is exiled in a foreign land Waiting for his redeemer (mashiah ben David)
Who will gather the nation that
has been scattered And remove its yoke of suffering
My elders, pray for me
That through grace I may return to my abode (eretz yisrael)

And peace be with members of my cohort
And with whoever harkens to my words
To my Rock, my Creator I cry out
That he may heal my sickness (pain):
And Halleluyah (praise God).

Source: National Sound Archives, Jerusalem fieldwork recordings of Avner Bahat Y2163. Text: Shalem Shabazi, found in Naomi and Avner Bahat, *Saperi Tama: The Diwan Songs of the Jews of Central Yemen* (Israel: Beth Hatefutsoth, 1995), p. 262. Translation by Professor Stanley Nash.

HAWWID MIN HINA [#15]

Hawwid min hina, ta^{c}aala ^{c}indina.	Stop over, come to us.
Yalla ana winta nhibbi ba^{c}dina.	Come on, let us love one another.
Gaana-l farakh zaala-l tarakh.	Joy is here, sorrow disappears.
Sadrii-n sharakh imta nistila.	My heart is enchanted. When shall we meet?

Source: 78 LP recording by Zaki Murrad (c1915–1920). Translation by Mohamed Shams.

BO'I BE-RINAH [#16]

Bo'i berina ya^{c}ala adina.	Come in Song, gentle graceful woman.
Leveiti ata ve-imakh eshkona.	To my house now and with you I will dwell.
Oyvekh barakh yish^{c}ekh parakh.	Your enemy fled your salvation blossomed.
Orakh zarakh eit lekhenna.	Your light shined, time to be bestowed to her.

Source: Hazzan Isaac Cabasso. Text from *Shir Usvakha, Hallel Ve-zimrah* (New York: The Sephardic Heritage Foundation Inc., 1964), pp. 156–157. Translation by Mark Kligman.

SHAV^{C}AT ANIYYIM [#17]

Shav^{c}at aniyyim ata tishma,	You hear the cry of the impoverished,
Tza^{c}akat hidal takshiv	You are attentive to the scream of the weak
ve-toshi^{c}a. Ve-khatuv:	and You give salvation. And it is written:
"Rannenu tzadikim ba-Adoshem,	"Joyfully exult in God, [you] righteous ones,
layisharim nava tehila."	for the upright, praise is fitting." (Psalm 33:1)
Befi yesharim titroemem;	Through the mouth of the upright You are exalted;
uvsiftei tzadikim titbarekh;	and with the lips of the right-eous You are blessed;
u-vilshon khasidim titkadash;	and by the tongue of the pious, You are sanctified,
u-vkerev kedoshim tithalal.	and in the core of the holy, You are extolled.

Source: Hazzan Isaac Cabasso. Text from *Siddur Kol Yaakov: Ke-Minhag Aram Tzoba* [Kol Yaakov Prayer book according to the customs of Aleppo], Rabbi David Bitton editor (New York: Sephardic Heritage Foundation Inc., 1995), p. 492.

LA MUERTE DEL DUQUE DE GANDIA [#18]

Mas arriva y mas arriva	Very high up
en la sivdad de Silivria,	in the city of Silivria,
hay havia pescadores	there were fishermen
pescando sus proverias.	fishing for the poor people.
Vieron venir tres caballos	They saw three knights arrive
haziendo gran polveria,	making a big cloud of dust,
vienieron cerca del rio	the knights came close to the river
a la mar lo echaria.	and threw something into the sea.

Echan ganchos y gancheras	The fishermen cast their hooks and anchors
por ver lo que les salia,	to see what was left for them,
les salio un duque de oro	what was left for them was a duke of gold,
hizho del rey paresia.	that appeared to be the king's son.
Si se lo traian vivo	If they fetched him alive
hombres grandes los haria,	rich men they would become,
si se lo traian muerto	if they fetched him dead
sus presentes les darian.	his gifts they would be given.
Camisa de holanda lleva	He wore a shirt of fine linen
camisa onde sirma y perla,	A shirt with silver thread and pearls,
anillo lleva en el dedo	he wore a ring on his finger
sien proves ricos hazia.	one hundred poor men he would make rich.

Source: Susana Weich Shahak collection National Sound Archives, Jerusalem YC2936/2. Text provided by Judith Cohen. Translation by Marilyn Mayo.

IRME QUERO MADRE A YERUSHALAIM [#19]

Irme quero madre a Yerushalayim	I want to go, mother, to Jerusalem,
y pasear las ervas y hartar me de eyas.	to walk on its pastures and stuff myself with them.
En el kotel maravi ha una ziyara	On the Western Wall there is a pilgrimage,
tudas mi deamandas ayi mas afirmean	all my demands there are fulfilled.
En el me arrimo yo, en el me abraco yo	On Him I trust, on Him I believe,
en el patron del mundo,	on the Master of the Universe,
en el sinyor del mundo.	on the Lord of the Universe.

Source: Susana Weich Shahak collection National Sound Archives, Jerusalem YC2936. Text provided by Judith Cohen. Translation from *Chants Judeo-Espangnols de la Mediterranee Orientale* (Inedit W260054), CD booklet Edwin Seroussi.

COPLA DE PURIM [#20]

Esta noche de Purim
no duermen los halwiyin
haziendo las halwinadas,
para las desposadas.

This Purim night
the sweets makers do not sleep
they are making sweets,
for the newlyweds.

Refrain:
Vivas tu, viva yo,
vivan todos los dzhudios,
viva la Reina Ester
que tanto plaser mos dió.

Long live you, long live me,
long live all the Jews,
long live Queen Esther
who gave us so much
pleasure.

Haman antes que muriera
llamó a su parentela
los puso en la cabeçera,

el día antes de Purím.

Before he died Haman
summoned his relatives
and placed them in a seat of
honor,
the day before Purim.

Y tu mi hizho Porata
vende la ropa barata
y no hables con quien trata,

en el día de Purim.

And you my son Porata
sell the rope cheap
and do not speak with those
who handle it,
on the day of Purim.

Dalfín mi hizho segundo
ansí tengas preto mundo

tuerto te vayas del mundo

en el dia de Purím.

Dalfin my second son
thus you shall possess a dark
world
twisted you shall go from the
world,
on the day of Purim.

Calla, tú, Zerah la loca
que a ti hablar no te toca
que por ti hissieron la horca,
en el día de Purím.

Hush, you, Zerah the crazy one
it is not your turn to talk
so for you they made the gallows,
on the day of Purim.

Y Shimshi el escribano

And Shimshi the scribe

se mataba con sus manos,
no deshaba hueso sano
en el día de Purim.

was killed with his own hands,
he did not leave a healthy bone
on the day of Purim.

Source: Susana Weich Shahak collection National Sound Archives, Jerusalem Y5773/10. Text provided by Judith Cohen. Translation by Marilyn Mayo and Nancy Wiener.

WEDDING SONGS [#21]

a. No me púsó mi madre cósa ninguna
la cara de esta novia cómo la luna.

La onza de la gracia,
y a cómo lo venderé

Ni lo vendo por onza ni por cuarterón

You did not arrange anything for me, mother
the face of this bride like the moon.

An ounce of charm, and how will you sell it?

I do not sell it by the ounce or by the quarter

b. La novia destrenza el pelo,
se désmaya el caballero.
Ay novía, vente a mi lado,
gozarás viciò y regalo.
Gozarás de buen marido,
quitarás ansiá y suspiro.

Ay, novía dela cara blanca,
Donde su novio se résmirara.

The bride lets down her hair,
the knight faints
Oh bride, come to my side,
you will enjoy vice and gifts.
You will enjoy a good husband,
you will get ride of anguish and sighs.
Oh, bride with the white face,
come where your husband breathes.

c. Ajuar nuevo delante vo lo pondré,

suegra y cunyada,
no tengáis que décir,
la nuestra novia
cenó y se echó dormir.
Anoche, mi madre,

I will place in front of you a new trousseau,
mother-in-law and sister-in-law,
you would not have to say,
that our bride
ate dinner and went to sleep.
Yesterday, my mother,

cenó y se echó a dormir,	she ate dinner and went to sleep,
sonyaba un suenyo,	and rang in a dream,
tan dulce era de decir,	so sweet it was said,
que se banyaba y a las orillas del Bir,	that she was bathing at the bank of the Bir,
vinía la ola y a mí me quervía llevar,	a wave came and it wanted to take me,
con amor, madre,	with love, mother,
con amor me iré a dormir.	with love, I will go to sleep.
d. Levantísme, madre, un lunes de manyana,	I would wake up, mother, on Monday morning,
fuérame al mercado,	and would go to the marker,
por ver como alborea, mi pastor.	to see how he rises my shepard.
Mercara un marido de honra y de fama,	He will buy a husband of honor and fame,
carpintero era, y maestro le llaman,	he was a carpenter, and they call him teacher,
ay, mi pastor.	oh my shepherd.
Maestro, maestro, arrégleme esta arca,	Teacher, teacher, fix this chest for me,
ha llave és de oro y la chapa de plata,	the key is gold and the pickax is silver,
ay mi pastor.	oh my shepherd.
e. Pase la novia andando,	The bride passes by walking,
galán trás de ella,	a handsome man behind her,
todo lo que la dice:	all that he says to her is:
si era doncella	if you were a maiden
y la onza de la gracia	and an ounce of charm,
y a cómo la venderé?	how will I sell it?
No la vendo por onza	I do not sell it by the ounce
ni por cuaterón,	or by the quarter,
se lo entrego a mi amado	I surrender it to you
de mi corazón.	Beloved of my heart.

f. [same text as c)]

g. Y fuérame a banyar a orillas del río, ahí encontré, madre, a mi lindo amigo, él me dió un abrazo, yo le dí cinco.	And I would go to bathe at the bank of the river, there I found, mother, my handsome friend, he gave me an embrace, I gave him five.
Por Dios, la neustra novia, cuerpo garrido, qué es lo que os ponís en escondido? si os ponéis albayarde u oro molido?	For God's sake, our bride, with the elegant body, what are you putting on in hiding? If you are putting on lead or powdered gold?
Tan bien que le parcis a vuestro marido.	How good you will look, to your husband.

Source: Susana Weich Shahak collection National Sound Archives, Jerusalem YC2261/11–19. Text: found in Susan Weich Shahak *Judeo-Spanish Moroccan Songs for the Life Cycle, Yuval Music Series* I (Jerusalem: The Jewish Music Research Centre, 1989). (a) p. 57; (b) p. 49; (c) p. 44; (d) p. 42; (e) p. 56; (f) p. 44; (g) p. 53. Translation by Marilyn Mayo.

LAS VENTANAS ALTAS AND *ADON OLOM* [#22]

Ventanas altas tienes tu, con velas amarillas, esta noche rogo al Dio, que me suvash arriva.	You have high windows, with yellow curtains, this night I pray to God, that you bring me upstairs.

Refrain:
Tirilaila, hop! tirilaila, hopa

En anillo que llevas tu, el diamante e smio, el kuyundzhu que lo hizo, es primo hermano mio.	The ring you wear, the diamond is mine, the jeweler that made it, is my first cousin.

Adon olam asher malakh,	Master of the universe who reigned,
beterem kol yetzir nivra.	before any being was created.
Le^{c}et na^{c}asa kekheftzo kol,	At the time when all was made by his will
azai melekh shmo nikra.	then as King was His name proclaimed.
Elohai hu, Elohai hu	He is my God, he is my God
Ve-akharei kikhlot hakol,	At the end when all shall cease to be,
levado yimlokh nora.	the revered God alone shall still reign.
Ve-hu haya ve-hu hove,	He was, and He is
ve-hu yiheyeh betif'ara.	and He will be in splendor.
Elohai hu, Elohai hu	He is my God, he is my God

Source: Susana Weich Shahak collection National Sound Archives, Jerusalem YC1188/5. Text for *Las Ventanas Altas* provided by Judith Cohen and translation by Marilyn Mayo. Translation of *Adon Olam*, *The Complete ArtScroll Siddur*, Rabbi Nosson Scherman translator (Brooklyn: Mesorah Publications, Ltd., 1984), p. 13.

CUANDO EL REY NIMROD [#23]

Cuando el rey Nimrod al campo salía,	When King Nimrod went out to the countryside,
mirava en el cielo y en la estreyeía.	he looked at looked up at the sky and stars.
Vido una lt santa en la giudería,	He saw a holy sign in the Jewish quarter,
que havia de nacer Avraham avinu.	that Abraham our father had been born.
Avraham avinu, padre querido,	Abraham our father, beloved father,
padre bendicho, luz de Israel.	blessed father, light of Israel.

Source: recording *Voice of the Turtle, The Time of Singing Has Come* (Titanic Records, 1985), side B #7. Translation by Marilyn Mayo.

SHABBEKHI YERUSHALAYIM [#24]

תְּהִלִּים

פרק קמז פסוקים יב-יג

יב) שַׁבְּחִי יְרוּשָׁלַיִם אֶת-יְהוָה
הַלְלִי אֱלֹהַיִךְ צִיּוֹן׃
יג) כִּי-חִזַּק בְּרִיחֵי שְׁעָרָיִךְ
בֵּרַךְ בָּנַיִךְ בְּקִרְבֵּךְ׃

Psalm 147:12–13

Shabbekhi yerushalayim et-Adoshem	O Jerusalem, glorify the Lord
haleli Elokayikh tziyon:	praise your God, O Zion.
Ki-khizzak berikhei sha[c]arayikh	For He made the bars of your gates strong,
berakh banaiyikh bekirbekh:	and blessed your children within you.

Source: Avihu Medina and Shimi Tavori, *Prakhei Gani* vol. 2. (ACUM CD 002), track 6. Text and translation: *Tanakh: A New Translation of the Holy Scriptures According to the Traditional Hebrew Text* (Philadelphia: The Jewish Publication Society, 1985), p. 1282.

HAPERAKH BEGANI [#25]

הפרח בגני

מיום אביב, בהיר וצח אותך, אני זוכר.
וכבר מאז, היטב ידעתי, שלא אוותר.
כי לי היית, בבת עיני בכל יום וכל ליל,
היית לי כמלאך האל, מתוך הערפל.
רציתי לבקש ידך, רציתי לך לאמר,

סוד אהבה שבלבבי, שמור מכל משמר.
רציתי לך לאמר אהבתי, אהבתי וניגמר,
אך לא העזתי, גם כשהיה כבר מאוחר.

פזמון: את עולמי עם שחר, את לי כל היום.
את עולמי בלילה, את החלום,
את בדמי, ברוחי, ולבבי,
את הניחוח המתוק, הפרח בגני.

מאז הלכת, מאז לא שבת, אני כה מעונה.
חיפשתי אחריך, אנה אנה עוד אפנה?
ביקשתי פה, שאלתי שם, ואין לי מענה.
אבל עדיין חלומות יפים, אני בונה.
מאז הלכת, יומי קודר, ארוך ומשעמם.
לשווא, רוצה אני לשכוח ולהית עלם
חיזרי מהר, כי בלעדייך עולמי שומם.
נדמו מיתרי קולי, וכינורי דומם.

Meyom aviv, behir ve-tzakh otakh, ani zokher.
u-khvar me'az, haitav yada^cti, shelo avater.
Ki li hayit, bavat eini bekol yom ve-kol leil,
Hayit li kemal'akh ha-Kel, metokh ha-arafel.
Ratziti levakesh yadekh, ratziti lakh lomar.
Sod ahava shevilvavi, shemor mikol mishmar.
Ratziti lakh lomar ahavti, ahavti ve-nigmar
Akh lo ha^cazti, gam keshehaya kevar me'ukhar.

Refrain: At olami im shakhar, at li kol hayom.
At olami belaila, at ha-khalom,
At bedami, berukhi, u-levavi,
At hanikho'akh hamatok, ha-perakh begani.

Me'az halakht, me'az lo shavt, ani ko me^cona.
khipasti akharayikh, ana ana od efna?
bikashti po, sha'alti sham, ve-ein li ma^cana.
Aval adayin khalomot yafim, ani bone.
Me'az halakht, yomi koder, arukh u-mishta^camem.

Leshav, rotze ani lishkoakh ve-lihiyot ilem
khizri maher, ki bil[c]adaykh olami shomem.
Nadmu maytrai koli, ve-kinori domem.

From a bright, shiny, spring day I remember you.
And even then I knew well, I won't give up on you.
For you have been the apple of my eye every night and every day,
You have been for me like an angel of God, merging from the mist.
I wanted to ask for your hand, wished to say to you,
'The secret of love is well kept within my heart."
But I never dared, even when it was too late for that.

Refrain: You are my world at dawn, you are my entire day.
You are my world at nighttime, you are my dream.
You're my spirit, in my blood, in my soul.
You are the sweet scent, the flower in my garden.

Since you left and never returned so tortured am I.
I searched for you everywhere, where shall I turn now?
I looked here, I asked there, no answers did I receive.
But still, beautiful dreams I create.
Since you left my day is dark, boring, and so long.
In vain I try to forget and to ignore
Quick! Return! For without you, my world is desolate.
Silent is my violin, mute my voice.

Source: Avihu Medina and Shimi Tavori, *Prakhei Gani* vol. 2., track 4 (Israel: ACUM C.D. 002, 1988). Music and Text by Avihu Medina. Translation by Amy Horowitz and Reuven Namdar.

EKHAD MI YODE[c]A [#26]

Who knows one? I know one: One is our God, in heaven and on earth.

Who knows two? I know two: two are the Tablets of the Covenant; One is our God, in heaven and on earth.

Who knows three? I know three: three are the Patriarchs; two are the Tablets of the Covenant; One is our God, in heaven and on earth.

Who knows four? I know four: four are the Matriarchs; three are the Patriarchs; two are the Tablets of the Covenant; One is our God, in heaven and on earth.

Who knows five? I know five: five are the books of Torah; four are the Matriarchs; three are the Patriarchs; two are the Tablets of the Covenant; One is our God, in heaven and on earth.

Who knows six? I know six: six are the Orders of the Mishnah; five are the books of Torah; four are the Matriarchs; three are the Patriarchs; two are the Tablets of the Covenant; One is God, in heaven and on earth.

Who knows seven? I know seven: seven are the days of the week; six are the Orders of the Mishnah; five are the books of the Torah; four are the Matriarchs; three are the Patriarchs; two are the Tablets of the Covenant; One is our God, in heaven and on earth.

Who know eight? I know eight: eight are the days of circumcision; seven are the days of the week; six are the Orders of the Mishnah; five are the books of Torah; four are the Matriarchs; three are the Patriarchs; two are the Tablets of the Covenant; One is our God, in heaven and on the earth.

Who know nine? I know nine: nine are the months of pregnancy; eight are the days of circumcision; seven are the days of the week; six are the Orders of the Mishnah; five are the books of the Torah; four are the Matriarchs; three are the Patriarchs; two are the Tablets of the Covenant; One is our God, in heaven and on the earth.

Who knows ten? I know ten: ten are the Ten Commandments; nine are the months of pregnancy; eight are the days of circumcision; seven are the days of the week; six are the Orders of the Mishnah; five are the books of the Torah; four are the Matriarchs; three are the Patriarchs; two are the Tablets of the Covenant; One is our God, in heaven and on earth.

Who knows eleven? I know eleven: eleven are the stars (in Joseph's dream); ten are the Ten Commandments; nine are the months of pregnancy; eight are the days of circumcision; seven are the days of the week; six are the Orders of the Mishnah; five are the books of the Torah; four are the Matriarchs; three are the Patriarchs; two are the Tablets of the Covenant; One is our God, in heaven and on earth.

Who knows thirteen? I know thirteen: thirteen are the attributes of God; twelve are the tribes; eleven are the stars (in Joseph's dream); ten are the Ten Commandments; nine are the months of pregnancy; eight are the days of circumcision; seven are the days of the week; six are the Orders of the Mishnah; five are the books of the Torah; four are the Matriarchs; three are the Patriarchs; two are the Tablets of the Covenant; One is our God in Heaven and on earth.

Source: #26 Isaac Jahanfard. Text translation: *The Family Haggadah*, Rabbi Nosson Scherman translator (Brooklyn Mesorah Publications, Ltd., 1981), pp. 86-89.

KEN SUPIESE Y ENTENDIENSE [#27]

Ken supiese y entendiense, alavar al Dio kreyense kualo es el uno? Uno es el Kriador, Baruch Hu Baruch shemo.

Ken supiese y entendiense, alavar al Dio kreyense kualo son loz dos? Dos Moshe y Aron, uno es el Kriador, Baruch Hu Baruch shemo.

Ken supiese y entendiense, alavar al Dio kreyense kualo son loz tres? Tres padrez muestroz son Avram Itzhak y Yaakov, dos Moshe y Aron, uno es el Kriador, Baruch Hu Baruch shemo.

Ken supiese y entendiense, alavar al Dio kreyense kualo son loz kuatro? Kuatro madrez muestraz son, Sara, Rivka, Lea, Rahel, tres padrez muestroz son Avram Itzhak y Yaakov, dos Moshe y Aron, uno es el Kriador, Baruch Hu Baruch shemo.

Ken supiese y entendiense, alavar al Dio kreyense kualo son loz sinko? Sinko livroz de la Ley, kuatro madrez muestraz son, Sara, Rivka, Lea, Rahel, tres padrez muestroz son Avram Itzhak y Yaakov, dos Moshe y Aron, uno es el Kriador, Baruch Hu Baruch shemo.

Ken supiese y entendiense, alavar al Dio kreyense kualo son loz seish? Seish diaz de la semana, sinko livroz de la Ley, kuatro madrez muestraz son, Sara, Rivka, Lea, Rahel, tres padrez muestroz son Avram Itzhak y Yaakov, dos Moshe y Aron, uno es el Kriador, Baruch Hu Baruch shemo.

Ken supiese y entendiense, alavar al Dio kreyense kualo son loz syete? Syete diaz kon Shabbat, seish diaz de la semana, sinko livroz de la Ley, kuatro madrez muestraz son, Sara, Rivka, Lea, Rahel, tres padrez muestroz son Avram Itzhak y Yaakov, dos Moshe y Aron, uno es el Kriador, Baruch Hu Baruch shemo.

Ken supiese y entendiense, alavar al Dio kreyense kualo son loz ocho? Ocho diaz de la mila, syete diaz kon Shabbat, seish diaz de la semana, sinko livroz de la Ley, kuatro madrez muestraz son, Sara, Rivka, Lea, Rahel, tres padrez muestroz son Avram Itzhak y Yaakov, dos Moshe y Aron, uno es el Kriador, Baruch Hu Baruch shemo.

Ken supiese y entendiense, alavar al Dio kreyense kualo son loz mueve? Mueve mezes de la prenyada, ocho diaz de la mila, syete diaz kon Shabbat, seish diaz de la semana, sinko livroz de la Ley, kuatro madrez muestraz son, Sara, Rivka, Lea, Rahel, tres padrez muestroz son Avram Itzhak y Yaakov, dos

Moshe y Aron, uno es el Kriador, Baruch Hu Baruch shemo.

Ken supiese y entendiense, alavar al Dio kreyense kualo son loz diez? Diez mandamientoz de la Ley, mueve mezes de la prenyada, ocho diaz de la mila, syete diaz kon Shabbat, seish diaz de la semana, sinko livroz de la Ley, kuatro madrez muestraz son, Sara, Rivka, Lea, Rahel, tres padrez muestroz son Avram Itzhak y Yaakov, dos Moshe y Aron, uno es el Kriador, Baruch Hu Baruch shemo.

Ken supiese y entendiense, alavar al Dio kreyense kualo son loz onsay? Onsay trivoz sin yosef, diez mandamientoz de la Ley, mueve mezes de la prenyada, ocho diaz de la mila, syete diaz kon Shabbat, seish diaz de la semana, sinko livroz de la Ley, kuatro madrez muestraz son, Sara, Rivka, Lea, Rahel, tres padrez muestroz son Avram Itzhak y Yaakov, dos Moshe y Aron, uno es el Kriador, Baruch Hu Baruch shemo.

Ken supiese y entendiense, alavar al Dio kreyense kualo son loz dosay? Dosay trivoz kon Yosef, onsay trivoz sin yosef, diez mandamientoz de la Ley, mueve mezes de la prenyada, ocho diaz de la mila, syete diaz kon Shabbat, seish diaz de la semana, sinko livroz de la Ley, kuatro madrez muestraz son, Sara, Rivka, Lea, Rahel, tres padrez muestroz son Avram Itzhak y Yaakov, dos Moshe y Aron, uno es el Kriador, Baruch Hu Baruch shemo.

Translation
Who knows one? One is the Creator, praise Him and praise His name.
Who knows two? Two are Moses and Aaron.
Who knows three? Three are the fathers: Abraham, Isaac and Jacob
Who knows four? Four are the mothers: Sarah, Rebecca, Leah and Rachel
Who knows five? Five books of the Law
Who knows six? Six are the weekdays
Who knows seven? Seven are the days including the Sabbath
Who knows eight? Eight are the days from birth to circumcision
Who knows nine? Nine are the months of pregnancy
Who knows ten? Ten are the commandments
Who knows eleven? Eleven are the tribes without Joseph
Who knows twelve? Twelve are the tribes including Joseph

Source: CD recording *A Different Night: A Passover Musical Anthology* Voice of the Turtle (Kol HaTor 018), track 11. Text in CD booklet by Judith Wachs, artistic director.

The following individuals provided valuable assistance in the collection of material for the CD: Ruth Freed and Gila Flam, from the National Sound Archives in Jerusalem. Assistance with Judeo-Spanish texts and translations, Judith Cohen and Marilyn Mayo. For translation of Hebrew texts, Stanley Nash and Amy Horowitz. Thanks to the following for general assistance in the compilation, typing, translation and editing of texts: Lina Barness, Paul Lewis, Rabbi Ira Rohde, Howard Sherman, and Nancy Wiener.

INDEX

C

F

N

O